SNAIL DOWN
WILTSHIRE

The Bronze Age Barrow Cemetery and Related Earthworks, in the parishes of Collingbourne Ducis and Collingbourne Kingston: Excavations, 1953, 1955 and 1957

by Nicholas Thomas

with contributions by

†Kenneth Annable, Marion Archibald, Paul Ashbee, Alex Bayliss, G H Bunting,
Arthur Cain, Juliet Clutton-Brock, †Ian Cornwall, Mark Corney, John Currey,
†Camilla Dickson, Anthony Duggan, E C Ellwood, David Field, Alex Gibson,
†Anthony Gunstone, Reg Jackson, †Peter A Jewell, Ian Longworth, Simon Mays,
Jonathan Musgrave, Deidre O'Sullivan, Frances Raymond, †J F S Stone,
D W Verity, Jacqui Watson and Robert Young

illustrations by Deborah Cunliffe, Nicholas Herepath, Andrew Howe, Ann Linge,
Frances Raymond and Nicholas Thomas

photographs by †G W G Allen, †Maurice Cookson, †Bret Guthrie, Vincent Megaw,
†J K St Joseph and Nicholas Thomas

**WILTSHIRE ARCHAEOLOGICAL AND NATURAL HISTORY SOCIETY
MONOGRAPH NO. 3
2005**

Published by the Wiltshire Archaeological and Natural History Society, 41 Long Street, Devizes, Wiltshire, SN10 1NS.

The publication of this volume has been generously funded by English Heritage.

First published 2005.

The plates are reproduced by permission of the following: Plate 1 Ashmolean Museum; Plates 2, 64A, 64B English Heritage; Plates 3, 5, 6, 8A, 8B, 11-12, 15, 17–28, 32-36, 41-55, 60 Nicholas Thomas; Plates 4, 7, 9-10, 13-14, 16, 29-31, 38, 40 Maurice Cookson; Plates 37, 39 Vincent Megaw; Plates 56-57 Bret Guthrie; Plate 58 A Duggan; Plate 59 American Journal of Opthalmology; Plate 61 E C Ellwood; Plates 65-67 Juliet Clutton-Brock and Peter A Jewell.

Front cover: Snail Down under Excavation, August 1953, looking southwards to Sidbury Hill. Oil painting by I P (Molly) Bewsher (Wiltshire Heritage Museum, DZSWS:2001.1010).
Back cover: Reproduction of map facing page 180 in R Colt Hoare, *Ancient Wiltshire,* Volume I, London, 1812.

ISBN 0 947723 12 9

Designed and typeset in Garamond by
Columns Design Ltd, Caversham, Reading, Berkshire
Printed in Great Britain by
Cromwell Press Ltd, Trowbridge, Wiltshire

For Susan, with Harriet, Amelia and Daniel;
who have long known Snail Down and borne its
study with great patience

CONTENTS

LIST OF ILLUSTRATIONS

LIST OF PLATES

Plates

Plates   Page No.

LIST OF TABLES

LIST OF DIAGRAMS

ABSTRACT

Snail Down is an Early Bronze Age barrow cemetery on Salisbury Plain, located 8 miles north-east of Stonehenge. Thirty-three mounds include examples of almost every type of Wessex barrow, as first defined by Sir Richard Colt Hoare and standardized by L V Grinsell. Barrows of bowl, bell, disc (two tumps), saucer and pond type were completely excavated between 1953 and 1957. Six contiguous mounds of scraped-up soil and another contained within a post ring, were examined in detail. Barrows tested by selective excavation included a ring-ditch (rare in Wessex) and a double bell-barrow whose princely copper-alloy grave-goods of ogival dagger and ring-headed pin have long been known.

The preferred burial rite at Snail Down was by cremation and disposal in burial pits of average size. One mound covered the base of a funeral pyre. Relatively modest grave-goods comprised a Food Vessel, Collared Urns, Accessory Vessels, a variety of beads, copper-alloy awls, flints and bonework. A trepanned cranial disc accompanied one burial. Ritual smashing of an urn provided a dramatic climax to another.

Structural and other features repeated among the barrows suggest that a broadly uniform burial tradition had been followed throughout the cemetery's lifetime, whose users were probably a single local community. A youth suffering from a form of tumor (*haemangioma*), added as an inhumation burial to a small mound on the berm of a bell-barrow, may have been a stranger to the region.

Radiocarbon determinations from charcoal and bone associated with some of the burials suggest that the Early Bronze Age cemetery could have been begun between 2140 and 1810 cal BC and ended between 1750 and 1440 cal BC, the use spanning between 150 and 600 years. A scheme is proposed for phasing the barrow cemetery.

Two neighbouring barrow mounds had been used to receive a small series of inhumation burials, one of which has been dated by radiocarbon assay to 1390–910 cal BC (GU-5305; 2920 ± 70 BP).

Stray sherds of Windmill Hill pottery were found in some barrows, and a weathered greenstone axe of Cornish origin. Remains of a Beaker settlement occurred beneath the row of scraped-up barrows, which account for the notable quantity of typical potsherds and flintwork incorporated in these and surrounding barrows. A battle-axe fragment of Group XIV camptonite from the Nuneaton district of Warwickshire may have had the same derivation.

The land around the cemetery is covered with the denuded remains of ancient fields, enclosures and trackways. Some of the fields may prove to underlie barrows. This relict landscape extends as far south as Amesbury. Its character was altered by the imposition of an extensive and striking layout of boundary ditches, first flat-bottomed (?later Bronze Age) and then of V shape (Iron Age); these earthworks represent changing regimes of land management spanning the last two millennia BC and extending through Romano-British times to the Middle Ages.

Animal bones throw light upon the livestock and dogs maintained by the Snail Down Early Bronze Age community and the wild animals they hunted. Remains of small mammals and vertebrates as well as land snails and charcoals provide evidence for the downland environment at the time of the barrows.

RÉSUMÉ

Le Snail Down est un cimetière de tertres funéraires de l'Age de bronze Ancien situé dans la plaine de Salisbury, à 8 milles au nord-est de Stonehenge. Parmi les trente-trois monticules, on trouve presque tous les types de tertres tumulaires du Wessex décrits dans la typologie initiale de Sir Richard Colt Hoare que L. V. Grinsell a ensuite standardisée. Entre 1953 et 1957, les fouilles ont permis de révéler des tertres de type réservoir, soucoupe, disque (deux petits monticules), cloche et cuvette. Six monticules contigus de terre rapportée des environs immédiats ainsi qu'un autre entouré d'un ceinture de pieux furent examinés en détail. Parmi les tertres choisis pour les fouilles, en figurait un entouré d'une rigole (rare dans le Wessex) et un autre à double cloche, connu depuis longtemps pour la beauté de la dague en ogive et de l'épingle à rête d'anneau en alliage de cuivre qu'on y avait retrouvés.

Le rite funéraire le plus répandu à Snail Down était la crémation puis la dispersion des cendres dans des fosses de taille moyenne. Un des monticules examinés recouvrait les restes d'un foyer funéraire. De ces modestes vestiges furent déterrés des récipients destinés à transporter la nourriture, des urnes à col, un conteneur à accessoires, un ensemble de colliers, des poinçons en alliage de cuivre, des silex, et des os travaillés. Dans une des tombes, on trouva aussi un disque cranien trépané; dans une autre, on retrouva une urne violemment brisée, le bris d'une urne servant alors à célébrer le rituel d'une autre.

Certains des traits d'ordre structurel ou d'une autre nature, communs à l'ensemble des tertres, suggèrent l'existence d'une tradition funéraire relativement uniforme qui aurait régulé la vie de ce cimetiè dont les utilisateurs appartenaient sans doute à la méme communauté locale. On a néanmoins retrouvé les traces d'un jeune atteint d'une forme de tumeur (*haemangioma*), dont les restes inhumés avaient été placés sur le petit dénivelé attenant au pied d'un tertre en cloche, ce qui pourrait indiquer qu'il eút été étranger à la région.

L'examen au carbone radioactif sur le charbon et les os retrouvés dans certaines des fosses tend à indiquer que l'utilisation d'un cimetière de type Age du Bronze Ancien aurait pu commencer entre 2140 et 1810 av J-C (en années calibrées) et prendre fin entre 1750 et 1440 av J-C (en années calibrées), s'étalant ainsi sur une période entre 150 et 600 années. Nous proposons ici un schéma d'analyse qui rende compte de la chronologie de l'évolution de ce cimetière de tertres.

Deux monticules assez proches ont accueilli les restes d'un petit nombre d'inhumations, et le carbone radioactif a permis d'en dater un d'entre 1390 et 910 av J-C (en annés calibrées). (GU-5305: 2920 +/− 70 BP).

Certains tertres ont révélé des tessons épars de poteries de Windmill Hill, ainsi qu'une hâche en pierre verte ancienne mais bien conservée provenant de Cornouailles. Les reliefs de la présence d'une communautè de Beaker, apparus sous la ligne des tertres de terre rapportée des environs immédiats, semblent expliquer la provenance d'une quantité non négligeable de tessons de poterie et de silex taillés trés caractéristiques retrouvés dans ces tertres et ceux environnants. Un fragment de hâche de combat en camptonite de GROUPE XIV provenant des alentours de Nuneaton dans le comté de Warwick pourrait être arrivé là de cette façon.

Le sol autour du cimetière garde la trace ancienne de champs, d'enclos et de chemins. Il est possible que certains de ces champs recèlent des tertres. Les reliquats de ce paysage ancien s'étendent vers le sud jusquà Amesbury. Son caractère s'est trouvé modifié par l'ajoût extensif et singulier d'un système de rigoles marquant ses limites: d'abord à fond plat (Age du Bronze Récent?) elles furent ensuite en forme de V (Age de Fer). Cette organisation des sols témoigne de l'évolution du mode de leur exploitation au cours de deux demiers millénaires, pendant toute la période Romano-Britannique et jusqu'au Moyen-Age.

Les os d'animaux donnet également une idée plus claire du bétail et des chiens que la communautè de Snail Down possédáit à l'Age du Bronze Ancien, et des animaux sauvages qu'ils chassaient. Les restes de petits mammifères et vertébrés mais aussi d'escargots de plaine et de divers charbons nous informent sur la nature des sols environnants à l'époque des tertres.

RESÜMEE

Snail Down ist ein Hügelgrab-Friedhof aus der frühen Bronzezeit, der sich auf der Salisbury Ebene 8 Meilen nord-östlich von Stonehenge befindet. Die dreiunddreißig Hügel repräsentieren Beispiele für fast jeden Typ des Wessex Hügelgrabes, so wie es erstmals durch Sir Richard Colt Hoare definiert und durch I. V. Grinsell standardisiert wurde. Zwischen 1953 und 1957 wurden Hügelgräber der Typen Kugel, Glocke, Scheibe (zwei kleine Hügel), Untertasse und Teich komplett ausgehoben. Sechs aneinander grenzende Hügel aus zusammengetragener Erde sowie ein weiterer, die von einem Ring aus Pfählen umfasst sind, wurden detailliert untersucht. Zu den Hügelgräbern, die durch selektive Ausgrabung getestet wurden, gehören ein Ringgraben (in Wessex selten) und ein Doppelglocken-Hügelgrab, dessen fürstliche kupferlegierte Grabesgaben – bestechend aus einem spitzbogigen Dolch und einer ringköpfigen Nadel - seit langem bekannt sind.

Der bevorzugte Bestattungsritus auf Snail Down war die Einäscherung und Entsorgung in Grabgruben von durchschmittlicher Größe. Jeweiles ein Hügel bedeckte den Boden eines Bestattungs-Scheiterhaufens. Relativ bescheidene Grabesbeigaben umfassten ein Nahrungsgefäß, eingefasste Urnen, Dekorgefäße, eine Vielzahl von Perlen, kupferlegierte Ahlen, Feuersteine und Knochenarbeiten. Während einer Bestattung eine trepanierte Schädeldecke beigefügt wurde, bot das rituelle Zerschlagen einer Urne den dramatischen Höhepunkt zu einer anderen.

Strukturelle und andere Merkmale, die sich bei den Hügelgräbern wiederholen, legen die Vermutung nahe, dass während der gesamten Bestehungszeit des Friedhofs, dessen Nutzer wahrscheinlich einer einzelnen Gemeinde angehörten, eine weitgehend gleichfömige Bestattungstradition befolgt wurde. Ein Jugendlicher, der an einer Tumorform (*haemangioma*) gelitten hatte und auf der kleinen Erhebung am Fuße eines Glocken-Hügelgrabes beigesetzt wurde, könnte fremd in der Region gewesen sein.

Bestimmungen mittels Radiokarbonmethode unter Verwendung von Kohle und Knochen, die mit einigen der Bestattungen in Verbindung gebracht werden, legen die Vermutung nahe, dass der frühe Bronzezeit Friedhof zwischen 2140 und 1810 ber.v.Chr angelegt und zwischen 1750 und 1440 ber.v.Chr. aufgegeben wurde und somit zwischen 150 und 600 Jahren lang genutzt wurde. Die vorliegende Arbeit schlägt ein Schema zur Chronologie und Datierung des Grabhügel-Friedhofs vor.

Zwei benachbarte Hügelgräber wurden dazu verwendet, eine kleine Serie von Beisetzungsbegräbnissen zu erhalten, von welchen eines durch Radiokarbonmethode auf den Zeitraum 1390-910 ber.v.Chr. datiert wurde (GU-5305:2920±70 BP).

In einigen Hügelgräbern fanden sich einzelne Scherben von Windmill Hill Töpferwaren, sowie eine verwitterte Grünstein-Axt kornischen Ursprungs. Unterhalb der Reihe von Hügelgräbern aus zusammengetragener Erde entdeckte man Überreste einer Beaker Siedlung, welche die beträchtliche Anzahl charakteristischer Topfscherben und Feuersteinarbeiten, die in diesen und umliegenden Hügelgräbern enthalten waren, erklären. Das Bruchstück einer Streitaxt aus de Gruppe XIV Camptonit aus dem Bezirk Nuneaton in Warwickshire könnte gleichen Ursprungs sein.

Das den Friedhof umgebende Land ist mit bloß gelegten Überresten altertümlicher Felder, Einfriedungen und Feldwege bedeckt. Es könnte sich herausstellen, dass einige der Felder unterhalb von Hügelgräbern liegen. Diese Landschaft voller Relikte erstreckt sich südlich bis Amesbury. Ihr Charakter wechselte durch die umfangreiche und bemerkenswerte Anlage von Grenzgräben, welche zunächst einen flachen Boden (späte Bronzezeit?) später jedoch eine V-Form (Eisenzeit) aufwiesen; diese Erdarbeiten repräsentieren die sich wandelnden Arten der Landbewirtschaftung in den letzen zwei Jahrtausenden vor Christus, während des Römisch-britischen Zeitalters bis ins Mittelalter hinein.

Tierknochen geben einerseits Aufschluss über den Viehbestand und die Hunde, welche von der Snail Down Gemeinde in der frühen Bronzezeit gchalten wurden, andererseits über die wilden Tiere, die sie gejaget haben. Überreste kleiner Säuge- und Wirbeltiere, wie auch Landschnecken und Kolhlezeichnungen, liefern Hinweise auf die Beschaffenheit der Umgebung zur Zeit der Hügelgräber.

ACKNOWLEDGEMENTS

Our work at Snail Down was dependent upon contributions from individuals, the majority of whom, alas, it is not possible to acknowledge individually because they were so many. Most were the diggers, who, for love of archaeology, had to find their way to Snail Down without much help from local public transport, camp in rugged conditions and face a not inconsiderable walk morning and night between camp site and Snail Down; who received only modest reimbursement of travel expenses or daily allowance but who were at least, we liked to think, well fed. Many have stayed in touch. Some became close friends. To all of them Charles Thomas and I extend our heartfelt thanks and our admiration for what they did.

My own first and special wish is to express adequate gratitude to Charles Thomas CBE and L V Grinsell OBE, the one for providing inspiration in his irresistible way, and for carrying so much of the day-to-day burden of running the dig, on and off site; to the other for introducing me to Snail Down one warm July day in 1952 and alerting me to the need for a programme of excavation and research there. But, like so many who feel a thrill every time they see a prehistoric barrow, I owe it to Leslie Grinsell for instructing me in the meaning of barrows, especially what can be called their surface architecture, and the need there is and continues to be to protect them and only to carry out carefully designed rescue programmes if a threat cannot be resisted. Because the circumstances surrounding the initiation of the Snail Down excavations are now a part of archaeological history, it has been thought justifiable to describe the process begun in 1952 and the way in which the excavations were carried out, at the beginning of the Introduction and not here. In that section I add further thanks to Leslie Grinsell and to Charles Thomas, explaining in detail the role played by the latter in our running of the excavations. It was wholly and delightfully appropriate that during the first season, on 9 August 1953 to be precise, Leslie Grinsell, with Charles Thomas in tow, discovered a hitherto unrecognised barrow on Snail Down; he noticed it first in Allen's air photograph (Pl 1) and located it on the ground, where its ditch was probed to establish with certainty that SPTA 2244 (see Concordance, below) could safely be mapped and listed. It was unfortunate that this discovery came too late for inclusion in Grinsell's Gazetteer of Wiltshire barrows for the *VCH* (1957).

My thanks go to the President and Council of the Wiltshire Archaeological and Natural History Society for allowing me to accept the Ministry of Public Buildings and Works' invitation to direct the excavations, with paid leave of absence from Devizes Museum for the purpose. During those periods my colleague Ken Annable ran the museum, supported, as always, by Frances and Albert Cole (Thomas 2003). More recently I have received invaluable and unstinted help and information from Dr Paul Robinson and Helen Goodman at Devizes Museum; and from Pamela Colman and Lorna Haycock in the Society's library. Members of the Society were also most generous in their practical support of our work, in the gift or loan of all sorts of equipment, as well as in their visits. Many became volunteers on site, among them Kate Forbes, Heather Benger and Owen Meyrick. Margaret Holmes lent her caravan so that I could be accommodated to a standard that was thought to be of sufficient dignity for an arrogant young curator.

To the then Chief Inspector of Ancient Monuments and Public Buildings at the Ministry of Works, B H St J O'Neil OBE, goes our gratitude for accepting the need for excavation and thereafter for placing the archaeological, scientific and clerical resources of his Department at our disposal. We were very pleased to receive site visits from him as well as from his colleagues John Hurst and Mike Thompson, who did much to ensure smooth financial support of the excavations and the generous supply of stationery, surveying equipment and films. Leo Biek and John Musty facilitated provision of the first radiocarbon determination (Site III) and metallographic analysis of the copper-alloy awls.

During the compilation of this excavation monograph Brian O'Neil's successors at what is now English Heritage have been exceptionally helpful, generous and constructive in all they have done; which has smoothed noticeably the path from field records to publication. Dr Robin Taylor organised the word processing of the initial manuscript, by Anna Eborall and Celsa Ward. Frank Gardiner found funds which enabled the small finds to be drawn; David Jordan further funds for a substantial run of ^{14}C determinations by Alex Bayliss (Section T) as well as the identification of a series of charcoals. This work was done by Dr G T Cook, Dr R A Housley and A J Walker. Camilla Dickson identified the charcoals (Part 2, Section S). Dr S Mays added further comment to Jonathan Musgrave's (Bristol) identification of the fetus from Site II. Members of English Heritage acted as referees of the final text during 1995 and I have been very glad to incorporate their suggestions and corrections in the text.

In 1993, preparation of the text for refereeing was supervised by Jan Summerfield, Finds Officer at English

Heritage (Portsmouth); when that process had been completed, further work was done to improve the text with the considerable help of Buzz Busby, also of English Heritage. Final word-processing and correcting was carried out by Sheila Keyte, from that office. The writer is greatly indebted to them all.

The Wiltshire Archaeological Society warmly acknowledges permission to excavate granted by the late Wilfred Cave MP (who visited the site during each season) and by the Ministry of Defence. Here its Defence Land Agent made every effort to meet our requirements, especially in a liaison role with the Army. Recently, John Loch, of that Agency, and his assistant Miss E J Dolman have provided us with an interesting history of the acquisition of Snail Down and its surroundings by the Ministry of Defence for military training, a complex process spread over several years.

Lt Col G J Hamilton DSO, GSOI, HQ Salisbury Plain District, is thanked for the loan of tents, beds and bedding and much else for our camp, and for filling in the excavations at the end of each season. In 1957 a new Army organisation, the School of Preliminary Education, supplied a work force to erect the tents behind the Crown Hotel at Everleigh. In that village, staff from the David Bruce Laboratories (Royal Army Medical Corps) gave much support in addition to welcome of a more sociable kind that reinforced the good spirit within our camp.

The contribution made by the Royal Commission on the Historical Monuments of England, through its Salisbury Office, was of the greatest importance. Under Collin Bowen OBE, and his colleague (and successor) Desmond Bonney, with Tony Pope and John Davies, the first detailed archaeological survey of Snail Down and its immediate environs was completed. This fieldwork provided the basis for Figure 2A, a plan of the area which was checked and re-surveyed in 1993, using new technology, by the current field staff at Salisbury (now Swindon), under its then head, Mark Corney, with David Field and Jo Donachie in the field. Deborah Cunliffe, Illustrator, drew Figures 1 and 2.

On the vexed problem of barrow numeration from Hoare to the present day, I am grateful for consultation with Roy Canham, of the Wiltshire Library and Museum Service, and his colleague Mrs Lesley Freke, as well as with David Field.

For me and for Charles Thomas, then so recently post-graduate students at the University of London Institute of Archaeology, it was a great comfort to feel that we could count on support and practical help from the many specialists there. Ian Cornwall was a tower of strength, visiting the barrows during our work and undertaking reports on soils and on the burials, cremations as well as inhumations, besides offering more general advice and information. In the Conservation Department, Ione Gedye, with Marjorie Maitland-Howard, helped solve several problems including conservation of the shale and amber beads. Maurice Cookson – Cookie – visited Snail Down and made a number of full-plate black-and-white photographs of a quality for which he was archaeologically renowned. Professor Gordon Childe came to see Snail Down in 1953.

Many scholars, including museum colleagues, gave freely of their knowledge and expertise. Those who contributed special reports to this monograph are acknowledged separately. Professor Richard Atkinson CBE visited the site in 1953 and kindly provided a means of calculating the yield of barrow ditches and the volumes of mounds and banks, from which we have been able to show whether the ditch surrounding a mound or contained within a bank, could have supplied enough material for such earthworks.

Through English Heritage, the School of Archaeological Studies at the University of Leicester undertook to supply a report on the flints from Snail Down (Part 2, Section G). Professor Richard Bradley, Department of Archaeology, University of Reading, kindly gave me access to the results of his Department's survey of the land between the rivers Avon and Winterbourne, Everleigh and Amesbury, within which the Snail Down barrows lie. Now published (Bradley *et al* 1994), this enables Snail Down to be viewed within a much broader context, an ancient landscape that survives amazingly intact not least because so much of this land remains within the care of the War Department and has thus been protected from the plough and other machinery of earthwork destruction. Their figure 1 includes broad indications of the earthworks and field systems within this landscape, with Snail Down towards its northern margin. I wish to thank, in particular, Frances Raymond, who read and corrected two drafts of my report on Sites VI and VII, proper interpretation of which depended so heavily upon the results of the Reading Survey in which she played an important part. She is also acknowledged below for her contribution on the later Bronze Age, Iron Age and some Romano-British pottery, Section E.

Paul Ashbee has written a comment on the archaeological significance of the radiocarbon determinations in Section T. It was entirely through his enthusiasm that I approached English Heritage with a request for such work, rather late in the day, and I am thankful to him for helping to add so directly and scientifically to the value of this report and to our knowledge of the order in which the barrow cemetery was extended during the third and second millennia BC.

In my search for excavation mementoes (Section U) I received help from Dr Paul Robinson and Helen Goodman, Clare Conybeare, Peter Saunders and Janet A Bell, Stanley Jenkins and his colleagues at Avebury Museum, and Edwina Proudfoot.

On several occasions I received assistance from colleagues at the City of Bristol Museum and Art Gallery: Ray Barnett, Roger Clark, Paul Elkin, David Eveleigh and Fiona Macalister. I am especially indebted to Martyn Heighton, Director of Leisure Services at Bristol, who allowed me considerable leave of absence during my last year at Bristol Museum to complete this report. Ann Linge, draughtsperson in the Museum's rescue archaeology unit (now Bristol and Region Archaeological Services), was responsible for drawing most of the pottery and the small finds as well as Figures 2A, 60 and 61. Frances Raymond made her own drawings of the later Bronze Age and Iron Age wares; most of the flints were drawn by Andy Howe.

Fiona Roe and Vincent Davies kindly supplied a new petrological identification of the greenstone axe from Site II which, with the battle-axe fragment from Site XIV, had been sliced and grouped in the fifties through the good offices of Dr F S Wallis and Dr J F S Stone.

I am pleased to acknowledge the general help provided by P Dorrell, Howard Hughes, Donald Grose, D D Mundy, J F S Stone and the staff of the library at the Society of Antiquaries of London.

I would like, particularly, to thank the following, who made an especial contribution to the excavations in the field: Duncan and Paddy Christie, Bryan Clausen, Ian Cossar, James Dyer, Kate Forbes, Bret Guthrie, Peter and Juliet Jewell, Vincent Megaw, Owen Meyrick, Mary-Jane Mountain, Gladys Pike and Barbara de Seyssel. Whereas the routine record photography was done by myself, we were privileged to receive visits from Maurice Cookson; and several images were provided by E Peacock (Devizes) and Colin Jordan (Luton). Ian Cossar and Vincent Megaw also helped with record photography.

Mrs Audrey Summers supplied a note (Section V) on the SPTA continuing vegetation study of Site I.

Whereas sole responsibility for errors and omissions is my own, I acknowledge with considerable gratitude the special part played in its preparation by Dr Isobel Smith. She devoted much time to a scholarly and detailed critique of the first draft, which improved the final text immeasurably.

This monograph has been written and compiled by me. It is my privilege to make clear, however, that the excavations were a joint collaboration with Professor Charles Thomas CBE FBA FSA. The division of our responsibilities in the field is explained fully in the first part of the introduction. Authorship of specialist reports is identified at the head of each.

Nicholas Thomas
Newlyn, Cornwall, Spring 2003

INTRODUCTION

*Our researches commenced in July 1805; and though they did not prove equally satisfactory with
those in the immediate neighbourhood of Stonehenge, yet they did not turn out
totally devoid of interest and novelty*

Sir Richard Colt Hoare (1812, 181)

THE SCOPE OF THE PROJECT AND ITS ORGANISATION

In July 1951 L V Grinsell alerted the President of the Wiltshire Archaeological and Natural History Society (WAS), R B Pugh, and Brian O'Neil, Chief Inspector of Ancient Monuments and Historic Buildings at the Ministry of Works, that the barrows on Snail Down were still suffering from military tank training. His correspondence with O'Neil won agreement in principle that excavation was advisable, together with better protection in the field. The latter was difficult to implement because legal control of ancient monuments by scheduling did not apply to sites on Crown land. O'Neil suggested that his Department would fund rescue excavation when a suitably trained archaeologist could be found for the work.

Exactly one year later, I was taken by Leslie Grinsell to see the barrows on Snail Down. I had become Curator of Devizes Museum (now Wiltshire Heritage Museum) on the first day of that July. Leslie Grinsell had equally recently moved to Bristol to assume Curatorship of the Department of Archaeology and Ethnography at the City Museum; his monumental work on the gazetteer of field monuments of the prehistoric, Roman and pagan Saxon periods for the Victoria County History of Wiltshire (Grinsell 1957) had just been completed, although he continued to be an occasional visitor to Devizes as long as details remained to be checked (*ibid* 1989, 23–24).

An excursion to Snail Down that August impressed us with the serious damage that the mounds had suffered and were continuing to suffer intermittently from military training with tanks. We felt that, with so much turf and subsoil ripped away by tank tracks, and often a deep channel ground down into the body of the larger mounds, wind, rain and frost in future years would continue a process begun before the outbreak of the Second World War. Brian O'Neil visited Snail Down with me that Autumn and it was accepted that the Ministry of Works would fund a programme of rescue excavations for at least three four-week seasons spread over five years. The first season was to take place in July and August 1953. The Society agreed to organise the excavation and release me, their Curator, to be its Director. This arrangement followed the model established between the Ministry of Works and the Ashmolean Museum, Oxford, for the excavations during the later forties and early fifties at Dorchester (Oxon: Atkinson *et al* 1951a; Whittle *et al* 1992).

Moving on to the present day, the greatest care is taken by the Ministry of Defence, through its Defence Land Agent at Durrington, to ensure that the Snail Down cemetery remains out of bounds to all military units training in the area. Peace has returned to this, one of the largest and finest barrow fields in the United Kingdom. Yet it is to be regretted that less concern has been shown to the often inconspicuous earthworks that surround the barrows and extend towards Sidbury Hill and beyond, particularly the rectangular layout of bank and ditch that encloses them, our Sites VI and VII, Enclosure A in Figure 2. The complex north-west corner of that earthwork, which was planned and excavated in 1957, has been heavily damaged in recent years and hidden beneath the improved surface given to the track that skirts the western side of Weather Hill Firs. Rescue excavation became a strong force in ensuring that the Snail Down barrows, at least, have received no further human damage. How seriously this is now taken is shown by the statutory protection afforded even to the spoil heaps of 1953 around Site I, which were left surrounding the completely cleared and unrestored disc-barrow so that future weathering of an exposed chalk surface and its re-colonisation by plants could be studied (Section V). They have become part of a scheduled ancient monument.

Rescue was the immediate purpose behind the excavations and their justification to the Ministry of Works, but scholarship was the principal spur. The Stourhead Collection at the Wiltshire Heritage Museum contained an incomparable series of later Neolithic and Early Bronze Age grave groups from barrows, about whose burial circumstances almost nothing was known. Detailed associations of objects, the sex of burials, ritual that happened around the grave before interment and barrow building, the internal structure of barrows, the shape of their ditches and the nature of the mounds' covering: about details such as these, of fundamental importance in our study of burial sites in Wiltshire, only very little was on record. For the most part we depended for information upon what Sir Richard Colt Hoare (1758–1838) had chosen to include in *Ancient Wiltshire* (1812, 1819) from the more detailed notes with which William Cunnington (1754–1810) had supplied him. Moreover, their excavations had been restricted to a central shaft, hardly ever opened out into an area excavation (the apparently extended trench at Bush Barrow (Crawford and Keiller 1928, pl XXXIIIa) was unusual). Complete excavation of a Wiltshire Bronze Age round barrow under modern conditions had hardly occurred: certainly not of a substantial mound and its surrounding ditch; not at all of special types like disc-barrows and saucers. Atkinson's work at the pond-barrow on Sheep Down (Dorset: Atkinson *et al* 1951) had been the first on that kind of barrow. The work of Ashbee, Greenfield, Vatcher, Christie and others lay ahead. This was one of the archaeological objectives behind the excavations we planned and which helped to dictate the sites we selected both for total clearance and for more restricted examination. Broadly put, we sought to uncover the full sequence of burial and ritual in a series of barrows, whose central grave goods had resided within the Stourhead Collection since the days of Hoare's and Cunnington's excavations about 1805. This great assemblage had been acquired by the Wiltshire Archaeological and Natural History Society in 1883 (Cunnington and Goddard 1896, i; Pugh 1953, 9, 20; Annable and Simpson 1964).

Our other objectives were to try to establish the order in which Snail Down's thirty-three mounds had been built, and over what period of time; and to study the relationship of the barrows to the enclosure – Enclosure A – that surrounded them.

Charles Thomas and I had been students of Professor V Gordon Childe at the University of London Institute of Archaeology. I completed my Diploma in 1952, Charles Thomas a year later his: it was natural that I should invite him to join me for three seasons of excavation at Snail Down. As an employee of the Wiltshire Archaeological and Natural History Society and Ministry of Works Site Supervisor, I took overall responsibility for the project. Charles Thomas was Assistant Supervisor and he also ran the tented camp that accommodated our labour force, up to about forty volunteers at any one time. A number of people who later achieved prominence in archaeology and related subjects cut some of their teeth at Snail Down, among them Peter Fowler, Vincent Megaw, James Dyer, Patricia Christie, the Higham brothers, Mary-Jane Mountain, Jeffrey May, Peter and Juliet Jewell, Ellen Macnamara, Bernard Wailes, David Ridgway, Bryan Clausen and Anthony Gunstone.

In 1953 we inhabited the Nissen huts of a Second World War prison camp immediately to the east of Lower House Farm, Everleigh, the home of Wilfred Cave, former MP for Devizes. Two student caterers from the Bath Academy of Domestic Science lived with us and provided all our meals. In 1955 and 1957 a tented camp was established in the paddock behind The Crown Hotel at Everleigh, where Hoare and Cunnington had stayed in 1805. Catering arrangements remained the same. Volunteers were charged less than £3 per week for full board and camping, and we paid a grant of up to £3, or wages of about 1/- (5p) per day, towards the costs of travel. The annual budget, excluding the Supervisors' fees, provided by the Ministry of Works was £350. The tented camp, including beds and bedding, was supplied in 1955 and 1957 by the Army, from their stores depot at Tidworth. Site huts, latrines and digging equipment were hired from F Rendell and Sons Ltd, and W E Chivers and Sons Ltd, both of Devizes. The Ministry of Works lent surveying equipment, gave stationery and photographic supplies and printed the films.

In consultation with the Ministry of Works, Charles Thomas and I decided what each four-week programme was to be; supervision of the sites to be involved was allocated between us. On occasion the work was directed jointly, for example Sites X-XIV in 1957. In the site reports that follow, I have indicated these allocations. All aspects of the work were carried out by the assembled team, including photography, where I held special responsibility for full coverage. In 1953 and 1955 we were fortunate to be visited by the late Maurice Cookson, of the University of London Institute of Archaeology: those of his images that are published here are acknowledged.

In 1955 and 1957 Collin Bowen, of the Royal Commission on the Historical Monuments of England (RCHME), Salisbury Office, with members of his staff, carried out a detailed survey of the Snail Down barrows. They established for the first time an accurate concept of the assortment of barrows on Snail Down and their inter-relationship, and the nature of the earthworks that surround them, traversed here and there by trackways and other features bearing little regard for this strikingly defined space. Their work provided the basis for a more exacting planning programme carried out under David Field in February 1993 using new technology. Figure 2 is the highly informative outcome, together with particular plans of Sites X-XIV with III and XVII, and Sites XIX and XXII (Figs 21, 33). During the course of this work in 1957, Collin Bowen discovered the pond-barrow, Site XVI. Our debt to these renowned field archaeologists is considerable.

THE PHYSICAL* AND ARCHAEOLOGICAL BACKGROUND

In the region of Salisbury, the River Avon and its four principal tributaries – Ebble, Nadder, Wylye and Bourne – radiate northwards and round to the west, dividing the Upper and Middle Chalk uplands of Salisbury Plain into a series of wedges of gently rolling open downs, defined quite sharply by their valleys. Along the north, the edge of this famous Wiltshire chalk country ends in a notable scarp, the ground falling rapidly from around 500ft into the Vale of Pewsey, whose Malmstone and sands of the Upper Greensand are revealed along an east-west geological upfold that breached the chalk. Lower Chalk fringes the southern edge of the Pewsey Vale. Two rivers have broken through the Vale's dramatically rising south side, the Avon itself and the Bourne to the east, and their valleys define one of these wedge-shaped areas of chalkland. Towards the northern end of this segment of Salisbury Plain occurs the barrow cemetery of Snail Down (SU 21785211, Site VIII). It lies within the shadow of Sidbury

* This description is based upon the essay 'The Physique of Wiltshire', by Joyce Gifford (1957, 1–20).

Hill, one of those rare, isolated High Summits, rising to 735ft OD, which characterise parts of the chalk uplands. Their surface deposits betray the former existence of a much higher plain of which they were once part, that was to become submerged by the Late Pliocene marine transgression.

Much of Salisbury Plain can be divided into a Higher Plain around the north and west, lying mainly between 650 and 450ft OD, and a Lower Plain at its heart, generally occurring within limits of 450/400 and 300/250ft OD. Sometimes the break in level between these two areas of chalkland is noticeable. Thus a marked scarp separates the region within which stands Snail Down from the Lower Plain that occupies the southern part of the land between Avon and Bourne. Beacon Hill Ridge marks a narrow final extension southwards from Sidbury Hill of the Higher Plain. Nine Mile River, a minor tributary that enters the Avon at Bulford, flows just to the west of this scarp.

A glance at the geological base of the distribution maps of the County in *A History of Wiltshire* (Gifford 1957) shows the location of the High Summits that comprise the third element of the Plain's chalklands. They lie for the most part above 650 ft OD and form a dramatic edge to the Plain where it finishes along the line of the Vale of Pewsey. Sidbury, as we have indicated, though isolated as a rounded hill, belongs to this aspect of the chalk of central Wiltshire. The top and sides of Sidbury are mantled with loamy red clay and shattered flints characteristic of the cover to much of the High Summits hereabouts. These deposits are spread mainly southwards from the Hill, but its northern slopes also carry such material, re-deposited by weathering.

Sidbury Hill dominates the country between Avon and Bourne. It has no rival until Easton Hill is encountered over five miles to the north, at the very edge of the Vale of Pewsey. A little further north-east, Wexford Down rises even higher, another relic of the High Summits. Southward it is possible to see Sidbury Hill from Woodhenge and from Stonehenge. Clearly visible within a region carrying a significant farming population in Neolithic and Bronze Age times, and witnessing from these early periods an exceptional concentration of religious monuments and burial mounds, long and round, it is reasonable to believe that Sidbury Hill would have been a special place to those living round about.

The Snail Down barrow cemetery evolved along the shallowly sloping north side of a slight combe which has creased the downland gently, westwards from the Bourne valley. Its head runs out below the crest of a ridge west of the cemetery, called Weather Hill. This combe contains drift gravel, which may explain the more flinty ancient land surface encountered beneath Site XIX on Snail Down (Fig 2), although there was no trace of gravel in the area of the pond-barrow, Site XVI.

The ground southwards rises gradually, before its much steeper elevation into Sidbury Hill. Immediately to the north of the cemetery the land levels off: it provides a false crest so that for those standing among the barrows it is impossible to see what lies beyond in that direction. Westward, another more distant crest, Weather Hill, conceals the road from Everleigh to Bulford and everything beyond. Southeastwards, however, the land is revealed widely, across the Bourne to the high ground of Warren Hill and that extensive range of rounded hills running south towards Winterslow.

Except to the southeast which is noticeably more wooded as the Bourne valley is approached, the region in which the Snail Down barrows are set supports open downland grasses and characteristic wild flowers and weeds, with light scattered scrub. The land is very well drained and lack of water must always have presented a problem in mixed farming. Two prominent dew ponds lying between Sites II and XVI (Fig 2), one circular, the other square, are witness to this shortage.

Yet trackways, criss-crossing Snail Down from early times until the outbreak of the Second World War, show how active the local farming community has always been here. Some of these tracks are shown in Figure 2, including one (T3) that has been carried on a shallow causeway across the lowest, and sometimes slightly damp part of the combe we have described. Until 1937, Snail Down lay in an area that was being farmed. Between 1937 and 1939 the region was acquired for military training by the Ministry of Defence (John Loch*, pers comm). But even before 1937, tanks had begun to use the main lines of barrows as a switchback affording useful – and irresistible – training for their crews (Loch, *ibid*). Early evidence of this activity can be seen in G W G Allen's famous air photograph of the cemetery taken from the south (Pl 1) in 1939 (Clark 1941, fig 92; Edwards 1984, fig 55). In recent years, with the use of tanks long since prohibited (although they operated around the northern skirts of Sidbury while our excavations were in progress), the area to the west of the barrows, about Weather Hill Firs, has become a parachute dropping zone. Snail Down today supports the kind of open downland vegetation that it has known for centuries. Essentially this is a regime of wild grasses sheltering those small flowers that make the chalkland such a delight. But a substantial population of rabbits has re-colonised the barrows and later earthworks since our excavations, and bushes and weeds have proliferated on and among the barrows: common elder (*Sambucus nigra*), blackthorn (*Prunus spinosa*) and hawthorn (*Crataegus monogyna*); and stinging nettles (*Urtica dioica*), ragwort (*Senecio jacobaea*) and thistles (*Circium repens* and *C. vulgare*). Several barrows are now suffering more from rabbits than from the military threats of former times.

Sidbury Hill supplies the nearest source of indigenous trees today. These include ash (*Fraxinus excelsior*), with some oak (*Quercus robur*) and sycamore (*Acer pseudoplatanus*): hawthorn, blackthorn and elder can also be found on the hill. On Cow Down, north-east of Sidbury, there is dogwood (*Cornus sanguinea*), and scrub that includes buckthorn (*Rhamnus cathartica*), as well as other species of bush and weed that are the product of a rabbit population occurring there too.

At the present time negotiations are in hand to give Snail Down and a much more extensive area southwards the status of a Site of Special Scientific Interest (Audrey Summers, pers comm).

---

* Senior Land Agent, Ministry of Defence, Defence Land Agent, Estate Office, Durrington, until 1995.

Snail Down got its name, we believe, from the profile of Site XIX, a massive double bell-barrow at the south-eastern corner of the cemetery (Fig 2). The northern of its two mounds is smaller and lower than the main mound and looks for all the world like a snail protruding from its shell when viewed from east or west. Otherwise, Snail Down supports a no larger population of land snails than any other part of the chalk downland of the Plain. Duchy of Lancaster documents in the Public Record Office give the name, Snayle down, for the first time in 1553 (Gover *et al* 1939, 345). Derivation of Sidbury Hill is less easy to explain. Shidbury and Chydebur' are recorded from 1325; Sydbury Hill in 1571. While derivation of the second element bury (OE burg, town, castle) is obvious enough, the first is not. Some bring it from the OE *scydd*, source of the modern word shed or small building (*ibid*, 343). Such structures may have existed on the hill, perhaps to shelter shepherds or swineherds, having sufficient prominence to give rise to a place-name. If, however, the first element was derived from the German *Schutt*, 'alluvial soil', 'bank of earth', 'mound', 'rubble' (Mawer *et al* 1929, 132–133) it provides an obvious reference to the Iron Age hill-fort whose substantial ramparts crown the hill.

The name Collingbourne refers to the upper part of the Bourne river: the stream of Col(l)a's people. It is first recorded in the early 10th century (Gover *et al* 1939, 345). Ducis derives from landholdings hereabouts of the earls (later dukes) of Lancaster (*ibid*, 343).

This wedge of the Plain between Avon and Bourne down to Salisbury undoubtedly supported a pioneer farming population from at least the fourth millennium BC (Piggott 1971, 48–49), but field monuments indicating such early settlement appear few. Grinsell's distribution map (1957, Map II) plots eight long barrows between the Pewsey Vale and Salisbury. Of these only two occur north of Sidbury. That at Weather Hill, which may have had a close neighbour now destroyed (*ibid*, 140, Fittleton 5 and 5a), lies nearest to Snail Down. At present the long barrow concentration occurs south of Sidbury, between Figheldean Field and Milston Down. Yet fieldworkers continue to remind us that our picture of ancient occupation hereabouts is incomplete. In recent years the double-entrance henge monument on Weather Hill, about 4400ft (1.3km) north-west of Snail Down, recorded on the SMR in 1980, has been surveyed (McOmish *et al* 2002, 33, 37)); and the RCHME team has been able to show that the Snail Down barrows are surrounded by traces of complex field systems. Both these discoveries have an important bearing upon the Beaker settlement lying beneath Sites X-XIV, and even upon the Middle Bronze Age sherds and the small inhumation cemetery added to Site XV, recovered during our excavations. David Field and Mark Corney have described the new survey below.

South of Sidbury Hill, it is principally the Lower Plain chalk that carries dense concentrations of round barrows (Grinsell 1957, Map V). North of Nine Mile River, great cemeteries occur on Silk Hill and above Choulston Farm, Figheldean. South of that stream, cemeteries on Brigmerston Down and Milston Down are outstanding (Fig 1), with major spreads of mounds above Bulford Camp and southwards of Durrington.

North of Sidbury the concentrations of barrows are less impressive (Fig 1). Nothing exceeds, even approaches, the monumentality of Snail Down. To the east, Cow Down (Collingbourne Ducis: Lukis 1867) offers a well-organised double alignment of barrows, ten bowls (two overlapping) pointing clearly towards Sidbury, with a second more minor row, but including a disc-barrow, on a parallel orientation immediately to the north. Northwards of Snail Down, the chalk downland contains a relatively insignificant number of round barrows. Of those shown in Ashbee's map (1986, 25, fig 1), only the Milton Lilbourne barrows and those at Pewsey Hill Farm (Vatcher, F de M, 1960), the Everleigh barrows and some on Bohune Down may claim to be cemeteries or barrow fields. The rest form a thin scatter of mainly isolated mounds.

Donation and Location of the Finds and the Excavation Archive from Snail Down

The artefacts and other finds and samples accumulated during the course of the Snail Down excavations have been deposited at the Wiltshire Heritage Museum as a gift through the courtesy of the Ministry of Defence (Thomas 1956, 181). Here they join the small series of objects found at the barrows by Hoare in 1805–1806, which together will provide data for future students of the Bronze Age, as well as an attractive, interesting selection of material for public display and education. The human and animal bones and the charcoals are included among the finds: snails and soil samples have not been preserved. Original plan and section drawings, site notebooks, diaries and an extensive archive of photographs (with their negatives) and slides are also to be found at the museum.

Snail Down, general bibliography

Published references to the excavated barrows have been listed at the beginning of each site description. The following general references have also been made to the cemetery and its related earthworks.

Hoare 1812; Clark 1941, pl 92; Grinsell 1953, 171; Hawkes 1954, 107; Thomas, A C, 1954; Grinsell 1958, 375; Thomas, S, 1965, pl 136; Fowler 1967, 34–35, 82, figs 16, 17; Grinsell and Dyer 1971, 66, No 53; Clayton 1976, 91; Thomas, N 1976, 228–232, figs 54–58, and pp 19, 21, 22, figs 6, 9 and 10; Bowen 1978, 118–119; Dyer 1981, 279–280, fig 27; Edwards 1984, 56, fig 55; Dyer 1997, 97–98, pl 34; Woodward 2000, *passim*, and fig 39, colour plate 15; Dyer 2001, 198.

Before this report went to press, *The Field Archaeology of the Salisbury Plain Training Area*, by David McOmish, David Field and Graham Brown was published (2002. Swindon: English Heritage). It contains numerous references to the Snail Down barrows and related earthworks; among illustrations, there is an important air photograph in colour, taken from the west (fig 2.26). Figure 2.18 includes a survey of the class II henge monument at Weather Hill, referred to in the Introduction to this Snail Down report.

Fig 1 Location of Snail Down and surrounding prehistoric monuments, RCHME, 1993, and the Reading Survey (Bradley *et al* 1994, fig 10). Letters A–D mark the corners of Enclosure A. Letters E, F, J, K mark the corners of Enclosure B.

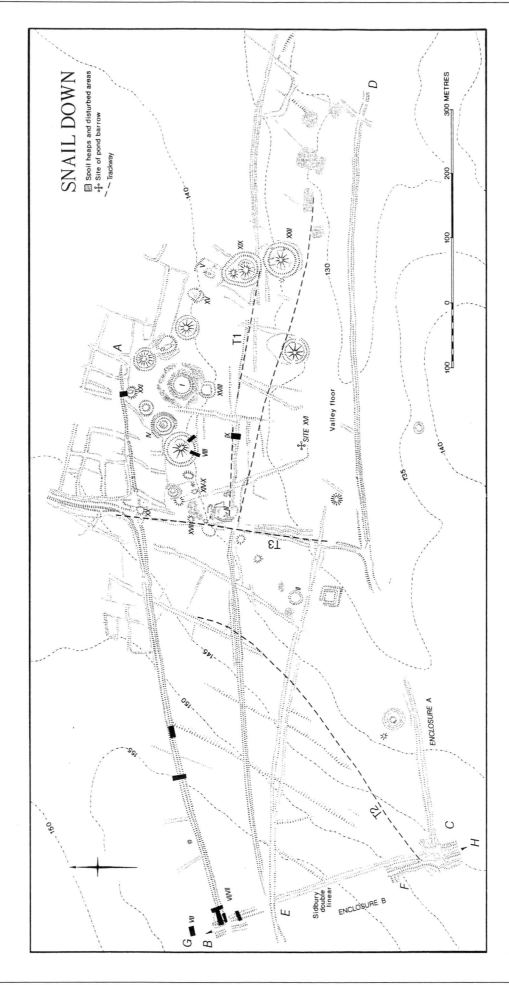

Fig 2 Snail Down, the barrow cemetery, related earthworks and underlying features (RCHME, 1993, incorporating RCHME 1957). Sections 9, 10 (Fig 20), respectively along and across side *AB* of Enclosure A, Site VI, are located 200–250m east of corner B of Enclosure A

SNAIL DOWN: CONCORDANCE OF BARROW AND EARTHWORK NUMBERS

Sir Richard Colt Hoare (1812, 180, plan), Canon E H Goddard (1914), L V Grinsell (1957; *VCH*), the Royal Commission on the Historical Monuments of England (RCHME), the County's Sites and Monuments Record (SMR), the Ministry of Defence's Salisbury Plain Training Area (SPTA) and our excavation programme 1953–1957 each produced a numbering system for some or all of the barrows on Snail Down. RCHME achieved the first comprehensive list of individually numbered mounds in 1957 (Fig 2A). It included the two barrows discovered during the course of our excavations, Site XVI and the saucer-barrow 2244, (shown in fig 2A as CD6c and CD6b respectively). RCHME established proper numeration of the two confused and confusing alignments between Sites III and VIII, our Sites X-XIV and those immediately N,

2220, 2231 and 2235 with Site XVII, where, before, even the VCH numeration had gone astray.

Throughout this monograph, barrows excavated in 1953–1957 are referred to by their site number in roman numerals (Sites I-XXII). All others carry their SPTA number in arabic. Thus Hoare's Hunter's Barrow is 2253. Table 1 sets out the six existing systems of numbers for Snail Down, together with our own; National Grid map references were supplied by RCHME. Table 2 does the same for linear and other features on Snail Down. Figure 2A locates the parish boundary dividing Collingbourne Ducis from Collingbourne Kingston and shows the SPTA number for every barrow. This plan of Snail Down, prepared by RCHME in 1953–1957, indicates all barrows as they appeared before excavation. It was published by H C Bowen in 1978 (115–123, fig 1).

Table 1   Snail Down: concordance of numbering schemes for barrows, and NG references

Barrows excavated, 1953–1957	Hoare, *Ancient Wiltshire* (1812) (1914)	*VCH (1957) subsuming Goddard*	Corrections, additions to VCH	RCHME (1957)	Wilts SMR (1975)	SPTA (1984)	National Grid references
I	18	CK18		12	SU 25 SW 626	2249	SU21875210
II	4	CK6		30	SU 25 SW 607	2213	SU21555194
III	?7 or 8	CK8		27	SU 25 SW 610	2224	SU21685205
IV	14	CK14		16	SU 25 SW 620	2245	SU21815214
V	23	–	CD3a	4	SU 25 SW 629	2266	SU22025208
VIII	13	CK13		17	SU 25 SW 619	2240	SU21785211
X	12	CK10		18	SU 25 SW 618	2237	SU21745210
XI	-	CK22		19	SU 25 SW 617	2234	SU21735210
XII	-	?CK23	CK23	20	SU 25 SW 616	2233	SU21715209
XIII	?8	?CK23	CK23a	21	SU 25 SW 615	2225	SU21715209
XIV	-	–	CK23b or ?CK24	22	SU 25 SW 615	2615	SU21705209
XV	22	CD3		5	SU 25 SW 628	2262	SU22025208
XVI	–	–	CD6c	8	SU 25 SW 633	2239	SU21775195
XVII	?7 or 8	CK25		25	SU 25 SW 611	2222	SU21675210
XVIII	20	CK17		13	SU 25 SW 627	2247	SU21865207
XIX	24	CD4		2	SU 25 SW 630	2268	SU22055202
XX	11	CK12		33	SU 25 SW 634	2229	SU21695217
XXI	16	CK16		14	SU 25 SW 622	2248	SU21865219
XXII	25, King Barrow	CD5		1	SU 25 SW 631	2269	SU22065196
	2	CK4		31	SU 25 SW 648	2207	SU21385179
	3	CK5		32	SU 25 SW 647	2205	SU21345181
	6	CK7		28	SU 25 SW 609	2217	SU21645202

Table 1   *Continued*

Barrows excavated, 1953–1957	Hoare, *Ancient Wiltshire* (1812)	*VCH (1957) subsuming Goddard (1914)*	Corrections, additions to VCH	RCHME (1957)	Wilts SMR (1975)	SPTA (1984)	National Grid references
	5	CK7a		29	SU 25 SW 608	2216	SU21625199
	?7 or 8	CK9		26	SU 25 SW 612	2220	SU21655207
	9	CK10a		24	SU 25 SW 613	2231	SU21705211
	10	CK11		23	SU 25 SW 614	2235	SU21725213
	15	CK15		15	SU 25 SW 621	2246	SU21845216
	17, Hunter's Barrow	CK19		11	SU 25 SW 623	2253	SU21925216
	19	CK20		7	SU 25 SW 624	2255	SU21945213
	1	CD1		10	SU 25 SW 649	2209	SU21415150
	21	CD2		6	SU 25 SW 625	2257	SU21975210
	26	CD6		3	SU 25 SW 632	2254	SU21935194
	–	–	CD6b	9	SU 25 SW 733	2244	SU21825175
	–	CD6a		–	SU 25 SW 646	2204	SU21315124

Table 2   Snail Down: concordance of numbering schemes for features other than barrows, and NG references

Type of site	Excavated sites 1953–1957	Wilts SMR	SPTA	NGR
Field system		SU 25 SW 701	2185	*c* SU21505240
Linear ditches	GH; VI VII	SU 25 SW 681	2181	SU21005210-SU21455080
	AB; VI	SU 25 SW 684	2191	SU21055201-SU21905215
	BC; VI VII	SU 25 SW 681	2181	SU21255145 (centre)
	CD	SU 25 SW 685	2197	SU21205179-SU22705180
Trackways	T1; IX (and III)	SU 25 SW 302	2219	SU21005195-SU22505195
	T2	SU 25 5W 785	2206	SU21165174-SU21555217
	T3; (XVII)	SU 25 SW 780	2242	SU22005310-SU21505140
Romano-British settlement		SU 25 SW 709	2274	SU21705235

A SURVEY OF THE EARTHWORKS
ON SNAIL DOWN

DAVID FIELD AND MARK CORNEY

INTRODUCTION AND BACKGROUND

The Snail Down Barrow cemetery and its environs represent one of the finest prehistoric funerary landscapes to survive in Wessex. Located 1.5km south-east of the village of Everleigh (NGR centre SU 218520), the complex lies within the range boundary of the Ministry of Defence's Salisbury Plain Training Area (SPTA). Initial fieldwork on the Down was carried out by the Royal Commission on the Historical Monuments of England during the 1950s and the area then revisited during the 1990s as part of the Commission's major survey of the earthworks in the military training area.

Set in open chalk downland, the cemetery comprises 33 barrows occupying a gentle south-facing slope towards the head of a valley, now dry, that gives access to the River Bourne, a kilometre distant to the east. The immediate environs contain a palimpsest of Wessex downland field archaeology, with Prehistoric to Romano-British field systems, linear ditches, trackways, quarries, and areas of 'ridge and furrow'. The earliest cartographic evidence here would appear to be in 1773, when Andrew's and Dury's *Map of Wiltshire* was published. At that time the area was depicted as open downland and the name 'Seven Barrows' appended. The first detailed investigation of Snail Down, however, was made by Colt Hoare (1812, 181–186, plan opp 180), who recorded the presence of 26 barrows, excavating a number of them, along with linear features and a 'British settlement'.

Use of the area by the military from the turn of the century, while protecting it from the ravages of agriculture, also produced the episode for which the site is best known, the tank tracks across the barrow mounds. A local shepherd (pers comm) was eyewitness to the event and recalled that the main damage resulted from a group of US Sherman tanks that drove across each barrow in turn when they were stationed nearby during WWII. However, air photographs indicate that vehicles had crossed the mounds before the war, and it may be that others subsequently followed, deepening and enhancing the ruts, leaving the barrows with gashes of up to 1m deep across them. Concern over this activity led to the excavation programme of the 1950s (discussed in this report) and prompted RCHME to produce a plan of the area (Bowen 1978, 118). This recorded the barrows as well as the surrounding linears at small scale. The pond-barrow and a saucer-barrow on the opposite hillslope were also discovered as a result of this fieldwork.

Although for the most part spared the ravages of modern agricultural methods, the complex has in the recent past been subject to severe damage by military vehicles. Such activity has now ceased and Snail Down forms part of the designated Archaeological Site Group (ASG) 11, which affords it protection as an environmentally sensitive area. Vehicle exclusion signs and incorporation of the site within the Everleigh air-dropping zone keep ground activity to a minimum, and damage now is restricted to that from rabbits and the growth of scrub.

The introduction of EDM survey equipment during the latter decades of the 20th century allowed large areas of archaeological landscape to be tackled to a degree not previously contemplated and a re-survey of Snail Down was conducted as part of the Commission's wider survey of earthworks on the SPTA. The surveyed area is bounded on three sides by linear ditches and on the fourth by an area of quarrying and includes a range of other earthworks, 'Celtic' fields, trackways, as well as bowl, bell, saucer, disc and pond barrows. As previously noted, the site occupies the head of a small dry valley, the lower parts of which are seasonally flooded and which in former times held a small stream issuing from springs close to the barrow group. Its gravels now occupy the valley floor.

THE BARROWS

The cemetery is arranged in a loose arc or crescent, with outliers to the south and southeast. Other isolated barrows lie within the immediate hinterland and just 1km to the southeast a further nucleated group on Cow Down are intervisible (Figs 1, 2). Together with a number of other groups they form part of a concentration situated around the base of the prominent Sidbury Hill, located c1km to the south, and they form part of an important wider concentration of some 300 isolated and grouped barrows situated between Wilsford (S) and Everleigh, mostly alongside the Avon and Nine Mile Rivers, that is among the densest in the country (Fleming 1971).

SPTA No	Type	Diameter (excluding ditch)	Height
2213 (Site II)	Saucer	15m	0.3m

Surrounded by a ditch, 3m wide by 0.5m deep. Central tump 7m diameter. Partly backfilled after excavation, with remains of spoil heaps to west, northeast and west: track encroaching on the south.

2216	Bowl	16m	1.5m

No ditch visible. Mound damaged by military vehicles to a depth of 0,5m.

2217	Bowl	19m	1.2m

No ditch visible. Mound damaged by military vehicles to a depth of 1m.

2224 (Site III)	Bell		

Almost completely removed by military and archaeological agencies. Site now marked by a confused mass of mounds and hollows. Arc of ditch recorded suggests a diameter of 35m. Damaged by military vehicles and the south edge overlain by a bank and track.(Site IX).

2222 (Site XVII)	Bowl	13m	1m

No ditch visible.

2220	Bowl	22m x 15m NNE-SSW	0.4m

Excavation hollow on summit; track (T3) encroaches upon the east side.

2231	Bowl	16m	1.5 m

No ditch visible and cut by 2235 on its east side.

2235	Bowl	17m	1.5m

Central tump 8m diameter and 0.4m high. Traces of a surrounding bank of uncertain date impinging on 2231.

2225	(Site XIII)	Bowl (site of)	

No trace on ground, but shallow scarps may represent excavation.

2233	(Site XII)	Bowl (site of)	

Possibly the mound to the south of 2231. If so it is a slightly oval bowl, with maximum measurements c14m x 9m x 0.4m high. No ditch visible. Appears to have been placed on or incorporated in a field lynchet or linear feature of early date (see below).

2234 (Site XI)	Bowl		

Possibly the small (5m diameter) mound east of 2233. No ditch visible and incorporated in a lynchet.

2237 (Site X)	Bowl	max 20m	0.9m

Slightly oval mound oriented NNE – SSW, maximum 20m by 15m

2240 (Site VIII)	Bell	29m	3.3m

Ditch 7m wide, 0.5m deep and separated from the mound by a 5–7m wide berm. Damaged by military vehicles to a depth of 1m. Irregularities in the southern arc of the ditch include a pre-war pit and excavation trenches of 1953 and 1957, with a spoilheap to the southwest.

2245 (Site IV)	Disc	35m	0.6m

Central mound is 14m diameter with an off-centre excavation hollow. Surrounded by a ditch 5m wide and 0.5m deep, with an external bank 4m wide and 0.5m high. Latter is absent on the southwest where it abuts 2240. Damaged by military vehicles.

2246	Bowl	24m	1.5m

Central tump or mound is 14m in diameter and 0.5m high with traces of a possible excavation hollow in the summit. No ditch visible.

2248 (Site XXI)	Bowl	19–21m	1.5m

Irregular central tump is 10–17m in diameter. No ditch visible.

2253	Bowl	25m	2.7m

'Hunter's Barrow'. Surrounded by ditch 6m wide and 0.5m deep. Depression in summit is old excavation (Hoare1812, 183–184). Damage from military vehicles has reached a depth of 1.5m.

2255	Bowl	30–33m	2.5m

An ovoid mound with an intermittent ditch, 5m wide and 0.5m deep. Mutilated by earlier excavations (pre-1953) and military vehicles.

2257	Bell	22m	3.6m

Berm 2m wide with ditch 7m wide and 0.5m deep. Damaged by military vehicles

2249 (Site I)	Disc (with two tumps)		

Platform diameter 25m with central tump 10m diameter and 0.3m high. Left open after excavation and surrounded by spoil heaps. Ditch 5m wide and 1m deep after excavation with traces of an external bank surviving on the southeast.

2247 (Site XVIII)	Bowl		

Disfigured by spoil from excavation of 2249. Probably original diameter 20m. Probable height 1.3m.

SPTA No	Type	Diameter (excluding ditch)	Height
2262 (Site XV)	Bowl	25–27m	1.3m

Slightly ovoid with a number of small trenches on the summit. No ditch visible.

2266 (Site V)	Saucer (or ring-ditch)	20–23m	0.3m

Slightly ovoid and damaged; Small, 9m diameter mound on south side may be derived from excavation spoil. Ditch 0.4m deep. Military vehicle damage has obscured the relationship with.

2268 (Site XIX)	Bell (twin)		

Conjoined mounds surrounded by a single ditch 8m wide and 0.7m deep. Northern mound 20m diameter and 1.5m high; southern mound, 24m in diameter and 3.9m high, appears to be set on a plinth 31m across. Both mounds separated from the ditch by a berm ranging from 1m to 3m in width. Ditch probably cuts into 2266. Mounds damaged by military vehicles.

2269 (Site XXII)	Bell	27m	3.9m

Christened 'King Barrow' by Colt Hoare (1812, 185–186). Mound sits on a plinth 31m across, separated from the ditch by a 6m wide berm. The ditch is 9m wide and 0.8m deep. A smaller mound, 0.5m high (now disfigured), overlies the berm to the north of the barrow. Damaged by military vehicles to a depth of 1m

2254	Bell	24m	3m

The ditch, 6m wide and 0.5m deep, is separated from the mound by a 1m wide berm. Indications of an external bank to the south and an irregular oval platform which may result from episodes of ploughing. Damage by military vehicles.

2239 (Site XVI)	Pond		

Very shallow ovoid depression with maximum diameter of 12m. Appears to be set within or incorporated in elements of a field system. Discovered by H C Bowen during survey of the area in 1957.

2229 (Site XX)	Bowl	23m	0.4m

Disfigured mound adjacent to linear ditch (Site VI). No surrounding ditch visible.

2205	Bowl	12m	0.5m

Small bowl barrow with shallow ditch 0.2m deep.

2207	Bowl	24m	2.2m

Ditch 5m wide, 0.3m deep. Mound infested with rabbits. Much shrub growth.

2244	Saucer	24m	0.3m

Discovered by L V Grinsell and Charles Thomas during the excavations in 1953. Very shallow with ditch 5m wide and 0.3m deep.

2209 (CD1 in Fig 2A) – has been omitted from this list.

THE BARROW CEMETERY

With the possible exception of barrows 2266, 2268, 2240 and 2245, none of the mounds or ditches intercut and the development of the cemetery cannot be conclusively demonstrated from the field evidence alone. The most striking feature of the barrow grouping is in the linear configuration incorporating the eight barrows 2207–2248. Aligned southwest to northeast, from the valley floor towards the false crest of the ridge, the spacing is relatively regular with the exception of 2240 (Site VIII), which impinges on the neighbouring disc 2245 (Site IV). The position of 2240 may also indicate respect for a pre-existing feature immediately to the southwest, which also appears to be used as the focus of a group of five small bowl-barrows (2237, 2234, 2233, 2225, 2615: Sites X-XIV) aligned west-southwest. Further mounds to the north strongly suggest that this was an important focal point in the funerary landscape. The cemetery itself is by no means prominently sited within the local landscape. The barrows are arranged right across the slope but avoid the

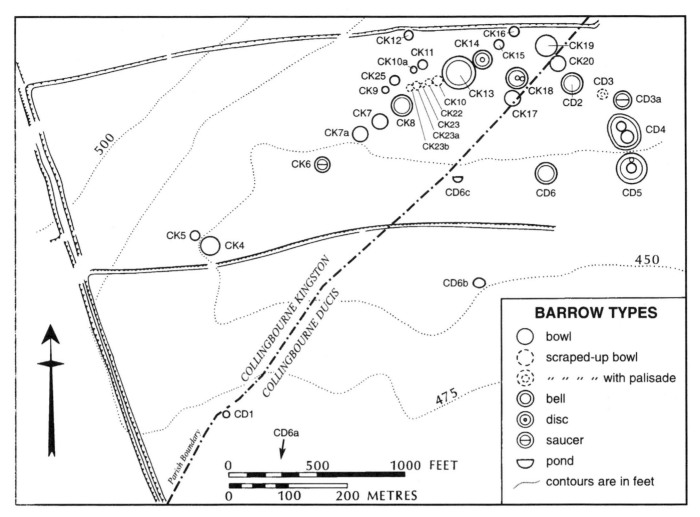

Fig 2A The barrows, lettered and numbered by Goddard and Grinsell according to parish; as surveyed by RCHME, 1953–1957 (Bowen, 1978, fig 1)

ultimate summit of the ridge and the lowest point on the valley floor. Only from the opposing slopes, or from the superior viewpoint of Sidbury Hill to the south can the complete layout of the cemetery be observed. Like other barrow cemeteries it may have been the springs and connection with water that provided the main focus of attention here.

POSSIBLE EARLY FIELDS OR ENCLOSURE

An intriguing feature lies immediately south of barrows 2231 and 2235. It resembles a fragment of early field system but is placed on a completely different alignment to those mentioned below. Crucially, it also appears to underlie small bowl-barrows 2233, 2234 and possibly 2231 and 2237 as well. It comprises a 30m length of shallow bank, 7m wide and little more than 0.2m high, aligned approximately west to east that underlies or abuts barrow 2237 in the east. In the west a further bank abuts it at right angles. This is broader, c11m wide and c25m long and it appears to underlie or abut barrow 2231. A double

lynchet on the same alignment can be traced south towards the valley floor for 170m. Whether this represents an early phase of field layout or of the cemetery itself is unclear.

ANCIENT FIELDS

The detailed survey recovered elements of a field system over the entire study area. Aligned southwest to northeast, the earthworks belong to an extensive co-axial field system covering at least 4 square km. On Snail Down the field boundaries take the form of low banks which have been reduced and spread by later ploughing. Now measuring up to 10m in width and a maximum of 0.3m in height, the banks define fields of rectangular form enclosing units of 0.3–0.5ha. The southwest to northeast elements are the more substantial with indications of lynchet formation. Cross divisions on a northwest to southeast alignment are staggered. The field system has been truncated by the linear ditches (Sites VI, VII) which enclose three sides of the barrow cemetery (see below). To the north of linear ditch VI (2191) (Fig 2, *AB*) the fields have well-developed lynchets surviving for up to 1m in height, suggesting continuity of cultivation or re-use after construction of the linear ditch. The field evidence points to some realignment or reorganisation of the field system, especially to the east of the north – south trackway T3 (2242). This can be traced within the barrow group, notably south of disc-barrow Site IV (2245), where a series of terraces and banks follow the later alignment. Further cultivation in the immediate vicinity of the barrows can be seen in the east part of the cemetery where boundaries abut or even encroach upon barrow ditches (cf nos 2248, 2253, 2255, 2262, 2266, 2268). Later ridge and furrow and modern cultivation have also occurred within the survey area, obscuring other points of detail.

LINEAR DITCHES

The barrow cemetery is enclosed on the north, west and south by elements of the linear ditch system which radiates from Sidbury Hill, a little over 1km to the south (Bradley *et al* 1994: McOmish *et al* 2002). The west side is formed by a double ditched 'spinal' linear (Fig 2, *BC*: 2181: Sites VI, VII;). Some 500m west of the cemetery, four subsidiary ditches form a staggered junction with the spinal element. Two (Fig 2, *AB* and *CD*: 2191 and 2197: Site VI), both surviving to *c* 6m wide and 1m deep with corresponding banks, run to the east, 300m apart, following the contour. The northern ditch (2191) can be traced for a distance of 800m along the false crest of the ridge, just avoiding the mound of barrow (2248; Site XXI) as it does so. The south ditch (2197) continues for a further 500m along the valley floor.

It has already been noted that the linear ditch system around the barrow cemetery postdates the establishment of the first phase of the field system. The southern linear (Fig 2, *CD*: 2197) curves slightly to the south to respect barrows 2205 and 2207. Detailed survey at the junction between the spinal and subsidiary ditches recorded a hollowed or quarried area, but this has been too seriously damaged by heavy military vehicles to be certain of its relationship to the respective ditches.

TRACKWAYS

A major embanked track, aligned north to south (2242: T3), 10m wide and 1m deep can be traced across the survey area. Crossing the northern linear (2191: Site VI) and carefully skirting barrow 2229 (Site XX), it continues south, between barrows 2231 and 2235, to cross the valley on a well-constructed causeway. The latter, 11m wide by 40m in length and with a shallow bank c3m wide to either side straddles the valley floor. Its purpose is unclear, but such a feature can only have been necessary if the valley bottom carried water at this point. The northern linear (2191) may have also been utilised to take traffic as the northern bank has been diverted to link in with Track 2242. Track 2242 can be traced south to an area of extensive quarrying, which may be associated with a brick kiln shown on the Andrews and Dury map of 1773.

Two further tracks aligned west to east, merit brief comment. After crossing the spinal linear 2232 at the same point, they divide. The northern example (2219: T1: Site IX), up to 7m wide, cuts across ancient field lynchets and the ditches of barrows 2224 and 2268 (Sites III and XIX). It may be making for an area of former gravel pits alongside the River Bourne, south of Leckford Bridge (NGR: SU 237518). The southern track, which is chronologically later than the northern example and may even be of military origin, runs southeastwards across ancient field boundaries before disappearing close to the valley floor.

QUARRIES

An extensive area of multi-period quarrying was noted to the east of the barrow cemetery along the northern side of the valley. Some of the resulting hollows have been smoothed by more recent cultivation. The quarrying itself may be of some antiquity.

POND

South of barrow 2213 is a sub-square dewpond, typical of those constructed during the 19th and early 20th centuries by the Cruse family of Imber (McOmish et al 2002). This example measures 19m by 16m and up to c1.5m deep, and spoil from construction and maintenance has been formed into an enclosing bank.

ROMANO-BRITISH SETTLEMENT

Colt Hoare (1812,178,181) noted the presence of an extensive Romano-British village to the north of the linear ditch 2238. The area has been ploughed in recent times and no trace of this can now be found. A number of shallow undulations can be seen amongst the realigned fields to the north of linear ditch 2191 and a few fragments of Romano-British pottery were observed in molehills in the area. A few hut stances may be present amongst the fields, but it is unlikely that settlement was extensive. Colt Hoare's map of the area also shows Romano-British settlement to the east of the barrow cemetery, but it is likely that he was referring to the quarry scoops there, which superficially resemble hut platforms. No pottery or other cultural indicators were noted in this latter area.

CONCLUSION

The RCHME survey demonstrated that the landscape archaeology of Snail Down is of considerable complexity. Earthworks attributable to one of the earliest phases of barrow construction can still be made out, as can successive phases of agricultural activity and land management. The Romano-British settlement described by Colt Hoare remains elusive, though the presence of potsherds on the surface hints at some local activity; realignment and reuse of the field system may have accompanied this. Industrial activity of unconfirmed, perhaps post-Roman, date, is present and a number of trackways, in places deeply rutted, cross the site, indicating that similar activities took place around Snail Down through to recent times.

METHOD

The survey was produced at a scale of 1:1000 and encompassed an area in excess of 60ha. Most of the archaeological and modern detail was recorded using a Wild TC 2000 EDM Total Stations survey system and data processed using Mathshop software. Additional measurements were made by taped offset. The resulting hachured plan (Fig 2), has had certain minor details omitted in the interests of clarity (all recovered detail is recorded on the field documents and may be consulted at the National Monuments Record Centre, Swindon).

PART 1: THE EXCAVATIONS, 1953–1957

EXCAVATION METHODOLOGY

Sites I-III and X-XVII were excavated virtually *in toto* using the quadrant system, sometimes adapted to suit the needs of a particular site such as Site I. Baulks were orientated broadly to the main points of the compass unless the state of the barrow necessitated otherwise. These systems are shown in the site plans. Baulk widths were 2 or 3 feet, depending usually upon barrow height. All finds were recorded three-dimensionally or else by layer number and general area within the site. The Snail Down Archive includes precise details of these procedures.

Where a site needed only trial excavation, to establish positions or settle points of detail, eg Sites IV, VI/VII, VIII, IX, XVIII-XXII, suitable trench systems were devised, as shown in their site plans.

Site V, levelled in Romano-British times, required a particular system of trenching, since it was virtually invisible on the ground. From the result of a single trial trench in 1953 (Figs 16, 17, section 1), a grid was laid out over half the estimated site. Using a selection of 4ft wide cuttings, 6ft apart and of appropriate lengths, the general course of the surrounding ditch was established. The approximate centre was cleared by expanding and joining some of these trenches. Only the northern half of the site was thus tested.

Throughout Part I, there are references to soil analysis carried out by I W Cornwall at the University of London Institute of Archaeology in the early sixties. These analyses and his comments are not published here, but their results are incorporated in the relevant site texts. They are available in the Archive.

SITE I

SPTA 2249: A DISC-BARROW WITH TWO MOUNDS

SUMMARY

A flat-bottomed ditch with outer bank, having an overall diameter of about 132ft, encircled the level space upon which two small mounds, central and eccentric, were set. Cremations buried in pits beneath the centres of the mounds had been disturbed. The pit beneath the eccentric mound was an immense oval hollow refilled with unweathered chalk. Each mound also contained within its material an intact cremation; one was accompanied by a copper-alloy awl. The two people buried in and under the eccentric mound may have been males; those from the central mound are unsexed. The four cremations and a small unsealed pit containing perhaps pyre sweepings that included a little cremated human bone, all placed along the same E/W alignment, were probably contemporary. Scattered pieces of unburnt human bone are thought to derive from corpses exposed in the vicinity. Beaker sherds, some sealed under the bank, and Grooved Ware from secondary positions, probably relate to the settlement under Sites X-XIV. Rim sherds from a Food Vessel and a Collared Vessel were also found.

INTRODUCTION

In 1953 Site I was covered by downland vegetation which in many places had been damaged by the passage of tracked vehicles. The surrounding bank was denuded but visible, like the silted-up ditch within. There were depressions at the centres of both mounds but no evidence that this disturbance was recent.

Sir Richard Colt Hoare and William Cunnington were at work among the barrows on Snail Down in 1805 and 1806 (Hoare 1812, plan opp. 180, No 18) but made no reference to this barrow, although it may have been they who dug the centres of its two mounds. L V Grinsell drew attention to Site I in his discussion papers on disc-barrows (1941, 84, fig 3; 1974, 80–82, 103, fig 1). Other references to Site I include Lukis 1867, 99 and pl II; Goddard 1914, 235 Collingbourne Kingston 18; Thomas and Thomas 1956, 130–134, fig 2; Grinsell 1957, 217, no 18; Stone 1958, pl 37; Biek 1963, 137, pl 14; Thomas, N 1965, 146; Fowler 1967, 34–35, figs 16, 17; Cunnington 1975, pl 21; Thomas 1976, 230; Dyer 1981, 279–280, fig 27; Burl 1987, 198; Dyer 1997, 97–98, pl 35.

The excavation, which resulted in clearance of the barrow to bedrock (Pl 4), lasted throughout the season of 1953; the writer was in charge during these five weeks, with a daily labour force of about 30 volunteers.

At the end of the dig the site was fenced off and left open so that the action of weather upon the chalk, the rate of silting in the ditch (sectioned in 1957, Figs 3, 4: section 5; Pl 8A), and the spread of vegetation across the area could be studied. This test was superseded by the construction of experimental earthworks on Overton Down and elsewhere under the auspices of the British Association for the Advancement of Science (Jewell 1963; Bell *et al* 1996). However, recording of the vegetation spread across the site continues (Section V).

DESCRIPTION

Pre-barrow Features and Settlement Remains

Three natural hollows in the chalk are interpreted as ancient tree-holes. One, originally sealed beneath the W half of the central burial mound, had been cleared out by those digging here before us ('tree-hole', Fig 5: section 2). The second, buried beneath the W edge of the eccentric mound, was filled with fine brown, chalk-flecked soil (layer 10, Fig 5: section 2). The Sweepings Pit (see below) had been dug into one end of the third, filled with pale brown loam (Fig 4, section 6: layer 13, and plan).

Owing to disturbance, an old land surface survived only beneath the N edge of the central mound and the W edge of the eccentric mound (layer 10: Fig 4, section 1; Fig 5, section 2). Preservation beneath the bank was variable: layer 10 was detectable as a pale brown soil on the N and S sides of section 1 and in section 3 (Fig 4), but generally less clearly than the drawings suggest. This buried surface stood more than 1ft above the present level of the central part of the barrow.

A spread of Beaker sherds and a few worked flints can probably be attributed to the settlement beneath Sites X-XIV (Figs 21, 24) although no structural features were found here, either under the bank or on the central plateau where a careful search revealed only the Sweepings Pit, which is more likely to have been associated with the use of the barrow. The 43 sherds include parts of at least two of Clarke's Southern British series Beakers (Part 2, Section C); they came mainly from the W side of the barrow and from various depths within the bank (distribution shown in Fig 3). Their relatively fresh condition suggests that they had been buried soon after breaking. The rim sherd of a Food Vessel (Section D, D1, Fig 43) lying near the base of the ditch and the concentration of Beaker sherds in the SW quadrant suggests that it may have fallen from the pre-bank surface and derive from the settlement beneath Sites X-XIV.

Only the 24 worked flints and waste recovered from the bank can be plausibly associated with the Beaker sherds; these comprise a scraper, a blade, twelve flakes and ten chunks (Part 2, Section G, G2, Fig 50). The scraper was incorporated within the outer edge of the bank in the SW quadrant. Evidence of post-constructional flint working on the site (below) indicates that few flints from the ditch or interior are likely to derive from the Beaker settlement.

The Burials (plan, Fig 3; sections, Figs 4, 5; Pl 7; Section A; Section L, L1, Fig 55)

Cremation 1, the primary burial under the **central mound**, had been completely disturbed. A very small quantity of burnt human bone and a little oak charcoal incorporated in the original filling were scattered on and just above the floor of the burial pit, presumably replaced by Hoare. The pit, just N of the mound centre, measured 3ft by 3ft and had been dug nearly vertically into the chalk to a depth of 1ft. The exact centres of both the mound and the barrow ditch fell within its area.

Cremation 2 was *in situ*, sandwiched in the midst of the central mound close to its E edge. The fairly compact mass of almost charcoal-free bone was roughly circular in plan, *c* 2–3in thick, with a maximum cross-measurement of *c* 6–7in. The bones, including chalk dust and chips, were well-integrated with the surrounding chalk rubble. A copper-alloy awl of the writer's Group 2B (Section L, L1, Fig 55) was recovered near the centre of the bone deposit. There was no indication that it had been buried with its handle.

Cremation 3, the disturbed primary burial beneath the eccentric mound, was a large deposit of burnt bone, possibly male, with some oak charcoal, that had been replaced, perhaps by Hoare, in one of several intrusions into the fill of the burial pit. The oval pit measured 21ft by 12½ft and was only just sealed by the mound heaped over it. The sides were sloping and the ill-defined floor dipped from N to S. Although it had been extensively robbed, much of the clean white chalk filling was preserved because of the 2ft to 3¼ft depth. In places the filling (Fig 5, layer 12) had been rammed solid and was almost indistinguishable from undisturbed bedrock. At other points it was so loose that it collapsed at a touch (Pl 7). The refill exactly resembled fresh quarried chalk and contained none of the turves or humus that must first have been dug out during its construction. There had been at least four

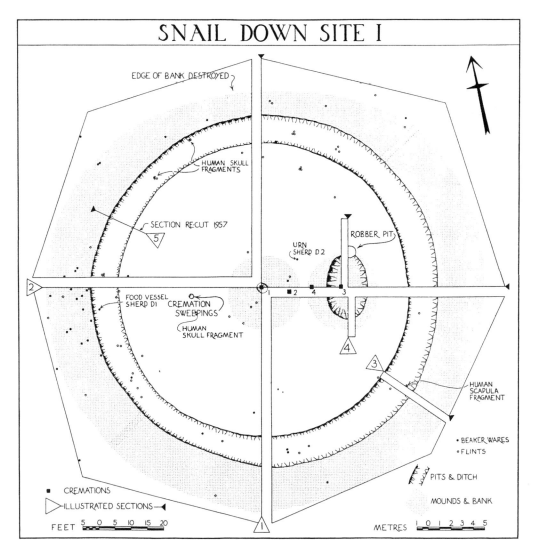

Fig 3   Site I, a disc-barrow with two mounds. Plan.

SNAIL DOWN SITE I

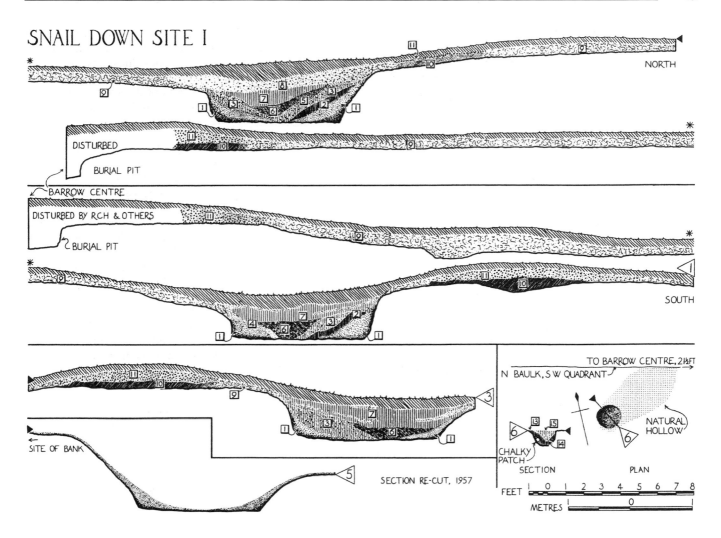

Fig 4   Site I, sections 1, 3. Plan of cremation sweepings pit and section 6. Section 5, 1957 re-cut of ditch silt.

robbings, but only three are indicated on the sections in Figure 5. A 1799 halfpenny was found in Robbing 1 (Section U, U2). The replaced Cremation 3 had been set at the base of Robbing 3 (Fig 5, sections 2 and 4) about 6in higher than the coin in Robbing 1.

Cremation 4 was *in situ* at the W edge of the rubble of the eccentric mound and in alignment with Cremations 1–3 (Fig 3; Fig 5, section 2). The bones, perhaps those of a male, were mixed with chalk dust and chips and a little oak charcoal. The deposit also resembled Cremation 2 in its size (*c* 2–3in by 6–8in) and roughly spherical but flattened shape. Although the deposit was closely associated with the mound material, the chalk immediately above it was noticeably less rubbly, more like a fine pale, chalky loam. This material was probably part of the original composition of the mound, but the possibility cannot be ruled out that the cremation may have been added after the mound was built.

The Sweepings Pit situated W of the central mound and nearly in alignment with Cremations 1–4, was a basin-shaped hollow, 1ft 4in in diameter at the top and 10in deep (Fig 4, section 6). The sides were lined with a greasy black substance which was almost solid charcoal, identified as Pomoideae (Section S), and contained a few

fragments of burnt human bone (Section A). The central filling was browner and included a few chalk chips. The contents had the appearance of sweepings and may have come from the funeral pyre for one of the cremations.

Cremations 1–4 included noticeably little charcoal, although charcoal was present in the upper filling of Robbing 3 in the eccentric mound and therefore associated indirectly with cremation 3. The mingling of burnt material with the bone in the Sweepings Pit was in strong contrast.

The Structures

The inner edge of the ditch (plan, Fig 3; sections, Figs 4, 5; Pls 4–6) described an almost perfect circle, 87½ft in diameter and centred on a point subsequently removed by the burial pit under the central mound. The outer edge was less regular. In profile the shape was uniform and in places rectangular, with flat bottom and vertical sides. The width at bottom varied from 7ft to 10½ft; the depth from the level of the old land surface was 2¾ft to 3½ft. The outer wall, still almost vertical in places, was nowhere less than 2½ft high. The somewhat sloping inner wall seldom exceeded a height of 1½ft.

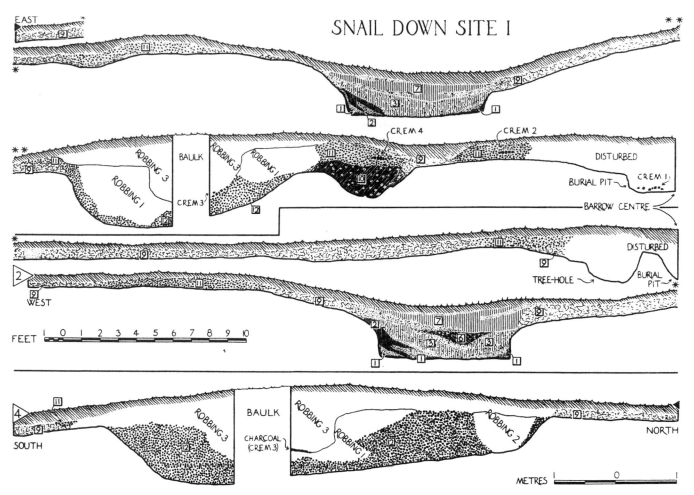

Fig 5   Site I, sections 2, 4.

Professor R J C Atkinson calculated (pers comm) that the ditch yielded 6600cu ft of chalk and soil. The maximum volume needed for the two mounds was *c* 2130cu ft and the remaining 4470cu ft could have provided a bank round the outer edge of the ditch 8ft 6in wide, a size commensurate with the dimensions of the bank in 1953.

No pick or wedge marks were seen on the walls or floor of the ditch.

The bank (Figs 4, 5, sections 1–3) comprised a dump of loose rubbly chalk mixed with humus (layer 11), 9ft to 11½ft broad and up to 1ft high above the old land surface. The inner side may have been retained by a wall of turves. A layer of almost chalk-free loam (layer 2, Figs 4, 5) resting upon the primary rubble eroded from the outer edge of the ditch seems best interpreted as the collapsed remains of such a structure. A section cut across the bank and ditch of Chiseldon G1, the disc-barrow on Burderop Down (Gingell 1992, 54–59, Fig 43) has indicated that there both the inner and the outer faces of the bank may have been revetted with turf.

The two mounds were almost perfectly circular in plan, with diameters of about 22½ft and maximum heights of 1 ft above the solid chalk (Figs 3–5; Pl 7). They were made of loose chalk rubble and humus (layer 11), resembling in texture and density the construction of the bank. As described above, the centres of both had been disturbed.

Post-construction Events

Four fragments of unburnt human bone were scattered in the ditch and on the plateau (positions shown on Fig 3: details in Section A, nos 1–4). Three were pieces of skull: one from the base of the topsoil on the plateau; the second from the floor of the ditch in the NW quadrant; the third at a higher level nearby. Part of a scapula lay on the ditch floor in the SE quadrant.

A small patch of oak charcoal occurred on the ditch floor in the NW quadrant.

As remarked above, most of the worked flints on the site were recovered from the ditch and plateau. They presumably include a number derived, like the Beaker sherds, from the pre-barrow settlement, but there is decisive evidence for post-construction flint knapping. Two nests comprising respectively 36 and 34 flakes were found on the floor of the ditch; each lay within an area of about 1sq ft, with some of the flakes touching each other. There was a third nest of 19 flakes in the upper ditch silt; a high proportion of other finds consisted of two to five flakes. They occurred at various levels in the ditch (Section G, Table 13). Scrapers G3 and G4 came from subsoil over the ditch in the SE and SW quadrants respectively. Eight nodules of burnt flint were distributed over the site.

The sherd from an Early Bronze Age Collared Vessel of Longworth's Secondary Series (Section D, D2,

Fig 43), lay in the subsoil close to the central mound (Fig 3). It is conceivable that this sherd may derive from an urn which once enclosed the cremation buried beneath this mound although no supporting evidence has survived.

The ditch sections (Figs 4, 5; full layer descriptions below) reflect an uninterrupted pattern of natural silting until the fill was complete. Layer 1, representing collapse of the upper edges of the ditch, and layer 2, apparently derived from a turf revetment along the inner face of the bank, would have formed within a few years. Figure 4, section 5 shows the amount of silt that had accumulated between clearing out the ditch in 1953 and redrawing its profile in 1957 after four winters, two of them severe. When the ditch was left open in 1953, all subsoils and turf had been removed from the barrow: the 1957 re-cut reflected the weathering of bedrock alone (Pl 8A). Layers 3 and 5 represent a generally slower silting, mainly derived from the outer side. These processes may have occurred over a period of ten to twenty years. Layers 6 and 7 were essentially slow silts, probably forming over several decades, if not centuries, although soil analysis shows that at no time did they become sufficiently immobile for a soil to develop. Layer 6 seems to have been a product of gradual bank spread. Layer 7 extended across the ditch almost everywhere and was noticeably free from chalky rainwash.

Layer 8 was present only round the N arc of the ditch (Fig 4, Section 1, North), coinciding with an abrupt narrowing of the bank. It represented bank material spread over the top of the ditch fill, presumably the result of ploughing. The RCHME survey of Snail Down (Fig 2) has revealed extensive ploughing among the barrows, perhaps from Early Bronze Age times, and Site I was probably damaged during some phase of this activity. The late date of the episode is evident from the position of layer 8, overlying layer 7.

Two sherds of late Iron Age pottery and 70 of Romano-British (Section E, *passim*; Section F, F1–4 and *passim*) were scattered over the site, almost all in topsoil or subsoil and more than half in the NW and SW quadrants.

REMARKS

The remains of at least four people were buried after cremation in this barrow, probably at roughly the same time. The alignment of the burials and the Sweepings Pit with its small collection of human ashes lends weight to the proposal that all were part of one barrow-building process.

Grinsell has summarized the traditional arguments for regarding disc-barrows as places of interment for females (1974, 86–87). Although neither Cremation 1 nor Cremation 2 could be sexed, the copper-alloy awl found with Cremation 2 belongs to the group of objects – beads, awls and small knives - that are considered more likely to have belonged to women than to men. The physical remains of Cremations 3 and 4 suggest that both may have been males.

The Sweepings Pit may have been a token deposit from the funeral pyre or pyres that had been fired away from the barrow. The human bone from this pit matches in quantity the deposits in the pits in the pond-barrow, Site XVI. Other Wiltshire barrows from which charcoal-filled pits are recorded include the disc-barrow, Chiseldon G1, on Burderop Down (Passmore 1929, 242), saucer-barrows at Down Farm, Pewsey (Vatcher 1960, 346) and a ditchless barrow on Overton Hill (Smith and Simpson 1966, 127; Fig 1). Bone was not present in these pits although the barrows contained cremated burials.

The scattered fragments of unburnt human bone (above) seem best interpreted in the light of other evidence from Snail Down that corpses were exposed or stored prior to cremation and burial (Sites III, XVI, XVII, XX). The phenomenon has been encountered elsewhere, for example at the Down Farm, Dorset, ring-ditch and also in later Bronze Age contexts (Barrett, *et al* 1991, 214).

The purpose of the great pit beneath the eccentric mound remains obscure. It had been dug, used and refilled during a short lapse of time since it contained only a rammed packing of unweathered chalk. Its elongated shape, shelving gently upwards at the N end, suggests that it could have accommodated a group of people – family mourners perhaps – during the final burial ceremonies. Alternatively, it may have been used to hold the corpses of the four people who were to be cremated and buried in the barrow. This suggestion is not unreasonable when considered in conjunction with the smaller 'empty' pits round Site III and the other evidence for temporary exposure of corpses on Snail Down described below and considered in Part 3. In size, though not in purpose, this pit recalls the inhumation burial pit at the centre of the South Glamorgan Beaker barrow, Sutton 268′N (Fox 1959, 65–66, figs 41, 42).

Around the S part of the ditch the bottom filling of slightly clayey silt (layer 1, Fig 4, section 1) appeared as a fairly hard, flat covering of the ditch floor. Although it seemed, at first, to correspond with reports of puddled surfaces caused perhaps by dancing in other barrows, eg Sutton 268′ (*ibid*, 98), it was more probably the result of poor drainage around this lower arc of the barrow and we concluded that there was no visible evidence for dancing or constant walking in the ditch of Site I during its period of use as a burial mound and focus for worship.

As indicated in Figure 3, the inner edge of the ditch was much more circular than the outer edge. The centre from which the ditch was laid out, presumably by peg and string, was removed when the central burial pit was dug, for they coincided. If the ditch had been begun before the burial pit was dug, it is reasonable to suppose that its circuit would have been perfectly symmetrical, for the centre would then have been available for check measurements. That this did not happen suggests that the barrow was built in the following sequence:

(1) Selection of barrow centre, driving in of peg there and marking out - using string and perhaps removal of a line of turf - at least along the inner edge of the ditch.
(2) Removal of central peg and construction of burial pit

in its place. (3) Construction of eccentric pit, assuming that this was contemporary. (4) Burial ceremony; pyres constructed away from the site of the barrow, cremations placed in pits. (5) Marking out of mounds. (6) Digging of ditch, erection of bank behind turf revetment and building of mounds over pits, incorporating extra cremations. Sweepings Pit dug and filled.

This sequence, in which the ditch was marked out early, but dug last, was repeated at Site III and seems to have been the normal practice on Snail Down and elsewhere in Wessex of the second millennium BC.

When completed, Site I would have appeared as a circular green plateau with two white chalky mounds, the whole surrounded by a blazing white ditch and bank, the latter perhaps separated by the thin green-brown line of a wall of turves.

The spoil around Site I, heaped up by excavation in 1953 and very chalky in appearance, had been overgrown completely with weeds and turf by 1957. The surrounding ditch of Site I and the larger plateau within, were taken down to solid chalk and left for study. When examined in 1967, this great expanse of white was still uncolonised by weeds and its overall appearance remained white. By 1994 the chalk had faded beneath a cover of weeds, but nothing resembling downland turf has yet developed (Pl 8B).

Figure 4
Detailed Description of Layers

Sections 1, 3, 5   Layers 1–8, ditch filling, including 1957 re-cut

Layer 1 Clean white chalk, filling angle between unweathered floor and lower walls of ditch. Chalk in form of nodules, in places loose and crumbly, elsewhere more compact but never solid. Formed the only silt exposed in section 5, re-excavated in 1957, which was beginning to support a thin vegetation by 1960 (Pl 8A, 1957, 8B,1994).
Layer 4 Essentially part of layer 1; found only in section 1. Much more compact white chalk.
Layer 2 Compact pale yellow soil; rested upon layer 1, on bank side of ditch only. In section 2 (Fig 5) in both ditch profiles it interrupted, and was covered by further deposition of layer 1.
Layer 3 Compact chalky soil, whiter than layer 2, more solid than layer 1, less solid than layer 4. Occurred mainly on bank side of ditch; in section 1 (N) it was continuous across ditch, likewise section 2, Fig 5.
Layer 5 In section 1 (N) only. A clean, fairly loose chalky rubble tip from both sides of ditch, failing to reach centre. Sealed layers 1–3.
Layer 6 Yellowish compact loam, less chalky than anything below it. No chalk chips.
Layer 7 Brown earth, less compact and darker than layer 6. No general scatter of chalk chips except for distinct slides from one or both sides of ditch and a concentration along top of layer. Continuous layer across ditch in most sections exposed.
Layer 8 Section 1 (N) only. Loose loam, with chalky rubble concentrated on bank side and thinning out towards inner side of ditch. Sealed ditch.

Sections 1, 3   Layers 9–11, make-up of mound and bank; and subsoils

Layer 9 Mixed chalk and dark brown loam, product of weathering and earthworm activity. Natural flints tending to concentrate towards base of layer. Graded slowly into undisturbed chalk. At edges of ditch, this layer ended sharply.
Layer 10 Ancient land surface sealed by bank and mound of barrow. Pale brown, freer of natural flints and chalk than layer 9. At edges, graded imperceptibly into latter. In section 1 (S) a natural hollow accounted for extra thickness.
Layer 11 Loose chalk rubble in matrix of brown loam, make-up of mounds and bank. In section 1 (S), part of layer 11 lay directly on the undisturbed chalk. Otherwise it rested on layer 10.

Section 6   Layers 13–15, filling of small pit and hollow; topsoil, undisturbed chalk

Layer 13 Pale brown loam filling natural hollow and cut by small pit. Resembled layer 10 above.
Layer 14 Almost black greasy soil. Contained much very fine charcoal, some burnt (human) bone and one patch of chalk.
Layer 15 Brown loam with darker patches and some chalk chips.
Topsoil Dark brown loam, almost no chalk or flints. Over ditches, where it was thickest it had accumulation of chalk specks and some flints at base, with occasional runs of chalk chips higher up.
Undisturbed Chalk Here firm and unmixed with clay. Bedded in layers 1–2in thick with short vertical and diagonal breaks occurring at intervals (Pl 6).

Figure 5
Detailed Description of Layers

Section 2   Layers 1–3, 6, 7, ditch-filling

Layer 1 Same as layer 1 Fig 4. In section 2 (E and W) accumulation of layer was interrupted by tip of layer 2 from bank side.
Layer 2 Same as layer 2, Fig 4. Only occurred on bank side of ditch.
Layer 3 Same as layer 3, Fig 4. Extended across ditch in both sections.
Layer 6 Same as layer 6, Fig 4. Section 2 (W) only.
Layer 7 Same as layer 7, Fig 4. A fairly considerable slide of chalky rainwash separates layer 7 from layers 3 and 6 in section 2 (W) only.

Sections 2, 4   Layers 9–12, make-up of mound and bank; filling of large pit; sub-soils

Layer 9 Same as layer 9, Fig 4. In section 2 (E) it separated mounds and constituted land surface beneath bank. In section 2 (W) formed land surface sealed by make-up of central mound.
Layer 10 Same as layer 10, Fig 4. Only occurs in section 2 (E) where natural hollow or tree-hole accounts for greater thickness of ancient land surface. Fine brown soil with chalk specks all through.
Layer 11 Same as layer 11, Fig 4. In section 2 (E) the bank sealed a shattered chalky sub-soil which did not

contain enough humus to resemble layer 10 and must be considered the same as layer 9.

Layer 12 Clean white chalk, rammed solid in most places, but quite loose in restricted areas: no clear pattern in variation of compaction. No earthy matrix or natural silting, but some areas where chalk was yellower and more like fine clay. No sharp break between base of layer 12 and undisturbed chalk. Upper part extensively robbed. Disturbed by at least three separate, unrecorded robbings.

Robbing 1 Removal of much of layer 12, probably before Cunnington and Hoare. Refill mainly dark and pale soils with one major concentration of compact pure chalk. Streaks of charcoal prominent. At base of refill, halfpenny of 1799 (Section U).

Robbing 2 Roughly circular pit cutting N edge of eccentric mound. Filled with clean light-brown earth.

Robbing 3 Later than Robbing 1, involving removal of some of its refill. At base (section 2 E), substantial cremation (C3) replaced by diggers. Refilling of Robbing 3 distinct layers of grey and brown soils, with more chalky lenses and patches. Charcoal streaks prominent, including one at base, close to redeposited cremation C3.

SITE II

SPTA 2213: A SAUCER-BARROW

SUMMARY

An almost level area with a diameter of about 55ft had been enclosed by a flat-floored ditch and an external bank. The overall diameter was about 92ft. The barrow contained five pits. Pit 1, at the centre, was 3ft across and 1ft deep, through whose floor a smaller pit had been dug. Pit 1 had been sealed by flints. Nine feet to the SW lay Pit 2, of identical shape but lacking a flint cover. Both contained burials after cremation; two Accessory Cups and an awl of copper alloy had been deposited in Pit 1 with an adult, perhaps female, burial. Filling in the upper part of Pit 2 included sherds of a Food Vessel, while with the burial itself, that of a juvenile, possibly female, there was a disc of bone which had been trepanned from the skull and not burnt. To the SE lay Pit 3, small and irregular, containing a Southern British Food Vessel inverted over an offering, perhaps of food. To its NE, Pit 4 contained the unburnt remains of a human foetus; E of that occurred Pit 5, an empty miniature replica of Pits 1 and 2. No conclusive evidence was found for mound material over the area within the ditch, yet it is probable that some form of covering had existed originally. A small heavily weathered axe of Cornish greenstone was found sealed by the bank at the NE. A radiocarbon assay of 5690 ± 90 BP was obtained for charcoal in the second burial pit.

INTRODUCTION

Site II was a saucer-barrow, where the diagnostic features of a circular ditch with external bank and apparently a low mound covering the space within the ditch could be made out in 1953 beneath the downland vegetation. It had suffered slight damage from armoured vehicles and its S edge had been overlaid by an E/W military track.

Hoare described the examination of this barrow, his No 4, in the following passage (1812, plan opp 180, No 4, and pl 22):

'. ... This is a low barrow encompassed by a circular ditch, and containing a cist within a cist. At the depth of one foot and a half we came to the first, which had been secured at the top by a covering of flints; it was nearly circular, and about three feet in diameter. Within this was another cist, more contracted in its size, but nearly of an equal depth, about 14ins. In this we found a most singular and novel interment of bones, very well burned; in throwing out of which with his shovel, our labourer surprised us with a beautiful and diminutive cup, which fortunately received no damage ... On pursuing our excavation, we discovered lower down another small cup most rudely formed, but resembling some others in our museum, and which seemed to have been protected by a wall of burned bones placed round it as a safeguard. Amongst the bones was a very delicate pointed pin of metal, bearing some slight indications of having been gilt. This interment appearing not to be in the centre of the mound, and observing a depression in the north-west side of it, we were induced to make another section, by which we discovered a large irregular cist, but no charred wood or signs of sepulture.'

Grinsell included Site II among the known saucer-barrows in his Wessex barrows paper of 1941 (88, 89). He and oth-ers further referred to it as follows: Cunnington and Goddard 1896, nos 104, 104a; Abercromby 1912, II, 118, pl 80, no 242; Goddard 1912, 149, no 226; *ibid,* 1914, 234, Collingbourne Kingston 6; Grinsell 1953, 171; Thomas and Thomas 1956, 134–137, fig 2; Grinsell 1957, 223; Biek 1963, 137, pl 14; Annable and Simpson 1964, 62–63, 117–118, nos 492, 501; Thomas, N, 1965, 145–146; Thomas, N, 1976, 229 and 21, fig 9, centre left, Accessory Cup; Warrilow 1980, Figs 12.1, 12.2.

On average, thirteen volunteers worked here daily for three weeks in 1953, under the direction of Charles Thomas. The barrow was backfilled at the end of the work.

DESCRIPTION

Pre-barrow Features and Settlement Remains

Two irregular hollows were recorded, one near the centre of the barrow, another at the NE and sealed beneath the bank ('tree hole', Figs 6, 7). The former had been cleared and re-filled with chalky loam by Hoare. The hollow beneath the bank (section 3 North-East, layer 6, Fig 7), containing mixed chalk and loam with flints concentrating towards its base, was cut by the barrow ditch, whose bottom fill at this point, layer 2, derived from it. On the surface of this hollow was found a small, noticeably weathered greenstone axe-head of Cornish origin (Fig 6; Section J, J1 and Fig 53). Both features we have interpreted as pre-barrow tree holes.

The barrow bank sealed an ancient land surface (section 3 North-East, section 2 West, layer 7, Fig 7). It was of brown chalky loam, natural flints tending to concentrate at its base.

No traces of the Beaker settlement located beneath Sites X–XIV were found here but the small quantity of

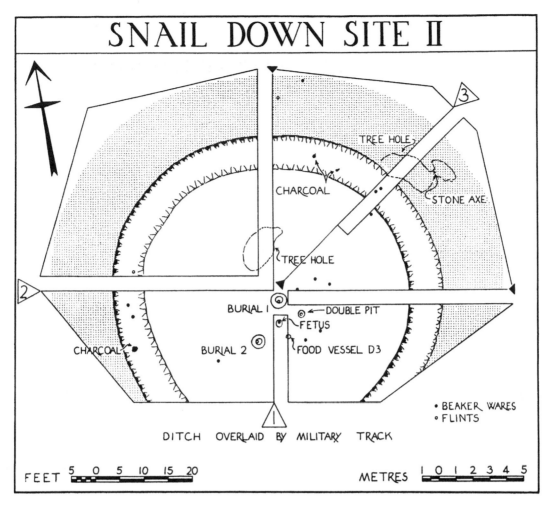

Fig 6   Site II, a saucer-barrow. Plan.

Beaker sherds from the upper filling of the ditch, as well as the greenstone axe sealed beneath the bank, could have been derived from the settlement.

The radiocarbon assay of 5690 ± 90 BP from charcoal associated with Burial 2 suggests that it may have been derived from a much earlier phase of occupation somewhere on Snail Down. Early Neolithic potsherds of Windmill Hill style and technology occurred among the assemblage of wares from the neighbouring mound of Site III (Section C) and the greenstone axe-head might also have been associated with such an episode.

Seven flint flakes, one retouched, were found among the natural flints in the central burial pit disturbed by Hoare (Section G). It is possible that these, like the Beaker sherds, may also have been derived from the settlement beneath Sites X–XIV; or even from the altogether earlier episode we have proposed in the history of Snail Down and incorporated when flints were gathered to fill the mouth of this burial pit.

The Burials and Associated Pits (plans, Figs 6, 8; sections, Figs 7, 8; Pls 9–12; burials, Section A, Cremations 5, 6, Inhumation 1; trepanned disc, Section B; radiocarbon determination, Section T; grave offerings, pottery, Section D, D4, D5, D7; copper alloy, Section L, L2; flint, Section G; excavation memento, Section U, U1).

Burial 1 (Cremation 5, Section A) comprised a small quantity of burnt bone of a young adult likely to have been female. It had been disturbed and replaced by Hoare in Pit 1. Charcoal (not identified) was present in the re-filled pit but the cremated bones were not noticeably darkened nor closely associated with charcoal and ash. This pit had a diameter at chalk surface of almost 3½ft and the upper part a depth of nearly 1½ft. Through the centre of its floor a circular extension had been dug to a further depth of 1ft and with a diameter of 15in. Hoare's 'cist within a cist' was well described.

The double pit had been excavated by Hoare with care, and, despite his surprising reference to the use of a shovel for the removal of such a delicate and personal deposit as burnt human bones, for the most part with a trowel. Its sides looked as fresh and unscraped as those in Burial Pit 2, which Hoare had not disturbed. On the floor of the lower pit, the mark of what appeared, nevertheless, to be the edge of a spade or shovel could have been made by the labourer who is described by Hoare (above) as throwing out one of the Accessory Cups while he was digging into it. The filling of Burial Pit 1 was streaky and parti-coloured (Pl 10), containing an unusually high proportion of unworked flints in the upper part and a concentration of cremated human bone at the bottom. The systematic return of its contents by Hoare reproduced

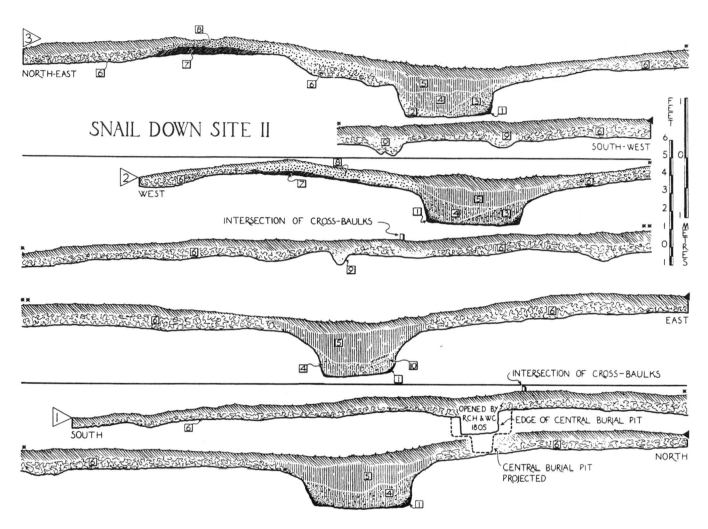

SNAIL DOWN SITE II

INTERSECTION OF CROSS-BAULKS

INTERSECTION OF CROSS-BAULKS

OPENED BY
RCH & WC
1805

EDGE OF CENTRAL BURIAL PIT

CENTRAL BURIAL PIT
PROJECTED

Fig 7   Site II, sections 1–3.

approximately its original filling, but lest posterity be deceived, he had placed a copper-alloy medalet inscribed 'Opened by Wᵐ Cunnington, 1805' on the floor of the lower pit (Section U, U1).*

Of the grave offerings deposited with Burial 1, the complete Accessory Cup (D4) and copper-alloy awl (L2) were removed by Hoare and became part of the Stourhead Collection (Cunnington and Goddard 1896, 104, 104a). This Cup appears to have been made with a fossil sea urchin in mind (for example the Upper Chalk species *Micraster corangiunum*, one of the two common-est fossils found in chalk country). The rim sherd, all that survives from a different style of Cup (D5), was recovered in 1953 from the infilling of the pit and may have come from the 'small cup' mentioned by Hoare (above).

Burial 2 belonged to a youthful individual, perhaps female, and was intact (Section A, Cremation 6). It had been placed at the bottom of a double pit only a little smaller than Pit 1 and in outline resembling it exactly (Pl 11). Around the SE side of its upper half, vertical

grooves were noted in the surface of the chalk which must represent pick or wedge marks left by the barrow builders.

Below the modern humus, the filling of the upper pit consisted of dark brown, fine organic soil, containing a few flints, scraps of cremated human bone and some sherds from the base and lower wall of a pot apparently of Food Vessel style (D7). The mouth of the lower part of this double pit had a filling, 3½in deep, of brown earth containing flints and more cremated human bone, mixed with ash and charcoal; below that, the fill was a much blacker soil with a greater concentration of cremated bone, together with ash, charcoal and natural flints. On the floor there was an unburnt disc of bone which had been trepanned from a human skull more likely female than male (Section B; Fig 38; Pl 60), presumably that of the person buried here (traces of the corresponding hole cannot be seen in the fragments of cremated skull that survived to be buried). Charcoals of *Corylus*, Pomoideae and *Quercus* (hazel, hawthorn/apple/rowan/whitebeam type, and oak) were submitted to the Scottish Universities

---

* Throughout this monograph, reference is made to Hoare as if he had been in charge, in the field, at the opening of each Snail Down barrow. R H Cunnington and Kenneth Woodbridge have established that on most occasions it was William Cunnington who exercised personal control of the excavation team and that Hoare's role was principally that of paymaster and, in due course (actually with commendable promptness) of pub-lisher (Cunnington 1975, 74, 88; Woodbridge 1970, Part 3 *passim*).

Research Centre at East Kilbride, Glasgow for radiocarbon assay, with the following result:

GU – 5301 5690 ± 90 BP); cal BC 4711–4460 (1 sigma); cal BC 4780 – 4350 (2 sigma).

This result, which suggests the use of some wood already ancient, is considered further in Section T. As suggested above, however, the charcoal may have been derived accidentally from earlier Neolithic activity hereabouts.

Burial 3 consisted of the unburnt remains of a human foetus, of about nine months (Section A, Inhumation 1). A small but wide selection of bones were scattered through the pale brown subsoil filling of a slightly ragged oval pit which lay 4ft 7in S of Burial 1 (Fig 6). This pit measured nearly 2 × 1¼ft at chalk surface and had a maximum depth of 1ft 2in. The filling was uniformly of soil not differing greatly from the topsoil: it included two small potsherds, one of unclassified Beaker, together with a larger bone, not human. Lacking stratigraphical evidence, we can only assume that this burial is contemporary with the other burials and features within the saucer-barrow. The two cremations here are likely to be those of women, so the inclusion of a foetus would not be inappropriate. Cremation 14 from the pit-within-a-pit at Site XVI was also of a young child (Section A).

A fourth pit was found, 5ft E of Burial 2 (Fig 8; Pl 12). It was roughly circular where it penetrated the chalk, about 15in in diameter. Two ragged channels, perhaps not man-made, led out from the chalk-cut pit as indicated in Fig 8. The upper edge of the pit had cut through the rotted chalk (layer 6, Fig 8), giving this part a diameter of 2–3ft. Its filling was a chalky loam, without charcoal or organic material. In the centre of the pit a Food Vessel (D3) had been carefully inverted over its contents of greyish soil. The Food Vessel was tilted slightly and its base was roughly flush with the upper edges of the chalk-cut pit.

The fifth pit lay about 5ft 7in SE of the central burial pit (Fig 6). It was located when that part of the central plateau had been cleared down to the undisturbed chalk. In its distinctive shape it resembled exactly, but in miniature, the pits-within-pits holding the two cremations in this barrow. Circular in plan, its upper, maximum diameter was about 1¾ft, narrowing slightly to a floor diameter of 1ft 1in. The upper part had been dug to a depth of 5in into solid chalk: through its floor a lower pit reached a maximum depth from chalk surface of 1ft. The upper diameter of this part was 7½in, narrowing to 6in at its base. The double pit contained what appeared to be pure topsoil. Only its shape linked it with Site II – and by inference with Site XVI. There the pit-within-a-pit was only a few inches larger and deeper.

The Structures

The ditch (plan, Fig 6, sections, Fig 7; Pl 9) appears to have been laid out from a centre which was close to the middle of the pit for Burial 1. From this point it had a maximum diameter of about 68ft. Along its floor, the width was 3¾–5ft. The original average depth of the ditch, measured from the surface of natural chalk where it had been preserved beneath the barrow bank, was almost 3¼ft (Fig 7, sections 1–3). The upper part of the inner wall of the ditch sloped more noticeably than that of the outer wall, whereas in the lower half of the ditch both walls were reasonably vertical. In plan, the outer edge of the ditch was a little more circular than the inner edge, for the latter was noticeably flattened along the NW.

Remains of a **bank** (Figs 6, 7, sections 1–3) outside the ditch, sealing an ancient land surface, were best preserved between the NE and W and were clear in section 3, NE and section 2, W. In the latter, the ancient land surface was about 8ft wide. In section 3 its outer edge lay 13ft beyond the upper, outer edge of the ditch, but at this point a large tree hole (above, Pre-barrow Features) separated bank from ditch. The tree hole filling was quite distinct from the brown loam of the ancient land surface, and was also sealed by material from the bank. Where preserved in sections 2 and 3, this consisted of a thin scatter of sludgy chalk and flints, nowhere more than 2–3in thick.

Wherever the site of the bank was cleared down to the undisturbed chalk, it was found that the latter appeared as a slight platform which, on average, was nearly 12in higher than the chalk surface outside the barrow and also the plateau within the ditch. Where this platform underlay the remains of an ancient land surface, as in sections 2 and 3, the width of the former exceeded the latter by about 5ft. The original breadth of the bank must therefore have been about 13ft. In section 1, N and section 2, E, the platform alone indicated the site of the surrounding bank. The surface of the natural chalk beneath the bank did not differ noticeably from that on the platform within the ditch or outside the barrow.

The plateau (Figs 6, 7; Pl 9) defined by ditch and bank was approximately circular, its centre located within the area of Burial Pit 1 and having an average diameter of 55ft. Although the land hereabouts sloped a little and was uneven, the sections indicated that the general level of this plateau was about 12in below the chalk surface at the

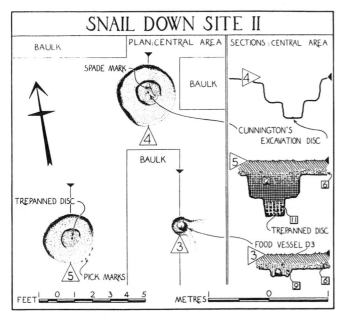

Fig 8   Site II, central area, burial pits, sections 3–5.

site of, or beneath the bank outside the barrow ditch. The surface of most of the plateau was roughly flat, but its edge had a gradual slope downwards caused by weathering and the rapid collapse of the upper inner wall of the ditch. It carried the usual natural sequence of turf, subsoil and weathered chalk on solid bedrock.

Post-construction Events

At two places in the NE quadrant, a small scatter of charcoal (not identified) occurred on the floor of the ditch (Fig 6). These were not the sites of fires since the chalk beneath them was unburnt. They contrasted with a more obvious hearth in the SW quadrant, where a hollow c 9in in diameter and 1½in deep had been scraped into the floor of the ditch and filled with grey ash. There was a hint from soil analysis that the ditch may have been cleaned early in its history.

When the ditch-silting process began, the bottom corners became filled with chalk (layer 1) which must represent the collapse of the upper edges soon after the ditch had been dug. Since Site II was built on chalk which contained much yellowish sludgy clay, the main prehistoric filling, represented by layers 3 and 4 (Fig 7), consisted of a compact mixture of clays and chalk which differed only a little from the earliest silt in the bottom corners and from the undisturbed chalk. They did not include the consistent bands of more loamy chalk in the outer half which suggested, in Site I, the presence of a turf retaining wall to the bank, nor was there a noticeable increase of chalky material along that side of the ditch caused by the return of some of the bank. A cluster of seven flints, two with secondary flaking, the others chunks, were found in the primary silt of the ditch at the W, close to the E/W baulk. A few sherds of Beaker pottery occurred, widely scattered, in the ditch, none below layer 5. Romano-British potsherds came from topsoil (Section F, F22 and *passim*).

REMARKS

Calculations for volume and density like those carried out on site I make it clear that the ditch of Site II provided more than enough material for its surrounding bank.

In depth, the ditches of Sites I and II were roughly alike, whereas the width of the ditch around Site I was generally twice that of the saucer-barrow. It has been suggested that the bank of the disc-barrow may have been revetted with turf at least around its inner edge, which would have made possible a surrounding earthwork of greater height. There was no evidence from the silting in the ditch of Site II that any such revetment had existed there.

The dimensions of Site II resemble those of other saucer-barrows in Wessex.

The only structural uncertainty about Site II concerned the form of its central area. When Grinsell examined the barrow during preparation of his *Gazetteer* for the *Victoria County History of Wiltshire* (1957), he con-

cluded that Site II had an internal mound with a maximum height of about 1ft. In 1805, moreover, Hoare had reported (above) that the mouth of the central burial pit had been reached at a depth of 1½ft, which implied that there had been more than the normal thickness of turf and subsoils overlying the natural chalk at the centre of the barrow. He also referred to Site II as ' … a low barrow … '.

Evidence from the burial pits and the hollow containing the inverted Food Vessel for the presence of a barrow mound was ambiguous. Hoare's report that the central pit had been 'secured at the top by a covering of flints' suggests some resemblance to Secondary Burial 1 on the berm of Site III (Pl 19), where a flint cairn had been heaped over and made to fill the mouth of a large burial urn let into a pit. There, we have assumed that the berm had been a ring of untouched Bronze-Age downland; that any burials dug into it therefore required protection and marking by a structure such as a flint cairn. Yet Hoare described the flints over Burial 1 as a covering not a cairn.

Neither the second burial pit at Site II, which was excavated without previous interference, nor the little hollow (or pit) holding the inverted Food Vessel, contained or were covered by any form of flint cairn or other material to protect them or signal their presence. These two features support our tentative conclusion that they may have been covered by a barrow mound, however slight. Certainly, the Food Vessel would not have survived complete, had it been left exposed to the elements. The abraded and incomplete sherds of a small Collared Vessel, D22, from Site XVII (Pl 50), which we believe to have been left thus exposed for a period, show how the relatively low-fired Bronze Age pots broke up and became scattered when so treated. Equally clearly, the filling of the Food Vessel pit was so loamy that it suggests a fairly chalk-free covering mound in that surrounding area at least.

Without a mound, Site II would have resembled Site V where the absence of a central covering was almost certain: there the area within the ditch looked level not domed. There, too, a pit dug into the solid chalk had required a puddled clay covering for its protection (Pl 27).

Our conclusion is that the saucer-barrow in the Snail Down cemetery probably had been covered by a slight mound. The flints filling the upper part of the central pit may have been no more than its topmost layer and not a cairn. What had become of this mound and what it had been made of must remain uncertain. In view of the sludgy nature of the natural chalk hereabouts, a low central barrow-covering which included turf and loam might have been returned, eventually, into its quarry ditch as silt, product of wind and rain, warm weather, frost and snow, without standing out noticeably in the latter's in-filling. Indeed, the generally even and uniform rate of ditch silting noted throughout the excavation may be accounted for by the presence of a slight central mound – a shallow covering of mixed clayey chalk and subsoil sufficient to obscure the downland turf and render Site II dirty white in colour with perhaps a cleaner-white surrounding ditch and outer bank. That in spite of such a mound this circular plateau had been weathered to below the level of the Bronze Age land surface beneath its surrounding bank may then be explained by the thicker and perhaps more compact construction of the latter. Site II seems, then, to have been a saucer-barrow within the normal definition of the type. Grinsell evidently estimated the original height of its mound correctly, even if nothing quantifiable remained for us to expose by excavation in 1953.

There was no evidence for the order in which burials and barrow building had taken place at Site II. We presume that the course of the ditch had been marked out in the turf by cord from a central post, which was then removed or destroyed when Burial Pit 1 was dug. If there had been a mound, it would have been derived from the surrounding ditch and constructed, like the bank, after the burial pits had been dug and filled, ceremonies completed and perhaps the Food Vessel placed upside down in its roughly scooped-out pit (see below).

The two cremation pits had not been filled up in the same way. According to Hoare, and to our examination of the material which he pushed back into the central pit, a relatively small quantity of clean cremated bone occupied the lower part of that double pit. Close to the top of this deposit, the complete Accessory Cup had been placed. Lower down a second Cup – put there first in the order of burial – had been carefully protected by bones selected to form a sort of surrounding wall. Somewhere among the cremated remains, perhaps near their base, an awl of copper alloy had been included. Much of the upper pit had been occupied by a mass of flints gathered from round about and during the start of ditch digging. They included ten worked flints (Section G, Table 15; Pl 10).

The second pit held a much larger cremation, closely mixed with the products both of the cremation process – wood ash, charcoal – and of the home – potsherds and humus-rich soil. A cranial disc, placed on the floor of the lower pit, was followed by a concentration of burnt human bone and unworked flints, gradually yielding to less humic earth as the filling process neared its end. Such material is likely to have been brought either from the site of the funeral pyre or else, perhaps, from the home of the person who was being buried. It was probably deposited loose in the lower pit, not in a bag like the cremation burial in Site XIV (Pl 34).

The two burial pits were so alike and their shape so unusual (see Part 3) that there must have been a close link in time between them, as there must, in time and usage, with Site XVI. Had their uppermost fillings been identical, they could have been seen as the product of a dual burial carried out simultaneously. The absence of a flint covering from Burial 2 and its off-central position support the possibility that the two pits may not have been strictly contemporary. Whatever the sequence, these pits, like that in Site XVI, appear to have been the work of one social group carefully following a set procedure in the process of burial after cremation at these two sites.

It proved impossible to establish the chronological position of the Food Vessel, upended over its presumed grave offering in a roughly made pit. Culturally, such a form of pot belonged to a context that included Beaker wares; an Accessory Cup like the complete one from Site II, with its Beaker-related comb-impressed decoration, confirmed their close relationship although the awl from the central pit was of a type never associated with Beakers (Section L). Nothing was found at Site II – except

perhaps the weather-worn Cornish greenstone axe – that need have been widely separated in time one from another, nor in cultural terms. It seems probable that the Food Vessel was deposited at the time the barrow was being built or else soon afterwards, and that its owner had enjoyed a relationship of some kind with the dead interred there, like that which prompted the burial of a broken, incomplete pot, admittedly in a secondary position, at the nearby bowl-barrow Site XVII.

Before 1953 no saucer-barrow in Wessex had been excavated completely, or even partially examined by modern methods. In 1958 three saucer-barrows were examined at Down Farm, Pewsey (F de M Vatcher 1960), and the following year a saucer-barrow at Fosbury, near Shalbourne was cleared (Johnston 1963). None yielded a central grave, nor did any of them contain features which resembled those of Site II at Snail Down. Indeed, the absence or rarity of burials linked these other barrows and set them apart from the rigidly central and thus conventional burial practice found at Site II. From information obtained by Hoare, Thurnam and others, it is clear that cremation was the rite almost invariably associated with burials in saucer-barrows, and a high proportion of them occurred at the centres of such burial mounds (Grinsell 1957, 222 – 224). At least four Wiltshire saucer-barrows have been found to contain secondary – or altogether later – burials (*ibid*).

Figure 7
Detailed description of layers

Sections 1, 2, 3   Layers 1–5, 10, ditch filling

Layer 1 Pure yellow-white chalk, more sludgy and compact than on other sites because of more clay-like consistency of natural chalk around Site II. Filled angles between lower walls and floor of ditch.

Layer 2 Found only in section 3, NE. Looser, more earthy chalk, derived from fill of ancient tree hole cut by barrow ditch.

Layer 3 Found in section 2, W and section 3, NE. Deposit of coarse silt containing more chalky rubble and flints than layer 4, which sealed it. An early silt, sealing layer 1 in both sections; derived from the inside.

Layer 10 Found only in section 2, E. This resembled layer 3, but its chalky rubble concentrated in three sloping tip-lines, separated by purer yellow loam.

Layer 4 Compact chalky loam, yellow-brown, with fairly heavy concentration of chalk and flint chips. Seals layers 1, 2, 3 and 10.

Layer 5 Upper ditch-fill, compact brown loam with thin scatter of chalk chips and flints. Sealed all previous layers.

Sections 1, 2, 3   Layers 6–9, make-up of bank and natural soils

Layer 6 Mixed chalk and loam, grading from modern humus above it to solid chalk below. Flints tending to concentrate at base. Rather more clay-like than on sites to the N and E because of nature of chalk hereabouts. In section 3, NE, this material filled an ancient tree hole.

Layer 7 Ancient land surface, a fairly clearly defined brown chalky loam sealed beneath bank surrounding barrow. Flints tending to concentrate at base.

Layer 8 Rubbly chalk sealing layer 7 and representing make-up of bank. Only preserved in section 2, W and 3, NE. In latter, overlay ancient tree hole as a diffuse scatter.

Layer 9 filling of small depressions. Several irregular hollows were found which interrupted layer 6. All filled with fairly chalk-free brown loam. In section 2, beneath intersection of cross-baulks, the hollow represented extreme edge of central burial pit.

Figure 8
Detailed description of layers

Sections 3, 5   Layers 9, 11, 12, pit-fillings

Layer 9 Brown loam with chalk chips and some flints. Interrupted layer 6 (Fig 7, sections 1–3) and filled small irregular pit containing inverted Food Vessel.

Layer 11 Filling of lower part of Burial Pit 2, section 5. Much cremated human bone mixed with soil, ash, charcoal dust and natural flints. Trepanned disc from skull at base. Upper part of this filling noticeably browner however and containing less cremated bone and wood ash.

Layer 12 Filling of upper part of Burial Pit 2, section 5. Parti-coloured, mainly dark-brown soil with chalk and flint chips, much charcoal, and potsherds, all thoroughly mixed. At top, became paler but still made sharp contrast with topsoil. This pit clearly cut layer 6.

Layer 6 Natural soil, as described above for sections 1–3. Cut by Burial Pit 2 and by Food vessel pit.

Section 4   Central burial pit

Mixed chalky earth, the infill of Hoare's excavation. Cunnnington's excavation disc at base. Fill included an unusually high concentration of natural flints.

SITE III

SPTA 2224: A BELL-BARROW

SUMMARY

Around 3490 ± 90 BP (NPL – 141) the centre for a bell-barrow was selected and a marking-out peg driven into the soil. When the edges of its surrounding ditch and the limit of its mound had been set out in the turf, a funeral pyre of oak logs and other wood was built 10ft to the N of the peg and perhaps at this stage a flimsy stake barricade, broken by a central gap, was erected just within the proposed edge of the barrow mound to the NW. A corpse, likely to have been that of a woman, was cremated upon the pyre. When the flames had died down and some of the charred embers deliberately scattered, the corpse's ashes were collected up in an urn (assuming Site III to be Hoare's No 7) and a shallow hole scraped to receive it just N of the marking-out peg for the barrow. Gangs of people then began to dig the ditch. Turves were heaped first, grass downwards, as special protection for the large urn which was projecting above the edge of its pit. Topsoil and subsoil followed until the core of the barrow was some 6ft high. The work was completed by a hard-packed jacket of clean chalk rubble, raising the height of the mound to above 8ft. Shortly afterwards, three elongated pits were dug at equal intervals around the outer edge of the ditch. Finally, and perhaps in association with them, two secondary burials after cremation were deposited in pits on the berm of the barrow in the SW quarter. They were contained in Collared Urns and each was covered by a heap of flints. In the first, had been buried a group of beads in faience, amber, jet, jet-shale and stone. The second appears subsequently (but still in ancient times) to have been emptied out and replaced in its pit, two small vessels added apparently to wedge it upright. A radiocarbon assay of 3440 ± 90 BP was obtained for Secondary Burial 1.

During Roman times a cart track, T1, connecting nearby farmsteads with the main road from *Sorviodunum* to *Cunetio* cut across the ditch and berm of this bell-barrow along its S margin.

INTRODUCTION

Site III was a bell-barrow, one of four examples of this type in the cemetery, and the smallest. It had been badly damaged by tracked vehicles; there was a broad hollow diametrically across the site, cutting down nearly 3ft into the mound and exposing about one quarter of the barrow to the elements. On either side of this rutted strip the barrow was covered with downland vegetation. A broad berm, which separated the base of the mound from its surrounding silted-up ditch, was clearly visible.

Hoare's account does not allow us to equate Site III with any of the mounds he examined because not all are numbered on his plan (1812, opp. 180). Number 6 is without doubt the bowl-barrow (2217) immediately SW of Site III; logically, Hoare's No 7 should be the adjacent symbol to the NW, our Site III. But his No 8 is depicted among the row of mounds immediately N, which includes Site XVII, and his No 7 could have been one of those. The identification must remain in doubt. Of Nos 7 and 8 Hoare wrote (1812, 183):

> In No 7 we discovered a large sepulchral urn rudely baked and containing an interment of burned bones. No 8 had a simple deposit of burned bones.

If Site III was Hoare's No 7, he removed the urn for we found no trace of it, nor has it survived. He left the bones behind and these we recovered. Outlines of an excavation pit at the centre of the barrow, presumed to be Hoare's, were clear in every section exposed in 1955. Tank tracks had destroyed its upper edges and it was not possible to discover whether it had been square or round. It narrowed in a series of steps, arriving at the burial pit

without damaging the ancient land surface immediately around it. It seems that this was a crater-like cutting, its sides kept clean cut. It had evidently been re-filled immediately, but not all the spoil had been replaced, for a considerable deposit lay on the S side of the barrow mound (Figs 10, 11, sections 2, 3).

Site III was included by Grinsell in his classic paper on bell-barrows published in 1934 (219, 229). Other references to it are as follows: Hoare 1812, plan opp. 180 (but not numbered), ?Nos 7 or 8, 183; Goddard 1914, 234, Collingbourne Kingston 8; Thomas and Thomas 1956, 137–139, fig 2; Atkinson 1957, 232; Grinsell 1957, 209; *ibid* 1958, 99, 102; Stone and Thomas 1957, 79; Annable and Simpson 1964, 63, 118, nos 504, 505; 64, 119, nos 515–518; S Thomas 1965, pls 137, 138; Thomas, N, 1976, 229, figs 54, 55, and 19, fig 6, Collared Urn; Longworth 1984, 285, Nos 1674–1676; Burl 1987, 196.

After excavation the spoil heaps were pushed back over the area of the barrow by military bulldozer, without any attempt at reconstruction. The work lasted for four weeks in 1955 under the direction of N Thomas. About thirty volunteers were present daily.

DESCRIPTION

Pre-barrow Features and Beaker Settlement Remains

The thickness and general appearance of the soil and subsoil beneath the barrow resembled that of today, allowing for compression by the superimposed mound. The soil upon which the barrow builders had stood was a compact chocolate loam. It was quite free of flints and chalk except for a concentration of the former at its base (clear in Pl 15). It had a fairly constant thickness of about 4in. Beneath it, the subsoil was composed of the usual grey jumbled soil, thoroughly mixed with chalk and flints. It contained a number of irregular hollows filled with more loamy soil which had probably held ancient tree and bush roots (eg Fig 10, sections 1 and 2; Fig 11, section 3). At the edge of the mound the ancient topsoil gradually thinned out and disappeared: the subsoil beneath it merged, without noticeable break, with the modern subsoil.

Numerous sherds of Beaker and associated domestic wares, and a few fragments of daub and Grooved Ware were recovered from the mound core of Site III (Section C). Sherds of earlier Neolithic plain wares (mainly in the mound core and land surface beneath) were included. Very few fragments could be joined together; few exceeded 1sq in in surface area. Though some sherds showed more wear than others, the majority was in fresh condition. More than one sherd matched fragments found on Sites X–XIV, which lay less than 100ft to the NE (Fig 21).

The horizontal distributions of Beaker and allied wares and of worked flint is shown in Figure 15. The following table indicates the amounts of such pottery and worked flint that came from the principal structural features of the bell-barrow:

This assemblage had the appearance of casual inclusion when the barrow ditch was being dug. We assume that it must have been lying about, in and just below the turf at that time, to become incorporated as the work proceeded. The horizontal distribution was not uniform. The mass of the material was concentrated in the NE quadrant of the mound, adjacent to the Beaker settlement beneath sites X–XIV, with some sherds and a noticeably higher concentration of flints in the opposite quadrant

One potsherd of earlier Neolithic (C9) and fifteen of Beaker wares were scattered over the ancient land surface together with 31 flints (Section G, Table 14). The Neolithic wares occurred at Site III alone. Together with the Cornish greenstone axe from Site II, a short distance to the SW, they represent an earlier occupation of this part of the down, of which no structural remains were uncovered during the excavations. The Beaker wares and the flints probably belonged to the settlement located immediately NE beneath Sites X–XIV.

A stakehole at the centre of the barrow and a slightly curved alignment of eleven similar holes N of it (Fig 9, 'marking-out peg'; Fig 12) might have belonged to a pre-barrow phase. It seems more likely, however, that they are from the earliest episode in the burial ceremonies which preceded construction of the barrow.

The Primary Burial, its Funeral Pyre and Related Structures (plan, Fig 12; sections, Figs 10 and 11; Pls 17, 18; burial, Section A, Cremation 7; radiocarbon determination, Section T).

On the land surface beneath the centre of the barrow, the remains of a **funeral pyre** were discovered, with a **burial pit** to the S and a **row of stake holes** to the NW.

The **burial pit** was found to occur exactly at the bottom of Hoare's presumed cutting. The large quantity of cremated bones which lay in it are probably those of an adult woman (Section A, Cremation 7). If Site III was Hoare's No 7 (see above), he had removed an urn from this pit but left behind the cremated human bones which had been contained within it. The pit was an irregular-sided oval, measuring c 4 × 3ft. It had been dug through the burnt land surface and subsoil but had only just penetrated the solid chalk (Fig 11, section 4). None of its original filling remained. During recent work (1994) on the primary cremation, a utilized blade flake, patinated white, was noticed among the bones and is omitted from Section G. This flake, 66.0m in length, retaining cortex along one edge, has been worked with minimal retouch into an end scraper.

On the NE edge of the pit there was a pile of flints, chalk, loam and ash roughly oval in shape and with a maximum thickness of about 5in (Fig 12). This deposit extended to the edge of the burial pit. The land surface beneath it was covered with the same wood ash that covered the central area. On the SW side of the burial pit, and separated from it by a space 2–3ft wide, was another elongated deposit roughly following the edge of the pit. This also lay on a land surface already covered by wood ash. The deposit itself was composed of earth and wood ash with much charcoal, including twiglets, some of which were standing on end. Flints and chalk were absent from this pile. These deposits were all that remained of the spoil produced when the burial pit had been made.

The area of land surface shown stippled in Figure 12 was found to be covered with wood ash. The soil itself was not baked hard or in any way altered by heat. The wood ash formed a patchy layer, nowhere more than 2in thick and in places almost disappearing. In plan, however,

Table 3   Identifiable Beaker and associated wares, and worked flints, stratified in Site III

	Potsherds	Worked Flint
Topsoil, subsoil, including berm	32	18
Chalk covering of barrow mound and earth/turf stack below	136	116
Ancient land surface at base of mound	31	59
Ditch filling	39	70
Three pits outside ditch	–	14
Secondary Burial 1	–	1
Secondary Burial 2	–	22
	238	300

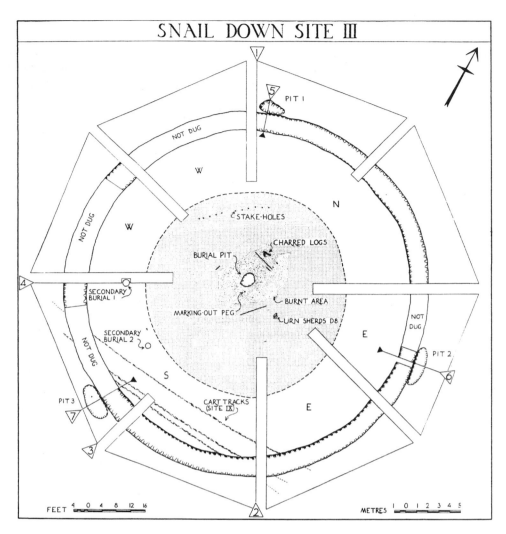

Fig 9   Site III, a bell-barrow. Plan. Course of Site IX cart tracks and hedge bank indicated.

it was concentrated in a roughly rectangular area measuring some 19ft x 11ft and beyond it the wood ash was absent. Besides grey ash, pieces of charcoal were scattered everywhere and increased in quantity towards the logs at the N end. Some of the charcoal fragments were large enough to be described as burnt twigs. All over this area small splinters and chips of burnt human bone occurred, together with a few pieces which were unburnt. These tended to concentrate around the S side of the burial pit.

At the N end of this ashy area a group of burnt timbers, A–K, was found which must represent the base of a **funeral pyre**. They formed a rectangular plan measuring 8ft × 3ft. As shown in Figure 12 by closer stippling, the land surface beneath and extending a little to the E of these logs was not just ashy but had been thoroughly burnt. It was coloured from white through grey to yellow and orange, yet this parti-coloured loam was nowhere more than about 3in thick. The area between the logs was filled with ash and smaller pieces of charcoal, some recognisable as twigs. Half a burnt hazel nut was found. Very fragmentary burnt human bone occurred in this ashy material. On the N edge of the pyre an unburnt lower incisor of a young adult was recovered (Section A, No 5).

The timbers of the pyre were orientated roughly E/W and lay in two groups. At the NW end of the deposit there were the charred remains of three short, stout logs, A–C, which overlapped. The largest, A, must originally have had a diameter of about 1ft. As discovered, they appeared as charcoal-lined voids. Clearly, the outsides of the logs had been preserved because they were partially burnt, whereas the unburnt centres had decayed completely, without becoming filled by earth. At first these logs were mistaken for wooden containers. The second group of timbers lay to the S and E. All appeared to be flatter and of solid charcoal, none wider than 3in nor thicker than 2in. As regular and straight as the plan (Fig 12) suggests, they may have been saplings or coppiced poles. At one point at the E end of the pyre a short length of wood, H, was found lying at right-angles to two other pieces and was on top of them. This provided the only evidence for a second layer of wood lying at an angle to the timbers on the land surface.

The group of three large logs had sunk into the old land surface and had just reached the subsoil. Some of the other logs had also burned their way down into the pre-barrow soil.

Two straight timbers, L, M, lay outside the area of land surface covered by ash. They had been thrown clear of the burnt area just described. The soil beneath them was quite unmarked by heat and unstained by ash. The

SNAIL DOWN SITE III

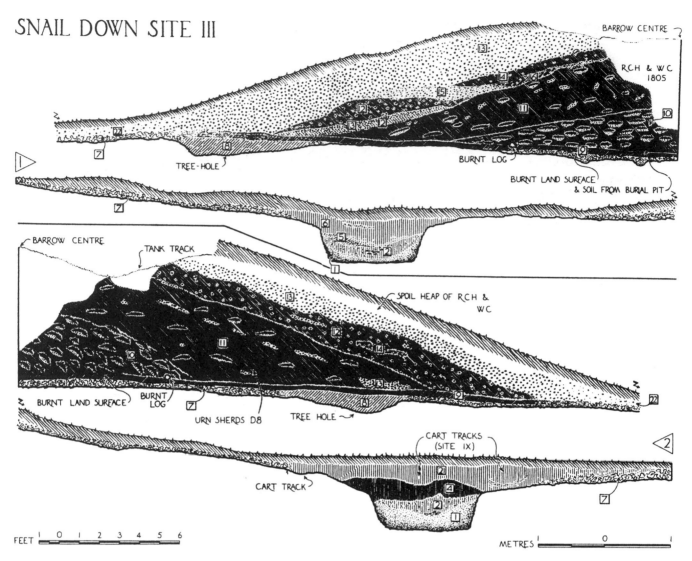

Fig 10   Site III, sections 1, 2, including Site IX.

timbers had evidently not been alight when deposited there. Identification of timbers A–M is given in Table 33, Section S.

Charcoal of *Quercus* (oak) was submitted to AERE Harwell and to the National Physics Laboratory in 1955 for radiocarbon assay, with the following results:

> HAR-61: 3540 ± 140 BP; cal BC 2125–1695 (1 sigma); cal BC 2290–1520 (2 sigma).
> HAR-13: 3500 ± 110 BP; cal BC 2010–1690 (1 sigma); cal BC 2140–1530 (2 sigma).
> NPL-141: 3490 ± 90 BP; cal BC 1935–1695 (1 sigma); cal BC 2115–1610 (2 sigma).

These results are considered further in Part 2, Section T.

To the SE of the burial pit a **single stake hole** was found extending into the undisturbed chalk. It was not observed running up into the barrow mound above, although this does not preclude the possibility that the stake had been upright when the mound was heaped over the burial area. The stake had been 2in in diameter, roughly pointed and driven 3in into the chalk. Its hole was filled with grey loam without trace of charcoal.

North-west of the burial area a **line of eleven stake holes** was found, running NE/SW for 20ft. They were fairly evenly spaced, 1–2ft apart. Between stakes 5 and 6 (Fig 12) there was a space nearly 4ft wide. Those numbered 1–5 formed an almost straight line whereas numbers 6–11 made a gentle curve. In diameter, they varied from 1½–3in and in depth (from chalk surface) from 1½–5in. The ends of some were almost straight, eg 5 and 6, 8, and 9; the rest showed evidence for sharpening. Their fillings were all a grey-brown loam, charcoal free. One of the stake holes (10) was discovered extending from the top of the old land surface; the others were not seen until the natural chalk had been reached.

THE BARROW STRUCTURES

In plan the **ditch** (Figs 9–11, 14; Pls 13, 24) described an almost perfect circle with a maximum diameter of 104ft (in Thomas and Thomas 1956, 137, it was given erroneously as 115ft). It had a fairly even width, at chalk

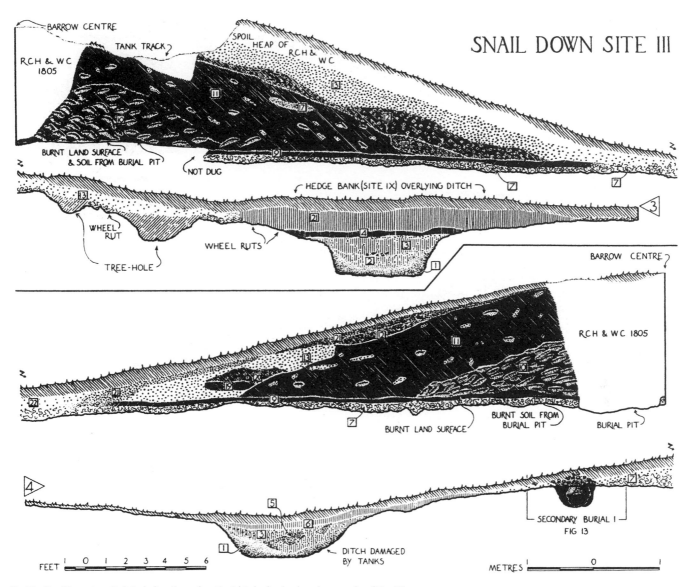

Fig 11   Site III, sections 3, 4, including Secondary Burial 1; hedge bank and cart tracks of Site IX.

surface, of about 4½–5ft and a depth, from the same level, of 2ft. Everywhere the floor of the ditch was flat, and its walls splayed out so slightly that originally they must have been vertical. Evidence for the base of a stake, found in the ancient land surface just to the S of the primary burial pit, proved to be so close to the estimated centre of this ditch circle that it may be presumed to be the point from which the latter was originally laid out (above).

A group of flints, five heavy roughing-out flakes, lay close together on the ditch floor near the SE corner of the S quadrant (Section G). Circumstance and precise location suggested that the latter was contemporary with the building of the barrow and probably to be associated with the work.

The **barrow mound** (plan, Fig 9; sections, Figs 10, 11; Pls 13–16) had been constructed in four distinct layers, corresponding to the order in which turf, humus, subsoil and solid chalk would have been thrown up when the surrounding ditch was dug. The top of the mound had been badly damaged by the passage of tracked vehicles and it was difficult to gauge its original height. This cannot have been far short of 8ft. The core of the mound was

a heap of dark chocolate-coloured soil (layer 10, all sections), greasy in texture and mottled with patches of orange, grey and almost black soils. It was thickly charged with charcoal specks and included some larger fragments. In plan this core was an irregular oval, distinctly pointed on its E side. It measured 24 × 20ft and its maximum original height must have been about 3ft. Within this highly coloured mound the outlines of turves were unmistakable: curved dark streaks averaging about 9in in length, with patches of greyer soil and chalk beneath – turves with the subsoil and chalk clinging to their roots (Pl 14). Specks of charcoal were noticeable. These turves had been stacked with the grass downwards. They tended to dip down, away from the central and highest point of the mound. Everywhere the edges of this turf core sealed the funeral pyre, the area of burning and the burial pit described above.

Layer 11 was a jacket of less turfy but still very humic soil which covered the central turf stack and formed a mound about 38ft in diameter and some 6ft high. The structure of individual turves was less distinct and this chocolate-coloured soil contained a number of

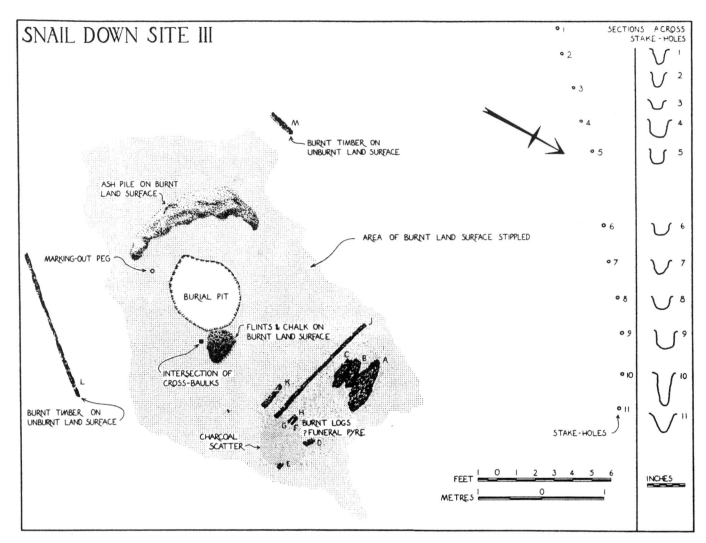

Fig 12   Site III, features associated with funeral pyre and central burial.

thin tips of chalk. Where turves were visible, they tended to lie horizontally.

Soil analysis confirmed that the material of the central stack was very high in humus content. Where samples were compared with those higher in the mound, eg from layer 12, it could be shown that the latter represented subsoil, whereas the greater humic content of the former suggested pure topsoil.

Throughout layers 10 and 11 there occurred a heavy scatter of mainly unworn potsherds, representing Beakers and allied wares, together with worked and unworked flint flakes. When their locations are plotted horizontally it can be seen that they were concentrated in the NE quarter of the mound, more sporadically towards the SW and everywhere less frequently on the berm and in the ditch (Fig 15). Table 3 (above) establishes that each of the principal structural elements making up Site III yielded its share of this material.

In contrast, one group of Collared Urn sherds was found lying close together and horizontally, about 9in above the ancient land surface in layer 11 (Fig 10, section 2, D8). These represented part of the wall and collar of a vessel which had been dropped – or deposited – and pressed flat during barrow building (Section D, Fig 45).

Attention is also drawn to a copper alloy object, N1 (Section N, Fig 59) whose apparent provenance within the barrow mound must be open to question.

Layer 12 sealed the turf and soil of the barrow core, and its outer edge almost coincided with the disappearance of the land surface beneath the barrow. Except where it had been damaged by the weight of military vehicles, this layer consisted of grey-brown soil, becoming increasingly chalky towards its top. It contained a number of streaks of darker soil which, as layers 14 and 16, became identical with the turf of layers 10 and 11 at the base of the mound. Around the northern sector of the mound, between the middle of the W quadrant and the octant baulk dividing quadrant N, layer 14 formed a noticeable, continuous spread over the upper part of the mound, separated from its core, layer 11, by a spread of more chalky soil, layer 16 (Fig 10, section 1; Pl 15). Layer 12 was irregular in thickness and composition. In section 2 (Fig 10) it was everywhere nearly 2ft thick. Elsewhere it was much thinner and in places had almost disappeared.

The mound reached its final height and diameter with a covering of unweathered chalk rubble (layer 13). In places this was about 2ft thick but elsewhere its thickness was less than 1ft (eg section 2, Fig 10). The base of the chalk was interleaved with the grey intermediate soils (layer 12) and even with pure turf and topsoil of the barrow's core (Fig 10, section 1; Pl 16). Its upper part, however, was pure white.

The diagnostic feature of a bell-barrow is the berm, or space skirting the mound and separating it from its surrounding ditch. The **berm** of Site III was clear on the ground before excavation. When dug (Pl 13), it was shown to have an average width of 17–18ft. It was covered by a normal thickness of downland turf, with below it a layer of jumbled grey soil with chalk chips and flints (layer 7). There was a concentration of natural flints at the base of the turf. Three sherds of Late Bronze Age Plain Ware (Section D, D9) occurred in layer 7, N Quad.

The berm sloped downwards towards the barrow ditch. On the S side, the outer edge of the berm was nearly 2ft lower than its inner edge where it joined the ancient land surface beneath the barrow. Elsewhere the drop was less noticeable, but since the Down here sloped from N to S, this was only to be expected. Everywhere, however, an average fall of 1–1½ft was recorded. This phenomenon, found wherever an ancient land surface was sealed beneath a bank or mound, has been discussed for Site I (above).

POST BARROW-CONSTRUCTION EVENTS

Three pits (plan, Fig 9; sections, Fig 14, 5–7) impinged upon the outer wall of the barrow ditch. They were spaced very nearly at equal intervals along its circumference.

Pit 1 had an irregular pear shape, its greatest width at chalk surface being nearly 4½ft and its length about 7 ft. Its maximum depth was nearly 3ft below the same surface and 1ft below the floor of the ditch at this point. Its sides were uneven but gently curved: its W end sloped up gradually but its E end became almost vertical.

Pit 2 was a more regular oval in plan, narrow with a fairly flat floor and evenly sloping sides and ends. It was 12ft long and about 3⅜ft wide where its sides were best defined. Its general depth was about 1½ft.

Pit 3 was the broadest. It was 10½ft long, 5ft wide with an overall depth of nearly 2ft. Its floor was flat but its sides and ends sloped up fairly sharply. The surfaces of all three pits were fresh and unweathered.

The ditch sections (Figs 10, 11, 14) suggest an uninterrupted pattern of natural silting until the fill was complete. The primary silt, layer 1, was a clean white chalk derived by weathering from the upper edges of the ditch. Secondary silts, layers 2, 3, 5 and 6, comprised a series of loams which became progressively more compact and chalky as they occurred deeper in the ditch.

The junctions between layers in the ditch were not as distinct as they were on Site I or on Site VIII, another bell-barrow (Fig 14, section 3), because the natural chalk beneath Site III approached the sludgy texture of that beneath Site II: soils and chalk tended to have much the same composition.

The fillings of the three pits and of the barrow ditch where they impinged upon each other were similar and indicated that their digging had followed closely upon the construction of the latter. It would seem that when the pits were dug, a low, narrow wall of chalk had been left separating them from the barrow ditch. Pit 1, however, went deeper than the ditch here and the outer wall of the latter was almost removed at the point of intersection (section 5, Fig 14). Because of this there was no primary chalk silt in the outer corner of the ditch here. In section 6 a considerable deposit of chalk in the outer half of the ditch suggested that this narrow separating wall had collapsed and weathered inwards into the ditch. In section 7 the primary chalk silt (layer 1, Fig 14) in the outer corner of the ditch was very slight, while there was a greater quantity of similar material near the bottom and on the inner side of the pit. Here the wall had evidently tumbled into the pit. The very loose chalk rubble on the floors of Pit 1 and the ditch beside it (section 5, layer 4, Fig 14) must represent a more sudden collapse of the wall in both directions. Layer 5 formed a compact chalky loam which filled the greater part of all the pits and the sections of ditch alongside them. It was heavily charged with chalk towards the outer half of each pit, suggesting the presence of spoil derived from the pits and heaped on their outer sides. There was also a distinct, but less noticeable increase of chalk in this layer towards the inner edge of the ditch. This would have been derived from the weathering of the ditch side. Nowhere was there a break in the upper fillings of pits and ditch. Pits followed ditch with an interval only long enough for the formation of a small amount of primary chalk silt in the latter. Soil analysis (in Site archive) of samples from section 5 confirmed that the filling of pits and ditch was natural, and that the pits had been dug soon after the ditch.

Where the bank of Site IX (below) overlay Pit 3 as well as the barrow ditch, a soil had formed across both features, confirming that the silting process had long since finished (section 2, Fig 10, section 7, Fig 14).

In all sections it was found that material from the mound had spread across nearly half the berm. This slip was almost 6in thick in section 3 (Fig 11) and here reached the ditch. Elsewhere the spread was much thinner. In section 4 (Fig 11) it was clearly cut by the pit for Secondary Burial 1 (below). The section across this burial (Fig 13, section 2) showed that subsequently the mound had continued to spread across the berm and up to the secondary burial: mound material covered its E edge.

Site III included two **secondary burials** of cremated human bones associated with Collared Urns and one with beads. Both occurred in the SW quarter of the berm (plans, Figs 9, 13; sections, Fig 13; Pls 19–23; Section A, Cremations 8, 9; urns, Section D, D10–D13, Figs 45, 46; beads, Section K, K1–K7, Fig 54).

Burial 1 (Section A, Cremation 8), lay about 34ft WSW of the barrow marking-out peg (above, Fig 9), nearly 5ft beyond the true edge of the barrow mound. Tank tracks lay on either side of it, obscuring the extent of its covering cairn of flints. A large Collared Urn (Section D, D10, Fig 45) was found standing upright in a pit which had been cut into the chalk to a depth of 1¼ft, with a maximum diameter of 2ft 2in. The walls of the pit were almost vertical and formed a fairly definite angle at their junction with the floor. On the E side of the pit its upper edge could be seen beginning at the top of the weathered natural chalk and was here sealed by later spreading of

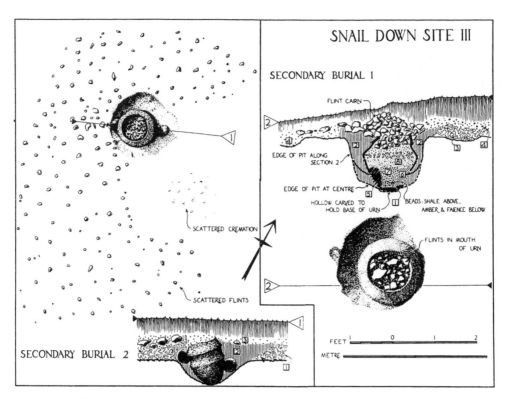

Fig 13   Site III, Secondary Burials 1 and 2, plans and sections 1, 2.

the barrow mound. On the W side the pit had been dug through material derived from the mound and here no subsequent debris from the latter had been deposited. The edge of the pit in the undisturbed chalk at the N and the W showed two distinct channels (Fig 13); elsewhere it was fairly regular and circular.

The urn had been placed against the E side of the pit, with its base set in a circular depression carefully cut into the floor of the pit to receive it (Fig 13; Pl 21). A similar hollow was also found in the central burial pit beneath Site XVII (below). The area between the urn and the sides of its pit had been filled with well-packed soil; around the W side, where the space to be filled was greatest, this was noticeably black and mixed with charcoal (Section S).

The urn had been placed in its pit intact and might just have projected above the contemporary ground level. As found, however, the weight of the flint cairn above it and the passage of army vehicles had compressed its collar and caused its lower half to bulge outwards (Pl 20). The cremated bones, perhaps of a child, had been placed at the bottom, forming a cylindrical heap 6in high and with distinct edges. This had been surrounded by soil, with a concentration of charcoal on the W. A thin scatter of small cremated bone fragments occurred throughout the earthy upper filling of the urn. The main mass of cremated bone contained brown patches which were tested for tannin and protein, in case they represented the remains of a leather container, for the compact appearance of the bone suggested that it had not been placed loose in the urn. No traces of leather were found, although this does not lessen the probability that the bones, once cool, had been put into a bag of some sort. Towards the base of the bone pile occurred a bead of amber, with fragments of another in stone, and one of

faience; three jet beads occurred about 1in higher up (Fig 13; Section K, K2-K7, Fig 54). The filling of the urn from its shoulder upwards comprised soil, chalk and charcoal, with an increasing quantity of flint nodules. At the mouth of the vessel and within the region of its collar the flints had been tight packed and interleaved, without bursting the rim. It was clear that such a packing was deliberate and not the result of subsequent pressure from above. The largest flints were reserved for the cairn which rose to a height of nearly 7in above the urn. This heap covered completely the urn pit but its original shape had been destroyed by the passage of army vehicles. In the scatter of flints from the cairn on its SE edge, one large shale or jet dumb-bell-shaped bead (Fig 54, K1) was found which may have formed part of an offering incorporated in the cairn. A thin spread of chalk from the barrow mound which overlay the edge of the cairn on the NE suggested that the mound had continued to spread after the deposition of Secondary Burial 1. Charcoals associated with the cremation included apple/hawthorn/rowan/whitebeam type, wild cherry/bird cherry type, and oak.

Charcoals of *Prunus avium/Padus* type, Pomoideae and *Quercus* (wild cherry/bird cherry type, hawthorn/apple/rowan/whitebeam type and oak) were submitted to Glasgow for radiocarbon assay with the following result:

GU-5302: 3440 ± 90 BP; cal BC 1886–1673 (1 sigma); cal BC 2020–1520 (2 sigma).

This result is considered further in Section T.

Burial 2 occurred nearly 20ft to the SE and was almost 32ft from the marking-out peg at the centre of the barrow. A Collared Urn (D11) lay tilted in a bowl-shaped pit which had a maximum diameter of 1ft 7in and a depth

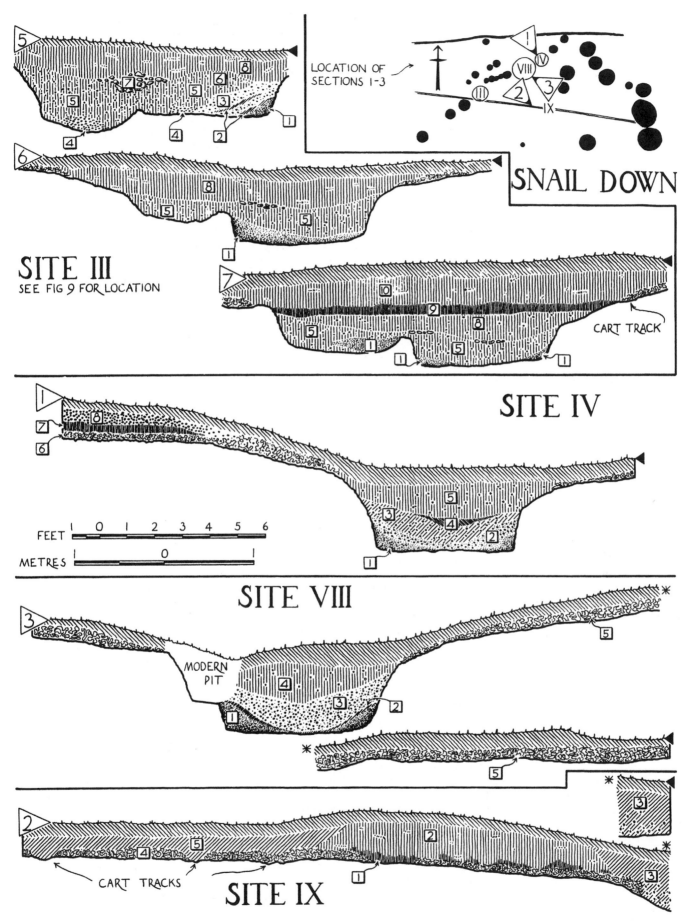

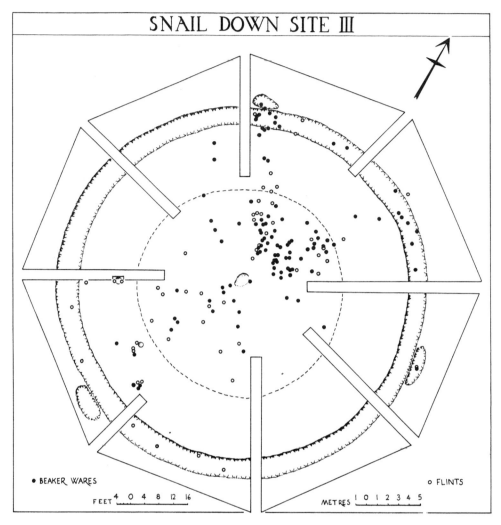

SNAIL DOWN SITE III

● BEAKER WARES   ○ FLINTS

FEET ⁴ 0 4 8 12 16   METRES ¹ 0 1 2 3 4 5

Fig 15   Site III, distribution of Beaker sherds and worked flints.

in solid chalk of 7in. The plan of the pit at chalk level was irregular, having distinct bulges on the N and E. Its sides sloped gently. The upper edge of the pit could be seen at the surface of the weathered chalk, giving it an original maximum depth of about 11in. The unweathered, intact Collared Urn stood uneasily in this pit, tilting towards the SW and clearly wedged into position by an equally complete Collared Vessel (D12) on the WSW and a Bipartite Vessel (D13) with damaged rim on the opposite side (Fig 13; Pls 22, 23; Section D, D11–D13, Fig 46). The three vessels contained fairly clean red loam identical to the material which filled the pit. Soil analysis revealed worm casts, while fragmentary snail shells in this filling confirmed its uniformity throughout the burial deposit and suggested that it was a natural accumulation. In addition, a worn sandstone pebble not native to Snail Down occurred in the top of the Collared Urn D11; what may have been fossilised droppings, perhaps of sheep, were found in the soil filling the Collared Vessel D12.

In the lower filling of the largest urn was a small quantity of burnt human bone, remains of a very young child (Section A, Cremation 9).

Additional cremated bone, but still not much more than a trace, lay scattered about, 2ft to the E of this pit. It occurred at the base of the chalky soil which sealed the

pit and represented the subsequent spread of mound material over this part of the berm. At the same level an unusual concentration of flint nodules occurred in an ill-defined arc around the N, W and S sides of the burial deposit (Fig 13). These also were thinly covered by the spread of the barrow mound. It seems not beyond belief to suggest that originally the largest urn, containing a cremation, had been covered by a flint cairn like that over Secondary Burial 1. Subsequently this cairn had been removed and spread around the W half of the burial area. The urn had been emptied, most of its contents scattered to the E and it had then been replaced in its pit, wedged in position by two small pots brought for this purpose or else originally part of the grave group. Thereafter, pit and urns seem to have become covered naturally, as soil analysis suggests, although their unweathered condition implies, on the contrary, that they must have received at least a slight covering of soil at the hands of those who enacted this curious circumstance.

Among the scattered flints from the cairn which covered this burial originally, 21 unworked flakes and a blade flake were recovered.

Site IX, a **bank** on the S side of the supposed Romano-British farm track T1 (Fig 2), was found to overlie the ditch of Site III and was examined at two points where the latter was sectioned (plan, Fig 9; sections, Figs 10: 2, 11: 3, 14: 7; Pl 24). Assuming a Romano-British date for this earthwork, it showed that at that period the barrow ditch had become silted up completely and that a soil had formed over it (Figs 10, 11, layer 4; 14, layer 9). The soil analysis of section 3 (Fig 11) established that the silting profile in the ditch, ending in a soil with Site IX on top of it (layer 21), was a well-established one, which must have been formed a considerable time before the superimposition of the bank.

On the S side of the mound (Figs 10, 11, sections 2 and 3), the remains of Hoare's spoil heap formed a deposit about 1ft in thickness which sealed layer 13.

REMARKS

Calculations described above, when applied to Site III, made it clear that the volume of turf and topsoil removed from the site of the ditch would have been sufficient to provide a turf core of the volume recorded beneath this bell-barrow. Enough chalk rubble could also have come from the ditch to cover the mound in the manner described above. In the *interim* report (Thomas and Thomas 1956, 139) it was suggested that the berm had probably been stripped down to the natural chalk when the barrow was built. This suggestion was not substantiated by our calculations for volume and is now withdrawn. When originally completed, Site III possessed a white hemispherical mound, separated from its equally white ditch by the berm's green ring of turf. This presupposes that, as the reports on snails (Section R), animal bones (Section Q) and soils have suggested, the Bronze Age vegetation cover on the Down resembled that of today. The berm served several purposes. Aesthetically it afforded a contrast between the mound and ditch, just as the flat grassy plateau defined by the ditch of any disc-barrow would have emphasised its chalk-white burial mound. Structurally it was a device to provide an imposing mound from a relatively shallow ditch. Thirdly it protected the barrow ditch from material which would slip from the sides of the mound.

The chalk covering was a notable feature of Site III. This could also be seen on Site VIII, where the tank track had exposed a section through the upper part of a much more substantial mound (Pl 3). Such jackets of whitening have been recorded on many bell- and bowl-barrows elsewhere in chalk country. Yet excavation of the massive double bell-barrow on Snail Down, Site XIX, showed that this covering layer had not been applied with such care: the section revealed that there the chalk crust had slipped from at least the upper part of the main mound (Pl 53) and was absent from the smaller mound. Nor was there any distinctive chalk covering to the bowl-barrow, Site XVII. Although a barrow ditch dug in chalk would naturally provide material to cover the barrow in the manner found on Site III, it is clear from the excavations at Snail Down that a dense, permanent white layer was not always desired (or achieved). It was evidently more than a structural feature made possible by local geology.

The barrow mound was probably built by people working in gangs. Evidence for this was clear at the junction of layers 12 and 13, the humic core and capping of chalk. Here there was much interleaving of soils and chalk rubble (Pl 16), as if some gangs had reached solid chalk in the ditch while others were still heaping soil.

Within the earthen core of the barrow mound, a subsidiary heap at the centre stood out clearly. It had been built over the burial pit and since this was shallow we may suppose that the first turves had been stacked carefully around the protruding urn to protect it from the great heap of earth and chalk which was to follow. Well-preserved turves were found also in Site XIX and appeared in the section exposed by tanks in Site VIII. They were not as distinct, however, in Site XVII.

The woman buried beneath Site III had been cremated on a pyre of oak and other wood (Section S). While the pyre was found to cover ground which had clearly been burnt by it, two timbers lay some distance to the S upon ground which was not burnt. This may be taken to suggest that when the pyre had burnt down it was scattered by those collecting the bones for burial. These had first been largely freed from charcoal – a practice noticed in many Bronze Age burials – and then placed in an urn. The burial pit was dug next. The spoil obtained from it was heaped first around the S edge and then, as the pit penetrated the chalk, in a pile just to the N. Both heaps sealed a land surface which was already covered with charcoal and ashes from the pyre.

The heaping of spoil from a burial pit around its edge as a deliberate act has been noticed elsewhere on Salisbury Plain and more widely throughout the British Isles (Part 3). It was also found at Site XVII (below). What is less frequently recorded was the careful separation of topsoil from subsoil during preparation of a burial pit. Whatever the explanation, it shows a nice distinction on the part of the grave diggers between the two principal layers beneath their feet, only to be expected of people whose livelihood was rooted in the soil. They did what came naturally when hollowing out the dead woman's burial pit. The generally ragged appearance of the central pit beneath Site III was also unusual. Its shape was irregular and no attempt had been made to copy the vertical sides and flat floor found in Secondary Burial 1 from this site and from Sites I, XIV, XV and XVII. It is possible, however, that at least in part the irregular plan of the pit can be attributed to Hoare's presumed clearance.

The line of stakes along the NW edge of the burial area is not easy to explain. It is possible that these may belong to the altogether earlier settlement found to underlie Sites X–XIV. The potsherds of Beaker and allied wares found in such profusion in the mound of Site III have been attributed to this source (above) and the stakes were not far from the mass of holes covered by Site XIV. Their regularity was, however, in strong contrast to the random scatter (Fig 21) of the settlement stake holes. If they belonged to Site III, they seem likely to have been associated with the primary burial. There was a central gap. Perhaps they represented a token entrance to this area reserved for the chief mourners, keeping out those less closely associated with the burial ceremonies? A parallel can be suggested, the ramp running into, and out of the ditch found beneath a barrow at Ysceifiog, Flintshire (Fox 1959, 4, fig 2, and 6–8), to which Sir Cyril Fox ascribed roughly the same purpose. Alternatively, this fence may have served to screen the mourners from the intensity of the flames (the missing central stake perhaps too short to penetrate the chalk like its neighbours). The feature is considered further in Part 3.

The discovery of three pits placed almost symmetrically along the outer circumference of the ditch emphasized the value of our decision to extend the excavation beyond the barrow ditch. Structurally, it was clear that the pits had been dug a short while after its construction. The material from them had been piled on their outer edge, whence it had returned during natural processes of silting. In view of their regular layout *vis-à-vis* the barrow ditch, it is presumed that the three pits were dug at one time – for the same purpose.

Soil analysis produced positive evidence that these pits had never contained corpses for any substantial period. Moreover, since only two secondary burials were found in Site III, it is difficult to connect the pits with the later burials directly. This feature, unique in barrow layout in Britain, was perhaps associated with those acts of ritual which must have occurred periodically after the burial of an important person. Since the three were contemporary, this particular act must have been an important one. There is no reason why it should not have been followed by one or both of the secondary interments. Perhaps for a short period corpses *were* extended in two of the pits prior to cremation. Pit 1 was noticeably more circular than the other two, and deeper. It could have served as an offering pit while Pits 2 and 3 were temporary receptacles for the dead.

If Pits 1–3 were not associated with the secondary cremations, they must represent the kind of subsequent act of worship which can be compared to the burial of Collared Vessel fragments in a pit in Site XVII (Pl 50). Each was an offering divorced from immediate human interment. It is possible also that the burial of the inverted Food Vessel in Site II represents the same behaviour (Pl 12).

Secondary Burials 1 and 2 were covered by small flint cairns and Collared Urns and Vessels were associated with both. Resemblances go no further. No 1 represented a straightforward burial of burnt bones in an urn accompanied by a wide variety of beads. In its first state No 2 was probably the same, although the pit containing the Collared Urn was no more than a depression in the solid chalk. Subsequently, the facts suggest removal of the cairn, emptying of the urn and its replacement in the pit supported now by two small pots. Such has no parallel in the archaeological record. The act was probably a sacred one: careful replacement of the urn does not look like the work of looters, a point we return to below (Part 3). Instead, it seems to represent yet another instance of post-burial ritual such as the digging of the pits around Site III and the deposit of a broken, incomplete vessel in Site XVII.

It was normal in the second millennium BC to cover burial pits with small cairns of flint or stone, especially when such secondary interments were not buried deep within the barrow's mound. Cremation Urns needed protection from the weather and from animals; and an element of secrecy may have made it necessary to hide the precise contents of a grave pit beneath such a covering. Although the pit found near the centre of Site V did not contain a burial, its contents were evidently so precious that it also had been given a deliberate covering – of

puddled clay – although this may not have been raised far, if at all, above the level of the surrounding land surface. The little pit containing Collared Vessel sherds in Site XVII, on the contrary, appeared to have been given no such protection.

The possibility that the three burials in Site III were contemporary needs to be recorded. Radiocarbon determinations for the funeral pyre and for charcoal from Secondary Burial 1 (Section T) would allow it, and it is also structurally permissible. The central burial was of a woman; the two others could have been her children. The presence of two flint cairns close together on what was to become part of the surrounding berm might have made it awkward for the barrow builders. But the notion cannot be ignored.

The Beaker sherds and other later Neolithic wares, along with the flints, which occurred at Site III in volume second only to that from Sites X–XIV, we interpret as having been associated with the settlement site below the latter barrows. These fragments of domestic rubbish were scraped up when the mound-building was proceeding. It is significant that, in distribution, the bulk of such finds in Site III came from that part of the bell-barrow nearest to Site XIV.

The occurrence beneath round barrows of domestic remains, where broken pottery was predominant, has been noted many times and commented upon at length by Gibson (1982, *passim* and below, Section C). The more precise significance of the Beaker settlement to the contemporary and later barrows on Snail Down receives final discussion in Part 3.

Figure 10
Detailed Description of Layers

Sections 1, 2   Layers 1–2, 5–6, ditch filling
Layer 1 Clean white chalk, filling angle between unweathered floor and lower walls of ditch. Hard and compact. In section 2, upper part had yellowish tinge; here layer 1 had exceptional thickness.
Layer 2 Grey-brown chalky loam with many chalk chips evenly scattered across ditch. Concentration of flint chips at or near base of layer.
Layer 5 Spread of rubbly chalk with compact chalk along its base, entering ditch from outside.
Layer 6. Deep brown loam, looser and darker at top, paler and more compact lower down. Contained distinct chalky spreads in section 1 and isolated chalk chips. Supported modern turf and humus, some natural flints concentrating along junction.

Section 2   Layers 4, 21, hedge bank of Site IX
Layer 4 Dark grey-brown compact loam with some natural flints along base. Top hollowed by cart track.
Layer 21 Very compact pale grey-brown loam, paler at base than at top. Almost free of chalk and flint chips. Compact trough S of ditch represented cart track.

Sections 1, 2   Layers 7–9, natural soils and ancient land surface
Layer 7 Undisturbed natural subsoil of Site III. Jumbled chalk and brownish loam, compacter under mound than elsewhere. Flints evenly scattered throughout.

Graded fairly evenly into solid chalk. Clearly cut by upper part of ditch and by cart tracks associated with Site IX in section 2.

Layer 8 Loose grey-brown loam, speckled with chalk chips. Contained scattered natural flints. Filled two hollows sealed by ancient land surface (9). Included specks of charcoal and some animal bones.

Layer 9 Dark brown slightly greasy loam, fairly free of chalk and natural flints. At centre of barrow (plan, Fig 12), top of layer 9 burnt red and black and covered with scattered charcoal, charred logs and heaps of ashy soil and chalky soil on S and N edges of burial pit . Died out under layer 13.

Sections 1, 2   Layers 10–16, make-up of barrow mound

Layer 10 Central stack of turves covering burial pit. Matrix of dark chocolate loam, containing turves – darker brown streaks, lighter on lower surface with patches of chalk here. In section 2, turves distinctly tilted down and outwards; in section 1, turves almost horizontal. Layer 10 sealed burnt land surface and heap of ashy soil (section 1). Specks of charcoal throughout layers 10, 11.

Layer 11 Matrix of dark chocolate loam, more parti-coloured than layer 10, with scattered turves, some showing chalk on underside. Also some thin streaks of chalk. All turves and chalk lenses tended to tilt down towards edge of mound, but less marked than in layer 10, section 2.

Layer 12 Fairly pale grey-brown loam, speckled with chalk chips, its lower half freer of chalk than the upper. Outer edge sealed ancient land surface (layer 9). Base of layer 12 in section 1 interrupted by layer 13 which extended across E half of W quadrant. Contained a thick spread of dark humic soil in section 2 (layer 14).

Layer 13 In both sections the main part of 13 constituted the layer of pure, compact chalky rubble covering the mound, and sealed by modern turf and humus: contained distinct patches of harder and softer chalk. It also included a thick spread of clean chalky rubble with clear-cut edges interrupting the initial deposition of layer 12 in section 1. In section 2 it formed a deposit on the ancient land surface near the edge of the upper turf core (layer 11). Varied in thickness from 2½ft (section 1) to 6in (section 2). Ancient land surface (9) died out under it.

Layer 14 Dark-brown humic soil lacking flints and chalk chips. Constituted a thick deposit separating upper turf core (11) and chalk barrow covering (13) at summit of mound in section 1. Appeared as insignificant spread in layer 12 in section 2.

Layer 15 Pale-brown chalky soil between layers 12 and 14/16, section 1 only.

Layer 16 Soft yellow-brown loam below layer 14, section 1 only.

Sections 1, 2   Layer 22, mound spread; ?Hoare's spoil

Layer 22 Brown loam, chalk content progressively thinner away from mound. Did not seal ancient land surface (9).

?Hoare's Spoil Heap Clear in section 2. Diffuse spread of chalky grey soil, extending as far as section 3 (Fig 11) and not present in octant E of section 1.

Figure 11
Detailed Description of Layers

Sections 3, 4   Layers 1–3, 5, 6, ditch filling
Layer 1 As for Fig 10.
Layer 2 As for Fig 10. Concentration of natural flints at centre of ditch in layer 2 (section 1, Fig 10) and at base of layer 2 in section 2, Fig 10, was on top of layer 2 in section 3 and at its base in section 4.
Layer 3 Compact brown soil with much scattered chalk.
Layer 5 Patches of compact chalk in layer 3, perhaps the result of tanks. Both layers untypical because of tank damage.
Layer 6 Grey compact soil, deposited by tank tracks.

Section 3   Layers 4, 21, hedge bank of Site IX
Layer 4 As for Fig 10 but thinner; noticeable line of chalk chips at base.
Layer 21 As for Fig 10.

Sections 3, 4   Layers 7, 9, natural soils and ancient land surface
Both layers as for Fig 10. Both cut by burial pit, section 4. Two prominent hollows filled by 7, sealed by 13, in section 3.

Sections 3, 4   Layers 10–13, 17–19, 21, make-up of barrow mound
Layer 10 As for Fig 10. In section 3, turves near centre of barrow sloped down towards edge of mound: higher in 10, turves more level. In section 4 all turves tended to slope down towards edge of mound.
Layers 11–13 As for Fig 10. Upper layers in section 4 damaged by tanks.
Layer 17 Light-brown patch of loam. Section 3 only.
Layer 18 Dark-chocolate soil resembling layer 11 but much more chalky. Section 3 only.
Layer 19 Brown soil almost free of chalk. Section 4 only.
Layer 20 Patch of more earthy chalk, section 4 only.
Layer 21 Top of 13, compressed and damaged by passage of tanks.
Layer 22, Mound spread. As for Fig 10. Cut by pit for Secondary Burial 1.
?Hoare's Spoil Heap As for Fig 10. Section 3 only.

Figure 13
Detailed Description of Layers

Secondary Burial 1 (section 2)
Layer 1 Fine white wood ash filling depression carved in floor of pit.
Layer 2 From floor of pit up to level of shoulder of urn, dense black ashy loam with much charcoal on W side, getting redder, with less charcoal, around E half of pit. Above shoulder of urn, loamy filling more evenly brown and free of charcoal.
Layer 3 Natural weathered chalk, well preserved on E side of burial and clearly cut by urn pit.
Layer 4 Spread of chalky material from barrow mound. Cut by urn pit but, on E side of section 2, shown to seal edge of urn pit after placing of burial.
Base of Urn contents Ash-free pale yellow soil, less than 1in thick.

Layer 5 Black soil with charcoal, around W side of cremation in lower part of urn.

Layer 6 Similar texture to above, but greyer in colour.

Layer 7 Cremation. A column of tight-packed burnt human bone, free of charcoal, but including small patches of bright brown soil. Beads of shale just above amber and faience at base of cremation.

Layer 8 Parti-coloured brown soil with charcoal and grey patches and small lumps of chalk. Sealed cremation and layers 5 and 6.

Flint Cairn Above layer 8 occurred first a band of small natural flint nodules, thicker on E side; then a flint-free deposit of ashy soil containing charcoal with very fragmentary cremated bone. Mouth of urn then filled with tight-packed, interlocking flint nodules, in an earthy matrix including chalk chips and traces of wood ash. This developed without break into remains (much damaged by tanks) of cairn of flints which covered urn and top of its pit, and extended above top of barrow mound spread around it.

Secondary Burial 2 (section 1)

Layer 1 Weathered natural chalk, cut by urn pit.

Layer 2 Clean reddish loam with some natural flints and animal bones. Filled urn pit and urns. Small patch of charcoal and wood ash beneath undecorated Vessel (D13) to N of large Collared Urn, and scattered burnt human bone in lower filling of largest urn.

Layer 3 More chalky soil representing spread of barrow mound. Sealed urn pit. Associated with concentration of flint nodules NW and SW of pots, and flecks of charcoal to W.

Figure 14
Detailed Description of Layers

Sections 5–7   Layers 1–10, filling of ditch and Pits 1–3

Layer 1 Compact chalk filling bottom corners of ditch, and one side of pit in section 7 (but here its deposition preceded by lower part of layer 5).

Layer 2 Two streaks of yellowish, more earthy chalk sealing layer 1 in section 5 and interleaved with layer 3 in this section.

Layer 3 In section 5 only. Fine pale-yellow loam impregnated with comminuted chalk. Less chalky than layer 1 beneath it but more chalky than normal ditch filling (layer 5) at this level.

Layer 4 Section 5 only. Loose chalk rubble at centre of ditch and of Pit 1, on natural chalk.

Layer 5 Main upper filling of pits and ditch. Brown loam charged with chalk and flints, in varying density as indicated in drawings. In section 5, this layer in pit more chalky than elsewhere, the chalk tending to fade towards outer edge of ditch (and inner edge of pit). Followed layer 4 below without break and no sharp change apparent as layer 5 entered ditch in this section. In section 6, density of chalk greatest towards outer edge of pit and inner edge of ditch. Likewise in section 7, where this material covered bottom of pit before layer 1 had started to accumulate, and eventually sealed layer 1.

Layer 6 Section 5 only. Deposit of pale loam with chalk, sealing layer 5 in middle of ditch and forming more gradual link between layers 5 and 8 than in other sections.

Layer 7 In all sections a thin scatter of loose flints separating layers 5 and 8, tending to concentrate above pit/ditch intersections. Heaviest deposit in section 5.

Layer 8 Uppermost pit and ditch-filling. Deep-brown loam with thin streaks of chalk, rather denser in section 7.

Layer 9 Section 7 only. Fine, deep grey-brown loam representing ancient land surface sealing pit and ditch when bank (Site IX) built across barrow here.

Layer 10 Section 7 only. Pale grey-brown loam, getting darker towards top: make-up of bank, Site IX. Some thin streaks of chalk in it.

SITE IV

SPTA 2245: A DISC-BARROW WITH CENTRAL MOUND

SUMMARY

The ditch of this disc-barrow was similar in shape to Site I, a little deeper and slightly narrower. Its bank, which preserved an ancient land surface, may have been separated from the ditch within by a slight berm; there was no evidence that it had ever been turf-revetted. A central burial after cremation had been disturbed before 1805.

INTRODUCTION

Site IV lay immediately NE of Site VIII, its ditch separated from that of the latter by a few feet. This disc-barrow was crossed by a broad tank track which had left it a greater ruin than any other site except the Hunter's Barrow (Fig 2). It was not possible to identify the actual mound; and the area where the bank of Site IV and ditch of Site VIII might have intersected had been destroyed. Only along the N and S areas of the site could its ditch and outer bank be seen.

Colt Hoare examined this barrow in 1805 and described the work in *Ancient Wiltshire* (1812) thus:

> 'No. 14 is a Druid barrow which had been opened before, as we found the ashes and bones of the original interment disturbed and jumbled together.' (plan, opp 180, No 14, 183).

Other references to Site IV include the following: Goddard 1914, 235, Collingbourne Kingston 14; Grinsell 1941, 108–109; Thomas and Thomas 1956, 140; Grinsell 1957, 217, No 14; *ibid* 1974, 103.

A point where the bank was well preserved on the NW side of the site was selected in 1953 and a trench was laid out across half of it and the ditch within, 5ft wide and 21ft long. Its purpose was to obtain comparative structural data for the study of the ditch and bank of Site I.

DESCRIPTION

Pre-barrow Features and Settlement Remains

No structures, potsherds or other traces of the Beaker settlement that lay to the W of Site VIII were found (Fig 2). The bank of Site IV preserved the remains of an ancient land surface (Fig 14, section 1; Pl 25). Upon *c* 4in of weathered natural chalk (layer 6) there was a diffuse layer of pale brown loam generally about 2in thick (layer 7). Along the E part of the cutting this soil increased in thickness, perhaps because of a tree-hole or other earth-filled disturbance in the natural chalk beyond the trench further E. This ancient soil contained many chalk chips, derived from the bank above by the activity of earthworms.

The Structures

The ditch (plan, Fig 2; section 1, Fig 14) was found to be $4\frac{1}{2}$ft deep (measured from the top of the ancient land surface), with a flat floor 5ft wide and sides which splayed out gently above the level of layers 1 and 2, to a width of about 8ft at the surface of the undisturbed chalk.

The bank (Fig 14; Pl 25), whose outer edge was not reached by the trench, showed as a fairly dense deposit of chalk rubble, in places nearly 6in thick. Its inner edge appeared distinctly, some 5ft from the outer side of the ditch. Between this edge of the bank and the ditch, the ancient soil extended for nearly 2ft as a fainter, more diffuse feature, with traces of rubbly chalk above it, separating modern turf from undisturbed subsoil. Then it died out and the chalk began to dip towards the ditch.

Beneath the bank, the chalk surface was $1\frac{1}{2}$ft higher than the modern turf on the plateau within the barrow ditch. It should be noted, however, that this area of the Down has a southward slope, which helps to accentuate the change in level between the ancient and modern land surfaces.

Post-construction Events

The bottom corners of the ditch were filled with clean, loose chalk rubble (layer 1), produced by the collapse of the upper walls of the ditch through natural weathering. Across the entire ditch, and sealing layer 1 on both sides, was a spread of much more condensed chalk (layer 2), which was thicker on the inside of the ditch. These layers, accumulating relatively rapidly, had preserved the ditch's original profile at its base, indicating, as elsewhere among the barrows on Snail Down, that their surrounding ditches had been dug with walls nearly vertical. Layer 3 was a compact yellow chalky deposit derived mainly from outside – the site of the bank. Where it covered the centre of the ditch, it was looser and more rubbly. Above it, layers 4 and 5 represented a slower, more earthy accumulation which filled the ditch to modern ground level. Layer 4 was paler brown and still chalky. Layer 5 was pure loam with a thick overall scatter of isolated chalk chips.

Two sherds, one of Romano-British ware, the other possibly pre-Roman, occurred in layer 5 of the upper ditch-filling.

REMARKS

The ditch-filling in general resembles that of Site I, particularly Figure 4, section 3. All the layers had been deposited by natural erosion, by wind and by rain. Layer 3 showed an increased thickness in the outer half of the ditch and was clearly derived from the bank. Layer 4 was not a true soil layer since it only filled the hollow along the centre of the ditch: it represented a pause in the levelling-up process. The primary rapid ditch-filling below it had ceased to happen: the slow secondary accumulation was to come on top of it.

The diffuse appearance of the ancient soil beneath the bank can be attributed to the activity of earthworms. On Site IV the process of transferring a buried soil to the surface by this means had never been completed, presumably because of the density of the bank rubble heaped on top of it. On Site I the land surface had been carried up through the bank until only a trace was visible in most sections.

Soil analysis demonstrated that the buried soils on Sites I and IV had become too degraded for comparisons to be possible. Their different states of preservation must be a reflection of the content and original thickness of the banks that covered them. Atkinson's calculations (pers comm) for volume of spoil from the ditch of Site IV show that it yielded about 5513cu ft. Its single mound probably required no more than c 293cu ft of make-up. The residue of ditch spoil, c 5220cu ft, would have provided a bank with a base width of 9.9ft, both broader and higher than that of Site I.

The section (Fig 14, 1) across the bank of Site IV showed that the soil beneath it extended towards the ditch for a short distance before dying out. From the evidence of only one trench, it seems safer to suggest that originally the chalk bank had extended across this also, but had been transferred to the ditch subsequently by natural weathering, rather than to postulate an earth and turf revetment to the bank like that deduced for Site I from stronger evidence. The silting in the ditch included no earthy layers in the outer half, such as one would expect from turf revetment to an external bank and which were actually found in the ditch of Site I. Allowing for the collapse and weathering of the upper edges of the ditch, the possibility exists that there may have been a space between bank and ditch which can only be interpreted as a berm, having a width of about 2–3 feet.

The ditch of Site IV was about 2ft narrower than that of Site I and about 1ft deeper. At the latter, there was no evidence to suggest a berm between the bank (with its turf revetment) and the edge of the ditch from which it had been derived.

Figure 14
Detailed Description of Layers

Section 1   Layers 1–5, filling of ditch
Layer 1 Loose chalk rubble, filling bottom corners of ditch.
Layer 2 More compact chalk rubble, extending across full width of ditch. Layers 1 and 2 had preserved original profiles of lower half of ditch.
Layer 3 Fine, compact, yellow chalky loam, containing areas of more chalky rubble in lower part: also contained isolated tips of purer chalk rubble.
Layer 4 Clean, yellow-brown earthy deposit filling naturally formed hollow along centre of ditch.
Layer 5 Medium-brown soil, evenly speckled with chalk chips throughout; lacked chalky slides or concentrations of rubble.

Section 1   Layers 6–8, make-up of bank and subsoils
Layer 6 Naturally weathered surface of undisturbed chalk bedrock, preserved beneath remains of bank of Site IV. Merged with more recent disintegrated chalk between inner edge of bank and outer edge of ditch.
Layer 7 Ancient soil sealed by barrow's bank. Diffuse pale chocolate-brown, containing even scatter of small chalk chips.
Layer 8 Fairly pure, concentrated chalk rubble forming bank of barrow.

SITE V

SPTA 2266: A RING-DITCH

SUMMARY

Site V was in all probability a ring-ditch with exterior bank, enclosing an apparently flat and oval area with a maximum diameter – ditch centre to ditch centre – of about 108ft. Near its centre, three pits were found: these lacked burials. The central pit contained chalk and chalky soil deposited alternately as if in handfuls from more than one container. It had been sealed by a distinctive plug of puddled chalk. Remains of a child, scattered at the base of topsoil immediately south of these pits, are considered likely to belong to the small later Bronze Age inhumation cemetery added to the neighbouring barrow, Site XV.

INTRODUCTION

It says much for Hoare's skill as a field worker that this site appeared on his plan of the barrow cemetery, for it had been all but levelled by ancient ploughing. It occurred on the NE side of the group, and, with Site XV, lay a little off the E line of mounds between the Hunter's Barrow (2253) and Site XXII (Figs 2, 2A). Its ditch showed as a very slight depression in the ground but neither central mound nor surrounding bank was visible. It was possible to see a positive lynchet, however, which had piled up around the NE side of the barrow. The S half was obscured by tank tracks.

There was no surface indication that Hoare had dug Site V but from the brief reference in *Ancient Wiltshire* (his No 23) we must suppose that he opened a trench near the centre. Of his work here and on Site XV (his No 22) he wrote (1812, plan opp 180, No 23, 185):

> 'The elevation of No. 22 is so slight and irregular, that doubts may be entertained if it was raised for sepulchral purposes, for on opening it, we could find no indicia of sepulture; and the same remarks may be applied to the next barrow, No. 23.'

Before excavation, Site V did not fit into the field classification of existing round barrows in Wessex, long since established by L V Grinsell (for example 1941, esp 77, fig 1). Lacking a central mound, it could be called neither saucer- nor bowl-barrow; it was rather too small in diameter to be a disc-barrow and it lacked a central tump. The excavation was undertaken to establish its place in the pattern of barrow types on Snail Down and also to discover its association with Site XV, its close neighbour to the W. As already indicated, moreover, it had been badly damaged by tracked vehicles.

Besides Hoare (above), the following references to Site V have been published: Goddard 1914, 230, Collingbourne Ducis 3a; Grinsell 1957, 167; Thomas and Thomas 1956, 140–141; Thomas, N, 1976, 230.

An important priority of this excavation was to establish the precise course of the ditch of Site V. Three trenches at the presumed centre were eventually opened out into a small area clearance and a group of three pits

was exposed. The S half of the barrow was not excavated in the time at our disposal because of disturbance by tank tracks, nor did it seem advisable to uncover the whole area within the ditch around the N half. Enough was done to establish the main structural features and to suggest the probability that no early prehistoric burials are to be found here.

The work lasted for fourteen days in 1955. An average of nine volunteers was present under the direction of Charles Thomas.

DESCRIPTION

Pre-barrow Features and Settlement Remains

No structures were found that could be attributed to activity hereabouts before Site V was built. Ploughing in possibly Romano-British times had removed most of the surrounding bank and the ancient land surface underneath.

A small sherd of Beaker ware was found lying on undisturbed chalk in the central area and it is possible that this may have been derived from the settlement beneath Sites X–XIV. The same could be suggested for the random scatter of flint waste material from the same general context (Section G).

The Structures

Three pits were found near the centre of Site V. Of these, the W pit (Fig 16; Fig 17, section 8) was the largest and lay nearest to the presumed centre of the barrow. It was oval in plan, with roughly cut sides and a flat floor. Its axes measured *c* 8 × 5ft and its depth from chalk level was about 2ft. The N end and both sides were nearly vertical, but at the S it sloped a little more gently. Its lowest filling comprised a layer (1) of loose chalk rubble which may have been the product of natural weathering and collapse over a very short period. The bulk of the filling consisted of compact chalk rubble (2) which was free of soil and other organic material.

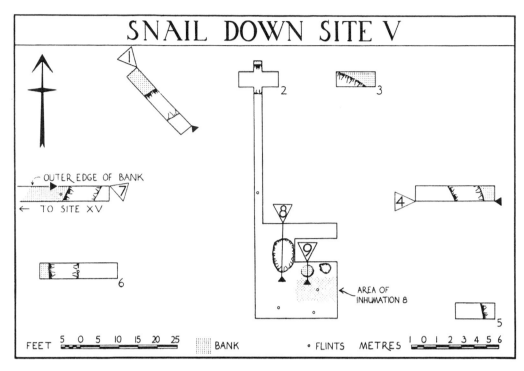

Fig 16   Site V, a ring-ditch. Plan, including position of Inhumation 8, later Bronze Age.

The central pit (Fig 16; Fig 17, section 9; Pls 27, 28) was circular, its diameter from chalk surface being about 3¼ft and its depth from the top of its puddled chalk dome (layer 5) *c* 2¼ft. The sides of this pit sloped down to a flat floor with a diameter of 1¼ft. Apart from an accumulation of clean, loose chalk in the S corner of the pit (layer 1) which appeared to be natural silt, the filling consisted of alternate but irregular layers of loose greyish chalk rubble (layer 3) and bands of almost black soil containing chalk (layer 2). These bands were 1–2in thick and most seemed to have been dumped from the S side of the pit during this deliberate act of infilling. When the pit had become full almost to chalk surface, an overall layer of compact chalk (layer 4) brought its contents close to the level of the ancient land surface. Finally, a layer of puddled chalk (layer 5; Pls 27, 28) was added to seal the mouth of the pit. At its centre this covering was about 2in thick. It was clear from the section, however, that the top of layer 5, had been removed, perhaps by ancient ploughing (layer 6). When first deposited, it may have been dome-shaped, standing above the level of the ancient surface. The domed effect shown in Plate 27 is misleading, since the weathered bedrock around it (layer 10) has been removed by excavation.

A third pit was found to the E of the two described above. It was no more than an irregular scrape into the subsoil, roughly 3ft in diameter and penetrating the chalk to a depth of 12in at its W end. It was filled with a mixture of chalk and reddish loam which, on Sites II and III for example, would have been characteristic of the filling of ancient tree and root holes. Here, however, some traces of charcoal were found at the bottom of the pit, which suggested that it may have been man-made.

The ditch (plan, Fig 16, sections, Fig 17; Pl 26) and remains of its bank were roughly oval in plan, their greatest diameter about 135ft. The ditch was uniform in general shape and size; its depth from the ancient chalk surface beneath the site of the bank was about 4ft and its width at chalk level around 8½ft. The flat, level ditch floor was 5–5½ft in average breadth. Undisturbed chalk hereabouts was hard and well bedded, like that beneath Site I (Pls 4, 6). This allowed the original diggers to achieve a smooth floor and perpendicular sides, with sharp angles at the junctions of walls and floor.

The bank of Site V (Figs 16, 17) had been removed completely by ploughing except for traces of rubble exposed in section 4. Wherever sections were dug across the ditch, however, the surface of the undisturbed chalk on the outside was found to be some 6in above that of the solid chalk within the ditch. This slight increase in height of the chalk beneath the site of the bank extended outwards for about 10ft in the cutting linking Sites V and XV (Fig 16, beyond section 7) and must represent approximately the original breadth of the bank. There was no evidence, from the ditch silt, that the bank had been revetted with turf like that of Site I, and it seemed probable that virtually no berm separated the inner edge of the bank from its ditch.

Post-construction Events

A roughly oval hole with sharply defined sides was dug into the S end of the W pit. Part of the original pit edge was cut away, accounting for its more gently sloping profile illustrated in Section 8. This intrusive pit had then been refilled with dark, humic and also chalky material (layers 3, 4, 7 and 5) which included a potsherd of prehistoric ware lacking diagnostic features. That the intrusion may have been ancient was suggested by the layer of

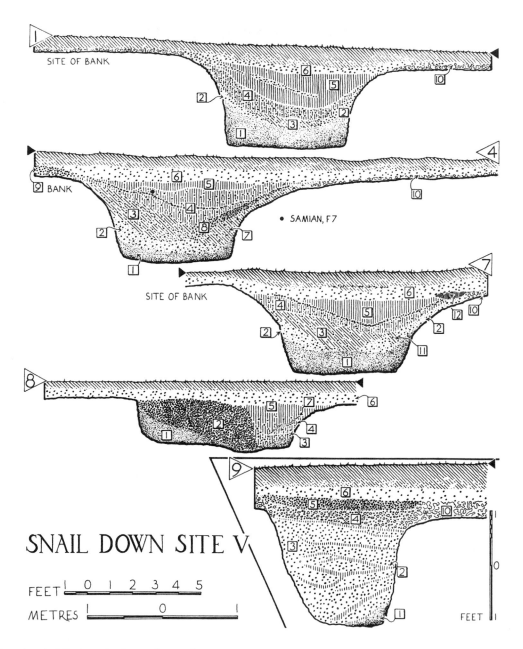

SITE OF BANK

BANK

SAMIAN, F7

SITE OF BANK

SNAIL DOWN SITE V

FEET | 0 1 2 3 4 5

METRES | 0 |

FEET

Fig 17 Site V, ditch sections 1, 4, 7; pit, section 8, central covered pit, section 9.

early plough soil (6) which overlay it and the rest of the pit.

Immediately S of the central and E pits (Fig 16), topsoil released a thin scatter of disturbed human bones that belonged to a child probably of the later Bronze Age – see below (Section A, Inhumation 8).

Of the ditch-filling, layers 1 and 2 had accumulated to a depth of more than twelve inches above the bottom of the ditch. It was clean, fairly loose chalk rubble, which had entered equally from each side, preserving the original profile of the lower half of the ditch. Layer 2 (Fig 17, all sections) appeared on both sides of the ditch overlying this primary silt, and was much more compact, less rubbly chalk. It must have taken longer to accumulate and was probably the result of wind and rain beating upon the upper walls of the ditch. The hollow formed by layer 2 along the centre of the ditch had been filled by a compact chalky deposit which was yellower in colour and clearly

contained a little humus. It would suggest that after the initial collapse of the upper edges of the ditch (layers 1, 2), soil from the now overhanging turf was being washed into the ditch (layer 3) together with more chalk from the upper ditch walls (section 4, layers 7, 8). With layer 4 appeared the first material derived from the bank. This was a thick deposit entering largely from the outside. Essentially of chalk and including soil, it extended across to the inner wall of the ditch and was fairly compact. Such an accumulation cannot have been rapid, and eventually it reached an angle of rest. Thereafter, layer 5 formed during a very much longer period. It was a compact fine loam with a high chalk content; in section 1, a thick tip of pure chalk rubble had slid in from the direction of the bank. The character of the upper filling of the ditch of Site V differed from that of all the other barrow ditches examined, because of the next and often deep layer (6), which separated the modern humus from layer 5, for it contained an unusual concentration of chalk chips and potsherds – the latter mainly of the later 1st-early 2nd centuries AD (Section F). This must represent agricultural activity hereabouts, which would have accounted for the development of a positive lynchet around this side of the barrow, referred to above.

Prehistoric finds were limited to an unstratified scatter of fourteen flint flakes (Section G), some indicated on the plan, Figure 16, and a small fragment of Beaker ware. There was a more noticeable quantity of Romano-British pottery associated probably with agricultural activity across the site which may have been responsible for its levelling. These wares, generally early Roman, are described in Section F. They occurred along the top of the ditch and mostly at the base of the topsoil. In section 4, one small sherd of Samian ware (F7), occurred in layer 5 (Fig 17), sealed beneath this early plough soil.

REMARKS

The central pit in Site V had a filling and a protective covering that represented a notable and particular human act. We have no means of interpreting the contents of the pit, despite I W Cornwall's considered attempts at soil analysis. It was evident, however, that after a short period during which the pit was open and attracting a little natural silting, it was then filled up to the level of the chalk surface with what appeared to be alternate deposits of chalky and of grey, more earthy material, that could have come in handfuls out of two or more containers, apparently from the S side. It was a ritual pit with a vengeance!

There are parallels for the sealing of such a pit beneath a domed structure, of which perhaps the closest formed the central – and only – feature of a small, oval mound in South Glamorgan, Six Wells 267', Llantwit Major (Fox 1959, 148–150). In detail, the shapes and fillings of the Snail Down and the Welsh pits differed: but in the domed clay covering of the latter the resemblance to that in Site V was remarkably close.

Within the Snail Down cemetery, the nearest resemblance to the clay cover sealing the central pit was the flint cairn heaped over Secondary Burial 1 at Site III. A similar cairn may have covered Secondary Burial 2 there and might also have closed the central burial pit at Site II.

There is at least one parallel, also, for the filling of a pit with contrasting streaky layers that suggests dumping from different pots, or by handfuls of different sorts of materials. This was the pit within a kerb-circle, barrow 6, at Metheral, Dartmoor, whose streaked contents were noted by the excavator (Hansford Worth 1937, 150).

The W and much the largest of the three pits within Site V bore some resemblance in shape and filling to the one beneath the eccentric tump of Site I. That it was sealed by the Romano-British ploughsoil ruled out interference to shape or filling by Hoare or other antiquaries. The natural accumulation of chalk rubble on its floor showed that it had been left open for a short period. Then came deliberate refilling with packed chalk rubble which differed from that in Site I only in the slight admixture of earth within it and in the absence of areas of loose chalk

which was a feature of the exceptional pit's filling in the disc-barrow (Site I). The large pit of Site V was tight-packed. Then, before the ancient ploughing that levelled the site, a smaller pit had been dug into its S end which altered its outline only a little. Since the shape of that interference was clean-cut, despite the relative instability of the chalk rubble into which it had been dug, the secondary pit had evidently been refilled without much delay. The accuracy with which it had been located at one end of the earlier pit suggested that the latter had been clearly visible when this happened.

The nature of the W and central pits supported the notion that they had not originally been covered by a mound.

If the larger W pit had some link with Site I, the pit dug into it, though lacking artefacts, at least recalls the digging of a much smaller pit into the edge of Site XVII, for the specific purpose of burying some worn sherds of a Collared Vessel (D22).

Silting of the ditch, which began with the undermining of sides and then the collapse of upper edges through natural agencies soon after the site had been completed (unless it was kept clean for some time by those who first built the place), demonstrated clearly that the main source of slower, subsequent infilling was the bank outside. There was virtually no indication of a mound within the ditch and the possibility must remain strong that the site lacked an overall covering for the three pits that lay close to its centre and apparently provided its *raison d'être*.

The evidence that was produced by our limited excavation suggested, then, that if Site V comprised no more than an oval space with pits, surrounded by a ditch with outer bank, it falls within a category of field monument called a ring-ditch, a form of burial or ritual structure well-known on river gravels like those of the upper Thames (Hamlin and Case 1963; Case *et al* 1966; Case and Whittle 1982 for example), but very rare on the Wessex chalk.

Case (Hamlin and Case 1963, 39–40) has described ring-ditches in the Oxford region as having a flat or oval space defined by an uninterrupted ditch with an outer bank (type 2a) or an inner bank (2b) or having a bank inside as well as outside the ditch (2c). Pits are a feature and nearly 50% of excavated ring-ditches have yielded burials.

Site V finds close comparison with ring-ditches of class 2a along the Thames. Its lack of a burial sets it a little apart, but its pits are appropriate to a ring-ditch and it is, of course, possible that burials remain to be found in this partly excavated site.

Fieldwork by the Royal Commission on the Historical Monuments of England (above: Earthwork Survey) confirmed our own finding that Site V may have been oval. This and other doubts, lingering despite excavation and field study, could be attributed to the barrow's subsequent history. Levelling of the site had taken place, apparently in Romano-British times. Early first-millennium AD farmers paid much less regard to the sanctity of the cemetery than later prehistoric cultivators whose boundary-ditch system (Sites VI, VII) was laid out and dug with careful respect for the barrows, even though the area was heavily cultivated. Site V became an early victim of the plough. Tank-training needs during the Second World War and for a short period thereafter paid even less regard to the barrows and caused further damage. A route for tracked vehicles was allowed to develop through the spaces between Sites V and XV and the great double bell-barrow to their S, Site XIX. This effectively put an end to any archaeological hope of revealing the true shape and character of Site V without the kind of massive effort that was not available to our group of volunteers in 1955. The latest survey of Snail Down (Fig 2) suggests, however, that the ditch of Site XIX may have clipped the already existing ditch of Site V.

If Site V may be oval in ground plan, an analogous structure on Snail Down lies 1360ft to the SW, CD6b. This was the small, possible saucer-barrow discovered by L V Grinsell and Charles Thomas in 1953 during the course of our work and surveyed by the RCHME (Fig 2A). Though much smaller, CD6b, which exercised considerable influence, we think, when the barrow cemetery took shape (Section 3), may have had the kind of association with Site V that Site II had with XVI and Site III with XVII, linkages that are considered in more detail below (Part 3, Fig 61).

If its oval shape harked back to what may have been one of the earliest barrow mounds (CD6b) on Snail Down, Site V's surrounding ditch and outer bank – probably its principal visual features – had been dug with the kind of precision and shape that distinguished the heyday of barrow-building on the Down, the time when bell-barrows like Sites III and XIX and XXII were being raised, and barrows of greater visual subtlety like I, II and IV, discs and saucer-barrows, were contributing variety to the great cemetery: Phase 4 of our chronological scheme for Snail Down (Part 3, Fig 61). The ditch of Site V was flat-floored and vertical-sided to an impressive degree, dug to a depth that made it a notable earthwork and providing a bank of white chalk rubble that would have added considerably to the structure's overall appearance.

The oval plan of Site V can be paralleled among Oxfordshire ring-ditches, for instance Nos 15 and 17 at Standlake (Case and Whittle 1982, 101), and No 3 at Hanborough (Case et al 1966, 16–19, fig 8, and others cited there, including examples among disc-barrows in Wiltshire and Dorset).

If Site V and possibly CD6b are the only examples of ring-ditches on Snail Down, this type of monument is, in proportion, even rarer elsewhere in Wiltshire, where Grinsell has recorded only six possible examples, Bulford 26 and perhaps 37 and Milston 8, 8a, 15a and 15b (1957, 217, 219, ibid 1974, 82), lying to the south. He saw these as disc-barrows lacking a central mound, although Milston 8, 15a and 15b appear to have raised central platforms. Moreover all except Bulford 37 exceed Site V in overall diameter, being closer to disc-barrows in size. It should be noted, however, that these analogous sites are all located within six miles of Snail Down.

Outside Wiltshire the only recorded ring-ditch in chalk country is barrow 17 within the Lambourn Seven cemetery in Berkshire (Case 1957, 23–25). Called a saucer-barrow by Case, it contained three Beaker-culture burials. Grinsell has failed to discover ring-ditches in Dorset or in Hampshire. The Snail Down ring-ditches, with those immediately south of Sidbury Hill, appear to be the only examples of this Thames Valley type of ritual and burial monument, their distributions linked by the lone example of Lambourn.

Omitting consideration of CD6b as a ring-ditch until it has been examined by excavation, Site V appears to be the only structure of its kind in the cemetery on Snail Down. Its uniqueness there could have accounted for its location a little to one side of the barrows' main alignment in that area of their grouping. Probably later in construction than Site XV (Part 3; Fig 60), it may nevertheless have been more closely associated with that early barrow than with the others at Snail Down and owed its special shape – its oval – and its construction as a ring-ditch to some tradition of burial and worship that had been superseded when the mass of the cemetery was developed.

There is a resemblance between Site V and the pond-barrow Site XVI (below). In our remarks about that site attention is drawn to circular stone-built monuments such as ring-cairns, which may have served similar purposes in Wales and the British Uplands (Lynch 1979, 1986). The inter-relationships between pond-barrows, ring-ditches and Highland Zone structures like ring-cairns are discussed further under Site XVI.

The inhumation of a child found below topsoil near the central and E pits had been thoroughly disturbed, probably by Romano-British ploughing, and was not associated with flints such as those that must have covered the inhumations added to neighbouring Site XV (Fig 25, inhumations I-V; Section A, Inhumations 3–7). Nevertheless their close proximity makes it likely that the remains from Site V represent an extension of the later Bronze Age cemetery added to Site XV around 1000 cal BC (Section A, inhumations 3–7; Section T, for radiocarbon dating).

Figure 17
Detailed Description of Layers

Section 1   Layers 1–6, 10, ditch and outer bank
Layer 1 Rapid silt, clean fairly loose rubbly chalk.
Layer 2 Very compact rainwashed chalk following sides of ditch and merging with layer 1. Formed trough along centre of ditch which was filled by layer 3.
Layer 3 Pale yellow, compact, earthy chalk at centre of ditch, filling hollow formed by layer 2.
Layer 4 Pale, compact, chalky loam, derived mainly from outer side of ditch and extending right across. At lowest point, in centre of ditch, included loose chalk rubble with some flints.
Layer 5 Light brown loan, hard and compact, containing tip of clean chalk rubble from outer edge of ditch (the equivalent occurred lower down in other exposures of this ditch-filling).
Layer 6 Darker brown, loose loam with scatter of chalk chips, a feature of the whole site.
Layer 10 Weathered natural chalk, the level on outside of ditch, beneath site of bank, 9–12in higher than that on inside.

Section 4   Layers 1–10, ditch, bank and central plateau
Layer 1 Rapid silt, clean fairly loose chalk rubble uniformly covering floor of ditch.
Layer 2 More compact, less rubbly chalk primary silt spreading across ditch mainly from outer side.

Layer 7 Light brown chalky earth with more distinct chalk fragments; inner side of ditch and preventing spread of layer 2.

Layer 8 Looser, small chalk rubble covering 7 and probably associated with it.

Layer 3 Pale yellow chalky soil filling trough left by layers 8, 2, and 7; became darker at its base.

Layer 4 Divided by a spread of chalk chips derived from the bank (layer 9): medium brown chalky soil below, similar but more powdery medium-to-dark soil above and yielding Samian sherd (Section F, F7).

Layer 5 Light brown, chalky, compact soil sealing most of ditch.

Layer 6 Darker brown loam with scattered chalk chips.

Layer 9 Compact rubbly chalk overlying bedrock, representing remains of bank. Not preserving an ancient land surface.

Layer 10 Weathered bedrock, undisturbed.

Section 7   Layers 1–6, 10–12, ditch

Layer 1 Primary rubbly chalk silt filling lowest part of ditch evenly.

Layer 2 More compact, less rubbly primary chalk silt, derived from ditch sides but not covering layer 1 completely.

Layer 11 Restricted area of disturbance from top of layer 2, inner side of ditch: loose brown loam.

Layer 3 Pale yellow compact soil filling channel formed by layer 2.

Layer 4 Pale-medium brown chalky soil derived mainly from outer side of ditch and spreading across it. Lens of loose chalk chips covering its upper surface.

Layer 5 Light brown, compact soil, chalky content but lacking loose chips.

Layer 12 Disturbance of upper surface of layer 5 at inner edge of ditch, darker brown, less chalky soil, not extending across cutting.

Layer 6 Darker brown, loose loam with scatter of chalk chips, extending across ditch as elsewhere on site. Seals layer 12.

Topsoil near base of topsoil a spread of chalky loam, not extending across cutting.

Section 8   Layers 1–7, W pit at centre of barrow

Layer 1 Loose clean chalk rubble.

Layer 2 Clean, more compact chalk rubble.

Layers 3, 4, 7, and 5 Filling of small pit dug into main pit: upper part, loose dark soil with thin even scatter of chalk chips; chalky tip ran in from S side, below which the intrusive pit-filling became progressively more chalky.

Layer 6 Loose brown loam with uneven scatter of chalk chips, covering pit and sealed by modern turf and topsoil.

Section 9   Layers 1–6, 10, pit at centre of barrow

Layer 1 Loose, clean chalk rubble in restricted deposit at bottom of pit.

Layer 2 Irregular streaks of grey soil mixed with fine chalk, occurring at intervals as roughly horizontal layers in pit: in plan the layers of this material did not always cover pit-fill from edge to edge.

Layer 3 Loose, fairly clean chalk rubble, interleaved with layer 2 to comprise fill of pit.

Layer 4 More compact chalk rubble, filling upper part of pit: contained some soil.

Layer 5 Very compact chalk, artificially puddled to form hard covering and slight dome to pit.

Layer 6 Loose brown loam with scatter of chalk chips: same as layer 6 in all other sections exposed.

Layer 10 Weathered natural chalk cut by pit.

SITES VI AND VII

ENCLOSURE DITCHES, CELTIC FIELDS AND TRACKWAYS, SPTA 2185, 2181, 2191, AND 2219, 2206, 2242

SUMMARY

Site VI was an enclosure of at least one hundred acres (c 40 hectares), having a V-shaped ditch generally 5ft deep, with a chalk rubble bank on the inner side. A thick accumulation of ancient ploughsoil occurred along the N edge of the V-ditch. The N side of the enclosure was shown to have respected the mound and ditch of a bowl-barrow, Site XX. Here, the bank of Site VI had been intersected by a series of tracks (T3) possibly associated with coins of the late fourth century AD. Between Site XX and the NW corner of this enclosure, the bank of Site VI was broken through by a trackway, T2, that had carried traffic across the Down.

At the NW corner it was shown that the ditch had superseded an earlier flat-bottomed ditch following the same course, and this in turn had been dug through a silt-filled ditch, also flat bottomed, but slighter. The latter, which ran N through Snail Down Square, a tree plantation, belonged to an earlier system, Site VII, not investigated further nor dated, but now explained by recent fieldwork (Bradley *et al* 1994, 132–134 and *passim*).

A scatter of potsherds in the region of Site XX and elsewhere suggested that Site VI had been laid out – its V-shaped ditch at least – by Middle Iron Age farmers during a striking reorganisation of a later Bronze Age system, and had continued in use probably until the end of the Iron Age. No respect had been shown for that barrow by their Romano-British descendants who may have had a settlement immediately to the N of Site XX and who seem also to have been farming the area extensively.

New surveys (Fig 2) have shown that Site VI overlies the denuded remains of field lynchets and other boundaries, some perhaps of the earlier Bronze Age, which fill Enclosure A and extend further to the N. It is possible that Site XVII overlies the edge of one of these fields. Traces of medieval ridge-and-furrow ploughing have also been identified within Enclosure A, which may have been a more recent agent in the denudation of this ancient agricultural palimpsest.

INTRODUCTION

Site VI (*ABCD* on plan, Fig 2) was a linear earthwork which defined a rectangular space roughly 1100ft wide and at least 3900ft long, an area of not less than 99 acres (*c* 40 hectares). It was designated Enclosure A. The E side of this enclosure has not been established: the slight banks starting at SU223518 and running NE have been shown by the Reading survey (Bradley *et al* 1994) and by RCHME to belong to the remains of Celtic fields and other complex earthworks that may have destroyed this side of Enclosure A. The barrow cemetery of Snail Down occupied the centre of the area so defined, with 2244 (Fig 2A) left outside to the S. Wherever visible, the bank of Site VI lay within its ditch; along the N side, *AB*, a slight rise suggested also the former existence of an outer bank.

In 1993 our knowledge of what lay within and around Enclosure A was increased beyond measure by the RCHME re-survey of the area. This is shown in Figure 2, with its broader context outlined in Figure 1, and is described by David Field and Mark Corney above. The results of the new survey have been incorporated within this account of Sites VI and VII, by their kind permission.

Side *AB* of Enclosure A lay along the S slope of a broad E/W ridge and ascended gently from the E towards its NW corner at *B*, the highest part of the downs hereabouts. Side *AB* skirted Site XXI, apparently having respect for its presence by carefully avoiding physical contact. Opposite Site XX there was a clear indication on the ground that Site VI curved N slightly to avoid the bowl-barrow there. At that point a long-established trackway, T3, coming up from the SW, branched to run on either side of XX (Figs 2, 18). It ran across the barrow ditch and broke through Site VI; here its prolonged use – it was recorded on the 1in OS map of 1808 – had created a marked spur which overlay the ditch of Site VI and extended almost to the N arc of the barrow ditch (Fig 18; section 6, Fig 19). Between that point and the NW corner, *B*, of Enclosure A, the earthwork has been interrupted by, or found to overlie, a series of field lynchets and associated boundary banks, all slight or denuded, which are described above, and shown in Figure 2. Our section 9 (Figs 2, 20) showed where one such lynchet, possibly used later as a trackway, has broken through the bank of Site VI.

From *B* (Fig 2), the W side of Enclosure A descended S in a gentle gradient to its SW corner at *C*. Almost everywhere along *BC* the bank was well preserved, but its associated ditch, facing W, was in places less evident. Indeed, for the first 230ft S of *B*, the ditch showed not at all, but instead there was a slight scarp to the W of its presumed line, running parallel but slightly out of alignment with both *B* and *EF*. About 230ft S of *B*, the earthworks were broken by a trackway, T1, which may have been in use since Romano-British times. Examined as Site IX during the course of our excavations (below), T1 ran almost E/W through the barrow cemetery. It entered between Sites XIX and XXII, overlay the ditch and berm of Site III along its S arc (Figs 9, 10, 33; sections,

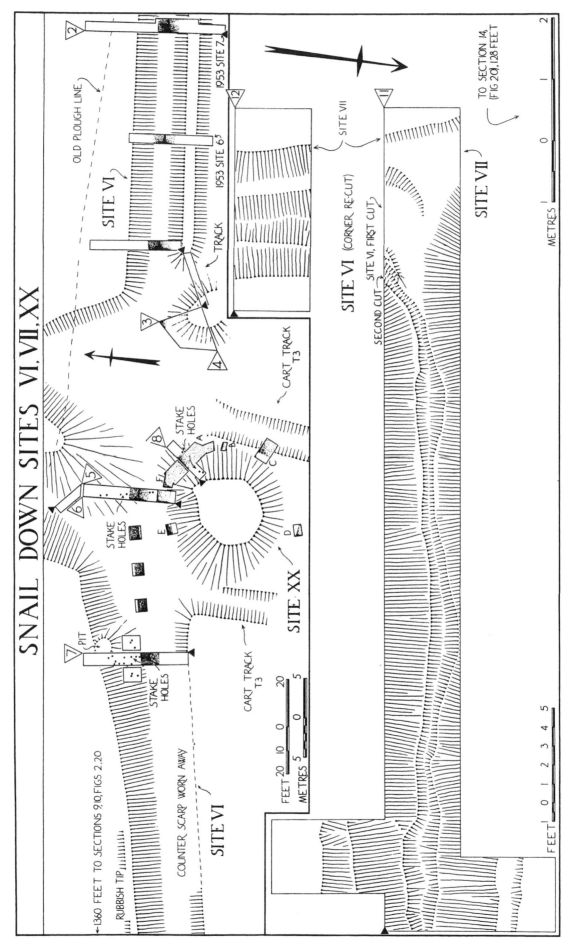

SNAIL DOWN SITES VI.VII.XX

Fig 18 Sites VI, VII and XX, linear ditches and bowl-barrow. Features around Site XX, including Cart Track T3; plan of Sites VI, VII, in NW corner of Enclosure A (Fig 2).

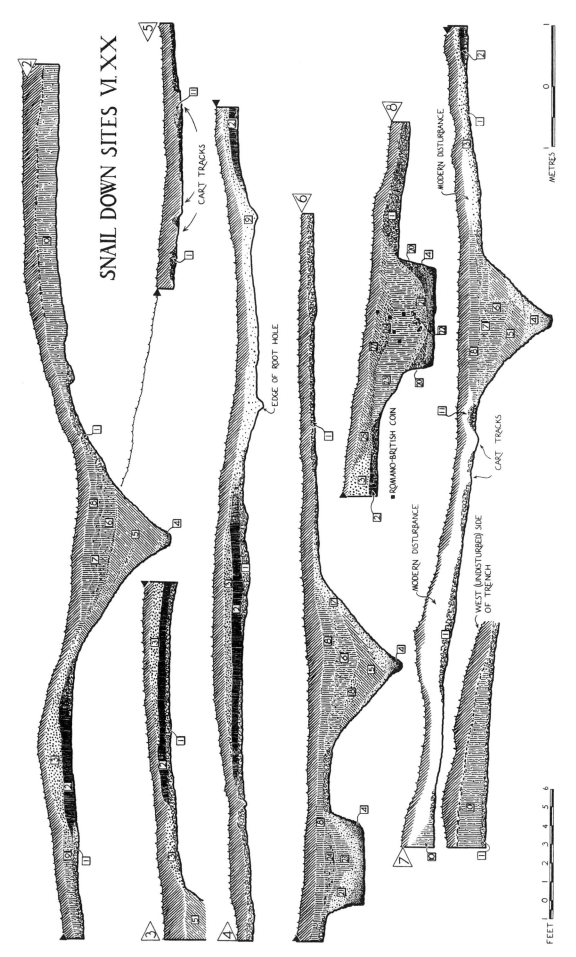

SNAIL DOWN SITES VI.XX

Fig 19 Sites VI, XX, sections 2–8. For Site VI, section 1, see Figure 35.

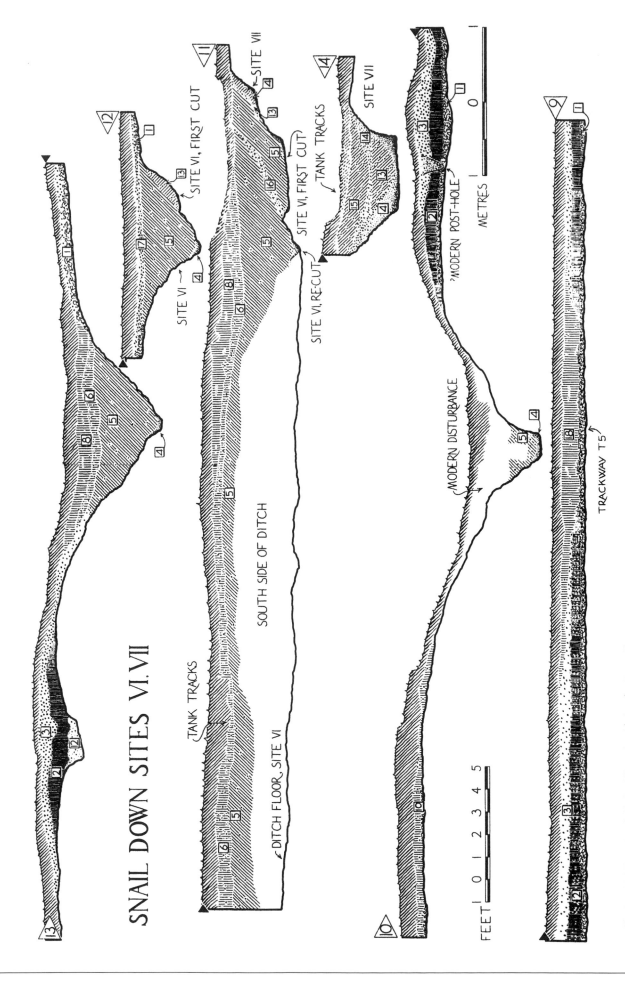

SNAIL DOWN SITES VI. VII

Fig 20 Sites VI, VII, sections 9–13; Site VII, section 14. See also Figure 35.

Figs 10, 11, 14; Pl 24) and ran on W across *BC* towards the settlement that is skirted by the Everleigh-Fittleton road, about SU194520 (Coombe Down in Bradley *et al* 1994, Fig 10). Where T1 crossed *BC* of Enclosure A, it has been worn down in recent times into a prominent hollow way, 4½ft deep and 20ft across, with steep sides (Fig 2). This modern wear is probably related to another track, still in use, which overlies the S arc of Site II and has been recorded on the 6in OS since at least the revised edition of 1906.

The E side of Enclosure B (*EFKJ*; Fig 1) ran parallel to *BC* and they seem to have been laid out so that their centres coincided. A space about 25ft wide separated the two lines of earthwork. Close to this common centre, early agriculture had been responsible for a break in both immediately S of a section where there was a noticeable change of direction in their otherwise straight alignment. It has been shown (Bradley *et al ibid*) that this great double earthwork, of which *BC/EF* are part, is almost certainly a Late Bronze/Early Iron Age development (*c* 8–5 century BC) of an earlier single bank and ditch which formed part of a system of territories whose communities used Late Bronze Age Plain Ware, dated to between 1200 and 800 BC.

Between *F* and *C* the earthworks have been obscured by the convergence of lynchets, a possible track-way (T2) and other agricultural features. T2 approached this junction from the SW and showed as a slight scarp on both sides of *FC/BC*. It was aligned upon its crossing point of *AB*, (Fig 20, section 9), which we have described above, adding that T2 probably originated as a lynchet. Figure 2, and David Field's and Mark Corney's account (above), indicate the extreme complexity of the S end of *BC* and the desirability of extended fieldwork in the immediate area.

At *C* the earthwork of Site VI (Enclosure A) turned E and followed the floor of a shallow gully traversing Snail Down. Its course here was sinuous, in order to avoid a prominent bowl-barrow (2207, with 2205 immediately NW), while maintaining a broadly parallel course to *AB*. Along most of this section the earthwork showed only as a ditch, 15ft wide at turf level and seldom more than 1ft in depth; here and there traces of a slight bank could be seen on the N side. A gap in this earthwork, 1570ft E of *C*, coincided with a prominent causeway to the N, crossing (and blocking) the gully floor and directed towards Site XX and the major crossing of *AB*. Part of Trackway T3, this feature was recorded on the OS 25in map. As we have already indicated, the recent surveys have shown that a group of Celtic fields and other features interrupt the E end of *CD* and may have destroyed the E side of Enclosure A.

Returning first to *B*, at this NW corner of Enclosure A a bank having a ditch on its W side, ran N for a distance of almost 1100ft, as recorded by O G S Crawford about 1925 and confirmed by the recent surveys. Hoare appeared to record the ditch for about 1700ft (1812, 180). It spanned a gully and ended at a scarp inextricably confused by local, possibly recent, disturbance and also by a series of earthworks spreading further N, which represent settlements, fields and a newly discovered henge monument and Early Iron Age enclosure (Fig 1). This earthwork, *BG* (Figs 1, 2), was designated Site VII. In Snail Down square (a tree planta-

tion), it showed as a bank in places 17ft wide and 2ft high with a ditch hollow on its W side. Excavation was to reveal that this ditch had a flat floor *c* 3ft wide, had been recut once and eventually superseded by the V-shaped ditch of Site VI, whose diggers had removed it where they met at *B*.

Sites VI and VII were part of a larger complex of earthworks. As we have seen, Enclosure B, *EFKJ* on the plan (Fig 1), lay immediately to the W, its E side utilising a length of the double earthwork which also formed the W side of Enclosure A. Enclosure B measured about 950 by 250yds, an area of *c* 52 acres (21 hectares). Its long axis, like that of Site VI, was E/W; its N and S sides, *EJ* and *FK*, were markedly curved, each bending S. Now badly denuded, it appeared that the position of its bank was variable. Along *EF* the bank lay to the E, outside the ditch, since it utilised the layout of the double earthwork; along parts of *FK* the bank appeared to have lain within. This enclosure contained no barrows, but there was a scattered group which included bell, bowl, disc and saucer forms immediately to the SW. Weather Hill, a local prominence, fell within the W part of Enclosure B. A disused dew pond impinged upon *FK*. There was a bell-barrow 750ft E of this intersection, which may have been used as a marker by those who dug the earthwork, since the latter changed direction at this point. Alternatively this change in direction may have been compelled by their desire to avoid damaging the pre-existing burial mound, an act of respect rather than field survey, discussed further below.

The W side of Enclosure B, *JK*, continued SW for about 900yds and then turned NW, dying out just short of the main road from Everleigh to Fittleton. A complex arrangement of Celtic fields used this ditch as their SE boundary, the whole group part of the Coombe Down settlement (Fig 1).

The earthworks in the area of Snail Down and Weather Hill have suffered much from military vehicles and trackways, and many important points of intersection have been obscured beyond recognition. The 6in OS maps (1901 edition) relating to this area, which were annotated by O G S Crawford around 1925 and are kept at Wiltshire Heritage Museum, are therefore of interest since they provide the only informed record of these earthworks before the land came under War Department control. Crawford observed that where the S extension of *JK* turned NW, it may have forked, a S branch running on to join up with the enclosures and celtic fields on Figheldean Down (Fig 1). He could have been confusing such an extension with some of the field lynchets recorded by the new surveys; alternatively his observation may have been of a feature that has now disappeared.

Crawford also recorded that *KJ* continued N for a short distance towards Weather Hill Firs. The 6in OS map of 1926, on the contrary, represented it as changing direction sharply at *J*, to run E almost parallel to *JE*. This interpretation was marked as 'Ditch (course of)' and was always difficult to understand in relation to the ground plan of Enclosure B and to Crawford's more likely suggestion. Here, too, a convincing explanation has come from Bradley *et al* 1994. They have located a boundary ditch linking Weather Hill with corner *J* of Enclosure B and stopping just N of that corner. That is the ditch whose eastward extension the OS incorrectly postulated, confused further, excusably, by the existence of celtic fields hereabouts. The ditch *JE* was sectioned both at *J* and between *J* and *E*. This revealed a symmetrical V-shaped excavation at both points, *c* 13ft wide and 4½ft deep, the former associated with Middle Iron Age pottery (*ibid*, 49).

Returning finally to Enclosure A, Site VI, a massive earthwork comprising a bank between two ditches with traces of an E bank here and there, extended SSE from point *C* on Site VI (*CH* on plan, Fig 2). It ran in an almost straight line across a valley and then climbed the steep slope to approach the main entrance of the Iron Age hillfort which crowns Sidbury Hill (Fig 1). This earthwork changed direction slightly once or twice before stopping abruptly 80ft short of the Iron Age ramparts. At a point 500 yds N of the hill-fort, *CH* was recorded as cutting across a disc-barrow (SPTA 2204), showing surprising insensitivity for prehistoric times. The intersection appears now to have been badly damaged, but Hoare remarked upon it particularly (see below) and his observation of this relationship has generally been accepted (Grinsell 1957, 217, CD6a, 255, no 95; *ibid* 1974, 103, no 6a). To Crawford, this length of N/S earthwork *BCH* was one structure comprising two banks and ditches, to whose W pair, *BC*, Enclosure B was attached. He recorded specifically that the E end of *KF* cut across the W ditch and bank of *BC* but stopped short of the bank and ditch immediately to the E. Presumably he saw enclosure A as appropriating this double earthwork as its W side in the same way. There was nevertheless an important difference between *HC* and *CB* that was still clearly apparent in the 1950s. The earthworks of the former were close-spaced, ditch-bank-ditch-small bank, while those of *CB* were separated by a gap 25ft wide (Fig 2). Before excavation we preferred to regard *BC* and *EF* as adjacent and probably contemporary sides of two enclosures, with earthworks *CH* as another structure altogether, possibly of later date. Part of our research design was to establish the relationship of Enclosure A, at least, to these complex earthworks. Whatever our conclusions of that time, this double earthwork has now been shown to be probably of one build, from its beginning on the N slope of Sidbury to our point *B*; and that it replaced an earlier series of single earthworks, for which our excavations provided important evidence (Bradley *et al* 1994, 41–47). Crawford's perceptive observation has been vindicated. Meanwhile, on-going fieldwork by RCHME along *BCH* is suggesting that it may have been built in sections, its precise character even more complex than our excavations revealed.

Hoare was the first to record the ditch system which we have just described (1812, plan opp 180, and 181).

'On quitting this fine eminence [i.e. Sidbury Hill], and descending into the plain towards Everley, our attention is attracted by a very bold, broad, and straight raised causeway issuing from the principal entrance of the camp, and directing its course towards Everley. In its structure it resembles so much the Roman roads, that I could almost suppose it had been formed after their model. This causeway extends in length 1 mile and 88yds, and its progress intersects in half a large Druid barrow, as will be seen on our map. It terminates in a valley, and immediately at a spot where there are several irregularities and excavations in the soil. With all the ardour and fancy of a zealous antiquary, I once fondly thought that here I might discover the traces of King Ina's palace, who according to tradition, had a country seat at Everley; but on digging into several of the banks, as well as into the hollow places, I could find no fragments even of stone, or any *indicia* of habitations. The origin and cause therefore of this singular bank and ditch must remain to be developed by some future and more fortunate antiquary.

A little on the south side of these excavations we meet two ancient banks and ditches, one of which crosses the trackway, and leads towards an extensive British village, and a large group of barrows.' [ie Snail Down]

Hoare's plan (back cover) must be treated only as an approximate representation of the earthworks in this region. He omitted the S side of Site VI (ie Enclosure A) altogether, and the N ditch of this site and the whole of Enclosure B were shown to be far more irregular in plan than even a casual inspection on the ground should have permitted.

The earthworks on Snail Down, as we have noted above, were considered again by O G S Crawford in 1928 (p 5). He recorded for the first time that *CH* was double, in which respect it differed from the other earthworks that radiate from Sidbury Hill. He also considered in some detail the relationship of barrows, fields and boundaries in this region, particularly to the W and S of Sidbury Hill, which will be discussed further below.

The next field-worker to be concerned with these earthworks was Professor C F C Hawkes, who examined their relationship to the ditches which underlay the ramparts of the Iron Age hill-fort on Quarley Hill, Hants (1939). He was able to show conclusively that one of the ditches on Quarley Hill (his Ditch 1) could be associated directly with the Deverel Rimbury (later second - millennium cal BC) settlements at Boscombe Down and Thorney Down and with the extensive network of ditches that covers the ridge to the E of the River Bourne. By inference it became clear that these earthworks were broadly contemporary with those to the W of the Bourne, including the system on Snail Down. Hawkes' description summarized the work which Dr J F S Stone had been doing at about the same time on the ditches and settlements at Roche Court (1932), Ford, Laverstock (1937a), Boscombe Down East (1937b) and Thorny Down (1937c).

The Snail Down ditches were discussed more directly by S Applebaum when he described the celtic field system on Figheldean Down, to the SW of Sidbury Hill, in 1954 (107ff, esp fig 1). Applebaum thought that a branch from Enclosure B (the SW extension of its W side, *JK*) was later than one group of celtic fields on Figheldean Down, and contemporary with others on its E side.

During the course of our excavations and subsequently, the RCHME studied the earthworks on Snail Down and produced a revised survey of them which is likely to remain the definitive statement of their layout (Figs 2 and 2A). It complements the work of Reading University (Bradley *et al* 1994) which sets Snail Down into a much wider archaeological context.** We now have an authoritative, scientifically based record of this extraordinarily well-preserved ancient agricultural landscape between the Bourne and the Avon, that is of national significance.

DESCRIPTION

The excavations, 1953–1957

A series of trenches (Figs 2, 18) was cut to establish profiles of Site VI at selected points along its N side (Fig 2, E trench symbol section 9, W symbol section 10, Fig 20), and to ascertain the behaviour of this ditch where it passed close to Sites XX and XXI, two of the cemetery barrows. The NW corner of the enclosure was cleared down to bedrock and further trenches were dug here (plan, Fig 18) to obtain profiles of the W side of Site VI and of Site VII, the ditch which extended N from Site VI (plan, Fig 2, *BG*). In all, 67ft of ditch silt was excavated from the N side of Site VI and 8ft was cleared from its W side. One trench was cut across the ditch of Site VII. The work lasted for three weeks during the 1957 season and one week in 1953; some fifteen volunteers took part and the directorship was shared.

The Ditch, Bank and Ploughsoil, Site VI (plans, Figs 1, 2, 18, 35; sections, Figs 18–20, 35; Pls 29–31.

Excavation in 1953 and 1957 provided the dimensions listed in Table 4 for the ditch of Site VI.

In profile the ditch was consistent. It was V-shaped, each side sloping at the same angle. The bottom of the ditch became a generally flat-floored slot about 9in wide and with nearly vertical sides. This slot was wider and less clearly defined in section 10 (Fig 20).

The material filling the ditch of Site VI was more uniform in colour and more compact than any other ditch silt examined on Snail Down except for that of Site VII. Essentially it comprised a pale buff loam, mainly very fine in grain size but including some larger chalk and flint fragments. Layers 6–8 were separated from layer 5 (which everywhere provided the main filling in the ditch) only by a gradual decrease in fine chalk content – and hence a dark-

ening in colour – as the modern humus was approached. Apart from a few thin, isolated chalky spreads, for example in section 2, Figure 19 and section 1, Figure 35, none of the filling seemed to have been derived from the bank. Loose chalk rubble was noticeably absent and the colour of layer 5 was uniform from one side of the ditch to the other.

The primary silt, layer 4 (layer 12, section 1, Fig 35) was nowhere as loose and rubbly as it was in the barrow ditches. Its presence was indicated only by an increase in the density of chalk towards the bottom of layer 5. It could hardly be detected at all in sections 11, 12, 10 and 13.

The bank of Site VI (layer 3) comprised a dump of chalky rubble mixed with loam, resting on a fairly well-marked land surface. The latter varied in width from 9–16ft and was everywhere 6–9in thick. In some cuttings it was found to be separated from the solid chalk by a layer of decayed chalk; elsewhere it lay directly upon bed-rock. More than one ancient tree or root hole was found beneath the ancient land surface. The bank itself had no revetment or other distinguishing features. In section 2 (Fig 19), where it was best preserved, it was a little over 12in in height and its chalk rubble composition was fairly concentrated. Here it tailed out gradually towards the barrow cemetery.

On the outer, or N side of the ditch of Site VI there was a thick accumulation of chalky, fairly compact loam (layer 10). The junction of its upper surface and the base of the modern humus was marked by a distinct line of flint chips. Layer 10 was well preserved in sections 2 and 7 (Fig 19) and in the two trenches between sections 3 and 2 (Fig 18, not illus). It showed more thinly, but unmistakably, in section 10, Figure 20. In colour, texture and chalk content this layer (10) generally resembled the main ditch filling of Sites VI and VII. The heavy concentration of natural flints on its surface was not exactly paralleled elsewhere in the excavations on Snail Down.

The Re-Cutting of Site VI (plan, Fig 18, lower half; sections 11, 12, Fig 20).

In 1957 the NW corner of Enclosure A was examined and a length of 44ft was excavated and planned (Fig 18, lower half; Fig 20, section 11). At the point where this ditch turned S, it was found that the outer or W side of an earlier ditch, here turning from E to S to follow the line of Site VI, had been left intact. This ditch had a flat floor. When Site

Table 4: ditch dimensions, Site VI		
Section	*Width* (at chalk surface)	*Depth* (at chalk surface)
11 (Fig 20, V-shaped ditch)	*c* 10ft (section not at right angles	*c* 2¾ft
12 (Fig 20)	*c* 7ft	2½ft
2 (Fig 19)	13ft	5¼ft
6 (Fig 19)	9ft	4¼ft
7 (Fig 19)	8ft	4¼ft
10 (Fig 20)	*c* 15ft (disturbed)	*c* 4¾ (disturbed)
13 (Fig 20)	11ft	4½ft
West of 2 (not illus)	14ft	5¼ft
East of 3 (not illus)	*c* 15ft	5½ft
1 (Fig 35, N of Site XXI)	11ft	5ft

**In the fifties, Collin Bowen and Desmond Bonney undertook the first survey of Snail Down, assisted by A L Pope and John Davies. In 1993, under Mark Corney, a new survey was made by David Field and Jo Donachie (above and Fig 2).

VI had been dug with its V-shaped profile, the earlier ditch had already silted up completely. This predecessor of Site VI was 3¼ft wide at its floor and about 3ft deep. The surviving side sloped outwards at an angle roughly parallel to the outer side of its V-shaped successor. The filling, a compact buff chalky loam, was identical with layer 5 of the V-shaped ditch. A sloping line of small chalk chips marked where the outer wall of the later ditch had been cut through the silt of the first ditch (Fig 20, section 11).

The same area of excavation also revealed that this predecessor of the V-shaped ditch of Site VI had itself been dug through a silted-up ditch of roughly the same shape and size, but running N/S, which is the earthwork designated Site VII. It is described below.

A second trench was excavated 80ft S of section 11 and here again the outer wall of the earlier ditch of Site VI remained intact (Fig 20, section 12). At this point the bottom corner of the ditch was less angular than that in section 11, and there was no sign of Site VII.

It is possible that the bulge in the walls of the V-shaped ditch in section 10, Figure 20, may also represent this earlier Site VI ditch. Here, if such inference is correct, the floor of the latter would have been nearly 7ft wide. The ditch in Section 10 had been badly damaged by a rabbit warren, however, and those digging for rabbits had removed all but the bottom 18in of silt from this part of Site VI. Little reliance can therefore be placed on this evidence that the earlier ditch of Site VI extended as far E as this; yet the possibility that the V-shaped ditch replaced the earlier ditch for much of its length must be strong.

Site VII (plans, Figs 2, 18; sections, 11, 14, Fig 20)

When section 11, Figure 20, was excavated, it was found that the two ditches of Site VI (the earlier having a flat floor) had cut through a ditch of even earlier date and flat-floored also. It was obvious from the plan (Fig 18) that this earliest ditch did not belong to the enclosure of Site VI since it lay almost at right angles to its N side. Instead, it was evidently part of the ditch that has been planned and observed since Hoare's time, a small earthwork continuing the line of double ditches from Sidbury Hill towards Everleigh and ending at a prominent scarp beyond Snail Down Square (above). This ditch was examined in Snail Down Square, where it could be seen as a slight hollow beneath a track used by military vehicles (Figs 2, 20, section 14). The ditch was found to be flat-floored, 3¼ft wide at this level and with a depth of about 2¼ft below solid chalk. The W wall of the ditch was vertical at its base and sloped outwards only slightly as it neared the chalk surface. Its E side was much less steep. In section 11 (Fig 20), the W side of this ditch sloped more noticeably, and here the ditch appeared to have been shallower, although damage to the natural chalk surface at the W end of the trench by military vehicles made this detail uncertain.

The filling of the ditch of Site VII had been heavily compressed by military vehicles so that its texture could not be reliably recorded. The layers of silt in it more closely resembled those in the barrow ditches, although layer 13 was close in colour to layer 5 in Site VI. The floor was covered with clean chalk (layer 4) derived from the collapsing upper walls of the ditch. This increased in

thickness on the E side and may have derived, in part, from a bank which must have existed along that side of the ditch. The greater part of Site VII was filled with a buff, chalky loam, layer 13, resembling layer 5 in Site VI. It was covered by a more chalky spread, 14, which again increased in volume on the E side. Above this, a less chalky layer, 15, covered the ditch, but its top has been damaged by the passage of military vehicles.

Layers 4 and 13 were represented in the fragment of this ditch which was found undamaged by Site VI in section 11 (Fig 20).

Relationship of Site VI to Sites XX and XXI (Figs 2, 18; Fig 19, section 6; Fig 35, section 1; Pl 31).

The plan of Sites VI and XX in Figure 18 makes it clear that the boundary ditch was diverted N in a gentle curve to avoid not only the mound of Site XX but also its ditch. Though at that time more than half filled with silt, the latter still evidently warranted respect. A space of about 3ft separated the ditch around the barrow from that of the boundary. The latter continued to curve E so that it just avoided the ditch and mound of another outlier of the barrow cemetery, Site XXI. Here (Fig 35) there was a gap of about 16ft between the two earthworks.

Opposite Site XX and, we presume, out of respect for that barrow, the builders of the boundary earthwork would have been faced with the problem of where to place the bank which followed the S edge of their ditch. Section 6, Figure 19, showed clearly that it was not dumped across the ditch of the barrow. The plan and section 8 (Figs 18, 19) indicated a dump of spoil – mainly compact buff loam with a capping of finer chalk (layers 26, 27) which was found on the NE side of Site XX and extending across its ditch at this point. The wide variety of finds sealed by the dump included a series of late fourth century Roman coins (Section P). These must have been dropped before this dump was heaped up, since they could not have drifted down naturally through such a thick deposit. From the correlation of Sites VI and VII with the ditches of probable later Bronze Age and Iron Age farmers S and SE of Sidbury Hill, already described, it is not chronologically possible that the dump overlying part of Site XX represented the bank of Site VI as originally constructed. The spoil obtained from the ditch of Site VI where it ran past the barrow was not located in the excavations of 1957. It might have been used to augment the Site VI bank to the E and W of Site XX. Here, however, the ground had been damaged by Trackway T3 and this cannot now be verified.

Opposite Site XXI there was a wider gap between the two earthworks; and the bank of Site VI was located in its normal position, immediately on the S side of its ditch. However, a narrow slot was found, penetrating the chalk to a depth of 1ft, which separated the S edge of the bank from the ditch surrounding Site XXI (Fig 35). The section indicates that the edge of the bank had spilled into the bottom of this small ditch. Clearly, it had been open at a time when the bank of Site VI had not consolidated, but was still spreading. At this point, the bank was 7½ft wide, somewhat narrower than elsewhere. It is possible that this shallow slot was dug as a marking-out ditch, indicating to the builders of Site VI the permitted S limit of their bank.

Later Fields, Trackways and Fencing (plans, Figs 2, 18; Figs 19–20, sections 5, 9).

Snail Down is criss-crossed with trackways and lynchets of various dates which have been plotted in Figure 2 and described above. One of these, T3, which crossed the S foot of the Down over a causeway (and here broke the earthwork *CD* of Site VI), skirted 2217 and 2220, overlay the ditch of Site XVII and ran each side of Site XX. At this point it cut across Site VI, carving a gap in its bank about 12ft wide and expanding further as it crossed the N edge of the boundary ditch. It left a conspicuous hollow in the area where VI skirted XX (Fig 19, section 5).

On the E side of Site XX, the bank of Site VI had been cut through twice by tracks which were branches of the main route just described. All were doubtless converging upon the Romano-British or earlier farmstead, believed to have stood on the level ground just to the N which was recorded by Hoare (1812, plan opp 180). Section 4, Figure 19, indicated the depth of the hollow which had been worn by the more easterly of these two tracks across Site VI. No wheel ruts were observed in the undisturbed chalk in section 4, but in section 5 these were prominent, two of them 7½ft apart measured from centre to centre, and on either side of these, as elsewhere in this section, there were areas of compact chalk sludge resting upon the bedrock, which had evidently been thrown up by the passage of vehicles in wet weather.

The excavation of sections 6 and 7 (Figs 18, 19) revealed a series of stakeholes which were not dated but which may be related to the ancient farming activity represented by the cart tracks described above. In section 6, these formed a straight line for a distance of 24ft and were apparently arranged in pairs, with wider spaces in between. They may have been designed to block the gap between Site XX and the tongue of undamaged ground to the N, defined by the hollowed tracks on either side of it. In section 7 a more random but extensive series of holes was found on the N side of the boundary ditch. Two roughly straight, short rows could be distinguished, but the scatter of holes on either side suggested that these alignments may be fortuitous. The stakeholes were all about 2in in diameter, up to 6in deep in the solid chalk and filled with loam slightly paler than the modern topsoil. Their ends were pointed and they had been rammed into the chalk.

The N side of the Site VI enclosure overlay and was also in association with field boundaries as well as the tracks described above. Section 9, Figure 20, showed that the bank of Site VI had been cut away, perhaps by a lynchet, reused as a trackway, which in 1957 could be seen running N at an acute angle to it (Fig 2). Here the ditch of Site VI had not been filled in.

The Finds and their Date (Pottery, Sections C, E, F, *passim*; bonework, Section H; flint, Section G; coins, Section P)

About fifty potsherds and a series of late Roman coins were found during the excavation of Sites VI, VII, XX and XXI. Most occurred in the cuttings adjacent to Site XX. The Roman coins and several of the Romano-British, Iron Age, later Bronze Age and Deverel Rimbury (Middle Bronze Age) potsherds were sealed beneath a dump of sludge which had been thrown up on the N side of Site

XX and covered its ditch at that point: the coins and sherds occurred above the earlier Bronze Age silt in the barrow ditch. Little Deverel Rimbury, later Bronze Age or Iron Age pottery was found anywhere else on Snail Down: its concentration in the area of the boundary earthworks, while marking some sort of association, may be more likely to reflect the presence of a Deverel Rimbury and Late Bronze Age settlement in the area, which pre-dates construction of Enclosure A, Site VI. It is not impossible that these sherds reflect the date of the fields underlying this enclosure. A significant group of Middle Iron Age sherds occurred low in the secondary ditch silt of Site VI, opposite Site XXI (Fig 35; Section E). The Late Iron Age pottery probably indicates the foundation of a succeeding settlement, which went on to develop in Roman times, as the occurrence of much Romano-British pottery and the coins testify.

One indeterminate potsherd of Romano-British fabric occurred about 2in below the layer of flints which covered a thick soil on the N side of Site VI (Fig 19, section 2, layer 10).

REMARKS

Two features exposed by the excavation of Site VI, the main filling of the ditch and the accumulation of chalky soil covered by a layer of flints which follows its N edge, require further comment. Soil analysis failed to explain how the ditch had become filled with such a uniform deposit of loam and chalk dust. This filling was quite unlike any deposit from the barrow ditches and was especially remarkable for the absence of primary silt in the form of chalk rubble, although it contained sufficient isolated chalk rubble and flints to rule out wind action as the sole agent in its deposition. It has been suggested by Dr Cornwall that damp conditions, perhaps coupled with frost, might account for the finely mixed, sludgy character of the chalk and loam filling. Occurrence of similar material in the linear ditches excavated by Reading University (Bradley *et al* 1994, 142–151 and *passim*) led them to propose that it related to a change of use of some of these ditches during the Iron Age: at that stage some were being used to define blocks of land for arable cultivation and it seems possible that the nature of their silting may have been the result of ploughing.

Such a high proportion of dusty chalk in a V-shaped ditch has been noted before in this region. Dr Stone remarked upon it when he sectioned a linear ditch on Easton Down (1937, 79–80) and again when examining earthworks of the same type a short distance to the E, on Roche Court Down, Winterslow (1932, 569–570). At Thorny Down he noted the same sort of filling (1937c, 642–646) and was able to show the part which rain had played in its formation. Similar chalky silt occurred in the angle ditch and linear ditch on Boscombe Down East (1937b, 468–469). In all these excavations, however, Dr Stone recorded the presence on the floors of his ditches of some loose chalk rubble.

The primary silt in the pre-Iron Age ditches on Quarley Hill appeared to correspond closely with that from Site VI (Hawkes 1939, 153, 156), for there the general absence of loose chalk rubble was also noted.

Only further excavation along the N edge of Site VI can throw light upon the thick deposit of compact, chalky loam which was found on that side of the linear ditch. In texture it resembled the filling of the ditch. It included no distinct layer of flints at its base nor did it seal a land surface. Our belief is that it represented an ancient plough soil, accumulating here at the edge of a field system whose S boundary was marked by Site VI. The line of tightly packed flints on top of this deposit must have been caused by subsequent ploughing of the soil above it. When such activity ceases, earthworms cause the flints to sink to the bottom of the layer, where they would pile up on the surface of the altogether harder lower soil. This could happen quickly (Atkinson 1956, 53–55) but once the flints had collected on top of the chalky loam and become tightly packed, it is unlikely that they would move further. The ploughing to the N of Snail Down which took place immediately before this layer began to form might, then, have occurred in Romano-British times. One Romano-British potsherd was found 2in below the flints in section 2 and the thick, chalky soil beneath it may have formed soon after Site VI was built, or at least re-cut, probably in the Middle Iron Age.

The dump of soil added to the NE flank of Site XX and covering its ditch must next be considered briefly. Its importance lay in the late Roman coins which were sealed beneath it. These, together with potsherds – Deverel Rimbury, later Bronze Age, Iron Age and Roman – had collected in the hollow which was all that remained of the ditch around Site XX. Since Site VI is prehistoric, this dump cannot represent its bank. The latter, as we have already suggested, may have been doubled in thickness on either side of Site XX, to absorb the material dug out from that length which ran past the barrow and avoid the necessity of defiling its mound or ditch.

While the tracks on either side of Site XX were in use, a good deal of chalky mud would have formed in wet weather. The dump of sludge, capped by clean chalk (Fig 19, section 8, layers 26, 27), which was added to the barrow with complete disregard for its sanctity can best be explained by the clearing of these cart tracks at intervals during the life of the Romano-British farmstead to the N and perhaps until much later. The 1in OS map of 1808 shows that this trackway was still in use at that date.

The most evocative aspect of Site VI was the very evident respect it paid to the barrow cemetery which it surrounded. Its builders knew what lay beneath those mounds. Respect for religious monuments – cursuses, henge monuments, barrows – was a notable characteristic of pre-Roman peoples in Britain. On Snail Down, the construction of Site VI can be understood at least in part as a means of preserving the area of the barrows from ploughing at that time. It may have been used for pasture alone. Such respectful land use, if we have judged it correctly, must be contrasted with the fields that were worked round the barrows at some earlier period. Their apparent denudation may actually indicate that they were not worked extensively before being superseded by Site VI. Thereafter, the agriculture within and around Enclosure A may largely have been Romano-British, when the barrows had lost some significance.

Other barrows in Wiltshire were also protected from prehistoric ploughing when, for example, they occurred in an area of celtic fields. The overlapping disc-barrows at Grafton provide one instance (Bowen 1961, 16, fig 2); on Marleycombe Hill, Bowerchalke, R C C Clay noted that a linear ditch (probably contemporary with our Site VI) deliberately skirted a group of earlier barrows (1927, 548, 551); and at Crawley Clump, near Winchester, O G S Crawford recorded that a small barrow cemetery was avoided by Celtic field lynchets (1928, 5).

This does not rule out the likelihood that many barrows were used as markers by later prehistoric agriculturalists when laying out boundary ditches. It seems clear that the S side of Enclosure B, to the W of Site VI, was deliberately curved S from its two ends almost (but not quite) to touch a bell-barrow. The mound must have been used as a boundary point and this would account for the otherwise curious bend S of both the long, parallel sides of that enclosure. But even here the earthwork did not make contact with the barrow nor intersect its ditch. In the same way, Sites XX and XXI seem to have been used as sighting points in deciding the precise course for the N side of Site VI, just as its S side apparently owed its position to the large mound (2207). But here also our plan, Figure 2, shows how the S side of Site VI curved to avoid contact with that barrow (2207).

On Snail Down, however, it was the elaboration of precautions to protect barrows which remains so striking. The care taken to avoid covering a silted up barrow ditch (Site XX) with bank materials, the digging of a marking-out ditch beside Site XXI (for such it must have been) to prevent the edge of the Site VI bank from running into the ditch of that barrow, indicate how close were these later prehistoric farmers to their predecessors, in spirit if not in time.

In the British archaeological record, damage to round barrows is rarely found before the Roman conquest. When Crawford observed in 1928 that the ditch extending SW from enclosure B to celtic fields on Figheldean Down cut through a barrow, he did so with surprise (ibid). All fieldworkers in this part of Wiltshire, however, from Hoare onwards, have been aware of the most dramatic and surprising instance of the desecration of a Bronze Age barrow of importance by a late prehistoric boundary ditch: the place below the northern slopes of Sidbury Hill where the double ditches referred to above – BH – cut through an isolated disc-barrow (2204), destroying half of it. The first notice of this quite unexpected intersection came from Hoare (1812, plan opp 180, and 181). A comment added by Crawford to his 6in map of the area in the Wiltshire Heritage Museum implies that he too saw the feature in the nineteen twenties, as, apparently, did Grinsell when confirming the intersection and measuring the surviving part of the barrow (1957, 217, No 6a). Military activity has further damaged it and RCHME have been unable to identify in detail and with certainty this strange superimposition. Such exceptions serve to reinforce the established behaviour of agriculturalists in ancient times: ancestral burial mounds were to be respected and protected.

The behaviour of those who drove their wagons or sledges across the berm of Site III (Pl 24) and skirted Sites XVII and XX with so little regard for them, piling mud on to the latter in wet weather to keep their tracks service-able, is also in striking contrast. Yet nothing represented this change of attitude more dramatically than the damage done by Ackling Dyke, an important Roman highway, to an enormous oval disc-barrow on Oakley Down (Dorset), one of the most prestigious Bronze Age barrow cemeteries in Wessex (Hoare 1812, plan opp 236; Crawford and Keiller 1928, fig 39, pl 31: Grinsell 1959, pl IIB, looking SW; Green 2000, pl 14). Here, perhaps, the slighting was deliberate, *imposition* of a system of roads upon a subject country with total disregard, in its building, for ancestral burial places and the like. The Roman attitude to the bar-rows on Oakley Down may thus have been an indirect acknowledgement of their sanctity up to that time.

Returning with this in mind to double ditches *BH* on Snail Down, which we now believe to be of Late Bronze Age construction in circumstances still to be fully explained, something more deliberate than mere disregard may have motivated such striking defiance of ancestors.

Reference has been made to the Reading University linear ditches research project (Bradley *et al* 1994). Its results, achieved through intense field survey and selective excavation, have established broadly the way in which the land between the Bourne and the Avon was exploited from Middle Bronze Age times until the Iron Age; and how Enclosures A and B on Snail Down can be fitted into a long-evolving, though by no means continuous scheme of ancient land management whose evidence is preserved hereabouts to an exceptional degree. Publication of this project has superseded our speculation of the fifties, in which the double ditches *BH*, for example, came to be regarded as probably mediaeval and so could be excused for the half-destruction of the disc-barrow below Sidbury. The survey's conclusions need receive here only enough notice to make clear the relationship between Snail Down's Enclosures A and B and the miles of related earthworks to the S, and the significance of our excavated findings to the Reading analysis of the later prehistory of this area of Wiltshire chalk downland.

Reading has proposed that at least the earliest ditch system in the region was a formal definition of territories; was the final indication within the countryside – white ditches, chalk rubble banks – of a process of land tenure whose roots had probably been established before the second millennium BC. To the Reading team such boundaries may not have been indicators to outsiders about ownership and trespass. Instead they gave guidance to the owners themselves about the traditional boundaries and limitations of their lands. Barrows, built at a time when such formal claims had not yet been inscribed upon the land in this striking way, now took their place within these more intensive systems of Bronze Age and Iron Age land ownership and use: they indicated the local people's age-old presence there, their ancestral entitlement to land. Having the bones of their forefathers beneath burial mounds carefully preserved among their fields, often dictating the layout of more obvious boundaries, lent authority to them.

Collection of surface finds by Reading during systematic field-walking as well as selective excavation have established a satisfactory chronology within which the boundary ditches as well as the open settlements and other features that have been recorded among them can be fitted. Towards the end of the Middle Bronze Age, a number of open settlements existed within the region, some of which appear to have replaced settlements that had been enclosed. In the Late Bronze Age, from around 1200 cal BC, the earlier linear boundary ditches were laid out – irregular, flat-bottomed, like those revealed at Sites VI and VII on Snail Down. Motivation for this earliest division of the land appears to have come from a need to emphasise territorial possession. In the process an essentially domestic landscape, wherein most aspects of life were reflected – settlements, agriculture, horticulture, management of livestock and the rest – became thus defined and enclosed. It seems to have been in the Iron Age, perhaps as late as the Middle Iron Age (*c* 400 cal BC), that some of these early ditches were re-cut, and re-cut again, with a carefully studied V-profile and more emphatic size. In this re-cutting, a piling of fresh chalk on to an old bank both heightened it and intensified its outward appearance and significance. Some lengths of ditch went out of use. This re-design of some of the earlier flat-floored ditches into a V-shaped form with a slot at the bottom (termed by some a cleaning slot) coincided with blocks of Celtic fields and may have been stimulated by new requirements for land use rather than a need to define territory. It is also now believed that in the Middle Iron Age certain small rectangular enclosures were new-built – with V-shaped ditches: Enclosures A and B on Snail Down may be examples. These major changes, which have been attributed to Iron Age times here, probably mark a period of intensified agriculture. They are matched elsewhere in the archaeological record by the large-scale use of storage pits to accommodate an increase in cereal production, to which recent excavations in the south of England bear striking testimony.

What needs to be emphasised is that major disruption and re-orientation seem to have taken place from about 800 cal BC, at the end of the phase during which Late Bronze Age Plain Ware was in use.

All Cannings Cross ceramics of the final Late Bronze Age and Early Iron Age were not found at Snail Down. After this apparent break in occupation history, Reading has proposed that settlement patterns may have changed, becoming centred upon high points in the landscape as well as shifting westwards towards the Avon valley. The story of late prehistoric occupation in our region did not resume until about the Middle Iron Age, *c* 400 cal BC, when more complex patterns of both enclosed and open settlements emerged. The Middle Iron Age construction that is proposed for Enclosures A (Site VI) and B at Snail Down was part of this process.

These enclosures are not alone, hereabouts, in perhaps having no contemporary celtic fields within them. Reading suggests that such earthworks and the re-cutting of others indicate a more intensive management of arable land and perhaps the careful husbanding of areas to be reserved for pasture. The RCHME survey of Enclosure A (Figs 1, 2) has shown how fields underlay and also abut upon the N side of Site VI. A build-up of ancient plough-soil along the N edge of side *AB* of Enclosure A, well-shown in our excavated sections (eg Fig 19, sections 2, 7), testified to the scale of plough agriculture *around* Enclosure A.

As well as adding further profiles of both flat-floored and V-profile ditches to the series recorded in the Reading survey, the Snail Down excavations have proved of value by recovering sherds of Deverel Rimbury (Middle Bronze Age) as well as Late Bronze Age Plain Wares (Section E). The material is the only direct evidence, at present, for Middle and later Bronze Age occupation N of Sidbury Hill.

Finally, the great double ditch *BH* has been shown by the Reading Survey to belong in all probability to the Late Bronze Age (800–600 cal BC), a stage when the earlier style of open settlements among fields had ceased, to be replaced in Wessex in due course by nucleated and enclosed settlements, managing an intensified agriculture. The earliest fortified settlement at Sidbury, perhaps the first phase of the hill-fort itself or else an earlier protective enclosure not yet discovered within or beneath the existing ramparts, may be associated with the double ditches *BH*. The Reading survey has been able to show that lengths of double ditch like *BH* occur within a much wider region of southern England at a time when some early hill-forts, like Sidbury perhaps, were being developed.

Changes of ditch shape to earthworks associated with second/first millennium BC land use are not limited to Wessex. In 1959 James Dyer excavated a series of flat-bottomed boundary ditches in Bedfordshire called Dray's Ditches (1961), which were attributed to the earlier Bronze Age by a scatter of Collared Vessel sherds. Here too a continuing need into the Iron Age was attested, since the flat-bottomed ditches were replaced by larger, V-shaped ditches early in that period. The history of Dray's Ditches affords a close parallel to the sequence of Sites VI and VII on Snail Down. Nor can it be without significance that the linear ditch at Boscombe Down East, which was shown by Stone to be earlier than a sub-rectangular enclosure there, had a flat floor (1937b, 471–473). It is noticeable, too, that at Quarley Hill one of Hawkes' earliest pre-Iron Age ditches, Ditch 2, had a flat floor for at least part of its course (1939, 154–156).

Figure 19
Detailed description of layers

(Figs 2, 18, for location of sections)

Section 2   Layers 1–10, bank, ditch and plough soil, Site VI (Enclosure A)

Layer 1 Weathered natural chalk, present in patches at edges of bank and on N side of ditch.

Layer 2 Ancient land surface beneath bank on S side of ditch. Fairly pale brown loam, some chalk and flint chips tending to concentrate towards base. Lying directly upon solid chalk bedrock except along edges where layer 1 intervened.

Layer 3 Bank make-up. At centre, concentrated pure chalk rubble. Upper part of bank contains increasing proportion of loam mixed with chalk rubble. Forward (N) half of bank increasingly of mixed loam and chalk as it approached ditch.

Layer 4 Pale-buff loam highly charged with powdered chalk, filling slot at bottom of ditch. Hardly distinguishable from layer 5.

Layer 5 Main ditch-fill. Very compact pale-buff loam. A few isolated chalk and flint chips and one distinct lens of chalk entering from bank. A second lens of small chalk rubble covered top of layer 5.

Layers 6–8 Darker-brown loam, sub-divided by decrease in quantity of larger chalk chips and general chalk content as turf and humus was approached.

Layer 9 Diffuse brown loan and chalk chips, increasing quantity of chalk chips as bank was approached. Upper part more chalk-free.

Layer 10 Very pale buff loam, less compact than layer 5 but more compact than layers 6–9. Darker in colour towards modern humus. Distinctive layer of flints and chalk chips along top, at junction with modern turf and topsoil. Noticeable increase in thickness of modern turf and soil over layer 10.

Section 3   Layers 1–3, 5, bank of Site VI and part of ditch.

Layers 1–2 The same as those in section 2, above.

Layer 3 Same as section 2. Between bank and ditch some bank rubble lay upon weathered natural chalk (layer 1) without intervening ancient land surface (layer 2).

Layer 5 Same as section 2. Here layers 6–8 could not be distinguished: the compact pale-buff loam of layer 5 lay immediately below modern turf and humus.

Section 4   Layers 1–3, 9, bank of Site VI cut by Trackway T3

Layers 1–3 Same as section 2, but bank rubble (layer 3) here more compact than in section 2.

Layer 9 Diffuse chalk chips mixed with pale brown loam: quantity of chalk increased where it approached bank of Site VI at each edge. Solid natural chalk underlay layer 9; one root hole and one natural hollow exposed, but no cart tracks.

Section 5   Layers 1 and 11, Trackway T3 on N side of ditch, Site VI

Layer 1 Weathered natural chalk, continuous at SE end of trench but broken by tracks at NW and in centre.

Layer 11 Patches of compact chalk, thrown up on to layer 1 by traffic forming this track.

Section 6   Layers 1, 4–6, 8, 17–18, ditch of Site VI; layers 4, 21, 23, 24, ditch of Site XX

Layer 1 Continuous layer of weathered natural chalk, cut by ditches of Sites VI and XX.

Layer 4 Compact chalky filling in slot at base of Site VI ditch and lower corners of Site XX: upper part finer chalk, lower part included more rubbly chalk.

Layer 5 Same as section 2, compact pale buff loam.

Layer 17 Fairly concentrated chalk mixed with pale-buff loam, entering mainly from N side of ditch but covering its inner (S) wall. The chalk lumps much smaller than layer 4.

Layer 18 Localised lens of pure chalk rubble entering from S side and overlying layer 5.

Layer 6 Very pale buff loam, some chalk evenly distributed. Darker at base, while top made uneven by root intrusions.

Layer 8 Dark-brown soil spreading evenly across ditches of Sites VI and XX. At its base over Site VI a thin spread of flints corresponding to those in layer 24, Site XX.

Layer 21 Looser chalk rubble mixed with pale yellow loam in ill-defined streaks. More entering from inner edge of barrow ditch.

Layer 23 Light-brown loam evenly mixed with small chalk chips. Particularly loose at centre.

Layer 24 Brown loam containing concentration of natural flints along base of layer. Barrow ditch overspread by layer 8.

Section 7   Layers 1–8, 10–11, bank, ditch and ploughsoil of Site VI

Layers 1–3 same as section 3, above. Ancient land surface (layer 2) disappeared between centre of bank and S (inner) edge of ditch but bank rubble above it (layer 3) ran up to ditch.

Layer 4 Thicker deposit than elsewhere of pure chalk rubble silt in bottom of ditch: more entered from bank (S) side than from N. Included tip of loose chalk rubble entering from S side.

Layer 5 Pale-buff compact loam with thin scatter of chalk chips. Upper part of this replaced by layer 6, which merged with it gradually. Layer 5 included a local chalky patch close to S wall of ditch.

Layer 6 Pale, almost white, compact loam highly charged with powdered chalk. Texture resembled layer 10, ancient ploughsoil. Merged gradually with layer 5 below.

Layer 7 Darker-brown loam, more chalky than layer 8 above; junction with layer 6, below, made uneven by action of roots.

Layer 8 Dark-brown loam, almost free of chalk: a line of chalk chips and natural flints at its base. Both edges damaged by modern disturbance.

Layer 10 Damaged by modern activity in section 7 but undisturbed (and shown in Fig 19) in W side of trench. Very pale compact buff soil, becoming almost white with powdered chalk towards base. Thin scatter of small chalk and flint chips all through. Thick line of natural flints along top, at junction with modern, noticeably thick, turf and humus.

Layer 11 Like section 5. Compact pure chalk, thrown up over layer 1 by wheels of vehicles driving across edge of ditch. Two cart tracks shown in section 7.

Figure 20
Detailed Description of Layers

(Figs 2, 18, for location of sections)

Section 13   Layers 1–6, 8, 12, bank and ditch *BC* of Site VI where it skirted W edge of Snail Down; cutting 80ft S of section 12

Layer 1 Weathered surface of natural chalk, present only at W end of trench where it was sealed by a thin spread of chalk rubble from damaged bank of *EB* (Fig 2).

Layer 2 Ancient land surface beneath bank, compact pale brown loam, thin scatter of small flint and chalk chips, concentrating towards base. Overlay soil-filled natural hollow (layer 12).

Layer 3 Bank make-up. Pure chalk rubble with some thin soil streaks. Highly compressed here by passage of military vehicles. Chalk spread into ditch where it overlay edge of layer 5 and was covered by part of layers 6 and 8.

Layer 4 Thin deposit of pure chalk sludge and rubble in slot at bottom of ditch.

Layer 5 Compact pale-buff loam; thin scatter of chalk and flint chips.

Layer 6 Paler than layer 8 and contained more chalk and flint chips. Less compact than layer 5 below it.

Layer 8 Darker than layer 6, paler than modern turf subsoil and included more chalk and flint chips than latter.

Layer 12 Fairly compact, pale chalky soil with some large chalk chips. Probably filling of an ancient tree hole.

Section 12   Layers 1, 4, 5, 13, 17, ditch of Site VI, 4ft S of section 11, including earlier phase

Layer 1 Same as section 13. Sealed on both edges of ditch by layer 17.

Layer 4 Same as section 13.

Layer 5 Same as section 13. Made clear contrast with layer 13 (earlier Site VI), showing it cutting latter.

Layer 17 Compact crushed chalk. Remains of bank of Site VI, or perhaps addition dragged across ditch by military vehicles.

Layer 13 Compact pale-brown buff loam; resembled layer 5 in texture but included higher concentration of chalk. Represented filling of Site VI, earlier phase.

Section 11   Layers 4–6, 8, 13, 16, longitudinal section of ditch of Site VI and transverse section after it had turned S and been re-cut; also section of remains of Site VII, here cut by earlier phase of Site VI

Layer 4 Small deposit of compact chalk rubble in slot at bottom of re-cut ditch of Site VI, and also in corners of flat-bottomed first ditch of Site VI, and of Site VII. More compact in VI than in VII.

Layer 13 Tip of more rubbly chalk overlying 4 and indicating line of first cutting of Site VI.

Layer 5 Same as section 13. Filled original and re-cut ditch of Site VI and was indistinguishable, being separated only by scatter of chalk and flint chips of layer 16.

Layer 16 Tip of chalk and flint chips coinciding with ridge of natural chalk on floor of ditch: represented debris caused by re-cutting ditch of Site VI.

Layers 6, 8 Same as section 13. At E end of section 11, layer 6, compressed by tracks of military vehicles. At W end, both layers and modern turf damaged by military vehicles

Section 14   Layers 4, 13–15, ditch of Site VII, examined in wood 128ft N of Section 11

Layer 4 Compact pure chalky sludge, including streaks of pale-yellow loam and of looser chalk chips. On W side of ditch, floor and corner covered by layer of pale-yellow loam, 3in thick in corner. Greater quantity of chalk had entered from E side of ditch: slightly more chalky towards top of layer on E side.

Layer 13 Pale compact loam, resembling main fill of V-ditches and flat bottomed ditch of Site VI.

Layer 14 Pale compact chalky loam spreading across ditch, increasing in thickness towards both sides.

Layer 15 Resembled layer 13, but slightly darker. Covered by thin compacted layer of mud caused by passage of military vehicles (Site VII here coincided with modern track).

Section 10   Layers 1–5, 10, bank, ditch and ploughsoil of Site VI, 760ft E of Section 11

Layer 1–5 Same as section 13. Ancient land surface (layer 2) thick and well preserved up to ditch edge. Most of ditch-filling disturbed by rabbit burrow. Layers 2 and 3 interrupted by post hole filled with fine, loose, grey-brown loam.

Layer 10 Compact, pale buff loam, with thin even scatter of chalk and flint chips. Resembled layer 10 section 2, Figure 19.

Section 9   Layers 1–3, 18, bank of Site VI cut by lynchet and possible trackway

Layers 1–2 Same as section 13. Ancient land surface, layer 2, interrupted by layer 18 but appeared in this as faint patches overlying layer 1.

Layer 3 Everywhere less compact than in section 13, 3.

Layer 18 Pale-brown loam, loose, with thin scatter of chalk and flint chips increasing in quantity towards base of layer. Interrupted layers 2, 3.

Section 1   Layers 1–4, 12–14, bank and ditch of Site VI opposite Site XXI

See Figure 35 and below, Site XXI.

SITE VIII

SPTA 2240: A BELL-BARROW

SUMMARY

The ditch surrounding Site VIII, the largest bell and visually the most significant barrow in the Snail Down cemetery, was found to resemble, in most respects, those around Sites III and XIX. No positive evidence was uncovered to indicate its chronological relationship with Sites IV or X, although there was enough to argue that its building had followed that of the latter. A sherd of Grooved Ware found casually in its tank-damaged top may have derived from the settlement sealed beneath Sites X-XIV where Beaker and Grooved Wares had been much in evidence.

INTRODUCTION

Site VIII was a bell-barrow, situated near the centre of the cemetery (Fig 2) and the largest, most dominating burial mound in the group. It had an overall diameter of about 150ft and a mound 11ft high, separated from its ditch by a berm of 25ft. A broad track ran across the centre line of the entire barrow, worn down deeply by military vehicles (Pl 3). This had cut destructively into the mound, removing much of its turf covering and damaging the upper archaeological layers. It had destroyed the critical area where the ditch of Site VIII may originally have intersected at least the bank of Site IV on the NE.

The section exposed by the tank track revealed that, beneath the modern turf over the mound, there was a covering of chalk like that at Site III and a more earthy core underneath. It was beneath this, presumably, that Hoare found his '*stratum* of black earth' (below).

Hoare cut a deep trench into Site VIII and recorded his work in *Ancient Wiltshire* (1812, plan opp 180, No 13, 183) as follows:-

'... No.13, a very large *tumulus*, in which we made a wide section to the depth of 12 feet, and the only thing worthy of remark was a *stratum* of black earth, 5 feet 9 inches from the surface, which pervaded the whole section'.

In addition, the following references to Site VIII are in print: Goddard 1914, 235, Collingbourne Kingston 13; Grinsell 1934, 219, pl XV, fig 10; Grinsell 1953, pl XIV, upper; Thomas and Thomas 1956, 142; Grinsell 1957, 209; Thomas, N, 1976, 230.

One trench was dug across the barrow ditch on its SW side in 1953 to compare its shape with those of Sites I, II and IV. In 1957 two more trenches were dug across the ditch, one on its W side and another on the SSE, in a search for evidence to establish the chronological relationship of this site to Site X, which lay immediately to its W. The trench illustrated in Figure 14 was on the SSE side of the barrow (Fig 2). J F Dyer and others directed these limited investigations during the seasons of 1953 and 1957.

DESCRIPTION

Pre-barrow Features and Settlement Remains

The trenches dug across the barrow ditch and part of its berm failed to reveal any remains of the settlement immediately to the W although the sherd of Grooved Ware picked up from the tank track across the mound (Section C, C55, Fig 40) can be attributed to that source. No remains of the ancient land surface were uncovered during this limited exploration.

The Barrow Structures

The **ditch** (plans Figs 2, 21; section 3: Fig 14, section 1: Fig 22; finds, Fig 40) had been dug to a depth of nearly 4ft from the present day chalk surface. Its depth from the ancient land surface must have been about 5ft. Its floor was flat and 5½ft in width; it was over 10ft wide at modern ground level.

Post-construction Events

The ditch-filling did not differ markedly from that of Site III, except that in every section exposed, a compact yellow chalky loam (layers 2, 10) covered the primary chalk silt in the bottom corners of the ditch. In section 1, Figure 22 (Fig 21 for location of section) this (layer 10) was not continuous across the ditch. In all other sections, however, it extended without interruption across the ditch-filling below. Layers 3, 4, 11 and 12 above it were unusually chalky and compact.

Section 3 (Fig 14) revealed a modern pit that had been dug into the outer edge of the ditch.

REMARKS

If Site X, and with it, presumably, Sites XI–XIV (below), had been built after Site VIII, such building activity is likely to have resulted in deposits of chalk or soil on the

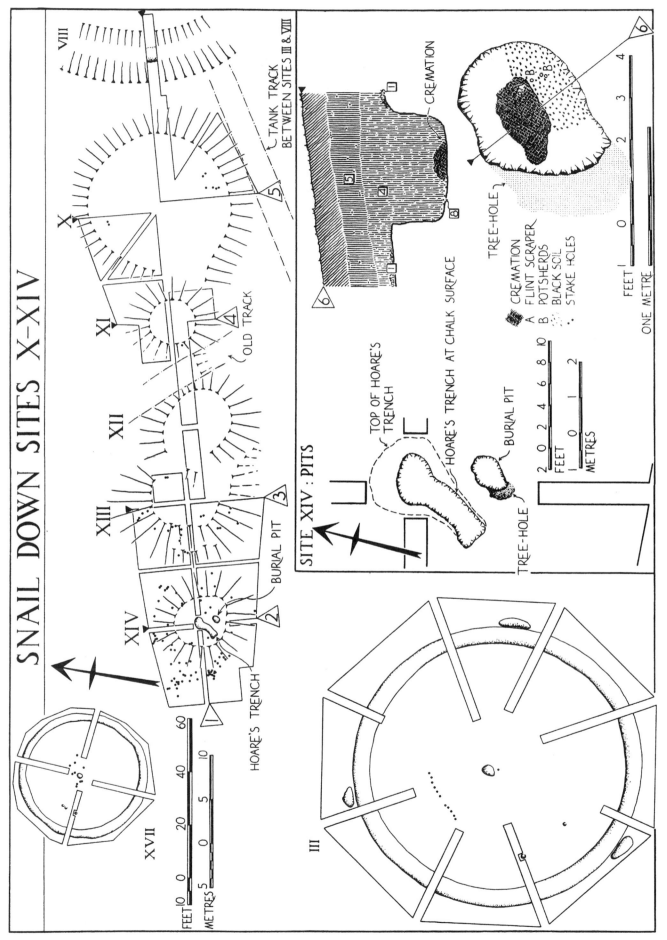

Fig 21   Sites X–XIV, scraped-up bowl-barrows overlying Beaker settlement. Plan, including Sites III, VIII, XVII; plan, section 6, burial pit in Site XIV.

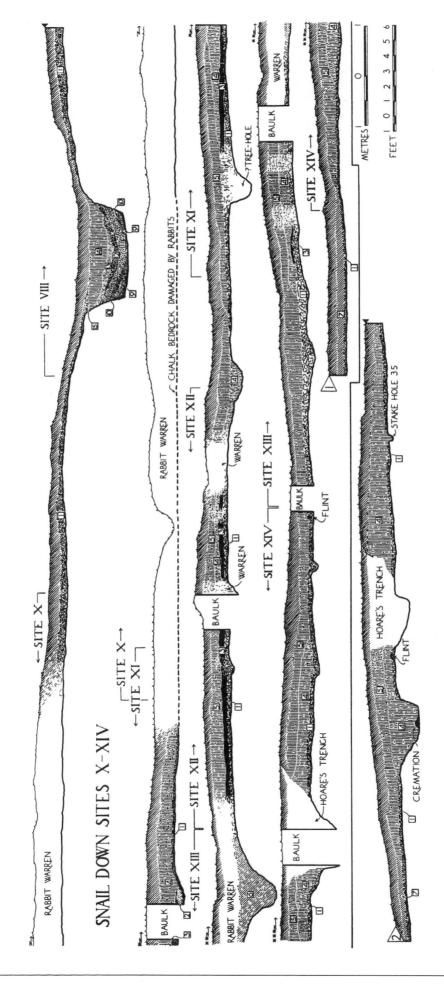

SNAIL DOWN SITES X–XIV

Fig 22 Sites VIII, X–XIV, sections 1, 2.

outer side of the ditch of this bell-barrow. However, no signs of such activity could be seen. It was thought at first that layers 3 and 4 might represent the construction of site X. A trench on the E side of Site VIII revealed the same feature, as did that on the S side; clearly these chalky layers were naturally derived and could not be considered as builders' debris from the adjacent barrows.

Assuming nevertheless that the building of Site X would have been recorded in the filling of the Site VIII ditch had the latter been already in existence, the absence of such evidence suggested that Site X was earlier in date. It was unfortunate that the relationship between Sites VIII and IV could not be tested by a trench on the E side where they were so close. The problem of priority in the building of the Snail Down cemetery is discussed in detail below (Part 3; Fig 60).

Site VIII remains undated. Its great size defeated Hoare and the character of its burials remains to be determined. The presence of burnt material in its earthy core suggests that, like Site III, it covered a cremated interment and, perhaps, a funeral pyre. In shape, its ditch was a well-dug example of the almost squared up surrounding quarry whose turf and bedrock chalk had been cut and extracted to build and whiten the mound within and, we must suppose, to exclude unpriviledged mortals from the sacred place of burial.

Figure 14
Detailed Description of Layers

Section 3   Layers 1–4, filling of barrow ditch, SE side.

Layer 1 Loose rubbly chalk, filling lower corners of ditch but not extending across ditch floor.

Layer 2 Compact yellowish clayey soil, spreading across ditch floor and sealing layer 1 in each corner.

Layer 3 Compact chalk, filling greater part of ditch; contained occasional streaks of more earthy chalk.

Layer 4 Medium brown soil speckled lightly with chalk chips. Less compact than 3.

Layer 5 Weathered chalk bedrock.

Figures 21, 22
Detailed Description of Layers

Section 1   Layers 9–15, filling of barrow ditch, adjacent to Site X.

Layer 9 Loose rubbly chalk, filling lower corners of ditch but not extending across ditch floor.

Layer 10 Compact yellowish clay soil corresponding to layer 2, section 3, Figure 14. In this section (1), however, it just failed to seal ditch floor and was slightly more earthy on outer side of ditch.

Layer 11 Compact chalk which, with layer 12, corresponded to layer 3 of section 3, Figure 14. Layer 11 was a little less compact than layer 12 above. This distinction not noted in section 3 (Fig 14).

Layer 12 Compact chalk, much more so than layer 11 but apparently part of same in-filling process of ditch.

Layer 13 Pale brown loam, fine chalk content higher than in layer 14 above.

Layer 14 Similar to layer 13 in texture, but deeper brown because of lower fine-chalk content. Included thin scatter of small chalk chips. Layers 13, 14 corresponded to layer 4 section 3, Figure 14.

Layer 15 Rubbly chalk, extending across most of ditch, beneath modern humus; derived from bedrock of outer, upper edge of ditch. Isolated phenomenon.

SITE IX

SPTA 2219: AN EARTHWORK AND TRACKWAY

SUMMARY

Where excavated, Site IX, part of Trackway T1, comprised a broad, low bank which in places encroached upon a series of wheel-ruts lying immediately to the N. Bank and tracks crossed the berm and ditch of Site III which, at that point, had already become silted up and covered by a mature soil. Romano-British pottery was found in the material of the bank in 1953.

INTRODUCTION

Site IX (Fig 2) was part of a complex trackway, T1, which traversed Snail Down from between Sites XIX and XXII on the E, to the point where, together with a modern military route overlying part of Site II (Fig 6), it crossed side *BC* of Enclosure A (Fig 2). Eastwards from the place where Site IX crossed a N/S lynchet, just W of the parish boundary (Fig 2; section 2, Fig 14), it has become incorporated within field lynchets and other features but its general course was aimed at the narrow gap between the double bell-barrow, Site XIX, and its S neighbour, Site XXII. Further E, RCHME have established its route as well as its double-ditch character (Fig 2).

A track following only approximately the line of Site IX between Sites XIX/XXII and Site III was noted in pencil by Crawford on his fields maps (now in the Wiltshire Heritage Museum) but he showed it as skirting 2217 instead of 2224 (Site III). It seems fairly certain, however, that Crawford's track was intended to indicate the line of our Trackway T1 (Fig 2).

Major Allan's air photograph of Snail Down (Pl 1) revealed T1's course clearly, including its continuation eastward from Sites XIX and XXII. No further notice was taken of it until a transverse trench was dug in 1953, with further work in 1955 (Thomas and Thomas 1956, 142–143), and a survey made of it by the RCHME in 1957 and then in greater detail in 1993.

During the course of the first season of excavations in 1953 it became clear that the barrow cemetery could not be examined in isolation from its surrounding earthworks and trackways, and a start was made in that year by digging a trench across Site IX, SSE of Site VIII (Fig 2). The track was examined again in 1955 during the excavation of Site III, since it cut across part of the ditch and berm of that site. In 1955, uncovering of cart ruts N of the bank overlaying the ditch and berm of Site III (Pl 24) led us to extend the 1953 trench a further 5ft to the N, to reveal similar ruts.

DESCRIPTION

The Structures and Cart Tracks

The bank (plans, Figs 2, 9; sections, Figs 10, 11, 14; Pl 24) was a generally flat-topped earthwork, differing from place to place only in width. Where it overlay the ditch of Site III (Fig 9), it sealed a clearly defined land surface. In the trench dug in 1953, SSE of Site VIII, the land surface sealed by the bank was patchy in appearance. Analysis revealed that this soil horizon was mature when the bank of Site IX was heaped over it. The pale colour and compact, almost clay-like character of the bank material suggested a high chalk content although this was not visible as nodules. The colouring was also patchy (Pl 24).

Beneath the earthwork in some places, and consistently to the N of it, there occurred a **series of ruts** which must have been made either by wheeled vehicles or by some form of sledge or travoys. These are indicated in sections 2 (Fig 10), 3 (Fig 11) and 7 (Fig 14) on Site III and in section 2 (Fig 14), the trench excavated in 1953. With the northernmost rut expressed as zero, the spaces between the centres of these ruts, from section to section, as shown in Table 5.

Table 5 Varying widths of cart tracks, Sites III, IX. Figures in italics represent ruts sealed beneath the bank of Site IX.

Site IX (1953), Figure 14	0–5½ft–8¼ft
Site III, section 2, Figure 10	0–6ft–10¼ft
Site III, section 3, Figure 11	0–7ft–8½ft–13¼ft–15½ft
Site III, section 7, Figure 14	0–2ft

All these ruts showed in the undisturbed chalk as very shallow soil-filled troughs 6–12in wide. Their distances apart gave some indication of the gauge of the wheels or runners of the vehicles that made them. Where they crossed the ditch of Site III (Fig 9) they tended to widen, as one would expect at a point where vehicles must have slid on the edge of the berm, especially in wet weather.

In the 1953 cutting across the bank SSE of Site VIII, four indeterminate sherds of Romano-British pottery were found, mostly close to bedrock. The bank overlying the ditch of Site III included one 1st century Samian fragment (Section F, F10).

REMARKS

Soil analysis failed to explain how the bank of Site IX had been developed. It may not have been a hedge bank since rootlets and root holes were absent. It is reasonable to suppose that it was associated with the ruts because they all followed the same course. Since it covered some of them, it may therefore have had more direct connection with ruts immediately beyond it to the N.

The intersection of Site IX and the track (T3) which ran nearly N/S, forking to pass Site XX and cross the ditch of Site VI, occurred to the SW of Site III but was not examined by excavation. The aerial photograph (Pl 1) seems to suggest that Site IX overlay it. The latter was probably associated with the supposed Romano-British settlement N of Enclosure A (Site VI) which was recorded by Hoare (1812, plan opp 180). Because of the Romano-British pottery found in the 1953 trench, it can tentatively be concluded that Site IX (ie the Trackway T1) was also Romano-British, linking some settlement further E with the known one c $1\frac{3}{4}$ miles W of Snail Down (Coombe Down, Fig 1).

It is difficult to separate the ruts into pairs and arrive at a uniform gauge for the vehicles that made them. Some may not have scored the chalk, while the land surface beneath the bank of Site IX could conceal additional ruts. Margary has drawn attention to this difficulty when discussing the width of ruts on Roman roads (1973, 22). There is a suggestion, however, that the northernmost ruts form a pair $5\frac{1}{2}$–7ft apart. Wheel-ruts $7\frac{1}{2}$ft apart were also uncovered when Trackway T3 was excavated as it ran on either side of Site XX towards a gap in the earthwork of Site VI at that point (Figs 2, 18). The normal gauge of Roman cart wheels was 4ft $8\frac{1}{2}$in. The ruts on Snail Down appeared to be generally in excess of that. The Wiltshire bow wagon of the last century was notable for the width of its body, which could be as much as 80in. In a series of bow wagons of Wessex type measured in the nineteen fifties (Jenkins 1961, 226–227), the gauge ranged between 63in and 79in (a specimen in Dorset). A wagon from Pewsham, Wilts, had tyres 6in wide, although the normal tyre for wagons in Wessex was 2–3in. The narrowest wheel gauge recorded in this survey was 50in for a Yorkshire box wagon. Wagons have been recorded only rarely in Britain in the lengthy period between later prehistoric times, when the wheels and wheel parts from Glastonbury, Newstead and elsewhere pointed to fully developed carts and wagons, and the 17th century. Yet there seems every reason to suppose that they were fairly widely used in medieval England, even if their wheels were perhaps solid. P Ashbee recorded a series of cart-ruts which had impinged upon the outer part of the filled-up ditch of bell-barrow G58 and bowl-barrow G61 on Earls Farm Down, Amesbury (1985, 44–46, figs 3–4, 54, fig 16). Some could be paired to a width of $4\frac{1}{2}$ft, nearly the

standard Roman gauge. Others, at 6–7ft, approximated more closely to those on Snail Down. A pair of cart tracks, not recognised at the time, straddled the berm and ditch of a bell-barrow on Oakley Down, Dorset (Parke 1955, 38, pls IIB, III). Its deep grooves were $5\frac{3}{4}$ft apart. Romano-British sherds and glass beads were secondary associations in the barrow. It is therefore likely that the tracks and associated bank constituting Site IX were made by wagons (or sledges) of a kind presumed to have been widespread in Britain from medieval times but whose origins may have been much more remote.

It is difficult to offer an explanation for the bank apparently associated with the tracks, or to show how it had been formed. It is possible that in wet seasons the tracks now sealed beneath the bank had become so deeply rutted that those using the route dumped turf, soil and perhaps chalk on top in an attempt to level and smooth their way across the Down. The tracks to the N could have been developed when this attempt at repair had failed, perhaps in a continuously wet season. When abandoned, the track thus repaired and widened might have appeared in due course as a slight earthwork. However, with natural flint available, it is curious that this metalling should have been ignored when repairing the first cart-track. Moreover, on open downland it is usual for people to follow ever-widening detours rather than attempt to level or repair an unmetalled track (Crawford 1953, frontispiece, and 70; note also his advice on studying Roman roads and trackways (*ibid*, 57)).

Here at present our attempt to explain the bank of Site IX must rest; until better-preserved or documented analogies are discovered, its purpose remains unsolved.

Figure 14
Detailed Description of Layers

Section 2   Layers 1, 2, 4, bank make-up, Site IX
Layer 1 Remains of old land surface, hard, compact loam like layer 2 but slightly darker brown; occurred as a disjointed layer at base of 2. Slight concentration of chalk and flint chips at base.
Layer 2 Hard, compact pale brown loam, free of flints and chalk chips except for short, thin runs of the latter as indicated in drawing.
Layer 4 Weathered natural chalk, cut in places by cart tracks.

Section 2   Layers 3, 5, soils against bank
Layer 3 Darker, less-compact brown loam on S side of bank. Became distinctly chalky at base where a hollow (perhaps a tree hole) appeared. Merged with layer 2, while oversailing its S slope.
Layer 5 Resembled 3. Overlay N slope of bank, layer 2, and merged gently with modern humus.

SITES X–XIV

SPTA 2237, 2234, 2233, 2225, 2615: DITCHLESS BOWL-BARROWS AND BEAKER SETTLEMENT

SUMMARY

The space between two bell-barrows, III and VIII, was occupied by a line of five earthen mounds of different sizes, their edges almost overlapping and their alignment conspicuously out of parallel with that of the main group of barrows on Snail Down. With Site XV, they may have been the earliest burial mounds to be raised on the Down. The W end of the row overlay part of an earlier settlement, and Beaker potsherds and other debris became incorporated in the mounds of Sites X–XIV, as they had in that of Site III and other sites close by. Presumably each mound had covered a burial but only one was found by excavation, off-centre in Site XIV. It was a cremation of a young adult, perhaps female, in a pit accompanied by a flint scraper and three urn sherds, two joining. The burial yielded a radiocarbon assay of 3555 ± 75 BP.

INTRODUCTION

This group of sites comprised five low and irregular mounds, apparently overlapping, which filled part of the space between Sites III and VIII. They had long been colonised by rabbits but had not suffered much damage from military vehicles. Surface inspection suggested that the mounds, like Site XV, lacked surrounding quarry ditches and had been built instead by scraping up turf and topsoil. A track, probably ancient, crossed the space between Sites XI and XII. The mounds were covered by downland turf made uneven and often broken through by rabbit burrows. There were also low bushes.

Hoare excavated at the centres of several barrows in the vicinity of Sites X-XIV but his plan of these (1812, opp 180) was inaccurate and it is difficult to allocate his Nos 8–10 precisely. His No 12, an unrewarding mound, was our Site X. Site XIII may have been his No 8. Site XIV produced clear evidence of a central trench penetrating the chalk which was probably dug by Hoare (but see below). No other work on these mounds has been recorded. In addition to Hoare, Sites X–XIV have been referred to by the following: Goddard 1914, 235, Collingbourne Kingston 10 only; Grinsell 1957, 168; Annable 1958, 5–6; Thomas 1976, 229–230; Gibson 1982, i, 37.

The chief reason for excavating Sites X–XIV was to establish their relationship one to another and also to attempt to show whether they were earlier or later than Sites III and VIII, the bell-barrows at each end of their line. The system of cuttings (Fig 21) in which the mounds were examined comprised a grid whose compartments conformed roughly to the differing sizes of the mounds and which provided a continuous section along the diameters of each. At the E end, one grid was extended to provide a section across the ditch of Site VIII. Early in the excavation of these mounds it became clear that rabbit burrows had damaged them too heavily for complete excavation to be worthwhile: even the solid chalk, as beneath Site XV, had been deeply scored by rabbits. The grids were not therefore cleared completely, and this accounts for the curious trench plan. The work was done during the first three weeks of the 1957 season under the direction of Nicholas and Charles Thomas and thirty to forty volunteers took part. The mounds were roughly restored by bulldozer at the end of the season.

DESCRIPTION

Pre-barrow Land Surface and Beaker Settlement

Traces of an ancient land surface were recorded beneath Sites XI, XII and XIII. Because of damage by rabbits it was poorly preserved; it may have been deliberately removed from beneath Sites X and XIV during construction of the other mounds. For convenience details are described site by site below and illustrated in Figures 22 and 23. Evidence for bush or tree holes came from Site XI (four; section 1, Fig 22) and XIII (several hollows, but their antiquity not established; section 1, Fig 22). Platforms of slightly raised, level chalk were recorded beneath each mound, where the ancient land surface had been protected from further weathering.

When the mounds of Sites X–XIV had been cleared down to the solid chalk, **111 stake holes** were located, their distribution shown in Figures 21 and 24. None was observed in the soil forming the base of the mounds; in the cleaned solid chalk, however, their circular, pale loam fillings were unmistakable (Pl 33, holes 8 and 9). Time allowed but seven to be emptied and their profiles examined. The diameters and depths (where sampled) of these holes ranged between 2–7in and 3–7in respectively.

The shapes of the holes were of two types, pointed and flat based. All were circular in plan except 74 and 98. All the pointed holes must have contained rammed stakes. However none of the post holes with flat bases contained packing, so presumably they too had contained driven stakes originally. In this process they may have become

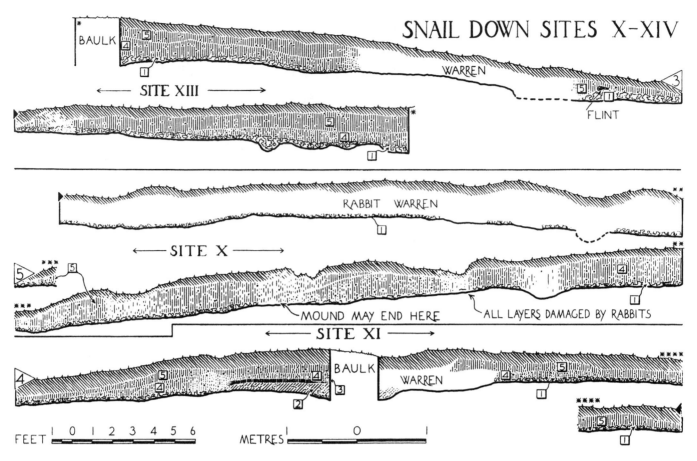

Fig 23   Sites X, XI, XIII, sections 3–5.

more blunted in final appearance than they had been before ramming started. A few of the larger holes were close together in pairs, for example 37 and 38, 45 and 46, 91 and 92. During excavation of 45 and 46 a small stake hole, 45A, was found running into the edge of 45. Several stake holes, examined by sectioning at the end of the excavation, were found to have a forked point, suggesting that the stakes had split while being driven into the chalk bedrock.

The fillings of all the holes were the same and were indistinguishable from the fine, pale compact loam of the mound cores: no charcoal or organic remains occurred in those dug out.

Although a recognisable overall plan fails to emerge from a study of these stake holes, it is possible to see two sides of a rectangle measuring $5\frac{1}{4}$ by $7\frac{3}{4}$ft in the arrangements of holes 6–15–16–18/18–17–12–4. Holes 73–76–77 and 75–79–81 form alignments, and there are a few pairs of large holes, which have already been described.

Stakes and posts like these must have formed part of a settlement whose builders were responsible for the broken Beakers and other wares and a general scatter of flint implements that were found in the make-up of Sites X–XIV. The volume of such domestic litter increased beneath Sites XIII and XIV, corresponding with the greater number of holes beneath those two mounds (Figs 21, 24). No well-preserved land surface with Beaker occupation debris *in situ* was found, however, because the surrounding area must have been divested of its turf and topsoil for

barrow building. Burnt flints and chalk in some quantity were recorded at the base of Site XIV in the area bounded by holes 40, 41, 35 and 38, but they could not be regarded as the remains of an intact hearth. Similar flints and burnt chalk occurred in quantity equal to that of the potsherds in the material of Sites XIII and XIV and clearly all must have derived from the settlement. In contrast with this evidence of occupation before the barrows were built, charcoal occurred in no significant quantity in the mound material nor were animal bones conspicuous.

A substantial quantity of sherds of Beaker and contemporary domestic wares together with five sherds of Collared Vessels, one from a Ridged Food Vessel and one from an Accessory Cup was recovered, scattered throughout Sites X, XI, XIII and XIV though only a very little came from the modern topsoil (Sections C, G, J). All were small, few decorated pieces seem to have come from the same pot and most were only slightly weathered. Their individual distribution beneath Sites XIII and Site XIV has been plotted in Figure 24. Sixty-two flint flakes and implements were scattered across Sites XIII and XIV, like the Beaker sherds, and their occurrence has also been recorded in Figure 24. Sites X(31) and XI(13) yielded a further 44 flints. The only unusual find, from Site XIV, was a flake from a stone battle-axe (Section J, J2, Fig 53). It had been made from camptonite, a good tool-making rock from the Nuneaton district of north Warwickshire, identified as Group XIV among the various rock sources now known to have been exploited in prehistoric times.

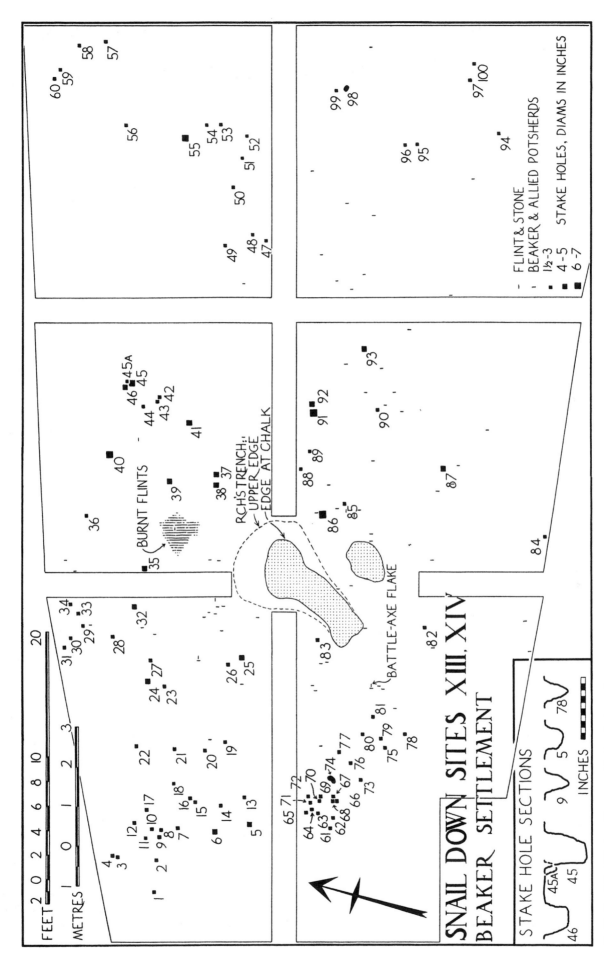

Fig 24 Sites XIII, XIV, plan of features and finds at Beaker settlement.

The unpatinated flint round scraper that had been placed with the cremation burial associated with Site XIV did not differ in appearance or in technique of manufacture from those associated with the Beaker settlement except that it alone was unpatinated.

THE BARROW STRUCTURES

Site X

No burial was located beneath Site X. This **mound** was the largest of the group, surface measurement giving it a diameter of 60–70ft (plan, Fig 21; sections, Figs 22, 23). It was also (with Site XI) the most nearly circular in plan. Its height was uniform with the others in the row, averaging 1¾ft above the level of the weathered natural chalk. Site X had, however, suffered more heavily than any of the other earthen mounds and little evidence remained of its original composition. In parts of the S half, as represented in section 5, Figure 23, the mound comprised pale brown compact loam with an even scatter of chalk chips (layer 4). There was no trace anywhere of an ancient land surface sealed beneath it and although the evidence was at best patchy, it seems possible that the Bronze Age turf and humus had already been removed, or at least heavily disturbed, when this mound was scraped up. In the N half of the site the underlying solid chalk showed as a slight but evident **raised plateau** where the mound had protected it from weathering (Fig 23, section 5). Measurement of this platform provided confirmation that the mound had an original diameter of *c* 60–70ft.

On the surface it seemed possible that the W edge of Site X was overlain by the E edge of Site XI. Excavation failed to settle this important point because at this junction both mounds had been destroyed by rabbits: the approximate area of overlap is indicated in section 1, Figure 22. On the ground the SW edge of Site X appeared to turn out somewhat, towards Site XI, but even this was not evidence for establishing the priority of one over the other.

In the SE quadrant of the mound a group of six **stake holes** (104–109, above) was found when the undisturbed chalk was cleared, and two more (110, 111) occurred near the N edge of the mound. These are considered to belong to the Beaker habitation site concentrated at the W end of the row and are described above.

A thin scatter of sherds of Beaker pottery and allied wares, and of flint implements and flakes occurred throughout the mound. They are presumed to belong to the occupation site sealed beneath these barrows, particularly beneath Sites XIII and XIV, and are described below (Sections C, D, G).

Site XI

No burial was found beneath Site XI. The **mound**, like that of Site X, was almost circular, having a diameter of about 35ft and a maximum height, above solid chalk, of 2ft (plan, Fig 21, sections, Figs 22, 23). The mound had suffered less than the others in the row. West of the N/S baulk which lay along its diameter, the mound preserved

an **ancient land surface** of deep buff, compact loam, fairly free of chalk chips and flints (layer 3). Above this lay the core, a pale brown loam, rather less compact than that of Site X, containing a thin and uniform scatter of chalk and flints (layer 4). Then above this the chalky loam became deeper in colour and here and there could be excavated as a distinct layer, though its junction with the core beneath was never sharp (layer 5). It contained more chalk and flints than the loam below; these may have been brought down to this level by earthworms working through the humus which lay above. East of the central N/S baulk this distinction between darker and lighter chalky loam was much less evident though it was sufficiently visible to be drawn in the S half of section 4 (Fig 23). In this sector of the barrow, the ancient land surface included more than 6in of flinty loam below the clean dark-buff band which marked the top of the prehistoric land surface. Beneath this the undisturbed chalk was firm, lacking the weathered surface encountered in most places on Snail Down (layer 1). This extra-thick ancient land surface and subsoil were probably associated with a hollow covered by, and extending N of, the main E/W baulk. It was however, also damaged by a rabbit burrow at this almost central point of the barrow (Figs 22, 23, sections 1, 4). The hollow may have been the remains of a **tree hole**, but one of extreme antiquity since the ancient land surface appeared to seal it. There were three other irregular tree holes beneath Site XI, one shown on the W edge in section 1 (Fig 22), a second in a similar position to the E and a third SE of the barrow's centre. None was sealed by the prehistoric land surface. That shown in section 1 had clearly broken up the land surface around it and its tree may have been standing shortly before the erection of this mound. The necessity to remove such a tree may explain the broken state of an otherwise well-preserved area of barrow mound and ancient subsoil at this point.

Little could be seen of a **raised platform** of natural chalk, protected from weathering because of the barrow mound placed upon it, like that beneath Site X, except around the S limits of Site XI. Here, as indicated in section 4 (Fig 23), there was a fairly distinct falling away of the undisturbed chalk beyond the edge of the ancient land surface; beneath the latter it was conspicuously level.

One stake hole, 103, from the Beaker settlement was found at the SW edge of the mound (Fig 21).

An **old track** (Figs 2, 21) was visible on the surface, running roughly NW/SE between Sites XI and XII, but it had left no traces below the modern turf. Nor was there any stratigraphical hint, at this point, of the priority of one of these mounds over the other. Their layers of make-up ran out exactly where it was hoped that a point of overlap might have occurred.

Beaker and other contemporary pottery was represented by a small scatter of sherds throughout the mound. Flint implements and flakes were also present and, like those from Site X, they can be accounted for by the proximity of the Beaker settlement to the W (Sections C, D, G).

Site XII

No burial was found beneath Site XII. The **mound** was so badly damaged by rabbits beyond the two trenches dug along its diameter that no more work was done upon it. Its perimeter appeared to be almost oval in plan, with long axes orientated NW/SE. Its maximum dimensions were about 45 by 50ft, with a height above solid chalk of almost 2ft near the centre. The NE edge had been cut into by the old track separating it from Site XI; around the W half, Site XII merged with its W neighbour, Site XIII. The resulting irregularity in shape, confused further by rabbit burrows, is suggested in Figure 21.

An **ancient land surface** was preserved beneath the mound, a layer of deep buff loam generally free of chalk chips and flints except along its base (Fig 22, section 1, layer 3), which was separated from the solid chalk by a few inches of weathered chalk and flints (layer 1). This dark land surface was preserved along the diameter of the barrow for a distance of 20ft and was slightly thicker and more distinct than that beneath Site XI. Above it, along the E half of the area examined, was deposited a thin layer of pale brown, compact loam (layer 4) containing an even scatter of small chalk chips and flints. Above this, and covering the ancient land surface along the W half of the mound, there was a darker loam, looser and with an even scatter of slightly larger fragments of chalk (layer 5).

The undisturbed chalk beneath Site XII showed a slight rise in level where it had been preserved beneath the mound of the barrow and this **level plateau** appeared to be marginally higher, overall, than that beneath Site XI.

A large rabbit warren had destroyed the archaeological layers at the junction of Site XII and its W neighbour XIII so that, despite the surface indications of an overlap, no evidence remains to show which barrow had been built first.

The cutting across Site XII failed to yield sherds or worked flints.

Site XIII

No burial was found beneath Site XIII. Except at the SE, where the **mound** merged with Site XII, its shape was clear on the surface (plans, Figs 21, 24; sections, Figs 22, 23; Pl 32). It had suffered heavily, however, from rabbits. Along its N/S diameter it measured about 57ft, but E/W it appeared to be much smaller. Probably its original shape was more oval than circular, like Site XII, but its junction with the latter made this difficult to assess. It had a height above solid chalk, at the centre, of just over 2ft.

The mound of Site XIII comprised all the features seen in Site XII (Figs 22, 23, sections 1, 3): traces of an ancient land surface of fairly dark buff loam with weathered chalk (layer 3) separating it from the solid bedrock (layer 1), then a layer of compact buff loam with an even scatter of chalk chips and flints about one foot thick (layer 4), followed by a covering of darker, less compact loam with rather more pieces of chalk and flints evenly distributed (layer 5). A jacket of downland turf, much cut up by rabbit burrows, covered the mound.

The **ancient land surface** beneath Site XIII was very poorly preserved, being visible only as indistinct, thin patches of darker buff soil in the W half of the mound: one such area is shown in section 1 (Fig 22). Overall, an area less than about one quarter of the base of the mound retained traces of this surface and it seemed clear that

when Site XIII was built the land which it was to cover had already been much cut up.

Beneath Site XIII there were slight traces of a **raised platform** of natural chalk which had weathered less than its surroundings. This could be seen clearly in section 1 where the W part of the barrow sloped down towards Site XIV.

A number of **irregular hollows** occurred close to the centre of Site XIII; one near its E edge is shown in Section 1 (Fig 22). No significance can now be placed upon them since all were filled with rabbit-derived material and none contained any archaeological evidence that it had originally been a burial pit or other artificial feature.

Indications in the field (Fig 21) suggested that Sites XIII and XIV may originally have met at one point, but hardly overlapped, and this was confirmed in the E/W section across the two sites (Fig 22, section 1). The approximate point of contact is shown in the section as occurring in the area of a N/S cross-baulk, but no evidence for an overlap could be seen. The upper mound material of both barrows appeared to the eye to be continuous from one to the other.

Numerous **stake holes** were found in the solid chalk (47–60, 94–102, Figs 21, 24), when the excavation had removed the mound material and the remains of the ancient land surface beneath. These had been made when stakes associated with the underlying settlement were rammed into the bedrock. None was recorded until the undisturbed chalk had been exposed and cleaned. Presumably they belonged to the greater scatter of stake holes beneath Site XIV to the W. Their plan, Figure 21, showed that in the area between these two mounds the number of stake holes lessened sharply. This suggested that the preservation must be attributed to the protection afforded by the barrow material on top of them, since otherwise all except the deepest holes would have been destroyed by weathering of the downland chalk surface.

Potsherds of Beaker and allied wares, with worked flints and flakes and animal bones, were scattered throughout the mound of Site XIII, in greater volume than that from Sites X-XII but exceeded by the archaeological material from Site XIV (Sections C, D, G). All can be attributed to the presence of the Beaker settlement sealed beneath the barrows, especially its neighbour to the W, Site XIV. A large base sherd of Collared Vessel came from layer 4. At the edge of the mound were six sherds of Middle and Late Bronze Age wares.

Site XIV

The Burial (plans, section, Fig 21; Pls 32, 34, 35; Section A, Cremation 10; pottery, Section D, D21; flint, Section G, G26, Fig 51). Site XIV covered a **pit** containing the cremated bones of a young adult, possibly female, the only burial recovered from these five barrows. It lay about 6ft S of the approximate centre of the mound. The pit was almost oval in shape, its W end a little irregular because here it ran into a deep, soil-filled excavation in the chalk, probably made by an ancient tree or bush. Its floor was flat and its walls, except at the SW end, were almost vertical (Fig 21, section 6). Maximum dimensions were $7\frac{1}{4}$ by $5\frac{1}{2}$ft; the flat floor was about $2\frac{1}{2}$ft below the surface of the solid chalk. Walls and floor of the pit were unweathered. A large patch of blackened soil and charcoal covered the SE quarter of the pit's floor to a depth of 1–2in (layer 8). Three plain sherds of Collared Urn lay on its surface (Fig 21, detailed plan, B; Section D, D21). Though placed separately, two of them have been found to join. The central part of the pit was covered by a human cremation which overlay the N edge of the burnt soil described above. In shape, the cremation was distinct and compact, elongated and coming towards a point at the W end, where the pieces of bone were noticeably larger than those at the opposite end (Pl 34; Fig 21). Although the bones were mixed with chalky soil and chalk fragments, charcoal (ash and oak) was scarce. An unpatinated flint scraper (G26, Fig 50) had been placed on top of the bones at their E end (Fig 21, detailed plan of pit, A). The pit was entirely filled with compact pale buff loam indistinguishable from that forming the core of the mound above (layer 4).

Charcoal of *Fraxinus* (ash) was submitted to Oxford for **accelerator dating** with the following result:

OxA-4178 3555 ± 75 BP; cal BC 2028–1777 (1 sigma); cal BC 2135–1699 (2 sigma). This result is considered further in Section T.

Site XIV had a well-preserved **mound**, almost circular in shape and disturbed by rabbits hardly at all. Its general diameter on the surface was about 37–40ft and at the centre it had a height above solid chalk of some 2ft (plans, Figs, 21, 24; sections, Fig 22; Pls 32, 34, 35).

There were no traces of an ancient land surface. Instead, the lower material of the mound (layer 4) lay directly upon the weathered surface of the chalk (Fig 22, sections 1, 2, layer 1). This lower mound material, as elsewhere among these five scraped-up barrows, comprised pale compact buff loam with only a slight scatter of fine chalk chips. It was charged with finely powdered chalk which gave it a slightly whitened appearance and must account for its pale colour. Here and there in the mound the pale buff loam was even paler, as if its powdered chalk content had increased. This slight variation in shade could not be defined sufficiently precisely to be planned and its significance remained obscure.

Around the S half of the mound the compact loam was covered by a darker brown soil (layer 5), less compact, which contained a slightly higher concentration of small chalk chips. North of the main E/W baulk across Site XIV this layer died out rapidly, the pale buff of the N half of the mound (layer 4) being thicker and capped directly by the modern humus and turf. The N/S section across Site XIV (Figs 21, 22) failed to show any of the deeper brown soil, though its disappearance was not in fact as sudden as this section might suggest. Eastwards from Site XIV, the brown soil continued apparently without interruption until it rose to cover the pale buff central core of Site XIII.

Site XIV was covered with unusually thick turf and humus; a distinct line of flints and chalk chips lay across its base.

Post-construction Events

The centre of the barrow contained an **elongated pit** which had been dug from a level less than halfway down the modern humus covering the barrow mound (Fig 21, detailed plan; Fig 22, sections 1, 2, 'Hoare's Trench'). Its NE end was almost circular where it penetrated the turf covering the barrow. The SW end was rectangular in plan and section. This pit penetrated the solid chalk, dipping down into it towards the N. Its filling was thoroughly mixed, including large lumps of solid chalk and remains of pieces of turf and humus (Pl 35; Fig 22). No traces of bone or artefacts were found in this filling.

Throughout the excavation and subsequently, this trench was assumed to have been the work of Hoare when he was at Snail Down in 1805. Only at Site XIV were we able to study precisely the shape of this kind of antiquarian excavation and the level of its upper edge in relation to the modern downland turf. It could be seen clearly that the upper edge had been cut from a level within the upper half of the present-day turf and that chalk chips representing spoil from this trench, on the gradual move downward through earthworm activity, occurred still within the upper half of the modern turf. This phenomenon – movement by earthworm action of material lying on the surface of soil or turf – was noted at Stonehenge by R J C Atkinson during his excavation of the nineteen fifties and sixties when he was studying physical evidence for the excavations of Lt Col W Hawley, which had been carried out immediately after the conclusion of the First World War (pers comm). Atkinson was able to show that layers of chalk chips which occurred at Stonehenge about half-way down from the surface of the modern turf were derived in all probability from Hawley's excavation spoil and had been buried to such a depth by earthworms over the course of some thirty years. That level, from excavations of the early nineteen twenties, corresponded with the level reached by spoil at Snail Down Site XIV which we had assumed to have been the work of Hoare in 1805. It seems therefore at least possible that the trench across the centre of Site XIV may have been dug in the twentieth century rather than the early nineteenth. As already indicated (above, introduction), we cannot be certain, from a reading of *Ancient Wiltshire*, which barrows in the area of Sites X–XIV had been dug by Hoare: Site XVII he left alone. Sites X–XIV, far less prepossessing even without their rabbit burrows, he may also have passed by (except, possibly, Site X) in favour of more interesting looking or larger mounds hereabouts. At Site I, the eccentric tump had suffered more than one assault from antiquarians and others over the years. In attributing Hoare's name to the central trench at Site XIV, and in using the shape of the trench as an indication of at least some care in his digging technique, we must bear the evidence from Stonehenge in mind and with it the possibility that this trench was not the work of Hoare, but of somebody (even a rabbiter) at a later date.

REMARKS

Excavation in 1955 and 1957 (Fig 21) revealed stake holes in varying numbers beneath Sites III, X, XI, XIII–XIV and XVII. No stake holes were discovered beneath any of the other Snail Down barrows during the three seasons on the

Down except *circles* of stakes beneath Sites XV, XVI and XIX; but those were clearly essential elements in the structure of those barrows and need not be included in this discussion. Despite the occurrence of Beaker potsherds in Sites I and II, we do not agree with Gibson (1982, i, 37) that such scatters of sherds should be considered as grounds for associating certain features of Sites I and II (the small pit containing ash and traces of cremated human bone in Site I, Figs 3, 4, for example) with the Beaker settlement. We prefer to suppose that the structural remains of the settlement were concentrated in the area of Sites XIII and XIV and to the W.

As indicated in Figures 21 and 24, the stake holes formed two distinct areas, one, the principal series, concentrated beneath Sites XIII and XIV, the other, more orderly and itself made up of two groups of holes, located beneath Sites III and XVII. There seems little doubt to us that the neat row of stake holes with a central gap beneath Site III was associated with funerary activities prior to the building of the barrow mound; and that the stake hole at the centre of that site may have been used in the barrow's marking-out process. This group of stake holes can, then, also be excluded from this discussion. For the same reason, the setting of stakes whose remains were found at the centre of Site XVII and were in use and, possibly, withdrawn before the digging of the central burial pit there, must have been associated with that site rather than with the Beaker settlement immediately to its SE. Structural remains of the Beaker settlement consisted, we suggest, of the stake holes beneath and around Sites X, XI, XIII and XIV, together with sherds of Beaker and allied wares, flint implements and flakes, perhaps the battle-axe fragment, and animal bones. Similar pottery and other material from Site III especially and from almost every other barrow examined during these seasons must be seen as debris from the Beaker settlement, some of it spread hundreds of yards from the complex centred upon Site XIV.

The land surface beneath Site XIV had been damaged when its top had been removed to provide mound material for one or another of the slightly earlier mounds among the X–XIV group so that all hope of finding an intact Beaker settlement surface was lost. Even the slight concentration of burnt flints and chalk bounded by stake holes 35, 38 and 39 was not convincing as the remains of a hearth.

The majority of these stake holes were concentrated around the W edge of Site XIV. It proved impossible to link any so as to outline convincing structures. Beyond a few pairs, the overall pattern appeared to be as random as it usually seems when Beaker settlement remains are excavated (Section C, introduction; Simpson 1971, *passim*).

Although potsherds and other artefacts were scattered in the general area of the stake holes, there was no marked coincidence, rather the reverse; sherds and flints occurred in smaller quantity than elsewhere in the major area of holes around the W arc of Site XIV. That said, the distribution of flints and sherds formed no obvious pattern. Many more sherds and flints had been incorporated into the mound of Site III than were found around Sites XIII/XIV: 190 sherds and 300 flints from Site III, 90 sherds and 109 flints from Sites X–XIV combined. Such concen-

trations raise the possibility that the centre of the Beaker settlement may lie between Sites III, XIV and XVII.

At Snail Down, the circumstance of barrow building had preserved ephemeral remains of an earlier settlement but without indicating anything of the form which these Beaker structures had taken. That they were flimsy was shown by the thinness of most of the stakes and the total absence of posts that had required the digging of larger holes and their chocking-up firmly with post packing. Local farmers' opinion in 1957 was that pointed stakes of some stoutness could be driven at least two feet into solid chalk hereabouts without excessive labour. Probably, short-lived farming settlements in Beaker times needed no stronger form of construction, unlike the great, permanent, timber buildings such as those at Marden, Durrington Walls, Woodhenge and elsewhere (Wainwright 1979, and refs. quoted there) which had also shown close association with Beaker users.

Most of the evidence for Beaker settlements of Snail Down type has been recovered in the form of potsherds and other artefacts only. Structures are rarely found. Snail Down has provided a welcome, but still enigmatic, addition to the small corpus of late third/early second millennium cal BC domestic sites from southern England, among which the closely similar remains at Downton, south of Salisbury, are at present the nearest (Rahtz 1962a, 123–127).

The first of several problems posed by Sites X–XIV concerns their chronological position within the cemetery. The Snail Down cemetery comprises two alignments of prominent ditched barrows (see Part 3, phases 4A and 4B, Fig 60) together with smaller mounds seemingly less deliberately placed. Spacing between barrows of phases 4A and 4B is irregular, gaps occurring between 2207 and Site II, Site II and 2216, between Site XXII and 2254; and between the latter and Site XVI, if those three barrows can be considered an alignment. Sites X–XIV form a short, contiguous row of insubstantial mounds between Sites III and VIII and out of alignment with the W half of the main cemetery, barrows 2207/Site IV (Figs 2, 21). It was hoped that the trench dug between Sites X and VIII would show which of those barrows had been built first. Unfortunately the filling of the ditch of Site VIII produced no such evidence (above). Although the gap between Site II and its neighbour to the N/E may be used to argue to the contrary, we have proposed below (Part 3) that some of the small mounds which occupy spaces between the major barrows were the earliest on Snail Down. At its beginning, the cemetery may have comprised isolated barrows (eg 2244, Sites XVIII and XXI) a pair (Sites V and XV) and a cluster (Sites X–XIV) subsequently incorporated within two alignments of majestic Wessex Culture barrows.

Preparation of the ground chosen for the site of a barrow must have been a normal preliminary procedure; trees and bushes removed, remains of old crops and other agricultural debris trodden down or removed; tall grass perhaps cut; derelict settlement structures cleared away. Usually the archaeological evidence is slight. Beneath Site XI, however there was enough to suggest that more than one tree or bush had been pulled up before the barrow was built there.

Sites X and XIV alone of this group of five yielded no trace of well-preserved land surfaces beneath their mounds. If all these barrows had been built originally by gathering turf and soil from round and about, the evidence suggests that Sites X and XIV, the mounds at either end of this row, were built last: their turf and subsoil had already gone to make up Sites XI-XIII. Sites III and XVII covered well-preserved land surfaces, so the soil-collecting for Site XIV did not go out in that direction.

Three of these mounds, XI, XIII and XIV, were cleared extensively or completely, yet only one, XIV, yielded a burial. Sites X and XII were not examined sufficiently for it to be certain that they were equally barren, but it seemed likely that extensive digging would have failed to reveal burials. Curiously, Hoare found *empty* pits beneath five of the mounds he dug at Snail Down; beneath six others, including our Sites V and X, he failed to find burials. If these sterile mounds can be considered as some form of cenotaph, it need not be so unlikely that four out of the five mounds under discussion never covered burials. Such a concentration of cenotaphs in one cemetery, at least eleven, and spread over the lifetime of that cemetery, is, however, unusual and worthy of particular note (see Part 3).

Finds from the burial pit beneath Site XIV provided evidence for a straight-forward sequence of interment. A pit was neatly dug, its edge impinging upon an old tree hole or soft spot in the chalk. No attempt was made to heap up the spoil from this pit around its edge as in Sites III or XVII: instead it must have been scattered. The burnt bones of a young adult, perhaps female, were brought to the spot in a bag: while the burial party carried its precious load across the Down the larger bones worked their way to the top of the container, the heavier dust and other extraneous material settling at the bottom. As drawn in Figure 21, the narrowed, W end of the supposed bag containing the bones would have been its mouth, the part held in the hand as it was carried to the pit for burial. A token sample from the funeral pyre, possibly, was scattered in one corner of the pit and the container of bones was laid down in the centre, overlying part of this burnt material which included three potsherds. A fresh unpatinated flint round scraper was put on top of the bones, then the burial-party set-to to cover the pit with scrapings from the surrounding downland and to form a heap over it. With no surrounding stake circle to guide them, nor apparently any marker beside the grave itself, its exact position may have been lost during the barrow-building, since the centre of the mound came to be several feet to the N. Site XIV provided the most convincing evidence from Snail Down that a cremation had been buried in a perishable container.

Alone among the flint implements found in Sites X–XIV, the flint scraper placed with the burial in Site XIV was unpatinated. The battle-axe fragment from this mound (Section J, J2) also appeared to be unweathered, its fractured surface still fresh and its ground surfaces smooth. This contrast in the condition of the flints added weight to the belief that the patinated pieces belonged, with the Beaker and other potsherds found in the mounds, to an altogether earlier period, to the settlement whose remains were represented by the scatter of stake holes. The battle-axe would have been at home in a Beaker context, though it could also have been wielded (and damaged) by the builders of Site XIV, particularly if

they were at work here, as we have argued above (and Part 3), early in the history of the cemetery.

Figure 21
Detailed Description of Layers

Section 6   Layers 1, 4, 5, 8, fill of burial pit and mound above
Layer 1 Surface of natural chalk, soft and weathered. Sides and floor of pit, clean firm chalk.

Layer 8 Blackened soil, liberally speckled with charcoal. Laid on clean floor of pit; covered in part by cremation.

Layer 4 Pale brown, compact loam, irregular scatter of chalk chips and natural flints. Filled pit, lay directly on cremation and layer 8 and extended without break into rest of layer 4 where it formed core of barrow.

Layer 5 Darker brown, less compact loam, irregular scatter of chalk chips and natural flints.

Figure 22
Detailed Description of Layers

Section 1   Layers 1–7, mounds, Sites X–XIV, layers 9–15, Site VIII
Layer 1 Surface of natural chalk, soft and weathered. Several natural flints over 1lb in weight embedded in layer. Not present at junction of Sites XI and XII.

Layer 2 Compact loam, as pale brown as layer 4 but containing more chalk chips and natural flints. Perhaps fill of ancient tree-hole (fragments of animal bone and a potsherd in fill).

Layer 3 Ancient land surface, deep buff band of chalk-free, compact loam with no noticeable concentration of chalk and flints at base: thick and clear in W half of Site XI and beneath Site XII, thin and patchy beneath Site XIII (not preserved in N/S section, Fig 23).

Layer 4 Pale brown, compact loam, irregular scatter of chalk chips and natural flints. Filled a hollow at E edge of Site XII and lay on chalk bedrock. Also formed core of its mound. Filled burial pit beneath Site XIV and formed core of this barrow.

Layer 5 Darker brown, less compact loam, irregular scatter of chalk chips and natural flints. North and E of 'Hoare's Trench' at centre of Site XIV, a concentration of flints and chalk chips along top of layer.

Layer 6 Filling of deep hollow at E edge of Site XIII. Pale brown loam, compact: contained more chalk than layer 4. May have been affected by rabbit warren above.

Layer 7 Deep brown, loose loam, resembling topsoil but containing thin scatter of small chalk chips. West end of Site XIV only.

Section 1   Layer 9–15, ditch, Site VIII. See site descripton above.

Section 2   Layers 1, 4, 5, 7, mound, Site XIV
Layer 1 Surface of natural chalk, soft and weathered. Several natural flints over 1lb in weight embedded in layer. Broken by stake hole 35, by burial pit and 'Hoare's Trench'.

Layer 4 Pale brown, compact loam, irregular scatter of chalk chips and natural flints. Filled burial pit, lying directly upon cremated bones. North of 'Hoare's Trench', concentration of chalk chips and flints along its top.

Layer 5 Darker brown, less compact loam, irregular scatter of chalk chips and natural flints.

Layer 7 Deep brown, loose loam, resembling topsoil but containing thin scatter of small chalk chips. West end of Site XIV only.

Figure 23
Detailed Description of Layers

Section 3   Layers 1, 4, 5, mound, Site XIII

Layer 1 Surface of natural chalk, soft and weathered: one patch extra thick and not removed (excavation at Snail Down included removal of weathered top of chalk, until more solid bedrock reached).

Layer 4 Pale brown, compact loam. Irregular scatter throughout of chalk chips and natural flints.

Layer 5 Darker brown, less compact loam. Irregular scatter throughout of chalk chips and natural flints including at least one slab over 1lb in weight.

Section 5   Layer 1, 4, 5, mound, Site X

Layer 1 Surface of natural chalk, soft and weathered. In places removed by rabbits.

Layer 4 Pale brown, compact loam, irregular scatter throughout of chalk chips and natural flints. Heavily damaged by rabbits.

Layer 5 Darker brown, less compact loam, irregular scatter throughout of chalk chips and natural flints.

Section 4   Layer 1–5, mound, Site XI

Layer 1 Surface of natural chalk, soft and weathered. Removed in places by rabbits.

Layer 2 Compact loam, as pale brown as layer 4 but with higher content of chalk chips and natural flints: probably the fill of ancient tree hole (yielded animal bone fragments and one potsherd). Overlain by layer 3.

Layer 3 Ancient land surface, deep buff band of chalk-free, compact loam. No noticeable concentration of chalk and flint chips along base.

Layer 4 Pale brown, compact loam, irregular scatter throughout of chalk chips and natural flints.

Layer 5 Deeper brown, less compact loam, irregular scatter of chalk chips and natural flints.

SITE XV

SPTA 2262: A SCRAPED-UP BOWL-BARROW WITH POST RING

SUMMARY

A pit containing the cremated bones of an adult of unknown sex lay beneath the NE part of a low mound of scraped-up turf and soil. A ring of posts some 50ft in diameter had been set within the mound; forty of the original post holes survived.

In the later Bronze Age, the bodies of four adults and a baby had been buried in shallow scoops in the S half of the mound, their crouched remains each covered by a rough layer of flints. Inhumation 8 from Site V (above) may have been an outlier of this cemetery.

INTRODUCTION

Site XV was a bowl-barrow but lacked visible evidence for a surrounding ditch. It lay about 120ft W of Site V (measured centre to centre). For many years it had been a rabbit warren (pers comm, the late W E Cave, MP), its turf covering badly cut up by those digging out rabbits and ferrets; in places the mound had collapsed into the burrows beneath.

Hoare found the mound of Site XV so slight and irregular that he doubted its antiquity; he dug here nevertheless but failed to recover a burial (1812, plan opp 180, No 22 and 185). Other references to Site XV are as follows: Goddard 1914, 230, Collingbourne Ducis 3; Thomas and Thomas 1956, 143–146 and fig; Grinsell 1957, 167; Ashbee 1959, 5–6, figs 2–3 and *passim; ibid* 1960, 60–65; Thomas 1976, 230.

A trial trench was cut into the E edge of the barrow as an extension to one of the cuttings across the ditch of Site V on its W side (Fig 16) to investigate a natural pipe of clay found in the chalk outside the ditch of the latter. This trench was incorporated into an irregularly outlined quadrant layout. Because the barrow had been so damaged by rabbits the baulks were not removed completely; otherwise the area occupied by the mound was cleared down to solid chalk.

The work lasted for seventeen days in 1955, about thirteen volunteers taking part under the direction of Charles Thomas.

DESCRIPTION

Pre-barrow Features

Because of the damage that the ancient land surface and underlying chalk had suffered from rabbits and rabbitters, no structural or natural features were identified beneath the barrow. It is possible that the unstratified Grooved Ware (Section C, C96–C99) may have belonged to an episode on this part of Snail Down before the barrow was built (see below).

The Burial (Figs 25, 26; Pl 39; Section A, Cremation 11). The **cremation pit**, the only certainly ancient feature within the post ring, was found on the W edge of the NE quadrant. This was a heavily damaged area of the barrow and the undisturbed chalk hereabouts was also badly weathered. The upper filling of the pit had been contaminated and contained the recent skeleton of a rabbit. However its lower half was intact, and the shape of the pit also remained unaltered. It was almost oval in plan, about 3½ft by 3ft and dug about 1¼ into solid chalk. Its sides were nearly vertical and smooth, its floor flat (Fig 26, Pl 39). The filling of the lower half comprised a central core of dark brown soil (layer 5), surrounded by compact small chalk rubble and silt (layer 4). A heap of cremated human bones lay on the floor in the E half of the pit, its W edge beneath part of the central earthy core, the rest covered by the surrounding chalk fill. The bones were not widely spread, and the pit-filling must have been carried out with some care so as to leave this as a heap almost 3in high on its W side.

The Structures

A **ring of at least forty post holes** (not forty-one, as described in Thomas and Thomas 1956, 144) was found around the mound, holes 1–36 forming an even curve from SE to NW, about 5ft within the edge of the mound as it exists today (plan, Fig 25; sections, Fig 26; Pls 36, 37). Around the NE half of the mound only four more holes were found, all lying approximately on one arc set about 3 ft beyond the arc of the other post ring: the gap between holes 37 and 1 and the irregular spacing of these outer post holes can probably be explained by destruction through weathering: the chalk bedrock hereabouts was unusually heavily decomposed. In addition, two post holes were found within the SW arc (22 and 25) and a small stake hole (18) occurred between holes 17 and 19. The post bases were exposed when the barrow mound had been cleared down to undisturbed chalk. They showed as distinct circles and ovals of dark grey-brown

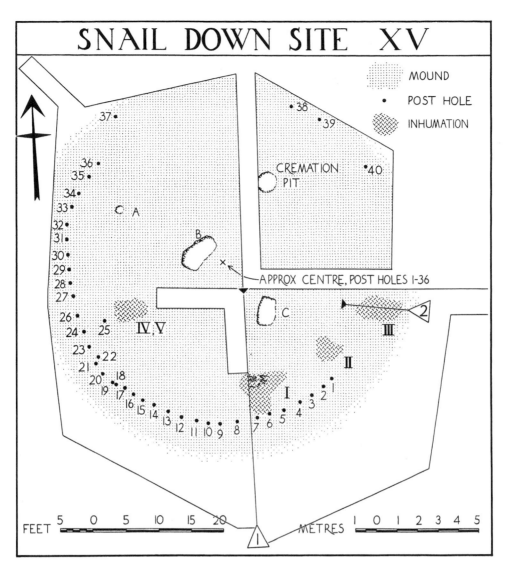

Fig 25   Site XV, scraped-up bowl-barrow with palisade. Plan, including inhumation burials of later Bronze Age indicated.

soil mixed with a small quantity of fine chalk chips representing rotted wood replaced by earthworm casts (Fig 26, layer 9; Pl 37). Nearly half the posts were oval in plan at chalk surface. Dimensions in inches, measured from solid chalk level, were as follows:

The range in depth of the post holes, 1 to 15in measured from undisturbed chalk, was remarkable (see Table 6). This can be explained by the unevenness today of solid chalk caused by rabbit damage.

Four post holes were sectioned by digging pits into chalk bedrock (Fig 26, Pl 37) and it was shown that the uprights had been set into prepared holes. Posts 7, 28 and 35 had pointed bases, but the end of post 15 was cut straight across and it could never have been driven thus into the solid chalk. The post packing everywhere comprised rammed chalk, some of it almost indistinguishable from decomposed natural chalk (Fig 26, layers 6, 8). Post 35 had been set against one side of its hole and held upright first by rammed chalk and then by a large flint stamped into the top (Pl 37). Its pit was deeper than most and the filling comprised less compact, more earthy rubble (Fig 26, layers 7, 8). Hole 18 alone contained an upright which appeared to have been rammed into place. The two inlying holes (22

and 25) and those around the N part of the circle (37–40) were of the same general size as the others.

In plan (Fig 25), posts 1–36 approximated closely to the circumference of a circle, its centre between pits B and C (see below), which had a radius of about $24\frac{1}{4}$ft. They were spaced on average some $2\frac{1}{4}$ft apart. Posts 37–40 lay close to an arc having a radius of $26\frac{3}{4}$ft from the same centre. Post 37 was farther from its arc than any other post and it is possible that there may have been an entrance there, 8ft wide, set out of alignment with the rest of the posts.

The position of post hole 1 was calculated before its excavation and was then exposed at the base of a complete section through the barrow in a relatively undisturbed area. Nevertheless no trace could be seen of a post presence in the mound. Hole 8 was also exposed at the base of a complete section through the barrow (the main N/S baulk) but its post also was invisible in the section. Posts were visible in the mound of Site XIX (below). Their absence from the mound of Site XV is perhaps further evidence of the completeness with which the material of this barrow had been turned over since its construction, because it was clear that the posts had never been pulled from their holes, but had rotted in position.

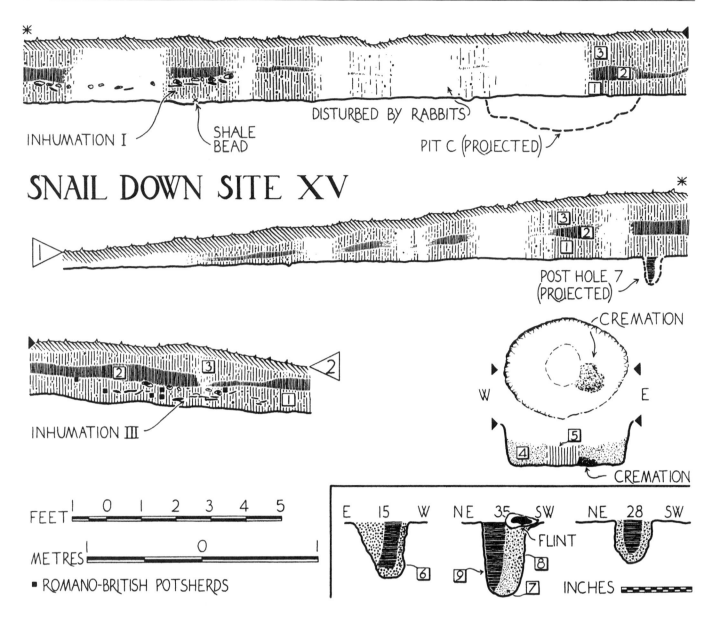

SNAIL DOWN SITE XV

Fig 26   Site XV, sections 1, 2; plan, section of cremation pit; Sections of post holes 15, 28, 35

Three non-burial pits were located within the post ring (Fig 25, A–C); they had been disturbed in recent times and their antiquity could not be established beyond doubt. **Pit A** was roughly hemispherical in shape, 1ft 2in in diameter and dug just over 1ft into the solid chalk. It was filled with chalky soil resembling layer 1 of the barrow mound (below). It contained neither archaeological material nor evidence for age or use.

Pit B was roughly sub-rectangular in shape, with a maximum length of 6¼ft and a width at its SW end of 3⅓ft. Its sides and floor were irregular but in cross-section its average profile was U-shaped. At each end its floor rose gradually to the chalk surface: at its NE end this pit reached a maximum depth of 1ft 8in. The mound above Pit B had been particularly heavily disturbed by rabbits and the original contents of the pit completely dug out by them. Its recent fill included shotgun cartridges and Romano-British potsherds: its original purpose and even its antiquity remained in doubt.

Pit C was sub-rectangular in shape, measuring roughly 4½ft by 2ft 10in. Its profile was irregular, the upper half dug about 6in into bedrock, with a central area sunk 4–6in deeper (Fig 26, section 1, profile of pit along major axis). When the overlying rabbit-damaged mound had been cleared down to the chalk, it was evident that at least two burrows had entered the pit (Pl 38). The top 6in of pit-filling, a medium-dark loam with large flints and chalk fragments, contained shotgun cartridges and another cartridge was found on the floor. Like Pit B, it had been turned over completely by those digging for rabbits. One of the pits may, however, have been the trench dug originally by Hoare.

The **mound** of Site XV (Figs 25, 26; Pls 36, 38) had a diameter of about 60ft and a height of some 2ft at its centre. As indicated in sections 1 and 2 (Fig 26) and in Pl 38, the material of the mound had been so turned over by rabbits and rabbitters that it was impossible to be certain of its original height, whether any of the inter-

Table 6 Dimensions in inches of holes in post ring of Site XV

Post No	Diam of post hole	Depth of post hole	Post No	Diam of post hole	Depth of post hole
1	4	12½	21	3½ × 3	4½
2	3	15	22	3	10
3	3	8½	23	3	8
4	3	8½	24	3½	7
5	3	8	25	4 × 2	6½
6	3½ × 3	10	26	3	12½
7	3 × 2½	9	27	3	8½
8	3 × 2½	3½	28	3	7½
9	3	4	29	3 × 2	4½
10	3 × 2½	5	30	3	9½
11	3	7½	31	3 × 2	9
12	4 × 3½	7½	32	3 × 2	7
13	3	7	33	2½ × 2	1
14	4 × 3½	7½	34	2½	7
15	4 × 3	9½	35	4	12
16	3 × 3	8½	36	2½ × 2	2
17	3½ × 3	10	37	2	3
18	1½	3	38	3½ × 3	1
19	3½	8	39	3	8½
20	3½ × 3	3	40	4 × 3	7

mittent layers were original or whether it sealed a land surface. Generally, the lower half of the mound was composed of a medium-brown, compact soil heavily mixed with fine and coarser chalk chips and natural flints, which lay directly upon fairly solid chalk bedrock (Fig 26, layer 1). There were no continuous or really convincing remains of an ancient land surface between it and solid chalk, though here and there the lower part of this soil was less chalky, as if the remains of a land surface were present. The accumulation of natural flints which is always found at the base of an undisturbed chalk soil profile was not obvious at the base of Site XV.

Layer 2 was the only clear and relatively intact deposit in Site XV. It comprised fairly loose, dark grey-brown loam, conspicuously free of chalk and flints. It sealed the secondary (later Bronze Age) inhumations (below) and evidently represented a turf-and-soil covering to the mound. It also sealed Romano-British potsherds. In appearance (colour and texture) it differed markedly from ancient land surfaces examined at Snail Down, for example beneath Site III, and it seemed fairly certain that layer 2 had been sealed and preserved in relatively recent times when layer 3 was spread over it.

Layer 3 was distinguishable from layer 1 beneath it only by being a little paler, consisting of loam mixed with chalk chips and flints. The amount of chalk varied from place to place, supporting our belief that this layer derived from digging connected with rabbitters. The original dumping of this layer must have been rapid, since the turf below it (layer 2) had evidently been sealed completely and at one time. Thereafter all three layers and the modern turf had been dug into and turned over, rabbit burrows penetrating the chalk even at

the centre of the barrow (Pls 36, 38) and shotgun cartridges turning up 9in below the top (natural chalk level) of pit C (below; Pl 38).

Thirteen sherds of Beaker and allied wares (Section C) were distributed apparently at random throughout the site. Examples occurred in each of the three layers that made up the barrow mound. One well-decorated sherd and a few less-diagnostic fragments probably represent an early European Bell Beaker (Section C, C101, Fig 41). Of much greater significance and interest were four sherds of Grooved Ware (ibid, C96–C99, Fig 41), in fabric and decorative style not represented elsewhere on Snail Down and certainly quite distinct from the other non-Beaker wares (some of which had grooved decoration) from Sites III and X-XIV to the NW.

A jet or shale dumb-bell-shaped bead of Wessex Early Bronze Age form (Section K, K8, Fig 54) was found at the base of the mound, below the area occupied by the knees of Skeleton I (Fig 26, section 1). Assuming a later Bronze Age period for the skeleton above it, this bead could have reached its place of discovery about the time of the barrow's construction: its position was less likely than that of the other finds to have been disturbed by rabbits. It matches exactly the bead associated with Secondary Burial 1 at Site III. A C14 determination helps place the building of that bell-barrow at 3490 ± 90 BP (Section T, below): the secondary burial was probably later, though by how much was not established.

Eleven pieces of worked flint came from the barrow, concentrated at various levels in the SE quadrant. None showed secondary working (Section G).

Two bone awls and another piece of worked bone (Section H, H3, H4, H7, Fig 52) occurred within the SE quadrant. Like almost all the prehistoric finds, their final resting places were the result of disturbance. They are forms of bone implement which are not easily datable, but in all probability they belonged to the first millennium BC and would post-date by a considerable period the construction of this barrow. A later Bronze Age parallel to H4 found recently in barrow West Overton G19 (Gill Swanton, pers comm) suggests that that implement at least could have been associated with the inhumations added to Site XV. It is even possible that some of them were associated with the marked concentration of Romano-British pottery and a spindle whorl from Site XV (Section F, *passim*; Section N, N9, Fig 59).

Remains of **five inhumations** were found in the S half of the barrow, all except Skeleton I scattered and almost destroyed by rabbits and rabbiters (Figs 25, 26, sections 1–2; Pl 40; Section A, Inhumations 3–7). They lay beneath layer 2, the turf line which divided the barrow horizontally into two parts. All the bones were in poor condition.

Skeleton I, probably the remains of an adult woman (Section A, Inhumation 3) had suffered least from rabbits although the skull had been removed and most of the bones were broken (Pl 40). It lay on its back, upper arms by its sides, right forearm slightly bent with hand in lap, left forearm missing. The legs had been placed with knees drawn up level with the waist; the lower parts of the legs were together and pressed against the thighs. Apart from a few individual bones the feet were missing. Skeleton I was surrounded, and originally covered, by an elongated pile of natural flints, orientated, like the skeleton, E/W, with an extension S which overlay post hole 6 (Fig 25). Few of the flints exceeded the size of a human fist and the majority were just pebbles; their concentration on and around the skeleton was unmistakable and they must represent the remains of a cairn which originally covered the corpse when it had been placed in its grave. This grave can have been no more than a shallow scoop since the burial lay immediately below the land surface (layer 2) which apparently represented the top of the barrow in ancient times. The regular outline of a grave could not be discerned beneath the flint cairn, but in view of the mixed and disturbed nature of the ground upon which the skeleton lay, this is not surprising. No grave goods were found with the skeleton.

Radiocarbon determination (Section T, 2920 ± 70 BP) has suggested that Skeleton I – and with it, by inference, the other four – belonged to the later Bronze Age. It seems probable that here we have an inhumation cemetery of a period and of a kind only rarely met with in British prehistory. To it, the child buried in nearby Site V (Fig 16; Inhumation 8) probably belongs.

Skeleton II lay about 13ft NE of Skeleton I (Inhumation 5), at the same level, just below the remains of layer 2. It consisted of a dispersed group of fragmentary human bones of which pieces of skull alone were recoverable. A concentration of natural flints represented the remains of a covering cairn (its rough outline indicated in Fig 25). The skull fragments belonged to a mature person, whose sex could not be ascertained.

Skeleton III, a further 10ft NE, lay across the line of the post circle which had left no trace around this arc (Inhumation 4). Dispersed and incomplete, the surviving bones were probably those of a mature female. They were associated with an elongated spread of natural flints whose E/W orientation suggested the direction in which the corpse must originally have been disposed (Fig 25). This burial also lay beneath layer 2; the concentration of Romano-British potsherds hereabouts included fragments sealed beneath layer 2 and occurring as low in the mound (layer 1) as the lowest part of the burial (Fig 26, section 2). Fragments of the bones of sheep, ox and pig occurred among the scanty remains of Skeleton III.

Skeleton IV, like Skeleton II, was represented only by a few scattered pieces of adult skull and other bones (Inhumation 6) and by a concentration of flints spread over a roughly oval area orientated E/W. These slight remains of a burial lay beneath layer 2. In the same area, but even more disturbed, were the remains of **Skeleton V** (Inhumation 7). An incomplete assemblage of bones indicated a baby of 18 months.

REMARKS

No certain explanation can be given for layers 1–3 in the make-up of Site XV because they had been too heavily damaged. Probably the original height of the mound was represented by the top of layer 2 and it must therefore have been a very low barrow. That its original top, layer 2, was covered over in modern times to develop a rabbit warren, is suggested by its thickness and relative continuity. The later Bronze Age deposition must have involved cutting through and disturbing the turf over the mound. In 1955, no trace of these insertions could be seen in this layer, but during the course of nearly three millennia it is likely that earthworms and other natural agencies could have removed such evidence.

In view of the uncertain antiquity of any of the layers revealed by excavation, we cannot now place too much significance upon the apparent absence of an ancient land surface at the base of the mound. Traces of a chalk-free level immediately above the undisturbed chalk were encountered, patchily, in many places. Although it could not be established that these were ancient or certainly the remains of an ancient soil, nevertheless that is what they may have been. Alternatively, it is not inconceivable that most of the ancient land surface was removed when the barrow was built, and then incorporated as mound make-up. Structurally, the mound of Site XV was likely to have resembled those of Sites X–XIV, and to have comprised scraped-up turf and chalky soil, but containing a ring of posts.

Post rings have been classified by Ashbee (1959). Site XV fell within his Category A2, a single ring of closely spaced posts, of which he listed nine examples in 1960. Ashbee also made a distinction between *peripheral* circles and those set well inside the original periphery of the mound, which he called *internal*. This Snail Down circle lay some 5ft within the existing edge of the mound, and even allowing for its spread as a rabbit warren, it seems that Site XV contained an *internal* post ring. Its purpose was likely to have been less functional than ritual.

The mound of Site XV was always so slight that its post ring would not have been needed as a revetment like those beneath Site XIX. There were no neighbouring barrows to protect from its spread (Site V was not near enough and may have been later in date: see below). Ashbee suggested that most internal post circles were withdrawn before construction of the mound above. It was clear, however, that the Snail Down posts (including those below Site XIX) rotted in position, the wood being replaced with fine soil by earthworms (above; Fig 26; Pl 37).

A ritual – that is, a non-functional – purpose for the post ring of Site XV would help to explain its absence from Sites X–XIV, whose mounds were otherwise identical. Burial practice evidently ordained that between Sites X–XIV the dangers of mounds coalescing was of no account, while for Site XV a different requirement had to be met by erecting a ring of posts which, in all probability, projected above the surface of the mound.

The SW half of the post ring approximated closely to a circle whose centre has been calculated and marked on the plan, Figure 25. The NE arc had roughly the same centre but greater radius. Since only four post holes survived here, it is possible that the post circle may have been incomplete. Assuming, nevertheless, that the remains are those of a complete circle, the change of radius for the two arcs is curious but not unknown in barrow post rings: plans of the majority of published examples tend to be irregular. At the time of the examination of Site XV, and in the *interim* report (Thomas and Thomas 1956, 144), it was suggested that the positions of holes 21 and 22 represented an overlap caused by the string, which must have been used to lay out the two arcs from a central post, becoming wrapped around this post and thus, at the completion of the task, falling short of its starting point which could have been hole 21. Study of the plan (Fig 25) makes this attractive suggestion unlikely since for the same reason hole 23 should also have fallen inside the arc. Instead, holes 22, 18 and 25 must be seen as additional to the main circle, for a purpose which is not clear from their arrangement.

There was a suggestion that the prehistoric pottery from this corner of Snail Down, and from Site XV in particular, was possibly a little earlier than that from the settlement beneath Sites X–XIV; and the Grooved Ware certainly found no parallel among the sherds associated with that settlement. From three seasons of extensive excavations, it was clear that the Grooved Ware of Longworth's Durrington Walls sub-style (Wainwright and Longworth 1971, 240–242) from Snail Down was concentrated beneath Site XV. Together with a few sherds of Mortlake ware (Section C) from Site XIX, European Bell Beaker sherds and associated, less diagnostic pot fragments, a different ceramic range emerged in and around Site XV. Whether Site XV was so closely associated with the Grooved Ware (whose well-preserved surfaces suggested that it had not been lying about for long before being incorporated in the mound) that we should consider XV a Grooved Ware burial mound is another question, which the excavation failed to answer. It suggests, however, that on one part of Snail Down (Sites X–XIV) people using English styles of Beaker and allied wares had settled, however briefly; while a few hundred yards SE a different group may have been present for a while,

possibly at a slightly earlier date. *Their* business could have been the building of barrow XV; or something else, which left broken pottery to be scraped up within the turf and soil of XV not so long after it had been discarded.

The jet or shale bead (K8), whose presence at the base of the mound and sealed beneath a later Bronze Age skeleton made it less obviously unstratified than the slightly earlier potsherds discussed above, may give an indication of the age of Site XV. It matched the shale dumb-bell-shaped bead (K1) from Secondary Burial 1, Site III, which could not have been placed there before the second half of the 16th century cal BC. Neither bead is thus early enough for association with Wiltshire Grooved Ware, whose central date lay about 2000 cal BC (*ibid*, 265–266). There was a strong resemblance, moreover, between the location of K8 and that of a similar bead from West Overton G6b (Smith and Simpson 1966, 126), presumed lost during construction of that mound.

Two other barrows in Wiltshire have yielded such beads as grave goods: a saucer-barrow in Durrington parish G14 (Annable and Simpson 1964, 51 and 106, Nos 275–277), where the burial may have been secondary; and two, but in wood, from a secondary burial in bell-barrow 5J on Net Down, Shrewton (Green and Rollo-Smith 1984, 309, fig 28).

The off-line position of XV within the SE line of Snail Down barrows has been used below to suggest that it belonged among the earliest barrows in the cemetery (Part 3; Phase 1A): closer, in period, to the use of Grooved Ware than to mature Wessex Bronze Age objects like the dumb-bell and related pestle beads. For that reason the Grooved Ware from XV may be a better indicator of its period of construction than the bead. And there, on present, uncertain evidence, the discussion has to rest.

The later Bronze Age inhumation cemetery and its significance is discussed further by Ashbee (Section T).

Figure 26
Detailed description of layers

Sections, 1, 2   Layers 1–3, make-up of barrow mound

Layer 1 Medium-brown, compact loam, unevenly mixed with small chalk chips and natural flints, slightly darker in colour than layer 3. In places, eg N end of Section 1 (near centre of barrow), bottom 4in free of chalk and flints, possibly representing remains of ancient land surface.

(NB The weathered chalk, illustrated in sections across other sites on Snail Down, is not recorded here because of the exceptionally deep weathering of the chalk beneath Site XV and its damaged state).

Layer 2 Deep grey-brown, fairly loose loam, free of chalk chips and flints in some areas, but containing varying quantities or narrow runs of chalk in others. Except where damaged by rabbits, it extended over layer 1 everywhere: average thickness *c* 4in, but varied greatly because of recent damage.

Layer 3 Resembled layer 1 in texture but contained more uneven amount of chalk chips and flints; generally paler in colour. Very uneven thickness, entirely due to recent disturbances.

rammed stakes. There may have been a gap in the fence facing SW – towards Sidbury Hill – but the surviving remains of the bank in this quadrant suggested that there was not a corresponding gap in the earthwork.

Traces of the bank of the pond-barrow lay immediately around its edge, and it is conceivable that the fence was no more than a low revetment incorporating hurdle work to preserve the chalky whiteness of the hollow from being stained by returning bank material. The overall appearance of this site when first built would have been a particularly white disc.

The three pits within the hollow contained soil, their chalk sides were fresh and it must be inferred that they had been filled very soon after digging. In Pits 1 and 2 this filling included a loose thin scatter of cremated human bone, with a more formal disposition in Pit 3, and it was followed immediately by soil until each of the holes was filled. The white hollow within the fence would, then, have contained three brown patches marking the sites of the pits. With the fence retaining the bank, this hollow could have remained thus white, with its pits standing out clearly to viewers as earth-filled hollows, for many years, as our continuing study of the weed colonisation at Site I is showing (above; Pl 8; Section V below). The earth filling the three pits would presumably have included weed and other pollen and in due course these must have become overgrown, changing from brownish soil marks to tufts of green. When the hollow of the pond-barrow eventually became grassed over and lost in the downland, an important source of this plant-spread would probably have been the humus filling these three pits, as it is also proving today from the re-filled central pits at Site I.

At the time of the excavation of Site XVI, only one other pond-barrow had been examined by modern means and the results made fully available, the site in Dorset at Winterbourne Steepleton where, on Sheep Down, a pond-barrow formed part of a small, compact barrow cemetery (Atkinson *et al* 1951). Here, the extensive excavation failed to reveal a fence or revetment within the bank, although Atkinson noted the presence of a chalk-free band of earth that followed its inner edge. At that time he suggested that this may have been deposited to fill up the awkward space between the inner edge of the bank and the ragged limits of a pavement of flints which filled the pond's hollow. It must be a possibility that this ring of earth represented the remains of a revetment to the bank. Beneath and around the edge of the pavement, thirty-five pits had been cut into the chalk. Of these, eleven contained token or complete cremations. Eight other pits were filled only with soil and fourteen yielded Collared Vessels or Food Vessels without remains of burials. The excavation of this Dorset pond-barrow drew attention to the likelihood that it was not just a burial ground but a place where pits were dug to hold offerings as well as burials and that here the practice was continued for some time after initial construction. To this extent its resemblance to Site XVI at Snail Down was close. Moreover both sites included cremations (and, in the Dorset site, two inhumations) of young children.

In 1989 Ashbee published the results of his excavation of the Wilsford Shaft (Ashbee *et al* 1989), which had begun as the routine excavation of what had been assumed to be a pond-barrow, Wilsford (S) 33a, an outlier of the great Normanton group of barrows S of Stonehenge (Grinsell 1957, 225). In this report, his exhaustive survey of pond-barrows, their locations, associations and their sizes, especially the diameters of their embanked hollows, established the essential characteristics of the type (Ashbee *ibid*, 139–143). His study confirmed the close association of pond-barrows with barrow cemeteries; but he was unable to identify any pond-barrows outside Wiltshire and Dorset.

More recent excavation has revealed the presence of two pond-barrows associated with the well-known cemetery at Barrow Hills, Radley (Oxon), on the Thames gravels (Barclay and Halpin 1999). To these can now also be added the full excavation of a substantial pond-barrow at Down Farm, Gussage St Michael (Dorset: Barrett *et al* 1991, 128–139).

The two pond-barrows excavated at Radley were located nearly 300ft apart, just beyond the SW end of the well-known double-linear group of sixteen barrows (Barclay and Halpin 1999, fig 1.2). They were close to Barrows 12 and 13, part of the parallel alignment formed by Barrows 12–16. One pond-barrow, 4583 (*ibid*, 52–55), had a diameter of about 15 ft within its surrounding bank, which has disappeared. It contained inhumations of an adult male and a juvenile. Finds included sherds of Beaker and Ground Ware. A radiocarbon determination for the adult showed that the burials belonged to the later Bronze Age, 1310–1000 cal BC (95% confidence).

Pond-barrow 4866 (*ibid*, 115–128) also lacked a surviving bank. Its pronounced hollow, over 21ft across, had been dug nearly 3ft into undisturbed gravel. Around its SE quarter, but well clear of a hypothetical bank, lay a rough arc of seven pits, five containing a crouched inhumation, and with cremations in the other two. The pond itself contained two cremations, of an adult male and of a young adult. A similar pit with the inhumation of a child associated with late Neolithic flints, lay equally spaced to the NW. Food Vessels were associated with some of these burials. Radiocarbon determinations showed a time range between 3320 ± 50 BP and 2490 ± 80 BP.

The Dorset pond-barrow at Down Farm, Gussage St Michael (diameter over 60 ft), had links variously with Snail Down Sites II and XVI, as well as with Radley 4583 and 4866, through its Collared Urn and Food Vessel finds and its pits-within-pits (Barrett *et al* 1991, 131, fig 4.10). Its burials comprised seven adult and three infant inhumations, with cremations of a further four infants.

At Down Farm, Radley and Winterbourne Steepleton, burials were concentrated around the edge and even outside the barrows (*ibid*, 137, fig 4.13). Here Snail Down XVI did not quite conform, with its three near-central pits.

At Winterbourne Stoke G47 (Gingell 1988, 58–63), excavation of the mound of a large disc-barrow revealed an early phase in which it resembled Site XVI. A ring of hurdlework retained a chalk bank with a flint wall outside that. There appeared to be an entrance at the E/SE. Then, or subsequently, an off-centre burial pit was dug to receive a cremation in a leather garment (*ibid*, 60, 63). This structure was not filled and sealed by the disc-barrow's central mound until the hurdling had started to collapse.

As to size, using surface measurement, more than half of the thirty-three pond-barrows Ashbee has recorded have a central hollow whose diameter falls within the general range of 32–46ft. Only four greatly exceed a breadth of 50ft: four others have diameters of about 20ft, to which Snail Down Site XVI, not recorded by Ashbee, and the Radley pond-barrows, may be added. They possessed roughly half the diameter of the Wilsford Shaft before its excavation had been begun and its so-far unique shaft revealed.

The cremated bones from the three pits in Site XVI seem to have been no more than token burials, two of them so slight that the bones could only be judged as human by inference. This pond-barrow may have been an enclosure first and only secondarily a location for burial. It could have been used as a place where corpses were laid for a period before cremation and final burial elsewhere, the three pits implying that it had served three burials. Since it is unlikely that it was covered by a roof, corpses would have been exposed here to the open air just as they could have been, we suggested, in the pits around Site III (above) and in (or on) the structure built at the centre of Site XVII (below). We can offer no further explanation for the minimal quantities of cremated bone returned for burial in Site XVI. The resemblance of Pit 3 to the two pits beneath the saucer-barrow, Site II establishes a strong link between those structures, though it should be noted that the bones from Pit 3 could not have belonged to either cremation from Site II, being of a very young child. An adult and a youth were buried beneath Site II (Section A, Cremations 5, 6). It is possible that the two corpses eventually burnt and buried in Site II might have been exposed within the Snail Down pond-barrow, but it seems unlikely that the scraps of burnt bone found in Pits 1 and 2 came from those cremations.

Double pits like the ones from Sites II and XVI have been found more recently in at least two other Wessex barrows, the pond-barrow at Down Farm (Dorset: above), and also in a small bowl-barrow at Rollestone Field, Shrewton (Green and Rollo-Smith 1984, 287 and fig 17). At the latter it was noticeable that the lower pits had been cut through the floors of their upper halves with no attempt at creating a symmetrical double pit. In that, they bore a particular resemblance to Pit 3 at Site XVI: at Snail Down II, as at Down Farm, Gussage St Michael (Dorset), upper and lower pits tended to have a common centre. The excavators at Barrow 25, Rollestone Field, believed that their double pits may have been re-used post pits, not then knowing of the parallels at Snail Down and now also at Down Farm. It seems clear that the post-pit hypothesis should be reconsidered. In Sussex, at Crowlink Barrow, Friston, a third instance of a double pit was recorded in 1852 (Figg 1852, 209:discussed further in Part 3).

Although double pits evidently had a wider currency – may have been a better-established form of cremation container – than had been thought when Snail Down II was excavated in 1953, we still believe that the occurrence of this rare form of double pit at two sites among the Snail Down barrows must mean that some form of relationship, chronological, cultural, existed between the saucer-barrow and the pond-barrow.

The Early Bronze Age period of the Snail Down pond-barrow, contemporary with the main phase of the cemetery, was established, then, by this link with Site II (which yielded Accessory Vessels and a Food Vessel in primary positions) and by the presence of Collared Vessel sherds and characteristic flint implements within its 'pond'. Site XVI, like other pond-barrows, belonged to the group of specialised structures, bell-barrows, disc-barrows, saucer-barrows, with their variants, which characterised the great barrow cemeteries of Wessex and were well-represented on Snail Down.

The principal characteristics of pond-barrows emerge thus:

(1) They had a fairly narrow range in size.
(2) A dished interior was the defining characteristic.
(3) Entrances through the surrounding bank were not included.
(4) In general burial was not a feature of the greater part of the dished area. It tended to take place around the edge and, especially, outside.
(5) Spreads of charcoal and dirty earth like those in some ring-cairns (see below) were not a feature of pond-barrows.
(6) Pond-barrows appear to have been left to weather and fill naturally when they had passed out of use. None has yet been found with an artificial filling or deliberately slighted.
(7) Pond-barrows were usually associated with barrow cemeteries, sometimes more than one to a group.
(8) Pond-barrows are the rarest class of special barrow in Wessex.

Finally, consideration has briefly to be given to the existence outside the South-of-England chalklands and river gravels of a type of site that appears to have had some relationship to pond-barrows and ring-ditches like Site V (above): the ring-cairns of Wales and the south west.

Through the work of Frances Lynch, A H Ward and others (discussion and bibliography in Ward 1988), it has become possible to understand ring-cairns, like pond-barrows and ring-ditches, as small arenas in which a variety of activities took place associated with funerary events or with token burial or, less commonly, with full-scale interment. Their overall structure – flat-floored, roughly circular walled or banked enclosures with one or, more rarely, two entrances – invites comparison with several features of pond-barrows and ring-ditches, granted the difference in building material between chalk or gravel, sometimes with fencing or stake rings, and stones with large slabs defining entrances and other major features. Ring-cairns tend to occur among burial cairns, though at a higher ratio than pond-barrows among other barrows in a group. Their internal diameters compare closely with the small to middle-sized ponds. Spreads of charcoal and dirty earth are a feature. When ring-cairns reached the end of their use they were usually filled in and entrances blocked.

In view of the *differences* between these three classes of monument, perhaps the case for analogy should not be pressed further. But sufficient common ground exists for it to be a reasonable belief that in pond-barrows, ring-ditches and ring-cairns we have one general class of funerary structure. It was closely associated in time and place with barrow and cairn cemeteries; and its usage combined token burial with other activities that are best explained as having to do with the more diverse treatment and worship of the Bronze Age dead that has come to light in recent years.

Figure 28
Detailed Description of Layers

Sections 1, 2   Layers 1–3, make-up of bank; and subsoils

Layer 1 Weathered chalk bedrock, solid chalk below.

Layer 2 Thin, faint and patchy traces of ancient soil sealed by bank above. Pale brown loam, more chalk-free than layer above.

Layer 3 Pale brown loam thinly mixed with chalk chips, representing remains of bank. Sealed traces of ancient land surface (layer 2) below.

Layers 4–6 Filling of pits and central hollow of pond-barrow.

Layer 4 Main filling of the three pits which had been dug from surface of layer 1: brown loam, slightly paler than that of layers 5 and 6, containing less chalk chips than layer 5. In Pit 1, floor covered by thin scatter of grey soil. All pit fillings included thin scatter of cremated bone: Pit 2 also contained noticeable scatter throughout of wood ash.

Layer 5 Mixed brown loam and chalk chips, darker in colour than 4. Represented spread of chalk rubble from bank. Sealed the three pits.

Layer 6 Main filling of hollow of pond-barrow: almost chalk-free brown loam, deeper in colour than 4–5.

SITE XVII

SPTA 2222: A BOWL-BARROW

SUMMARY

Site XVII was a bowl-barrow whose surrounding ditch had a maximum diameter of 48ft. The mound was intact. Central burial had been preceded by construction of an irregularly shaped wooden structure, upon, or within which a corpse may have been exposed. Cremation of an adult male took place elsewhere. The timber structure was eventually removed and a burial pit dug beneath it, topsoil and subsoil carefully separated. In the floor of the pit a saucer-shaped depression had been carved. This roughly fitted the base of a large Collared Urn of Longworth's Secondary Series, which may have stood in the pit for some time before burial finally took place. That ceremony involved removal of the urn, deposit of burnt material over the floor of the pit, replacement and then deliberate smashing of the urn. After that the cremation was put in the pit and the barrow built. Later, three small pits were dug into the W margin of the mound, one of them containing fragments of a small Collared Vessel, also of Longworth's Secondary Series. Possibly in Roman times the W arc of the ditch and that part of the mound were damaged when the route of Trackway T3 became established, N/S, across Snail Down. The central burial yielded an anomalous radiocarbon determination of 5310 ± 70BP; from the pit on the W edge of the mound containing Collared Vessel sherds came a radiocarbon determination of 3480 ± 70BP.

INTRODUCTION

Site XVII appeared to be a small, typical bowl-barrow. It lay just over 100ft WNW of Site XIV. Trackway T3, which ran N to cross the linear ditch (Site VI) by Site XX, cut across the ditch and W edge of the mound. The barrow was covered with well-preserved downland turf and there was no evidence that animals had burrowed into it, as they had its neighbours to the SE; nor could any sign be seen on the surface of disturbance by earlier antiquaries.

Hoare plotted but did not number this barrow on his published plan of Snail Down (1812, plan opp. 180). In 1957, having excavated examples of all types of specialised Wessex barrow, we felt justified in devoting the last fortnight of the final season to the complete excavation of a bowl-barrow. Site XVII was chosen because it appeared to have been untouched and was small. We also wished to see if remains of the Beaker occupation beneath Sites X–XIV extended this far. In our interim report of 1956 (Thomas and Thomas, 131, fig 1), this barrow was shown, incorrectly, as having a scraped-up mound.

The following additional references have been made to Site XVII: Grinsell 1957, 169; Annable 1958, 6–7; Biek 1963, 250; Annable and Simpson 1964, 64, 119, and 121, Nos 510, 533; Thomas 1976, 230; Longworth 1984, Nos 1678, 1679.

The barrow was cleared to bedrock during the course of seventeen days; about twelve volunteers took part, under the supervision of the late Professor Peter Jewell and N Thomas.

DESCRIPTION

Pre-barrow Features and Beaker Settlement Remains

The barrow mound preserved a land surface roughly 32ft in diameter (edges shown on plan, Fig 29). The bedrock beneath was unusually uneven for Snail Down and the ancient land surface covering this circular area was accordingly irregular and in places particularly thin. The absence of flints and chalk lumps within it suggested that the downland hereabouts had not been disturbed, at least for some considerable time prior to erection of the barrow.

There was, however, a noticeable deposit of pale grey loam with a darker soil above it, which extended for most of the length of the N/S baulk and had a less-easily distinguished E/W width of some 12ft (Fig 30, Section 1, N, layers 3, 4; not distinguished in Section 2, W; or Section 1, S, but undoubtedly present; Pl 44). The burial pit's upper edge occurred level with the top of this layer, charcoal and other debris associated with the pit also appearing on top of layer 4. Clearly, its deposition occurred before the digging of the burial pit and the other related structures. Its significance is considered further below.

The stake holes found around the central burial features are likely to have belonged to the burial process and not to the Beaker settlement situated a short distance SE (Fig 21). Excavation suggests a distinction between the array of settlement stake holes and those of the structures underlying Sites III and XVII. Sixteen identifiable sherds of Beaker must however represent its proximity to the settlement (Section C, C104-C110). Some occurred in the barrow ditch, especially layers 9 and 11, others mainly at the base of the mound. One sherd was incorporated in the filling of the burial pit.

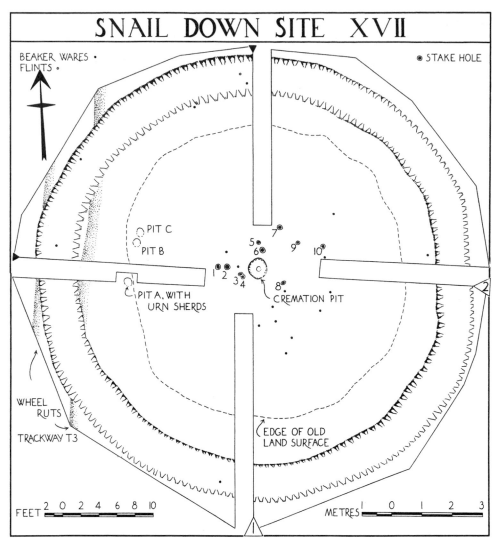

Fig 29   Site XVII, a bowl-barrow. Plan, including wheel ruts of Trackway T3.

The Burial: preliminary episode

(Plans, Figs 29, 31; section, Fig 30; Pl 46)

The first stage in the burial of the ashes of a young adult, probably male, was the erection of ten stakes, driven into bedrock around the site of the burial pit (Figs 29–31). The depth and shape of each stake hole was calculated by careful probing, and holes 1 and 2 were excavated completely and then sectioned in bedrock (Pl 46). All the stakes were roughly cylindrical, narrowing to blunt points: hole 2, however, was sharply pointed.

Their dimensions and depths in solid chalk, in inches, were as shown in Table 7.

The fillings of the stake holes differed. Most contained clean, pale-buff chalky loam, close in colour and texture to the ancient land surface material. Hole 9 contained a large amount of fine charcoal with buff loam while hole 5 contained darker loam, mixed with charcoal flecks.

In plan, these ten holes formed an irregular, elongated layout, occurring mainly to the E and W of the burial pit site which did not, itself, occupy the centre of this cluster of timbers. The roughly diamond-shaped area they defined measured about 11 × 6ft.

The positions of holes 5 and 6 were covered by the N pile of spoil from the burial pit. Much of the charcoal in

Stake No	Diameter	Depth in chalk	Stake No	Diameter	Depth in chalk
1	$3\frac{1}{2} \times 4$	9	6	$3\frac{1}{2} \times 5$	$4\frac{1}{2}$
2	$4\frac{1}{2}$	12	7	3	4
3	$2\frac{1}{2} \times 3$	6	8	$2\frac{1}{2} \times 3$	$2\frac{1}{2}$
4	$2\frac{1}{2}$	5	9	$2 \times 1\frac{1}{2}$	2
5	$2\frac{1}{2}$	5	10	$3 \times 2\frac{1}{2}$	$2\frac{1}{2}$

Table 7 Dimensions and depths in inches of stake holes around central grave

SNAIL DOWN SITE XVII

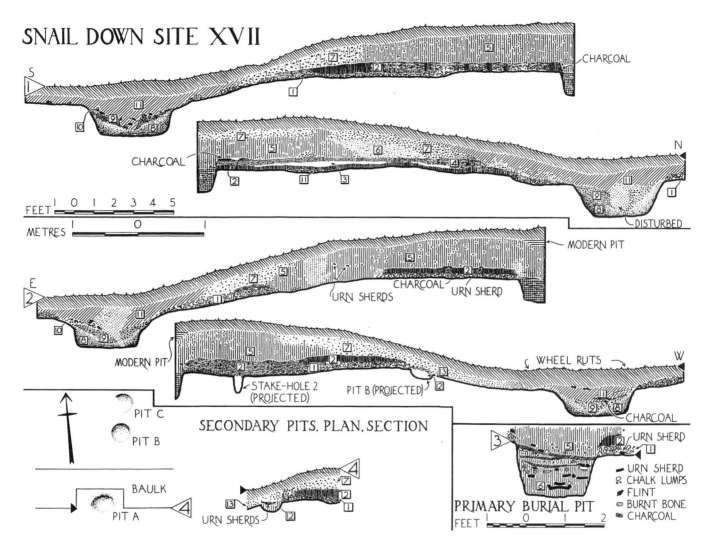

Fig 30   Site XVII, sections 1, 2; section 3, central cremation pit. Plan of Pits A-C with section 4.

hole 9 may also be explained by spill from a charcoal scatter in the area of this stake when it was withdrawn. No trace of any of the stakes occurred in the ancient land surface or higher up in the mound, although their soil-filled holes would have been very difficult to see in the former, and it seemed probable that all were pulled out before the burial pit was dug.

The presence of numerous bones of small rodents the size of voles was recorded on the ancient land surface in the area of the burial pit, particularly in the S half of the barrow, as well as higher up in the mound and within the pit itself. Some may have been carried down to this level by a burrowing animal whose tunnel was noted during the excavation in the immediate vicinity of the burial pit, and could therefore be modern. But at least two compact masses of bones, resembling pellets disgorged by birds of prey such as buzzards, were found at ancient ground level 2ft S of stake holes 1 and 2 (Fig 31) and were certainly not later than the burial activity (report on these pellets, Section Q). Since such bone clusters would disintegrate soon after deposit unless covered up quickly, it seems likely that they were disgorged shortly before the mound was built.

The Burial: grave pit and burial ceremony
(Plans, Figs 29, 31; sections, Fig 30; Pls 45, 47–49; Section A, Cremation 15; Collared Urn, section D, D23, Fig 47)

The cremated bones of an **adult, probably male,** had been interred in a **grave pit** at the centre of Site XVII. It lay at the centre of the barrow and had been dug from the level of the top of layer 4 (Fig 30, Section 1, N). At this level its mouth was roughly D-shaped in plan, the straight W side about 2ft long and overall diameter about the same. The pit was dug down into the bedrock to a total depth (from layer 4) of just over $1\frac{3}{4}$ft, of which about $1\frac{1}{4}$ were in solid chalk. It had not been dug with particular care; in the chalk its plan was roughly circular, about 2ft across, and its walls narrowed unevenly to a level floor measuring c $1\frac{3}{4}$ x $1\frac{1}{2}$ft. The most carefully-made part was a **saucer-shaped depression** carved in its floor, which measured 6in in diameter and penetrated the chalk to a depth of almost 1in (Pl 49). This feature resembled that found in the pit of Secondary Burial 1, Site III, and in both instances the depressions fitted the bases of the urns found buried in them. The angle formed by the floor and walls of the burial pit was not cut sharply, nor was the

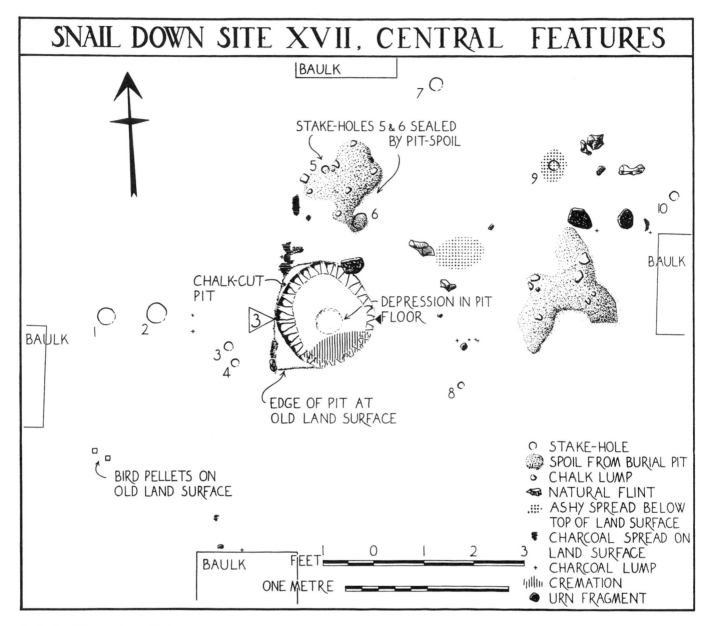

SNAIL DOWN SITE XVII, CENTRAL FEATURES

BAULK

STAKE-HOLES 5 & 6 SEALED BY PIT-SPOIL

CHALK-CUT PIT

DEPRESSION IN PIT FLOOR

BAULK

BAULK

EDGE OF PIT AT OLD LAND SURFACE

BIRD PELLETS ON OLD LAND SURFACE

○ STAKE-HOLE
SPOIL FROM BURIAL PIT
⊙ CHALK LUMP
NATURAL FLINT
ASHY SPREAD BELOW TOP OF LAND SURFACE
CHARCOAL SPREAD ON LAND SURFACE
+ CHARCOAL LUMP
CREMATION
URN FRAGMENT

BAULK

FEET

ONE METRE

0   1   2   3

Fig 31   Site XVII, plan of central burial features.

floor made absolutely flat. Several almost glassy-smooth marks were noted on the wall of the pit and at its base, which appeared to have been made by an adze of polished stone or of metal.

The **spoil** taken when digging out the burial pit was piled on the contemporary Bronze Age land surface as it had been in Site III (Fig 12). At site XVII, rather less care had been taken to separate topsoil from subsoil, although it was clear (eg Pl 45) that the heap to the E was much more earthy than that to the N, which was mainly of chalk rubble. Both had been heaped well clear of the edges of the pit (Fig 31). Flints and large chalk lumps occurred in both spoil heaps, which stood up to 3in above the level of the surrounding ground. Although no calculations were made, it is clear that the pit would have yielded more material than the volume found in these heaps.

Other features of the spoil derived from the original digging of the burial pit were noted. The N spoil heap

covered the holes of **two stakes** from the preliminary structure described above (Plan, Fig 31, 5 and 6), and it was clear that the stakes did not run up through this heap. The ground surface beneath both heaps was free of charcoal, but charcoal had been scattered over the N heap and a sherd of the urn found broken and buried in the central pit lay on top of the spoil heap to the E of the burial pit.

At two places immediately NE of the burial pit, spreads of ashy material mixed with charcoal were incorporated within the soil forming this layer (Fig 31, plan; Fig 30, layer 4) and lying some 2in below the surface on which the urn sherds and other features associated with the pit occurred. Subsequently, much more charcoal was spread around the area of the central pit after it had been dug. Apart from the ashy spreads referred to above, the area covered by the mound was free of charcoal and other human debris until the burial pit had been dug.

No funeral pyre or other fire had been lit at or near the centre of Site XVII. The corpse had been cremated elsewhere. When the bones and a large Collared Urn were prepared for final burial, however, a considerable quantity of charcoal, burnt soil and dirty, ashy material was included. Moreover, charcoal and ashes had been scattered in thin patches all over the central area (Fig 31) and particularly around and in the pit itself, whose sides had become stained with the dirty material. The woods represented include hazel, hawthorn/apple/ rowan/white-beam type and wild cherry/bird-cherry type.

When the time had arrived for the cremation and urn to be buried, the bottom of the pit was first covered with a deposit of brown loam mixed with ash and charcoal (Fig 30, section 3, part of layer 6). Upon that the Collared Urn was set, level and upright, slightly off centre to the N (Pl 48). At this stage in filling the pit we suppose that the urn, which may previously have stood in the empty pit and now was no longer in good condition (see below), had been deliberately smashed. No sherds occurred below the level of the base, but above it lay the greater part of the vessel, packed together in large pieces and spreading over the NE wall of the pit and out in a scatter over the ancient land-surface to the NE (Fig 31; Pls 45, 47). More ashy loam, which included yellow, charcoal-free patches (layer 6), was then dumped into the pit, covering the remains of the urn. Next, a large concentrated heap of cremated human bones was placed in the SW quarter of the pit, on top of the broken urn and clearly separated from it (the bones, that is, had not been in the urn when it was broken), and the rest of the pit then filled to the level of the surface of the solid chalk. This filling (Fig 30, layer 6, upper) now included more distinct spreads of dark, charcoal-filled soil separated by irregular patches of yellower loam. Urn fragments occurred throughout this upper filling but always concentrated towards the NE quarter. That much trampling took place during the filling of the pit is shown by the occurrence of a small urn sherd, burnt bone and charcoal directly upon solid chalk just W of the pit edge, having reached that level by being pressed through the soil and subsoil of the contemporary land surface.

A few small rodent bones were found, scattered in the yellower patches of soil in the upper filling of the pit.

As indicated in the section across the pit (Fig 30, section 3), its blackened earthy filling did not reach the level of the land surface but only to the chalk bedrock (although charcoal extended up the sides of the pit and onto the land surface in places). The base of the mound (layer 5), charcoal-free loam, lay directly upon the burial material in the pit and filled its upper 4–6in to the level of the ancient land surface.

Charcoals of *Prunus avium/Padus* type, Pomoideae and *Corylus* (wild cherry/bird cherry type, hawthorn, apple and rowan/whitebeam and hazel) were submitted to Glasgow for radiocarbon assay, with the following result:

GU-5303 5310 ± 70 BP; cal BC 4241–4007 (1 sigma); cal BC 4340–3990 (2 sigma).

This result is anomalous, since it is at least a thousand years older than expected for a barrow whose central burial was associated with a Secondary Series Collared Urn of the Early Bronze Age. The funeral pyre for this cremation may have incorporated ancient wood, although oak, the only wood likely to have survived for so long, was not recorded here. An even greater dating anomaly

was recorded at Site II (above) and we return to the problem in Section T.

The Barrow Structures
(Plan, Fig 29; sections, fig 30; Pls 43, 44)

The **ditch** which surrounded Site XVII was circular, laid out from a centre which appeared to have been in the area occupied by the S half of the burial pit, perhaps a few inches S of the saucer-shaped hollow scraped out at its centre (plan, Fig 29; sections, Fig 30; Pl 43). This ditch had a maximum diameter of about 48ft. In plan, it had been dug with less care than those of sites I-III. Around the W arc and at the SE, the ditch seemed to have been excavated in a series of short, almost straight sections, while around the opposite quarters of its circuit it approximated more to a true circle. The ditch itself had a width, at floor level, of about 3ft and a depth, from solid chalk, of 1½–2ft.

The **mound** comprised a core of fairly pale loam (layer 5) which was piled to a height of 1–1½ft above the Bronze Age land surface (layer 2) at the centre of the barrow. Generally, this soil was parti-coloured, containing indistinct patches and spreads of slightly paler, more chalky material. No separate decayed turves could be distinguished as they had been in Sites III and XIX (Pls 14–16, 55). Those mounds also differed considerably in appearance, since the mound core of XVII included a scatter of small chalk chips throughout, in very variable proportions (Pls 43, 44), whereas in the other sites the distinction between the turves and earthy core, and the chalk above, was marked.

Around the edges of this earthy mound, there was a concentration of chalk rubble (layer 7), here and there covering more finely broken chalk and chalky loam (layer 6). Layers 6 and 7 represented the outer chalky covering to the mound, derived from its surrounding ditch in the manner well represented on Snail Down by Sites III and XIX, and elsewhere in chalk country wherever barrows were enclosed by a ditch. At Site XVII, however, this chalk crust had been dispersed almost everywhere and spread down through the mound except around its edge, particularly around the N arc of the mound, where it remained concentrated.

Measured from the centre, the outer edge of the earthy core of the mound had a radius of about 9–10ft. In the arc of the NW quadrant, however, this radius decreased to about 8ft. The first stage of the barrow was thus not placed centrally within its surrounding ditch, and the chalk which followed had a correspondingly wider space to fill between the mound and inner edge of the ditch. The berm which the sections record at the W end of the E/W baulk and at the N end of the N/S baulk may have been a feature of the barrow when completed: not all of it need be attributed to the later trackway (T3) (Figs 2, 29) which impinged upon the edge of the mound around this arc, as well as the ditch.

Mound core and chalk rubble sealed a land-surface (described above) about 32ft in diameter (Fig 29). Outside the edge of the chalk crust around the mound, the surface of the bedrock sloped steeply to the inner edge of the ditch; generally there was a space or berm about 3ft wide between mound and ditch, all of it steeply weathered.

Around the W arc of the barrow this space was about twice as wide. Here, however, the Romano-British or later N/S trackway T3 had cut across the barrow mound and ditch (Fig 29) and the extra width of the berm could be attributed to damage from this relatively ancient feature.

The Secondary Series Collared Urn found smashed in the central burial pit is fully described in Section D, D23, Figure 47. The flintwork was mainly waste material but included two scrapers, both in topsoil. It was evenly distributed throughout the site (Section G).

Post-construction Events

The ditch filling was everywhere the product of natural weathering, the bottom corners and floor being covered by clean, chalky rubble (layer 8), almost always compacted and bound by chalky rainwashed material. The filling above this comprised very pale, fine loam heavily charged with chalk dust, sometimes including large loose flints and chalk at its centre (layer 9). The uppermost part of the ditch was filled with looser brown loam, containing only a little chalk as small, hard chips (layer 11). This general sequence was occasionally interrupted by runs of chalk chips entering from either side of the ditch (layer 10).

In the NW arc of the ditch, between $4\frac{3}{4}$ft and $6\frac{1}{4}$ft N of the E/W baulk, a considerable concentration of charcoal occurred at a depth of $1\frac{1}{3}$–$1\frac{1}{2}$ft below modern turf, towards the base of layer 11 (Fig 30, Section 2, W). This spread of charcoal lay close to Pits A–C (Fig 29; see below), which also contained much charcoal.

Three shallow pits had been dug into the edge of the mound on its W side (plan, Figs 29, 30; sections, Fig 30; Pl 50; Collared Vessel, Section D, D22, Fig 47)

Pit A was semi-circular in section and in plan oval, about 1ft 2in in maximum width and dug into the solid chalk to a depth of some 6in. It was filled with dark-brown loam including a thin scatter of fine chalk chips and mixed throughout with comminuted charcoal of hazel and hawthorn/apple/rowan/whitebeam type. Towards the top of this earthy filling (Fig 30, Section 4, layer 12) two substantial weathered, fragments of a small Collared Vessel had been carefully and deliberately packed, each with inside uppermost, the larger fragment overlying the smaller, with the collar on each facing the centre of the barrow (Pl 50). The base and part of the wall and collar were missing and the edges of the surviving fragments were rounded and weathered. It was clear that this pit had been dug from the level of the top of the chalk crust of the mound and that the latter was cut through by the pit (Fig 30, Section 4). Subsequently, earth mixed with rubble from the crust had spread across the top of the pit (layer 13).

Pit B was hemispherical, 11in in diameter and dug into solid chalk to a depth of about 2in. It lay $3\frac{3}{4}$ft north of Pit A and was filled with dark grey-brown loam mixed with a proportion of charcoal similar to that in Pit A. On its floor lay a few small crumbs of cremated bone, insufficient for identification but apparently human.

Pit C lay about 6in N of Pit B. It had a maximum diameter of 10in and a depth in the bedrock of under 2in. Its SW edge had left no impression in the chalk: it was more a semi-circular scoop dug sloping towards the NW.

The earth filling its lower part was browner than in Pits A and B yet it contained much more pure charcoal (hawthorn/apple/rowan/whitebeam type) among the soil. No burnt bone was found in it.

No trace of Pits B and C was seen until bedrock had been reached. Hereabouts the edge of the mound had been broken up and hollowed by the early track (T3) which impinged upon it, and this made it uncertain whether these pits were sealed by the mound or had been inserted (Fig 30, Section 2, layer 13). Pit A had escaped damage from the track and was clearly later than the construction of the mound.

Charcoal of Pomoideae (which included hawthorn, apple and rowan/whitebeam) from Pit A was submitted to Oxford for accelerator dating with the following result:

> OxA-4179 3480 ± 70 BP; cal BC 1896–1705 (1 sigma), cal BC 2020–1640 (2 sigma).

This estimate is consistent with an Early Bronze Age period for the sherds of Secondary Series Collared Vessel found in Pit A. A determination within this range or a little earlier had been expected, also, for the central burial (above), hence the level of anomaly for that result. These results are considered further in Section T.

As already mentioned, the **supposed Romano-British trackway, T3,** lay across the W margin of Site XVII (Figs 2, 29; Fig 30, section 2, W). It left its impression in the ditch and also along the edge of the mound. Here the chalky covering (Fig 30, layer 13) had been finely crushed and in part made to merge with the weathered bedrock below.

The fragmentary and weathered Secondary Series Collared Vessel found in Pit A is fully described in Section D, D22, Figure 47. A few scraps of indeterminate R-B pottery occurred in superficial positions in the barrow. Two flint scrapers and 40 flakes were recovered from various parts of the barrow (Section G).

REMARKS

The earliest man-made feature beneath Site XVII was the elongated spread of dark-brown loam with lighter grey soil beneath (layers 4 and 3) which was found lying on the ancient land surface roughly parallel with the N/S baulk across the barrow and extending for a few feet on either side. Unfortunately the full character of this spread was not appreciated until the main cross-baulks were being studied and drawn. It is clear, however, that these two layers were spread before anything else happened on the site: they were cut through by the burial pit, and they underlay the charcoal which was only scattered hereabouts when the burial ceremony had begun. Layers 4 and 3 appeared to represent turf, with vegetation uppermost and chalk subsoil downwards, laid in one thickness upon the ancient land surface. Early in 1993 the RCHME re-surveyed the Down and found traces of cultivation possibly underlying several barrows (above; Fig 2). The orientation of these faint earthworks is NE/SW and this coincides approximately with the shallow ridge of soils covering the ancient land surface and underlying the N/S baulk across the barrow. Layers 4 and 3 could be remains of pre-barrow cultivation, attributable to the Beaker settlement immediately to the SE, or to other agriculture earlier than the cemetery. Although no Beaker or allied sherds were directly associated, this tentative interpretation supports rare but increasing evidence, some of it circumstantial, that Beaker-using people in the south of England cultivated fields. They may even have begun to introduce land boundaries, whose successors two millennia later can be seen in earthworks such as Sites VI ands VII on Snail Down (Case 1995, 15; and pers comm).

The ten stakes driven into the ground around the central area where the burial pit was to be dug conformed to no obvious plan. However, it is possible to visualise a gathering of upright posts, some quite sturdy, their upper parts perhaps painted and carved, serving some ritual or decorative function.

Alternatively, these holes might represent the remains of a flimsy, raggedly-designed building or enclosure, stakes 2, 6, 7, and 7, 9, 10 forming the two N sides of such a structure, with stakes 1 and 5 as reinforcements or replacements. Stake 8 formed the fourth corner, with stakes 3 and 4 (one replacing the other?) making a solid SW wall with an open SE side between stakes 8 and 10. Such a structure need not have been a building: it could have formed the framework of a platform raised above ground, in plan a parallelogram, on which, for instance, the body of the dead person could have been exposed.

Groups of posts or stakes set apparently at random around a grave are not conspicuous in the archaeological record. Commoner are single posts or pairs close to a grave. Beside the mortuary house beneath barrow IX at Beaulieu (Hants: C M Piggott 1943, 17–19) the corpse had been laid close to an upright. Other single posts and pairs of posts have been found associated with graves at Amesbury G70 (Christie 1964, 32, fig 2, and 35), at West Overton G6b (Smith and Simpson 1966, 124, fig 2 and 129), Winterbourne Stoke G30 (Christie 1963, 375, fig 3, and 377) and, in Dorset, at Kinson Barrow 3 (Knocker 1959, 137, fig 4) and at Crichel Down (Piggot and Piggott 1944, 74, fig 22). Beneath Stanton Harcourt King Barrow, Oxon (Harden and Treweeks 1945, 24–25, 30), a post had been set up among the timbers constituting a funeral pyre.

Study by Peter Jewell (Section Q) of the bird pellets found among the central features of Site XVII has added considerably to our knowledge of what happened before the barrow was built. It seems that the wooden uprights offered convenient perches for large birds of prey such as buzzards or kites: more pellets were recovered from Site XIX, whose mounds were ringed by wooden uprights which must have afforded a similar attraction to such birds. If the posts at Site XVII had been set up for only a few days, with the barrow-builders perhaps encamped nearby for a burial ceremony which was to be completed quickly, it is unlikely that these shy birds of prey would have used the posts even at night. Instead, the presence of the bird pellets suggests that there may have been a considerable interval between the erection of the posts and the next stage of the burial, a period in which the Down may have been deserted by the people whose cemetery occurred there.

The precise composition of the pellets from Site XVII and from Site XIX belonged to the summer and autumn; these burials took place at a time of year for which corroborative evidence has come from other ritual sites, notably harvest time at Pond Cairn, South Glamorgan (Fox 1959, 122–123), and, less certainly, at Silbury Hill (Whittle 1997, 43–44, 46) high summer. This rare evidence at Snail Down pointed to summer and autumn as the time when Bronze Age people may have been accustomed to bury their dead, the harvest safely garnered, weather still warm and the days long for the arduous and devoted work that was to be done.

The condition of the large Collared Urn found smashed in the central pit supports our belief that this burial ceremony was prolonged. The urn's upper part had suffered considerably from weathering before its interment. Less than half the collar survived; everywhere its decoration was blurred and the condition of the collar sherds was extremely friable. By contrast, the lower two-thirds of the pot were in perfect condition. The state of this vessel suggested that it had been exposed in the open for some while, and it is not beyond belief that its previous resting place could have been in the empty burial pit. With a height of 17in, its collar would have been exposed to the weather, while its lower half was protected within the pit.

Care in the disposal of spoil from the burial pit resembled the treatment of spoil from the central grave beneath Site III. Both suggested the work of people tied closely to the soil, who paid meticulous regard to the sacred minutiae of burial ceremonial during the interring of their dead. This detail served, also, to associate both sites in time as well as in tradition, though an even closer resemblance between the pit of XVII to that of Secondary Burial I in Site III argued more strongly for the priority of at least the construction of III over XVII. In the floor of both pits, a saucer-shaped hollow had been carved, as if to accommodate and steady the base of the large urn found in each. Such a detail has never been recorded before. Found twice in the Snail Down cemetery, it implied continuity of burial practice and argued, with other evidence, that this cemetery was essentially the work of one community. Occurring moreover, beneath neighbouring barrows, one an outlier of a main row and later in date, it suggested that, within a cemetery, the precise location of barrows was carefully calculated, seldom random.

Spoil from burial pits heaped just clear of their edges has been found before and we have documented it below (Part 3).

The most dramatic act in the burial ceremony at Site XVII was without doubt the breaking of the large urn. This splendid vessel, its collar weathered and perhaps even incomplete, had been placed in the pit whose floor had first been covered with 2–3in of soil and ashes, and demolished by a series of sharp blows, sending sherds northeastwards for a distance of up to 6ft, another sherd ending up almost the same distance to the S. Small pieces came to rest on top of each spoil heap from the burial pit. Most of the vessel remained in the pit, lying against the E wall with two or three large pieces on the uppermost edge of the pit (Pls 47, 48). Sherds from opposite sides of the vessel were pressed against each other and it seemed clear that the vessel had been empty when smashed. Subsequently, some of the fragments were further scattered within the pit when the cremation and the rest of the filling was added.

This ritualistic assault upon the urn, for which it is unsatisfactory to substitute the less evocative explanation of an accident, or even the clumsy burial of fragments, need not have required excessive energy from the person to whom the task had been given. Two or three sharp raps from a heavy tool or club delivered with only a short swing of the forearm would probably have been sufficient to reduce a large, heavy, low-fired Collared Urn to fragments, with a few pieces flying some distance away.

Further evidence for ritual breakage, or at least regard for the sanctity of a broken and incomplete vessel, came from Pit A, one of three pits all of which were likely to have been dug at some considerable distance in time from the burial of the large urn. Pieces of a small bi-partite Collared Vessel had been carefully packed near the top of the pit. Perhaps this was a relic from the original burial ceremony, or had been left at the barrow with an offering (of flowers even?) soon after building, to be buried much later as a pious act connected with tidying the site, or reconsecrating it. Pits B and C, like A, contained much charcoal, and in the ditch next to them a spread of charcoal occurred also. This material lay high up in it (layer 11, depth 1⅓–1½ft from modern turf; Fig 30, section 2, W) and a time to be measured in years must be allowed for the ditch to have acquired so much silt before this charcoal was deposited and with it, by inference, Pits B and C to be constructed. Pit A could be seen, by its stratigraphical position, to have been dug after the barrow mound had started to spread.

Unequivocal evidence for deliberate on-the-spot breakage of objects to be buried with the dead is hardly ever recorded from barrow excavations in the British Isles. L V Grinsell has made a study of the phenomenon, his most mature statement appearing in 1975 (Chap 7, *passim*; see also 1953, 36–37). Of twelve principal reasons which he adduces for breaking or damaging funerary objects, the one generally accepted as the most likely explanation for the evidence found in Britain is the ritual killing of an object so that, its spirit thus released, it could accompany the deceased to the after-life. This appears to suit the circumstances recorded at Site XVII. Had the urn *contained* the cremation it accompanied, it would have been curious to break it – disturbing to its content, much of which might thus have been ejected from the burial pit designed to contain it. But to have deposited and smashed the urn and then place the cremation – perhaps in a bag – within its shattered remains can be seen as a logical and emphatic way of consigning both to a new life and another world.

Indisputable proof of an intentional act of breakage at a Bronze Age barrow site appears to be restricted to Snail Down XVII. But only a little less certain are instances of the breaking of arrowheads mounted in their shafts in Yorkshire and Glamorgan quoted by Grinsell, together with the group of obviously broken bronze axeheads from a barrow on Combe Hill, Jevington, Sussex (Curwen 1954, 151, Pl xiv). Nor is there reason to doubt Fox's discovery of the *sherds* of a complete Beaker, packed carefully around the head of a male buried at barrow Sutton 268', South Glamorgan (Fox 1959, 67).

More convincing is the evidence for burial of already damaged or incomplete objects, a category to which the remains of the small Collared Vessel from Pit A belong. From Wiltshire the most obvious example of this aspect of the practice is the still unexplained, twisted bronze object with a few links of its chain, found by Hoare in a bell-barrow, his Wilsford 18 (Wilsford G58: Thomas 1954, 326–330). That grave find also included a bone knife handle which had been buried without its metal blade.

A very small quantity of burnt bone, assumed to be human, was found in Pit B. In quantity it resembled the token deposits in Pits 1 and 2 at Site XVI and it seems unlikely that with Pits A-C we are dealing with a secondary burial. Possibly, this burnt material and damaged vessel D22 represented sweepings from the site of the original funeral pyre, collected or at least buried, for some unknown reason a considerable time after that event. Small pits containing such token deposits from the funeral pyre have been found occasionally beneath barrows, usually in a primary position (discussed further, Part 3). The charcoal-filled pit from Site I is explained in this way and the possibility that it was secondary also, though still containing a token deposit from one of the original pyres like that postulated for Pit B, has already been discussed. These intriguing possibilities we cannot take further: Pits A-C are one of several features which established Site XVII as perhaps the most interesting among the barrows so far examined on Snail Down.

The excavation revealed that the earth core of the barrow mound was not a true circle, a greater space between its edge and the ditch existing around its NW quarter than elsewhere. Here the chalk rubble which went on top had to be correspondingly broader to bring the final mound almost up to the ditch edge. Probably the S and E ends of our main sections give a truer picture of the structural intentions of the barrow-builders: the space between mound and ditch was here mainly the product of weathering and the overall appearance allows the barrow to be described as a bowl- not a small bell-barrow.

Very little of the chalk covering survived over the main part of the mound, though it was thick and solid around the edge. Some of this must have slid from the top of the mound. Most of the chalk has, however, been spread through the mound, making its earth core more chalky than that, for example, in Sites III or XIX. The main agent in this dissemination of chalk must have been earthworms. Evidently the chalk over Sites III and XIX was so thick and solid that earthworms imprisoned in the soil beneath were unable to get through it and it remained intact until the present day. Site XVII was much smaller, particularly its ditch, and the chalky covering must always have been thin, especially with the extra space to cover around the NW. An inch or two of chalk, always perhaps a little earthy, could easily have been carried down into the mound by the quantity of earthworms which such a central core would have harboured.

In the excavation of the barrows at Snail Down, Site XVII is of special importance because it yielded much material undamaged by earlier antiquaries. In particular it has emphasised how Bronze Age burial practice could involve acts spread over a considerable period of time while yet maintaining a sense of continuity.

Figure 30
Detailed description of layers

Sections 1, 2   Layers 1–2, ancient land surface

Layer 1 Weathered natural chalk, tending to occur in hollows in the bedrock which was unusually uneven beneath this barrow. Certain surface areas of level bedrock also weathered, however, eg section 2, E.

Layer 2 Ancient undisturbed soil forming Bronze Age land surface. Thin, buff loam almost free of flints and chalk chips. Unusually thick around centre in NW quadrant: here difficult to distinguish from layer 4.

Layers 3–7, mound of barrow

Layer 3 Thin spread of very pale grey-brown loam, almost free of chalk and flints; in plan occurred irregularly along line of N/S baulk, with width up to 12ft; edges too indistinct to be planned.

Layer 4 In plan coincided with layer 3, overlying it and probably associated with it: resembled layer 2 but a little paler: also almost free of chalk chips and flints. Cut by upper edge of burial pit.

Layer 5 Core of mound, redder-brown than layer 2, with diffuse and uneven scatter of chalk chips and flints. In places, distinct patches of chalk chips, eg section 1, N, on top of layer 4. Some slight spreads of fine charcoal.

Layer 6 Compact small chalk chips in matrix of pale-grey, fine loam, occurring in isolated area in NW quadrant (section 1, N).

Layer 7 Loose, rubbly chalk in pale red-brown loamy matrix: chalk concentrated around edges of mound, very diffuse over central area; proportion of chalk to loam differing widely from area to area (fairly thick chalk crust over mound in NW quadrant, almost absent in S half of barrow).

Layers 8–11, ditch filling

Layer 8 Compact chalk rubble in matrix of greyish powdered chalk, filling bottom corners of ditch everywhere: more compact in some areas than in others.

Layer 9 compact greyish chalky soil, no individual chalk chips. Frequently disturbed by rabbits.

Layer 10 Loose run of chalk chips and flints, differing in intensity from area to area, often entering ditch noticeably from outer side.

Layer 11 Loose red-brown loam, almost free of chalk and flints. Frequently disturbed by rabbits.

Section 3   Layers 1, 2, ancient land surface cut by burial pit

Layer 1 Weathered chalk bedrock, one urn sherd, charcoal and chips of cremated bone pressed down into it.

Layer 2 Soil of natural profile, cut by upper edge of burial pit.

Section 3   Layers 6, 5, filling of central burial pit

Layer 6 Lower pit filling. Brown loam with a little chalk; ash and charcoal haphazardly throughout. Upper pit filling similar but included series of almost black ash and charcoal-laden spreads, with cremation at their base. More lumps of chalk and flints in upper filling. Some charcoal extended up and over on to ancient land surface.

Layer 5 Base of barrow mound. Pale brown loam with uneven distribution of chalk chips. Lay directly on uppermost ashy spread filling mouth of pit at bedrock level.

Section 4   Layers 1, 2, 7, 12, 13, Pit A, cut through edge of mound; and Pits B and C

Layers 1, 2 Weathered bedrock with ancient land surface on top, preserved by chalky crust of mound.

Layer 7 Chalk rubble forming crust to earth core of mound. Cut by Pit A.

Layer 12 Filling of Pit A, dark grey-brown loam with finely comminuted charcoal all through. Slight spread of fine chalk over top and in upper fill of pit. Sherds of small Collared Vessel packed together near top, but covered by small amount of fine chalk in upper part of pit. Filling of Pits A and B identical. In Pit C, loam less grey but more charcoal, less comminuted.

Layer 13 Brown loam, resembling topsoil but a little more compact, spreading over top of Pit A; well-charged with finely powdered chalk chips. Caused by hollow-way (T3) across W edges of barrow and ditch. Merged imperceptibly with weathered natural chalk here.

SITE XVIII

SPTA 2247: A BOWL-BARROW

SUMMARY

A slightly oval bowl-barrow, about 4ft high in Hoare's day, had been raised over a central burial pit dug 3ft into solid chalk. It contained a Collared Urn of Longworth's primary series, which had been placed upright and to one side of the pit and filled with cremated bones. The mound's chalky covering, subsequently removed, we suggest, by rabbitters, had been derived from an unusually narrow, slot-like surrounding ditch, which found its only recorded parallel among the Snail Down barrows at Site XXI.

INTRODUCTION

Site XVIII was a bowl-barrow lying immediately to the S of Site I, their edges separated by a little over 10ft. Obscured by tall weeds and bushes, the mound had evidently long been a rabbit warren. Despite the dense overgrowth and disturbances, however, it could be seen to be low and flattened, and the slight hollow of a surrounding ditch was just visible.

Hoare (1812, plan opp 180, No 20, 184) excavated this mound, presumably at its centre, and found a burial pit cut into the chalk to a depth of 3ft. He recorded that at this point the chalk surface occurred 4ft below modern turf. In the pit was a cremation, contained in a Collared Urn standing upright and set close to one side of the pit. This elegant and complete vessel belongs to I H Longworth's Primary Series of Collared Urns (Section D, D24, Fig 43). An excavation memento of our type 1 (Section U) was left here by Hoare (*ibid*).

Other references to Site XVIII are as follows: Cunnington and Goddard 1896, 67–68, no 255; Abercromby 1912, II, pl 64, no 24; Goddard 1914, 235, Collingbourne Kingston 17; Grinsell 1957, 168, No 17, and 235; Annable 1958, 7; Longworth 1961, 295, no 72; Annable and Simpson 1964, 66 and 122, no 540; Thomas 1976, 230; Longworth 1984, no 1677.

At a late stage of the final season it was decided to section the ditch and part of the mound to examine the structure of the barrow, since surface features suggested the unusual combination here of a ditched barrow inhabited by rabbits. Our purpose was to determine why, at this site, the chalk from the ditch had not, apparently, afforded protection against rabbits as it had everywhere else on the Down. The work occupied about six volunteers for five days.

DESCRIPTION

Pre-barrow Features and Settlement Remains

The limited excavation failed to reveal an ancient land surface other than weathered bedrock. Two sherds of Beaker ware occurred in topsoil and these might have been derived from the Beaker settlement to the WNW.

The Burial

As already indicated, cremated bones, in a Primary Series Collared Urn, had been placed to one side of a pit dug 3ft into bedrock at the centre of the barrow. The bones were not removed by Hoare or re-discovered in 1957.

The Structures

Time did not allow the production of a detailed site plan (the outline in Fig 32 is only approximate). The damage which the mound had sustained from rabbits also made planning extremely difficult, hampered as it was in addition by heavy weed infestation. Nevertheless our survey of the excavated features and probed areas suggested that unlike the other barrows examined on Snail Down (except Site V), Site XVIII may not have been circular.

The **surrounding ditch** had been cut into solid chalk to a depth of 4½–4ft (Fig 32; Pl 52). Noticeably slot-like, the width of the ditch at floor level was only 1-2ft, expanding by weathering to 4–5ft at chalk surface. The ditch floor had been very carefully cut flat, making a sharp angle with the walls.

This ditch, so carefully cut to shape, defined a **plateau** noticeably level but only approximately circular. The edges had been scarped by weathering hardly at all. In sections 1 and 3 it was noticeable that, where Snail Down naturally begins to slope S, the chalk surface of the S sector of the plateau protected by the barrow mound stood over 1ft above the solid chalk outside its ditch (Pl 51).

The **mound** had an average maximum diameter of *c* 65ft and a general height above solid bedrock of almost 2ft. It had suffered extensively from rabbits; the evidence from the only cutting (No 1) to expose a substantial part of it failed to establish how far any of this material remained undisturbed. It was clear, however, that the chalk bedrock had been weathered to a depth of more than 6in in places (layer 1). In section 1, the brown soil comprising the bulk of the mound (layer 6) included dis-

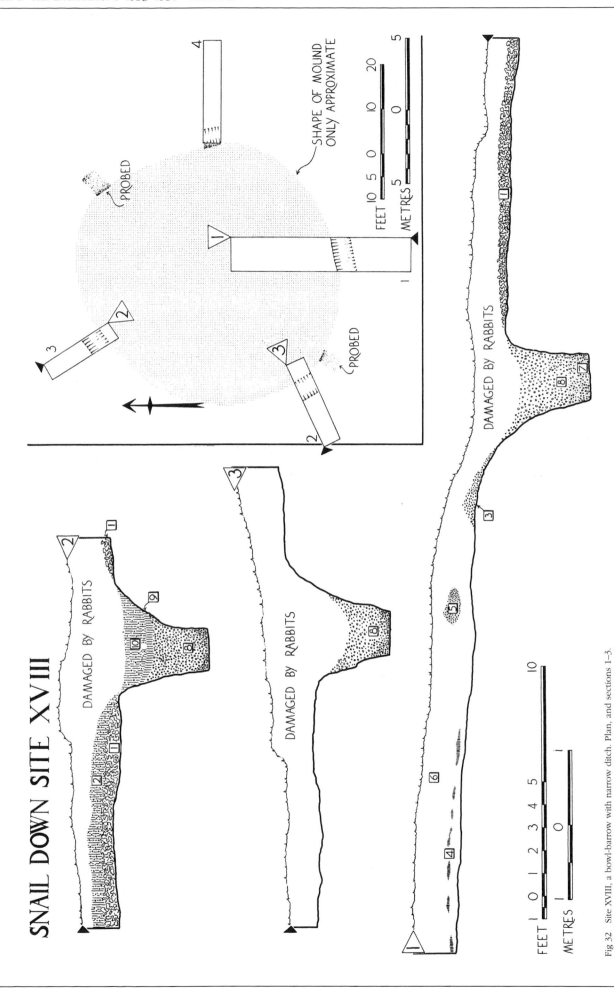

SNAIL DOWN SITE XVIII

Fig 32   Site XVIII, a bowl-barrow with narrow ditch. Plan, and sections 1–3.

tinct darker brown patches, mostly about 9in across, with chalk chips attached to their undersides. These were concentrated at a level (layer 4) just above solid chalk but were also present throughout the remains of the mound. They appeared to represent small turves and artificial dumps of soil with which the mound had been made up. Despite the damage, it was also possible to make out that its upper half included sufficient chalk chips and powdered chalk to suggest that originally at least some of the contents of the ditch had been spread over the earthy mound within.

At one point, as indicated in Section 1, a large patch of pure chalk occurred midway between the top of the mound and bedrock (layer 5; Pl 51). It did not extend across the cutting and may have been produced by rabbits.

More evidently structural, a spread of chalk rubble mixed with some soil extended across cutting 1 following the inner, weathered edge of the ditch (Fig 32, layer 3). On the level plateau it had a width of about 2ft and it extended forward to cover the uppermost slope of the ditch wall. This feature, which lay directly upon bedrock, was not recorded in sections 2 or 3.

The Primary Series Collared Urn from the central grave is described and discussed by Longworth in Section D (D24, Fig 43). Seven featureless sherds of Collared Vessel fabric were recovered in topsoil. Here also two flint flakes were found in the topsoil (Section G).

Post-construction Events

Everywhere the lowest filling in the ditch (layers 7, 8) comprised lumps of fine chalk, often loose to the touch and the pieces occasionally almost fist-sized. Its original upper limit was preserved only in section 2 where a thin, buff-coloured band of fine soil (layer 9) ran across the ditch from edge to edge. Above this in the same section the secondary filling (layer 10) consisted of pale brown soil with lighter patches and mixed small chalk chips. Here, only a little of this layer had survived the depredation of rabbits, but enough to suggest the kind of upper filling which the ditch must originally have contained.

REMARKS

The lower 1½–2ft of the walls of the barrow ditch were unweathered, making a sharp angle with the narrow, flat floor. The loose, pure chalk of layer 7, which filled at least the lower half of the ditch, must have fallen in from the upper walls at the first frost after its construction and it is likely that within one or two years of completion, the surrounding ditch would have been half-filled with chalk. The soil which covered this in cutting 3, section 2, can be seen to represent that point in the silting of the ditch when collapse of the exposed chalk beneath the turf and topsoil had undermined the latter and the soil beneath the turf followed the chalk silt into the ditch. Above this the undisturbed filling in section 2 was more

mixed, soil with chalk lumps representing the slower silting process which followed the first rapid weathering of the raw ditch sides. Thereafter the record had been destroyed by rabbits.

The inner wall of the ditch sloped at a noticeably greater angle than the outer, which came close to the vertical. Nevertheless the plateau covered by the barrow mound was conspicuously flat until close to the inner edge of this ditch, as if the tail of the mound had been carefully constructed and had stayed in place. This would have protected the plateau from the sort of re-shaping by weathering seen clearly in Sites I, II and XVII, preserving for some time the outlines originally envisaged by the barrow's builders. In view of this it would appear that the less steep inner slope of the ditch was part of the design of the barrow and not the result of weathering. No evidence, however, was found in cutting 1 for the existence of a revetment for the mound with the exception of a slight concentration of diffuse chalk rubble (layer 3) along its edge and lying directly upon undisturbed chalk. This feature was not found in cuttings 2 or 3 and could have been produced by rabbits. Nevertheless, it coincided so closely with the change of angle in the undisturbed chalk between the unusually level barrow-platform and the inner slope of the ditch that its function as a revetment, or at least a deliberate concentration of chalk rubble around the edge of the mound, must remain a possibility.

Enough of the mound survived in cutting 1, section 1 to show that its core had been made of turves, presumably cut at the start of ditch-digging. Many could be traced individually in the exposed section, with scraps of chalk adhering to their undersides. The turves had evidently been laid grass upwards. There was also sufficient chalk rubble and chalky soil in the mound, particularly in its upper half and around its edge, to imply the former existence of a deposit of chalk rubble over the turfy core of the barrow.

Yet Hoare had recorded that the mound was about 4ft high, from turf to chalk bedrock, when he excavated its centre in 1805. That would have made the barrow over twice its present height. Had his measurement in *Ancient Wiltshire* been a printing error for 1¾ft (and this must remain an unverifiable possibility), or had his measurement included the depth of the burial pit, his height for the mound would have accorded well with ours. Taking his account, however, at its face value, we can only suggest that Site XVIII may have been selected as a rabbit warren earlier this century, or last, and its upper half removed in the process and scattered. Major Allen's great air photograph of Snail Down, taken shortly before outbreak of the Second World War (Pl 1), makes it clear that at that time Site XVIII was suffering from rabbits and rabbiting more drastically than any other barrow within the cemetery. It is at least possible that such activities could have caused the destruction and disappearance of the upper half of the mound, leaving the kind of unevenly flat-topped barrow that was recorded in 1957.

The slight concentration of rubbly chalk soil around the edge of the mound in at least one cutting may have been the less disturbed remains of a chalk covering, reinforced here, perhaps, in order to prevent its spread into a surrounding ditch whose particular shape was in need of special protection against too-rapid silting.

From the evidence of thirty-six barrows in Wiltshire excavated and published from 1965, it is clear that, on average, the depth of burial pits in the chalk, whether small and designed for cremations, or appropriately larger for inhumations, coffins and other structures, varies between 1–2ft and sometimes considerably beyond; the deepest recorded among this survey of barrows was 7½ft (2.25m), at Shrewton (Green and Rollo-Smith 1984, 275–279, fig 12). There, it was noted that the barrow, 5k, was the earliest within the series of burial mounds on Net Down. Although the cremation pit at Snail Down XVIII was not deep by their standards, there may be enough evidence from Wiltshire to suggest that, if Hoare's observation was correct, the pit of Site XVIII was of an above-average depth; and that the series of deeper pits beneath Wiltshire round barrows tended to be associated more often with Beakers than with Collared Urns or Food Vessels or with other Wessex Bronze Age objects such as beads and bronzes.

On Snail Down the ditch around Site XVIII had narrowness and depth in proportions which were echoed only in the ditch of Site XXI (Fig 35). No other barrows so far excavated had ditch floors so narrow. Excavation also revealed the possibility that Site XVIII was unusual in having a plan which was not truly circular. Hereabouts only the small saucer-barrow to the S of the main group, beyond the boundary ditch CD (Fig 2, 2244), and the ring-ditch Site V, are similarly irregular or oval in plan. The early Collared Urn from Site XVIII and the actual position within the cemetery of Sites V (with XV), XVIII and XXI, will be used in the general discussion (Part 3) to suggest that they may have been the earliest barrows in the cemetery. Although a gravel subsoil must always have made it difficult to dig narrow slot-like ditches comparable to those of Sites XVIII and XXI, the ditch surrounding Site V at Dorchester on Thames, Oxon (Atkinson et al 1951, 43–47, figs 20, 21) as well as the linear ditches forming a cursus-like monument at North Stoke, Oxon (Case and Whittle 1982, 62–66, figs 35, 36) show that when the occasion demanded it, ditches of this particular form could be dug. That both sites belonged to the Neolithic (North Stoke radiocarbon determination 4672 ± 49 BP) indicates a possible ancestry for the ditch form at Snail Down. Before the stage, approximating perhaps to Wessex II, when the main group of barrows was built at Snail Down (Part 3; Fig 60), it seems that the fashion for broad, relatively shallow surrounding ditches, laid out as nearly circular as possible, had not arisen. So also may we contrast the deep pit beneath Site XVIII, if Hoare's account is to be relied upon, with the relatively small, shallow, burial pits

beneath Sites I, III, XIV and XVII. It had been dug into solid bedrock to more than twice the depth of most of them.

Figure 32
Detailed description of layers

Sections 1–3   Layers 1, 2, 4, ancient land surfaces

Layer 1 Weathered natural chalk. Inexplicably absent beneath mound in section 1 and everywhere in section 3, it was conspicuous outside the ditch in sections 1 and 2. Surface of chalk bedrock generally very even beneath and around Site XVIII, except where channelled by rabbits.

Layer 2 Outside ditch in section 2, an unusually deep weathering of bedrock: layer 2 represented this chalk further broken by root action.

Layer 4 Indistinct level of elongated, darker brown patches with traces of chalk on undersides, following a line about 6in above bedrock but dying out roughly 12ft inside the surrounding ditch. Similar traces of turves noted throughout layer 6.

Layers 3, 5, 6, mound material

Layer 3 Spread of clean chalk rubble lying directly on bedrock and following inner edge of ditch, section 1 only.

Layer 5 Isolated patch of concentrated chalk rubble in a chalky matrix, extending less than 2ft into trench. Possibly derived from rabbit activity.

Layer 6 Pale brown loam, heavily damaged by rabbits, containing uneven scatter of chalk rubble and powdered chalk. Here and there, throughout, thin darker brown patches of soil with chalk on undersides, similar to those in layer 4 but not occurring in a distinct level.

Layers 7–10, ditch filling

Layer 7 Very loose chalk rubble, sometimes falling away to the touch, occupying lowest foot of ditch in section 1.

Layer 8 Similar to layer 7 but not quite so loose. Nevertheless represented a very rapid accumulation of pure chalk. Top damaged by rabbits in sections 1, 3.

Layer 9 Section 2 only. Very pale yellow-brown soil, almost devoid of chalk, covering layer 8 and running from edge to edge of ditch.

Layer 10 Section 2 only. Pale brown soil, darker than layer 9, filling upper part of ditch. Even mixture of chalk throughout.

SITE XIX

SPTA 2268:A DOUBLE BELL-BARROW

SUMMARY

The burial ceremony followed cremation of at least two corpses at or near the site and included deposit of the only prestigious grave-goods so far found at Snail Down. The bigger mound was built first, to cover the richly provided cremation in its large wooden coffin; turf for the purpose was stripped from the area immediately to the N which was to be covered by the smaller mound soon afterwards. The turf core of each mound was stacked within a circle of short quite stout stakes, whose principal purpose may have been to indicate the precise shape each mound was to take, and the relationship of one to the other. The surrounding ditch yielded a final covering of chalk for the two mounds enhancing the outward appearance of what may have been regarded as the most important burial in the cemetery. A burnt timber from near the base of the main mound yielded a radiocarbon determination of 3330 ± 80 BP.

INTRODUCTION

Site XIX was a double bell-barrow with enclosing ditch pear-shaped in plan. One mound was larger than the other and the space between them had become filled through subsequent mound settlement, so that when seen in profile from a distance this imposing structure looked not unlike a snail with its head extended outside its shell. Snail Down may owe its name to the distinctive appearance of Site XIX (above, Introduction).

The earthworks were covered by downland turf but a wide track had been worn through it into the undisturbed upper layers of the barrow by repeated passage of military vehicles along its main axis. A tank route at right-angles also filled the space between Site XIX and the double bell-barrow immediately to the S, Site XXII. Both routes obscured the surrounding ditch of Site XIX along its N and S arcs (plan, Fig 33). In addition, some probably ancient rutting had damaged the berm and inner edge of the ditch around its S side, caused by Trackway T1, which was associated further W with Site IX (above) and had also damaged the berm of site III (Fig 9) as it ran E/W across the Down.

L V Grinsell first emphasised the importance of Site XIX in 1934 (p 218). In addition, the following references to this double bell-barrow have been published: Hoare 1812, plan opp. 180, No 24, 185; Thurnam 1871, 454, pl 35, fig 4; Evans 1881, 242, 366, fig 449; Cunnington and Goddard 1896, nos 116, 128; Abercromby 1912, pl 60, no 029b; Goddard 1912, 119, no 15, 154, no 271; *ibid* 1914, 230, Collingbourne Ducis 4; Grinsell 1934, 218; Piggott 1938, 87, fig 18, Wessex Grave no 54; Grinsell 1941, 80, fig 2 and *passim*; *ibid* 1957, 213; Annable 1958, 7; Annable and Simpson 1964, 47, 101, nos 193–194; Piggott 1973, 370, fig 22, A1, 2; Gerloff 1975, 105, 250, pl 49, D; Thomas 1976, 230.

Excavation on a very small scale was carried out during 1957, to ascertain whether the barrow with its two mounds was of one period of construction. The work lasted for a week and about 12 volunteers took part under the overall supervision of Peter Jewell and Bret Guthrie.

DESCRIPTION

Pre-barrow Features and Settlement Remains

This limited excavation produced no evidence for earlier occupation except for a scatter of Peterborough and Beaker sherds within the barrow mounds. The ancient soil preserved beneath the south mound and beneath the weathered chalk and soil filling the space between the two mounds contained more flinty gravel and clayey soil than usual beneath barrows on Snail Down. This may reflect Site XIX's position near the floor of the shallow combe defining the S edge of Snail Down, which contains drift gravel (Introduction, above).

The Burials

Hoare excavated at the centres of both mounds in 1805 (*op cit*) and described his work as follows:

'No 24 is a very large barrow, 97 feet 16 (*sic*) inches in diameter, and 11 feet 4 inches in depth from the summit to the floor, on which we found a very perfect interment of bones minutely burned, and enclosed in wood, which we traced very satisfactorily for the extent of six feet in length, and more than three in breadth. Within this wooden chest, or perhaps the more simple trunk of a tree, were the fragments of a beautiful little cup. The bones being tinged with green, we were led to suppose that we should find some articles of brass, and we were not disappointed in our expectations, for we shortly took out a spear head with three rivets, similar in form to those we had found on former occasions; and from the mouldering remains of wood, adhering to it, we clearly perceived that it had been carefully protected by a scabbard. Close to this spear head lay another singular instrument of brass, which was also secured in a sheath of wood lined with cloth, the web of which could still be distinguished. ... This barrow is surrounded

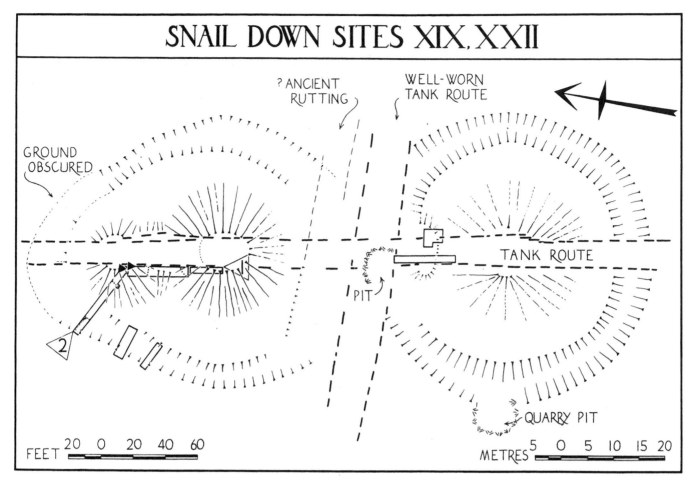

Fig 33   Sites XIX, XXII, double bell-barrow and bell-barrow with added mound. Plans, including Trackway T1 and 1939–45 tank route

with a ditch, enclosing a smaller mound, which contained a simple but large interment of burned bones, perhaps of the slave or dependent of the chieftain who was buried in the larger one, as in both instances the same system of interment was adopted.'

The 'beautiful little cup' has not survived, but the dagger and ring-headed pin remain and are described in Section M, M1 and M2, Figure 56, Plates 62–64.

The Structures

One complete profile of the **ditch** was obtained in section 2 and its upper edges were identified in two other cuttings at the point where it swung outwards to skirt the W side of the large mound (Figs 33, 34; Pl 54).

Overall dimensions of Site XIX were difficult to calculate because of damage inflicted by the tank route along its main axis. The maximum diameter of the surrounding ditch, measured E/W was about 175ft; its N/S length approximately 205ft.

The ditch is typical of those around the Phase 4 barrows (Part 3, below) on Snail Down, flat-bottomed, originally vertical-sided and generally monumental. At chalk surface this ditch was about 10ft wide, narrowing to about 6ft at floor level. Its depth, measured from the solid

chalk outside, was about 3½ft. In section 2, the inner edge of the ditch was separated from the original edge of the north mound by a berm at least 16ft wide. Surface indications and the location of the true course of the ditch in the other two ditch sections suggested that the berm around the larger mound may have been over 40ft wide.

Each mound was surrounded by a **single ring of stakes,** whose holes were revealed when bedrock had been reached. At the S end of Section 1, the **holes of four stakes** were found, spaced about 2ft 2in apart and lying on an arc which presumably followed the outer edge of the mound. Except for hole 5 all were circular, 2½in in diameter at chalk surface. Hole 5 measured 2 x 3in and was 4in deep from the same level: hole 6 was 3½in deeper and the other two (probed, not excavated) were approximately the same. In shape, holes 5 and 6 were similar, cylindrical and tapering gradually to rounded ends. Careful excavation of hole 6 revealed that the pointed end of this stake had begun to split as it was hammered into the chalk.

Like the larger (south) mound, the smaller had also been ringed around by a **single ring of short stakes** of which four were exposed in section 1 and four more in section 2. These were all set about 1¾ft apart, a little closer than those around the other mound. They measured 2–2½in in diameter. Nos 1 and 5, which were traced in the main sections (section 1, Fig 34) penetrated the chalk to a

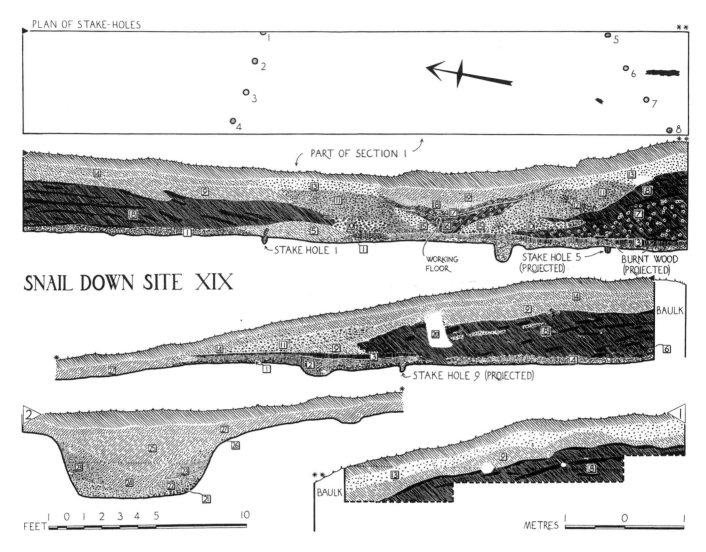

PLAN OF STAKE-HOLES

PART OF SECTION I

SNAIL DOWN SITE XIX

STAKE HOLE I
WORKING FLOOR
STAKE HOLE 5 (PROJECTED)
BURNT WOOD (PROJECTED)

BAULK

STAKE HOLE 9 (PROJECTED)

BAULK

FEET 1 0 1 2 3 4 5   10

METRES 1   0   1

Fig 34   Site XIX, sections 1, 2, including plan of stake rings.

depth of 4½in. No 9 (section 2) was 5½in deep in chalk. A slight change in the texture of their filling enabled the upper part of stakes 1 and 12 (not illustrated) to be traced into the mound for a distance of 9in from their points. It could be seen that the stakes had been bent outwards (Fig 34; Pl 54, stake 1) and their upper ends cut straight across. They had therefore been driven in to a total depth of some 7in from the surface on which the mound builders were standing (layer 1) and half of this was into loose subsoil. No trace of stakes occurred above the point shown in section 1 and it is probable that these represented the complete stakes.

Outside the stake circle around the north mound, a **low bank** of brown soil filled with flints and small chalk chips occurred in sections 1 and 2; in section 1 (layer 5) it extended within the stakes for about 1½ft and had an overall width of about 6ft. In section 2 (layer 9) it began about 2ft beyond the stake circle and had a width of 4–5ft (in section 2 it is illustrated – Fig 34 – as an increase of chalk chips at the outer edge of layer 9). This slight bank preserved a complete ancient soil profile (layers 1–3): evidently the stake circle around the smaller mound marked the area within which the turf itself had apparently been removed before the mound had been raised.

The **south mound** had a diameter of about 82ft and a maximum surviving height of some 9½ft above the ancient land surface which it covered (Figs 33, 34, Pl 53). The N/S tank route had removed much material from the top of the mound, and its original height would have been at least one foot more.

As exposed in section 1, this mound preserved an ancient land surface whose clayey, flint-free upper layer (layer 3) covered a more jumbled weathered chalk bedrock (layer 1) containing flints among the fragmented chalk. This undisturbed layer was interrupted from just within the stake circle (below) which presumably enclosed the whole mound; it became less clayey, more gritty because of an increase in flint fragments. About 2ft within the stake circle a rough piece of burnt wood measuring (inches) 21¾ by 4½ and 1½ thick, lay on the original land surface which here was not itself burnt. A second piece, measuring (inches) 6 x 3 x 1 lay outside, just beyond stakehole 7 (Fig 34, section 1). These were of oak. Charcoal from the larger piece was submitted to Glasgow for radiocarbon determination, with the following result:

GU-5304 3330 ± 80 BP; cal BC 1737–1521 (1 sigma); cal BC 1875–1440 (2 sigma).

The result is considered further in Section T.

The edge of the mound was exposed at ancient ground level; the extension of section 1 southwards towards its centre only examined its upper 2–3½ft. At the edge, however, within the stake circle but spilling out beyond it for 4–5ft, the lowest structure of the mound comprised parti-coloured soil (layer 7) in which the individual turves could not be seen clearly although the material evidently included topsoil. However it incorporated a high proportion of natural flints, small and medium in size (up to about the volume of a hen's egg) which gave it a speckled appearance and a loose, rough texture in strong contrast to the make-up of the smaller mound (Pl 54) and to that of sites III and XVII.

The layer above (layer 8), however, which was traced almost to the centre of the mound, lacked these flints and retained clearer traces of turves, though not concentrated as they were in the smaller mound or in Site III. As far as could be seen, and as indicated in the section (Fig 34) they lay roughly horizontally over the top of the mound and dipped down around its sides.

The mound had next been covered (layer 9) by paler brown soil with an even mixture of small chalk chips and natural flints whose loose structure and lighter, more uniform colour set it apart from the turfy, less chalky material below. Above this, and mingled with it at their junction, came the outer jacket (layer 13) of chalk rubble. In the section excavated, layer 9 covered only the upper slopes of the mound, not being present in the area exposed in the main trench of Section 1.

The chalk rubble covering the south mound was generally thin and diffuse, everywhere mixed with fine, pale brown loam. In places it was at least twelve inches thick, noticeably on the top of the mound (Pl 53), but elsewhere, particularly on the middle slopes towards the NW side, it almost disappeared.

Opposite the north mound, however, the chalk covering increased not only in thickness but also in hardness and in the density of pure chalk, with its accompanying whiteness. Layer 10, interleaved between the ancient land surface and the mass of this chalk, was of loose rubble and included some soil; and layer 12, higher up, was also an isolated patch of loose rubble. Otherwise the chalky covering (layer 11) was homogeneous and extremely hard. Layer 15, the outermost spread of the chalk mound-covering, was also compact and likely to have been part of the original covering.

The **north mound** had an estimated maximum diameter of 55ft and a height of 4½ft from solid chalk (Fig 34, Pls 53, 54). Low in relation to its diameter, it had a gently domed profile with a broad almost flat top.

The land surface preserved beneath this mound (layer 1) apparently represented subsoil and weathered chalk only; there was no trace of the slightly clay-like layer which, beneath the larger mound, occurred on top of this and was interpreted as downland turf with its undisturbed soil profile below. This subsoil at the base of the north mound comprised mixed dark brown soil, flints and chalk which contrasted sharply with the turfy soil of the mound above it.

The lower part of the north mound consisted of stacked turf (layer 8), possibly placed with grass downwards, although this detail, so clear in Site III, was less certain here. The turves, some of them strips at least 2ft long, generally lay horizontally except at the edge of the mound where they dipped, following its contours. Very few flints were included in layer 8, and only a little chalk. There was a slight scatter of charcoal fragments throughout this and the layer above, with a concentration of charcoal at the base of the mound on the S side. In section 2, at a point which must have been fairly close to the central burial, layer 8 covered the edge of a heap of turfy material (layer 6) distinguished by a high concentration of small chalk chips. The main part of the heap lay apparently towards the NE and the centre of the mound. Above layer 8 came a more evenly coloured layer (layer 9) of compact paler-brown soil with a general scatter of mainly small chalk chips and a few flints.

Here and there in the turf stack but particularly at its top, just below the chalk covering (layer 14), small groups of tiny animal bones occurred which resembled those from the ancient land surface beneath Site XVII (Section Q, below). It is possible, however, that these may have been introduced in recent times: traces of a small animal burrow occurred in the top of the mound and the age of the bones is in doubt.

The north mound was capped by a layer of chalk (14) of which only a thin and diffuse scatter of small and medium chips survived. This chalky spread merged gradually into the upper half of layer 9 below it and accounted for the generally high chalk content of that layer. At the outer end of section 2 there was an increased accumulation of pure loose chalk rubble (layer 11) around the lower slope of the mound, equal in density to the chalk between the two mounds in section 1 though looser than all except layer 15. Between the two mounds there had been a massive build-up of compact chalk against the side of the N mound, including at least one lens of loose chalk (layers 11, 10) equal to that around the base of the larger mound immediately to the S. This chalk deposit sealed a land surface with complete soil profile below it (layers 1, 3) like that beneath the chalk in section 2.

Hoare recovered from Site XIX the most chieftainly grave group yet found among the Snail Down barrows. The ogival dagger and ring-headed copper-alloy pin are described below (Section M, M1, M2) with full bibliography. A broken Accessory Cup has not survived. Sherds of Peterborough and Beaker wares were found thinly scattered through the north mound. These sherds are described in Section C, C113-C119. Forty-five flint implements and flakes occurred within the two mounds, in three contexts: ancient land surface, turf mound cores and chalky coverings. Implements included two scrapers, an awl and a serrated flake. Near the base of layer 9 in the north mound, at the point shown in section 2 (Fig 34) by a large flint symbol, a pile of about eight flints occurred, each weighing some 2–4lbs, two of them apparently large crude choppers.* A Beaker sherd and a scatter of chalk were associated with these flints. All the flints are described in Section G, Figures 50, 51. A single unburnt

---

*Regrettably, these two crude chopping tools have not survived. They were noted carefully at the time but not drawn.

adult human molar was recovered from the earthen core of the north mound (Section A, III, 6). It may have come from the corpse ultimately cremated and buried beneath this mound and is thus of interest in helping to establish the adult age of that burial.

Post-construction Events

The filling of the ditch consisted of loose chalk rubble in the bottom inner angle (layer 21) with an accumulation above that of loose small chalk spreading across the ditch (layer 22), its upper extremes becoming a more compact chalk wash (23). Secondary filling, entering the ditch equally from both sides, consisted first of chalky-brown soil (24) and then of less-chalky, deeper-brown soil (25) which included a lens of loose chalk rubble entering the ditch from inside (26). Covering the whole ditch came the base of the modern soil profile, which included many small chalk chips (27).

The space between the north and south mounds was filled by a dense accumulation of chalk whose composition varied from loose rubble (layer 15) to very fine silt (layer 18) (Fig 34, Pl 53). All these layers covered the pre-barrow natural soil profile which extended without interruption across the space between the two stake circles (layers 1, 3).

On top of layer 16, concentrated along the W side of section 1 but extending across the trench, occurred a considerable scatter of struck flint flakes (Fig 34, section 1, 'working floor') including a small proportion of tools (Section G, Fig 50), with animal bones, one Beaker sherd and a sherd of Iron Age bead-rim pottery*. No charcoal was present but clearly the deposit represented part of a later prehistoric working area in a spot sheltered by the two barrow mounds.

REMARKS

The limited objectives of this excavation, to see if both mounds were contemporary with their surrounding ditch and to compare their mound structures with the other large mound excavated on Snail Down, Site III, were achieved.

Section 2 and the two incomplete cuttings across the ditch to the W (Fig 34) suggested that Site XIX had one continuous ditch and not interlocking ditches surrounding mounds of two different periods. Section 1 provided an additional check that no barrow ditches ran between the two mounds, as they did, for example, at Amesbury G72, a bowl-barrow overlapped by a saucer-barrow (Ashbee 1985, 62, fig 25, 63–67).

The space between the two mounds and the area occupied by the larger mound were found to be covered by an intact ancient soil. The ground beneath the smaller mound had, however, been considerably altered, either by

prolonged trampling or, more probably, by the removal of the turf covering. This interference with the natural profile had occurred only within the stake circle: the land beneath the chalky outer covering around the edge of the mound was found to be intact. From this it was inferred that although the stake circles around the two mounds may have been set out at the same time, part of a complicated exercise in field geometry in which, presumably, the ditch was also planned, the larger mound was built first and incorporated turves and topsoil removed from the area within the smaller stake circle. The building of the latter probably followed at once: certainly the soil profile sealed by the base of its chalk outer covering was exactly the same as that beneath the larger mound and was indeed continuous between the two mounds.

This brief examination of Site XIX showed that the double barrow was of one construction, the larger mound built first and perhaps the whole operation prolonged. If ancient, the presence of pellets of birds of prey in the make-up of the smaller mound provided evidence that there were periods when those building the barrow had deserted the site. The double bell-barrow at Radley (Oxon), which incorporated an earlier Beaker burial, was also probably a one-period structure (Williams 1948, 8–9; Barclay and Halpin 1999, 153–156), the space between its mounds filled by an apparently artificial ridge of earth and gravel which resembled the chalk linking the two mounds of Site XIX. The latter, however, is considered here to have been the result of natural weathering and silting (below). Snail Down XIX and Radley 4 and 4A have shown, by excavation, that there was in the Early Bronze Age an architectural distinction between double barrows which were built at one time, their surrounding ditch continuous and of oval or pear-shaped plan, and those where a later barrow was linked to an earlier one by an encircling ditch or, as at Amesbury G72, by a penannular ditch, in physical contact with an arc of the already existing barrow ditch.

The problem of the source of the massive stack of turves in the smaller mound was raised but not solved by these trenches. Presumably the larger mound would have incorporated the turf from the whole of the ditch area as well as from the base of the other mound. The intact land surface sealed by the accumulation of chalk between the mounds showed that, as we have suggested for other special barrows on Snail Down such as sites I and III, the berm was left with its downland covering in place. Much, at least, of the turf and soil for the smaller mound must, then, have been collected from outside the area of the barrow ditch.

Comparison of the lower turf core of the larger mound, layer 7, with that of its upper turf, layer 8 and the lower core of the smaller mound, layer 8, afforded a contrast which may have reflected two different sources of material, since layer 7 of the larger mound contained much more flint than the other turfy layers, and the structure of the individual turves in layer 7 was not so distinct as in layer 8 here or in the smaller mound. It seems just possible that this mixed, flinty material (layer 7) came

---

*This sherd has not survived. It was carefully recorded at the time, and examined closely because of the rarity of such wares here. There is no need to doubt either its discovery in that location or its probably late Iron Age character.

from within the staked-out circle of the smaller mound, following some activity in that area which had caused excessive trampling and break-up of the natural soil cover. If this was so, then turf from this spot would have been heaped up to form the base of the larger mound at the beginning of its construction and not, as would otherwise have appeared more probable, at a later stage to increase its height. As an alternative, the turves forming the inner core of the larger mound may have been brought from elsewhere, before the turf over the site of the double-barrow ditch was removed.

The presence of a circle of stakes around the turf core of each mound requires explanation. These had been driven only a short way into the chalk and their original lengths were about 9–12in. Comparison with circles of stakes found surrounding the turf core of a bell-barrow on Farncombe Down, Berks (Rahtz 1962, 4–11, fig 7) showed that the Site XIX stakes had been forced a much shorter distance into solid chalk ($4\frac{1}{2}$–$5\frac{1}{2}$in against $13\frac{1}{4}$in average) although the stakes at both sites were of similar diameter. The estimated original length of the Farncombe Down stakes was about $4\frac{1}{2}$–6ft and the excavator conjectured that they had formed a vertical revetment to a drum-like turf structure, the spaces between them (about 2ft) being linked with some kind of wickerwork. Their layout would have been suited to such a function. In contrast, the stakes around the Snail Down XIX mounds were probably structurally functionless; they were too shallow in the solid chalk and too short above ground to have acted as a useful revetment. Moreover two of them, examined in profile above the level of the ancient ground surface, had been pushed outwards either by pressure of the mound within, or else by accident during turf-stacking (Pl 54). The Farncombe stakes, probably held together by wicker-work above ground, still stood vertically (represented by voids) when excavated. On this analogy the leaning posts in Site XIX must have been freestanding and unjoined above ground. A similar contrast could be seen in the '28ft circle' beneath the Sheeplays 293′ barrow (South Glamorgan), where stakes had been driven 10–12in into the ground and extended above the land surface, tied together in some way, to a height of at least 2ft (Fox 1959, 134–135).

It should not be forgotten, nevertheless, that at Sheeplays 293′ Fox found evidence for a hasty repair to the NW arc of the turf stack at the centre of that barrow, for which a curved row of short stakes closely resembling those at Site XIX had been driven into the edge of the structure without penetrating the ancient land surface. With such an insecure foundation they too had been bent outwards by pressure from the mound within (*ibid*, 137, fig 68).

Like Farncombe Down, Sheeplays 293′ and also Snail Down Site XV, the stake circles of Site XIX were *internal*, by Ashbee's definition (1960, 62), the stakes originally being concealed by outer layers of the mound. And it is clear that all these circles had been standing when their barrow mounds were heaped over them.

If not structural, then the purpose served by the Site XIX circles may have been to indicate exactly the positions and shapes of the two mounds within the area to be enclosed by the ditch. Site XIX was, however, no ordinary barrow. It was a double bell-barrow in which one mound was almost twice the size of the other; the width of the berm varied correspondingly and there was a space between the two mounds so that their outlines could remain distinct. A good way to achieve that specialised form would have been to set out the limits of the two earth cores on the ground by driving in short upright stakes. It appeared that, for some reason, a slight external annular bank accompanied the N circle, whose stakes were also set a little closer than those of the other. That the area thus surrounded may have taken on an added significance was suggested by the possibility that turf from exactly within the smaller circle was used to form the base of the turf core of the larger mound.

It must surely have been the intention of the builders of Site XIX to keep the two mounds distinct, yet today they are joined by a saddle of compact chalk about $3\frac{1}{2}$ft high. The structure of this saddle, revealed in section 1, comprised hard, fine chalk in thick deposits (layers 10–12) which ran up against the earth-and-turf core of each mound and were partly interleaved with them. Probably layers 10 and 11 of both mounds were part of the original construction and had been joined together subsequently, through natural processes of weathering and soil movement, by layers 15–18. The juxtaposition of the two mounds had prevented the chalk from being dispersed more widely and so it gradually built up into the saddle. Section 2 revealed a similar accumulation around the foot of the smaller mound on its NW side: here, however, there had been nothing to prevent the chalk from spreading more widely (some of it into the ditch) and the chalk was therefore thinner than between the mounds and less compact. All this chalk nevertheless contrasted strongly with the scanty chalk covering to the upper half of each mound (layers 13, 14): since it preserved an ancient land surface it could not have been entirely the product of slip from the upper surfaces of the mound. Some of it must have been the base of the original covering. Allowing for settlement and spread of the mounds and their chalky coverings, only a few feet could have separated them when they had been completed. This space must have begun to silt up, and the mounds run together at their closest point, fairly soon after construction so that the land surface sealed beneath them showed no variation between the annular bank around the N mound and the core of the larger mound. Layer 15 perhaps represented the first real movement of chalk after completion of the barrow; layer 16 then accumulated much more slowly and its top provided a convenient surface for people who came here to flake flint implements in a sheltered spot. The sherd of Iron Age bead-rim pottery found among the flints (above) suggested that layer 16 may have been building up for over one thousand years. The chalky spread between the two mounds continued with layers 17 and 18. The saddle and the upper part of each mound was finally linked by a spread of loose chalk rubble with soil, (layers 13, 14, 19), differentiated only by slight variations in the proportions of chalk to dark earth, all of it loosened and worked through by earthworms from the pure chalk-free topsoil above.

The Iron Age sherd may indicate an unusually late date for the working of flint on Snail Down.

Comparison of Plates 13, 43 and 53 shows how marked was the difference between the thick chalk outer covering of Site III and the outer chalky layer over Sites XVII and XIX. The dispersal of the chalk crust of site XVII has been attributed to the work of earthworms incorporated in the mound and an originally thin spread of chalk from a small ditch. The limited excavation of Site XIX was less successful in establishing a reason why the greater part of both mounds appeared to have been covered so relatively thinly with chalk from the massive surrounding ditch.

Figure 34
Detailed Description of Layers

Section 1 Layers 1, 3; Section 2 Layers 1–4, ancient land surface and sub-soil

Section 1

Layer 1 Weathered chalk mixed in places with brown loam, merging into solid chalk bedrock. Solid chalk included irregular pockets filled with this weathered material eg beneath chalk crust of larger mound, N of stakehole 5.

Layer 3 Beneath larger mound, within area of stake circle; compact, slightly clayey dark brown soil free of flints and chalk chips. Outside stake circle but sealed by chalk crust (layers 10–13) layer 3 less compact and full of small flints and chalk chips. Layer 3 continued between chalk crust of larger mound and earth core of smaller, but was here free of chalk chips and flints and was paler and less compact than under mound within stake circle.

Section 2

Layer 1 Weathered chalk above solid chalk bedrock.

Layer 2 Pale brown soil mixed with chalk chips and broken flints, also filling irregularities in layer 1 and bedrock.

Layer 3 Dark brown clayey soil, free of chalk chips and flints. Disappeared within stake circle.

Layer 4 Parti-coloured brown loam with scattered small chalk chips and flints: distinct from turves and soil of core of mound. Its base merged with decayed chalk bedrock (layer 1).

Section 1   Layer 7, 8, core of larger mound

Layer 7 Edge of mound core, abundant indistinct traces of turves showing as slightly darker marks within dark brown earthy matrix. Structure of turves much less distinct than in layer 8. Also, layer 7 heavily charged with natural flints and small chalk chips, which did not occur in layer 8 above or in the smaller mound. Slight scatter of small charcoal scraps throughout layers 7 and 8.

Layers 8 Similar earthy mound material to layer 7 but free of flints and chalk. Turf structure also clearer, particularly in extension of main cutting to centre of larger mound: suggestion that turves piled upside down (but not as clear as in Site III).

Section 1   Layers 5, 8, 9; Section 2 Layers 6, 8, 9, core of smaller mound

Layer 8 Medium brown soil, slight even scatter of chalk and flints chips, full of darker brown streaks lying horizontally near centre of mound, or tilted down towards edges, representing turves of irregular length and size. Lighter patches may have been subsoil attached to turves or dumped separately. Possibility that turves were mostly stacked grass downwards. Scatter of small charcoal scraps throughout layer, with slight concentration at base of mound just within stake circle in section 1.

In section 2, near top of layer 8, slight spread of chalk and flint chips sloping down towards ditch: just above, concentration of eight heavy flint blocks including two crude chopping tools, and potsherd.

Layer 9 Paler, compact brown soil with increased volume of small chalk chips and flints and absence of dark brown turf structure. Around base of smaller mound opposite ditch (section 2), an increase of small chalk chips and flints: probably the equivalent of more distinct annular bank in section 1, layer 5.

Layer 5 In section 1, concentration of chalk chips and flints in coarse-textured medium brown soil, occurring as bank on outside of stake circle and extending just within it. Probably equivalent of less-concentrated chalk and flints at base of layer 9 opposite ditch in section 2.

Section 2

Layer 6 At inner end of section 2, at base; edge of turf dump containing concentration of small chalk chips, in contrast to rest of layer 8 above.

Section 1 Layers 10–13, chalk covering to larger mound

Layer 10 Very loose chalk rubble, interleaved with earthy mound make-up, at base of mound.

Layer 11 Very compact almost pure white chalk lumps cemented with chalky wash into homogeneous mass.

Layer 12 Interruption of layer 11, an isolated run of chalk rubble sloping down towards centre of barrow; much looser than layer 11.

Layer 13 Looser chalk rubble mixed with pale brown loam: fairly compact but very uneven proportion of chalk to loam. Generally much more earthy than chalk covering to Site III; but more concentrated than on smaller mound of site XlX.

Section 1 Layer 10, 11, 13, 14; Section 2 Layers 11, 14, 20, chalk covering to smaller mound.

Layer 10 Lens of loose chalk rubble incorporated in layer 11 and interleaved with mound layer 8.

Layer 11 In section 1, resembled layer 11 on larger mound: very compact clean chalk lumps cemented by chalky wash into homogeneous mass. In section 2, layer 11 much less compact and homogeneous.

Layer 13 Fairly loose chalk rubble in dark earthy matrix, merging into top of layer 11.

Layer 14 Very slight scatter of small chalk chips in dark earthy matrix. In section 1, increased in chalk content sharply to become layer 13. In section 2 chalk increased slightly in volume towards outer edge of mound but chalk chips had pea-like texture.

Layer 20 (section 2 only) Isolated column of chalky material extending into earthen mound: ?animal burrow.

Section 1 Layers 15–19, filling of space between mounds

Layer 15 Crisp granular chalk rubble, distinguished by looseness from layer 11.

Layer 16 Compact pale-buff chalky wash with a few chalk lumps, preserving ancient land surface (layer 3). Flint-working floor on surface.

Layer 17 Thin lens of more granular chalk wash extending across space between mounds. Sealed working floor.

Layer 18 Fine, compact, pale buff chalky soil.

Layer 19 Darker, less compact soil heavily charged with small chalk lumps.

Section 2 Layers 21–27, filling of ditch

Layer 21 Very loose chalk rubble in bottom inner angle of ditch.

Layer 22 Chalk chips, smaller than in layer 21 and not so loose, spreading across ditch.

Layer 23 Compact pale buff chalky wash, on both sides of ditch.

Layer 24 Small chalk chips in matrix of pale brown soil, filling centre of ditch.

Layer 25 Upper ditch-fill, medium brown soil with almost no chalk, but containing lens of concentrated chalk rubble (layer 26) entering from within.

Layer 27 Loose dark brown soil mixed with small chalk, covering top of ditch and extending across berm.

SITE XX

SPTA 2229: A BOWL-BARROW AND TRACKWAY T3

SUMMARY

Site XX was apparently a cenotaph bowl-barrow. It had a chalky covering and was surrounded by a broad, flat-floored ditch of the kind associated with Phase 4 at Snail Down, the principal period of barrow-building there. The barrow was earlier than the boundary ditch, Site VI. The material constituting the spur overlying the ditch at the NE sealed late Roman coins and is more likely to have been associated with the cart-tracks skirting the barrow than with the construction of Site VI, which is considered to be Middle Iron Age.

INTRODUCTION

A bowl-barrow occupying a critical position in the layout of the post-cemetery ditch system (Sites VI/VII) and flanked by hollow ways of even later agricultural activity on the slightly higher ground to the N (Trackway T3), Site XX comprised a mound with noticeably level top, about 55ft in diameter within its ditch and just over 2ft high. There was an apparent extension to the NE, perhaps associated with a tongue of ground on the N side of the linear ditch (Site VI), which had evidently been formed by the trackway skirting the barrow and crossing Site VI. A slight dip at the centre of the mound probably represented Hoare's examination of the barrow. The site was generally free of undergrowth, being covered by healthy downland turf undisturbed by rabbits. In our interim report of 1956 (Thomas and Thomas 1956, 131, fig 1) Site XX was shown, incorrectly, as having a scraped-up mound.

Hoare investigated this barrow (his No. 11) and found '... a vacant cist' (1812, plan opp. 180, No 11, 183). Other references to Site XX include Goddard 1914, 235, Collingbourne Kingston 12; Grinsell 1957, 168; Annable 1958, 8.

The **ditch** of Site XX was examined as part of our investigation of the linear earthwork Site VI and its relationship both to this barrow and also to Trackway T3 crossing it at this point. A major cutting (sections 5, 6, Fig 18) was laid out to run N from the edge of the barrow mound to the N edge of Site VI, to study the appearance of the latter at its nearest point to the barrow. A second cutting (section 8) was laid out along, and immediately to the E of, the crest of the extension of the barrow northeastwards, referred to above; its purpose was to establish the character and date of this spur, especially its relationship to Site VI. Both these cuttings were taken to bedrock. Section 8 was extended laterally, E and W, cuttings A and F, to expose more of a deposit found at a depth of 2–2½ft in the barrow ditch (Fig 19 section 8, layer 22), which was thought at the time to represent a man-made pavement. It was not cleared below this feature. Four other cuttings B-E were dug to the same level or to chalk-surface, in order to see if the feature described above continued around the circuit of the ditch, and to trace exactly the edges of the barrow ditch for planning purposes. The work was part of a three-week session on Sites VI and VII in 1957.

DESCRIPTION

Pre-barrow Features and Settlement Remains

No features were identified which could be related to the Beaker settlement a short distance to the S. A single Beaker sherd probably originated from that source and a flaked flint axe may have had the same origin.

The Burial

Hoare found a presumably central pit beneath Site XX (above) and reported that it was empty.

The Structures

The ditch of Site XX (plans, Figs 2, 18; sections 6, 8, Fig 19; Pl 31) was flat-floored, 4¼–5¼ft wide, sides originally nearly vertical, expanding to a width of 5½–8ft at chalk surface. Its overall diameter was *c* 65ft; depth from the surface of the eroded chalk was 2–2¾ft.

The SW end of cutting 8 extended 2½ft into the **barrow mound** whose centre stood 2–3ft above bedrock. It was found to comprise fairly dense chalk rubble (layer 3), more concentrated than in the mound of Site XVII. It overlay a well-preserved ancient land surface (section 8, Fig 19, layer 2). At the inner end of the cutting this surface was nearly 6in thick, consisting of medium brown loam with a slight amount of small chalk chips scattered evenly through it.

Post-construction Events

The ditch sides and floor were covered with chalk silt, fairly loose and rubbly against the undisturbed chalk (layer 4, sections 6, 8). In section 8, one large natural flint lay on top of layer 4, near the centre of the ditch. Above this (layer 20), the primary silt remained chalky but was much more compact. In section 6, layer 21 was less compact than layer 4 below it and both were less compressed than layer 20 in section 8. The upper part of the ditch in section 8 was filled with a compact buff loam (layer 23) which had a distinct concentration of natural flints at its base, mixed with a variety of potsherds, some late Roman coins and other finds, which followed the circuit of the ditch. This accumulation of dense loam may have caused the compression of layers 4 and 20, beneath. In section 6, layer 23 occupied an equivalent position but it was much thinner and less dense. Above layer 23 in section 8 there occurred a distinctive spread of pure chalk rubble, containing a similar scatter of associated finds. This layer 26, with 27 above it, formed the main part of the spur projecting NE from the edge of the barrow mound and it died out to the E and W of section 8; it was absent in section 6. Layer 26 comprised fairly pure, compact chalk with some looser chalk rubble in places. Layer 27 contained much small chalk rubble but it was less compact, containing a higher proportion of medium brown loam and modern rootlets. On the inside of the ditch, there was a deposit of brown soil mixed with small chips of chalk, layer 25, which merged gradually with layer 23 below it but was in marked contrast to the barrow mound material (layer 3) and with the dump of chalk forming the spur (layer 26, 27), which appeared to overlie it. Layers 26 and 27 were not represented in section 6 since that cutting lay clear of the slight spur represented by these layers. Instead, the usual slowly accumulating upper layers found in most of the Snail Down barrows were recorded. A light brown chalky loam, layer 23, covered the quick silt (4 and 21), but here it was more dense than in the ditches of the other excavated barrows; looser brown flinty soil, layer 24, occurred above it, with layer 8, dark brown soil with some chalk chips, sealing the top of the ditch and extending across the ditch of Site VI immediately to the N.

At the base of layer 23 in section 8, as indicated above, there occurred a concentration of flint nodules and some bones and potsherds which was exposed horizontally along a 24ft run of the barrow ditch in the cuttings around the E half of the barrow. At first thought to be a man-made feature, it became clear in due course that this represented a natural accumulation which had formed in the angle of rest of the lower layers of silt in the ditch. Among the animal bones in this material were fragments of a human skull, teeth and other parts of a skeleton (Section A, Inhumation 9). Their place within this complex part of Snail Down's history could not be shown.

The objects (pottery, section C, C120, Section E, *passim*, inc E6–E8, E12–E13, Section F, *passim*, inc F19; worked flint, Section G; worked bone, Section H, H2, H5, H6; Roman coins, Section P, P1–P12) recovered from the cuttings across the ditch of Site XX, particularly from cutting 8 with its extensions and from the soundings around the S arc of the ditch, included virtually every period represented on Snail Down. Beaker sherds, Late Neolithic/Early Bronze Age flints and sherds of Middle Bronze Age Ware and Late Bronze Age Plain Ware occurred at the base of layer 22, among an accumulation of natural flints along the centre line of the ditch. The pale buff loam (layer 23) between these flints and the upper chalky rubble, layers 26, 27, yielded mainly Late Bronze Age Plain Ware and flint implements including a flaked axe, with Romano-British sherds, 4th century AD coins and Iron Age wares in its upper half.

REMARKS

Such a small-scale excavation, with a limited objective, could not be expected to shed much light on the nature of the barrow itself. It was clear, however, that from the relatively large surrounding ditch enough chalk could have been extracted to provide a fairly dense white covering to the mound. Greater effort had been made to whiten Site XX than had been made on Site XVII, whose ditch was narrower and shallower (Fig 30). At least the edge of the very chalky mound – whose core was not reached by our cutting – had inhibited earthworm activity in the ancient soil preserved beneath it and this was distinct and relatively unsorted.

The ditch exhibited a silting process which resembled that in most of the barrow ditches at Snail Down, early weathering filling its lower corners, with clean chalk rubble extending across the floor. However, the compact fine buff loam of section 8, layer 23 and section 6, layer 23 was only readily matched in the main filling of Site VI, the boundary ditch skirting this barrow. The excavation and subsequent laboratory analysis failed to explain the source of this very fine-grained, compact loam but it seems possible that wind action was in part responsible. A change in climate could have occurred between the construction of barrows and that of the boundary system but if this accounts for the different sort of filling of Site VI, it is hard to believe that Site XX was also much later in date than the other barrows in the cemetery. The problem can only be solved by further work in this interesting area of the Down. The upper filling contained a higher concentration of artefacts than in any comparable cutting elsewhere on the Down because of its proximity to Site VI and the presumed Romano-British cart tracks (T3) which skirted Site XX. The spur, or dump of chalky material which was heaped across the barrow ditch at the NE, must have been related to these tracks rather than to Site VI, sealing as it did material including coins dated to the late 4th century AD (Section P). It could, for example, have been the product of repeated scraping and removal of mud from the cart tracks which crossed Site VI at this point. The presence of three late Roman coins so noticeably lower in the ditch filling than the other coins, occurring well down in layer 23, can best be explained by earthworm activity. It seems unlikely that the mud-scraping activity which we have related to the track T3 and which resulted in layers 26 and 27 can have been distinctly later than the 4th century AD date of these coins.

There can be little doubt that Site XX was earlier in date than Site VI. As we have already suggested, Site XX seemed to have been used as a marker by those digging Site VI, forming a lay-out point for their boundary ditch. Where the two virtually coincided, Site VI curved N slightly to avoid an intersection with the ditch of Site XX. About 3½ft separated the ditches (Pl 31, Figs 18, 19), a space too narrow to take the bank of spoil derived from Site VI and which everywhere else was heaped along its S edge. Our excavations failed to reveal where the spoil from Site VI was piled in the area of the barrow: not, almost certainly, on the barrow mound itself; nor across the barrow ditch to form the spur which we examined. That sealed Roman coins and was clearly too late by over half a millennium for an acceptable date for Site VI. Possibly the Site VI ditch spoil was spread less carefully to the E and W of Site XX, to become dispersed and no longer evident by the passage of vehicles along each branch of T3, where it cut across Site VI here. The dump of chalk and soil examined in section 4 (Fig 19) may have been derived in part from the length of Site VI ditch that skirted Site XX.

Hoare's description of the burial features preserved beneath the mound of Site XX was less equivocal than it had been for other barrows that he examined on Snail Down. Site XX has to be regarded as a genuine cenotaph, its central grave pit found; and found to be empty. The cenotaph barrows at Snail Down are discussed in Part 3.

Figure 19
Detailed description of layers

Section 6   Layers 4, 21, 23, 24, 8, filling of barrow ditch away from overlying spur

Layer 4 Fairly loose clean chalk rubble covering floor and filling lower corners of ditch.

Layer 21 Clean chalky rubble, looser than layer 4 below.

Layer 23 Pale, fairly compact brown soil, whitened by fine chalk content. Much looser along centre of ditch where flint content increased. Generally resembled layer 23 in Section 8 but a thinner deposit.

Layer 24 Slightly darker brown soil, loose and with high natural content of unworked flints.

Layer 8 Dark brown soil speckled with chalk chips mixed with flints.

Section 8   Layers 1–3, mound

Layer 1 Weathered chalk, nearly 1ft thick on outer side of barrow ditch, much thinner beneath ancient land surface sealed by barrow mound.

Layer 2 Ancient land surface beneath barrow mound. Medium brown soil, very thin scatter of small flint and chalk chips throughout. Upper surface marked clearly by mound rubble dumped upon it.

Layer 3 Mound of barrow, concentrated chalk rubble mixed with small amount of pale brown soil.

Layers 4, 20, 21–23, 25–27, ditch filling and superimposed spur.

Layer 4 Silt in corners and on floor of ditch; fairly loose, clean chalk rubble without soil.

Layer 20 Clean chalk rubble, more compressed than layer 4 and mixed with less rubbly chalk.

Layer 21 Fine chalk, less compressed than layer 20 and lacking rubble.

Layer 22 Concentration of unworked flints, with some artefacts, at angle of rest of primary silt (layers 20, 21), near centre of ditch: a natural feature.

Layer 23 Compact pale buff chalky loam filling upper part of ditch. Slightly more chalky in appearance on inner side, perhaps deriving from rubble of mound. A few small chalk and flint chips scattered throughout.

Layer 26 Concentrated layer of chalk rubble in a chalky matrix, sealing much of layer 23 below. Some looser rubble in places.

Layer 27 More diffuse chalky rubble in a medium brown loamy matrix.

Layer 25 Medium brown, fairly loose loam mixed with chalk chips, underlying layers 26 and 27 and merging imperceptibly with top of layer 23.

SITE XXI

SPTA 2248: A BOWL-BARROW

SUMMARY

Site XXI was established as a bowl-barrow by the discovery of a surrounding ditch. Noticeably narrow and deep, its specialised form linked Site XXI with Site XVIII. A slight linear ditch found to run between Sites XXI and VI was probably broadly contemporary with the latter. It is suggested that this feature may have been dug to ensure protection of the barrow when the adjacent boundary earthwork was constructed.

INTRODUCTION

Site XXI was a bowl-barrow, its ditch not evident prior to excavation. The barrow mound, which was some 60ft in diameter and 2–3ft high, had been damaged by rabbits and supported a growth of tussocky grass and small bushes that obscured its features.

The mound was examined by Hoare and numbered 16 on his plan: '... in no. 16 was a deposit of burned bones within a cist' (1812, plan opp. 180, No 16, 183). Other references to Site XXI are the following: Goddard 1914, 235, Collingbourne Kingston 16; Grinsell 1957, 168; Annable 1958, 8.

One trench was dug northwards from the presumed edge of the barrow to cross Site VI, whose bank lay about 17ft N of the edge of the barrow at this point. An additional cutting and an extension at right angles to the main cutting were made to examine the small ditch which was found to lie between the bank of Site VI and the ditch of Site XXI. The work lasted four days and was carried out by five volunteers.

The purpose of this limited exploration was to compare the relationship of Site VI to Site XXI, following our examination of the linear earthwork as it ran past Site XX, some 190yds to the W. At the latter near-intersection, the barrow and linear ditches were so close that there had not been room to continue the bank of Site VI between them, and our excavation there never resolved what the builders of Site VI had done with the bank material in that area. By Site XXI, there was sufficient space for a bank and it differed little in width and structure from the bank of Site VI elsewhere on Snail Down. We also wished to check the presence of a ditch around the barrow and, if it proved to exist, its shape.

DESCRIPTION

Pre-barrow Features and Settlement Remains

This limited examination revealed no trace of the Beaker settlement to the SW nor of any other earlier features. The roughed-out flint axe from low in the ditch of Site VI here may have been associated with the Beaker, or even pre-Beaker activity on Snail Down. Two Neolithic sherds from topsoil might have had the same origin.

Section 1 did not extend far enough to reveal a land surface beneath the barrow mound. Under the bank of Site VI an ancient surface was uncovered (Fig 35, section 1). It comprised almost chalk-free loam (layer 2) overlying weathered natural chalk (layer 1).

The Burial

Hoare reported a burial after cremation in a pit, presumed to have been central. It was not uncovered in 1957.

The Structures

The **barrow ditch** (plans, Figs 2, 35; section, Fig 35) had a depth of 3½ft from the present-day chalk surface. Its floor, noticeably flat in the short length exposed by excavation, was 1¼ft wide. The width of the ditch at chalk surface measured 8½ft. However, 3½ft of this was accounted for by the very gradual slope of the inner edge before it dipped steeply – like the outer wall – to its floor. By projecting upwards the line of the lower walls of the ditch, where their original angles of slope had been protected by primary weathering material, it was possible to calculate an original width, at chalk surface, of *c* 2½ft for this feature.

No artefacts were recovered from the barrow structure during the excavation of Site XXI.

Post-construction Events

The lower half of the ditch was filled with loose chalk rubble (layer 6). The upper filling comprised progressively paler loam mixed with chalk chips (layers 7–9).

Across the space between the ditch of Site XXI and the bank of Site VI, where the two sites lay closest to each other, ran a linear feature here described as a **marker-ditch** (plan, section, Fig 35). In section 1 its width, at chalk surface, was almost 2½ft and its depth *c* 1ft. Here its profile was U-shaped, both walls originally not far from the vertical.

The course of the marker-ditch was followed for a distance of 18½ft by extending section 1 NE and by digging

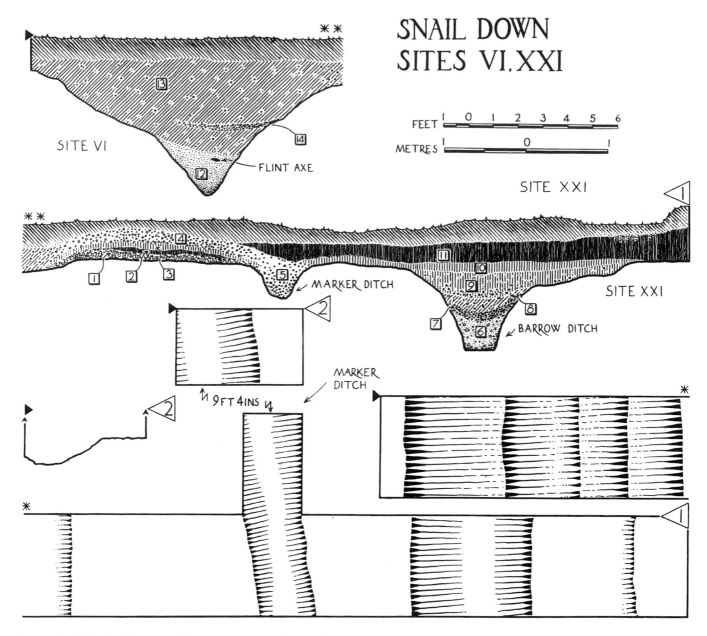

Fig 35   Sites VI, XXI (Fig 2 for location), plan, sections 1,2 (see also Fig 19).

another cutting a further 9ft to the NE (Fig 35, section 2). The ditch became a little shallower and its profile much more open, the further it extended from the point of near-contact between Sites VI and XXI.

The **ditch** of Site VI here as elsewhere in the excavations (Figs 19, 20; Pls 29–31) was V-shaped, with a maximum depth from chalk surface of about 5ft. Its inner wall showed a distinct break in the angle of slope at a point almost 22ft above its floor. This break in angle, above which the outer side of the ditch widened sharply, coincided with the surface of the lowest silt in the ditch.

The **bank** of Site VI occupied the space of about 92t which lay between the marker-ditch just described and the V-shaped ditch of Site VI. Its construction was exactly the same as that revealed in other sections across this great boundary earthwork (Figs 19, 20). On the ancient land-surface lay a spread of slightly more chalky, yellower soil followed by pure chalk rubble (layers 3, 4).

Southwards, this chalk rubble ran down across the N wall of the marker-ditch separating it from Site XXI and on to its floor. Northwards the rubble of the Site VI bank gradually spread and merged with the upper pale buff filling of its ditch.

The filling of the ditch comprised (layer 12) primary, fairly loose buff loam mixed with chalk lumps, which were derived mainly from the outer side. Just below its surface lay a small chipped flint axe roughout (Fig 35; Section G, G16, Fig 51). Above this the rest of the ditch was filled uniformly with compact pale buff loam (layer 13) containing a slight, even scatter of small chalk chips, increasing towards the top where some of the rubble from the bank had spread into the ditch. One thin lens of pure chalk (layer 14) occurred low down in this main ditch filling, derived from its inner wall.

The marker-ditch was filled with fairly compact, pale brown loam heavily charged with chalk chips (layer

5); these became noticeably more rubbly towards the bottom and appeared to derive from the chalky rubble and loam forming the core of the bank of Site VI (layer 4). Along the N side of the marker-ditch, the material forming the ancient land surface beneath the bank of Site VI (layers 2, 3) merged imperceptibly with the upper, more loamy filling of that ditch.

A soil had formed across the top of the barrow ditch (layer 10), which was preserved by a fresh dumping of soil, layer 11, presumably the work of those digging out rabbits which seem to have infested this barrow for some years. Layer 11 was a deep brown soil with only a little chalk, while below it layer 10 was almost as dark but contained many small chalk chips. The modern turf and the humus which covered the space between the barrow mound and the bank of Site VI were irregular in thickness, the activity of rabbits and their catchers evidently continuing to the present day.

The soil profile represented by layers 10 and 11 ran over the inner tail of the bank of Site VI but clearly the rabbit colony had never extended into Site VI.

REMARKS

The filling in the ditch of the bowl-barrow, Site XXI, offered the kind of profile to be expected of a narrow, almost vertical-sided ditch which had been left to silt up naturally. The lower half contained a deposit mainly of chalk which must have fallen from its upper walls fairly soon after the barrow had been built. Its upper fill was more compact and earthy, product of much slower weathering.

The chief interest of this ditch, apart from establishing that Site XXI was a bowl-barrow, lay in its close resemblance to the slot-like, but deeper ditch of Site XVIII, lying 400ft due S (Fig 32; Pl 52). As discussed below (Part 3), there may be some grounds for suggesting that both barrows had been built early in the history of the Snail Down cemetery.

The discovery of what we have termed the marker-ditch provided us with a feature apparently broadly contemporary with Site VI; from its occurrence between the earthwork and the barrow, we conjecture that it was related to both, acting perhaps as some form of protection of one from the building of the other, in the way that the little ditch around the Heelstone at Stonehenge may have been dug to indicate the necessity for respect and preservation during construction of the later ditches of the Avenue (Atkinson 1956, 66–67).

The filling of the marker-ditch clearly derived from its N side and, where the two features were at their closest, the rubbly earth forming the bank of Site VI had run without a break into the marker-ditch. The latter must have been open and almost unsilted when Site VI was being built.

Our work at Sites XX and XXI showed in two different ways how deep was the concern of those who built the boundary ditch to avoid impinging upon these outliers of the barrow cemetery. Along the N side of Enclosure A (Fig 2) this ditch and bank, for some reason, ran particularly close to the barrows. The ditch only just avoided Site XX and the bank at that point had to be placed elsewhere. Certainly, the builders of Site VI did not put the spoil from their ditch on the mound of Site XX or across the line of its ditch. The same regard was shown for Site XXI, where a guideline in the form of a length of ditch was dug to keep the bank of Site VI from spreading across to the barrow ditch.

In profile, the noticeable break in slope of the upper walls of the ditch of Site VI, which coincides with a slide of chalky rubble (Fig 35, layer 14) suggests the possibility that the boundary ditch may have been cleared out in part and given a shallow, U-profile, quite unlike its original V-form. In this it resembles possible changes in profile of Site VI elsewhere along its northern side, for example sections 10 and 13 (Figs 2, 20). It has already been shown that the original profile of this boundary ditch, referred to as Site VII (Fig 20, sections 11, 12, 14), had been flat floored, then re-dug the same, before being given its striking V-profile (Site VI). Clearly, Site VI, Enclosure A (Fig 2) enjoyed a long life and re-diggings are to be expected, even if the original profile became thereby totally altered.

Site XXI remained intact until relatively recent times, when its mound was thoroughly despoiled by people digging for rabbits; layer 11 must represent their activities, covered eventually by a modern soil and downland turf.

Figure 35
Detailed description of layers

Section 1   Layers 6–11, ditch-filling of Site XXI
Layer 6 Loose rubbly chalk with some finer chalk, filling lower half of ditch.
Layer 7 Compact chalk, the rubble set in a fine chalk matrix.
Layer 8 Dark brown soil with even scatter of chalk chips, filling upper part of barrow ditch.
Layer 9 Paler brown or buff soil, compact in upper part, containing more chalk chips in lowest 4in along full width of ditch. Upper part extended inwards to fill the shallow, uppermost ditch where its inner edge sloped up to chalk surface very gradually.
Layer 10 Dark brown, almost black, soil, fairly loose and lacking chalk chips, sealing barrow ditch and extending over inner tail of bank of Site VI.
Layer 11 Deep brown soil with thin scatter of small chalk chips. Preserved layer 10; possibly 19th-20th century product of rabbitting.

Layers 1–5, bank of Site VI and filling of marker-ditch.
Layer 1 Weathered natural chalk surface beneath bank of Site VI.
Layer 2 Ancient land surface, thin layer of pale brown soil on weathered bedrock. Contained a small quantity of scattered chalk and flint chips.
Layer 3 Slightly darker brown soil mixed with a little scattered chalk, merging gradually with layer 2 below.
Layer 4 Rubbly chalk in a matrix of finer chalk and some pale buff soil.

Layer 5 Filling of marker-ditch: in its lower half, rather more chalk-rubbly soil, becoming finer and more compact chalky soil in upper half. Along N upper edge (ie nearer side to bank of Site VI), layers 2–4 of bank of latter merged gradually with the marker-ditch filling.

Layers 12–14, filling of ditch of Site VI

Layer 12 Fairly loose buff soil mixed with chalk lumps and natural flints, the latter (including a small flint roughout axe-head), concentrating at the top of the layer and following the long axis of the ditch, on its S half.

Layer 13 Uniform, compact, pale-buff soil filling upper half of ditch. Fairly even scatter of small chalk throughout.

Layers 14 Lens of almost pure chalk, entering the ditch from its S side, at a low level of layer 13 and not extending across ditch.

SITE XXII

SPTA 2269: A BELL-BARROW WITH EXTRA MOUND

SUMMARY

A small and damaged oval mound located on the berm of a bell-barrow, on its N side, was proved to be ancient, probably contemporary with the main barrow mound. The crouched skeleton of a young male of the Early Bronze Age, wearing some beads including a sea shell, had been inserted into it as a secondary burial. Bone from the skeleton yielded a radio-carbon determination of 3485 ± 110 BP.

INTRODUCTION

Site XXII is a bell-barrow of some grandeur, occupying what was probably a crucial position at one end of the eastern of the two alignments of barrows which constitute the essential layout of the cemetery. It had a mound 85ft in diameter and (1951) *c* 13ft high, which was separated from its surrounding ditch by a berm *c* 22ft wide. The ditch averaged 22ft in width at modern ground surface and sank about 2ft along its central line. A main tank route crossed the barrow along a near N/S axis and another, E/W, together with Trackway T1, has damaged the N arc of its ditch where there was a space between this barrow and Site XIX (Figs 2, 33).

On the N side, a small elongated mound apparently measuring about 30 × 19ft (it had been damaged by military vehicles) and 1–2ft high occupied almost the whole width of the berm. Probably it had originally been placed symmetrically between the base of the mound and the inner edge of the ditch. By 1957 it was damaged and distorted by the tank tracks which traversed the barrow; its N edge had merged with the barrow ditch at the point where they lay closest. When L V Grinsell recorded his examination of Site XXII in 1951, he described the mound on the berm as circular, 18ft in diameter, 2½ft high and damaged by tanks (1957, 209). Allen's air photograph (Ashmolean Museum SD 1085) of 1933 suggests strongly that the small mound was circular; SD 1087 of 1939 (Pl 1) supports that belief. The four mounds of Sites XIX and XXII are in alignment (Fig 33).

On the W side, a quarry pit about 35ft in diameter impinged upon the outer edge of the ditch. On the N side, almost opposite the mound on the berm referred to above, a similar, but slightly smaller pit also interrupted the outer ditch edge and extended across more of the silt-filled ditch than the pit to the W. Allen's air photographs of 1933 and 1939 make it clear that whereas the W pit looked long-dug in 1933, the N pit did not exist in 1933 or 1939. It must have been made during the nineteen forties and has itself suffered from the E/W tank route that remained in use until about 1950. Trackway T1 was well-established by 1933.

Site XXII was covered by rich downland turf except where military vehicles had worn a broad track across the whole monument, penetrating its covering of white chalk rubble.

Site XXII was examined by Hoare (1812, plan opp. 180, No 25, 185), who commented on the result of his work as follows:

> 'No 25. This *tumulus*, from its superior size, might justly be denominated the King Barrow. It is finely fossed round, and measures from its summit to the floor, thirteen feet; yet though we made a very large section in it, and undermined it on every side, we could discover no symptom whatever of burial … '.

Other publications include: Goddard 1914, 230 Collingbourne Ducis 5; Grinsell 1934, 219; *ibid* 1941, 80, fig 2; *ibid* 1957, 209; Annable 1958, 8; Thomas 1976, 230, fig 56.

For recording and planning purposes, it was necessary to test the relationship of the small elongated mound on the N side of the berm to the quarry pit which lay roughly opposite it on the outer side of the ditch: on field evidence, it was at least possible that the mound – like the quarry pit – was recent, especially since Hoare made no mention of it. A trench 40 x 4ft was laid out, roughly following the central line of the tank route crossing the barrow and including this mound. It was excavated to bedrock but it was found that the barrow structure had been so crushed and distorted by the military track that no man-made features could be distinguished. The sections exposed in the trench sides were too damaged to draw. In pursuit of the same objective a rectangular cutting with a short extension to part of the W side, was dug, therefore, on the E side of the route and just beyond it, exposing an area close to the centre of the elongated mound. The N half of this area, including the extension, was cleared to bedrock: the S half was excavated to the ancient land surface, where evidence was uncovered which enabled us to achieve our objective without digging further.

The work lasted three days at the end of the season, four volunteers taking part under Bret Guthrie.

DESCRIPTION

Pre-barrow Features and Settlement Remains

The ancient land surface comprised slightly greasy brown soil almost devoid of flints and chalk (Fig 36, section 1,

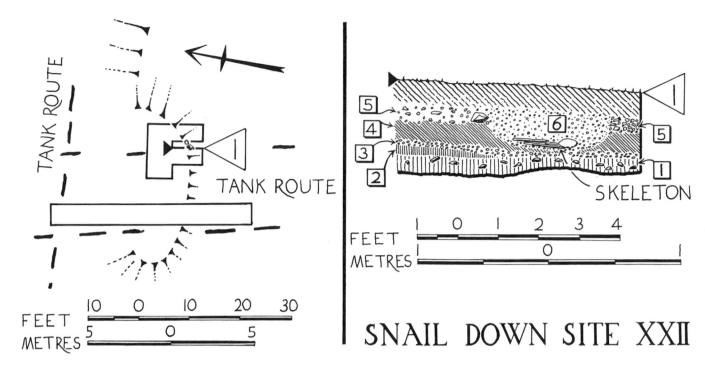

Fig 36   Site XXII, plan of Early Bronze Age burial, Inhumation 2, and section 1.

layer 2), which overlay a deeper deposit of pale brown soil containing a fairly heavy, even scatter of natural flints and chalk chips (layer 1).

No traces were found of earlier settlement remains or of natural features.

The Structure

A small oval mound (plans, Figs 2, 33, 36; section, Fig 36) had been placed upon the ancient land surface covering the berm of the bell-barrow. The source of its make-up was not established. It comprised, first, a thin scatter of small chalk chips (layer 3). Then came compact buff soil mixed with some chalk and flints (layer 4), about 6in thick, with a similar thickness of fairly dense chalk rubble overlying it and originally forming a whitened covering (layers 5). Above that was modern turf and topsoil.

Post-construction Events

The Secondary Burial (Section, Fig 36; Pls 56, 57; beads, Section K, K9–K11, Figs 37, 54; anatomical report, Section A, Inhumation 2, Pls 58, 59)

At the SE edge of the mound, an almost vertical-sided **oval pit** had been dug through layers 5 and 4 to the surface of layer 3 (Fig 36, section 1). Its fill, layer 6, consisted of a mixture of chalk rubble and buff soil which was paler and more chalky than layer 4 of the mound, which it penetrated. The pit contained the **tightly contracted corpse of a youth**, probably male. The body had been placed on its right side, the left shoulder and that half of the body extending just forward of the right. The head was to the N and the skeleton's main axis aligned NE/SW. The skull

was tilted back slightly, as if looking upward as well as forward. The lower jaw had fallen open a little and been displaced back slightly as well as towards one side.

The body had been laid to rest with its back straight, upper arms down in front of the chest then bent at the elbows so that both hands were before the face, left placed over right. The finger bones had loosened and fallen away before a detailed record of the hands' precise relationship to each other could be made. The thighs were drawn up sharply so that the knees lay opposite the chest. The left knee covered and almost touched the left elbow; the right knee was immediately forward of the left. The shins had been directed downwards again and pressed close together. Feet were in direct contact with the pelvic region, in such a position that the left foot underlay the right, its heel below the ankle of the latter. The right foot pointed upwards with its long axis so nearly parallel to its tibia that force might have been necessary to establish it at that angle. The left foot, below it, had been placed at an angle of over 90° to its shin (Pls 56, 57).

Beneath the right side of the lower jaw, three beads were found in a line and not quite touching each other (Fig 37; Section K, K9–K11, Fig 54). Nearest to the vertebrae, its pierced umbo facing the spine, lay a cockle shell with its inner surface on the ground. Beyond it was a cylindrical amber bead with an oval bead of the same material beyond that. These beads may have constituted a token necklace, their weight just sufficient to cause them to hang down as the corpse was manoeuvred into position over its grave and so come to rest beneath the right side of the face.

The bones of this sixteen to eighteen-year-old were well-preserved, suggesting normal good health (Section A, Inhumation 2). Yet there was one exception. The lad was suffering from a tumour of a kind known as a *haemangioma*, in the region of the left eye. Not malignant, it was

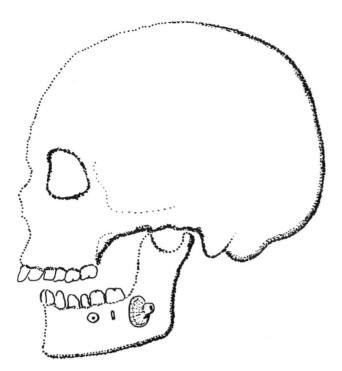

Fig 37 Site XXII, skull of Inhumation 2, showing position of beads (1-r, K9, K10, K11) lying between lower right jaw and land surface. Scale of beads exaggerated.

unlikely to have been the cause of death: but for a few years before he died the youth would have suffered, at the least, from impaired vision through that eye (Pls 58, 59). Some three-and-a-half millennia after his burial, he passed into medical history by becoming the earliest person on record to have suffered from that form of disease.

One femur of the skeleton was submitted to Oxford for accelerator dating, with the following result:

OxA-4211 3485 ± 110 BP; cal BC 1950–1680 (1 sigma); cal BC 2134–1520 (2 sigma).

This result, which indicates an Early Bronze Age period for the burial, is considered further in Section T.

REMARKS

The oval mound on the berm of the bell-barrow preserved a land surface which appeared ancient. There was a clear visual and textural difference between it and land surfaces of relatively recent date at Snail Down that have been accidentally preserved by being buried. There was unlikely to be any link, therefore, between the oval mound and the quarry pit close to it, on the opposite side of the barrow ditch.

If, then, ancient, the oval mound can be assumed to be broadly contemporary with the bell-barrow, though there was no evidence to show whether a lengthy period of time had elapsed between construction of the main mound and ditch and the raising of this small oval feature upon its berm.

That the oval mound covered a land surface on the berm gave confirmatory evidence for the supposition, at Site III for example, that the berms of most bell-barrows

were not cleared to bedrock as part of the barrow-building operation, but were left as green annular rings, emphasising the contrast between the whitened mounds and their quarry ditches and the surrounding downland.

It was clear from the excavation, and confirmed in the drawn section and photograph (Fig 36; Pl 56) that this juvenile inhumation had been inserted into the oval mound, thus constituting a secondary not a primary burial. The skeleton lay in a pit at the edge of the mound, whose filling contrasted clearly with the upper chalky material and the brown soil below, into which it had been dug: there was no doubt that the burial of the corpse was not the reason for which the mound had been raised. That reason we failed to identify.

Apart from the later Bronze Age inhumations added to Sites V and XV (Section A, Inhumations 3–8) and the fetus from Site II (*ibid*, Inhumation 1), the skeleton from Site XXII was the only one to be found at Snail Down during the campaigns of 1953–1957 and, with the foetus, the only certain Early Bronze Age one so far on record from the cemetery. With such a clear preference for cremation here, the presence of just one near-adult inhumation suggests that some special circumstance surrounded its burial. The tightly flexed attitude of the skeleton indicated that the corpse may have been bound in that position, or had been placed there in a tight-fitting container which kept the limbs close to the trunk. Such a circumstance could support the proposal that this particular burial had been made by people not otherwise associated with the Snail Down cemetery, a separate group on the move through the area, perhaps, and overtaken by the death of one of their young people. The necklace he wore, with its sea-shell pendant, gave an indication that they may have been strangers here. That they inhumed the boy at a period when cremation was becoming the normal rite, may also suggest that they were on the move and had not the time to devote to burning him.

During the excavation of the skeleton no evidence was found to suggest that any of the bones were out of position or ends of limbs out of joint: but the tightly contracted attitude of arms and legs was noteworthy. Recent discoveries of Bronze Age inhumations beneath barrows in Wiltshire have emphasised the contrast in disposition of an unburnt corpse between fully extended (rare), lightly flexed, crouched in an attitude of sleep or tightly contracted like that from XXII. At barrow G30 among the Cursus group at Stonehenge, the excavator recorded an equally tightly trussed, youthful skeleton buried in the primary silt of the bell-barrow's ditch (Christie 1963, pl III). Ashbee recovered a skeleton similarly treated beneath barrow G51 within the same group; its compactness was more extreme, however, since its feet had been ruptured to force it into the grave (Ashbee 1978, 17, fig 9, pl 6). Two of the inhumations found at Crichel Down (Dorset) were noticeably tightly trussed. The limbs of the corpse from barrow 5 had been pulled together until a number of joints had been disarticulated, though perhaps made easier because of decomposition; a corpse had also been pressed into a tightly fitting grave pit beneath barrow 9 (Piggott and Piggott 1944, 68–69, pl VIIIa; 72, pl Xa). The almost violent handling of corpses to meet the needs of transport or disposal below ground in pits of pre-ordained size was evidently accepted burial practice.

The orientation of the skeleton, whose head lay at the NE and feet at the SW, followed common practice among earlier Bronze Age people. This has been demonstrated clearly by Burl (1987, 166, table 14), who showed that while all cardinal points had their followers among communities at this time, most heads went to the N, NE or E when inhumation was being practised. Inter-cardinal points other than NE tended to be avoided.

Apart from Snail Down Site XXII, no bell-barrow has yet been found upon whose berm a burial mound of some kind had been added, either as part of the original design or subsequently. For bell-barrows to have been built double where two mounds were enclosed within one ditch as an original design, was common enough (Grinsell 1941, 80, fig 2). Double bell-barrows existed with identical mounds and with mounds differing considerably in size. Snail Down Site XIX was an example of the latter. Excavation has revealed that while some double bell-barrow ditches were continuous and symmetrical in plan (Snail Down XIX), others were not because the bell-barrow mounds were of two periods or represented a change of mind by the builders, eg Radley, 4/4A (Oxon: Williams 1948, 8–9). Bowl-barrow builders chose from the same set of options when designing a double version of their type of burial mound. The excavation of Snail Down XXII failed to reveal by how great a span of time the building of the main mound and the small, perhaps oval one, heaped up on the N arc of its berm, had been separated. There was no reason why they should not have been contemporary. Nor was there any evidence to show that the small mound had been originally for burial purposes. The skeleton found in it was intrusive and not at all central.

Perhaps the closest structural parallel to this double bell-barrow is to be seen at the Winterbourne Stoke Cross-Roads cemetery, where the ditch of bell-barrow Winterbourne Stoke G4 is overlapped by a pond-barrow G3a (well-shown, for example, in RCHME 1979, pls 2, 3). Here, the pond-barrow has an overall diameter of nearly seventy feet, much too large to have occupied the twenty-one-foot berm of the bell-barrow. At Winterbourne Stoke, the pond-barrow was evidently later than the bell-barrow with which its builders made deliberate contact. The circumstances surrounding the construction of the small mound at Snail Down XXII seem to have been quite different.

Figure 36
Detailed description of layers

Section 1 Layers 1–5, make-up of mound and ancient land surface.

Layer 1 Medium brown soil with fairly heavy even scatter of flints and chalk chips, forming ancient subsoil. Overlying weathered chalk.

Layer 2 Slightly darker brown soil, greasy in texture and lacking flints or chalk, becoming less definite towards the edge of the oval mound.

Layer 3 Thin concentrated spread of more chalky soil across layers 1 and 2.

Layer 4 Fairly compact buff soil containing an uneven scatter of flints and chalk chips, forming core of oval mound.

Layer 5 Fairly dense layer of chalky soil with some flints, covering oval mound beneath modern topsoil but interrupted by patches of less chalky soil.

Layer 6 Filling of inhumation pit

Layer 6 Buff loam with chalk and flints, paler than layer 4, more chalky than layer 5. Represents the filling of a pit containing an inhumation, dug through layers 5 and 4. Ran out just beyond head of skeleton. Here the SE edge of the mound became almost free of chalk.

Plate 1   Snail Down, looking N, 4 June 1939. The first tank tracks visible traversing the main barrows (G W G Allen: Archive No 1087; Copyright the Ashmolean Museum, Oxford).

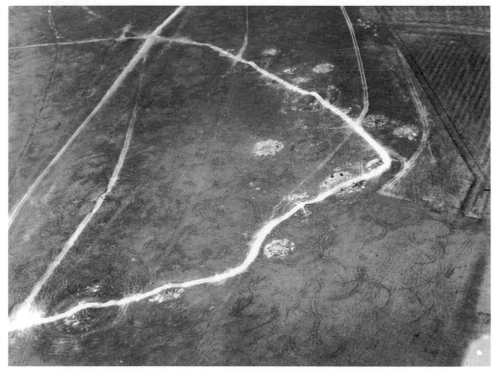

Plate 2   Snail Down, about 1950, looking W. Tank damage at its maximum. Note also smaller barrows (eight visible) heavily damaged by rabbit burrows (English Heritage).

Plate 3   Site VIII, the great bell-barrow, looking W. Its E-W surface axis ruined by tank traverse (Nicholas Thomas).

Plate 4   Site I, looking NW. The disc-barrow's encircling ditch (Maurice Cookson).

Plate 5   Site I, E face, N/S baulk. The ditch filling, looking W (ranging rod shown in Snail Down photographs is 6ft long) (Nicholas Thomas).

Plate 6   Site I, SW quadrant. Natural bedding and layering of chalk exposed in lower wall and floor of ditch. Scale, inches (Nicholas Thomas).

Plate 7   Site I, filling of pit beneath eccentric mound, showing robbing pits. Looking NE (Maurice Cookson).

Plate 8A   Site I, SW quadrant, looking S. Accumulation of weathered chalk in ditch by August 1957. This Site remains open (see Section V) (Nicholas Thomas).

Plate 8B   The same view, 1994 (Nicholas Thomas).

Plate 9   Site II, looking S to Sidbury Hill. Right-hand figure (Charles Thomas) kneels beside central burial pit (Maurice Cookson).

Plate 10   Site II, central burial pit with Hoare's backfilling sectioned. Scale, inches/centimetres. Looking W (Maurice Cookson).

Plate 11   Site II, burial pit in SW quadrant after excavation. Scale in lower pit in inches (Nicholas Thomas).

Plate 12 Site II, SE quadrant, inverted Food Vessel D3 against N/S baulk, looking W. Ring-building of vessel indicated where parts of wall and base have become detached. Scale, inches (Nicholas Thomas).

Plate 13 Site III, looking S to Sidbury Hill, baulks remaining. Figures stand on berm. Chalk covering of mound evident (Maurice Cookson).

Plate 14   Site III, W half, E/W baulk, S face. Hoare's trench cutting through earth mound and central turf heap to locate central grave. Chalk covering here almost removed by tanks (Maurice Cookson).

Plate 15   Site III, S half, N/S baulk, W face. Mound make-up with chalk covering. Note concentration of flints along base of ancient land surface (Nicholas Thomas).

Plate 16   Site III, N half, N/S baulk, E face. Interleaving of chalk and earth; Hoare's trench visible to left. Funeral pyre appearing on lower level of ancient ground surface (below highest recording peg) (Maurice Cookson).

Plate 17   Site III, burial area exposed, looking S. Pole separates pyre logs from cremation pit (earth spoil beyond, chalky spoil near pole). Isolated timbers top left. See Figure 12 (Nicholas Thomas).

Plate 18   Site III, main group of oak pyre logs on ancient land surface. Scale, inches. Looking W. See Figure 12 (Nicholas Thomas).

Plate 19   Site III, Secondary Burial 1, its flint-covered urn (D10) revealed between tank tracks. Scale, inches/centimetres. Looking NE (Nicholas Thomas).

Plate 20   Site III, Secondary Burial 1 (Cremation 8), crushed Collared Urn in pit: solid chalk excavated to reveal pit shape. Scale, inches/centimetres. Looking NW (Nicholas Thomas).

Plate 21   Site III, Secondary Burial 1 (Cremation 8), pit cleared to reveal depression carved into floor to receive base of Urn. Scale, inches (Nicholas Thomas).

Plate 22   Site III, Secondary Burial 2 (Cremation 9), looking N. Traces of scattered flint cairn to left (Nicholas Thomas).

Plate 23   Site III, Secondary Burial 2 (Cremation 9), looking S. Collared Urn (D11) steadied in pit by Accessory Vessels D12, D13. Flints from cairn to right. Scale, inches (Nicholas. Thomas).

Plate 24   Site III, S part of barrow looking E. Foreground, bank of Site IX overlies barrow ditch, with cart tracks, left, across berm. Figure in distance stands beside section 2 across Site IX. See Figs 2, 14 (Maurice Cookson).

Plate 25   Site IV, section through inner part of bank of disc-barrow, looking NW. Residual ancient land surface beneath concentrated chalk rubble bank. Scale, inches (Nicholas Thomas).

Plate 26   Site V, section across filled ditch of ring-ditch, bank originally to left. Upper chalk spreads the result of ?Romano-British cultivation and levelling. Cutting 1, section 1, NE face. See Figure 17 (Nicholas Thomas).

Plate 27   Site V, central pit, looking W. Puddled chalk covering revealed when surrounding chalk cleared to bedrock. Near scale, inches (Nicholas Thomas).

Plate 28   Site V, *idem*, looking W. Most of chalk covering removed, to reveal streaky pit-filling. Scale, inches/centimetres (Nicholas Thomas).

Plate 29   Site VI, linear earthwork, section 2, looking S. Ditch with slot at base, and bank beyond. See Figure 19 (Maurice Cookson).

Plate 30   Site VI, same section, looking NW to ploughsoil along outer edge of ditch (Maurice Cookson).

Plate 31   Sites VI and XX, section 6 (location, Fig 18) looking W. Rectangular profile of bowl-barrow ditch (left) with V-shaped linear ditch curving to avoid it. Outer edge of V-ditch in boxes beyond (Maurice Cookson).

Plate 32   Sites X-XIV, looking NE, Sites VIII and X in background. Figure kneels behind cremation pit of Site XIV; pegs in stake holes of Beaker settlement (Nicholas Thomas).

Plate 33   Site XIV, Beaker settlement stake holes 9 (left), 8. Scale, inches/centimetres (Nicholas Thomas).

Plate 34   Site XIV, SE quarter, cremation pit with cremation, probably in a bag. E face of N/S baulk. Scale, inches/centimetres (Nicholas Thomas).

Plate 35   Site XIV, central area looking NE. Pole stands in Hoare's trench penetrating bedrock. Cremation pit in front of figure (Nicholas Thomas).

PART 2: HUMAN REMAINS, ARTEFACTS, ANIMAL BONES AND THE ENVIRONMENT

FINDS AND SAMPLES FROM SNAIL DOWN, 1805–1806 AND 1953–1957

Artefacts described in some of Sections A–U are given a running number within each Section, prefixed with the letter of that Section. Thus F20 is the Gallo-Belgic dish sherd described in Section F on the Romano-British wares from Snail Down. Illustrated objects also carry their Section's letter and number.

Throughout Sections A–U, the following abbreviations for dimensions have been used: d, depth; diam, diameter; h, height; th, thickness; wt, weight; w, width. Dimensions are maximum unless stated otherwise. Objects which include numbers prefixed with DZSWS belong to the Wiltshire Heritage Museum and are already within their catalogue. All the finds from the excavations of 1953–1957, together with the paper and photograph archives, have been deposited in the Wiltshire Heritage Museum.

A THE HUMAN CREMATIONS, INHUMATION BURIALS AND FRAGMENTS

G H Bunting, D W Verity, Ian Cornwall, Anthony Duggan, Simon Mays, Jonathan Musgrave and Nicholas Thomas

I CREMATION BURIALS

By G H Bunting and D W Verity, with Ian Cornwall

Site I, disc-barrow

Cremation 1, central mound, primary burial, disturbed by Hoare.

Fragmentary, burnt human remains, mostly long-bone and skull fragments. Age and sex unknown.

Weight: 49.1g.

Cremation 2, central mound, intact satellite or secondary burial.

Fragmentary, burnt human remains. Age and sex unknown.

Weight: 225.0g

Cremation 3, eccentric mound, intact burial.

Burnt, highly fragmentary human remains. Identifiable elements include humerus, ulna, vertebrae and skull. Parts of the maxilla and a mandibular condyle are of adult size. Some pieces of skull retain evidence of un-closed sutures, including the trace of a metopic suture. Adult, cranial morphology suggests possibly male.

Weight: 1717.3g

Cremation 4, eccentric mound, disturbed by Hoare

Burnt, fragmentary human remains. Identified elements include radius, femur, humerus, ulna, clavicle, manubrium, phalanges, vertebrae, tibia, scapula and skull. Cranial sutures are generally un-closed, but the presence of alveoli for the third molars in the mandible and maxilla are indicative of an adult individual. Skull morphology is suggestive of male sex.

Weight: 586.0g

Cremated bone, pit on central plateau

Among the soil and charcoal from the small pit on the central plateau (Fig 3, Cremation Sweepings) was found a scatter of cremated human bone. It appears to belong to a juvenile or young adult. These remains may have been derived from the site of a funeral pyre and should probably be associated with one of the cremations from this barrow, probably either cremations 1 or 2 in view of the adult appearance of Cremations 3 and 4. They are not, therefore, treated as a separate cremation. Weight: 17.7g.

Site II, saucer-barrow

Cremation 5, in primary pit, disturbed by Hoare

Burnt, highly fragmented human remains. Identifiable elements include humerus, tibia, radius, metapodials, phalanges and skull (including the maxilla and the margin of an orbit); also eight roots of teeth (including M^3 with roots not fully closed) indicating an age probably in the early twenties. This is consistent with the open sutures evident in the skull fragments. The gracility of the cranial fragments is perhaps suggestive of female sex.

Weight: 1193.9g.

Cremation 6, in off-centre pit, intact (see also Section B, cranial disc)

Burnt, fragmentary human remains. Identified elements include fragments of cranial vault, mandible, maxilla and petrous parts of temporal bones. The cranial sutures are not closed and the epiphyses of the long bones are not generally completely fused to their shafts. The teeth show little wear. Probably an adolescent or young adult, sex unknown (but the cranial disc, Section B, considered possibly female).

Weight: 1053.6g. Associated with charcoals of hazel, apple / hawthorn / rowan / whitebeam type and oak.

Site III, bell-barrow

Cremation 7, in primary pit, disturbed by Hoare

Burnt, fragmented human remains representing all parts of the skeleton. Partial obliteration of skull sutures and the fusion of epiphyses to their shafts indicates adult status. Female sex is suggested by the general lightness of the cranial bones and the small mastoid processes.

Weight: 1309.9g. Associated with seeds, including a hazel nut and charcoal of oak logs and saplings from a funeral pyre.

Cremation 8, Secondary Burial 1, intact

Burnt, highly fragmented human remains with few identifiable pieces. Parts of canine and a premolar with open roots suggest a child.

Weight: 1547.9g. Associated with charcoals of apple/hawthorn/rowan/whitebeam type, wild cherry/bird cherry type, oak and unidentified wood.

Cremation 9, Secondary Burial 2, scattered in ancient times

Burnt, highly fragmentary human remains. The long-bone pieces are small in diameter, skull fragments thin with open sutures. Erupted deciduous incisors, a canine, and unerupted deciduous molars together indicate an age of about 1.5 – 2 years.

Weight: 73.6g.

Site XIV, scraped-up barrow

Cremation 10, in primary pit, intact

Burnt, fragmentary human remains. All long bones appear to be represented, the axial skeleton by pelvis, scapula, vertebrae and sacrum, the extremities by phalanges and a calcaneum. There is a large number of skull fragments. The epiphyses are fused and the dentition is adult with an M^3 recently erupted with very little wear. These observations are consistent with early adulthood. The morphology of the supra-orbital region of the frontal bone and the nuchal crest of the occipital bone suggest female sex.

Weight: 3086.1g. Associated with charcoals of ash and oak.

Site XV, scraped-up barrow with post ring

Cremation 11, in primary pit, intact

Burnt, fragmentary human remains. A metapodial of a bird (cf pigeon) was also present. Most parts of the skeleton are represented. Age adult, sex unknown.

Weight: 1653.3g

Site XVI, pond-barrow

Pits 1 and 2

Cremations 12, 13. These yielded very small quantities of ash and unidentifiable bone fragments, probably cremated and not certainly human.

Weights: 4.8g, 2.2g respectively

Pit 3

Cremation 14. Burnt, fragmentary human remains. The skull was very thin, with open sutures. Long bones were small and light. One germ of a deciduous molar survived. Young child of unknown sex.

Weight: 55.4g

Site XVII, bowl-barrow

Cremation 15, primary burial in central pit

Burnt, fragmentary human bone. Most parts of the skeleton are represented. The tooth roots are fully closed.

Cranial suture closure is not advanced. These observations are consistent with an individual in young adulthood (i.e. about 18–30 years). The skull shows robust mastoid processes, and there is no evidence of a pre-auricular sulcus on the surviving iliac fragments. A well-built young adult, probably male.

Weight: 899.3g. Associated with charcoals of hazel, apple / hawthorn / rowan / whitebeam type and wild cherry/bird-cherry type.

A commentary on the cremations
(by Nicholas Thomas)

Data for weights of bone from adult cremations found in 31 barrows excavated in Wiltshire and published since 1945 suggest that about 66% weighed less than 1000g, 23% weighed between 1000 and 2000g and 11% over 2000g (sources mainly in *WAM*). The 3980g of bone from cremation 2, barrow 1, at Cowlam Wold (Yorkshire, Humberside: Watts and Rahtz 1984, 28) appears to be exceptional, although it compares with Snail Down XIV, cremation 10 (3086g), as well as with a modern adult cremation (below).

At Snail Down, of eight certain adult cremations, two (25%) weighed less than 1000g, five (63%) between 1 and 2kg and one exceeded 2000g. Although the figures are too few to be significant, it can be remarked that, so far, Snail Down has yielded rather more cremations than usual within the range of 1–2kg. Such data might tentatively suggest that those cremating their dead for burial in this cemetery made more than average attempts to gather up a substantial amount of burnt bone for the grave.

In modern cremation practice (personal information, Bristol crematorium), the bones of an adult will be reduced to a weight of about 2750–3600g. For a 10-stone male, according to Ian Cornwall (Christie 1967, 364), the weight when cremated would be about 4400kg. It follows that the material excavated from an average Bronze Age cremation is considerably less than the full amount of burnt bone which would have been produced by the cremation of the body.

Inspection of the remains from the fifteen cremations and the sweeping from the pit in Site I indicates that bone fragments range in colour from creamy white to deep grey. The absence of charcoal from all but 8, 10, 12 and the Sweepings Pit was striking. Cremation 7 retained a small number of conspicuously black bone fragments from an otherwise creamy-white bone assemblage.

II BRONZE AGE INHUMATION BURIALS

Site II, saucer-barrow

Inhumation 1 (by Simon Mays). A handful of bones representing a perinatal infant, from small pit S of central cremation pit (Fig 6).

First recognised by Juliet Clutton-Brock and Jonathan Musgrave, the remains consist mainly of skull fragments, although parts of the axis vertebra, one metacarpal and a few long-bone fragments are also present. The bone surfaces have suffered some erosion whilst in the soil. One tooth is present, a crown of a deciduous maxillary central incisor. Its state of development (the crown was almost complete) suggests that the infant died in the perinatal period. It is not possible to determine whether the infant was stillborn or died soon after birth.

Comment *by Nicholas Thomas*

An Early Bronze Age perinatal infant burial is an unusual discovery. Whilst no comprehensive search has been undertaken, especially beyond Wiltshire and Dorset (Wales and Scotland were not investigated), only six such have been noted. One, in a Middle Bronze Age context, was found at Manor Farm, Borwick, Lancs (Olivier 1987, 162). A second came from a ring-ditch at Warren Farm, Milton Keynes, Bucks (Green 1975, 96–97) and a third from among the five to seven burials from Winterbourne Stoke G39 (Gingell 1988, 75), where there were traces of bones designated 'neonate' in an otherwise adult cremation. The fourth occurred in Barrow IV, Marshfield, Glos (Gettins *et al* 1953, 36) ; and what may have been two more in a pit in the Sheep Down pond-barrow in Dorset (Atkinson *et al* 1951, 5–7).

Site XXII, bell-barrow with added mound

Inhumation 2 (by Ian Cornwall and Anthony Duggan). Secondary burial of an adolescent. Plan, section, Figure 36; Plates 56–59.

The Skeleton *(by Ian Cornwall)*

The remains represent an almost complete inhumation.

Age: approximately 16–18 years, based on epiphysial fusion and development of third molars.

Sex: Possibly male, based on pelvic morphology.

Stature: 147.5cm (if male), 143.9cm (if female). Estimated from long-bone lengths (including epiphyses), using the formulae (for adults) of Dupertius and Haddon (1951).

The tumour *(by Anthony Duggan)*

The orbital aspect of the left orbital plate of the frontal bone is covered by a roughly triangular area with its apex lying medially, consisting of alternating erosion and proliferation of bone. The lesion has a honeycomb appearance and is densest in its middle part, thinning out towards the edges. The erosions are clear cut, the large ones being circular, the smaller ones resembling minute canaliculi. These channels vary in thickness and diameter from pinpoint to about 0.5mm and are separated by a lace-work of bony proliferation, many of the walls being serpiginous and threadlike.

Examination of the intracranial surface of the orbital plate by reflection shows no abnormality and the pathological change has not, therefore, involved its whole thickness, but has been produced by a purely intraorbital condition.

It is possible that this lesion was due to pressure from a tumour consisting of small blood vessels, known as a *haemangioma*, which could cause alternating erosion and proliferation of bony substance, thus leaving its impression upon the orbital plate. A *haemangioma* in this position might arise either from the periosteal vessels or from vascular connective tissue behind the lachrymal gland.

Plate 58 includes a photograph of a *haemangioma* taken from a human orbit, from which it will be seen that the surface configuration of such a tumour is not unlike the mirror image of the Snail Down specimen.

Such a tumour would have been present for several years at least, to give rise to these changes, and would have impaired vision and given rise to diplopia and restricted movement of the eyeball (Pl 59). It is not possible to say whether total blindness would have been present as the size of the growth is impossible to estimate. It is unlikely that such a tumour would have been in any way malignant, or that it would have contributed towards death other than by inflicting physical handicap.

III ISOLATED HUMAN REMAINS, UNBURNT, MAINLY BRONZE AGE

(by Jonathan Musgrave)

Site I, disc-barrow

Isolated human bones, plan, Figure 3
1 Small parietal fragment from the skull of an adult, mature but not very old. SW quadrant, central plateau, S of Sweepings Pit, subsoil, depth 6in.
2 Large skull fragment from a right parietal; the subject probably adult but not very old. NW quadrant, in silt at outer edge of ditch floor, layer 1, depth 2ft 3in.
3 Skull fragment of left temporal with external auditory meatus and mastoid process. NW quadrant, centre of ditch, base of layer 8, depth 1ft 6in.
4 Fragment of a right scapula with spine, glenoid fossa and coracoid process. Includes part of an unfused acromial epiphysis. SE quadrant, outer edge of ditch, layer 1, depth 2ft 4in.

Site III, bell-barrow

5 Lower incisor of a young adult, fairly unworn. On ancient land surface immediately N of funeral pyre, Figure 12.

Site XIX, double bell-barrow

6 Probable lower left first permanent molar, moderately worn (Brothwell 1981, wear stages 3+C4). N mound, earthy core, layer 8, Figure 34.

IV INHUMATION BURIALS, ALL PROBABLY LATER BRONZE AGE

(by Ian Cornwall and Jonathan Musgrave)

Site XV, scraped-up barrow with post ring

Secondary burials (plan, Fig 25; Pl 40) (**inhumations 3–5 by Ian Cornwall**).

Inhumation 3 (plan, Fig 25, Skeleton I; Pl 40). Remains of one individual, the skull is missing. Adult; general skeletal gracility suggests female sex.

This skeleton was radiocarbon dated (Section T) and attributed to the end of the second millennium cal BC. By inference, the other inhumation remains from Sites XV and V (4–8) are also considered to belong to the later Bronze Age.

Inhumation 4 (plan, Fig 25, Skeleton III). Comparatively few remains of a robust adult. An almost complete left ilium bears traces of a preauricular sulcus which suggests female sex. Associated with these remains were a sheep humerus and metatarsal, a cattle mandible and lumbar vertebra fragments, and two pig molar germs.

Inhumation 5 (plan, Fig 25, Skeleton II). Skull fragments only. They are light and thin but their proportions suggest maturity.

Inhumation 6 (plan, Fig 25, Skeleton IV) (**inhumations 6–9 by Jonathan Musgrave**). Scattered remains probably of one adult, age range 25–35, comprising eight cranial vault fragments, showing little sutural closure, left proximal end of ulna, one rib fragment, one left patella, four proximal toe phalanges and one unidentified cancellous fragment; three incisor teeth, two premolars and one upper and one lower molar, all well-worn.

Inhumation 7 (plan, Fig 25, Skeleton V). Scattered among bones of inhumation 6, the remains of a baby of *c* 18 months, comprising a fragment of atlas vertebra and an uncalcified molar crown, together with the greater part of the right half of a mandible.

Site V, ring-ditch

Inhumation 8 (plan, Fig 16). Scattered remains of a child aged about four, consisting of a modest collection of fragments from the vault of the skull together with most of the left mandible; also five vertebral and four rib fragments. Topsoil.

Site XX, bowl-barrow ditch; but perhaps associated with Site VI, Middle Iron Age enclosure.

Inhumation 9. Skull fragments, pieces of occipital bone including inion, with pronounced nuchal markings, and fragments of parietal bone, heavy, with incompletely ossified sutures. Three teeth were present: canine, incisor and pre-molar, all fairly well worn. Two molar fragments were also present. Section 8, layer 21, depth 2ft 2in (Fig 19).

B THE TREPANNED CRANIAL DISC FROM SITE II

Ian Cornwall with Nicholas Thomas

INTRODUCTION

Among the cremated bones in Pit 2 of Site II was a disc of unburnt bone which had been shaped thus during the process of removal from a human skull in an operation called trepanation. This was submitted to I W Cornwall for study.

SNAIL DOWN SITE II

A roughly elliptical cranial disc, 3.25 × 2.60cm, 3.5mm thick, apparently unburnt. Figure 38; Plate 60. DZSWS: 1955.213.

The specimen is too small to locate with certainty, but is probably from a parietal bone and, if undistorted, perhaps from just posterior to the middle part of the coronal suture.

The disc is very thin, perhaps an indication of female sex. It does not appear to have been heated to a high temperature, but there is a slight cracking of the outer surface which may be due to some degree of heating and consequent shrinkage on cooling.

Cut-marks are clearly discernible on the outer table; the overlapping ends of the resulting groove, not quite coincident, being visible on the inner, only. This feature shows clearly in the illustrations. There are two small (ancient) pressure-flake scars on the opposite edge of the inner side, suggesting that the point of the tool was twice inserted at different points in order to lever up the loosened disc, which leverage gave rise to the final tension-fracture of the thin bridge which still separated the not quite coincident ends of the cut.

Comment (by Nicholas Thomas)

Over one hundred instances of trepanation in European prehistory have now been recorded, from southern Sweden to Portugal. As Piggott showed half a century ago (1940, Fig 2), principal concentrations occur in central and in southern France.

South-eastern England proves also to be a notable area in this distribution. Snail Down Site II, Amesbury Barrow 51 (Ashbee 1978, 46–53) and Amesbury Barrow 71 (Christie 1967, 361–362) are important Bronze Age additions to Piggott's list; the two probable trepanations found by Ashbee at Fussell's Lodge long barrow (Wiltshire) (Ashbee 1966, 59–60) are another, of considerably earlier date.

According to Piggott's register (1940, 124–127), all except one were associated with inhumation burials. The exception, an early find from Moret, France, is described ambiguously and does not certainly belong to the cremated skull fragments that are mentioned.

If the trepanned disc from Snail Down II came from the corpse with whose burnt bones it was found, it appears to be the only known instance of the operation on a person who was accorded cremation rather than inhumation burial. The cranial disc itself had been carefully kept aside when the corpse was burnt; then added to the bones after they had cooled sufficiently to affect it only slightly.

Despite a search of the accompanying cremation from Site II, no pieces of burnt skull were found preserving the parts from which the disc had been trepanned. We shall never know whether the female from Site II had survived her perilous operation.

The evidence published so far has paid little heed to the sex of prehistoric people who underwent trepanation. Those from Crichel Down (Piggott 1940, 112–113, pls 8, 9) and from Amesbury Barrows 51 and 71 were male, as was an example from Fussell's Lodge. The teenager buried in a short cist at Mount Stuart, Bute (Ashbee 1978, 52) showed an abnormality of the skull which may have

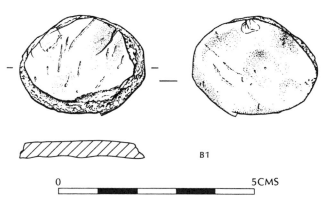

Fig 38 Trepanned cranial disc, Site II

been in part the result of a scraping away of the bone. This person was certainly female.

Trepanning is the oldest known surgical operation. More instances of this perilous procedure have been recorded from the Neolithic than from any other period. Preliminary stages included cutting the skin and soft tissue beneath. One of three methods was then selected to remove a disc of bone from the skull: sawing, to extract a square or rectangular piece; drilling and connecting the drilled holes; or by cutting and scraping a groove, without damaging the *dura mater* immediately beneath the skull. This, the least unsafe trepanning technique, was preferred among prehistoric practitioners in Britain. No evidence has survived to indicate the use of anaesthesia, or the consciousness or otherwise of the patient (Parker *et al* 1986, *passim*).

Cornwall has drawn attention to the trepanning techniques involved in the Snail Down operation: first,

very careful cutting of a groove to define the disc using, no doubt, a succession of sharp flint flakes; and then a delicate levering at different points, which led eventually to removal of the cranial disc. Small flake scars on the inner surface of the disc left by this process are noticeable. Similar grooving to outline the shape and size of the disc and then to remove it has been recorded at Amesbury Barrow 51. The likeness one to the other of the Amesbury 51 and Crichel Down cranial discs led Ashbee to wonder whether the two operations had been carried out by the same person. Their generally circular to oval shape recalls that of the Snail Down disc and is in contrast with the squarer void left by the Amesbury 71 trepanning. At present it must suffice to emphasise the immense difficulty of achieving a successful trepanning at this remote time and speculate no further about how widespread the skills may have been among communities in Wessex and other areas of lowland England.

C THE NEOLITHIC AND BRONZE AGE POTTERY FROM THE BEAKER SETTLEMENT

ALEX GIBSON

INTRODUCTION

Shortly before his death, David Clarke had prepared a note on the Beaker sherds from the barrow material and the pre-barrow occupation deposits at Snail Down. This was reassessed by the present writer in 1979 as part of his PhD study of Beaker domestic assemblages (Gibson 1982). Consequently, the writer was invited to contribute to the report by the excavator and, as a result, David Clarke's original report has been augmented and up-dated. Some minor overlap occurs with Frances Raymond's report on the later prehistoric wares (Section E). Cross-references have been made where necessary.

The pottery from the site falls into five main categories. In addition to the Beaker material which forms by far the largest assemblage, there is also an element of residual earlier Bronze Age potsherds, particularly from Collared Urns. With the exception of the earlier Neolithic material, the other main categories may probably be broadly contemporary; the presence of Grooved Ware, Peterborough Ware and Collared Urn sherds on mainly Beaker-associated domestic sites is well-paralleled (Gibson 1982), although strict association in such contexts can rarely be proven.

NEOLITHIC

Earlier Neolithic

The pottery constituting this category consists of a small, tentatively identified, assemblage of sherds from Site III. Formal characteristics such as belly carinations or diagnostic rim forms are absent from the group, though two sherds representing a large portion of an apparently straight-sided neck and simple upright rim were noted (C9). Unlike the majority of the other material from the pre-barrow contexts at Snail Down, these earlier Neolithic sherds contain shell opening agents similar to a large proportion of the earlier material (29.5%) from Windmill Hill (Smith 1965a, 46).

Grooved Ware

Sherds of Grooved Ware, or possible Grooved Ware, have been recognised from Sites I, III, VIII and XV. Though the majority of sherds are small, comparatively few are decorated in any way other than by parallel grooves; and no vessels are reconstructable. Site XV produced the most diagnostic Grooved Ware in the form of C96 and C99. These sherds are both probably from barrel-shaped vessels and the zonal decoration, in-filled with impressions, suggests that they belong to the Durrington Walls sub-style of Grooved Ware as defined by Wainwright and Longworth (1971). This is, perhaps, to be expected from the geographical location of Snail Down.

Peterborough Ware

Pottery from this ceramic tradition has been noted at Sites III, X, XIV and XIX; the first three sites, located at or near to the presumed nucleus of the Beaker settlement, and the fourth at the other side of the cemetery. The sherds from X and XIV are undecorated and are tentatively identified only by their coarse, fairly soft fabric containing abundant coarsely crushed calcined flint opening agents. Of the eight sherd groups from Site III, only two are decorated and the rest are again tentatively identified by fabric. The decorated sherds (C10 and C11) are both patterned lightly, one with twisted cord and the other with slight incisions. This might suggest that they are from early in the stylistic sequence of later Neolithic impressed ware, such as the decorated phases of the Windmill Hill sequence (C11) or the Ebbsfleet sub-style of the Peterborough tradition (C10). The sherds from Site XIX are almost all decorated and include a flat-topped rim sherd (C116). The decoration comprises whipped-cord maggots (C114), bird-bone impressions (C115, C117), whipped-cord impression (C116), stabs and fingernail impressions (C113). Once again, few formal traits are recognisable, but the abundance of decoration suggests that the sherds may be from the Mortlake sub-style of the Peterborough tradition and thus stylistically later than the potsherds from the settlement area.*

BEAKER

The Beaker material falls into two categories. The first comprises a small number of sherds from All-Over-Cord-decorated vessels (AOC), possibly some from European Bell Beakers (E) and possibly a few sherds of vessels from their domestic repertoires comprising mainly fine, undecorated sherds and vessels with sparse finger-nail impressions (see Clarke 1970). This material is early in Clarke's stylistic sequence and would be assigned to steps 1–3 in Lanting and van der Waals's scheme (Lanting and van der Waals, 1972). According to these typologies, this material might date to 2400–1900 cal BC, but the assemblage is scanty and probably residual to the main phase of deposition.

The second category, in contrast, comprises more than 400 sherds of Beakers from Clarke's Southern British Series (S2–4) and much domestic ware clearly derived from an occupation deposit represented by the complex of stake holes below Barrows X-XIV. This fairly homogeneous assemblage would equate to Lanting and van der Waals's step 5 or later and might, perhaps date to 2000–1700 cal BC. However, the growing corpus of Beaker-associated radiocarbon dates suggests that the chronological separating provided by these two assemblages may be more apparent than real in view of the lack of any obvious chronological coherence in either Clarke's or Lanting and van der Waals's stylistic sequences (Kinnes, Gibson *et al*, 1991).

Phase I: The Stylistically Earlier Material, E and AOC (steps 1–3)

Four sherds of AOC Beakers (Site III, C40; XIV, C69; XVIII, C111; XIX, C118) have been recovered from barrows which were strung right across the excavated area. To these might perhaps be added three or four undiagnostic sherds possibly from stylistically early and contemporary European Bell Beakers from Barrows III (C32), XV (C101) and XIX. These few fragments, scraped up into the mound material of the later barrows, may possibly represent the fringes of a domestic scatter or hint at a manuring process on fields near to a settlement. The material is, however, too scanty to allow a tighter assessment and need not necessarily even be domestic in origin.

Phase II: The Southern British Phase (steps 5–7)

This phase contains clear traces of a small domestic site, incorporating Southern Beakers, and partly recovered from the post hole complex beneath Barrows X–XIV. The structural evidence for this settlement was preserved in varying states of erosion, and the debris and artefactual evidence for the occupation of the site was scraped into the material of the later barrows, zoning outwards over a radius of *c* 250m from its main focus. Approximately 220 sherds were recovered from Barrow III, *c* 90 in Barrow XIV, *c* 30 in Barrow X and under 20 sherds in Barrows I, II, XIII, XVII, and XVIII. The majority of the flint artefacts recovered from the mound material of Sites X-XIV probably came from this domestic site, including the fragment of a battle-axe of Group XIV, Nuneaton Camptonite (Section J, J2, Fig 53).

The pottery debris from this settlement at Snail Down is typical of Beaker domestic assemblages elsewhere in Britain in that it mainly comprises a few small sherds each from a large number of vessels. The estimation of minimum numbers of individual vessels suggests that fragments of over thirty fine-ware beakers are represented including at least one handled Beaker (C51) from Site III. These are accompanied by sherds of more than twenty fingernail- and fingertip-impressed coarse-ware Beakers, of which at least two were heavy-duty vessels or giant Pot-beakers (C16, C41).

The rusticated pottery can be divided into five main types:

1. regular fingernail impressions
   (a) alone
   (b) with cordons
2. random fingernail impressions
3. paired fingernail impressions (crowsfoot)
4. fingertip impressions
5. stabbed decoration including oval, triangular, sub-circular and sharp-pointed toothed-comb impressions.

A single undecorated Beaker is recognisable from sherds within the assemblage and this, combined with the variety of rustication techniques used, is typical of stylistically later Beaker domestic assemblages (Gibson 1982).

The decorated fine-ware Beakers are predominantly comb-impressed, with a clear preference for bar-chevron-decorated necks, and bellies with ladder-filled zones. Traces of vertical decoration have been noted within the assemblage as have large filled triangles and floating lozenges, suggesting broad decorative zones on at least some vessels. This is a preference which, together with markedly funnel-shaped necks, is distinctive of the Southern Series of necked Beakers in Wessex, South Wales and Southern Ireland, as opposed to the preferred cylindrical necks and hexagon motifs of the eastern

---

*This report was written in 1990 as an up-date to an earlier version (1981) which itself was based on an original report by the late David Clarke. Since 1990 our perception of the Peterborough ancestry of earlier Bronze Age Food Vessels and Collared Urns has been questioned by the critical analysis of existing (and the acquisition of more, reliable) radiocarbon dates (Gibson & Kinnes 1997). It would now appear that the Fengate style of Peterborough Ware was already fully formed by 3000 Cal BC, almost a millennium earlier than the available dates for Collared Urns. It seems unlikely that the peculiar and unstable Fengate form should last, unaltered, for this length of time. The shared stylistic features of the two ceramics remain remarkable, however, and archaeological research must now be directed to explaining these similarities in light of the apparent chronological separation.

counties. Herringbone, lattice, ermine and floating-lozenge motifs are also recognisable within the assemblage, the latter becoming more common in the later phases of the Southern tradition (S3 and S4). The incised or scored decoration on some sherds also suggests a later element; however the failure of the stylistic sequences to match the growing radiocarbon absolute chronology has already been mentioned and must always be considered in such mixed assemblages.

Particularly noteworthy is C52 from Site III, a comb-decorated fine-ware vessel in a thin, pink fabric exhibiting traces of a circular scar on the outer surface. The scar is typical of those left by firing spalls, roughly circular discs of clay blown off the surface of the vessel during firing and usually caused by a build up of water vapour in the fabric. This is generally a result of fabric containing too few opening agents and/or too rapid a rise in firing temperature. Firing wasters such as this are only rarely identified in prehistoric pottery assemblages.

BRONZE AGE POTTERY

The majority of sherds assigned to this category, and in particular to the Collared Urn tradition, are once more tentatively identified chiefly on the grounds of fabric and especially because, macroscopically, the fabric differs significantly from those found in the other categories already discussed. In particular, a large sherd from Site XI (C61) is decorated with bird-bone impressions as might be expected in a Peterborough assemblage, but the fabric differs from the other Peterborough sherds and in any case the close relationship of Collared Urn to Peterborough Ware is well-known (Longworth 1984; Gibson 1982; 1986). The sherd decorated with round-toothed comb impressions from Site XIII (Section D, D18) is almost certainly Urn and may have resembled the comb-decorated Urns from Site III, Secondary Burial 2 (D11, D12; Fig 46). This Collared Urn identification is also the most likely for the shoulder carination from a tripartite vessel from Site XVIII. Sherd C92 from Site XIV may also be from a tripartite vessel, but the fineness of the fabric and characteristic stabbing below the carination suggests that it may be more likely to be from a southern Vase Food Vessel, similar to that from Winterbourne Stoke G24 or Winterbourne Stoke G14 (Annable and Simpson 1964, 62, nos 488 and 496).

One sherd from Site XIV (C93) is a base sherd decorated with small triangular stabs and, by its small size and fine fabric, may represent a fragment of an Accessory Vessel.

CATALOGUE OF ILLUSTRATED SHERDS

Notes

All fabric descriptions have been done macroscopically and are therefore general and subjective. They may be confirmed/rejected by future microscopic analysis. In the descriptions of context, unless indicated otherwise, the last, Arabic, numeral is the layer number as shown on the drawn sections. For some sites, where indicated, it is followed by a dimension in inches ('in'), which represents the approximate depth of the find from modern turf level.

The assemblage of potsherds associated with the Beaker settlement, including the pieces described in this catalogue, weighed approximately 2509g. Sherds described in the catalogue are illustrated in Figures 39–42. Sherd C112 appears in Figure 48 as E1.

Site I

Beaker

C1 Six body sherds in a hard, red fabric. Decorated with multiple horizontal comb impressions. SW Quad, bank, 11. Figure 39.
C2 Base-angle sherd in a red-brown fabric with a black core. Undecorated. SW Quad, central area, 9. Figure 39.
C3 Rim and body sherds in a hard, reddish-brown and well-fired fabric with calcined-flint inclusions. Decorated externally with combed vertical triangles/chevrons. SW, NW Quads, bank, 11. Figure 39.
C4 Two sherds from the neck angle. Decorated in the neck with five horizontal lines of comb impressions and on the belly with three lines of the same technique. There is an undecorated band 9mm wide in the waist angle. SW Quad, bank, 11. Figure 39.
C5 Sherd in a hard, well-fired fabric with red-brown surfaces and a black core. Decorated externally with comb impressions in what appears to be a running filled-chevron motif. SW Quad, bank, 11. Figure 39.
C6 Base angle, probably Beaker, in a red-brown fabric with a black core. Traces of possible oblique-line decoration on the outer surface, but too abraded to be certain. SW Quad, bank 11. Figure 39.
C7 Six sherds (three joining) possibly from the same vessel. From the rounded belly of a Beaker in a reddish-brown, hard fabric. Decorated with broad multiple zones of oblique incised lines, some combed, and ermine motif. SE, SW, NW Quad, bank, 9, 11. Figure 39.

Site II

Beaker

C8 Sherd from the belly of a Beaker. Pink and porous fabric with grey-brown surfaces and sparse calcined-flint inclusions. Sherd *c* 6mm thick. 12 lines of (?) horizontal combed herringbone motif visible. SW Quad, ditch, topsoil. Figure 39.

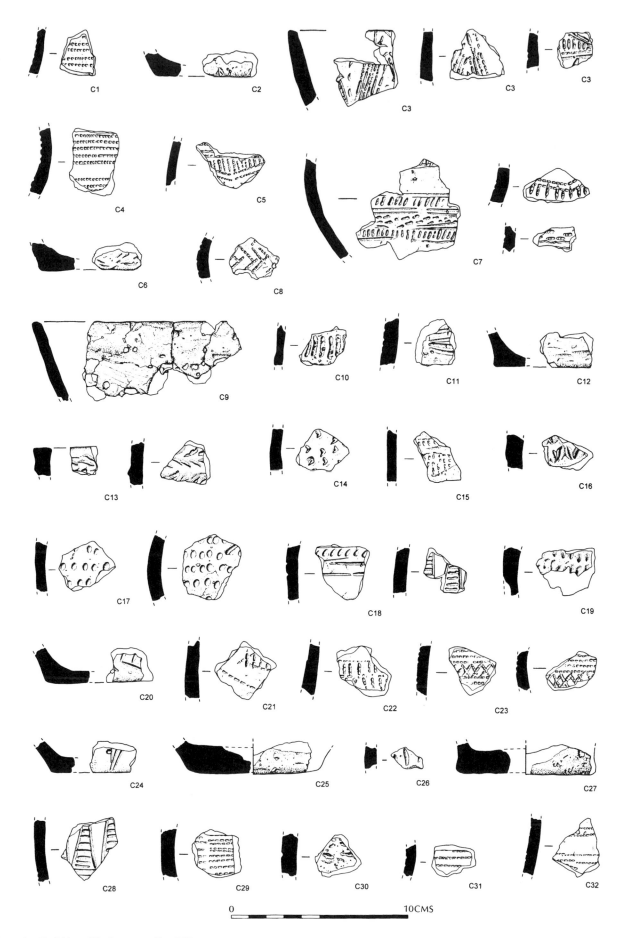

Fig 39 Earlier Neolithic and Beaker wares, Sites I-III.

Site III

Because of the size and complexity of its structure, as well as the large number of individual finds recorded, the barrow has been divided into nine areas, to which sherds have been allocated in the catalogue, as follows:

I   Turf and topsoil over whole site.
II   Spoil thrown out by Colt Hoare
III Chalk crust covering mound (layers 12, 13, 15, 18, 21).
IV   Earth and turves of mound core (layers 10, 11, 14).
V   Ancient land surface (layer 9).
VI   Berm (layers 7, 22)
VII Ditch (layers 1–6)
VIII Pits 1–3
IX   Area outside ditch (layer 7).

Where possible, sherds have been allocated layer numbers within these finds areas (cf Figs 10, 11).

Neolithic Plain Ware

C9 Two conjoining rim sherds from a straight-necked, undecorated bowl. Possible earlier Neolithic. The fabric is fine and well-fired with grey-brown surfaces and black core; shell inclusions. S Quad, VI, 7 (tree hole). Figure 39.

Neolithic impressed ware

C10 Sherd in a hard, calcined-flint-filled fabric with grey-brown surfaces; five short, slightly curved, twisted cord-impressed lines. Possibly from the neck of an Ebbsfleet vessel. N Quad, IV, 14. Figure 39.
C11 Sherd in a black fabric with calcareous inclusions; four converging horizontal, lightly incised lines. Possibly from a bowl in the Southern Decorated Bowl tradition. N Quad, IV, 11. Figure 39.

Beaker

C12 Base sherd in a pink-brown fabric; undecorated. N Quad, III, 13. Figure 39.
C13 Rim and body sherds similar to C60 (Site XI) and C75 and C80 (Site XIV). All N Quad, III, 13; IV, 14; IV, 15 respectively. Figure 39.
C14 Six sherds in a pink, well-fired fabric; decorated externally with random triangular stabs. Very similar to C58, C81, C82 and C89. Possibly the same vessel. All N Quad, III, 13; VII, 6; VII, 2; V, 9; mound, general, VII, 6. Figure 39.
C15 Sherd in a light brown fabric with traces of a coil break. Abraded but apparently comb-decorated with opposed filled triangles. N Quad, VII, 6. Figure 39.
C16 Two sheds in a thin, red, well-fired fabric; horizontal rows of paired-fingernail impressions. Both S Quad, II. Figure 39.
C17 Thirteen sherds in a similar red-brown fabric with grey core and finely crushed calcined-flint inclusion. Decoration comprises horizontal lines of close-set and shallow oval impressions, probably bird bone.

Possibly three vessels represented by these sherds. All N Quad except two (S Quad) and one (W Quad). Locations: IV, 14; VII, 6; VI, within Urn, Sec Burial 1; III, 13; VII, 2; VII, 1; IV, 16; IV, 16; V, 9; V, 9; IV, 10; V, 9; VI, 7. Figure 39.
C18 Four sherds in a similar pink, well-fired fabric; decorated with incised ladder pattern. One close to C28. All N Quad, IV, 14; IV, 14; VII, 6; VI, 7. Figure 39.
C19 Single sherd in an orange, fairly soft fabric decorated with short, vertical, oval stabs. N Quad, VII, 2. Figure 39.
C20 Two sherds including a base sherd in a pink-brown fabric; traces of vertical comb-impressed lines incised at base. Both N Quad, IV, 14, III, 13. Figure 39.
C21 Large body sherd in a pink-brown, well-fired fabric; comb-filled chevron or lozenge decoration. N Quad, III, 12. Figure 39.
C22 Two joining sherds in a pink-brown fabric; traces of horizontal and vertical comb-impressed lines. N Quad, III, 16. Figure 39.
C23 Three sherds in a pink-brown, hard, well-fired fabric; zones of comb-impressed cross-hatching bordered by multiple horizontal lines. All N Quad, IV, 16; V, 9; V, 9. Figure 39.
C24 Base sherd in a pink fabric; incised decoration forming base of a tall pendant triangle. Close to C33. N Quad, VII, 6. Figure 39.
C25 Base sherd in a pink fabric with a grey interior. Undecorated. Diameter 73mm. N Quad, III, 13. Figure 39.
C26 Two sherds in a hard, brown fabric, decorated with single fingernail impressions. Both N Quad, IV, 13. Figure 39.
C27 Base sherd in a pink-brown fabric. Undecorated. Diameter 80mm. S Quad, IV, 11. Figure 39.
C28 Sherd in a pink-brown, fine and well-fired fabric; deep, incised, filled-pendant triangles. Close to C18. N Quad, IV, 11. Figure 39.
C29 Sherd in a pink-brown fabric; eight horizontal comb-impressed lines. N Quad, IV, 11. Figure 39.
C30 Sherd with a red-brown exterior, grey interior and core. Contains abundant finely crushed calcined-flint inclusions. Decorated with paired fingernail impressions. N Quad, VII, 6. Figure 39.
C31 Sherd in a pink-brown fabric; traces of horizontal comb-impressed lines. N Quad, IV, 14. Figure 39.
C32 Sherd in a pink-brown fabric; traces of horizontal comb-impressed lines and an undecorated zone. N Quad, IV, 11. Figure 39.
C33 Sherd in a pink fabric with grey inner surface; multiple incisions, probably representing a filled-triangular motif. Close to C24. N Quad, IV, 13. Figure 40.
C34 Sherd in a pink fabric; traces of combed decoration probably forming multiple chevrons. N Quad, V, 9. Figure 40.
C35 Pink, well-fired sherd with finely crushed calcined-flint inclusions. Decorated with comb impressions forming shallow, filled-pendant chevrons. N Quad, III, 13. Figure 40.
C36 Pink-brown sherd in a fine, well-fired fabric with a soapy-textured finish. Decorated with two zones of vertical impressions (ladder motif) separated by multiple faint comb impressions. N Quad, III, 13. Figure 40.

Fig 40   Beaker wares, Sites III, X, XI, XIII, XIV; Grooved Ware, Sites VIII, X.

C37 Pink-brown sherd in a well-fired fabric and dark core. Decorated with a zone of abraded ladder motif made by tooth-ended implement between lightly incised groove and line of near-contiguous finger-tip impressions. N Quad, III, 13. Figure 40.

C38 Base sherd in a pink-brown fabric; traces of filled-triangle comb-impressed motif. N Quad, III, 13. Figure 40.

C39 Sherd with orange-brown surfaces and a black core. Decorated with paired-fingertip impressions. N Quad, IV, 11. Figure 40.

C40 Sherd in grey fabric; decorated with a single line of twisted-cord impression. N Quad, I. Figure 40.

C41 Two sherds in a brown fabric with finely crushed calcined-flint inclusions. Decorated with vertical lines of paired-fingernail impressions. Both N Quad, VI, 7; IV, 10. Figure 40.

C42 Sherd with a brown outer surface, dark-grey inner surface and hard, well-fired fabric. The decoration comprises two zones of comb-impressed ladder motif. N Quad, VI, 7. Figure 40.

C43 Sherd in a pink-brown, well-fired fabric with calcined-flint inclusions. Decorated with comb impressions forming filled opposed triangles or lozenges. S Quad, IV, 9. Figure 40.

C44 Base sherd in a pink-brown fabric; traces of horizontal and vertical comb-impressed lines; base *c* 71mm in diameter. S Quad, IV, 9. Figure 40.

C45 Sherd in a well-fired fabric with red surfaces; decorated with horizontal and vertical impressions made with a comb having large, rectangular teeth. S Quad, IV, 9. Figure 40.

C46 Well-fired sherd in a pink fabric with black interior surface. Decorated externally with pairs of fingernail impressions arranged in a crowfoot motif. W Quad, IV, 11. Figure 40.

C47 Rim sherd in a light-brown fabric with grey core. The decoration comprises two zones of ladder motif, with maggots along top of rim. W Quad, IV, 11. Figure 40.

C48 Base sherd in a pink fabric; a single, deep horizontal groove above the base. Diameter *c* 80mm. W Quad, IV, 11. Figure 40.

C49 Sherd in a pink-brown, well-fired fabric with finely crushed calcined-flint inclusions. Decorated with comb impressions forming horizontal lines below traces of a zone of opposed multiple chevrons. E Quad, IV, 11. Figure 40.

C50 Two conjoining sherds in a red-brown fabric with crushed calcined-flint opening agents. Decorated with rows of vertical fingernail impressions. Both W Quad, VI, 7. Figure 40.

C51 Sherd in a pink-brown fabric. Undecorated. Probably includes the springing of a handle. S Quad, IV, 11. Figure 40.

C52 Sherd in a pink-brown fabric with traces of horizontal comb-impressed lines. External scar represents traces of a firing spall. Central area, IV, 11. Figure 40.

C53 Rim sherd in a hard, well-fired pink fabric; decorated with a zone of comb-impressed ladder motif. N Quad, V, 9. Figure 40.

C54 Base sherd in a hard fabric with a pink exterior and brown interior. Probably undecorated. W Quad, IV, 11. Figure 40.

Site VIII

Grooved Ware

C55 Small sherd in a pink fabric with some finely crushed calcined-flint and grog inclusions. Decorated externally with two shallow but clearly defined grooves. Modern disturbance, top of mound. Figure 40.

Site X

Because of its damaged state, only the SE and NW Quadrants of this mound were excavated. In the catalogue, the sherds are located first by letters indicating one or other of these areas, followed by the layers in which they were found, detailed in Figures 22 and 23, and their depth from the surface in inches. Beneath the barrow's ragged topsoil, the N half of the mound that was excavated had been turned over by rabbits: the S half, though damaged, preserved traces of mound deposits but no ancient land surface.

Grooved Ware

C56 Small grey sherd with a coil-break visible in the fabric. Decorated externally with two shallow but clearly-defined grooves. SE Quad, 4, 16in. Figure 40.

Beaker

C57 Base-angle sherd in a dark brown, gritty fabric with abundant finely crushed inclusions. Decorated externally with carelessly executed paired-fingernail impressions. From a rusticated Beaker. SE Quad, beyond Mound, 1. Figure 40.

C58 Sherd in light-brown, fine and well-fired fabric. Decorated externally with apparently random or broadly linear triangular impressions. Probably from a rusticated Beaker. Cf C14, C81, C82, C89. SE Quad, 4, 20 in. Figure 40.

Site XI

Beaker

C59 Sherd in a fine, dark-brown fabric exhibiting a zone of toothed-comb decoration comprising a band of cross-hatching bordered (?) above by two horizontal lines. SE Quad, mound edge, 4, 9 in. Figure 40.

C60 Sherd with a red-brown outer surface and grey-brown inner surface. Decorated with horizontal lines of paired-fingernail herringbone emphasising raised cordons. From a rusticated Beaker with pronounced plastic decoration. Cf C13, C75, C80. SE Quad, beyond mound, 5, topsoil. Figure 40.

Grooved Ware

C61 Large, slightly gritty sherd with a grey-brown outer surface, brown inner surface and black core. Join-void visible in the breaks. Decorated externally with bird-bone impressions. Possibly Peterborough, but differs in fabric from the other Peterborough sherds. N edge of mound, 5, 9in. Figure 40.

Site XIII

Beaker

C62 Sherd in a fine, well-fired fabric with a brown outer surface, grey inner surface and core. The decoration comprises close-set, vertical, filled triangles executed with a fine comb. SW Quad, beyond mound, 5, 15in. Figure 40.

C63 Two sherds in a deep red, hard, well-fired fabric. Possible base angle and wall sherd of a rusticated vessel decorated with horizontal rows of regularly spaced sub-triangular stabs (probably bird bone). SW Quad, edge of mound, 5, 10in; ibid, base of 5, 12in. Figure 40.

C64 Sherd in a red-brown, fine fabric from the belly of a round-bodied vessel. Decorated externally with comb-impressed, filled, floating lozenges. Probably from an S3 vessel. Ibid, 5, 9in. Figure 40.

Other

C65 Coarse sherd with brown surfaces and a black core. Contains abundant, finely crushed calcined-flint inclusions which have erupted both surfaces, giving a gritty feel. Decorated externally with a horizontal row of impressions (indeterminate) arranged in a herring-bone motif. Deverel Rimbury Ware. NW Quad, edge of mound, 5, 12in. Section E, E3. Figure 40.

C66 Three sherds plus fragments of pottery with red surfaces, black core, and large calcined-flint inclusions up to 7mm across. One sherd has short vertical impressions externally (possibly fingernail or bird bone). Beaker and Deverel Rimbury wares. SW Quad, edge of mound, 4, 12in; ibid; NW Quad, edge of mound, 5, 12in. Section E, E4. Figure 48.

Site XIV

Beaker

C67 Sherd in a hard, reddish-brown fabric, from the waist of a necked Beaker decorated with two zones of ladder motif separated from each other by a line of combed impressions. The verticals in the motif appear to be fingernail impressions. The comb used had broad, rectangular teeth. Cf C68. SW Quad, 5, 14in. Figure 40.

C68 Sherd similar to C67 above, but from the belly of a necked Beaker. Also decorated with combed ladder motif but there are hints of a narrow undecorated band at or just above the maximum belly diameter. Possibly from the same vessel as C67 above. SW Quad, 5, 14in. Figure 40.

C69 Fine sherd in a dark-brown fabric; decorated with three encircling twisted-cord lines. SW Quad, 4, 30in. Figure 40.

C70 Rim sherd from the neck of a barrel-necked vessel in a fine, brown fabric. Decorated externally with a zone of ladder motif bordered above and below by three lines of comb impressions. The verticals of the motif appear to be fingernail impressions. SW Quad, topsoil over mound. Figure 40.

C71 Flat-topped rim sherd in dark-brown fabric; decorated externally with three or four lines of carelessly applied comb impressions. Below this there is an undecorated band. SW Quad, topsoil over mound. Figure 40.

C72 Sherd in a hard fabric with red-brown outer surface and black inner surface. The decoration comprises two narrow zones of ladder motif, abraded, but apparently comb-impressed. SE Quad, 5, 6in. Figure 40.

C73 Sherd in a fairly soft fabric, orange exterior and dark-grey interior. Decorated on the outer surface with two pairs of fingernail impressions. Probably from a fingernail-rusticated Beaker. Possibly same pot as C88. SW Quad, 4, 14in. Figure 41.

C74 Two sherds in a brown, gritty fabric with abundant finely-crushed, calcined-flint inclusions. Decorated with fingernail impressions. SW Quad, 4, 14in; SE Quad, 5, 12in. Figure 41.

C75 Sherd in a red-brown well-fired fabric; decorated with paired-fingernail herringbone, raising horizontal ribs around the neck of the vessel. Similar to C13, C60 and probably the same vessel as C80. SW Quad, 5, 12in. Figure 41.

C76 Two sherds in a dark-brown fabric; abraded comb decoration forming large filled triangles. NW Quad, 5 or 4. Figure 41.

C77 Sherd in fine, red-brown fabric, hard and well-fired. Decorated with apparently random fingernail impressions. From the upper part of a straight-necked vessel. NW Quad, 4, 12in. Figure 41.

C78 Sherd with dark-brown surfaces and an orange core, in a fine and well-fired fabric. Decorated with a zone of opposed filled triangles in deeply impressed comb. Cf C91. NW Quad, 4, 12in. Figure 41.

C79 Two rim sherds from the same pot in a grey-brown fabric; decorated with two zones of combed ladder motif. From the neck of a barrel-necked vessel. SW Quad, 4; SE Quad, 4, 16in. Figure 41.

C80 Two sherds of fingernail-rusticated Beaker with heavy plastic decoration. Probably same vessel as C13, C60 and C75. SE Quad, 4, 16in; 5, 18in. Figure 41.

C81 Two sherds, one a base sherd, in a light brown fabric decorated with regular rows of small oval or sub-triangular stabs. Probably from the same vessel. SE Quad, 1, 21 in; Hoare's trench. Figure 41.

C82 Sherd in a pink, well-fired fabric; decorated with random triangular impressions. Like C58, and C89 below. SE Quad, 1, 21in. Figure 41.

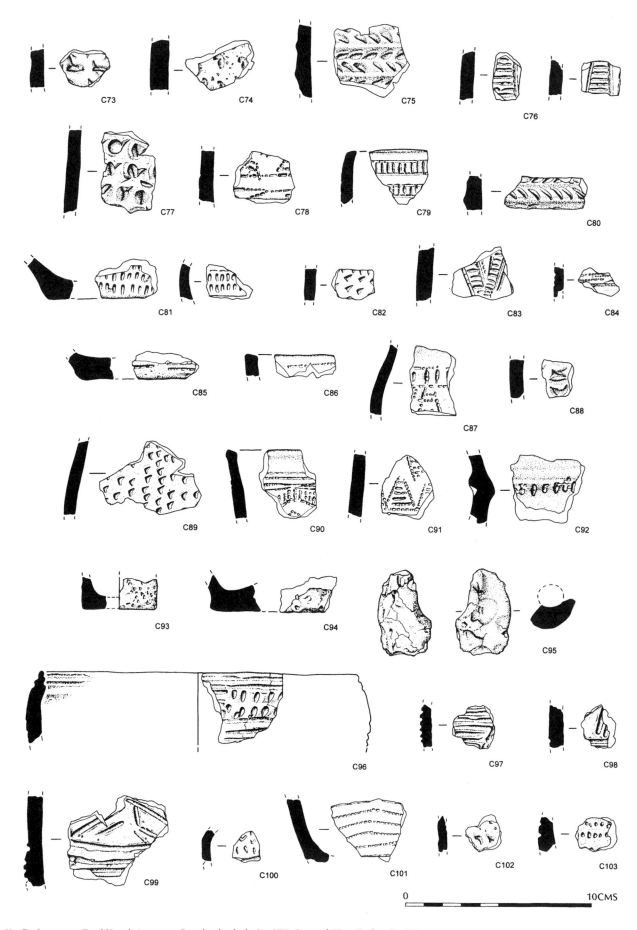

Fig 41 Beaker wares, Food Vessel, Accessory Cup sherds, daub, Site XIV; Grooved Ware, Beaker, Site XV.

C83 Sherd in a grey-brown fabric with traces of coil breaks in the fractures. Decorated externally with two converging ladder motifs executed in toothed comb. NW Quad, 1, 15in. Figure 41.

C84 Sherd in brown, fine fabric with traces of a coil break. Decorated externally with four overlapping but broadly parallel combed lines. NW Quad, 1, 15in. Figure 41.

C85 Base-angle sherd in a soft fabric with orange-brown surfaces and a black core. The fabric contains abundant calcined flint. Decorated with two encircling combed lines. SW Quad, 1, 18in. Figure 41.

C86 Flat-topped rim sherd with orange outer surface, black core and brown inner surface. An abraded line of comb impressions is visible on the outside. NW Quad, mound. Figure 41.

C87 Fine, well-fired sherd in a pink fabric with combed decoration. Motifs visible appear to be a zone of broad ladder motif above a zone of filled triangles. From the upper part of belly of a necked Beaker. SE Quad, 4, 18in. Figure 41.

C88 Small sherd in a pink fabric decorated externally with large, well-defined paired-fingernail impressions. Perhaps same pot as C73. SW Quad, 1, 25in. Figure 41.

C89 Restored sherd in a fairly soft, orange fabric. Decorated with vertical rows of triangular impressions. Similar to C14, C58, C81 and C82. SE Quad, 4, 23in. Figure 41.

C90 Rim sherd in an orange-brown fabric from a necked Beaker. The rim is slightly bevelled internally. Decoration, combed, comprises three horizontal lines bordering filled chevrons, possibly forming a broad zone of reserved running-chevron decoration. SW Quad, Hoare's trench. Figure 41.

C91 Large sherd in a light-brown fabric. Decorated with a zone of opposed filled triangles in deeply impressed comb. Similar to C78 but in a different fabric. SW Quad, Hoare's trench. Figure 41.

Food Vessel

C92 Fragment in a red-brown, well-fired fabric from near the rim of a tripartite vessel. Externally, a cordon in the neck is emphasised by a row of vertical bird-bone impressions placed below the cordon. NE Quad, 4, 9in. Figure 41.

Accessory Cup

C93 Base sherd in a hard, grey fabric from a miniature vessel with small, profuse, triangular stabs decorating the outer surface. The vessel had a base diameter of 40mm and thin walls suggesting that it may be from an Accessory Cup. SE Quad, 5, 9in. Section D, D20. Figure 41.

Other

C94 Base sherd in a coarse, calcined-flint-filled fabric with orange outer and grey-brown inner surface. The

central part of the base interior is thickening. Possibly Beaker. SW Quad, 5, 10in. Figure 41.

Daub

C95 Fragments of daub with wattle impressions clearly visible. SW Quad, 1, 18in. Figure 41.

Site XV

Grooved Ware

C96 Rim sherd in a grey-brown well-fired fabric, from a barrel-shaped vessel, rim diameter 170mm. The decoration comprises two grooves internally, immediately below the rim. Externally, two rows of vertical sub-triangular impressions (probably bird bone) are bordered above by two and below by three horizontal grooves. Join voids are visible in the fabric. SE Quad, disturbed, close to Inhumation 3 (Skeleton I) Figure 41.

C97 Sherd in a black, well-fired fabric; decorated externally with six deeply cut grooves. NW Quad, base of turf. Figure 41.

C98 Sherd decorated with horizontal and oblique grooves. Probably the same vessel as C102. NW Quad, base of turf. Figure 41.

C99 Sherd in a grey-black, porous fabric. The decoration comprises converging grooves forming a (?) triangular panel filled with haphazard herringbone grooving. Topsoil. Figure 41.

Beaker

C100 Sherd in a red-brown fabric with a dark core. Externally decorated with small, oblique, (?)fingernail impressions. SE Quad, close to Inhumation 6 (Skeleton II) Figure 41.

C101 Sherd in a hard, dark-brown fabric, slightly porous in section and with finely crushed inclusions. The sherd comes from near the base angle of the pot and is decorated externally with four horizontal slightly curved lines of comb impressions. The joins between individual comb-lengths are clearly visible. SW Quad, disturbed, close to Skeleton IV. Figure 41.

C102 Thin, abraded sherd with red outer surface, black inner surface and black core. Row of abraded, possibly fingernail impressions. Cf C98. Possibly Beaker. Topsoil. Figure 41.

Other

C103 Grey sherd with red inner surface and calcined-flint inclusions. Decorated externally with two horizontal rows of sub-circular stabs. Probably earlier Bronze Age. NW Quad, N half, disturbed. Figure 41.

Site XVII

Beaker

C104 Sherd in a red, well-fired fabric with a grey inner surface. Faint angular stab impressions, perhaps in rows. SW Quad, ditch, 11. Figure 42.

C105 Sherd of rusticated Beaker in a pink, hard and well-fired fabric; decorated externally with four horizontal rows of regularly spaced, single, vertical fingernail impressions. NW Quad, ditch, 9, 14in. Figure 42.

C106 Sherd in a red, well-fired fabric. Combed decoration externally comprising what appears to be an element of filled-chevron motif. NW Quad, 4, 24in. Figure 42.

C107 Sherd in a hard, red fabric; decorated externally with combed cross-hatching. SE Quad, 2, 28in. Figure 42.

C108 Sherd from the neck of a vessel in a pinkish-grey fabric, hard and well-fired. Decorated externally with impressions made with a comb having large, rectangular teeth and with short, vertical fingernail impressions. The decoration consists of a zone of ladder motif bordered, at a distance, by horizontal lines. Overlaps in the individual lengths of comb are plainly visible. SE Quad, 5, 17in. Figure 42.

C109 Sherd in a grey, well-fired fabric; decorated with coarse-comb herringbone impressions. Central burial pit, 5. Figure 42.

C110 Body sherd from a round-bellied pot in a hard, brown fabric with abundant finely-crushed calcined-flint inclusions. Decorated externally with vertical rows of regularly spaced shallow fingernail or bird-bone impressions. Probably from a fairly fine and small rusticated Beaker. NE Quad, 9, outer edge of ditch. Figure 42.

Site XVIII

Beaker

C111 Small body sherd in a fine waxy-textured red fabric. Decorated externally with three horizontal twisted-cord impressions. Cutting 1, topsoil. Figure 42.

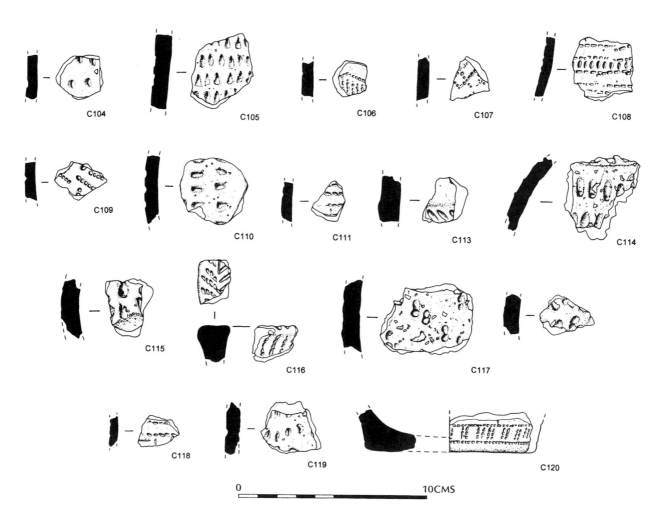

C104 C105 C106 C107 C108 C109 C110 C111 C113 C114 C115 C116 C117 C118 C119 C120

0   10CMS

Fig 42   Beaker wares, Site XVII; Beaker, Collared Vessel, Site XVIII; Peterborough Ware, Beaker, Site XIX; Beaker, Site XX.

Collared Urn

C112 Possible Collared Urn fabric. Fine, well-fired and pink throughout. Possible but faint whipped-cord maggot impressions on the outer surface. Cutting 1, topsoil. Section E, E1. Figure 48.

Site XIX

Peterborough Ware

C113 Sherd in a slightly porous fabric with a pink outer and grey inner surface. Decorated with a row of oblique fingernail impressions. Topsoil. Figure 42.

C114 Large sherd in a coarse, pink fabric with large calcined-flint inclusions many of which have erupted the outer surface. Abraded decoration appears to consist of whipped-cord impressions arranged as a single horizontal line at the top of the sherd and two rows of vertical maggots below. N Mound, section2, 8. Figure 42.

C115 Sherd in a pink-brown fabric with grey inner surface. Decorated with two large, deep bird-bone impressions. N Mound, section 1, 8. Figure 42.

C116 Rim sherd in a grey fabric with calcined-flint inclusions. Flat-topped rim decorated on the top with a row of herringbone motif formed by short twisted-cord impressions. An oblique row of the same technique is found inside the rim. There is no trace of

external decoration. N Mound, section 1, 8, 27in. Figure 42.

C117 Two coarse sherds in a fabric with pink outer and grey inner surfaces. Abundant large calcined-flint inclusions up to 8mm across. Decoration consists of traces of two rows of bird-bone impressions. N Mound, section 2, 8, 29in. Figure 42.

Beaker

C118 Sherd in a light-brown, fine fabric decorated externally with two rows of twisted-cord impressions. Possibly from an AOC Beaker. N Mound, section 1, 5, 39in. Figure 42.

C119 Sherd with brown surfaces and a black core in a fairly coarse calcined-flint-filled fabric. Decorated externally with shallow fingernail impressions. Possibly rusticated Beaker. N Mound, section 1, 8. Figure 42.

Site XX

Beaker

C120 Base sherd in a hard, pink, well-fired fabric with crushed shell inclusions. Base diameter c 90mm. The decoration consists of combed impressions arranged to form a single zone of ladder motif. Ditch, section 8, 21, 3ft. Figure 42.

D COLLARED URNS, FOOD VESSELS AND ACCESSORY CUPS AND VESSELS FROM THE BARROWS

Ian Longworth

THE COLLARED VESSELS

The Collared Vessels from the cemetery show considerable variation in form, less so in decoration. On typological grounds the urn containing the (probable) primary burial in Barrow XVIII discovered by Colt Hoare is likely to be the earliest, since this belongs to the Primary Series and stands close to ancestral Fengate forms. The decorative patterns used are identical to those on another Vessel of the Primary Series found in a barrow at Penmaenmawr, Dwygyfylchi, Gwynedd (Longworth 1984, 2095) though on this the hurdling ornament has been applied to the collar rather than the neck.

Excluding the urn extracted by Hoare in 1805 from Site III, which may well have been of Collared form but about which nothing was recorded, the remaining Vessels, where sufficient survives to allow comment, all belong to the Secondary Series. The majority of these (six out of seven) carrying traits typical of the south-eastern style of that tradition – twisted cord horseshoes on the shoulder (D8 and D23); horizontal lines on the collar (D11); point-toothed comb decoration (D11, D12 and D24) and form BIII (D22). Exceptionally the Vessel accompanying the primary burial in XVII (D23) carries, in addition to the twisted cord horseshoes, a row of jabbed impressions on the shoulder, a feature otherwise typical of the north-western style.

Throughout the tradition, identical pairs of Collared Vessels are absolutely rare, so the general similarity in form and disposition of the decoration on Vessels D10 and D23 and again in form (but not in size) between the associated Vessels D11 and D12 is striking. It is also perhaps worth noting that the relatively rare use of pattern D (Longworth *ibid*, fig 9), when found, is usually, as on D11, applied in rough-and-ready fashion (cf in twisted cord on an Urn from Stanton Moor 7, Derbys (Longworth *ibid*, 315) or in comb on a Vessel from Micheldever, Hants (*ibid*, 624). Indeed the majority of patterns when made with a point-toothed comb appear carelessly achieved, though well-formed schemes can occasionally be found as, for example, on a Vessel from Hutton Cranswick, Humberside, (*ibid*, 723).

The proportions, though not the precise size, of Urns D10 and D23 are very similar to the Urn from Winterslow 21, Wilts (*ibid*, 1739) which carries an almost identical scheme of decoration to another Vessel from the Snail Down Cemetery, D8. This was associated with a very similar necklace composed of amber, jet and faience beads to that found with Urn D10, suggesting that some features of custom and belief were shared by those engaged in burying their dead at these two sites.

ACCESSORY CUPS

The slightly inturned tub-shape of Cup D4, though simple, is not particularly common, but Cups of this form do not cluster in any geographical grouping. Undecorated examples from Wiltshire include Ford, Laverstock (Stone 1937a, pl 111) and Temple Down (Annable and Simpson 1964, 64 and 120, 523) and examples occur sporadically further afield, for example undecorated from Ampton, Suffolk (Kinnes and Longworth 1985, UN 50:2) and Durham (*ibid*, UN 6:3), the former certainly, the latter probably associated with Collared Urn burials (for a full list of such associations see Longworth 1984, 53, Cup type e). The use of a point-toothed comb is not particularly common on this class of Cup and their distribution is dispersed eg Lambourne CCLXXXIX (Kinnes and Longworth 1985, 289:5); Tynings Farm, Cheddar, Somerset (University of Bristol Spelaeological Society Museum) and as far afield as Santoft, near Cawthorn, North Yorkshire (Sheffield Museum J 93–876).

Little can be said of the second Cup recovered by Hoare from Site II, D5. This had clearly been found intact but little now survives. The marked internal rim can be found on a number of Cups, all of which share a form which is broad and squat eg Bishops Cannings 62a, Wilts (Thurnam 1871, 360, fig 38), Melbourne 24 (Cambs: Stevenson 1987, 8, figs 2,3) and Middleton and Smerrill 4 (Derbys: Longworth 1984, 283), the last associated with a Collared Urn and bronze awl.

ACCESSORY VESSEL
(with Secondary Burial 2, Site III, D13)

Examples of Vessels of varying shape probably in current use as domestic ware are occasionally found in association with Collared Vessels (Longworth 1984, 50). The form of this pot is not dissimilar to the neck and body of a normal Collared Vessel but without the collar. A very similar Vessel came from West Ashby, Lincolnshire (N Field 1985, 121, 122, fig 13, 3) though here the rim has been strengthened internally.

FOOD VESSELS

A decorated rim sherd from Site I, D1, belongs to a Food Vessel probably of bipartite form with concave neck and everted rim, similar to the Vessel from Knowle, Little Bedwyn (Annable and Simpson 1964, 67 and 124, 557). The form is sometimes found with decoration on the inner surface of the rim and over the neck as on a Vessel from the Cae Mickney cemetery, Llanidan, Anglesey (Lynch 1970, 161, fig 55, 5) though here without the internal moulding.

The bipartite Food Vessel from Site II, D3, is ubiquitous in both plain and decorated forms, with a widespread distribution. The body sherds D7 could well have come from a similar Vessel since on these the body decoration is often not taken down the whole way to the base.

Site XIV produced a wall sherd of Ridged Food Vessel (C92, Fig 41) of the type in which body decoration consists of simple impressions made either with a blunt instrument or occasionally cord and confined either to the edges of the multiple ridges or, leaving the ridges plain, as a single row of decoration in the multiple grooves. Too little survives, however, to establish the precise form of this Vessel.

SITE I

D1 Rim sherd of Food Vessel of well-fired paste, pale chocolate brown externally, patchy brown to grey on the internal surface becoming grey to darker brown towards the lower margin of the sherd. Core black.
Decoration: made with a fine twisted cord. On the internal moulding, three horizontal lines above lozenges. On the external surface, lozenges beneath three horizontal lines and above the remains of two horizontal lines. (Fig 43).
SW Quadrant, outer half of ditch, section 2, layer 3, d 2ft.
DZSWS: 1955.213; Thomas and Thomas 1956, 134.

D2 Rim sherd of Collared Vessel of well-fired paste, deep red-brown externally. Core, orange outer, black inner. Internal surface dark red-brown, patchy grey/black on the rim bevel.
Decoration: on the internal rim bevel, two coarse twisted cord horizontal lines. On the collar, remains of a single coarse twisted cord horizontal line survives. (Fig 43).
NE Quadrant, central plateau, between mounds, section 2, layer 9, d 1ft.
DZSWS: 1955.213; Thomas and Thomas *ibid*.

SITE II

D3 Food Vessel   Complete
Diameter of mouth: 10.9cm
Height: 10.8cm
Diameter of base: 6.25cm
Of coarse paste with large flint inclusions and possible grog. Patchy pale orange brown externally, with greyer brown and black patches on the rim. Interior similar with some patches of greyer brown. Core orange near the surface.
Undecorated. (Fig 44).
SE Quadrant, section 6, inverted over possible food offering in small pit (Fig 8, section 3; Pl 12).
DZSWS: 1955.213; DM259; Thomas and Thomas *ibid*; Annable and Simpson 1964, 62 and 117, 492.

D4 Accessory Cup   Complete
Diameter of mouth: 3.6cm
Height: 3.4cm
Diameter of base: 2.9cm
Of well-fired paste, uneven chocolate brown externally with areas of wall almost black clearly discoloured by exclusion of air during firing. Internally and on rim similar to external surface with area of dark brown shading into black at wall/base join.
Decoration: Externally, vertical lines of point-toothed comb-impressions and faintly along rim. (Fig 44).
Primary cremation burial in pit with second Accessory Cup (D5) accompanied by cremation and copper alloy awl (L2, Fig 55).
Hoare 1812, 182–183, Pl 22; DZSWS: STHEAD.104; Abercromby 1912, II, pl 80, 242; Thomas and Thomas 1956, 134; Annable and Simpson 1964, 63 and 118, 501; Warrilow 1980, fig 12.2.

D5 Two joining sherds from Accessory Cup, of well-fired paste. Reddish pale chocolate brown on both surfaces. Core black. Diameter of mouth 3.1cm.
Decoration: on top of rim, diagonal impressions. (Fig 44).
See D4.
DZSWS: 1955.213.

D6 Four plain sherds including base angle of Bronze Age fabric, perhaps Late Bronze Age Plain Ware (see also Section E).
Topsoil.

D7 Eight sherds (three joining) from the base and lower body of a Food Vessel, of fairly well-fired coarse paste, externally patchy grey-brown. Core black. Internally similar to external surface but grey/black brown where interior wall turns into base.
Decoration: remains of short diagonal twisted cord lines to form ? herring-bone pattern. (Fig 44).
From eccentric burial pit.
Thomas and Thomas 1956, 135.

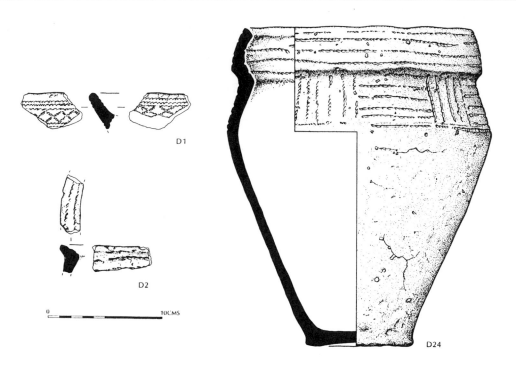

Fig 43 Food Vessel, Collared Vessel sherds, Site I; Collared Urn, Site XVIII.

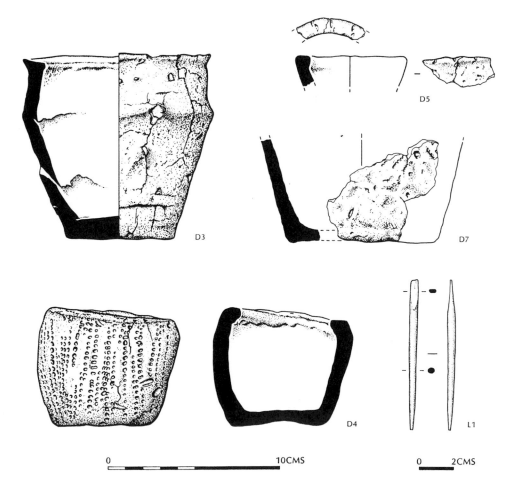

Fig 44 Food Vessel and sherds, Accessory Cup and sherds, copper alloy awl (L2), Site II (see also Fig 55).

SITE III

D8   Sherds, including fragments of collar, neck and shoulder, of a Collared Vessel of fairly well-fired paste.

Externally pale chocolate brown becoming more orange-brown at rim and collar interior. Core, outer orange, inner black. Internally below the collar grey/black.

Secondary Series, Form IC, South Eastern Style.
Dimensions:
Height (surviving): *c* 15.3cm
Decoration: on the internal rim bevel, faint twisted cord horizontal lines. On the collar, twisted cord hurdle pattern beneath a single horizontal twisted cord line. On the shoulder, twisted cord horseshoes. (Fig 45).

Quadrant E, section 2, layer 11, d 5ft, near ancient land surface sealed by mound (Fig 10, section 2).
Thomas and Thomas 1956, 139; Longworth 1984, 1676.

D9   Three sherds, Collared Urn fabric. Perhaps Late Bronze Age Plain Ware.
Undecorated.
N Quadrant, berm, layer 7.

D10   Collared Urn, restored but distorted with much of rim missing.
Secondary Series, form IV.
Dimensions:
Diameter of mouth: *c* 34.3cm
Height: 45.2cm
Diameter of base: 15.25cm
Of quite well-fired paste with some flint and grog. Externally smoothed particularly at neck. Externally deep, slightly reddish chocolate with patches of grey-brown to black on collar and neck. Internally, deep grey-brown patchy. Core black to inner black, outer orange.
Decoration: on the internal bevel, two twisted cord lines crossed by vertical lines. On the collar, twisted cord filled triangles enclosed by pairs of horizontal twisted cord lines. On the shoulder a single twisted cord horizontal line crossed by short vertical cord lines. (Fig 45).
Secondary Burial 1 (Cremation 8) on berm (Fig 11, section 4, Fig 13, section 2; Pls 19, 20).
DZSWS: 1955.214; Thomas and Thomas 1956, 138; Annable and Simpson 1964, 64 and 119, 515; Longworth 1984, 1673.

D11   Collared Urn complete save for part of upper collar. Of fairly well-fired coarse paste, roughly smoothed.

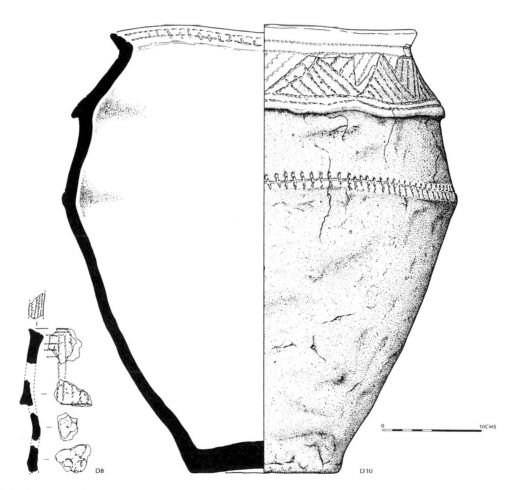

Fig 45   Collared Vessel sherds, Site III; Collared Urn, Secondary Burial I, Site III.

Externally uneven deep red-brown with patches of deep red, especially on the collar. Internal surface of collar and neck similar but darker brown to grey black on body. Core orange.

Secondary Series, South Eastern Style, Form I/II.

Dimensions:

Diameter of mouth: 21.4 cm
Height: 29.1 cm
Diameter of base: 14.1 cm

Decoration: on the inside of the rim, short diagonal toothed-comb lines. On the collar, open rectangles in point-toothed comb. (Fig 46).

Secondary Burial 2 (Cremation 9) on the berm (Fig 13, section 1; Pls 22, 23).

DZSWS: 1955.214; Thomas and Thomas 1956, 138; Annable and Simpson 1964, 63 and 118, 504; Longworth 1984, 1674.

D12 Collared Vessel, complete save for small fragment of rim. Of well-fired paste, roughly smoothed but with some inclusions erupting through the surface. Externally, pale chocolate brown with some black and darker brown patches. Internal surface similar but in some areas becoming deep orange. Outer part of core, orange.

Secondary Series, South Eastern Style, Form IA.

Dimensions:

Diameter of mouth: 8.7cm
Height: 8.9cm
Diameter of base: 5.4cm

Decoration: on the inside of the rim, occasional point-toothed comb short diagonal lines. On the collar, irregular horizontal lines in point-toothed comb-impressions. (Fig 46).

Secondary Burial 2 on the berm (Fig 13, section 1; Pls 22, 23).

See D11 and D13.

DZSWS: 1955.214; Thomas and Thomas 1956, 138; Annable and Simpson 1964, 63 and 118, No 505; Longworth 1984, No 1675.

D13 Bipartite Vessel, complete. Of well-fired paste with some flint inclusions erupting through the surface. Roughly smoothed. Externally, uneven orange brown, pale chocolate brown, to grey brown. Two-thirds of upper body tending to black. Internally uneven pale chocolate brown, redder in patches especially around upper third. At rim, core is orange brown.

Dimensions:

Diameter of mouth: 8.7cm
Height: 10.4cm
Diameter of base: 7.3cm

Undecorated. (Fig 46).

Secondary Burial 2 (Cremation 9) on the berm (Fig 13, section 1; Pls 22, 23)

See D11 and D12.

DZSWS: 1955.214; Thomas and Thomas 1956, 138; Annable and Simpson 1964, 66 and 122, 543; Longworth 1984, 1674.

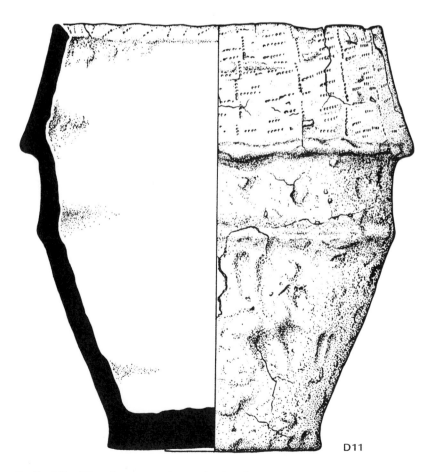

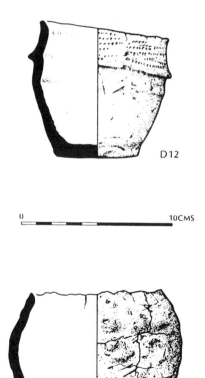

D12

0   10CMS

D11

D13

Fig 46   Collared Urns, Bipartite Vessel, Secondary Burial 2, Site III.

SITE X

D14 Undecorated base angle of Collared Vessel of fairly soft paste, externally orange-brown, internally black with black core.
Unstratified from mound.

D15 Undecorated base sherd of Collared Vessel, of paste similar to D14.
Unstratified from mound.

SITE XI

D16 Undecorated wall sherd of Collared Vessel, pink surfaces with grey core.
SE Quadrant, layer 4, d 16in.

D17 Undecorated wall sherd of Collared Vessel, pink surfaces with grey core.
SE Quadrant, beyond mound, layer 1, bedrock.

SITE XIII

D18 Sherd from collar of Collared Vessel of sandy fabric, brown on collar.
Decoration: on the collar, lines of point-toothed comb-impressions.
SW Quadrant, topsoil.

SITE XIV

D19 Sherd of Ridged Food Vessel of well-fired fabric, red to brown in colour.
Decoration: on (or below) an external cordon a row of deep vertical impressions. (Fig 41, C92).
NE Quadrant, layer 4, d 9in
Section C, C92.

D20 Base angle of Accessory Cup (diameter of base: 3.9cm) of well-fired paste, grey in colour.
Decoration: on the external surface, stabs. (Fig 41, C93).
SE Quadrant, layer 5, d 9in.
Section C, C93.

D21 Three undecorated wall sherds from the body of a Collared Vessel.
Cremation pit (Fig 21, section 6).

SITE XVII

D22 Collared Vessel. About two thirds of Vessel represented but most of collar lost. Of quite well-fired, coarse paste. Externally, grey/dark brown with small area of redder brown on collar. Internally, similar

with some areas deep brown. Core black becoming medium chocolate brown at the collar.
Secondary Series, South Eastern Style, Form BIII.
Dimensions:
Diameter of mouth: 10.1cm
Height: 12.3cm
Diameter of base: 7.2cm
Decoration: on the collar, fine diagonal twisted cord lines enclosed between single twisted cord lines. (Fig 47).
Secondary deposit at edge of mound, in pit, unaccompanied (Fig 30, section 4; Pl 50).
DZSWS: 1960.10; Thomas and Thomas 1958, 7; Annable and Simpson 1964, 65 and 121, 533; Longworth 1984, 1679.

D23 Collared Urn, restored. Most of the body and two thirds of the neck survive but only parts of the collar and very little of the rim.
Secondary Series, North Western/South Eastern Style, Form II.
Dimensions:
Diameter of mouth: *c* 34.4cm
Height: *c* 44.3cm
Diameter of base: 15.1cm
Of quite well-fired paste with flint and grog inclusions. Externally well smoothed. Externally, deep chocolate brown to black on neck and parts of collar becoming paler on the body. Internally, deep chocolate brown to black brown but paler near the base.
Decoration: on the internal rim bevel, traces of perhaps a single twisted cord line. On the collar, a filled-triangle pattern, perhaps multiple vertical chevron, in twisted cord bounded below (and perhaps above) by a single twisted cord. On the shoulder, twisted cord horseshoes above a row of jabbed impressions. (Fig 47). Deliberately broken and placed near base of pit, then cremation placed in and over its remains. (Fig 30, section 3; Pls 47, 48).
DZSWS: 1960.10.4; Thomas and Thomas 1958, 7: Annable and Simpson 1964, 64 and 119, 510; Longworth 1984, 1678.

SITE XVIII

D24 Collared Urn, complete save for small fragment of rim. Of rather soft paste tempered with flint and grog, surfaces well smoothed. Externally slightly uneven greyish brown with two greyer areas from shoulder to base, one adjacent to large area of orange-redness, the result of variable conditions in the firing. Internally similar but greyer on body. Outer core at collar, deep grey-chocolate brown to orange.
Primary Series, South Eastern Style, Form IB.
Dimension:
Diameter of mouth: 20.4cm
Height: 28.5cm
Diameter of base: 9.5cm
Decoration: on the internal moulding and on the collar, horizontal twisted cord lines. On the neck,

twisted cord hurdle pattern above a single horizontal twisted cord line on the shoulder. (Fig 43).
At centre. At one edge of pit cut into chalk, upright, containing cremation.

Hoare 1812, 184; DZSWS: STHEAD.255; Thomas and Thomas 1958, 7; Annable and Simpson 1964, 66 and 122, 540; Longworth 1984, 1677.

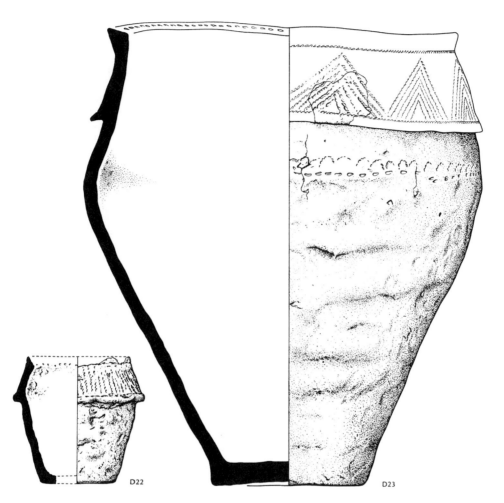

D22

D23

Fig 47   Collared urn, Collared Vessel, Site XVII.

E BRONZE AGE, IRON AGE AND ROMANO-BRITISH POTTERY ASSOCIATED WITH THE LINEAR DITCH SYSTEM, SITES VI AND VII, AND LATER AGRICULTURE

FRANCES RAYMOND

INTRODUCTION AND METHODOLOGY

This report is concerned with an assemblage of 112 sherds, weighing 1.049kg, which represent many different ceramic phases, beginning with the Early Bronze Age and ending sometime during the Early Romano-British period. Some minor, unavoidable overlap occurs with the extensive report on the Beaker settlement pottery by Alex Gibson (Section C) and, by Kenneth Annable, on Romano-British pottery (Section F). Cross-references have been made where necessary. The condition, size and scattered distribution of sherds in primary contexts is more consistent with chance loss than with deliberate deposition. Two groups of material, the Late Bronze Age Plain Ware and the Late Iron Age to Early Romano-British assemblage, are most likely to be derived from settlements in the vicinity of the barrow cemetery. The Early and Middle Bronze Age pottery may also have a similar origin, although the additional funerary role of ceramics during these periods complicates an attempt to reconstruct the general circumstances which led to the deposition of a few small sherds.

Although most of the pottery discussed below indicates vague and uncertain activity within and adjacent to the barrow cemetery, which cannot be related directly to a structural phase, there is one notable exception. This takes the form of the reconstruction of the northern boundary of Enclosure A, Site VI, as a V-shaped linear ditch, an event which is associated with sherds of Middle Iron Age date.

Before embarking on a more detailed account, there are a few general methods which have been applied to the ceramics, regardless of chronology. All vessel fragments with diagnostic features have been illustrated and will be discussed in the appropriate section. Many of the fabrics are identical to those recovered from other sites in the vicinity of Snail Down during the Reading Linear Ditches Project (Raymond 1994). To avoid repetition these have not been described again, but, for the purposes of cross-referencing, the same codes are used in this report,

while the bibliographic references for the detailed descriptions are given in Table 8. Wares which are at present unique to Snail Down have been assigned codes according to the same method. Briefly, a series of letters arranged in alphabetical order precedes a colon. These are the initials of the inclusions present in individual fabrics. They include: C chalk; F – flint; fe – iron minerals; G – grog; M – mica; Q – quartz conglomerate; S – quartz sand; Sa – sarsen; sh – shell; and V – voids. The colon is succeeded by a date or style attribution. These comprise BKR – Beaker; DR – Deverel Rimbury (Middle Bronze Age); LBA – Late Bronze Age Plain Ware; IA - Iron Age of uncertain phasing; IA-RB – Late Iron Age to Early Romano-British; RB Romano-British of uncertain phasing; and Indet – prehistoric sherds of indeterminate chronology. The numbers which mark the end of each code are employed simply to distinguish between wares which share the same inclusions, but in contrasting quantities and/or sizes. These numbers continue the sequence begun during the Reading Linear Ditches Project (Raymond *ibid*). All new fabrics are described in Table 9.

THE EARLY BRONZE AGE POTTERY

This includes the remains of four Beakers represented by four small and abraded sherds, weighing only 28 grammes. The illustrated example, E1 (all sherds are illustrated in Fig 48), was recovered from the topsoil over a bowl-barrow (Site XVIII). It is decorated with relatively unusual motifs, although unfortunately the orientation and position of the sherd in relation to the original vessel is uncertain. The same fabric (feGS: BKR/4), used in the construction of this sherd, E1, occurs on other sites in the vicinity (Raymond *ibid*, table 23). The information relating to the style of these other examples is minimal, but some were certainly decorated with motifs which contrasted with the sherd from Snail Down. This observation finds similar echoes in the Stonehenge area, where single fabrics were used to produce Beakers of contrasting styles (Cleal and Raymond 1990, 238).

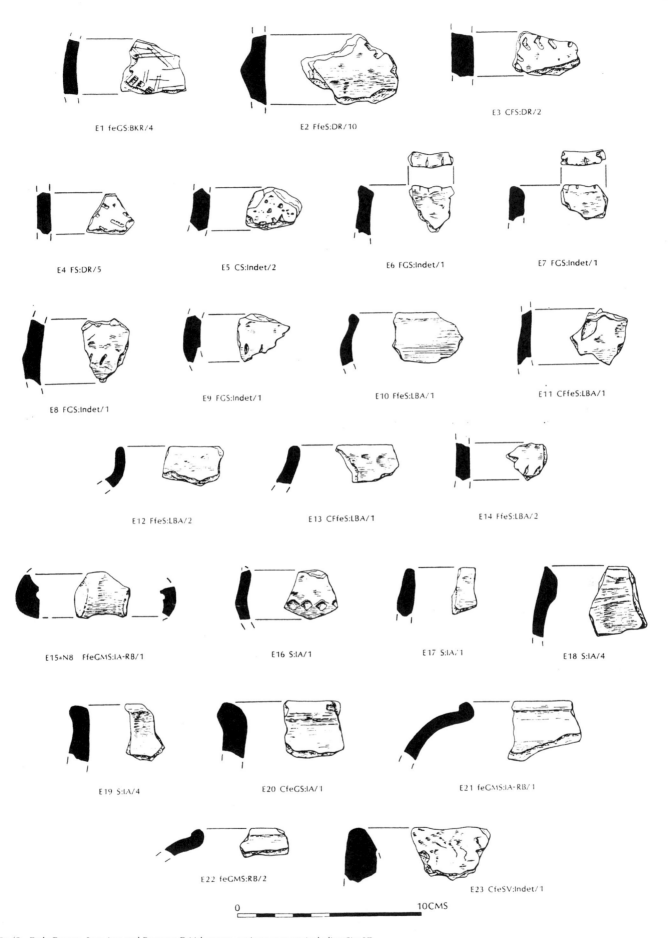

E1 feGS:BKR/4

E2 FfeS:DR/10

E3 CFS:DR/2

E4 FS:DR/5

E5 CS:Indet/2

E6 FGS:Indet/1

E7 FGS:Indet/1

E8 FGS:Indet/1

E9 FGS:Indet/1

E10 FfeS:LBA/1

E11 CFfeS:LBA/1

E12 FfeS:LBA/2

E13 CFfeS:LBA/1

E14 FfeS:LBA/2

E15=N8 FfeGMS:IA-RB/1

E16 S:IA/1

E17 S:IA/1

E18 S:IA/4

E19 S:IA/4

E20 CfeGS:IA/1

E21 feGMS:IA-RB/1

E22 feGMS:RB/2

E23 CfeSV:Indet/1

0   10CMS

Fig 48 Early Bronze, Iron Age and Romano-British wares, various contexts including Site VI.

Two of the other sherds are decorated, but these have not been illustrated owing to the uninformative nature of the motifs. The first, made from a sandy ware (feS: Indet/2), is decorated with a single linear impression and was recovered from the edge of the barrow mound overlying the Beaker settlement (Site XIII), which also yielded a second undecorated fragment in a fabric (GS; BKR/1) found on other sites in the area (Raymond *ibid*, table 23). The second sherd came from the infill of the Romano-British or later cart track (Site VI, section 4, layer 9; Figs 18, 19); it is in extremely poor condition, but displays faint traces of point and rectangular toothed comb impressions. The only remarkable feature is its fabric (FfeMS: BKR/1), which contains a moderate quantity of mica, a relatively uncommon inclusion in other Beakers from the area, although it occurs in some of the wares recovered from the environs of Stonehenge (Cleal and Raymond 1990, 238). The Beaker fabrics which form the subject of this report are all slightly unusual. Two contain no grog (FfeMS: BKR/1; feS: Indet/2), one has very little (feGS:BKR/4), while two are tempered with fairly high quantities of sand (feS: Indet/2; GS: BKR/1).

A fifth vessel, represented by a single decorated sherd (E5; Fig 48), is also included in this section. It was recovered from the old land surface, sealed by the bank of the linear ditch running along the northern side of the barrow cemetery. The sherd is fairly abraded and this, together with the Late Bronze Age date for the initial construction of linear ditches (Bradley *et al* 1994), means that it is most likely to be residual. The proposed dating for this particular fragment of pottery is in any case not entirely certain. There is no information concerning vessel form, while neither the decoration nor the fabric is entirely diagnostic, although both find their closest parallels within assemblages of Early Bronze Age date.

THE MIDDLE BRONZE AGE (DEVEREL RIMBURY) POTTERY

The Middle Bronze Age assemblage (Fig 48), consists of thirteen sherds, weighing 117 grammes, which came from at least five different vessels. Three of these, being represented by fragments with diagnostic features, are illustrated (E2–E4). Two (E3 and E4) came from the edge of one of the mounds overlying the Beaker settlement (Site XIII). The stratigraphic association between these sherds and the two fragments of Beaker should be regarded with some caution. The presence of a single sherd of Late Bronze Age Plain Ware in the same context suggests that there may have been some disturbance along the perimeter of the barrow mound. It is possible that one of the vessels (E4) was produced at a time when Deverel Rimbury ceramics were emerging as a new style in the area. Although there is no clue as to the form of the vessel, the impressed comb motifs would be more usual in an Early Bronze Age context. However, the fabric is typical of the Middle Bronze Age and seems to have been a fairly common ware throughout this period, being used to produce Deverel Rimbury vessels, probably Barrel Urns, on other sites in the vicinity of Snail Down (Raymond *ibid*).

The remaining eleven Middle Bronze Age sherds were all recovered from the topsoil, one associated with a barrow (Site XI) at the eastern edge of the Beaker settlement; another from Site VII, Section 14 (Fig 20) and the remainder, including E2, from the area around Site XX, where later activity, associated with Iron Age and Romano-British pottery, had resulted in a great deal of chronological mixing. This same area also produced sherds of Late Bronze Age Plain Ware and although the stratigraphic relationship has been lost, it repeats an association which has been noted on a number of settlements close to Snail Down (Bradley *et al, ibid*). This may be yet another example of a diffuse open settlement, substantially of Late Bronze Age date, but with origins towards the end of the Middle Bronze Age. In the absence of structural evidence this must of course remain conjectural, although the quantities of pottery are entirely consistent with the amounts recovered from the fringes of such sites (Bradley *et al, ibid*). In the case of Snail Down, the most likely location is somewhere to the north of the barrow cemetery.

The Deverel Rimbury fabrics include three examples (CFS: DR/2; F: DR/2; and FS: DR/5) which have a relatively widespread distribution (Raymond *ibid*, table 23). This is a pattern which is replicated by a number of fine wares in the area, but which contrasts markedly with the confined distribution of coarse wares (Raymond *ibid*). The two new fabrics (FfeS: DR/10 and FS: DR/10) identified at Snail Down fall entirely within the expected range of wares common during the Middle Bronze Age.

THE LATE BRONZE AGE PLAIN WARE

At Snail Down the Late Bronze Age is marked by nineteen sherds, weighing 106 grammes and representing a minimum of ten vessels. Nine of the illustrated sherds (E6–E14, Fig 48) belong to this period. Fourteen sherds were recovered from the vicinity of Site XX, all but four from residual contexts, where they were associated with Middle Bronze Age, Iron Age and Early Romano-British pottery (E9–E13). The exceptions came from the tertiary silts and from the top of the primary silt of the bowl-barrow Site XX and included three of the illustrated examples (E6–E8). Four further sherds were associated with the tops and edges of barrow mounds (Sites II, III, XIII and XIV). The example from Site XIV is illustrated (E14).

The last of the nineteen Late Bronze Age sherds has some relevance in providing a general date for the origin of the linear ditches. It was stratified in the bank on the south side of the linear ditch marking the northern boundary of Enclosure A. This suggests that the bank was constructed sometime after Plain Ware had become established as a new ceramic style. This again is consistent with the dates for other linear ditches in the area (Bradley *et al, ibid*). In this case the time lapse between the deposition of the sherd and its incorporation in the bank is of course impossible to demonstrate.

The Late Bronze Age Plain Ware from Snail Down shares a number of features with assemblages derived from nearby settlements (Raymond *ibid*). Such traits include rim and upper vessel profiles; the restrained nature of the decoration, which is confined to the tops of rims and shoulders; and the fabrics. On sites with larger assemblages there are a number of subtle differences which emerges from this background of general similarity. It would appear that these contrasts between the ceramics are congruent with different settlements and with the territories defined by linear ditches (Raymond *ibid*). The assemblage from Snail Down is far too small to support a detailed level of interpretation, but it would appear to contrast with contemporary pottery in one fairly striking way. It is the only site where the Late Bronze Age ceramics are decorated with finger-nail impressions. Elsewhere finger-tip, or finger-nail marks set within finger-tip impressions were the usual decorative techniques employed during this period (Raymond *ibid*). Once again we may be seeing an example of the way in which a local community was drawing on a shared repertoire of ideas about style and technology, but was using this knowledge in a very individual and creative manner.

There is a second analogy with other sites in the area, but this time it is a chronological parallel. There is no indication of any activity occurring at the very end of the Bronze Age when All Cannings Cross ceramics were being used. Elsewhere the beginning of this phase is marked by an abandonment of settlement (Bradley *et al, ibid*), an event which may well have taken place in the vicinity of Snail Down.

THE IRON AGE POTTERY

Most of the sherds of Iron Age date (Fig 48) are undiagnostic and cannot be assigned to a specific phase within this general period, although there are a few exceptions. The earliest recognisable example is represented by a single sherd (E16), which finds its closest parallels within Early Iron Age assemblages. Although there are other undiagnostic fragments of vessels made from the same fabric represented at Snail Down, at present the longevity of this ware in the locality is unknown, in spite of its relatively widespread distribution (Raymond *ibid*, table 32). The main relevance of this sherd, which comes from the topsoil containing pottery of Middle Bronze Age to Romano-British date at Site XX and Site VI nearby, is that it indicates the commencement of another phase of activity in the vicinity of Snail Down, even if its nature is obscure and its scale minimal.

The only securely stratified sherds, unaccompanied by either earlier or later material, are of Middle Iron Age date and come from the V-shaped re-cut of the linear ditch which forms the northern boundary of Enclosure A close to Site XXI (section 1, Fig 35). In total, five sherds in fairly fresh condition, weighing 62 grammes, and representing a minimum of two vessels, were recovered. The illustrated example (E20) is from the secondary silts of this ditch, which also incorporated two featureless fragments of pottery, one in the same fabric. Two further sherds in an identical ware to E20 were recovered from the lower secondary silts, 6in above the primary fill of the ditch. Apart from the fabric, the surface treatment of these sherds is entirely con-

sistent with a Middle Iron Age date. There are obviously many taphonomic problems concerning the origin of artefacts incorporated in ditch silts. However, the evidence suggests a relatively short interval between the beginning of the silting, following the reconstruction of the linear ditch, and the inclusion of the pottery. Once again, the time lapse between the deposition of the sherds and their incorporation in the linear ditch is unknown.

The remaining Iron Age pottery consists of twenty-four sherds, weighing 161 grammes, and representing a minimum of seven vessels. It is of uncertain phasing and includes three of the illustrated vessels (E17–E19). Many of the fabrics appear to have been produced over a long period and are not diagnostic of any particular style.

These sherds were all recovered from various contexts in the vicinity of Site XX. Seventeen were associated with Late Iron Age and Early Romano-British pottery. Fifteen of these sherds were from the topsoil and one was from the tertiary silts of the bowl-barrow, Site XX. The final sherd associated with Early Romano-British pottery was at the base of the bank adjacent to the linear ditch marking the northern boundary of Enclosure A, overlying the ditch of Site XX (section 8, layer 23; Figs 18, 19). However, the proximity of this feature to the Romano-British cart track and to the field system in this location may well indicate that the bank in this area was a product of Romano-British cultivation and not the remains of the earlier linear boundary. The other seven sherds were associated Iron Age pottery alone. They were recovered from two contexts dug in 1953, a buried ploughsoil (Site VI, section 2, layer 10; Figs 18, 19); and a spread of bank material adjacent to the linear ditch marking the northern boundary of Enclosure A.

THE LATE IRON AGE AND EARLY ROMANO-BRITISH POTTERY

The pottery belonging to this phase consists of twenty-one sherds, weighing 148 grammes, and representing a minimum of nine vessels, including the two illustrated bead-rim jars (E21–E22, Fig 48). There appears to be a continuity in the use of a number of fabrics between the Iron Age and Early Romano-British periods (FfeGMS: IA-RB/I; feGMS: IA/l; feGS: IA/6; feGS: IA/7; S: IA/l; S: IA/2; S: IA/4; and CFfeMS: Indet/1). At least one of these wares (S: IA/1) had a long currency, with its origins in the Early Iron Age. Although the quantity and size of inclusions within fabrics remained unchanged, by the Early Romano-British period raised firing temperatures and the evidence for wheel-thrown pottery had substantially altered the appearance of these wares. Even though the data are slight they may indicate that alterations in technology were taking place at long-established production centres. At Snail Down the assemblage is small and the contexts mixed, so that it is not possible to trace the development of ceramic technology, nor to date the observed changes with any accuracy. For this reason the majority of sherds has been assigned to a broad phase between the end of the Iron Age and the end of the Early Romano-British period.

The pottery of this general date is all derived from the area around Site XX; fourteen of the sherds including the two bead rim jars (E21, E22) were found in the top-soil. Three came from the tertiary silts of Site VI, NE of Site XX, and two from the lower ditch fill of the bowl-barrow, Site XX. One was excavated from the upper fill of the linear ditch marking the northern edge of Enclosure A (Site VI, section 2, layer 5; Figs 18, 19), while the last of the sherds came from the base of the bank associated with this same boundary (Site XX, bank overlying barrow ditch, section 8, base of layer 23; Figs 18, 19). Its significance has been discussed already in the preceding section.

IMPORTED AND INDETERMINATE ROMANO-BRITISH POTTERY

This is represented by a total of thirteen sherds, weighing 262 grammes, which were all recovered from the vicinity of Site XX, with the exception of a single fragment from the topsoil over another bowl-barrow (Site XVIII). The only identifiable sherd was Savernake Ware from the spread of bank material associated with the northern linear ditch of Enclosure A (Site VI, unpublished section, W of section 2; Fig 18). One of the sherds came from the tertiary silts of the barrow at Site XX (section 8, base of layer 23, Figs 18, 19), but the remainder were found within the topsoil.

POTTERY OF INDETERMINATE DATE

This is represented by nine sherds, weighing 154 grammes, which come from at least five different vessels, one of which is illustrated (E23, Fig 48). Although none of the sherds is diagnostic, all the fabrics are prehistoric (Cfe: Indet/l; CfeSV: Indet/l; FfeGS: Indet/l; QS: Indet/I and Ssa: Indet/1). They were recovered from topsoil contexts which produced ceramics of many different dates, including Romano-British wares.

Table 8   Bibliographic references to pottery fabrics described during the Linear Ditches Project

Fabric Code	Reference (Raymond 1994)
feGS: BKR/4	Appendix 2, Table 29
GS: BKR/1	Appendix 2, Table 29
CFS: DR/2	Appendix 2, Table 29
F: DR/2	Appendix 2, Table 29
FS: DR/5	Appendix 2, Table 29
CFfeS: LBA/1	Appendix 2, Table 30
Ffes: LBA/1	Appendix 2, Table 30
FfeS: LBA/2	Appendix 2, Table 30
FfeS: LBA/3	Appendix 2, Table 30
FfeS: LBA/5	Appendix 2, Table 30
Ffes: LBA/6	Appendix 2, Table 30
CfeGS: IA/1	Appendix 2, Table 31
FS: IA/8	Appendix 2, Table 31
feGMS: IA-RB/1	Appendix 2, Table 31
feGS: IA/6	Appendix 2, Table 31
feGS: IA/7	Appendix 2, Table 31
S: IA/1	Appendix 2, Table 31
S: IA/2	Appendix 2, Table 31
S: IA/4	Appendix 2, Table 31
FGS: Indet/1	Appendix 2, Table 31

Table 9   The type, quantity and size range of inclusions, used as criteria to define individual fabrics

Fabric	Chalk % Size (mm)	Flint % Size (mm)	Iron Minerals % Size (mm)	Grog % Size (mm)	Mica % Size (mm)	Quartz Conglom % Size (mm)	Quartz Sand % Size (mm)	Sarsen % Size (mm)	Shell % Size (mm)	Voids (plant) % Size (mm)
FfeMS: Bkr/1		2 0.5–3	7 0.0–0.1		10 <0.03–0.06		2 0.06–0.2			
FfeS: DR/10		20 0.1–5	10 <0.03–0.1				10 0.1–0.7			
FS: DR/10		25 0.2–3					2 0.3–0.8			
FGS: IA/4		5 0.3–0.8		15 0.5–2			40 0.03–0.7			
Ssh: IA/1							40 0.1–0.5		3 0.1–7	
FfeGMS: IA-RB/1		2 0.5–2	10 <0.03–0.3	2 0.3–0.5	5 <0.03		20 0.03–0.2			
FeGMS: RB/2			5 0.03–0.06	10 0.4–6	2 <0.03		3 0.03–0.05			
CFfeMS: Indet/1	2 0.1–1	3 0.5–5	10 <0.03–0.1		5 <0.03–0.2		20 0.03–1			
Cfe: Indet/1	25 0.1–5		3 0.03–0.1							
CfeSV: Indet/1	2 0.5–4		7 0.03–0.01				40 <0.03–0.03			10 3–7 long
CS: Indet/2	3 0.05–1						20 0.1–0.4			
FfeGS: Indet/1		5 0.5–5	5 <0.03–4	7 0.15–0.3			10 0.15–0.4			
FeS: Indet/2			10 <0.03–0.15				40 0.06–0.4			
QS: Indet/1						15 0.1–3	40 0.1–0.5			
SSsa: Indet/1							40 0.03–0.4	7 0.4–8		

Pottery illustrated in Figure 48, including fabric codes

E1 Body sherd, Beaker. feGS: BKR/4. Site XVIII, topsoil. Section C, C112 (considered possibly Collared Urn).

E2 Body sherd, with rib or lug, Middle Bronze Age. FfeS: DR/10. Site VI, linear ditch cutting, E of section 4, topsoil.

E3 Body sherd, Middle Bronze Age. CFS: DR2. Site XIII, NW Quadrant, edge of mound, layer 5, d 12in. Section C, C65.

E4 Body sherd, possibly Middle Bronze Age. FS: DR/5. Site XIII, SW Quadrant, edge of mound, layer 4, d 12in. Section C, C66.

E5 Body sherd, indeterminate. CS: Indet/2. Site VI, inner edge of bank on S side of linear ditch, W of Site XXI.

E6 Rim sherd, probably Late Bronze Age Plain Ware but just possibly Middle Bronze Age. FGS: Indet/1. Site XX, section 8, layer 23, d 15in.

E7 Rim sherd, probably Late Bronze Age Plain Ware but just possibly Middle Bronze Age. FGS: Indet/1. Site XX, section 8, base of layer 23.

E8 Body sherd with decorated shoulder, Late Bronze Age Plain Ware. FGS: Indet/1. Site XX, section 8, base of layer 23, d 2ft.

E9 Body sherd with decorated shoulder, Late Bronze Age Plain Ware. FGS: Indet/1. Site VI, unstratified.

E10 Rim sherd, Late Bronze Age Plain Ware. FfeS: LBA/1. Site VI, section 7, NW of Site XX, topsoil.

E11 Body sherd, Late Bronze Age Plain Ware. CFfeS: LBA/1. Cutting NE of Site XX, across bank and ditch of Site VI, at base of bank.

E12 Rim sherd, Late Bronze Age Plain Ware. FfeS: LBA2. Site XX, section 8, topsoil.

E13 Rim sherd, Late Bronze Age Plain Ware. CFfeS: LBA/1. Site XX, section 8, topsoil.

E14 Body sherd, Late Bronze Age Plain Ware. FfeS: LBA/2. Site XIV, SW Quadrant, section 2, layer 5, top of barrow mound.

E15 Possibly half a spindlewhorl, Iron Age. FfeGMS: IA-RB/1. Site VI, section 7, topsoil. See also Section N, N8.

E16 Body sherd, decorated shoulder, perhaps earlier Iron Age. S: IA/1. Cutting NE of Site XX, across bank and ditch of Site VI, topsoil.

E17 Rim sherd, Iron Age. S: IA/1. Cutting NE of Site XX, across bank and ditch of Site VI, topsoil.

E18 Rim sherd, Iron Age. S: IA/4. Cutting NE of Site XX, across bank and ditch of Site VI, topsoil.

E19 Rim sherd, Iron Age. S: IA/4. Site VI, section 3, layer 3, bank rubble.

E20 Rim sherd, Iron Age. CfeGS: IA/1. Site VI, N of Site XXI, section 1, layer 14, d 2ft 7in.

E21 Bead-rim sherd, Early Romano-British. FeGMS: IA-RB/1. Cutting NE of Site XX, across bank and ditch of Site VI, topsoil.

E22 Bead-rim sherd, Early Romano-British. FeGMS: RB/2. Cutting NE of Site XX, across bank and ditch of Site VI, topsoil.

E23 Possibly daub. CfeSV: Indet/1. Cutting NE of Site XX, across bank and ditch of Site VI, topsoil.

F ROMANO-BRITISH POTTERY DERIVED FROM AGRICULTURE AROUND THE BARROW CEMETERY

Kenneth Annable

INTRODUCTION

In the course of excavations within the Snail Down barrow cemetery, a quantity of Romano-British pottery, including sherds of Samian ware, was recovered from the upper levels of sixteen individual sites as follows: Sites I–VII, IX–XVI and XVII, represented by bell-, bowl-, disc-, saucer- and pond-barrows and a ring-ditch; Sites VI and VII formed part of a linear earthwork; and Site IX, a hedge bank and cart track.

In all, 361 sherds of coarse pottery came to light, of which forty-six were rim pieces; in addition there were nineteen Samian fragments, amongst them four rims, bringing the overall total to 380.

A further small amount of Romano-British pottery occurred among the prehistoric sherds associated with the linear ditch system, Site VI, and are included in Frances Raymond's report, Section E above. Fabric analysis was made of those pieces.

SAMIAN WARE

The Samian group was recorded from eight sites: – I, III, V–VII, IX, XV and XVI. All the fragments were small or tiny in size and, almost without exception, considerably abraded with much of the surface glaze weathered away. Amongst the rims, very little of each vessel wall remained. All the vessels represented are plain forms, and are listed below but not illustrated.*

Site I (four sherds)

F1 Plate, either Drag 18 or 18/31. Central Gaulish. Probably from Les Maitres de Veyre kilns. Late 1st-early 2nd century. NW Quadrant, ditch, 7.

F2 Probably a cup, Drag 33, or an enclosed vessel. Likely source Lezoux. Early-mid 2nd century. NW Quadrant, ditch, 7.

F3 Form unrecognisable. Possibly South Gaulish. 1st century. NW Quadrant, ditch, 3.

F4 As last. Possibly South Gaulish. 1st century. NE Quadrant, eccentric mound, 11.

Site III (single sherd)

F5 Form uncertain. South Gaulish. 1st century. N Quadrant, berm, 7.

Site V (three sherds)

F6 Cup, possibly Drag 33. Probably South Gaulish, *c* AD 50–90. Central area, 6 (eg section 8, Fig 17).

F7 Form uncertain. South Gaulish, La Graufesenque. 1st century. E ditch, section 4, 4, depth 1ft 8in (Fig 17).

Site VI (two sherds)

F8 Form uncertain. South Gaulish, La Graufesenque. 1st century. Section 2, 7.

F9 Cup, Drag 27 or plate, Drag 18. South Gaulish, La Graufesenque. 1st century. E of section 2, ditch (not illustrated), depth 1ft.

Site IX (single sherd)

F10 Form uncertain. South Gaulish, La Graufesenque. 1st century. Bank crossing Site III.

Site XV (five sherds)

F11 Drag 27. Probably Central Gaulish. 1st-mid 2nd century. NE Quadrant, disturbed.

F12 Bowl or plate. South Gaulish, La Graufesenque. 1st century. NE Quadrant, disturbed.

* I am indebted to Barbara Davies, City of Lincoln Archaeological Unit, for her identification of the Samian pottery.

F13 Base of cup? South Gaulish, Montans kilns. 1st century. SE Quadrant, below turf, disturbed.

F14 Form uncertain. Possibly Central Gaulish. 1st-2nd century. SE Quadrant, below turf, disturbed.

F15 Bowl or plate. South Gaulish. 1st century. SE Quadrant, below turf, disturbed.

F16 Form uncertain. South Gaulish, La Graufesenque. 1st century. SE Quadrant, below turf.

Site XVI (two sherds)

F17 Plate. Drag 18 or 18/31. From Les Maitres de Veyre kilns. Late 1st-early 2nd century. NE Quadrant, outer edge of bank, 3.

F18 Plate. Drag 18 or 18/31. As last. Late 1st-early 2nd century. SE Quadrant, topsoil.

Site XX (one sherd)

F19 Bowl or plate. South Gaulish. 1st century. Section 8, 26.

Coarse Pottery

With few exceptions, the coarse sherds were much abraded at face and edges; many were small, with little of each vessel wall remaining with the rims. The general condition of the Snail Down assemblage, both native wares and Samian, points to the subsequent utilisation of the cemetery area by a neighbouring Romano-British farming community, the sherds recovered being spread across the region through the normal process of manuring to become broken and abraded by weathering and plough action.

Amongst the series, the majority vessel forms consist of small to medium-size jars or bowls with curved rims, in an almost invariably sandy fabric, fired grey buff/brown at surface and generally buff/brown at core. Twenty-nine rims of the type were recorded, spread across most of the sites examined; one example (Site XV) was tempered with tiny white flint grits. Figure 49, F21–F25.

As already implied above, the lack of diagnostic features (eg larger body sherds retaining rims or bases) makes close dating of this type of vessel almost impossi-

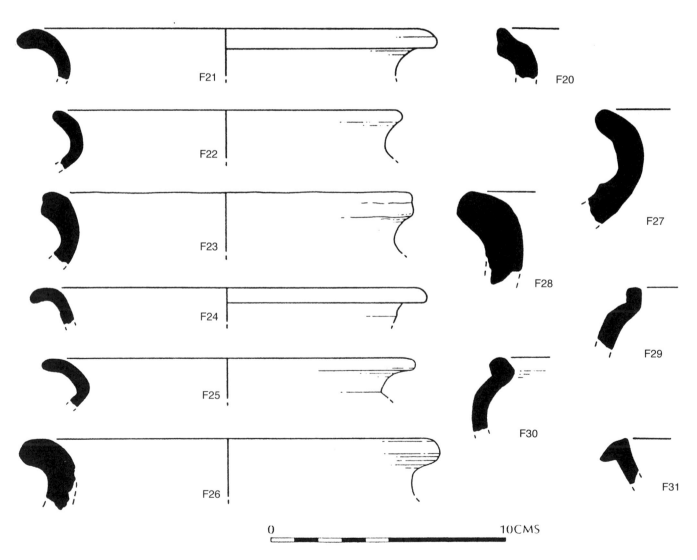

Fig 49   Romano-British wares, Sites I, II, III, V, VI, X, XV.

ble, particularly as the form is one that continued with little change throughout the Roman period.

Comparable rim types have, however, been recorded from a number of sites in the county, notably a Roman well at Mildenhall (*Cunetio*), near Marlborough, (Annable 1966a, 15, fig 2, nos 2–4, 24, 35, 38), back-filled *c* AD 60; a late 'Celtic' rubbish heap at Oare, near Marlborough (Swan 1975, fig 4, nos 40, 46, 48), the recovered material dating to the second half of the first century, and a Roman pottery industry in the Savernake Forest, (Annable 1962, 151, fig 5, nos 28, 31, 33), which also began production *c* AD 60.

Moreover, from Sites I, V and X, came body sherds with wall grooves, and from Sites V and VI, with neck cordons; both are decorative features common in the pre-Roman Iron Age, but continuing into the Roman period, and clearly linked with the curved rim jar/bowl group. They are likewise of common occurrence amongst the products of the above-mentioned sites (Annable 1966a, 16, fig 3, nos 40, 43; Swan 1975, fig 4, 44, 45).

Also within the same chronological context were:

(a) Thicker, heavier rims and body sherds, representing large storage jars with curved rims (Sites I–III, V–VI, XIV–XV) in either a coarse, native fabric, occasionally pitted, and fired orange/buff throughout, or a finer fabric, fired pale grey at surface, with orange-buff core. One or two of these sherds are again tempered with whitish crushed flint grits (Annable 1962, 151, fig 5, nos 13, 21, with bead and curved rims; Annable 1966a, 16, fig 3, no 41; 17, fig 4, no 67; Swan 1975, fig 3, 30). Figure 49, F26–F28.

(b) Three bead-rim jar rims (Sites V, VI, X) in a sandy fabric fired grey to grey/buff core and surface. Figure 49, F29, F30.

(c) A single rim of a Gallo-Belgic dish in a fine, smoothed fabric, fired pale cream throughout (Site I). Figure 49, F20. The above three vessel forms are likewise illustrated amongst the pottery assemblages from Oare, Mildenhall and Savernake Forest.

From the obviously close relationship between the preponderance of the pottery spread across the Snail Down cemetery and the Marlborough group of sites referred to, (amply confirmed by a close examination of the sherd fabrics of the entire assemblage), it must be concluded that the main occupational phase in the vicinity of the cemetery occurred within the second half of the first century AD.

Furthermore, confirmation is provided by the evidence of the Samian wares. Of the nineteen dated sherds, thirteen, more than two-thirds of the total, fall within the same date bracket. However, the remaining half-dozen fragments are assigned between the late-first to mid-second centuries, and these prompt the suggestion of a continuing, if perhaps diminishing occupation beyond the first century. But there seems little to support this hypothesis amongst the coarse-ware rims apart from a single pie-dish with triangular rim section, a form that begins to appear in the early second century (Greene 1976, 59,

fig 6, nos 97–98; 65), and a sherd of a ?Severn Valley handled tankard (possibly a local copy), another vessel type in common use within the second century. On the other hand there is little difficulty in accepting that the curved-rim jars continued in use into the second century. Similar jar/bowl types with comparable rims forming part of the deposit from Wanborough, Wilts (Greene 1976, 56–58, figs 3–5 *passim*) and dated AD 120, compare well with the Snail Down types and those recorded amongst the ceramic repertoire of the Marlborough group. There remains also the more precise evidence of the Samian sherds which it is difficult to gainsay.

Present amongst the Romano-British coarse wares was a group of ten sherds which might be thought to raise the possibility of a secondary occupation of the area within the later phases of the Roman period. The late types, considerably weathered, included four sherds (Sites I, III, XV, XVI) of New Forest colour-coated wares (Swan 1973, 120), dating from the late third century onwards; a single sherd (?Oxford ware) with colour coat and rouletted decoration; two flanged-bowl rims (Sites I, XV) – late third/fourth century types of this long-lived form (Fig 49, F31) and a single cooking-jar rim fragment (Site VI), the rim extending beyond the maximum girth of the vessel (another late vessel hardly appearing before the late third-fourth centuries).

Can this small group be thought to represent a late phase of Roman occupation near the cemetery? The relationship between the mass of the sherd fabrics throughout the assemblage and the early vessel rim types has been noted. Thus of themselves these few late rims comprise manifestly too small a group to constitute a settlement; it seems reasonable, therefore, to consider them simply as intrusive sherds dropped at random by visitors passing across the Down during the later phases of the Romano-British period.

The Illustrated Romano-British Pottery, Figure 49

F20 Gallo-Belgic dish. Site I, NE Quadrant, ditch, 7.

F21 Curved-rim jar. Site I, SE Quadrant, ditch, 7.

F22 Curved-rim jar. Site II, NE Quadrant, ditch, topsoil.

F23 Curved-rim jar. Site III, N Quadrant, unstratified.

F24 Curved-rim jar. Site V, central area, topsoil.

F25 Curved-rim jar. Site XV, SE Quadrant, below turf.

F26 Storage jar with heavy rim. Site V, topsoil.

F27 Large storage jar with heavy rim. Site X, SE Quadrant, topsoil.

F28 Large storage jar with heavy rim. Site XV, SE Quadrant, below turf.

F29 Bead-rim bowl. Site V, central area, 6.

F30 Bead-rim bowl. Site VI, section 2, top of 3.

F31 Flanged-rim bowl. Site XV, SE Quadrant, below turf.

(The single number at the end of some of the locations above refers to the layer number in the relevant illustrated sections)

G THE FLINT

ROBERT YOUNG AND DEIRDRE O'SULLIVAN

INTRODUCTION

The material was initially examined by Andrew Howe in 1980 in the course of his project work for the then certificate, now MA, in Post-Excavation Studies in the School of Archaeological Studies, University of Leicester. We have subsequently re-analysed the material and broadened the scope of the discussion. However, we have used some of Howe's original drawings in this report as they are of such high quality. Additional material has been drawn by Nicholas Herepath and Ann Linge. Deirdre O'Sullivan produced the tables and graphs on the Excel and Cricket Graph packages available at Leicester.

The data including measurements have been stored as a database in both Dbase 4 and Excel file formats, in the site archive. Measurements refer to maximum dimensions in accordance with standard practice in lithic studies (Saville 1980, Wilson 1980, Young 1987). Terminology adopted is generally in accordance with that recommended by Healey (forthcoming). The category of waste material is taken to include miscellaneous chips and chunks as well as all types of non-retouched or unutilised flakes. All cores and tool types, and a generous sample of miscellaneous retouched/utilised pieces have been illustrated, and are numbered G1–G47 in Figures 50 and 51.

GENERAL REMARKS

Most of the flint from Snail Down is of good quality, with many pieces still retaining a fine, sharp edge. Virtually all of it shows heavy grey-white recortication; where flint colour can be observed, this ranges from blue-grey to dark grey/black. Primary nodule cortex is usually soft and chalky and off-white/buff in colour.

The quantity of material varies considerably from site to site although excavation policy required the recording of every recognised piece of struck flint. Table 10 indicates a notable lack of cores, a point to which we return in the general discussion.

A total of 987 pieces was examined by the authors and Table 10 gives a breakdown of numbers and classifi-cation of types of material recorded by site. Three sites (I, III and XIX) produced reasonably large assemblages (ie 150+ items) and these are considered in greatest detail. Length: breadth ratios have not been plotted for those sites with less than 10 complete flakes. No flint was recovered from Sites IV, VIII, IX, XII and XX.

SITE I

A total of 178 pieces was recovered. Their distribution through the site stratigraphy is shown in Table 11. With the exception of 12 finds of burnt flint (7%) all have some degree of recortication and 81 pieces (45%) show some trace of cortex.

Core

One core was recorded (Fig 50, G1). This is a single platform core, flakes removed around part of the circumference (Table 26). The core is on a large primary flake and retains much fawn/buff cortex on its unworked faces.

Scrapers

Three scrapers were recorded. The first (Fig 50, G2) is an end scraper on the distal end of a thick, heavy, secondary flake, with a plain butt and pronounced bulb of percussion. The flake is totally recorticated and retains a patch of hard fawn/buff cortex on its dorsal face. Steeply retouched by hard-hammer direct percussion; the working edge has many small hinge fractures.

The second scraper is discoidal, on a totally recorticated, inner, flake with a plain butt and pronounced bulb of percussion (Fig 50, G3). The dorsal face shows blade-like scars from previous removals, and the piece has been retouched around the circumference by a hard hammer, using direct percussion. Many small hinge fractures are visible on the working edge.

The third is a side and end scraper on a totally recorticated, probably secondary flake, with a fawn/buff cortex-like inclusion on its dorsal face (Fig 50, G4). It has

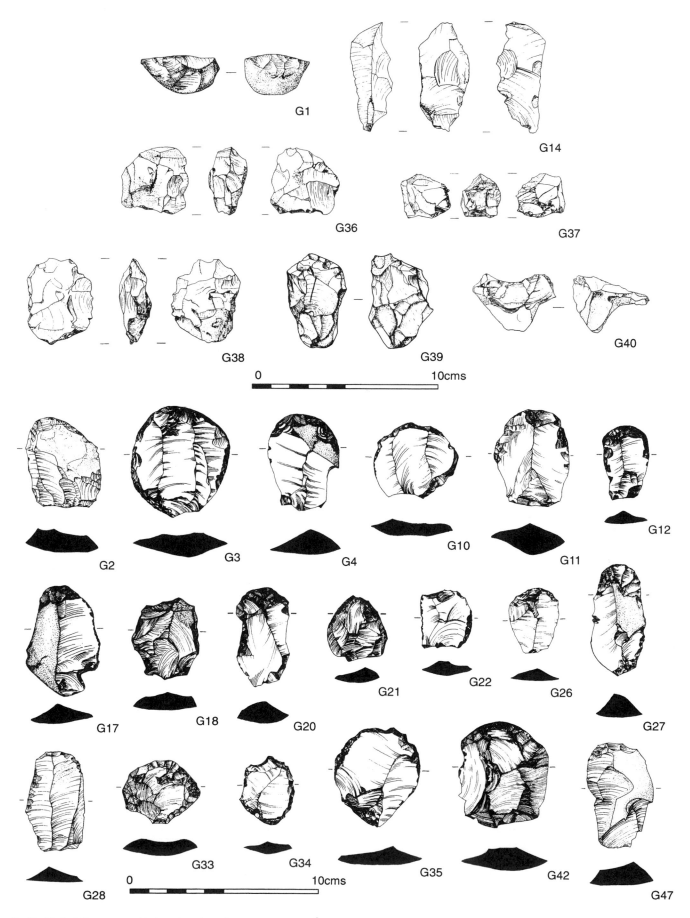

Fig 50   Worked flint, scrapers, blade tools, various sites.

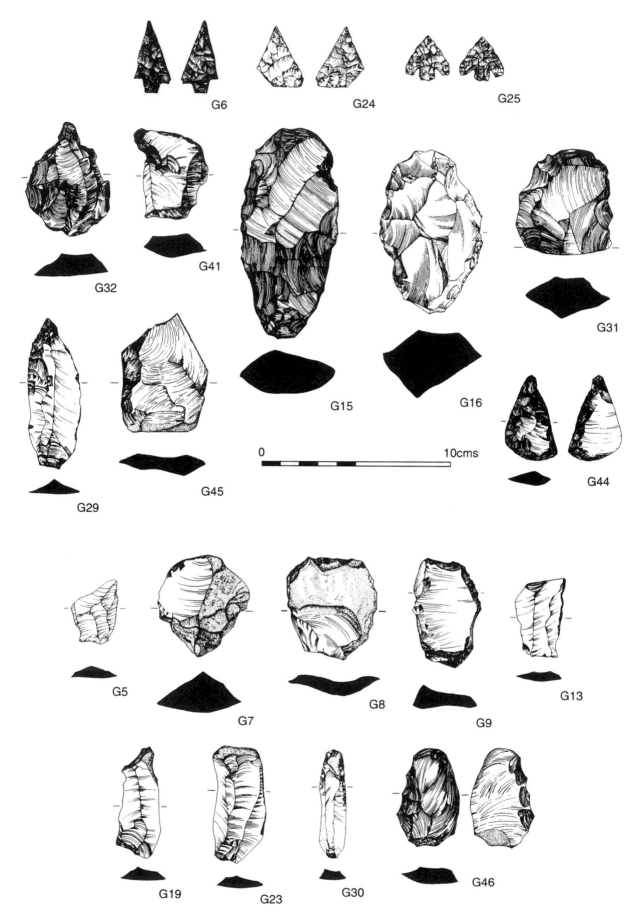

Fig 51   Worked flint, arrowheads, core tools, cores, various sites.

Table 10 Distribution of flint types across the sites at Snail Down

Site	Arrow Head	Axe	Awl	Scraper	Knife	Saw	Ret Blade	Blade	Ret Flake	Prim Flake	Sec Flake	Tert Flake	Core Trim Flake	Core	Chip	Chunk	Total Worked Flint	Unmodified	Total
Site I				3				9	1	5	64	74	1	1	5	15	178		178
Site II	1								4		7	4				4	20	5	25
Site III				3			1	6	3	17	71	167			1	11	280	20	300
Site V								2			2	9		1			14		14
Site VI/VII		2		1			1	2	1		2	1				3	14		14
Site X				1			3	2			8	15				1	30	1	31
Site XI				1				1			3	7	1				13		13
Site XIII				2			1	3		1	8	5	1			5	26	1	27
Site XIV	2			3	1		2	1	6		5	7				9	36	2	38
Site XV								3			1	6	1				11		11
Site XVI		1	1	1				1	3		10	25				2	44	4	48
Site XVII				2					1		10	28					41	3	44
Site XVIII											1	1					2		2
Site XIX			2	2		1		4	2	10	55	101	1	5	2	42	227	14	241
Site XXI				1													1		1
Total	3	3	3	20	1	1	8	34	21	33	247	450	5	7	8	92	937	50	987

Table 11   Distribution of flint types by context, Site I

SITE I Context (Layer nos, Figs 4, 5)	Scraper	Blade	Flake	Ret Flake	Prim Flake	Sec Flake	Tert Flake	Core Trim Core	Chip	Chunk	Total
11	1			2	1	13				10	27
10,11		1									1
7	1	2			8	14			2	1	28
2,3					6	2					8
1		2	1	3	38	26			1	4	75
9	1				1	6					8
Topsoil		1			5	6	1	1			14
3					3	2					5
3,6,7		1									1
6		2				4			1		7
3,6,7					1	1			1		3
1,3						1					1
Total	3	9	1	5	63	75	1	1	5	15	178

a plain butt, pronounced bulb of percussion, and retouch around the left edge and distal end by hard-hammer, direct percussion. The dorsal face shows uni-directional flake scars from previous removals. The flake is thick and heavy and may have been taken from the core in an effort to remove the cortex-like inclusion.

Blades

Nine retouched blades were recorded, three on secondary removals, six on tertiary or inner flakes. Of these, five are broken; one retains a cortical butt, two are plain and two faceted. One has a hinge termination at the distal end; three retain cortex on their dorsal faces. All have total white recortication. None is illustrated. Complete examples measure from 46–97mm in length (mean length 74mm) and in breadth from 16–38mm (mean breadth 30mm).

Miscellaneous Retouched Pieces

A totally white recorticated inner flake, with a plain butt and pronounced bulb of percussion shows possible utilisation/serration on the right edge distal end (Fig 51, G5).

Waste Material

Under this heading (Table 10) 166 pieces are classified. Six secondary and 15 tertiary flakes are incomplete. D1: a–d (for Diagrams D1–D9, see end of Section G) show length/breadth data for complete flakes of all classes. D1: a gives a breakdown of the two variables by flake type and indicates that secondary flakes tend to be larger than inner or tertiary removals. D1: b–d show length/breadth data for all complete flakes and indicate that the tendency

is for flakes to be longer than they are broad. However, D1: d shows that few reach true blade-like proportions. Data on striking platforms/butts and bulb types is set out in Table 12; the great majority of butts are plain on this site. There is a slight preponderance of pronounced bulbs of percussion over diffuse types.

SITE II

Twenty-five pieces of flint and two non-local, rounded pebbles were recorded from this site. The stratigraphic distribution of the material is indicated in the table below. Where visible, the flint is blue/grey-black in colour but most pieces show white recortication. Twelve finds retain fawn/buff cortex to a greater or lesser degree.

Arrowhead

One was recorded (Fig 51, G6). This is a barbed and tanged example of Green's Sutton Type a (Green 1980, 50–51). It is made on an inner flake which has total white recortication, and has been bifacially worked with shallow invasive retouch, possibly by pressure flaking. The tang is squat and the barbs vestigial.

Miscellaneous Retouched Pieces

Four retouched/utilised flakes were recorded, three are secondary flakes retaining cortex on their dorsal faces, one is an inner flake. Three have plain butts, one is faceted. Two have pronounced bulbs of percussion; the other two have diffuse bulbs. In length they range from 32–66mm (mean length 52mm) and in breadth from 19–45mm (mean breadth 31mm). (Fig 51, G7-G9)

Table 12 Butt and bulb types, Site I

| Context | Flake Type | Platform Type | | | Bulb Type | |
		Plain	Cortical	Faceted	Pronounced	Diffuse
Topsoil						
	Primary					
	Secondary	1	2	1	4	
	Tertiary	6		1	6	1
Subsoil						
	Primary					
	Secondary	1				1
	Tertiary	6			4	2
Bank						
	Primary	1		1	1	1
	Secondary	1			1	
	Tertiary	4		1	2	3
Ditch						
	Primary	1	1	1	1	2
	Secondary	47	4	4	28	27
	Tertiary	39	1	7	23	24
Mound						
	Primary					
	Secondary					
	Tertiary	2		2	3	1
Total		109	8	18	73	62

Table 13 Distribution of flint types by context, Site II

Context (layers, Figs 7, 8)	Arrow-Head	Ret Flake	Sec Flake	Tert Flake	Chunk	Unmodified	Total
Topsoil	1	2	1	1		1	6
4,5		1					1
1,3/4			2		4	1	7
Burial 1		1	4	2		3	10
Burial 2				1			1
Total	1	4	7	4	4	5	25

Waste Material

The remaining 20 pieces are classified under this heading. All the flakes are complete. The length/breadth measurements and ratios of complete flakes, including retouched pieces, are shown in D2: a-c. The retouched pieces are generally narrower and longer than the unretouched flakes, although the total number (15) is too small for significant comparison.

SITE III

A total of 300 flints was distributed throughout the site as shown in Table 14. Site III is one of the few Snail Down barrows where there is sufficient material to deserve some analysis by context, and the material from different deposits has been considered separately. Information about the striking platform/butts and bulb types for waste flakes from all contexts is set out in Table 15.

Topsoil

Eighteen pieces were recorded under this heading.

Waste material

All can be classified as waste material. The total includes one chunk, two natural/unmodified pieces, one waste flake. These are not discussed further. Of the 14 extant waste flakes, one primary, one tertiary flake are broken at the bulbar end. The 12 complete flakes range in length from 22–45mm (mean length 35mm) and in breadth from 20–57mm (mean breadth 30mm). Details on butt and bulb types are contained in Table 15 below.

Table 14   Distribution of flint types by context, Site III
(ALS: ancient land surface)

Context	Scraper	Ret Blade	Blade	Ret Flake	Prim Flake	Sec Flake	Tert Flake	Chip	Chunk	Unmod	Total
Topsoil					2	1	12		1	2	18
Mound	2		2		5	30	69	1	2	5	116
Ditch	1		2	1	5	19	26		7	9	70
Pyre		1		1	2	3	19			2	28
Pit 1					1	3	4				8
Pit 2			1								1
Pit 3						3	2				5
Urn 1							1				1
Urn 2			1		2	7	11			1	22
ALS						5	23		1	1	31
Total	3	1	6	3	17	71	167	1	11	20	300

Table 15   Butt and bulb types, Site III

Context	Flake Type	Platform Type		Bulb Type		
		Plain	Cortical	Faceted	Pronounced	Diffuse
Topsoil	Primary		1			1
	Secondary	1			1	
	Tertiary	11			4	7
Mound	Primary	4	2		2	4
	Secondary	24	6	2	19	13
	Tertiary	75		2	55	22
Ditch	Primary	2	3		2	3
	Secondary	13	6		12	7
	Tertiary	17		5	10	12
Funeral Pyre	Primary	2			2	
	Secondary	2	1		2	1
	Tertiary	17			11	6
Pit 1	Primary	1			1	
	Secondary	1		2	2	1
	Tertiary	3		1	2	2
Pit 3	Primary					
	Secondary	3			3	
	Tertiary	2			2	
Urn 1	Primary					
	Secondary					
	Tertiary	1				1
Urn 2	Primary		2		1	1
	Secondary	5	2		4	3
	Tertiary	10		1	4	7
ALS	Primary					
	Secondary	4			4	
	Tertiary	12		2	5	9
Total		210	23	15	148	100

The mound

One hundred and sixteen pieces were recovered from the mound and related contexts.

Scrapers

Two were recorded, both made on inner flakes with plain butts and pronounced bulbs. G10 is a short end scraper, G11 is a long end scraper (Fig 50).

Blades

Two unretouched examples were recorded. Both are inner removals with plain butts and pronounced bulbs of percussion (46 × 26 × 6mm; 49 × 19 × 9mm).

Waste Material

The remaining pieces can be classified under this heading and the total includes one chip, three chunks and ten natural/unmodified pieces (including five pot-lid flakes). Of the remaining flakes, ten are broken at the distal end, eleven at the bulbar end. Where information survives, butt and bulb types are shown in Table 15. Complete flakes range from 11–81mm (mean length 36mm), in breadth from 14–95mm (mean breadth 30mm).

The ditch

Seventy pieces of flint were recorded from the ditch.

Scraper

One was recorded (Fig 50, G12), on a tertiary flake with plain butt and pronounced bulb of percussion; retouch around distal end and right and left edges. There is also inverse retouch on both edges.

Blades

Two broken, unretouched examples, both on inner removals. One retains plain butt, pronounced bulb of percussion. Not illustrated.

Miscellaneous Retouched/Utilised Flakes

One was recorded (not illustrated), an inner flake with plain butt and pronounced bulb of percussion (72 × 75 × 27mm). Trace of possible utilisation at distal end.

Waste Material

This constitutes the remainder of the material from the ditch and the total includes seven chunks, four natural/ unmodified pieces, five rounded, probably flint, pebbles. Two flakes are broken at their distal ends, three at bulbar end. The evidence for bulb and butt types is classified in Table 15. Complete flakes range in length from 16–86mm (mean length 43mm) and in breadth from 15–72mm (mean breadth 37mm).

The funeral pyre

There were 28 pieces of flint from this context, broadly equivalent to the ancient land surface context recorded below.

Retouched Blade

G13 (Fig 51) was on a tertiary removal, broken at bulbar end. Both edges show retouch/utilisation.

Miscellaneous Retouched/Utilised Flakes

One, not illustrated, was an inner flake with plain butt and pronounced bulb. Both edges show traces of utilisation (41 × 25 × 10mm).

Waste Material

The remaining pieces can be classified under this heading; the total includes two natural/unmodified pieces (one of which is a pot-lid flake). Of the twenty five flakes, five are broken, three at the bulbar, two at the distal ends. Butt and bulb types are shown in Table 15. Complete flakes range in length from 11–47mm (mean length 32mm) and in breadth from 10–39mm (mean breadth 22mm).

The pits

Pit 1

Eight retouched flakes were recorded. Seven are complete, one is broken at the distal end; butt and bulb types are shown in Table 15. Flakes range in length from 20–58mm (mean length 38mm) and in breadth from 13–37mm (mean breadth 27mm).

Pit 2

One retouched blade was an inner removal with plain butt and diffuse bulb of percussion.

Pit 3

Five flakes were recorded, four complete, one broken at the distal end. Complete flakes range in length from 22–34mm (mean length 28mm) and in breadth from 20–47mm (mean breadth 34mm).

The Urns

(Secondary Burials 1, 2)

Urn 1

One retouched inner flake, hinge termination at distal end.

Urn 2

Twenty-two pieces of flint.

Blade

One example, broken at its distal end. It retains a plain butt and diffuse bulb of percussion.

Waste Material

The total includes one unmodified/natural lump of flint. Of the 20 flakes, two are broken at the distal end, one is broken at the bulbar end. Butt and bulb types are shown in Table 15. Complete flakes from this context range in length from 19–86mm (mean length 41mm) and in breadth from 13–74mm (mean breadth 33mm).

The ancient land surface

Thirty-one pieces were recorded from the ancient land surface (Table 14); see also Funeral Pyre above.

Miscellaneous Retouched/Utilised Pieces

One was recorded (not illustrated), a tertiary flake with plain butt, diffuse bulb of percussion, utilised/retouched on the right edge of dorsal face, distal end.

Waste Material

The remaining pieces include one chunk and one natural/unmodified piece which are not discussed further. Of the 28 flakes, nine are broken at the bulbar end, one at the distal end (for butt and bulb types, Table 15). The 18 complete flakes range in length from 23–103mm (mean length 43mm) and in breadth from 12–48mm (mean breadth 27mm).

The Waste Material – a General Comment

In view of the fairly small size of the stratified groups from Site III the metrical data for complete waste flakes from the site have been plotted together (D3: a–d). An examination of these data shows that most of the flakes are fairly squat; very few reach blade-like proportions. It was hoped that some diversity might be observed, especially between the size range of the material from the ancient land surface and that from the rest of the site, and that this might shed some light on broader chronological issues (see general discussion below). However, no such differences can be shown. This may be simply a reflection of sample size.

SITE V

Fourteen pieces of flint were recovered from this site, all from chalk below the turf layer (Figure 17, layer 6). All are heavily recorticated; three retain fawn cortex.

Core

One core fragment (Fig 50, G14) was found (Table 26).

Blade

Two fragmentary, unretouched examples, one with plain butt and pronounced bulb.

Waste Material

The remaining pieces are all waste flakes and include two secondary removals and nine inner flakes. Two are broken. Ten retain plain butts, one has a cortical butt. Six have pronounced bulbs, five have diffuse bulbs of percussion. In size the complete examples range in length from 28–65mm (mean length 44mm) and in breadth from 12–41mm (mean breadth 28mm). Because of the small number of complete pieces, the length/breadth data have not been plotted.

SITES VI/VII (ENCLOSURE A) AND SITES XX, XXI

Fourteen pieces of flint were examined from these sites and their locations through the sites' stratigraphy is shown in Table 16. All except two pieces have heavy, white, recortication. Flint colour where visible is blue-grey/black. Six pieces retain smooth, fawn cortex.

Axes

Two unfinished flint axe rough-outs were recorded. Figure 51, G15 (Site XX), is oval in shape, with the beginnings of a pointed butt and broader cutting edge. It has been bifacially worked probably by soft hammer, using direct percussion and shows clear evidence for alternate flaking to create the cutting edge around its circumfer-

Table 16   Distribution of flint types of context, Sites VI/VII and XX

Context (Layer numbers, Figs 18, 19, 35)	Axe	Scraper	Ret Blade	Blade	Ret Flake	Sec Flake	Tert Flake	Chunk	Total
Site VI, section 7; topsoil					1				1
Site VI, section 3; 5				1					1
Site XX, section 8; topsoil			1	1		1		1	4
Site XX, section 8; 22	1					1			2
Site XX, section 8; 23							1	2	3
Site VI, opp Site XXI, section 1; 13	1	1							2
Site VI, opp Site XXI, section 1; 12	1								1
Total	3	1	1	2	1	2	1	3	14

ence. The edges are abraded and have many small hinge fractures.

Figure 51, G16 (Site VI, opposite Site XXI; Fig 35) is a smaller artefact, and much cruder in its technology. It is roughly oval and shows evidence for alternate flaking around its circumference. The abraded edges have small hinge fractures.

Scraper

One was recorded (Fig 50, G17), a side and end scraper on a secondary flake retaining cortical butt, fawn cortex on dorsal face, pronounced bulb of percussion. The tool has been retouched on the right edge and around the distal end.

Blades

Three complete blades, on tertiary removals, all have plain butts. Two have pronounced bulbs, one a diffuse bulb of percussion. One shows evidence for utilisation on both edges.

Retouched flake

One was recorded, slight retouch on edges (not illustrated). This is a secondary flake with buff/fawn cortex on its dorsal face, retaining a plain butt and pronounced bulb of percussion (45 × 44 × 12mm).

Waste Material

The remaining seven pieces include three chunks which are not discussed further. Two waste flakes are secondary, two are tertiary removals. All, with one exception which has a facetted butt, have plain butts, pronounced bulbs. One has a hinge fracture at distal end. Flakes range from 29–47mm in length (mean length 37mm) and in breadth from 22–60mm (mean breadth 39mm). The small number of complete dimensions have not been plotted.

SITE X

Thirty-one pieces of flint, including one unmodified, natural piece, were recovered: their stratigraphic distribution is shown in Table 17 below (the trench layout for Sites X–XIV, adapted from a quadrant system, comprised a series of exposed areas N and S of an E/W baulk across the diameters of the five barrows, Fig 21).

All finds with the exception of one piece have total heavy white recortication. Eleven pieces (35% of the total) retain cortex to a greater or lesser degree.

Scraper

One (Fig 50, G18), on distal end and left edge of tertiary flake, plain butt, pronounced bulb of percussion.

Blades

Five blades were found. Four are inner removals, one a secondary removal. Four show diffuse bulbs of percussion, one has pronounced bulb. One has cortical butt, two are plain, two are faceted. Three examples show retouch/utilisation on one or both edges. Only one example is illustrated (Fig 51, G19). This has been retouched across left edge at distal end. Three complete blades range in length from 49–59mm and in breadth from 22–27mm.

Waste Material

There were 24 pieces, one chunk, eight secondary, fifteen tertiary flakes. All but one of the flakes are complete. Nineteen show plain butts, the remainder are faceted. Fifteen show diffuse, eight show pronounced, bulbs of percussion. These data might indicate greater emphasis on soft-hammer, direct, percussion in production of flakes from this site. Complete flakes range from 31–68mm in

Table 17   Distribution of flint types by context, Site X

Context (layer numbers, Figs 22, 23)	Scraper	Ret Blade	Blade	Sec Flake	Flake	Tert Chunk	Unmod	Total
Area 1S:								
Topsoil		2		7	10	1		20
5		1	1		1			3
4 (base)	1							1
Area 2N:								
Topsoil					2			2
Disturbed			1	1	2		1	5
Total	1	3	2	8	15	1	1	31

length (mean length 52.3mm) and from 19–65mm in breadth (mean breadth 38mm). Analysis of length/breadth data is given in D4: a-c. The diagrams indicate that the majority of the material is generally squat in terms of its overall morphology. There seems to be no evidence for an attempt to produce blade-like removals.

SITE XI

Thirteen flints were recovered from this site and their stratigraphic distribution is shown in Table 18.

All show heavy, white recortication; three pieces retain fawn, nodule cortex.

Scraper

An end scraper was recorded (Fig 50, G20), made on an inner flake, plain butt, pronounced bulb of percussion. Retouch is on left edge, dorsal face.

Blade

An inner removal blade, with plain butt, pronounced bulb of percussion (44 × 19 × 8mm).

Waste Material

The remaining eleven finds are flakes. Three are secondary flakes, eight are inner removals. Nine of these are complete and show plain butts, pronounced bulbs of percussion. One is a core trimming/rejuvenation flake. Complete flakes range in length from 32–85mm (mean length 41mm) and in breadth from 28–61mm (mean breadth 32mm). The number of complete measurements available is too small to justify detailed plotting.

SITE XIII

This barrow produced 26 pieces of struck flint and one unmodified, natural fragment of flint. Their stratigraphic distribution can be seen in Table 19. All, with the exception of one flake, show heavy, white recortication. Nine pieces retain cortex varying from smooth to rough, pitted in texture and buff/fawn/brown in colour.

Scrapers

Two were recorded (Fig 50, G21, G22). G21 is an end scraper, on an inner flake, plain butt, pronounced bulb of percussion. It was probably removed by hard-hammer direct percussion; totally recorticated. G22, a side scraper,

Table 18   Distribution of flint types by context, Site XI

Context (layer numbers, Figs 22, 23)	Scraper	Blade	Sec Flake	Tert Flake	Core Trim Flake	Total
Area 2N: topsoil			2	1	1	4
Area 2S: 4	1		1	4		6
Area 3S: topsoil		1		1		2
E-W Baulk 4				1		1
Total	1	1	3	7	1	13

Table 19   Distribution of flint types by context, Site XIII.

Context (layer numbers, Figs 22, 23)	Scraper	Ret Blade	Blade	Prim Flake	Sec Flake	Tert Flake	Core Trim Flake	Chunk	Unmod	Total
Area 4N: topsoil	1									1
Area 5S: topsoil		1			2					3
Area 5S: 5					1					1
Area 5N: topsoil			3	1	2	1	1			8
Area 5N: 5	1				2	4		5	1	13
Area 5N: disturbed					1					1
Total	2	1	3	1	8	5	1	5	1	27

is also on an inner flake. It has a plain butt, pronounced bulb of percussion, total white recortication.

Blades

Four were recovered, one complete example (Fig 51, G23) is illustrated. The three broken pieces are tertiary or inner removals, the complete example is a secondary removal. All heavily recorticated; plain butts, pronounced bulbs of percussion. The complete example retains rough nodular cortex on distal end, dorsal face; retouching on its right edge.

Waste Material

Of the remaining pieces, omitting the natural fragment, there were five chunks and 15 flakes. One primary flake, eight secondary flakes, six inner removals (including one core trimming flake, not illustrated) make up this last figure. Thirteen flakes are complete, ranging in length from 24–74mm (mean length 40.3mm) and in breadth from 22–50mm (mean breadth 37.2mm). These data are presented in histogram form in D5: a–c. Dimensions tend

to confirm the general trend from the other barrows on the site, an emphasis on squat flakes with little attempt to produce blade-like removals.

SITE XIV

Thirty-eight pieces of flint, including two natural unmodified pieces were recovered from contexts shown in Table 20. All, with one exception, show heavy white recortication. Seventeen pieces (c 45%) retain cortex to a varying degree; in eight examples this cortex is hard, rough and pitted. Eleven pieces (c 29%) show signs of thermal damage.

Arrowheads

Two were recorded (Fig 51, G24, G25). G24 has been made on an inner flake and is triangular in shape. It has been bi-facially retouched, possibly by pressure flaking; broken at its base on right-hand edge. Perhaps an unfin-

Table 20   Distribution of flint types by context, Site XIV

Context (layer Numbers, Figs 21, 22)	Arrow-Head	Scraper	Knife	Ret Blade	Blade	Ret Flake	Sec Flake	Tert Flake	Chunk	Unmod	Total
Area 5N: 5				1							1
Area 5N: base of 4							1				1
Area 5S: 4	1										1
Area 5S: Cremation pit (Fig 21)		1							6		7
Area 5S: 5						1	2	3			6
Area 5S: Base of 4		1									1
Area 6N: top of 4	1										1
Area 6N: Topsoil					1	1	1				3
Area 6N: 5			1								1
Area 6S: 5		1		1		3	1	3	3	2	14
Area 6S: base of 5						1		1			2
Total	2	3	1	2	1	6	5	7	9	2	38

ished barbed and tanged arrowhead. G25 is a complete, bifacially retouched, barbed and tanged arrowhead of Green's Sutton Type b, one of the commonest forms in Britain (Green 1980, 119). Made on an inner flake.

Scrapers

Of three examples (Fig 50, G26, G27, G28), G26 is of interest as it comes from the cremation pit (Fig 21). It is an end scraper on an unrecorticated inner flake, broken transversely but irregularly at the bulbar end. G27 is an end scraper on a secondary flake retaining cortex on the right edge of its dorsal face; plain butt, pronounced bulb of percussion. G28 is an end scraper on an inner flake with thermal spalling on its distal end and on its bulbar face; plain butt, diffuse bulb of percussion.

Knife

This (Fig 51, G29) has been made on an inner flake; plain butt, diffuse bulb of percussion, retouched on the left edge, dorsal face. Both edges show signs of use.

Blades

Two were unretouched examples, one an inner removal with plain butt, diffuse bulb. It measures 79 × 28 ×10mm. The other is a secondary removal with plain butt, pronounced bulb of percussion. It retains fawn cortex on its dorsal face and measures 77 × 23 × 9mm. The retouched blade (Fig 51, G30) is a secondary removal with cortex on dorsal face; faceted butt, diffuse bulb of percussion, shallow retouch on both edges and around distal end.

Miscellaneous Retouched Pieces

Four secondary, two inner flakes show varying degrees of retouch (not illustrated).

Waste Material

Nine chunks, two natural/unmodified pieces of flint, are not discussed further. One tertiary flake is broken at the bulbar end. Of the remaining complete flakes, four are secondary, eight are tertiary removals. Ten retain plain

butts, one has faceted butt, one retains cortical butt. Seven have pronounced bulbs, five have diffuse bulbs of percussion. Complete flakes range from 42–80mm (mean length 55mm) and in breadth from 24–61mm (mean breadth 37mm). Length and breadth data for complete flakes are shown in D6: a–c.

SITE XV

Three blades, 8 flakes were found at Site XV; their stratigraphic location can be seen in Table 21. All show heavy, white, recortication, two retain cortex. No diagnostic tool types were recovered and none of the finds is illustrated.

Blades

Two blades are on tertiary/inner removals; the third is a secondary example. One inner blade broken at bulbar end. One of the two complete blades (109 × 34 × 20mm) has cortical butt, diffuse bulb of percussion, terminates in a hinge fracture; the other (74 × 31 × 8mm) has plain butt, pronounced bulb. Secondary blade has buff/fawn cortex on dorsal face.

Waste Material

Seven flakes are complete and range in length from 29–62mm (mean length 48mm) and in breadth from 22–42mm (mean breadth 30.2m). All with one exception are tertiary/inner removals. The single core-trimming flake has been struck in the same plane as its core's striking platform. The number of complete flakes does not justify detailed presentation of length/breadth data.

SITE XVI

This was the largest of the 'small' assemblages, with a total of 48 pieces, including four natural/unmodified. All show heavy white recortication. Ten of the struck pieces (23%) retain smooth fawn/grey/brown nodule cortex. Stratigraphic distribution of the material is shown in Table 22.

Table 21   Distribution of flint types by context, Site XV

Context (layers Fig 26)	Blade	Sec Flake	Tert Flake	Core Trim Flake	Total
SE Quad: disturbed	1	1	2	1	5
NW Quad: topsoil	1		2		3
SE Quad: skeleton 1	1		2		3
Total	3	1	6	1	11

Table 22   Distribution of flint types by context, Site XVI

Context (layers, Fig 28)	Axe	Awl	Scraper	Blade	Ret Flake	Sec Flake	Tert Flake	Chunk	Unmod	Total
Topsoil	1	1			1	4	7	1		15
Pit 3				1	1	2	3		1	8
NE Quad: 6						1	4	1		6
NE Quad: 5						2	6			8
NE Quad: Pit 1					1				1	2
SW Quad: topsoil			1		1	5			2	9
Total	1	1	1	1	3	10	25	2	4	48

Axe

Fragment of butt end of unpolished flint axe, oval section; alternate, bifacial working (Fig 51, G31).

Awl

One (Fig 51, G32), on an inner flake. Retouched to form boring point at bulbar end.

Scraper

Short end scraper (Fig 50, G33), made on inner flake with faceted butt, pronounced bulb.

Blade

Unretouched blade, an inner removal with plain butt, diffuse bulb of percussion, hinge termination (34 × 13 × 4mm).

Miscellaneous Retouched Flakes

Three examples were recorded: none is illustrated. One is an inner flake, plain butt, diffuse bulb of percussion, hinge termination, bifacial retouching on both edges; measures 36 × 30 × 7mm. The other two examples are a secondary and an inner flake. One has cortical butt, pronounced bulb, the other retains faceted butt, diffuse bulb of percussion. Former measures 55 × 26 × 8mm; traces of retouch/utilisation on right edge. Latter measures 43 × 44 × 9mm; patch of inverse retouch/utilisation on left edge, bulbar face.

Waste Material

There were 37 pieces of waste. Two were chunks, one retaining a patch of nodule cortex. Ten secondary, 25 inner flakes were recorded. Of these, one secondary flake and eight inner flakes are broken. Twenty-three flakes retain plain butts, four are cortical, five are faceted. Twelve have pronounced bulbs of percussion, twenty have diffuse bulbs. Five examples have hinge terminations at the distal end. Complete flakes range from 27–85mm in length (mean length 44mm) and in breadth from 16–56mm (mean breadth 31mm). Breakdown of these data is contained in D7: a–c.

SITE XVII

This site produced 42 flints, including two natural and unmodified. All show heavy white recortication; eight examples (c 20%) retain fawn, smooth, nodular cortex. Stratigraphical distribution of the material is shown in Table 23 below.

Scrapers

G34 (Fig 50), a side and end scraper on inner flake, faceted butt, diffuse bulb of percussion; steeply retouched around its circumference. G35 (Fig 50), an end scraper on distal end of inner flake; plain butt, diffuse bulb of percussion.

Table 23   Distribution of flint types by context, Site XVII

Context (layers, Fig 30)	Scraper	Ret Flake	Sec Flake	Tert Flake	Unmod	Total
NE Quad: topsoil	1			1		2
NE Quad: 2		1	3	8		12
NE Quad Ditch: 11			6	17		23
NE Quad Ditch: 8	1					1
NW Quad: Below chalk crust				1	2	3
NW Quad: 5				1		1
Total	2	1	9	28	2	42

Miscellaneous Retouched/Utilised Pieces

An inner flake with plain butt, diffuse bulb of percussion, hinge termination at distal end (58 × 54 × 16mm). Traces of utilisation on right edge of distal end, dorsal face (not illustrated).

Waste Material

Waste material consists of nine complete secondary flakes, 23 complete, five broken tertiary flakes.

Seven secondary flakes have plain butts, three retain cortical butts. Six show diffuse bulbs of percussion, three have pronounced bulbs. Twenty tertiary flakes have plain butts, four have facetted butts; seventeen have pronounced, seven have diffuse bulbs of percussion. Reduction sequences of the raw material explain occurrence of cortical butts among secondary flakes and absence among inner flakes. Two secondary flakes, twelve inner flakes have hinge terminations at distal ends. Complete secondary flakes range from 23–76mm in length (mean length 47mm), and in breadth from 26–56mm (mean breadth 34mm). Complete inner flakes range from 15–61mm in length (mean length 34mm) and from 16–81mm in breadth (mean breadth of 32mm). A breakdown of length/breadth data is shown in D8: a–c.

SITE XVIII

Two flint flakes were found, in disturbed soil, one a secondary flake, broken transversely at bulbar end, retaining hard, fawn cortex on dorsal face, with hinge termination. The other a tertiary flake with plain butt, pronounced bulb.

SITE XIX

This site produced 237 pieces of flint, including ten unmodified/natural pieces. Table 24 gives a breakdown of the major artefact types and their distribution through the site stratigraphy. Flint came from three major contexts: working floor between barrow mounds, levels below working floor, the barrow itself.

The working floor

This area produced 128 flints including three unmodified/natural pieces (two pot lid flakes, one lump). All show heavy, white, recortication; 60 struck pieces (48%) retain cortex.

Cores

Five cores were recorded from Site XIX. Their attributes with those from Sites I and V are shown in Table 26.

Borers/Awls

One example (Fig 51, G41), on an inner flake, plain butt, diffuse bulb of percussion, retouched at distal end.

Waste Material

The waste material consists of thirteen irregular chunks and 106 flakes. Details of their type are recorded in Table 24. One primary flake, three secondary flakes, nine inner flakes are broken. Surviving butt and bulb types are classified in Table 25. Data suggest that hard-hammer direct percussion was the main technique in flake removal.

The complete primary flakes range in length from 18–54mm (mean length 38mm) and in breadth from 20–85mm (mean breadth 43mm). The 38 complete secondary flakes range from 17–82mm in length (mean length 47mm) and in breadth from 14–67mm (mean breadth 35mm). The 46 complete inner flakes range in length from 11–62mm (mean length 37mm) and in breadth from 10–88mm (mean breadth 30mm). Length/breadth ratios of complete flakes have been plotted as a separate scattergram for this context (D9: a–e).

Table 24 Distribution of flint types by context, Site XIX

Contexts (Section 1, Fig 34)	Awl	Scraper	Saw	Blade	Ret Flake	Prim Flake	Sec Flake	Tert Flake	Core Trim Flake	Core	Chip	Chunk	Unmod	Total
1: W. 17, 16	1					7	40	58	1	5		13	3	128
1: below W. 16				1		3	12	16			2	27	7	68
1: N mound, 8		1	1	2	1		3	23						31
1: S mound, 8	1				1			1				2		5
1: S mound, 13		1		1				2						4
ALS								1						1
Total	2	2	1	4	2	10	55	101	1	5	2	42	10	237

(W = working floor: ALS = ancient land surfaces: 8, 13, 16, 17 = layer numbers, Figure 34)

Table 25   Butt and bulb types, Site XIX

Context	Flake Type	Platform Type			Bulb Type	
		Plain	Cortical	Faceted	Pronounced	Diffuse
Working Floor	Primary	3	3	2	4	
	Secondary	26	15	34	6	1
	Tertiary	32	14	46		
Below Working Floor	Primary	1	1		1	1
	Secondary	9	2		5	6
	Tertiary	14	1	2	8	9
Barrow	Primary	Primary				
	Secondary	3			3	
	Tertiary	23		2	21	4
Total		111	36	86	48	21

Table 26   Dimensions and weights (grams) of cores

Site	Illustration	Type	Length	Breadth	Thickness	Weight
Site I	Fig 50: G1	Single-platform	40	41	22	32.7
Site V	Fig 50: G14	Core fragment				
Site XIX	Fig 50: G36	Keeled	72	78	38	154
	Fig 50: G37	Multi-platform	48	45	38	91
	Fig 50: G38	Single-platform	88	65	34	173.9
	Fig 50: G39	Single-platform	70	103	56	413
	Fig 50: G40	Keeled	47	65	34	103

Below the working floor

Sixty-eight pieces were recorded from below the working floor (Fig 34, layer 16, lower). They include 27 chunks, two chips, five unmodified/natural 'pot lid' removals and two natural/unmodified lumps. Of the remaining 32 flakes, eight are broken (two at bulbar end, six at distal end). Surviving butt and bulb types are shown in Table 25. Complete flakes range in length from 24–71mm (mean length 41mm), in breadth from 12–65mm (mean breadth 35mm).

The barrow

The remaining 50 pieces come from chalk crust (layer 13) and earth core (layer 8) of the site.

Scrapers

Two were recorded. G42 (Fig 50) is on distal end of inner flake with plain butt, pronounced bulb. G43 (not illustrated, now missing) is on distal end of inner flake, with faceted butt, diffuse bulb of percussion.

Awl/Borer

One possible example, (Fig 51, G44), on inner flake. Bi-facially worked, shallow retouch around circumference on dorsal face. Also inverse retouch on right edge and across base.

Saw/Serrated flake

One was recorded (Fig 51, G45), on secondary flake retaining buff cortex, plain butt, pronounced bulb. Fine serrations visible on both faces of right edge; also retouch on left edge.

Blades

Three unretouched blades, one a small bladelet broken at both ends. Of the two other examples, one (56 × 22 × 9mm) is a tertiary removal, the other (61 × 18 × 6mm) a secondary removal. Both have plain butts, pronounced bulbs.

Retouched/Utilised Flakes

There were two, one (Fig 51, G46) illustrated. Both are inner flakes, plain butts, pronounced bulbs of percussion. Illustrated example shows traces of utilisation on both edges. The other piece, broken at the distal end, shows evidence for retouch/utilisation on both edges.

Waste Material

Forty-one pieces classified as waste include two chunks, not discussed further. Of 31 flakes, four (three inner flakes, one secondary removal) are broken at distal end, one (an inner flake) at bulbar end. Surviving butt and bulb types are classified in Table 24. Complete flakes range in length from 25–60mm (mean length 41mm) and in breadth from 13–88mm (mean breadth 30mm). These data are considered further below.

SITE XX

See under VI/VII

SITE XXI

One piece of flint, a scraper (not illustrated), came from the edge, barrow mound, but possibly from enclosure ditch (Site VI) opposite, upper ditch fill. The scraper was made on distal end of secondary flake. Shows heavy, white, recortication; retains patch of buff/fawn cortex on dorsal face at left edge. Plain but crushed butt, pronounced bulb of percussion.

General comments

The material from Snail Down combines elements from funerary, domestic and industrial deposits, and ranges from artefacts deliberately deposited in graves to waste material discarded at a production site. In the process of barrow construction some flints may have been redeposited but the generally fresh state of the material suggests that it has not been extensively exposed or reworked. The assemblage is not very large by the standards of comparable barrow complexes, and statistical data have been compiled for the purposes of general comparison with other sites, rather than as a means of refining any internal site chronologies. The most striking feature of the assemblage when viewed as a whole is the lack of cores, matched by a shortage of primary flakes. The evidence for primary production of lithic material is virtually limited to Site XIX. This may imply some social restriction of production on site, which is surprising in view of the existence of a settlement beneath Sites X–XIV.

It has recently been suggested that the finds of flint-working debris in long barrow ditches might represent a symbolic attempt to 'close down' the sites as ritual monuments (Philips and Thomas 1989). However, the barrow ditches themselves would have provided ready-made quarries for raw material and this point should not be overlooked in any consideration of the nature of the overall assemblage. The lack of cores and primary flakes makes further discussion of this point difficult.

It is obvious from the study of butt and bulb types that both hard-hammer direct percussion and soft-hammer direct percussion were the main flaking techniques. As data for Sites I, III and XIX (those sites with the largest samples of material) show, the representation of these techniques varies across the barrow group.

A consideration of the data on length/breadth measurements for complete flakes from all sites shows that very few flakes reach blade-like proportions, with most of the groups of material conforming to Ford's (1987) criteria for broad Bronze Age date. The overall trend from all the excavated Snail Down barrows conforms to the generalised pattern from sites such as West Kennet Avenue (Smith 1965a) and other Bronze Age sites in Wessex such as Amesbury Barrow G71 (Saville 1980a, 3–9).

As Pitts and Jacobi have shown, and as has been borne out by other workers in the area, there is a tendency for the morphology of waste flakes to change over time in the south of England, with a general trend from blade-like proportions to shorter squatter flakes (Pitts and Jacobi 1979; Healey and Robertson Mackay 1983; Ford *et al* 1984).

Some twenty scrapers were recorded from various locations across the barrow group (see Table 10). None of these is exceptional, though one or two show evidence for skilful knapping and none would be out of place on any Late Neolithic/Bronze Age site in the south of England. The fact that scrapers are the only significant tool type recorded is of interest. This may simply reflect the fact that scrapers are easy to identify and so are regularly collected, but their numbers might suggest that the majority of the lithic material on the sites came from domestic contexts.

The three arrowhead forms recorded are equally common in terms of their regular occurrence on Bronze Age sites in the south of England. The Sutton Type b, barbed and tanged example from Site XIV is one of the commonest forms known in the south.

The two axe roughouts associated with the linear ditch, Site VI, could be Neolithic and are probably residual in the area. This is also the most likely explanation for the axe fragment from the topsoil of Site XVI.

The lithic assemblages from Snail Down are much as might be expected from a barrow group of this type and date, with clear evidence for some domestic activity in the vicinity, but there are limited indications of actual manufacture/production processes.

Figure 50
Cores and Scrapers

Cores

G1, core, SDI; G14, core fragment, SDV; G36, keeled core, SDXIX; G37, multi-platform core, SDXIX; G38, single-platform core, SDXIX; G39, single-platform core, SDXIX; G40, keeled core, SDXIX

Scrapers

G2, end scraper, SDI; G3, discoidal scraper, SDI; G4, side and end scraper, SDI; G12, long end scraper, SDIII; G10, short end scraper, SDIII; G11, long end scraper, SDIII; G17, side and end scraper, SDVI/VII; G18, scraper, SDX; G20, end scraper, SDXI; G21, end scraper, SDXIII; G22, side scraper, SDXIII; G26, scraper, SDXIV; G27, scraper, SDXIV; G28, scraper, SDXIV; G33, short end scraper, SDXVI; G34, scraper, SDXVII; G35, scraper, SDXVII; G42, scraper, SDXIX; G47, scraper, SDXXI (or VI)

Figure 51
Implements and Projectile Points; Miscellaneous retouched pieces

Implements and Projectile Points
G6, b-and–t arrowhead, SDII; G24, triangular arrowhead, SDXIV; G25, b-and–t arrowhead, SDXIV; G32, awl, SDXVI; G41, awl, SDXIX; G15, large axe rough-out, SDVI; G16, small axe rough-out, SDVI; G31, axe fragment, SDXVI; G29, knife, SDXIV; G45, saw, SDXIX; G44, ? Awl, SDXIX

Miscellaneous retouched pieces
G5, ?utilised inner flake, SDI; G7-G9, retouched secondary flakes, SDII; G13, utilised flake, SDIII; G19, retouched blade, SDX; G23, retouched blade, SDXIII; G30, retouched blade, SDXIV; G46, retouched flake, SDXIX

DIAGRAMS

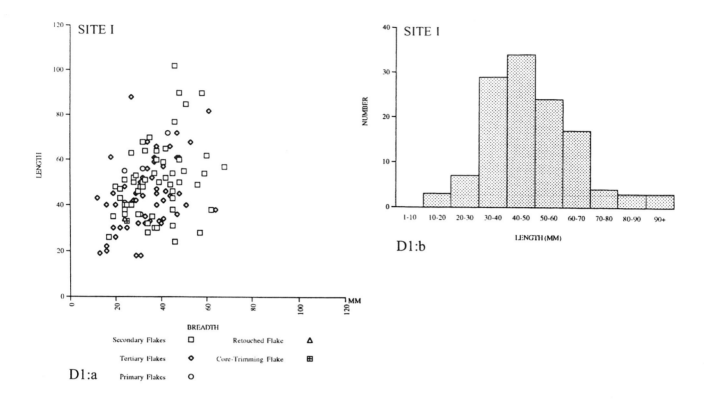

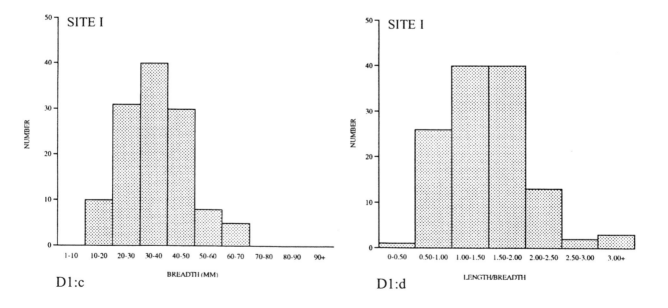

Diagram 1: a–d Length and breadth data, complete flakes, Site I
    a: scattergram, length:breadth ratio distribution by type of flake.
    b: histogram, length of all complete flakes.
    c: histogram, breadth of all complete flakes.
    d: histogram, length/breadth of all complete flakes.

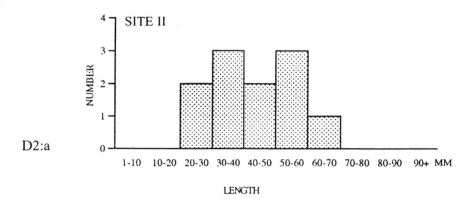

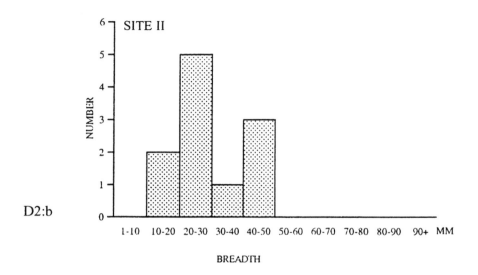

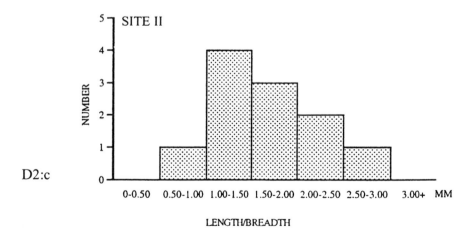

Diagram 2: a–c Length and breadth data, complete flakes, Site II
      a: histogram, length of all complete flakes.
      b: histogram, breadth of all complete flakes.
      c: histogram, length/breadth of all complete flakes.

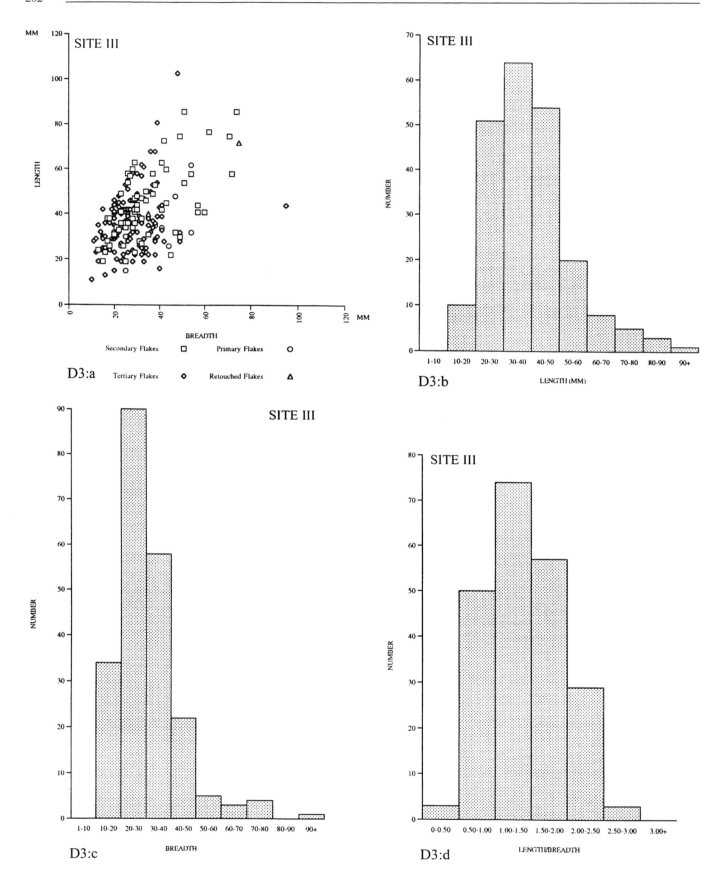

Diagram 3: a–d Length and breadth data, complete flakes, Site III
    a: scattergram, length:breadth ratio distribution by type of flake.
    b: histogram, length of all complete flakes.
    c: histogram, breadth of all complete flakes.
    d: histogram, length/breadth of all complete flakes

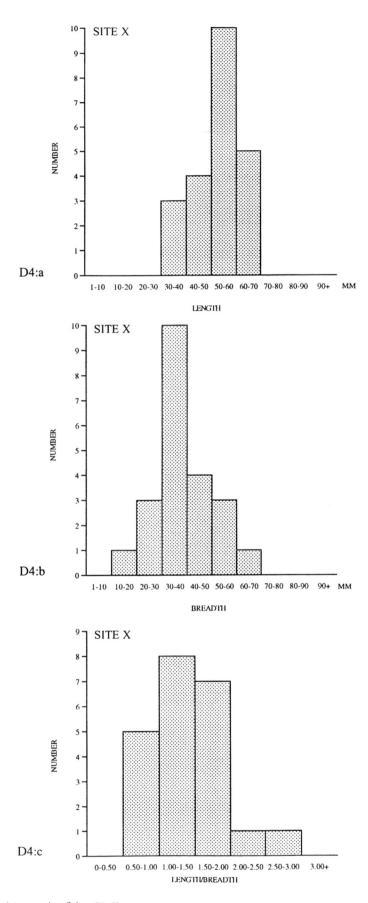

Diagram 4: a–c Length and breadth data, complete flakes, Site X
    a: histogram, length of all complete flakes.
    b: histogram, breadth of all complete flakes.
    c: histogram, length/breadth of all complete flakes.

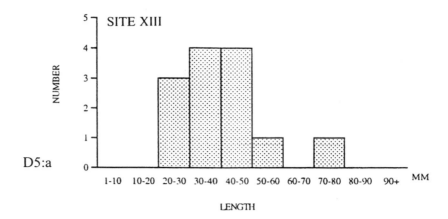

D5:a

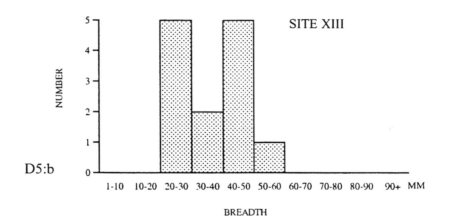

D5:b

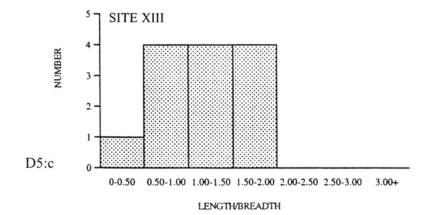

D5:c

Diagram 5: a–c Length and breadth data, complete flakes, Site XIII
    a: histogram, length of all complete flakes.
    b: histogram, breadth of all complete flakes.
    c: histogram, length/breadth of all complete flakes.

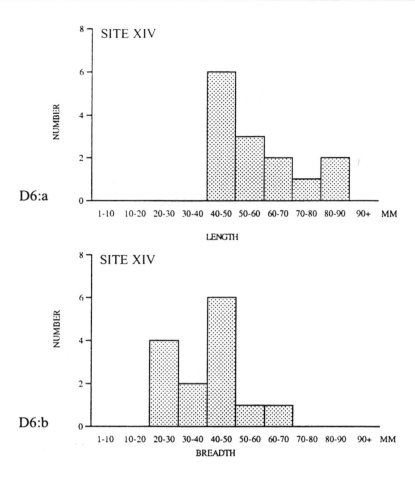

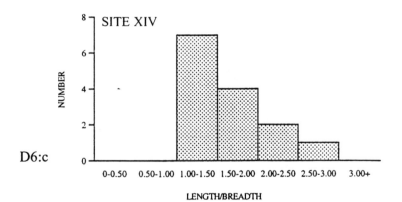

Diagram 6: a–c Length and breadth data, complete flakes, Site XIV
    a: histogram, length of all complete flakes.
    b: histogram, breadth of all complete flakes.
    c: histogram, length/breadth of all complete flakes.

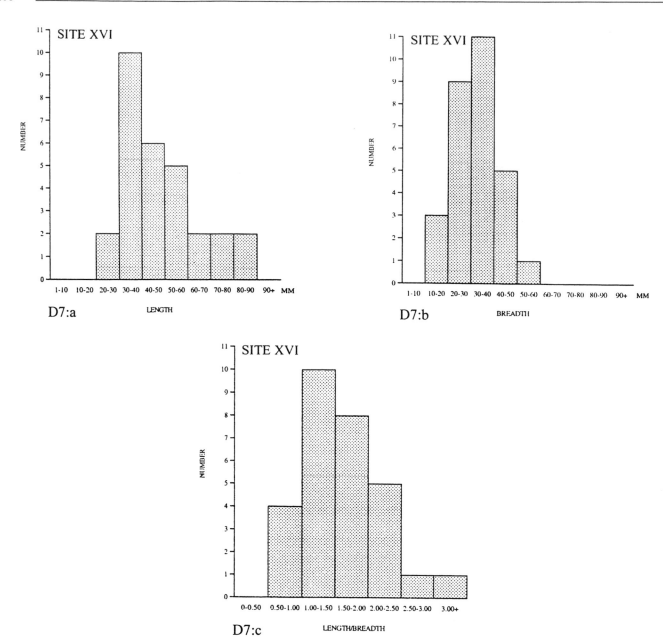

Diagram 7: a–c Length and breadth data, complete flakes, Site XVI
    a: histogram, length of all complete flakes.
    b: histogram, breadth of all complete flakes.
    c: histogram, length/breadth of all complete flakes.

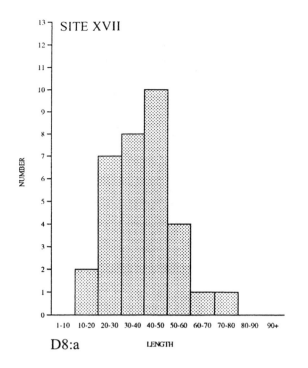

D8:a

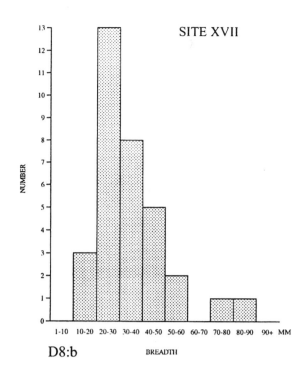

D8:b

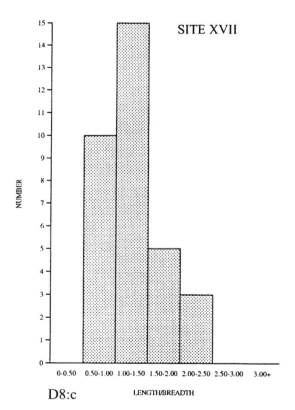

D8:c

Diagram 8: a–c Length and breadth data, complete flakes, Site XVII
a: histogram, length of all complete flakes.
b: histogram, breadth of all complete flakes.
c: histogram, length/breadth of all complete flakes.

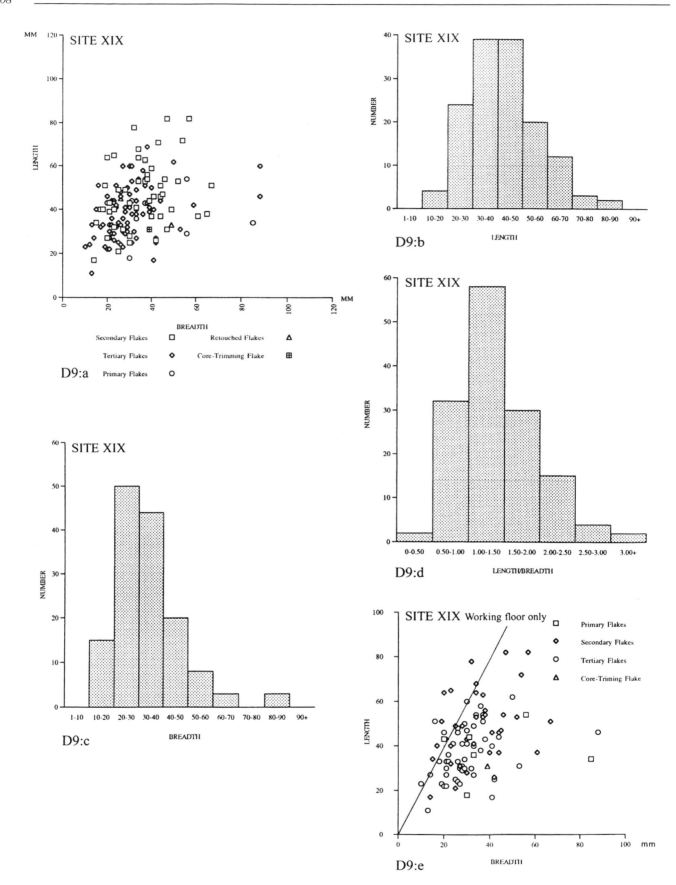

Diagram 9: a–e Length and breadth data, complete flakes, Site XIX
    a: scattergram, length:breadth ratio distribution by type of flake.
    b: histogram, breadth of all complete flakes.
    c: histogram, breadth of all complete flakes.
    d: histogram, length/breadth of all complete flakes.
    e: scattergram, length: breadth ratio distribution by type of flake, working floor only

H WORKED BONE

Nicholas Thomas

Seven bone implements were recovered during the excavation, which were not related closely to barrows or burials. In addition, a series of bone objects was found by Hoare in the primary grave pit (but probably a cenotaph) beneath SPTA2207. These are described and illustrated separately (Section M, Fig 56). The non-sepulchral bonework of 1953–1957 is described first, followed by notes on its typology, chronology and methods of manufacture. Animal identification has been done by Juliet Clutton-Brock. H1-H7 are illustrated in Figure 52.

H1 **Pointed end of a pendant or pin.** Cut from the metapodial of an artiodactyl and ground to a point, with a shallow U-section (see H2). Butt-end lost. L 5.4cm; Figure 52. Site XIII, S half, modern turf. When complete, would probably have resembled M7 (Fig 56).

H2 **Bone-working residue.** Proximal end of a hollow left metacarpal of a sheep. Both broad sides grooved longitudinally to divide the bone eventually into two, for production, in all probability, of a pair of pendants or pins of the type represented by H1. Marks along the surfaces of these grooves suggest that they were made by cutting, perhaps using flint flakes or saw blades. L 6.7cm. Figure 52. Site XX, section 8, base of layer 23.

H3 **Awl,** complete; made on the distal end of a sheep's metatarsal, probably left side. Hollow. Condyles retained to form butt. Length 9.3cm. Figure 52. Site XV, SE Quadrant, outside post ring, disturbed area; d 1ft. Attenuated and very sharp point made most probably by grinding; in the process the whole implement has acquired an almost rectangular cross-section. It has not been perforated nor hollowed intentionally. Weathering has removed all trace of surface treatment or polishing save at the extreme point, which is polished. Though this type of implement is classified as a gouge, it could never have been used in that way, being too pointed. As a leather-worker's awl, however, or as a borer for some other relatively soft material, it would have been ideal, the condyles at the butt providing an appropriate grip.

H4 **?Awl,** complete except for tip but slightly weathered: made from a long bone shaft of sheep or roe deer size. Condyles removed by cutting across the bone. Cut marks indicate that this neat operation was done with a series of short cuts and regularly rotating the bone. No final grinding was attempted. Traces of three short shallow grooves across the bone, beginning 8mm from the proximal end and almost on the plane of the gouge edges, perhaps represent earlier attempts to cut off the condyles: or indicate butchery marks, or else the result of usage. Weathering has obscured the precise means by which the gouge blade was opened out; grinding presumably. There are traces of longitudinal grinding marks along the shaft. Hollowed probably intentionally. L 7.4cm; l of gouge blade 4.3cm; diam 1cm. Figure 52. Site XV, SW Quadrant, base of turf and modern humus.

At All Cannings Cross, where similar objects occurred, Mrs Cunnington classified those with end removed and no rivet hole as Class C (1923, 82, pl 8, figs 14–19). Figure 17, which includes some cross-cuts like H4, is particularly close. A shorter but otherwise close parallel, attributed to the later Bronze Age, has come from a barrow, West Overton G19, associated with a cremation (Gill Swanton, pers comm). A less-precise analogue from the Wilsford Shaft (Wilsford G33A), of the later Bronze Age also, is of greater diameter and has a much shorter, blunter blade: its opposite end is apparently missing (Ashbee *et al* 1989, 49–50, figs 46, 47).

H5 **?Gouge**, point damaged, made at the distal end of a tibia, probably sheep, right side. Butt broken across raggedly, and no perforation. Hollow but not bored. Whole surface bears traces of smoothing in the form of slight facets, longitudinal and narrow; here and there polishing apparent. Along one side, from centre to butt, a pair of finely incised lines or scratches, converging towards butt. Gouge blade formed by an oblique cut, ground down, whose steep angle, in contrast to H3, has exposed only a short opening into the bone. L 10.2cm. Figure 52. Site XX, section 8, base of layer 23.

In Mrs Cunnington's classification of such pieces among the bonework at All Cannings Cross (Cunnington 1923, 85ff), this is of Class E (see also Wheeler 1943, 303ff). A related piece came from the upper filling of the Wilsford Shaft (Wilsford G 33a: (Ashbee *ibid*, 49, fig 46, 6).

H6 **Bone-working residue**: probably the distal end of a sheep's metatarsal, left side. Has been roughly broken

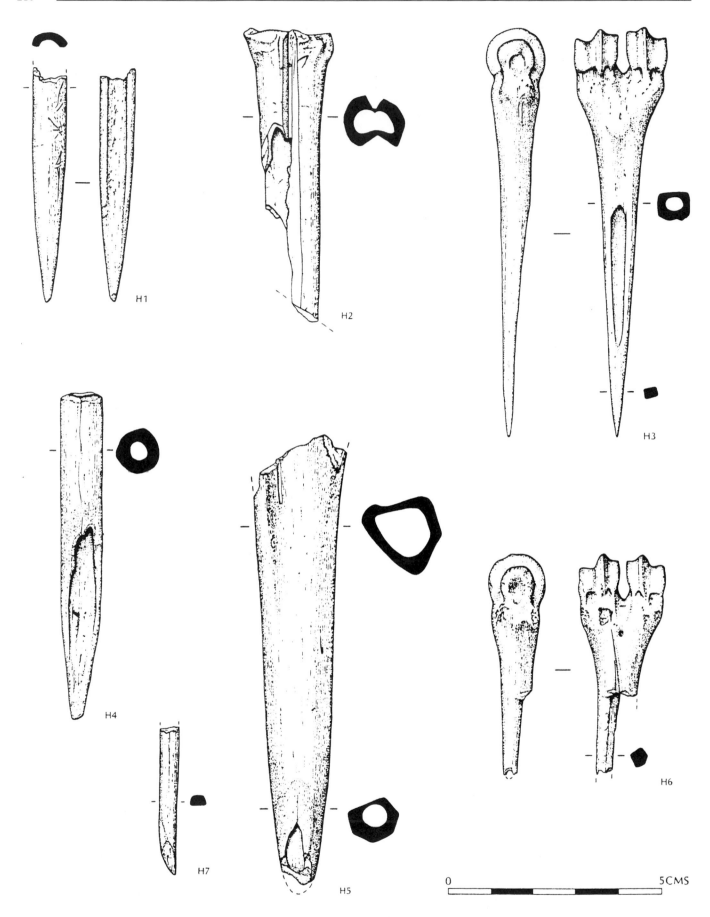

Fig 52   Worked bone, Sites XIII, XV, XX.

across from a point 3.2cm from its distal end, apparently during process of carving two prongs which were eyed needles in the making. End of one needle survives, its eye already bored but then broken at that point. Other needle prong, if such it was, has been detached. On both broad sides of the bone, beginning immediately below condyles, traces of cutting and grinding processes by which the bone was divided into two needle prongs can be seen. L 5cm. Figure 52. Site XX, NW arc of barrow, cutting E, base of topsoil.

H7 Part of **solid bone pin with oblique-pointed end**. Made on sliver of bone, possibly from shaft of a sheep's metapodial. Shaped and polished all over to give oval cross-section. L 3.4cm. Figure 52. Site XV, SE Quadrant, within post ring; topsoil. Traces of polishing on pin and its point suggest that asymmetrical shape was a deliberate design, not the result of a break.

TYPOLOGY, CHRONOLOGY AND MANUFACTURE

The Snail Down bonework was made from the metacarpals, metatarsals and a tibia of sheep. Juliet Clutton-Brock considered but ruled out the use of roe deer bone. The grave-group from 2207 also included plain pins of antler. These various implements represent some of the main categories of small bone tool and ornament found in pre-Roman Britain:

1 **Short featureless pins** made on solid slivers of bone or antler and more obviously for ornament than for use as borers. Impossible to date closely out of context, Snail Down H7 may belong to the early second millennium cal BC, if truly associated with Site XV. A series occurred at All Cannings Cross, of the earlier Iron Age (Cunnington 1923, pl 13, 3–6).

2. **Points made on split metacarpals or metatarsals**, usually perforated at the butt-end, which also retains traces of the bone's articulating surface; the generally accepted use is as pendants rather than for coarse sewing. They are more closely datable, occurring frequently in Early Bronze Age contexts. Snail Down HI may have been associated with the construction of Site XIII or else derived from the Beaker settlement beneath; the similar (complete) pendant from 2207 (M7, Fig 56) can be placed in the early second millennium cal BC. The practice of splitting sheep's long bones to make ornaments with a trough-shaped cross section was more common during the Neolithic and Early Bronze Age than at other times in our prehistory.

Examples of the type – not always perforated – have come from Windmill Hill (Smith 1965a, 128, B9–13), Woodhenge (Cunnington 1929, 107, pl 19A, 4) and Maiden Castle (Wheeler 1943, 181, fig 48, 1). Another has been found at an earthwork west of Badbury Rings (Dorset), beneath the second phase bank at this site (Gingell 1988, 75, fig 12). The largest single series of such points was found in the celebrated Neolithic/Early Bronze Age 'Bone' barrow at Upton

Lovell, G2a, at least forty-one such points, apparently graded in size to form a collar, although their use as a fringe to a skirt should not be ruled out (Piggott 1962, 93–97, pl 1). There the associated stone tools included battle-axes, polished flint axe-heads, stone rubbers (Thomas 1966, 2, fig 1) and a grooved whetstone, together with shale beads and a bronze awl.

Unperforated points within this series, which were represented among the bone ornaments at Upton Lovell, occurred at Amesbury barrow G39, at the top of the mound whose primary grave yielded amber and jet beads when Cunnington excavated there in ?1808 (Ashbee 1981, 24, fig 8, 3).

These pendants are distinct in the treatment of their heads from the fine series of ring-headed pins made similarly on split sheep metapodials from the Wilsford Shaft (Ashbee *et al* 1989, 48–49, figs 45, 46), which came from the waterlogged lowest fill and thus from within the Middle Bronze Age. They can also be distinguished from bone pins with plain, solid (not U-sectioned) shafts, whose heads are equally plain and carry a small perforation, sometimes drilled from both sides, like the one from Long Crichel, Barrow 7 (Dorset), accompanying an earlier Bronze Age inhumation (Green *et al* 1983, 50, fig 7).

A perforated pendant of the series, with a bronze ogival dagger of Gerloff's Type Camerton (1975, pl 18, 188), was found in an urn containing a cremation at Wimborne St Giles G20, Dorset (Annable and Simpson 1964, 55 and 109, nos 349–350). To these the two Snail Down pendants, H1 and M7, can now be added, together with H2 which is in the process of being split to provide blanks for two such pendants.

3 **Eyed needles for sewing** are characteristic of the Iron Age, occurring within that context at Maiden Castle, All Cannings Cross and on most Iron Age sites where bone was well preserved. A needle of this type has, however, been found in a grave-group from Barrow H3 at Amesbury Park (Annable and Simpson 1964, 53 and 108, nos 322–324), while another came from the lower, waterlogged infills of the Wilsford Shaft, (Ashbee *ibid*, fig 46, 5) ; but earlier Bronze Age examples are not common. Snail Down H6, a residue from which such pins may have been made, was not found in a datable context.

4 There is an ill-understood series of **gouge-like points** fashioned on one or other end of sheep metacarpals and metatarsals. These, like the needles of category 3, belonged essentially to the Iron Age. Longitudinal boring of the implement has sometimes been claimed, in addition (frequently and unequivocally) to a smaller transverse perforation near the butt; this, if it is a hole for a wooden peg, would have allowed the object to be firmly hafted. Probably the process of prolonged burial accounts for their hollow centres. Cunliffe (1991, 446, fig 17.1, 6–11) has described hafted examples as pin beaters used in the weaving process. Snail Down H3 belongs in general to this group. It is unusual in retaining the condyles at the distal end (but cf Cunnington 1923, pl 9, 8), a factor which would have prevented it from being hafted. The gouge element is sharper, longer and more elegantly shaped than most and its use as an awl seems obvious. Snail Down H4 is of the same category, but less common because its end has been cut off.

Though characteristic of the Iron Age, two exceptionally short examples should be noted from the later Bronze Age settlement on Itford Hill, Sussex (Burstow and Holleyman 1958, 204–205, fig 29). And an even closer parallel came from a Beaker occupation area covered by the barrow mound of Avebury G55 (Smith 1965, 35, fig 5.10, and 38).

5. Gouges were also made on the tibiae of sheep. These were sturdier; from the nature of the bone they lacked the narrow tube shape of category 4. The gouge end was shorter and the butt often left rough. Snail Down H5 is typical. Similar pieces have come from later Bronze Age sites, for example the enclosures on Boscombe Down East, (Stone 1937b, 466–489, pl vi), and Ogbourne Down, (C M Piggott 1942, 56, fig 6, 17), as well as from Iron Age sites like Fyfield Bavant Down, (Clay 1924, 481, pl IX) and All Cannings Cross, (Cunnington 1923, pl 13, 12, but perforated).

The working of these small bone implements and pins was by cutting, grinding, boring and polishing, using flint blades and saws, awls and perhaps gravers, with fine-grained hones and sand of various textures. Metal knives could also have been used. Fresh animal bone is, however, notoriously hard and grinding may have been more productive than cutting.

H2 exhibits evidence of the adaptation of a form of the then ancient groove-and-splinter technique for making harpoon heads and long pins of antler. It shows longitudinal channels on opposite sides of a sheep's metacarpal, from which, eventually, two U-shaped blanks could have been produced and made into pins or pendants like Snail Down H1. This Mesolithic technique had enjoyed a long life. At the Mount Pleasant, Dorset, henge monument (Wainwright

1979, 173 and fig 78), a strip of antler had been removed using this method; and from Long Crichel Barrow 5, Dorset, came a small ox metatarsal bearing two deep, longitudinal incisions which were considered to be the first stage in the manufacture of a bone pin (Green *et al* 1983, 48). It occurred in the phase 1 ditch, belonging to the Beaker period.

Snail Down H6 shows that bone sewing needles were sometimes shaped and the eye bored before being removed from the parent bone. In the Snail Down instance, one needle may have been detached successfully: boring the eye on the other – always the most difficult process – caused it to break at that point. A later Iron Age settlement at Fisherton, Salisbury, yielded a similar piece of needle-maker's debris (Stevens 1934, 611, B33, fig 9).

The finding of two pieces of bone-worker's debris close together (H2, H6) suggests the presence nearby of a workshop and a settlement. H5, also from the same general context, reinforces this impression. That these three belong to categories of small bone object that have come, elsewhere, from sites dated variously within the last two millennia BC, from later Neolithic until the end of the Iron Age, confirms the difficulty of close dating for common types made from one source of raw material – sheep long bone.

At Snail Down, the presence of H2, H5 and H6 on the northern edge of the barrow cemetery seems to reflect the respect shown to the barrows by later prehistoric people using the Down: the debris of domestic occupation was not generally allowed to be spread over the barrow area. In all probability the three bone pieces were associated with people who were responsible for Sites VI and VII in one or another of their phases.

Fig 53 Stone axe, Site II, battle-axe fragment, Site XIV.

J STONE TOOLS AND SARSEN

Nicholas Thomas

J1 **Stone axe-head**, heavily weathered, almost no original ground surface remaining. Blade at an acute angle to upper line possibly through use and re-sharpening. Butt less carefully completed. Oval cross-section. The blade edge is rounded and blunt partly through weathering. The axe is unusually thick for its length. Material: greenstone (Evens *et al* 1962, 259, no 868), almost certainly an epidiorite of probably Cornish origin (Vin Davis, *in litt*, June 1992). L 7.2cm; d 4.75cm; w 3.35cm. Figure 53. Site II, NE Quadrant, section 3, layer 6, d 16in.

J2 **Stone battle-axe fragment**. Part of the side and gradual curve round to top (or bottom: the fragment is too small to be precise). Narrower end perhaps close to blade, as the figure suggests, but it lacks certainty; no trace of presumed shaft hole. Original surfaces well-smoothed, almost polished in places; colour patchily green and pale cream. Material: camptonite, Group XIV, from the silts in the Cambrian beds near Nuneaton, Warwicks (Shotton 1959, 135–137; Evens *et al* 1962, 220, 263, no 1059; Evens *et al* 1972, 263). L 7.2cm. Figure 53. Site XIV, SW Quadrant, layer 5, d 14in.

Group XIV was a source of good implement-making stone that was exploited by later Neolithic and earlier Bronze Age communities principally in the West Midlands, as Shotton showed in 1959. Its distribution further afield, especially to the south-west, appears to have been slight: the Snail Down fragment and a complete piece from Codford St Peter barrow G5, both battle-axes (Evens *et al* 1962, 248, 263, nos 297 and 1059). The current published total of Camptonite battle-axes and axe-hammers is fourteen.

In 1966 Roe proposed, on the grounds of form, that Group XIV battle-axes were likely to prove to be of Early Bronze Age date and that associations with Food Vessels and early Wessex graves were to be expected, not with Beakers. This might suggest that the Snail Down fragment belonged to the construction of Sites X-XIV rather than with the domestic Beaker settlement they sealed. Yet we have argued (Part 3) that Sites X-XIV may have been close in time to the Beaker remains: and recently a battle-axe of Group XIV has come to light at Long Eaton (Derbys) that belongs to Roe's proposed earliest form of battle-axe, her Stage I (Moore and Cummins 1974, 65; Roe 1966, 205–207), having well-established association with Beakers. The Snail Down battle-axe fragment could therefore have been dropped at any stage of the activity around Sites X-XIV and what lay beneath.

J3 **Stone flake**, humanly struck; rectangular shape; non-bulbar face shows the scar for a similar flake, as well as a patinated, unflaked area. Triangular cross-section. Material: sarsen. L 8.3cm; w 5.55cm; th 2.3cm. Not illustrated. Site XX, section 8, layer 23.

Two other small, amorphous pieces were recorded, one from topsoil on Site III, a second from the base of Site XI. Raymond has shown (Section E, Table 11), that sarsen is a rare inclusion in pottery within the region.

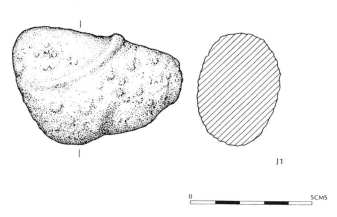

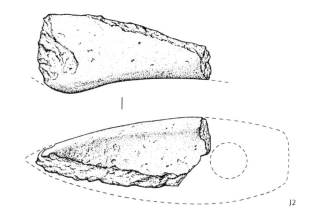

0   5CMS

Fig 53   Stone axe, Site II, battle-axe fragment, Site XIV.

K BEADS FROM BURIALS IN SITES III, XV AND XXII

NICHOLAS THOMAS, WITH A NOTE BY J F S STONE

Beads were recovered from three barrows: a token prestige necklace of five different materials from Site III Secondary Burial 1, a single bead found unassociated at the base of Site XV, and from Site XXII a group of three beads, two ambers and a sea shell. All are illustrated in Figure 54. We are indebted to Ray Barnett, Bristol City Museum and Art Gallery, for help with identification and naming of shells.

SITE III

K1 **Dumb-bell-shaped pendant bead**. Unweathered and retaining good polish. Body cylindrical with concave wall; top and bottom of equal size and slightly domed. Shallow V-perforation drilled through body nearer to one end. Closely akin to K8. Material: probably jet. H 14mm; diam 12mm. Diam of perf 2.5mm. Found in cairn material associated with Secondary Burial 1 (Cremation 8) but disturbed in wartime by passage of military vehicles.

K2 **Short biconical bead,** narrow perforation. Surface slightly weathered. Material: jet. L of perf 4.4mm; diam 7.1mm; diam of perf 2mm. DM1788. Annable and Simpson 1964, 64 and 119, no 517.

K3 **Short biconical bead**, similar to K2 but slightly longer; perforation also wider, surface slightly weathered. Material: jet. L of perf 4.7mm; diam 7.3mm; diam of perf 3mm. DM1788. Annable and Simpson *ibid.*

K4 **Short biconical bead,** larger than K2, K3 but of similar type. Surface slightly weathered. Material: jet. L of perf 8mm; diam 9.9mm; diam of perf 3.4mm. DMI788. Annable and Simpson *ibid.*

Beads K2–K4 were analysed by Bussell *et al* (1982, 30, nos 60–62) and found to be jet. All the jet/shale beads were viewed (by NT) under a X10 lens. Nos K2–K4 and K8 were slightly too weathered to preserve marks of manufacture. K1, in mint condition and well polished, showed file marks running in various directions on top and bottom, and consistently at right-angles to the long axis around its concave wall, as would be expected.

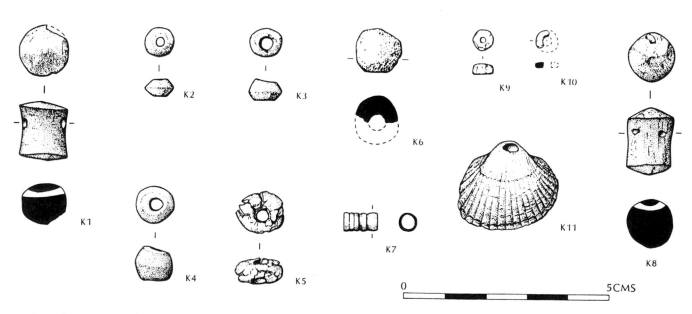

Fig 54   Beads, various materials: K1-K7, Site III, Secondary Burial 1; K9-K11, Site XXII, Inhumation 2; K8, Site XV.

K5 **Flattened globular bead**, perforation through thinnest part. Heavily weathered. Material: amber. L of perf 5.9mm; diam *c* 11mm; diam of perf 2.4mm. DM1788. Annable and Simpson *ibid*, no 518 (second bead not of amber – see below, K6); Beck and Shennan 1991, 153 (but one bead not amber, see below).

K6 **Globular bead**, broken. Material: soft, cream-coloured stone. L of perf 11mm; diam *c* 11.4mm; diam of perf *c* 3mm. DM1788. Annable and Simpson *ibid*, 518, but incorrectly called amber.

K7 **Segmented bead**, complete but fragmented. Five segments. Material: glassy faience. L 7.9mm; diam 4.6mm; diam of perf 3mm. Stone and Thomas 1957, 79; Annable and Simpson *ibid*, 516 (through confusion caused by the writer [NT], the wrong faience bead was shown in Annable and Simpson: correct bead illustrated in this report, Fig 54). Beads K2–K7 found at three different levels within the Collared Urn of Secondary Burial 1: probably deposited loose, not as a strung necklet. It is presumed that these were associated with bead K1 as part of the same offering.

SITE XV

K8 **Dumb-bell-shaped pendant bead**, close in shape and size to K1. Slightly weathered. Body less concave-sided, ends raised into more prominent points. Perforation drilled with a more sharply angled V shape. Beads K1 and K8 could have been made by the same hand. Material possibly lignite. H 1.7mm, diam 1.2cm; diam of perf 1.8mm. Found at base of barrow mound, below later Bronze Age Skeleton I; not, therefore, close to primary cremation burial (Fig 25).

SITE XXII

K9 **Almost circular disc-bead**, upper and lower surfaces flat, edge formed as if in a series of microscopic straight sections. Narrow perforation. Material: amber. L of perf 2mm; diam 5.6mm; diam of perf 1mm.

K10 Fragment of a **bead** possibly resembling K9, therefore disc shaped. Material: amber. Dimensions similar to K9.

K11 **Pendant** made from a sea shell indistinguishable from the modern cockle (*Cardium edule* L.). The umbo pierced, apparently, by careful cutting rather than drilling. W 2.5cm; diam of perf 4mm.

DISCUSSION

Jet, jet/shale, amber, faience, stone, shell and bone: so far only fossils and glass and metals are missing from the range of natural and man-made materials for beads and pendants used by the community when burying its dead at Snail Down. The beadwork from most Wessex cemeteries and individual burials that have yielded these personal ornaments shows a similar range. It is seen again in the unexpectedly comprehensive series of beads from West Kennet chambered tomb, these probably belonging to the later history of the long barrow and the ancillary building such as an ossuary that may have been involved (Piggott 1962a, 51–53, fig 18, amber noticeably absent; and 75).

All materials for beads at Snail Down except stone and bone are exotic – brought in from outside the region – faience, amber, jet/shale and shell. The segmented faience bead, K7, which *could* have been made in Wiltshire, was submitted to J F S Stone soon after its discovery in 1955 and he wrote the following note in March 1956.

'Faience bead from Snail Down Bell-Barrow Site III

The single segmented faience bead, found with beads of amber and shale accompanying a secondary cremation in a large Collared Urn, is representative of the well-known type of segmented bead found in a number of barrows in Wessex, and especially those of Salisbury Plain (Beck and Stone 1936, 215). It possesses five segments, is 7.9mm long, 4.6mm in diameter, and has the usual large perforation which in this instance is 3mm in diameter.

In colour the bead is light green, and the coloured glaze appears to have penetrated the core completely which is composed of large grains of quartz. It is in fact not normal faience at all but consists of another variety known as 'Glassy Faience' or Lucas's variant E (Lucas 1948, 188), in the making of which pre-made powdered glass, coloured with copper compound, was mixed directly with powdered quartz and then, after moulding, fired in a furnace. The composition is thus homogeneous throughout and the quartz grains appear to be floating in a lake of glass, as distinct from normal faience where the powdered glaze was used as an external slip to coat a pre-made colourless quartz core. The surface of this type of faience is therefore not usually glossy or glass-like, as in normal faience, but somewhat porous looking.

It is of interest, too, that during firing this Snail Down bead came into contact with a little colourless glass which still adheres as a small patch over two of the segments.

Glassy faience beads are very rare in Wiltshire – this is in fact the first I have seen and recognised as such possibly because of its fragmentary state. They are rare too in the south of England, the only other example being a necklace of six beads from Frampton, Dorset (Fox and Stone 1951, 30). In Scotland and the north, however, they are more common, and the recently discovered necklace from the Mound of the Hostages, Tara, Republic of Ireland, is composed of beads of the same material (O'Ríordáin 1956, 170; Stone and Thomas 1957, 79 for the Snail Down bead).

This Snail Down bead is thus of considerable interest, and its position in the heartland of the Wessex Culture, which acquired segmented beads only and not star or quoit forms which lie peripherally and around the coasts, strongly suggests that the two varieties of faience are contemporary and were acquired from an eastern Mediterranean source at the same time.

Glassy faience segmented beads are known from Malta where they are dated 1450–1350 BC and from Leopoldsdorf near Vienna. They seem to be common in Egypt during the XVIIIth Dynasty, especially at Tell el Amarna (1380–1350 BC). The evidence at present suggests that the main movement of faience beads to the west and north, through the Mediterranean, took place during the fourteenth century BC, and that their dispersion as trade beads was possibly in some way connected with Mycenaean trade expeditions.'

Since 1956, when Stone described the Snail Down bead, these faience objects found in the British Isles and in Europe have undergone detailed reassessment. Even today, however, it is still impossible to perceive any chronological or cultural significance in the two types of faience.

Since Dr Stone's time, a fruitful line of enquiry has been the application of neutron activation and X-ray analysis (Aspinall *et al* 1972; Aspinall and Warren 1973). This work has identified the constituents of faience beads and revealed a difference between those of the British Isles and Central Europe, and the Near East (Harding and Warren 1973). Such results seem to reinforce the contention of present-day scholars that faience beads of segmented, star and quoit styles could have been manufactured in the British Isles as part of the now well-established manufacture of beads in glass (Guido *et al* 1984).

Faience beads remain a rare type of find in Wessex graves. Until Green and Rollo-Smith published the faience quoit bead from Net Down Barrow 5L in 1984 (310–311, fig 29, 10), no quoit or other faience beads except segmented had been found in Wiltshire; and from Wessex more widely only one star bead and one quoit in faience, in Dorset, near Dorchester (Stone and Thomas 1957, 82). In southern England and the Republic of Ireland, only nineteen faience beads appear to have been recorded since 1945:

Wiltshire

Amesbury, New Barn Down G61a (Ashbee 1985, 74–75, figs 38, 39, 5, 8; 81, 89). Two segmented beads.
Shrewton, Net Down 5L (Green and Rollo-Smith 1984, 310–311, fig 29, 8–10). Two segmented, one quoit bead.
Snail Down, Site III (this report). One segmented bead, glassy faience.

Isle of Wight

Arreton Down (Alexander and Ozannes 1960, 275–276, fig 6, 5). One segmented bead.

Devon

Shaugh Moor, Ring Cairn 2 (Wainwright *et al* 1979, 26–27, fig 13). Ten fragments making up seven segmented beads.

Isles of Scilly

Knackyboy Cairn, St Martin's (O'Neil 1952, 30–34). Star bead, associated with seven glass beads.

Republic of Ireland

Mound of the Hostages, Tara (Co Meath: O'Ríordáin 1956, 163–173, pl XXIII). Four segmented beads, glassy faience.

The pair of jet/shale dumb-bell beads from Snail Down, K1, K8, are a rare form and may have come from the same workshop. Traces of working by some form of fine grinding all over the bead from Site III are not usually so well preserved. Unfortunately this pair was not included in the recent programme of analysis by X-ray fluorescence and its raw material has not been characterised more closely (Bussell, *et al* 1982, 27–32). The only known parallels to the Snail Down beads, three from Hoare's excavation of Durrington G14 (Annable and Simpson 1964, 51 and 106, nos 275–277), were shown to be non-jet.

Two other beads discovered since 1945 also resemble the Snail Down beads closely but are of wood: part of a composite necklace found with a female secondary inhumation in bell-barrow 5J on Net Down, Shrewton (Green and Rollo-Smith 1984, 309, fig 28). They differ principally in having more sharply domed lower ends; and uppers with cruciform engraved decoration. Although the report refers to them as toggles, clearly they were intended as beads since, like the others under discussion, the shallow V perforation is closer to one end (here decorated), so that the beads all hang down comfortably when threaded.

One other form of jet/shale bead was found at Snail Down, three examples of a biconical bead, nos K2-K4, identified as of jet. A distinction should be made between *short* biconicals like these, less than 1cm in length or else length broadly the same as diameter, and similar beads two to three times the length. Such should be called *long* biconicals: the largest from the Wessex grave Upton Lovell G2a can represent that type (Annable and Simpson 1964, 49 and 104, no 252). Biconicals in the great jet/shale crescentic necklaces from northern England and Scotland, eg Mount Stuart, Bute (Clarke *et al* 1985, 156, fig 4.90), are invariably long biconicals. Short jet/shale biconicals are rare. Recent finds are few, but include West Overton G6b (Smith and Simpson 1966, 131,

132, fig 4, 2), much larger but short in proportion to diameter; and Wigber Low, Derbys (Collis 1983, 67, no 4159, there described as a ring, in jet/shale).

A small number is illustrated in Annable and Simpson 1964, eg nos 250, 251, 341, 391, 498. Further north, jet/shale examples occurred in a necklet from Calais Wold Barrow 114 (East Yorks, Humberside: Mortimer 1905, 169, pl 54, fig 426), associated with faience.

Snail Down K5 is one of three amber beads from the cemetery. It can be described as flattened globular, to separate the form from fully globular beads. It is perforated through the narrower plane: Ashbee (1981, 15–16) has distinguished between beads that are end perforated or edge perforated, and ovoid beads whose perforation, like Snail Down K5, can be said to be vertical (beads are of course strung horizontally). Recent finds of this type in Wiltshire include Amesbury G61a, New Barn Down (Ashbee 1985, 73, 75, figs 38, 39), with a primary cremation in a well-furnished female Wessex grave; Winterbourne Stoke G38, with the primary cremation in a Collared Urn (Gingell 1988, 49, 51, fig 28, 2), and Winterbourne Stoke G47 (*ibid*, 60, 61, fig 38, 5, 6) with the primary cremation of a well-provided Wessex grave. The type was made in jet/shale – for example West Kennet (Piggott 1962, 52, 53, fig 18, 8) as well as in amber, and occurs frequently in Wessex graves and elsewhere in a range of sizes.

The two very small amber beads from Site XXII, K9 and K10 (the latter only a fragment) are disc-shaped. The form is not well-known in this prized material, occurring more frequently in jet/shale, in a range of sizes. A recent find in jet/shale was made in Winterbourne Stoke G47 (Gingell 1988, 61, fig 38, 7); many years ago Preshute G1a yielded a substantial necklace in graded discs probably of lignite (Annable and Simpson 1964, 47 and 101, no 203). Most recently, fifty-five such beads in stone have been found with a Beaker burial at Chilbolton, Hants (Russell, 1990, 159–160, fig 4). True disc beads in amber, where both faces are flat and edges squared off, are rare: but the distinction between such discs and flattened globulars like those in the amber crescentic collar from Upton Lovell G2c (Annable and Simpson *ibid*, 48 and 103, no 227) is probably too slight to pursue.

We may be sure of a Baltic source for the Snail Down amber, but via our east coasts (Beck and Shennan, 1991, 27 and *passim*). A weathered, rounded lump brought to Devizes Museum in 1956 (1956.232) was a beach pebble of amber, the size roughly of a duck's egg (wt 79.6g). It appears to have escaped Beck and Shennan's attention. Found on the surface at East Coulston, below the northern edge of Salisbury Plain, at ST951544, it should perhaps be placed alongside the only other recorded lumps of beach amber from Britain, from Gough's Cave, Cheddar Gorge (Somerset) and from Cresswell Crags, Derbys (Beck and Shennan *ibid*, 197, 198, figs 11.3 (5) and 11.4 (1)). The Cheddar lump came from an Upper Palaeolithic Cresswellian context: the piece from Derbyshire was found in that cave only by repute (*ibid*, 152, 154). At least the Derbyshire and Wiltshire pieces might perhaps be regarded as raw material brought from an east-coast location and lost or deposited somewhere near where Bronze Age amber objects were being made. Such an overwhelming concentration of amber beads in Early Bronze Age

Wiltshire and a little further afield (*ibid*, 72, fig 6.1) makes the likelihood of Wessex workshops exploiting east-coast beach amber a strong possibility.

One incomplete bead from Snail Down, K6, is apparently of soft stone; it has not been analysed. Suitable stone must have been available in most parts of the country including Wiltshire. Of all the Snail Down beads this one alone may have come from a local material. Besides the Chilbolton beads mentioned above, four stone beads are illustrated in Annable and Simpson *ibid*, nos 337 and 338, biconicals from Wilsford G46; no 400, a small ring bead from Amesbury G48; no 479, a similar bead from Warminster G13; and a cylindrical bead of chalk from Preshute G1a, no 198. More recently a globular chalk bead was found associated with a necklace of mixed materials including faience in barrow 5L, Net Down, Shrewton (Green and Rollo-Smith 1984, 310–311, fig 29): and three from the Arreton Down barrow, IOW (Alexander *et al* 1960, 275–276, fig 6, 6, 7). Thurnam's excavation of the rearmost chamber at West Kennet yielded a large stone bead among the later Neolithic material (Piggott 1962, 52–53, fig 18, 14).

Though suitable soft stone must have been easy to obtain, stone beads are not found commonly in Wessex graves.

Shells perforated for use as beads or as precious objects are also not common. Search of the literature reveals that freshwater shells and land snail shells were not generally so used: shells from the sea coasts on the contrary were greatly prized. In the following short and not comprehensive list of sea shells from British Neolithic and Bronze Age burials, the cockle from Site XXII, K11, appears to be a new species for a bead:

Wiltshire

Aldbourne G12 (Kinnes and Longworth 1985, 128–129, no 285). Globular shell bead, not identifiable.

Amesbury, New Barn Down G61a (Ashbee 1985, 73–75, figs 38, 39; 81). *Trivia arctica* (Montagu), the Cowrie found in British waters.

Collingbourne Ducis, Snail Down, Site XXII (this report, K11, Fig 54). *Cardium edule* (L.). The Common Cockle.

Shrewton, Net Down 5J (Green and Rollo-Smith 1984, 309, fig 28). *Littorina littoralis* (L.), the flat Periwinkle.

Shrewton, Net Down 5L (*ibid*, 310, fig 29). *Littorina littoralis* (L.), the flat Periwinkle.

Avebury G22, West Kennet long barrow (Piggott 1962, 51–53, fig 18, 15–19). *Dentalium vulgare* (da Costa), the Tusk-shell; *Littorina littorea* (L.), the Winkle; *Cypraea* sp., a Cowrie species (likely to be the Cowrie found in British waters, *Trivia* sp.); *Nassarius reticulatus* (L.), a Dog-whelk; *Nucella lapillus* (L.), the Common Dog-whelk.

Wiltshire generally: Hoare recorded finding *Nerita*: this is probably the British freshwater species *Theodoxus fluviotilis*, which belongs to the family of Nerites but is not in the genus *Nerita*.

Hoare also recorded *Dentalium*, the Tusk-shell (1812, 114).

Dorset

Dorchester, a barrow near (Warne 1866, iii, 45; Thurnam 1871, 534–535). *Cypraea* sp, a Cowrie species (see above, West Kennet).

Hampshire

Rockbourne Down (S and C M Piggott 1945, 157). *Littorina littoralis* (L.), the Flat Periwinkle.

Berkshire

Lambourn Long Barrow (Wymer 1966, 8–9, fig 6). *Nucella lapillus* (L.), the Common Dog Whelk.

Gloucestershire

Nympsfield Long Barrow (Clifford 1938, 191, fig 2; 203 and 210). *Nucella lapillus* (L.), *ibid*. Considered unique in a British tomb in 1938.

Yorkshire

Fimber C33, the Church Hill barrow (Humberside: Mortimer 1905, 190, pl 63, fig 480). *Pecten*, perhaps *Pecten maximus* (L.), the Great Scallop.

Langton, North Yorkshire (Kinnes and Longworth 1985, 32). *Trivia arctica* (Montagu), the Cowrie common in British waters; *Littorina obtusata*, the Flat Periwinkle; *Dentalium entalis* (L.) the Tusk-shell.

Of all these shells, only *Nerita* might have come from inland waters. The rest are marine molluscs. They could all have been picked up on sandy (Cowries, Cockles, Scallops) or rocky (Winkle, Dog-Whelk, Periwinkles) shores. Tusk-shells are usually hard to find as they burrow in sand off-shore: and fragile too, so that they are often broken by the time they have been washed up on a beach.

The fragmentary tooth probably of a Mako shark *(Isurus oxyrhinchus)*, from a bell-barrow at Sutton Veney (Johnston 1980, 43), a rare British visitor in off-shore waters, may also have been picked from a beached carcass. Remains from sea fish and shells were carefully collected and distributed far inland in the earlier Bronze Age and before that.

L EARLY BRONZE AGE COPPER-ALLOY AWLS FROM SITES I AND II, WITH METAL ANALYSIS AND CLASSIFICATION

Nicholas Thomas, with a note by E C Ellwood

L1 **Copper-alloy single-ended awl**, Group 2B (below). L 4.5cm; diam 2mm. Figure 55. Found with Cremation 2 in the central mound, Site I (plan, section, Figs 3, 5). Patinated dark green, with a surface of almost glass-like smoothness. This is in essence a thin, straight rod of circular cross-section, tapering gradually to a point, of which the extremity has been broken across in antiquity. For a distance of 11.0mm, the thicker end of the rod has been filed down on two opposite sides to form a very slightly asymmetrical, chisel-shaped tang which would have been pressed into a small handle of wood or bone. One side of this filed-down end was polished at the Tin Research Institute to see whether the awl had been heated by inclusion in the funeral pyre (below). It is not now possible, therefore, to say whether the tang had originally been symmetrical.

That this tang had been filed down to its present shape can be seen from an examination of its unpolished side. Under a 210 hand lens, minute striations are visible running across the long axis of the tang's surface and also across its other two, more rounded surfaces. No such file marks appear along the rest of the awl. Metallographic analysis has established that at least the basic form of both Snail Down awls was achieved by casting and then by cold-working, probably by hammering; they were annealed at least once to make it possible for working by hand to continue. In such a way each awl must have been changed from a cylindrical rod to a pointed one, with a tang formed at one end by a combination of hammering and filing.

Similar transverse file marks are clearly visible on the tang of a Group 2B awl from disc-barrow Milton Lilbourne 1 (Ashbee 1986, 56–57, fig 30, 1, fig 31). The lopsidedness of that tang suggests that most of the filing had been done from one side. Curiously, the description makes little mention of the filing process, concentrating instead upon other evidence (eg fig 31) which established hammering as an important element in the manufacture of the awl.

L2 **Copper-alloy single-ended awl**, Group 2C (below). L 5.1cm; diam 1.6mm. Figure 55. Stourhead Coll 104a; Goddard 1912, 149, no 226. Found with a

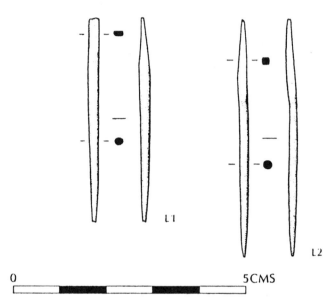

Fig 55 Early Bronze Age copper alloy awls: L1, Site I, cremation 2; L2, Site II, central burial pit (see also Fig 44).

cremation and other grave goods in the central burial pit, Site II, by Hoare in 1805. Patinated deep green, with yellow-brown areas along the lengths of the awl. One surface of the four-sided tang polished for metallographic examination.

This implement, thinner than the awl from Site I, has a circular cross-section, tapering more suddenly towards a point which is intact. The opposite end has been formed into a four-sided tang probably by hammering combined with filing. Fine file-marks can be seen running across the long axis of the tang on its three patinated sides. The end of the tang was left rough.

A metallographic examination of both Snail Down awls and, for comparison, the awl now in Bristol City Museum from Marshfield Barrow III, Glos (Gettins *et al* 1953, 37–38) was made by E C Ellwood, Chief Metallurgist at the Tin Research Institute, Greenford, Middlesex in 1955. The principal aim was to establish whether the awls had been through their respective funeral pyres; during the course of this limited piece of research, light was thrown upon the method of manufacture of each awl. Mr Ellwood kindly reported as follows:*

'Bronze Awls, Snail Down Barrows: and Marshfield Barrow III (Glos)

Snail Down Site II, L2. A metallographic examination was carried out on the surface of the square shank after suitable polishing and etching.

The material consisted of small-grained crystals of the alpha solid solution with non-metallic inclusions drawn out along the length of the awl, indicating mechanical working. The alpha solid solution showed annealing twins and deformation lines running in different directions in different crystals. It may be stated quite definitely that the awl was made by working down a small casting or portion of a casting, probably by hammering, that the metal was annealed at least once to remove the hardening produced by working, and that it was finally hardened by working. The evidence of this final hardening still remains and it would have been removed by heating to a temperature of 350–400°C. This indicates that it has not been subjected to temperatures above this since it was last hammered. The various features of the structure of the metal are shown in Plate 61a and b.

Snail Down Site I, L1. A similar examination was carried out on the second awl. The main features were exactly the same as described for the awl from Site II, except that the inclusions were not drawn out to the same extent and the grains were somewhat larger, as shown in Plate 61c.

Bronze Awl, Marshfield Barrow III

A metallographic examination of this specimen was carried out on a transverse section taken from about the centre of the awl. The grain size was larger than that of either of the other awls examined, but again the evidence of the method of manufacture and the persistence of the cold-worked structure was similar.

This section was taken remote from the hammered flats, which indicates that the whole of the awl was hardened and strengthened by cold working. The structure is illustrated in Plate 61d.

Micro-hardness tests were carried out and the results obtained are shown in Table 27. These results substantiate the deductions made from the examination of the micro-structure regarding the residual strain hardening of the bronze. However, the degree of strain hardening cannot be estimated without knowing the composition of the metal.'

A funeral pyre of wood might reach a temperature of almost 1000°C. When a reconstructed Iron Age style of timber *house* was burnt down experimentally at the Butser Ancient Farm Project (Hants) recently, the thirty-minute conflagration reached this temperature (P J Reynolds: *pers*

Table 27   Micro-hardness of awls from Snail Down and Marshfield (Glos)

Identity	Load	DPN	Average
Snail Down, L2	10g	172	
	10g	186	181.3
	10g	186	
Snail Down, L1	10g	165	
	10g	172	171.6
	10g	178	
Marshfield Barrow III	10g	146.3	
	10g	146.3	149.2
	10g	155.0	

comm 1992). The melting point of a typical (10%) tin bronze of the Bronze Age is just over 1000°C and could thus be reached during the course of a human cremation. As Mr Ellwood has shown, the evidence for cold working which he could still detect in all three awls, would have been lost had they been submitted to heat above a temperature of 350–400°C. Clearly, they had been kept from the flames. Their presence among cremated bones may reflect their use in fastening the bags in which, most probably, the burnt human bones were buried, although their shortness did not make them an ideal kind of fastener. More probably, awls were placed with these three burials because they were, very likely, of women; and the evidence shows that in the earlier Bronze Age an awl was considered an appropriate accompaniment for a woman who was to be buried (see further below).

BRONZE AGE AWLS IN BRITAIN AND IRELAND

Three groups of awls are found in these islands.

Group 1 is double pointed with a central swelling or maximum thickness. One point formed the business end, the other was pushed into a handle. There is evidence that both ends were used for business. Group 1 is associated characteristically with Beakers of several styles – so far with Clarke's groups E, N2, N/NR-FN? and S4 (Clarke 1970). It also occurs with objects commonly associated with Beakers. Where the metal has been analysed, Group 1 awls usually prove to be of non-alloyed copper.

Group 2 comprises single-pointed instruments that can be subdivided through the ways in which one end was fashioned into a tang that could be fitted into a handle. Associated grave goods are commonly Collared Urns, Food Vessels and the kind of bronzes and other things usually found with them.

Where the evidence permits, awls of both groups were generally the accompaniment to a female burial. Awls could be the sole object with a burial (eg Snail Down I) or else part of a grave group (Snail Down II).

---

* This report was written in July, 1955, in response to a request from L Biek, of the then Ministry of Works and Planning (Biek 1963, 137, pl 14).

The wide range of objects found with awls in graves can readily be appreciated by perusing the illustrations of grave groups in Annable and Simpson (1964); and their range in type and size on p 113.

Group 3. Certain awls stand out because of exceptional size. Incorporating the types in Groups 1 and 2, they are nevertheless felt to be different or serving a different craft; and some belong to the Middle or later Bronze Age.

Awls of Group 1 are found in four minor variations:

1A Square cross section throughout. Type specimen: Thickthorn, Dorset (Clarke 1970, 288, fig 65, E184; Drew and Piggott 1936, 80, fig 2, awl not illustrated).

1B Square centre, each pointed half circular in cross section. Type specimen: Carrickinab, Co Down (Collins and Evans 1968, 19, 23–24, fig 3).

1C Circular section throughout. Type specimen: Rudstone IV, Yorks ER, North Humberside (Kinnes and Longworth 1985, 61, no 62, Burial 4).

1D Square centre, one end with circular cross section, the other squared. Type specimen: Kirkaldy, Fife (Clarke 1970, 406, fig 1014, S4 1655).

Awls of Group 2 are single pointed: The four recognisable varieties are defined by the way in which the tang (for fitting into a handle) has been worked. The cross section of the business end is always circular. Analysis of the metal usually indicates a copper alloy.

2A Chisel-ended tang made by hammering the end of a circular-sectioned rod from both sides and squashing it so that it is expanded slightly beyond the maximum width of the rod. Type specimen: Sutton Veney G11c (Annable and Simpson 1964, 60 and 116, no 466). A particularly clear example of this hammering and squashing process came recently from Amesbury G61a (Ashbee 1985, 74–75, figs 38, 39).

2B Chisel-ended tang finished by filing and grinding so that its maximum width does not exceed that of the business end. Type specimen: Snail Down Ll (Fig 55). When the writer first published his scheme for awls (Collins and Evans 1968, *ibid*) he inadvertently named the Site II awl as type specimen for 2B, where the Site I awl had been intended.

2C Square-sectioned tang, tapering only slightly; its end remains squared. Gradual transition to circular business end. Type specimen: Snail Down L2 (Fig 55; Annable and Simpson 1964, 63, associated with no 501 but omitted from catalogue).

2D Awl expands noticeably at transition from tang to business end. Tang usually chisel ended. This is the most developed form of awl. Type specimen: Winterbourne Stoke G28 (Annable and Simpson 1964, 62 and 117, no 486).

In the writer's definition of awl types for the Carrickinab report (Collins and Evans *ibid*) he suggested a fifth type within Group 2A-2E, which had a circular section and no special tang. He does not now accept the existence of such a type.

Awls of Group 3 are notable for their exceptional size. Maximum thickness can exceed 3mm, which, with their greater length, makes them readily distinguishable from the delicate little implements of Groups 1 and 2. This difference is demonstrated clearly by the three awls found in the rich Wessex grave Preshute G1a (Annable and Simpson 1964, 47 and 101, nos 205–207). No 206 is probably Group 2D, no 207 is Group 2B, no 205 is an altogether more substantial implement and is typical of Group 3. Its purpose must have been different from that for which Groups 1 and 2 were designed. In the Carrickinab report scheme for awls, the Preshute awl was included among Group 2(2F): here it has been preferred to include it in Group 3(3D).

As the collection in Wiltshire Heritage Museum makes clear, the large awls of Group 3 can be both double and single ended (Annable and Simpson 1964, nos 415, 416 and 419 the former; 205, 364 and 429 the latter). If the majority of these pieces belongs to the earlier Bronze Age, some of Group 3 may nevertheless have been made in the Middle, and certainly the later Bronze Age. The following three varieties were distinguished in the Carrickinab report, where it was not made clear enough, however, that types 3A and 3B were double pointed – enlarged versions of Group 1 – while 3C was essentially a chisel-tanged single-pointed awl.

3A Central expansion, tapering symmetrically to two points: square cross-section throughout. Type specimen: Upper Upham House, Aldbourne (Ashmolean Museum, Oxford, no 1955.147).

3B Central square section, one end worked into a chisel-ended tang, the other into a business end with circular section. Type specimen: R Thames at Richmond (British Museum W.G.1765).

3C (in a re-ordering of the Carrickinab awl report) Square central expansion, both points developed with circular cross-sections. Type specimen: Wiltshire Heritage Museum no 416 (Annable and Simpson 1964, 58 and 113, no provenance).

3D Single-pointed awl, the tang chisel shaped, business end circular sectioned: essentially an enlarged form of Group 2B. Type specimen: Thorndon (Suffolk) Late Bronze Age hoard (*Inventaria Archaeologica* GB 11, 5). This is the type of Preshute G1a (Annable and Simpson 1964, 47, no 205; and no 364 from Wilsford G42, a bell-barrow in the Lake group whose rich Wessex grave yielded also the large, glass bead – 'stone' in Annable and Simpson 1964, 56 and 110, no 364 – described properly and published in 1984; Guido *et al*). There acknowledgement is given to William Cunnington III and E H Goddard who recorded it as of glass in their catalogue of the Stourhead Collection in 1896 (47, no 174c; the awl no 174a).

Not all 3D awls can be allocated to the later Bronze Age. There is no questioning the Wessex Culture phase for the 3D awl from Preshute G1a, burial mound of one of the most nobly accoutred ladies yet found in Wiltshire. But what of the closely similar awl from Wilsford G42? Of its Wessex Culture associations, the only survivor from Hoare's excavation is the bead which has been established as being of sealing-wax-red glass. The Wilsford G42 awl should be regarded as broadly contemporary with the large awl from Preshute G1a.

The requirement for a type of awl that was more sturdy than the relatively frail pieces of Groups 1 and 2 certainly began in the earlier Bronze Age. It continued, however, unlike those earlier Groups, and joined the repertoire of later Bronze Age craftsmens' small hand tools.

In use, most awls were fitted into a handle. Usually the size of a little finger where the evidence survives, in southern England these were of wood or bone. A very few were of bronze, perhaps cast as one with the awl. The Stourhead Collection includes an unprovenanced awl, the remains of whose carefully shaped wooden handle has a collar close to its mouth which would have helped the user to force the awl forward (Annable and Simpson 1964, 58 and 113, no 420). The wooden collar is echoed in a bone example from the well-known and princely dagger-grave group beneath bell-barrow Winterbourne Stoke G5 (*ibid*, 50 and 105, nos 263–266). A close bone parallel to that came from Site 5, a ring-ditch, at City Farm, Hanborough, Oxon (Case *et al* 1966, 65, fig 25, 9). The awl is of Group 2B. Remains of a handle presumed to have been of wood surrounding the tang of an awl from Barrow 23, Rollestone Field, are too slight to indicate its exterior form, while being clear evidence that awls were often – perhaps usually – buried in their handles (Green and Rollo-Smith 1984, 308, fig 27). Contrast between corrosion products on the tangs and on the business ends of the three awls from Preshute G1a also establishes that those instruments were similarly handled when placed in the grave (Annable and Simpson 1964, 47 and 101, nos 205–207). The uniformly smooth patination on the Snail Down awls, as upon so many, indicates on the contrary that handles were sometimes removed before burial, perhaps as a form of ritual killing; unless more awls than we think were used without handles. From northern England, Mortimer illustrated four awls to which he added the outlines of somewhat larger handles of different shapes. These reconstructions were based upon observation made while his 'prickers' were being excavated. The awl from Life Hill Barrow 294 (East Yorks, Humberside) has an extended oval shape with slight swelling at the hand end and no collar for a finger rest (1905, 204, pl 66, fig 500e). Handle outlines for awls from Aldro Barrow 116 and from Huggate and Warter Wold Barrows 249 and 254 indicate a bulbar swelling to fit into the hand's palm, making them closely akin to modern bradawls and engraving tools (*ibid*, 54 and pl 12, fig 97; 315 and pl 119, fig 935; 320 and pl 122, fig 954).

A bronze awl cast as one with its handle, as claimed by Mortimer, was found in Barrow C37 of the Garton Slack group, deposited apparently with a black flint flake in a bag (*ibid*, 262 and pl 92, fig 728). In shape, this awl with its handle closely resembles the unprovenanced wooden handled awl at Devizes (Annable and Simpson 1964, 113, no 420). Mortimer (1905, 262) made reference to another all bronze awl-and-handle apparently found by Thurnam in a barrow near West Kennet and now lost (Thurnam 1860, 329 and fig). This has continued to cause confusion, as explained by Annable and Simpson (1964, 52 and 55, nos 299 and 360). They fail, however, to explain their interpretation of Thurnam's drawing as of a bronze awl in a bone handle. Mortimer was not in doubt that the handle was metal, writing as if he may have seen it.

How awls of Groups 1 and 2 were used remains uncertain. That many were associated with women (but not all) suggests some domestic craft. Most are so narrow that they do not appear appropriate for piercing leather prior to sewing since the hole they made would have been so small. They could have been used for decorating leather by pricking or scoring it, although this is not usual leather-working practice (Hodges 1964, 152). Tattooing has been considered as a possible use for the sharper, more delicate needles; and therefore an activity performed usually by women. The discovery of a uniquely preserved corpse of an Early Bronze Age man in the Hauslabjoch glacier on the Austro-Italian border, whose body appears to retain traces of some form of skin ornament, may prove to uphold such a use (Spindler 1994, 169–173).

There is no doubt that awls were an important possession and accompaniment for the dead and required careful protection. A Group 1 awl (drawing and text do not allow further classification) from bowl-barrow Amesbury G51, associated with a necked, late-phase Beaker of Stage 6 and a male inhumation, had been placed carefully upon a slip of antler which the excavator saw as being there for protection of its two well-formed points (Ashbee 1978, 20, fig 12, 1 and 2). Other implements with that burial established their owner as a leather-worker.

M GRAVE-GROUPS RECOVERED BY HOARE AND CUNNINGTON IN 1805: SITE II (HOARE 4), SITE XIX (HOARE 24), SPTA 2207 (HOARE 2) AND SPTA 2253 (HOARE 17, THE HUNTER'S BARROW)

Nicholas Thomas and Jacqui Watson

In describing the following groups of grave-goods that are part of the Stourhead Collection at the Wiltshire Heritage Museum (Cunnington and Goddard 1896), the archaeological contexts for those from Sites II and XIX are to be found under the relevant excavation reports above. The others – for 2207 and 2253 – are summarised below.

SITE II, HOARE 4

An **Accessory Cup** together with a **rim fragment of a second Cup** and a **copper-alloy awl** are described in Sections D and L, by I H Longworth and N Thomas respectively; Figures 44, 55.

SITE XIX, HOARE 24

M1 Bronze ogival dagger of Gerloff's Type Camerton, retaining two stout rivets (plug- rivets). Material: copper-alloy. Analysis has shown 86.6% copper, 13.2% tin and six other trace elements. It belongs to Group FG within the current programme of analysis of European Bronze Age bronzework (Gerloff 1975, 268, no 184; Britton 1961, 46, no 28). L 13.2cm; w 4.6cm; th 6.5mm; l of rivet (median line) 1.4cm; diam of rivet 9mm. Figure 57; Plates 62–64. Thurnam 1871, pl 35, fig 4; Evans 1881, 242; Goddard 1912, 119, no 15; Piggott 1938, 87, fig 18, Wessex Culture Grave 54; ApSimon 1954, 59, no 24; Annable and Simpson 1964, 47 and 101, no 194; Gerloff 1975, 105, no 184, pl 49; DZSWS: STHEAD.128. The shallow-curved heel exhibits an irregular central notch, for the third rivet, mentioned by Hoare (1812, 185), which has not survived. The blade's cross-section shows a thick convex midrib lacking decoration, with three clearly defined contiguous ribs

each side and extending to within 42mm of the blade's tip. Outside these, and reaching virtually to the point, are two pairs of shallower hollows and ridges which define the weapon's hollow-ground cutting edges. On both faces of the heel, the contiguous ribs have been flattened out into not much more than shallow lines between the mark left by the hilt's mouth and the two rivets, beyond which they do not extend. The tip of the blade has a rounded point. As our drawing (Fig 56), and the drawings in Annable and Simpson and Gerloff show (1964, 101, no 194; 1975, pl 49), one cutting edge of this dagger is noticeably more sinuous – ogival – than the other: this is a result of the casting process, not of uneven whetting.

The pair of sturdy rivets, known as plug-rivets, have the usual slightly domed heads, slanted appropriately to fit flush with the sloping surfaces of the hilt whose attachment to the blade they secured.

Arguably the most interesting aspect of the dagger blade are the traces it retains of its hilt end and the sheath in which it was buried. Such, mere marks on the bronze surface, are almost all that we now have of one of the most complex mixed-media crafts practised by Bronze Age people – wood, bone, horn, bronze, amber, sometimes gold and tin, and leatherwork – whose mastery enabled the leaders of society to demonstrate their status through possession of a bronze dagger with, often, ornamented hilt, sheath and belt or baldric. The use of glue is implicit though it has never survived: and stainers, with punching and slitting, may have supplied a decorative finish to almost everything, though once again we are left with guesswork.

None of the drawings published hitherto does justice to the visible traces of sheath and hilt, although Annable and Simpson indicate the shape of the sheath's mouthpiece (omitted in Gerloff's drawing but mentioned in her text). Both faces of this dagger blade show the usual form of hilt end: a shallow curve interrupted at its centre by a more or less semi-

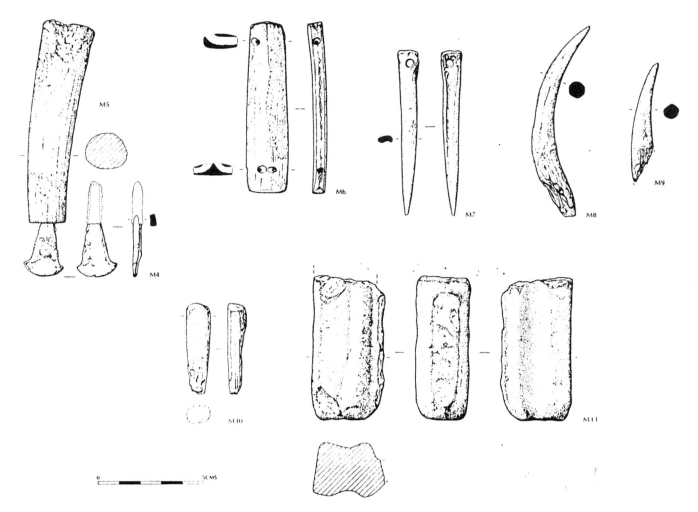

Fig 56   Early Bronze Age bone and stonework and copper-alloy chisel, central pit, bowl-barrow SPTA 2207 (Hoare 2).

circular indentation large enough to act as a thumb rest when the dagger was being used. Nothing survived of the rest of the hilt, including the rivet that is presumed to have been located within the notch in the outline of the heel. If the hilt had been broken off in an act of ritual 'killing', we would expect the surviving rivets to appear twisted, instead of occupying their original positions unchanged and showing no sign of strain.

On both faces, the blade's heel retains traces of an evenly curved line closely following the heel's irregular edge. This is interpreted as an indication of where, for some reason, the inside of the hilt ended its close contact with the heel. We cannot now tell whether the hilt had been carved from one piece or made in two longitudinal halves, brought together to enclose the blade's heel and held in place by three rivets and, perhaps, glued and bound decoratively with leather thong.

A wooden mouthpiece has been attached to the top of the sheath so that its grain lies at right angles to the rest of the sheath's outer wooden casing. These contrasting features are shown clearly in the drawings (Fig 57). The width of the mouthpiece is 8mm. Traces of the wooden scabbard, best preserved along its midrib, extend virtually to the blade's tip. When the dagger was fully sheathed, there would have been a gap of some 6mm between the mouthpiece and the line of the handle's mouth. The blade's surface in this space bears, nevertheless, prominent traces of the kind of rough surface deposit that must represent a lining to the scabbard. Were this deposit to have been the product solely of corrosion, or salts produced from the blade's copper alloy, we would expect to see something similar at the butt. But, as we have emphasised (drawings and plates likewise), this is not so. We conclude that the deposit belongs in some way to the sheath: and that, therefore, the sheath's lining must have extended beyond the mouthpiece and made a close fit with the end of the hilt, including its thumb-rest indentation. This is a feature of the sheath that occurs on almost all daggers that have been recovered from graves in chalk country. When Audrey Henshall studied a series of Scottish knives and daggers some of which retained traces of sheaths and hilts (1968), she was able to show that, when found, the dagger from Kirkcaldy (Fife) had been jammed so well into its sheath (much survived) that the mouth of the latter enclosed the end of the dagger hilt including the lower pair of rivets (*ibid*, 186–187 and 179, no 9). A fur sheath which also extended over the hilt's end has been found in a barrow at West Ashby (Lincs) (Field 1985, 124–126).

The dagger blade was submitted to the English Heritage Centre for Archaeology, Portsmouth, in 2001, for analysis of the organic material preserved upon it. The following report has been compiled by Jacqui Watson.

Organic additions

The hilt of the dagger M1 was made from horn, and has a clearly visible omega-shaped hilt-line (Fig 57; Pls 62, 63). The mineral-preserved remains of horn on the dagger are insufficient to confirm whether the hilt was made from a single piece of horn or two plates held together by the rivets at the top of the blade. These rivets indicate the thickness of the hilt at this point as being about 12.5mm (Fig 57). In the photograph published in 1964 (Annable and Simpson 1964, plate for no 194) the impression of a textile is clearly visible in the corrosion on the right-hand rivet, but it was not noticeable on recent examination.

In addition to traces of the hilt, there are remains of the organic sheath preserved on the blade. The most noticeable is a wooden strip that corresponds to the scabbard mouth, which was made from *Fraxinus* sp. (ash), and has a radial surface with the grain aligned across the width of the blade, as indicated in Figure 57. Using the scanning electron microscope (SEM) the condition of the copper-preserved wood can be seen (Pl 64), where almost all of the structure has been replaced by copper salts, and the wood structure itself has largely dissolved. Both sections illustrate just over 1 year's growth, and it is possible to make out the large spring vessels and compare them with the typical twinned vessels at the end of the growing season that are associated with ash. The original shape of this sheath mouth could easily have been fashioned using a metal knife or flint blade, working with the grain to pare off slivers of wood.

There are no recognisable remains on the blade to suggest what the main part of the sheath was made from, but it is assumed to have been of leather like other examples (see below).

Comparison with other daggers

Most of the hilts with omega-shaped hilt-lines that have been identified, appear to be made from one piece of horn or wood, the latter sometimes ornately decorated with pins in gold or tin, or small copper-alloy rivets. The dagger from Lockington, Leicestershire, has a horn hilt with omega-shaped hilt-line also, attached with four rivets and with a much larger blade (Hughes 2000). Although not described as such in the catalogue, the dagger from Winterbourne Stoke G4 (Annable and Simpson 1964, 48, no 220, 102) appears to have a horn hilt. The hilt of the dagger from Amesbury G58 is also known to be of horn (Ashbee 1985, 67–68, figs 33, 35). The dagger from Wilsford G56 (*ibid*, 44, no 159, 98) has a horn hilt but with three rivets attaching the hilt to the blade and with a wooden mouthpiece. In the case of the dagger from Wilsford G5, Bush Barrow (*ibid*, 45, no 170, 99) the horn hilt was attached to the blade with six rivets. The principal

daggers in the Wiltshire Heritage Museum's collection have been published with enlarged photographs of their hilts and the top of the blades (*ibid*, plates for nos 159, 169, 170, 194, 220, 266).

The dagger from Hove, Sussex has a horn handle with an omega-shaped hilt line attached to the blade with two copper alloy rivets. It also appears to have wood across the top of the blade, very like the scabbard mouthpiece on the Snail barrow dagger (Clarke et al 1985, 117, fig 4.45; Cat, 97.3).

Audrey Henshall's corpus of dagger graves (1968) from Scotland includes seven daggers with omega-shaped hilt-lines. Four of these have been identified as being made wholly or in part of horn, and the description of a fifth implies use of the same material. Where present, the rivets indicate that the hilts are between 9–12mm thick at the top the blades.

The dagger from Bargeroosterveld, Drenthe, Netherlands, has a single-piece horn hilt attached with 4 bronze rivets and decorated with grooves and tin nails. (Clarke *et al* 1985, 148, fig 4.83; 226, fig 5.64; Cat 170).

Where the evidence remains, construction of the sheaths is even more variable than the hilts. The sheath of the dagger from Wilsford G56 still has the remains of a wood mouthpiece; the rest of the sheath was recorded by Colt Hoare as being lined with textile. In the case of the dagger from Wilsford G5, Bush Barrow (Annable and Simpson 1964, 45, no 170, 99), traces of an animal pelt are clearly visible on the blade. The dagger from Lockington had a sheath made of wood lined with an animal pelt, and with a resin on the outside of the wood (Hughes 2000). From Barrow Hills, Oxfordshire, a piece of decorated resin or very degraded leather was found with knife-dagger M8 and it is thought to be the remains of a decorated sheath (Barclay and Halpin 1999, 145).

In the Scottish examples, Henshall (1968) details both wood and animal skin sheaths. The dagger from Gilchorn, Angus (178, 191) has a wooden scabbard that extends into the omega-shaped void in the hilt-line. The wooden mouthpiece of the Snail Down example does not interlock in this way, although it has been suggested above that the sheath's lining may have projected beyond its mouthpiece, to fill that space. Another dagger with traces of a wooden sheath comes from Gask Hill, Collesie, Fife (*ibid*, 186, 185). Leather sheaths on the other hand seem to be common, but still of complex construction and often decorated. The dagger from Ashgrove, Fife (*ibid*, 184, 182) had a sheath made from animal skin with lines of sewing that created ribs. In the case of the dagger from Kirkaldy, Fife (*ibid*, 186, 179) the sheath was made from two layers of animal skin stitched together with gut, and had a sheath mount made from horn. The Auchterhouse dagger (*ibid*, 180, 188) has the remains of a black substance on the blade, thought to be degraded animal skin.

Hoare seems to imply (1812, 185) that the dagger sheath from Site XIX had been lined with cloth. He made this assertion more than once of daggers he unearthed and we believe that either he was confusing the lining deposit described above with cloth, or else, more likely, he meant that dagger and scabbard had further been *wrapped* in cloth. Cloth buried in contact with copper alloy usually leaves a clear trace – notice it on the Bush

Barrow axe blade (Annable and Simpson *ibid*, no 178, plate). The blade from Site XIX bears no such traces today. But it *does* carry a slight indication of cloth on one rivet head, shown clearly in Annable and Simpson's plate of 1964, but not hitherto remarked upon and now (2001) almost invisible (cf this report, Pl 63).

Hoare recorded, also, that the pin from Site XIX (below, Section M, M2) had been contained in its own wooden case and that *this* had been cloth-lined. The pin was cleaned (in the writer's time at Devizes, to reveal its full decoration, not hitherto recorded), but before that it bore no trace of cloth.

Bronze Age daggers of the different types found with burials in Britain have been studied exhaustively by Sabine Gerloff (1975). The dagger from Site XIX is her no. 184 and belongs to Type Camerton, of which some thirty such blades are known. Its period of use covers the second phase of the Wessex Culture. While essentially British in general character, it is clearly related to a family of ogival-bladed daggers that was current in Switzerland, the Rhone, Middle Rhine and northern France, during the stage when Early gave way to Middle Bronze Age within the fourteenth century cal BC.

M2   **Ring-headed pin with two free-cast rings**. Material: probably copper alloy. L 16.1cm; th of shaft 6mm; diams of fixed rings 19mm; diams of loose rings 1.5cm, 1.6cm. Figure 56; Plates 62,63. Evans 1881, 366, fig 449; Goddard 1912, 154, no 271; Piggott 1938, 87, fig 18, Wessex Culture Grave 54; Annable and Simpson 1964, 47 and 101, no 193; Gerloff 1975, 121, pl 49; DZSWS: STHEAD.116, provenance incorrect. The long, plain, gradually tapering shaft, its point now damaged, has been cast with two circular rings at its thicker end. The cross-section of the shaft is circular; those of the rings forming the head are D-shaped, with almost a square section where they merge into the top of the shaft. Hanging from each of these rings is a slightly smaller, thinner ring, that swings freely and would have rattled slightly when the wearer walked. Much more irregular in outline, thickness and even size, the loose rings have an almost circular cross-section.

The top of the pin shaft, its fixed and its loose rings, have been decorated with lightly incised nicks and dots. The edges of all four rings have simple, oblique nicks, evenly spaced; where the two fixed rings merge together, a line of dots marks the junction on both faces of the pin, with a roughly V-shaped addition of dots at the lower end of the fusion. Immediately below the fixed rings, the pin shaft has been decorated with a loose scheme of zig-zags for a length of about 15mm. It is not possible to say whether the decoration was part of the original casting or added afterwards. It seems at least possible that the decoration on the pin and its heads was cast, while that on the loose rings was added. None of the rings shows any sign of the kind of wear that might have been expected had the pin been long in use. That this striking ornament was greatly prized is suggested by the care with which it was buried in its own box, wrapped for good measure in cloth, as Hoare has told us (1812, 185, pl XXIII).

Gerloff has studied the pin in detail because of its association with the ogival dagger from the same grave and its value as dating evidence (1975, 110–112, 120–121). Like the parallels for her Types Camerton and Snowshill daggers, similar pins have been found in Switzerland, the Rhone, north Italy, southern Germany and the Middle Rhine, with a version in silver from Brittany. Annable and Simpson have drawn attention to another close likeness found at Novy Budzov in Poland (1964, 26). These two sources include a full bibliography. It can be added that the casting of free rings within other loops and rings was also done on the so-called Wilsford 'Standard', found apparently with a primary inhumation that was well-provided with other grave goods, at the base of bell-barrow Wilsford G58 (Thomas 1954, 326–330; Annable and Simpson 1964, 47 and 102, no 211). The three rings cast together as a chain and at the same time to a sturdy loop on the 'Standard' are circular and accurately made, unlike those on our pin; and, through whatever they were holding or attached to, have caused noticeable wear to the loop of the 'Standard'.

M3   **Accessory Cup**. This was found by Hoare within the chest or tree-trunk coffin containing the cremation burial. He describes it as ' … the fragments of a beautiful little cup'. Unfortunately the cup was not illustrated in *Ancient Wiltshire* nor has it survived. From Hoare's words we may assume that we have classified it correctly; 'beautiful' may be taken to imply that it was decorated.

Not enough of these vessels has been recovered from modern excavation for us to know whether the burials they accompanied favoured one sex more than the other. The presence of a dagger in Site XIX suggests that a male had been buried there.

SPTA 2207, HOARE 2

The following objects, found in a central grave but lacking all traces of a burial (see Part 3, section 11), were described in detail by the writer in 1954 (317–320). Only brief comment and new drawings are added here.

M4, M5   Miniature copper-alloy axe-head fitted into a red-deer antler handle for use as a hand-tool. Axe-head l 4.5cm. Figure 56. Evans 1872, 144; ibid 1881, 163, fig 189; Goddard 1912, 146, no 209; Annable and Simpson 1964, 57 and 112, nos 382, 387; DZSWS: STHEAD.95. We here emphasise its possible function as a leather worker's knife. The end of the handle, though now roughened, shows no sign of damage and we must suppose that this tool was used by drawing (ie cutting) or pushing (gentle chiselling) without being driven by mallet or other force.

Miniature axe-heads, those with a length not exceeding about 50mm, are rare. Two similar axe-heads have been recorded from Wiltshire:

1   Wilsford G64, bowl-barrow (Annable and Simpson 1964, 52 and 107, no 315), l 5.2cm.

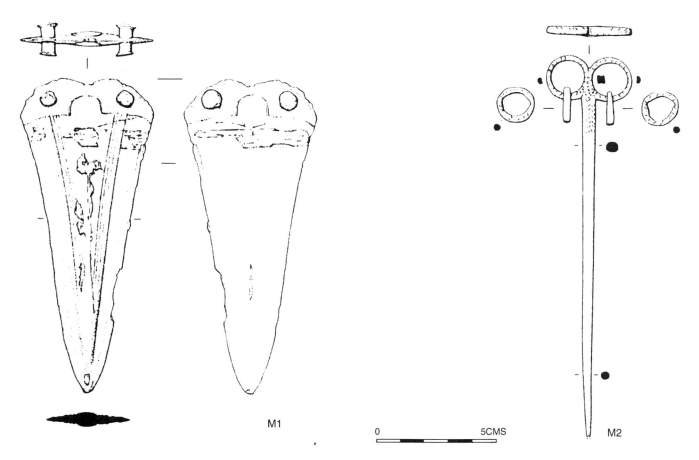

Fig 57   Early Bronze Age copper-alloy dagger and pin, central burial, double bell-barrow, Site XIX.

2 Unprovenanced, probably Wiltshire (*ibid*, 57 and 111, no 381), l 3.3cm

Three other axe-heads from the region are only a little larger:

    3 Wilsford G58, bell-barrow (*ibid*, 47 and 102, no 213), l 8.4cm.

    4 Unprovenanced, probably Wiltshire (*ibid*, 52 and 107, no 299), l 7.0cm.

    5 Breach Farm Barrow, South Glamorgan (Grimes 1938, 113, fig 4), l 8.4cm.

M6 **Perforated bone plate**, made from ox-sized rib, edges trimmed. Figure 56. Evans 1872, 382; Annable and Simpson *ibid*, 57 and 112, no 383; DZSWS: STHEAD.96. While its use as a bone equivalent of a necklace spacer plate remains most likely, it could possibly have done service as an archer's wristguard. When fresh, the perforations would have been strong enough to withstand the return of a bow string.

M7 **Perforated bone pin**, made from the proximal end of a sheep (or roe deer) metatarsal. Figure 56. Annable and Simpson *ibid*, no 389; DZSWS: STHEAD.98. This type has been discussed above (Section H), where it was shown to belong most obviously to the Early Bronze Age.

M8, M9 **Two bone points**, made from untrimmed tines of roe deer antler, broad ends gnawed. Figure 56. Annable and Simpson *ibid*, nos 385, 386; DZSWS: STHEAD, 98a (longer), 98b respectively.

M10 **Possible bone pin**. Perhaps antler. Figure 56. Annable and Simpson *ibid*, no 388; DZSWS: STHEAD.98c. Re-examination suggests strongly that it is the remains of a thick pin, shaft and point weathered away, the head worked into a slightly flattened convex end. It is too narrow, thick and blunt to have been a leather worker's spatula (Smith and Simpson 1966, 134–141).

M11 **Grooved whetstone**. Figure 56. Evans 1872, 241; Annable and Simpson *ibid*, no 384; DZSWS: STHEAD.97. Made of weathered Bath Stone (Great Oolite age) from the Bath district, this craft tool is one of only two recorded examples having more than one groove. Newall was able to list fifteen grooved whetstones in 1932 (1932, 456–458). Since the Second World War a grooved whetstone of ferruginous sandstone has been found in Barrow V at West Heath, Sussex (Drewett 1985, 58, fig 24 and microfiche, p 14). The important example from Breach Farm, South Glamorgan (Grimes 1938, 113, fig 4) was a pre-war addition to Newall's list.

M12 **Grooved whetstone**. Hoare apparently found a second hone of this specialised kind here, for he likened it to the one which he found among several stone hones within the Bone Barrow at Upton Lovell, G2(a) (1812, 75–76, Pl vi). It has not survived.

M13 **Whetstone**. Hoare recorded the presence of a hone in unused condition, of 'freestone'. It has not survived.

M14 **Hone**. This was said by Hoare to be of a 'blueish colour'. It also has not survived.

For reasons elaborated below (Part 3), we regard these objects as a votive deposit rather than a grave group. Though placed, according to Hoare, in a grave pit, the absence of a burial and the precise location of the covering barrow mound suggest that this site could have been more to do with dedicating the major alignment of barrows that would follow; less with a corpse – ?of a craftsman – whose body was not available for burial on Snail Down.

SPTA 2253, HOARE 17, THE HUNTER'S BARROW

When Hoare tackled this large bowl-barrow he found that its upper part had already been dug into and, by repute, had yielded a quantity of beads. Nevertheless its centre was sufficiently undisturbed for Hoare to make one of his more poignant Bronze Age discoveries. First, the skeleton of a small dog was unearthed within three feet of the surface. The primary burial lay intact on the ancient land surface, 8ft 10in below modern surface, and Hoare proposed that one was the companion of the other. It would appear that the cremated bones and ashes, ' … piled up in a small heap … ', had been deposited in a container; and on the ground, not in a burial pit. The presence of 'ashes' may refer to a high charcoal content rather than finely comminuted bone. This heap was surrounded by 'a circular wreath of horns of the red deer'. Among the bones and ashes of the cremation were five flint arrowheads and a small red pebble (Hoare 1812, 183, Pl XXII). Three arrowheads survive and, with the pebble, are illustrated and described here (Fig 58).

M15 **Barbed-and-tanged arrowhead**, pale honey-coloured flint, some mottling; patches of grey/white patination. Ends of barbs straight, angled upwards (towards point). End of tang roughly pointed. Ends of barbs and tang in alignment. Part of original flake surface survives on one face. L (from tip to end of tang) 3.9cm; w 2.7cm. Figure 58. Evans 1872, 343; Annable and Simpson 1964, 57 and 112, no 397; Green 1980, 354, no 256; DZSWS: STHEAD.105.

M16 **Barbed-and-tanged arrowhead**, mottled medium-brown flint, patches of grey/white patination. Partly translucent. Ends of barbs straight and angled upwards: tang extends below their line and has shallow convex end. L 3.7cm; w 2.7cm. Figure 58. Evans *ibid*; Annable and Simpson *ibid*, no 398; Green *ibid*; DZSWS: STHEAD.106.

M17 **Barbed-and-tanged arrowhead**, pale honey-coloured flint, yellow and less translucent than M15. Patches of grey/white patination, less than M15 or M16. One barb damaged probably in manufacture and completed as a short, convex-ended stump. The other's end is straight, angled upwards. Tang extends below surviving complete barb and has convex end. L 3.9cm; w 3.0cm. Figure 58. Evans *ibid*;

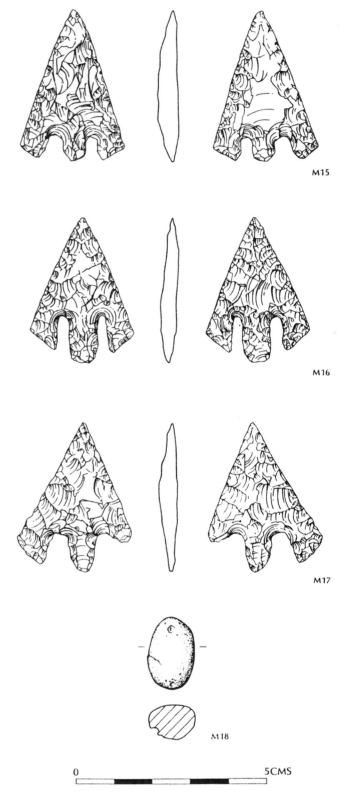

M15

M16

M17

M18

0   5CMS

Fig 58   Early Bronze Age arrowheads and pebble, central burial, bowl-barrow SPTA 2253 (Hoare 17), the Hunter's Barrow.

Annable and Simpson *ibid*, no 396; Green *ibid*; DZSWS: STHEAD.106. Arrowheads M15 and M16 belong to Green's Conygar type: M17, on the grounds of the different barb, to his Sutton b form. Both are broadly contemporary; but whereas Sutton arrowheads occur more frequently in Beaker contexts, especially in graves, the exceptionally finely finished, not-everyday arrowheads of Conygar form are found more usually in graves with associations that include Food Vessels and Collared Urns. None has yet been found with a Beaker. In essence, the Hunter's Barrow arrowheads belong to the full Early Bronze Age, and in their forms and finish represent arrowhead manufacture at its finest in Britain, before the decline in archery that came about by the end of this period.

M18 **Naturally shaped pebble**, roughly oval; medium red/brown. Material: silica-cemented medium/coarse quartz sandstone. A second, slightly larger and more irregular pebble of exactly the same material occurred in the upper ditch silts of Site XX (section 8, Fig 19). It is not possible to locate the source of this quartz sandstone. L (of M18) 1.8cm; w 1.2cm. Figure 58. Evans *ibid*, 419; Annable and Simpson *ibid*, 57, not numbered nor illustrated; DZSWS: STHEAD.108, where it was conjectured, incorrectly, as being of red jasper.

N MISCELLANEOUS ARTEFACTS, PREHISTORIC AND LATER

Nicholas Thomas, with a note by Reg Jackson

N1 **Metal object**, cast; complete in itself but intended to be an attachment. In the form of a bluntly pointed acorn, surrounded by fleshy leaves, four upstanding and four with tips rolled downwards, the whole design springing from a circular base formed into three sharply detailed ribs. Two equally crisp grooves run around the tip of the acorn-shaped central core. From the base extends a cylindrical feature, less in diameter and bearing a roughly arranged series of surrounding grooves, not screw threads, which end in a pad-shaped terminal. A hole, *c* 3mm in diameter, has been drilled (? or cast) centrally and cleanly through this projection or tang. A second, narrower, rougher drilling has been made at right angles (? after casting), which penetrates the first drilling almost at its centre and does not go further. A similar rough drilling has been made opposite, which fails to interrupt the first hole.

Material: copper alloy, patinated. L 5.05cm; w 2cm; diam of tang 1.1cm; l of tang 1.3cm. Fig 59. Site III, Quadrant Sb, layer 11, earthy barrow core, above central turf stack and (apparently) sealed by chalk crust.

These details of context have been given at length because, according to excavation records, this object appears to have been found well-stratified within the barrow mound and sealed by the chalk crust. In the excavation finds book and on the object's finds bag (no 196) it was placed in layer D, the upper earthy core of the mound and only just outside the central turf stack heaped over the burial pit. At the time, the attention of the site director (NT) was not drawn to it and his note books and day book make no reference to it. The object seems, simply, to have been found in an Early Bronze Age context, recorded and bagged according to the system and not commented upon until the site and its finds were prepared for publication. A practical joke is unlikely but cannot be ruled out. More probably, the excavators misinterpreted the object's precise location as they dug.

Superficially the object's decoration is related to the acanthus leaf and its overall appearance is classical. F K Annable, to whom it was shown, does not see it as Roman. Eighteenth or even nineteenth century AD might be more generally acceptable for such a mysterious object. Patination favours an earlier period, such as Romano-British, although it would be wrong to rule out the centuries in between. Chalk behaves so kindly to copper-alloy objects that, in the writer's opinion, the surface appearance of the object *could* be the result of prolonged burial – even burial since the earlier Bronze Age.

If this object was contemporary with the central Early Bronze Age cremation it would be quite without parallel from Britain, lying even further outside the range of objects found regularly with barrow burials and elsewhere than the tanged, twisted-bar bronze object with attached rings found apparently in an Early Bronze Age context beneath bell-barrow Wilsford G58 (Annable and Simpson 1964, 47 and 102, no 211 – 'bronze two-pronged object'; Ashbee and ApSimon in Thomas 1954, 326–330, proposing an ancestry within the third millennium BC in Central Anatolia, and serving as the top to a 'standard').

As, then, to date and authenticity, the Snail Down object appears to be Early Bronze Age on the evidence of the excavation record; but it is difficult to accept it as that because of its uniqueness and it seems therefore more likely to be Roman or later and intrusive.

The purpose served by the Snail Down object remains equally unknown. The supposed tang, with peg- or rivet-hole, perhaps reinforced or repaired twice by added holes, implies that the object was attached to something else, such as furniture, by a peg, and was decorative; or else a knob handle. Less likely may have been its use as a plumb-bob: modern examples usually carry a much sharper point than the rounded top to the acorn form within the leaves. And whereas one good hole through the opposite end would have been perfect for a plumb-line, it would not explain the other holes drilled into the tang.

This unfortunately seems to be as far as any discussion on dating and function can be carried until an analogue from a reliable context has been found.

N2 **Arrowhead**, hollow socket. Two thin, pointed barbs, one broken, lie close to the socket.

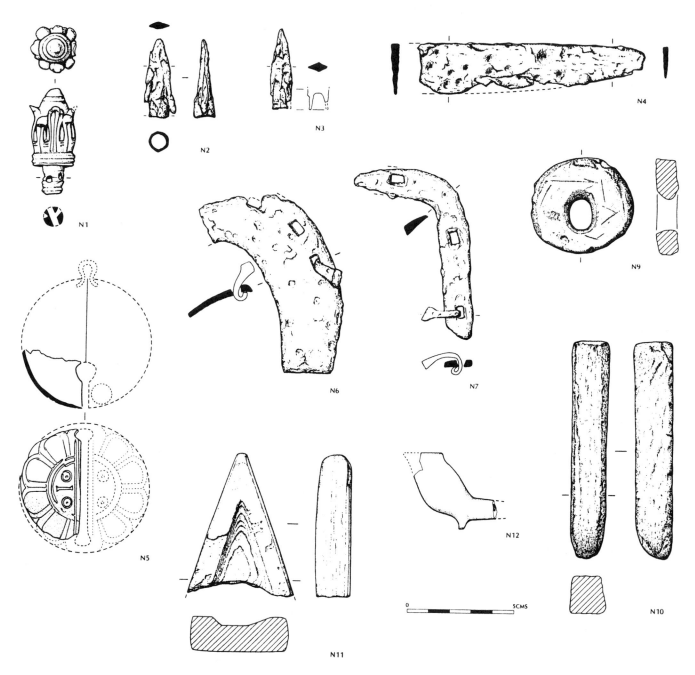

Fig 59   Miscellaneous prehistoric and later objects, various sites.

Material: iron, corroded. L 3.7cm; diam of socket at least 9mm; l of barb 1.2cm. Fig 59. Site III, Quadrant Wa, layer 6, humus below turf over ditch.

This is very close in size and detail to N3 below.

N3 **Arrowhead**, hollow socket. Two thin, pointed barbs, pressed against socket.

Material: iron, corroded. L 3.7cm; diam of socket 9mm; l of barbs 8mm. Fig 59. Site XIV, Quadrant NW, layer 7, d 9in below turf.

The types and development of iron arrow-heads, military and civilian, were discussed in some detail by Ward-Perkins in the *Medieval Catalogue* of the London Museum (1940, 65–73). The Snail Down heads conform to type 16, socketed with barbs close to the socket and not projecting below its base. The

shape is seen as one of several whose use was generally for hunting not war. In a variety of the type, from Breedon-on-the-Hill (Leics), the barbs start much closer to the socket's tip (Wacher 1964, 131–132, fig 4, 1). In date these heads belong generally to the fourteenth and fifteenth centuries but may have come into use earlier and continued, also, into post-medieval times. The rather larger example of the type found at Threave Castle, Galloway, came from a context dated 1455–1640 (Good and Tabraham 1981, 112, 114, fig 12, 107). Pitt-Rivers (1890, 19, pl XX, 2, 10) suggested that this short, heavy type of head, a quarrel, was for use with crossbows rather than longbows. They appeared in England *c* 1200, but, inferior to longbows, were never adopted widely here. The context of Pitt-

Rivers' published quarrels was King John's House, Tollard Royal (Wilts), a medieval house with a lengthy history of use and development. They were not closely datable there.

N4 **Knife blade**, handle end missing, heavily corroded. Single edge; back of knife almost straight, cutting edge may originally have been slightly convex. Cross-section triangular. Both faces of blade probably flat.

Material: iron, corroded. Surviving l 10.8cm; th of back 4mm. Fig 59. Site III, Quadrant Nb, layer 13, top of chalk crust.

Such simple knife blades were current from Iron Age times; this piece might be as old as that; or less than one hundred years. Its context shows that in all probability it was left in the turf and drifted down until coming to rest on top of the mound's chalky cover. The blade could have been dropped by Cunnington and found such a resting place since 1805.

N5 **Rumbler bell fragment**, probably for sheep. Originally spherical, with a suspension loop at the top and, in the lower half of the sphere, a slit with circular openings at each end, part of one retained here. A metal ball would have been incorporated within the sphere to jangle when the animal moved. Lower half has cast, traditional decoration of petal-like arcades around two half-moon shapes, one each side of the slit, which contain the initials of the bell-maker. The letter I (or J) between circled stops is preserved.

Material: copper alloy, probably bronze bell-metal. L 5.15cm; original diam 6cm. Fig 59. Site III, Quadrant Na, humus below turf, d 6in.

Many rumbler bells were made at Aldbourne (Wilts) and often carry the signature RW for Robert Wells (1764–1792). They range in diameter from not much more than *c* 3cms to about 10cm and an extensive series is held – and displayed – at the Wiltshire Heritage Museum. This collection includes at least one pair of large bells mounted on a frame for wearing by a packhorse (Cunnington and Goddard 1934, 272, M134).

The museum has a complete rumbler identical in size and detail to the Snail Down fragment, with maker's initials IB (DZSWS: 1982.15). These letters may stand for James Burrough of Devizes, active *c* 1750. But the Museum also possesses a similar bell signed IS. And it appears that IB bells are known from Aldbourne as well as from Oxfordshire (Paul Robinson, pers comm). We can only conclude that the Snail Down rumbler might have carried a signature IB; and it *might* have been the Devizes maker James Burrough.

Whoever the maker, when this bell cracked on Snail Down and fell silent, its owner suffered a tiresome loss.

N6 **Half a horseshoe**. Only one branch present; not clear whether the plain calkin end is complete (it lacks a calkin). Outer surface slightly convex, inner side equally concave. Three rectangular nail holes survive, one retaining its square-headed nail.

Material: wrought iron. Max l 9.9cm; max w 3.35cm; wt *c* 2oz. Fig 59. Site III, Quadrant Ea, base of topsoil over ditch.

N7 **Half a shoe**, possibly for a donkey or mule. Calkin end perhaps incomplete. In plan unusually squared as it turns to cover the toe. Three rectangular nail holes, one retaining a slim, rectangular-headed nail. Flat in crosssection, outer surface edges slightly rounded.

Material: wrought iron. L between surviving ends 9.3cm; w 1.5cm; th 4mm; wt *c* 1oz. Fig 59. Site VIII, outer edge of ditch, on bedrock, d 9in.

Horseshoes are notoriously difficult to date outside an attributable context. N6 appears to be from a working horseshoe which, when complete, was akin to keyhole shoes of the sixteenth or seventeenth centuries. N7 is noticeably narrower and slighter, with an unusual squared corner that suggests that it was made to fit a deformed hoof (or even to repair a farm worker's boot?). Its proportions would suit a mule or donkey, both of which were used by country people up to the twentieth century. The nails in N6 and N7 are of 'Mustad' pattern, supplied widely to British farriers by a Swedish firm of that name whose centre of distribution is at Portishead (Somerset). The date of these nails and shoes is likely to be later nineteenth to early twentieth century.

N8 **Spindle whorl**, pottery, broken in half along the perforation. For details of ware, context and fabric, see Section E, E15; the same object; Fig 48. This is a well-known southern English form, with slightly domed ends and concave sides, cylindrical perforation. It occurred at All Cannings Cross (Cunnington 1923, pl 25, 6, 10); and at Maiden Castle, from Wheeler's Iron Age B levels (1943, 294–295, fig 99, 9).

N9 **Spindle whorl**, flat faces and roughly squared edge. Oval perforation carved through, slightly off-centre.

Material: chalk. D 4.85cm; th 1.3cm; diam of perforation 1.3cm. Fig 59. Site XV, NW Quadrant, base of turf.

In view of the numerous Romano-British potsherds in this heavily disturbed barrow, the spindle whorl is likely to be of Roman date.

N10 **Whetstone**, probably complete. Rectangular in cross-section, angles not quite at 90°; two corners fairly sharp, two more rounded. One end squared off, the other carefully rounded down to an oblique nose. Not much evidence of surface wear through use.

Material: micaceous sandstone, fine grained; perhaps from the Upper Greensand fringing Salisbury Plain. L 10.1cm; w 1.6cm. Fig 59. Site XIX, smaller (N) mound, layer 14, top of chalk crust. Not a closely datable type of object when divorced from an identifiable context as here, this whetstone is unlikely to belong to the period of the barrows. Its relative coarseness makes it a rough sharpener, not one for a fine edge tool.

N11 **Fragmentary stone object**, original shape not obvious. Very carefully finished flat surfaces, well polished on the ? base, sides and facetted point. The ? upper surface bears an equally carefully hollowed recess, concave rather than flat in section. In carving this hollow, the banded nature of the stone has been revealed; and because of it the surface containing the recess is slightly less smooth, and lacks the fine polish on the rest of the object.

Material: silty limestone, possibly from the Tisbury/Chilmark area. L 68.5mm; th 16.5mm; d of recess 4mm. Fig 59. Site VI, section 2, layer 8, near centre of ditch, depth 11in.

The archaeological context suggests that this object is unlikely to be pre-Roman, although uncertainty as to date must remain. Pre-Roman communities in southern England lacked a tradition for carving stone containers and it is therefore improbable that it is, for example, an ancient palette or similar shallow receptacle. That the whole object has been so carefully finished and polished, including the surviving blunt-pointed end, implies that it was an object in the round and not, for example, an inlay for furniture. But for the superior exterior finish, it could be considered as part of a mould. Having surfaces in such fine, unweathered condition, it is perhaps most likely that this enigmatic fragment falls chronologically within the last two centuries of our era.

N12 **Clay Tobacco pipe bowl with spur**, stem missing. Fig 59. Site III, Quadrant Na, berm, layer 22.

Description by Reg Jackson

The bowl does not bear a maker's mark. However, it may be dated by style to *c* 1690–1710. The bowl form also indicates that it was made in Wiltshire. A comparison can be formed with published tobacco pipes made in Marlborough and Salisbury, for example:

Atkinson 1965, 91, fig 2, bowl form R, made by John Greenland, active in Salisbury in the early eighteenth century; *ibid* 1970, 182, fig 2, no 17, made by William Hurd who was working *c* 1690–1700 in Marlborough.

The pipe bowl was found on the berm on the north-east side of the bell-barrow, just below modern turf and humus. That side of the mound was sheltered from the prevailing wind, a place where such as a shepherd might have paused for a smoke – and broken his pipe. The pipe is too early to have belonged to any of Hoare's men of 1805.

P THE ROMAN COINS, SITES VI, XVI AND XX

Marion Archibald

Twelve Roman coins were found in 1957 during the examination of Site XX to determine its relationship with the linear ditch immediately to the north, Site VI. This work included excavating sections 6 and 8 (Figs 18, 19); the latter was extended into a small area excavation to record the nature of chalky deposits heaped over the ditch of Site XX at this point (Fig 19). These, which sealed Roman coins, Romano-British pottery and other late finds, were probably the result of constantly clearing chalky mud from a trackway running up and around Site XX from the south, T3 (Fig 2), and crossing Site VI. A Romano-British settlement or farmstead may lie to the north, associated perhaps with the ancient fields that extend northwards from Site VI.

The following Roman coins were recovered during this work; they give some indication of the late Roman period when Trackway T3 was in use. Where the archaeological context for each coin is noted, 'section' refers to the published section, the number following being the layer number on that section. This is followed by an indication of the coin's depth from modern turf.

P1 VALENTINIAN I
GLORIA ROMANORVM
Lyons 367–375 AD
LRBC II, 361a
Site XX, section 8, 23, d 1¾ft.

P2 VALENTINIAN I
GLORIA ROMANORVM
Arles 367–375 AD
LRBC II, 479
Site VI, section 6, topsoil

P3 VALENTINIAN I
GLORIA ROMANORVM
Mint uncertain. 364–378 AD
Site XX, section 8, 23, d 1½ft

P4 VALENTINIAN I or VALENS
SECVRITAS REIPVBLICAE
Arles 364–367 AD
LRBC II, 485 or 486
Site XX, section 8, 23, d 1¾ft

P5 VALENTINIAN I
SECVRITAS REIPVBLICAE
Siscia 367–375 AD
LRBC II, 1414 or 1415
Site XX, section 8, 23, d 1¾ft

P6 THEODOSIVS I
VOT X MVLT XX
Rome 364–367 AD
LRBC II, 767
Site XX, section 8, 23, d 1¾ft

P7 THEODOSIVS I (probably)
SALVS REIPVBLICAE
Nicomedia 388–395 AD
Site XX, section 8, 23, d 1½ft

P8 GRATIAN
GLORIA ROMANORVM
Lyons 367–375 AD
LRBC II, 308
Site XX, section 8, 23, d 2¼ft

P9 GRATIAN
GLORIA ROMANORVM
Arles 367–375 AD
LRBC II, 505 or 529
Site XX, section 8, 23, d 2½ft

P10 GRATIAN
SECVRITAS REIPVBLICAE
Arles 375–378 AD
LRBC II, 533
Site VI, section 6, 1, base of topsoil

P11 GRATIAN
SECVRITAS REIPVBLICAE
Lyons 375–378 AD
LRBC II, 366
Site XX, section 8, 23, d 2½ft

P12 ARCADIVS
VICTORIA AVGGG
Trier 388–392 AD
LRBC II, 170
Site XX, section 8, 23, d 2½ft

One other Roman coin was found, at the pond-barrow, Site XVI

P13 DIVA FAUSTINA
PIETAS AVG SC
Rome 141 AD or later
BMC 1474 (very worn)
Probably deposited in the mid-3rd century
Site XVI, NE Quadrant, within bank, layer 6, d 9in.

[BMC: H Mattingly, *A Catalogue of the Roman Coins in the British Museum: The Coins of the Roman Empire, Vol IV, Antoninus Pius To Commodus*. 2nd Edition, London 1968.
LRBC: R A G Carson, P V Hill and J P C Kent, *Late-Roman Bronze Coinage AD 324–498*, London 1960.]

Q REMAINS OF THE WILD AND DOMESTIC ANIMALS

Juliet Clutton-Brock and Peter Jewell

INTRODUCTION

Animal bones were recovered from thirteen of the sites excavated at Snail Down*. No one site yielded a particularly large number of bones, nor within any given site were there enough bones to allow different layers in that site (a barrow ditch, for example) to be treated separately. The sites concerned are shown in Figure 60, where the absolute numbers, and the percentages by species, of bone remains and teeth found in the excavation of each site are presented. It will be seen that the total number of bone fragments from some sites is very small and such inadequate samples could not usefully have been examined separately. For this reason the remains from all sites have been treated here as a single faunal assemblage. It seems reasonable to do this as all the sites except VI/VII are of earlier Bronze Age date. Sites VI/VII were not barrows but linear ditches of later Bronze Age and Early/Middle Iron Age date. It was not possible to detect from the bones any differences in the size or types of animal present at these sites and so they have not been excluded from the general analysis.

The material consists predominantly of large bone fragments most of which can be assigned to the appropriate species, but few are useful for measurement. There are some whole bones, however, and where measurements could be taken these have been tabulated in the text. The percentage numbers in the whole collection of the principal animals represented were:

Ox	51
Sheep/Goat	24
Pig	8
Horse	7
Roe Deer	5
Dog	3
Red Deer	2
	100%

Besides these remains there were a few bones of hare and fox. The ox bones were from wild cattle (aurochs) and domestic cattle, but the horse and pig animals cannot be certainly identified as wild or domestic. The remains of large mammals will, therefore, be dealt with simply in systematic order.

As well as the remains so far discussed, a large number of bones of small vertebrates was also recovered from the barrows. This was an unprecedented discovery and these finds and their interpretation will be discussed in a separate section of this report.

DOMESTIC ANIMALS AND LARGE WILD MAMMALS

Dog

The remains of dog from Snail Down consist of eight mandibular rami, and the basal part of a skull that includes the occipital bone, the foramen magnum and the occipital condyles. In addition, from Site I there is a collection of dog bones which most probably represents a single animal: vertebrae, the pelvic girdle, the radii and numerous fragmentary post-cranial bones.

Seven of the mandibles are from animals of approximately the same size, that is about the size of, say, a Welsh sheepdog. Mandible X 4** is smaller than the others. The teeth are relatively large and are somewhat compacted in all the jaws. This is a condition that is very commonly found in primitive domestic dogs in Europe. The teeth are larger than those of similar-sized present-day dogs and closer in size to those of the European wolf from whom the dogs must have been, at least in part, descended. The jaws, however, are considerably shorter in overall length than those of the wolf, and it is this

---

*Note: The identification of the animal remains from Snail Down was made in the early 1960s and the report was written in 1964. A few minor alterations have been made and references added in 1991 but the bones have not been re-examined for this publication. Where no decimal point is indicated, the measurement was made to the nearest mm.

**In this report, the Roman numeral is the barrow number, the Arabic the find number in the site field find books.

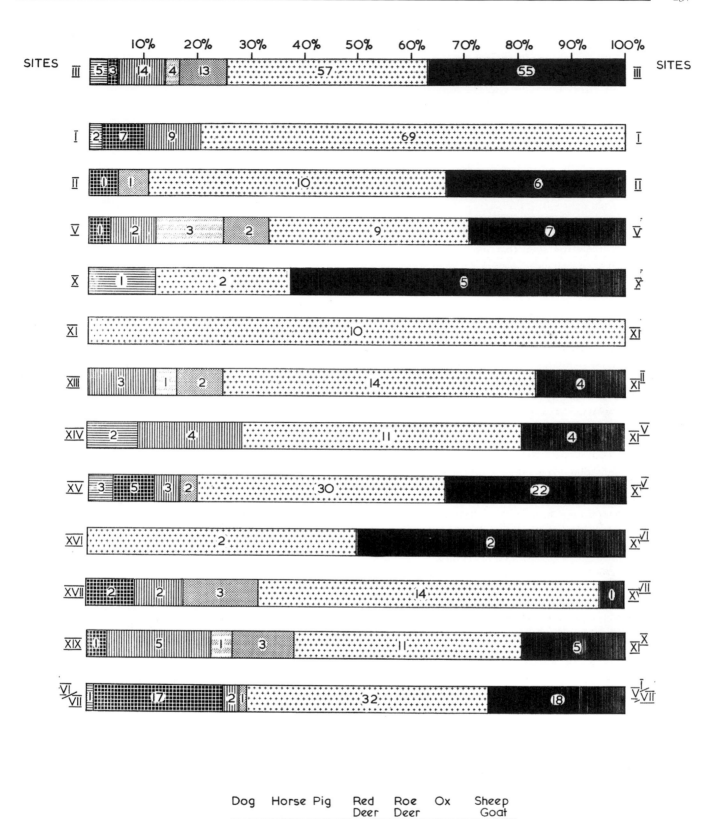

Fig 60   Absolute numbers and percentages of bone fragments and teeth from Snail Down.

feature that gives rise to the compaction of the teeth. The relative proportions of canid jaws and teeth have been discussed by Clutton-Brock (1962) and Harcourt (1974).

One of the mandibles from Snail Down, III 115, shows signs of periodontal disease (Clutton-Brock 1962 a). This is a disease of the bone of the jaw which particularly afflicts animals that have been fed on sloppy foods (King 1948). It is very commonly found in domestic animals and in animals that have been kept in captivity but it is very rare in wild animals. In the mandible from Snail Down, the diseased part of the bone lies between the third and fourth lower premolars and around the anterior edge of the carnassial tooth (Pl 67).

The dog jaws from Snail Down have been compared (Table 28) with those from the Neolithic site of Windmill Hill. It will be seen that the Snail Down dogs had, on the average, slightly larger carnassial teeth than those from Windmill Hill.

Complete list of the dog remains by sites

Site I

335	Right mandibular ramus with all the cheek teeth except P1 and M3. The bone is charred.
215	Right mandibular ramus with P4, M1 and M2.
No number	Large numbers of fragmentary bones of dog which most probably all come from one individual. The only complete bones are the radii and their length is 149mm. The left mandibular ramus is also present. The bones show spots of charring.

Site III

25 and 115	Complete mandible found in the ditch fill. Left ramus has the canine, P4, M1 and M2. The right ramus has the canine, P2, P4, M1 and M2. The teeth and bone show spots of

charring. Periodontal disease of the bone can be seen around the sockets of both first molars (the carnassial teeth) (Pl 67).

180	Part of a left horizontal ramus without teeth. The tooth row is straight but the sockets are somewhat compacted. The bone is charred.
No number	Part of the right horizontal ramus of a mandible with P2, P3, P4 and M1.

Site X

4	Right mandibular ramus with M1. This jaw bone is smaller than all the other dog jaws and the ramus is more curved.

Site XIV

No number	One upper first molar.
No number	One premolar.

Site XV

90	One occiput.
36	One upper right molar 1.
No number	One maxillary fragment with P3. Measurements of the mandibles and teeth are given in Table 29.

Site XX

322	Right mandibular ramus with P2, P4, M1 and M2.

If the added individual lengths of the teeth P1–M3 are expressed as a percentage of the directly measured length of the cheek tooth row, then this index can be used to show the degree of crowding of the teeth. This figure is given in the last column of Table 29 for the dog jaws from Snail Down.

Table 28 Lengths of the lower first molar (the carnassial tooth) of dog jaws from Snail Down and Windmill Hill

	Snail Down			Windmill Hill	
Tooth		Length of lower Molar 1 (mm)		Jaw	Length of lower Molar 1 (mm)
I	335	23.90		Mounted skeleton	20.85
I	215	22.90		B.173	19.65
I	?	21.00		B.22	18.65
III	25	23.00		B.108	19.80
				?	19.50
III		24.00		B.124	18.35
X	4	20.00		B.161	20.75
XX	322	21.90		B.17	20.70
				B.204	23.50
	mean 22.39			mean 20.19	
	Range for 7 teeth – 20.00–24.00mm			Range for 9 teeth – 18.65–23.50mm	

Table 29 Measurements of the dog mandibles to show the size of the teeth and the degree of crowding. Where the teeth are missing their size has been estimated by measuring the lengths of the sockets.

Site and Number	Depth of mandible (mm)*	Length of cheek teeth row (mm)†	Length P1 (mm)	Length P2 (mm)	Length P3 (mm)	Length P4 (mm)	Length M1 (mm)	Length M2 (mm)	Length M3 (mm)	Degree of crowding
I 335	21.3	72.8	5.0	10.0	11.5	13.3	23.9	9.4	5.0	108%
I 215	23.5	-	-	-	-	13.0	22.9	10.3	5.0	-
I no number	20.0	72.6	4.5	9.3	10.5	12.4	21.0	8.3	4.5	97%
III 25	20.5	73.0	4.8	9.2	11.5	12.7	23.0	9.5	4.2	96%
III 180	-	-	4.8	9.0	11.2	12.3	-	-	-	-
III no number	-	-	-	-	12.0	12.8	24.0	10.0	-	-
X 4	18.5	67.8	4.5	8.6	10.2	10.8	20.0	9.5	4.2	99.5%
XX 322	22.0	70.8	4.5	9.0	11.2	12.0	21.9	9.0	4.0	101%

* Measured below the fourth pre-molar.
† Measured from the anterior edge of the socket of P1 to the posterior edge of the socket of M3.

Horse

Small numbers of the bones and teeth of horses were found throughout the sites and make up 7% of the whole collection of large mammal remains. The bones are small and probably represent early domestic ponies, remains of which begin to appear in the archaeological record in the Late Neolithic (Clutton-Brock and Burleigh 1991).

Measurements of the more complete bones are given below.

Measurements of horse bones

Scapula

I 328   Length of the scapula head – 56mm.
         Width of the scapula head – 46mm.

Humerus

VI/VII   Maximum width of distal articular surface – 72.5mm.

Radius

III 260   Maximum width of distal articular surface – 64.5mm.

Metacarpals Maximum width of distal articular surface

I 333A   40mm.
II 21   40mm.

Tibiae Maximum width of distal articular surface

?   69mm.
III 27   64.1mm.
VI/VII 354 67.4mm.

Pig

Pig bones and teeth make up 8% of the total number of animal remains. It is not possible to say whether these bones represent wild or domesticated animals. They may be from the wild boar, *Sus scrofa* L. which was hunted for food or they may be from domesticated pigs that were bred from the wild boar. It is often possible to tell from the shape of the skull and sometimes from the size of the teeth which type is represented. The ranges of tooth size in wild and domestic pigs overlap but large male wild boars have distinctively large teeth. In the case of the Snail Down specimens, however, there are no skull bones and the teeth are not so large that they can be definitely identified as wild boars.

Miller (1912), measuring nine skulls, quotes a range of 29.0–47.0mm for the lengths of lower third molars of *Sus scrofa*. The three lower third molars from Snail Down measure 36mm, 32.4mm and 34.1mm. Measurements of the lengths of lower third molars of nine present-day domestic pigs fall within the range 32.8–36.4mm.

Measurements of the bones and teeth from Snail Down were taken from the more complete specimens and are given below. Besides the remains of adult animals there was a jaw of a foetal or new-born pig.

Measurements of the pig bones and teeth

Upper second molars

I 264   Length 17.3mm, a much worn tooth.
III 199   Length 19.3mm, unworn.
XV ?   Length 22.7mm, fairly worn.

Lower third molars

XIV ?   Length 32.4mm, unworn.
XIV ?   Length 34.1mm, fairly worn.

Mandibles

XV 83   The third molar is just erupting.
          Length of third molar – 36mm.
          Length of second molar – 34.1mm.

Mandibles

I 121   Only the symphysial part of this mandible is present. The canines are small and most probably this was a female pig. Maximum width of the mandible measured externally, between the canines, is 40.6mm.

Scapula

I 20   Minimum width of neck – 18.75mm.

Radius

III 51   Width of the proximal articular surface – 21.5mm.

Tibiae

I 47   Width of distal articular surface – 28.8mm.
III 82   Width of distal articular surface – 28.3mm.

Talus

No Number Maximum length of talus – 45.7mm.

Cattle

The cattle bones show a remarkably wide range of size and on close examination it is evident that particular bones may be allotted to two distinct size groups (Pl 65). There are, for example, a few small astragali but a fragment of one very large one; there are two very large, robust, 1st phalanges amongst other much smaller ones; and the same contrast is seen in a pair of hoof cores. Of the many fragments of the radius, two very large distal ends (equal in size to those of a large modern bull) contrast with eight small proximal ends, two of which are very small.

The evidence points to two distinct types of cattle being present, the most likely explanation being that the bones are those of both wild aurochs (*Bos primigenius*) and of domestic oxen. To examine this possibility a metrical analysis was made of cattle bones from earlier (Neolithic) and later sites, together with the aurochs bones from Star Carr (Clark 1954, 70–95), and the results of this investigation (Jewell 1962, 1963a) show conclusively that both *Bos primigenius* and much smaller domestic cattle are present. A particularly striking match was found between the metacarpal bones from Star Carr (The Natural History Museum collection) and the large metacarpals from Snail Down. The latter are only slightly smaller than the metacarpals of the aurochs from Lowe's Farm, Cambs (Shawcross and Higgs 1961) that is dated to the Early Bronze Age. The largest metacarpal fragment (Table 30) from Snail Down is very wide but flattened antero-posteriorly and is probably from a bull aurochs whilst an almost complete but slender specimen (Pl 65, top row, 3rd from left) is certainly from a cow. A detached metacarpal epiphysis from an aurochs calf is present; it is outside the size range of the domestic ox. Another close comparison can be made with the aurochs of mid-Atlantic age from East Ham (Banks 1961) where the measured bones of the appendicular skeleton are the same size as those from Snail Down. The *Bos primigenius* remains were not confined to any one site but occurred in I, III, V, XIV, XV and XIX.

Measurements of the cattle bones are presented in Table 30. All the bones are broken except the smaller bones of the appendicular skeleton. The distal ends of the humeri show a gradation in size, but not very large ones are present, and the fragments of tibiae are all very small. There is one basal fragment of a horn core which is complete where attached to the skull; its circumference here is 128mm, which is small, but it will be from a young animal. In general the domestic ox material from Snail Down is comparable with that from other broadly contemporary sites and the animals were evidently of the typical small stature. An examination of the charts in Jewell (1962, 1963a), where measurements of cattle bones from sites of the Neolithic to the Middle Ages are set out, suggests that the Bronze Age Snail Down animals were not yet reduced to the minute size of the later Iron Age. On the other hand, the large type of domestic cattle of the Neolithic age are no longer in evidence. Because the sample is small, however, such inferences can only be tentative.

Table 30   Measurements of cattle bones (nearest mm)

Metatarsal	I 221									
Width distal articulation	52									

Metacarpals	XV	III 105	I 278	XV 78	I 312	I 41	XIV 228	V 16		
Length	–	–	–	–	–	242	256	241		
Width distal articulation	59	50	55	54	82	81	77	68		

The separate distal epiphysis from a young animal has a width of 63mm

Talus	XV 63	XV 77	XX 322							
Length	65	62	60							

First Phalanges	XV	XIX 288	XIII 236		I 327	I 367	XV	XIX	III 20	XV 48
Length	81	78	60		55	65	56	61	53	55

Humerus	II 41	I 349	I 276	I 255	II 14					
Width distal articulation	87	74	67	81	73					

Radius	I 39	XVII 66	III 35	III 40	I 276	XV 30	XVII 69	VI/VII 95	XV 67	
Width distal end	96	89	–	–	–	–	–	–	–	
Width proximal end	–	–	68	80+	69	63+	71	67	75	

Tibia	I 326	I 282	III 258	III 27						
Width distal end	67	56	51	54						

Horn core	XVII 96									
Circumference base	128									

Sheep/Goat

It is extremely difficult to distinguish the post-cranial skeletal bones and the teeth of sheep from those of goats when the primitive domesticated animals are concerned*. The skulls and horn cores can be separated and the scapulae and metapodial bones only if they are complete enough to give length and width measurements. There are no horn cores or skull bones amongst the Snail Down remains and very few complete limb bones. One identifiable scapula proves that sheep is certainly present. It is not known whether goat is present or if so in what proportion, so all these bones and teeth have been grouped under the heading sheep/goat.

Remains of sheep/goat make up a quarter of the total number of animal bones. Measurements were taken wherever possible and they are listed below.

Measurements of the sheep/goat bones and teeth

Scapula

XV 33   This bone is certainly sheep.
Maximum length of scapula head – 26.8mm.
Maximum width of scapula head – 20.4mm.
Minimum width of neck – 18.2mm.

Humerus

I 90   This bone is most probably sheep. It is complete.
Length of humerus – 115mm.
Width of shaft at mid-point – 13mm.
Width of distal articular surface – 27mm.

Radii (complete)

III 5   Complete radius.
Length of bone – 136mm.
Width of shaft at mid-point – 14mm.
Width of proximal articular surface – 28.6mm.
Width of distal articular surface – 24.4mm.

Proximal ends of radii	Width of proximal articular surface
III 242	27mm.
III 108	27.3mm.
III 42	27.65mm.
XIII 258	27.6mm.
XIV 204	27.45mm.
XV 36	25.7mm.

Distal end of radius	Width of distal articular surface
II 25	25.6mm.

Proximal ends of metacarpals	Width of proximal articular surface
III 50	22.4mm.
VI/VII 298	18.8mm.

Distal end of metacarpal	Width of distal articular surface
II 98	20mm.

Tibiae

Distal ends	Width of distal articular surface
I 353	27.0mm.
III 49	25.0mm.
III 50	23.8mm.
III 105	20.3mm.
III 3	23.0mm.
XV 36	27.5mm.
XVI 57	23.0mm.
XVII 58	22.8mm.
XVII 114	23.0mm.

Metatarsals

III 105 Complete bone. Most probably a female sheep.
Width of proximal articular surface – 19.0mm.
Width of distal articular surface – 22.8mm.
Minimum width of shaft – 11.0mm.
Maximum length of bone – 113mm.

Proximal ends of metatarsals	Width of proximal articular surface
II 9	22.2mm.
III 50	18.0mm.
V 9	17.4mm.

Tali	Maximum length	Maximum width of inferior surface
I 263	27mm	18.3mm.
XV 56	30.2mm	18.7mm.

Red Deer *Cervus elaphus L*

Only a few bones and pieces of antler of red deer were found at Snail Down. Site III produced a proximal end of a metatarsal bone, one first and one second phalanx and one antler tine. There were a few fragments of bone from Sites V, XIII and XIX. It is, however, peculiarly difficult to

---

*When this report was prepared in the early 1960s the criteria for distinguishing sheep and goat were only just being developed and were not available for reference (see Boessneck, Müller and Teichert 1964 and Boessneck 1969). Accordingly the remains of these animals from Snail Down were not separated into sheep and goat.

distinguish some red deer bones from those of small cattle and it is quite possible that other fragments have been wrongly identified.

Metatarsal	Width of proximal articular surface
III 218	35mm.

Roe Deer *Capreolus capreolus* L.

The roe deer is represented in larger numbers than red deer. There are nearly as many roe deer bones as horse bones, and it is probable that this species was frequently hunted for meat.

It is often difficult to distinguish post-cranial skeletal bones of roe deer from those of sheep and goat so a definite figure for the numbers present cannot be given.

Metacarpal	Width of proximal articular surface
XVII 56	19.8mm.

Metatarsals	Width of distal articular surface
I 23	23.7mm.
III 47	25mm.

Small mammals and other small vertebrates

Most of these remains came from sites XVII and XIX and were found at the level of the ancient land surface, although a few were found at places in, or on, the turf stack. The remains were evidently deposited at the time of construction of the barrows. The finds were in the form of aggregates of small bones including mammals, toad, lizard and slow-worm and there can be no doubt that they are the remains of the pellets disgorged by some raptorial bird. A clue to the origin of these pellets was given when ancient stake holes were found in the old land surface under the barrows. Standing stakes, erected by the barrow builders, must have formed attractive perches for the birds. If a guess is to be given what kind of bird was involved, then buzzard or kite seems the most likely choice.

Six species of small mammal were identified in the pellets and included the mole, water vole, short-tailed vole, long-tailed field mouse, common shrew and pygmy shrew. The minimum numbers of individuals were ascertained by counting the most abundant bone or tooth of right or left side for each species. The results are set out in Table 31.

The remains of the water vole include a few crania that are complete in the maxillary and orbital region, but always lack the occipital region. Other skulls are more fragmentary, although a large number of mandibles was obtained. Teeth and limb bones are plentiful. The skull bones were compared with *Arvicola amphibius amphibius*, *A.a. reta* (the form found in northern Britain) and *A. sherman* (the continental form). No evidence was found to distinguish the Bronze Age specimens from the form found in the south of Britain today – *A.a. amphibius*. A large collection of skulls of this species are available for measurement at The Natural History Museum and graphs were prepared to correlate some dimensions of the cranium (particularly the ratio of frontal width to inter-orbital constriction) and mandibular length to body weight. On the basis of these graphs the body weights of the Bronze Age specimens can be estimated, and from these, in turn, the state of maturity of the animals can be ascertained using the data presented by Perry (1943). The majority of the Bronze Age water voles that became items of prey were either juveniles or young adults, estimated to have been between 80 and 220 grams in body weight.

Of the three species of field and small scrubland rodents that occur in England today, the short-tailed vole, the field mouse and the bank vole, only two are represented in the Bronze Age collection (Table 31) and the short-tailed field vole is dominant. This animal is characteristic of open grassland. In order to see what species live on Snail Down at the present time, thirty Longworth traps were set on and about the barrows during a weekend in late November, 1958; the traps were down for two nights.

Several short-tailed voles and field mice were captured but, as in Bronze Age times, the bank vole was apparently absent.

Table 31   Small mammal prey from Early Bronze Age pellets

Minimum number of individuals

	Barrow XVII	Barrow Modern XIX	Longworth traps
Mole (*Talpa europea*)	4		15
Water vole (*Arvicola amphibius*)	20	2	
Short-tailed vole (*Microtus agrestis*)	6	40	3
Field mouse (*Apodemus sylvaticus*)	1	2	3
Common shrew (*Sorex araneus*)	2	4	2
Pygmy shrew (*Sorex minutus*)	0	2	0
Bank vole (*Clethrionomys glareolus*)	0	0	0

COMMENT

Economy

The reasons for treating the bones, pooled from all sites, as a single faunal assemblage have been mentioned in the introduction. We have made no attempt to assess the 'minimum number of individuals' at each site, again because the number of bones is too small to allow this to be a useful procedure. The chart, (Fig 60), is, therefore, compiled from the information from all the reasonably large bone fragments. Animal bones in a barrow site must have a more diverse origin than those, for example, in a settlement midden, and there may be no justification for using a calculation of the minimum number of individuals. Some support for the assertion that the proportions ascribed to the species in Fig 60 are correct is gained from the fact that for many of the sites the proportions are similar. Apart from the fact that so many of the bones were smashed (presumably carried out to extract the marrow), an additional hazard is indicated by the gnawed condition of many of them. Plate 66 shows the deep pitting of the ends of a bone caused by powerful gnawing, probably by a dog, but it is as well to bear in mind that the wolf and fox would additionally act as scavengers.

It is clear that the meat-producing aspect of the economy was dominated by the husbandry of cattle. Fifty-one per cent of all bone fragments were from cattle and twenty-four per cent from sheep or goat. But, because of the differences in body size, the contribution of ox meat would, of course, be proportionately much greater. If the horse and pig bones are all from domestic animals, then the amount of meat derived from wild mammals appears to have been insignificant. Interestingly enough, amongst the hunted species it would again have been cattle that were most important. The huge size of the aurochs made a single individual equivalent to a large number of red and roe deer.

Environment

The bird pellet remains may give some indication of the environment at the time of barrow construction. The most puzzling question posed by the finds is what were water voles doing on the top of Salisbury Plain in the Bronze Age? The Plain is a free-draining chalk upland and the nearest water to Snail Down is the River Avon *c* 4 miles away. In England today the water vole is fairly strictly a water-side animal and the buzzard, for instance, would not normally hunt over nearly such great distances (Moore 1957, and pers comm). Is it possible that conditions were wetter in the Bronze Age and that active streams ran higher in the chalk? On the contrary, the Bronze Age falls into the Sub-Boreal climatic phase and is generally considered to have been more continental, with drier summers than at present, although wetter interludes, represented by recurrence surfaces in the formation of bogs, did occur. On the other hand perhaps the status of *Arvicola* has changed considerably in the last 3000 years. On the Continent there are sub-species of *Arvicola* of the *sherman* group that live a fossorial existence far away from water. Something of this kind has been reported to happen at one place in England – on Read's Island in the Humber (Southern and Crowcroft 1956). Here it is suggested that the wide distribution of the voles over the entire island is made possible by the absence of rabbit, rat and mole. It is significant that neither the rabbit nor rat formed part of the British fauna in Bronze Age times. It is suggested, therefore, that in the absence of these species and in the resulting different ecological conditions, the British water vole commonly occupied dry habitats.

Open grassland is suggested by the large numbers of short-tailed voles represented and the field mouse would also be present in such a habitat. The absence of the bank vole is a complementary and significant fact as this species prefers scrub or bracken-covered areas and shuns the open. It is absent in the area today (Table 31).

Barrow XVII and Barrow XIX are distinct entities and many decades may have separated their construction. Yet in both cases the bulk of the prey represented in the pellets is formed by the larger small mammals, either the water vole or the mole. Because these species are more easily caught by birds of prey when the ground cover is well grown, compared with the smaller mice and shrews, pellets of such composition are characteristics of summer and autumn (for evidence in relation to the Tawny owl, see Southern 1954). Strong support for the suggestion that the pellets were formed in summer or autumn can be seen in the high proportion of juvenile and immature animals of all species that occur in the pellets. Evidence for the season of the year at which activities were carried out in prehistoric times is sparse, and some of the biological indicators have been discussed by Jewell (1958). It seems that pellet-remains may be of the greatest assistance in this respect and these minute remains are well worth recovering and recording.

R THE MOLLUSCAN MATERIAL

Arthur Cain, with John Currey

INTRODUCTION

(by Nicholas Thomas)

Samples of the larger, readily visible snail shells encountered during the course of excavations were recorded and preserved for future study. In those years we had not learned to appreciate the much greater importance of microscopic mollusca as indicators of environmental change and such collecting was not done. Dr Currey and Dr Cain approached NT initially, since they were conducting research into the field genetics of snails *Cepaea nemoralis* and *hortensis*; in particular the stability of populations over long periods of time. Their studies had already covered Wiltshire sites such as Avebury, Windmill Hill, The Sanctuary and Woodhenge; and also Abingdon causewayed camp (Oxon). They wished to examine our Bronze Age snail remains in connection with this aspect of their enquiries. Dr Cain's Snail Down report identifies, and comments upon, all our macroscopic mollusca; special detail has been included on *nemoralis* and *hortensis*. The report has not been changed since its compilation during 1962–1963.

THE REPORT

The following snails were recorded from Sites I, III, XI, XV, XVII and XX. Where layer numbers are quoted for context, these can be identified using the relevant published sections.

Site I

	Mollusc	Number Preserved	Comment
14	*Pomatias elegans* (Müller)	4	
	Cepaea nemoralis (L.)	1	unbanded 00000
	Context: NE quadrant, eccentric mound, Robbing 3.		
2	*Pomatias elegans* (Müller)	7+	
	Cepaea hortensis (Müller)	1	five-banded 1(234)5
	Helicella itala (L.)	5	
	Context: NE quadrant, central mound, Hoare's excavation re-fill.		
3	*Pomatias elegans* (Müller)	2	
	Cochlicopa sp	2	
	Pupilla muscorum (L.)	5	
	Vallonia costata	1	
	Cepaea nemoralis (L.)	3	one pink-banded 00300, one pink 00300S (spread-banded), one yellow 00000 – periostracum still attached – modern
	Context: NW quadrant, bank make-up, 11.		
4	*Cepaea nemoralis* (L.)	2	both pink 00300, with periostracum – modern
	Helicella virgata (da Costa)	3	modern
	Helicella itala (L.)	12	
	Context: NW quadrant, ditch, 7.		
5	*Cepaea nemoralis* (L.)	1	pink 00300, no periostracum but very well preserved
	Context: NW quadrant, ditch, 7.		

	Mollusc	Number Preserved	Comment
6	*Pomatias elegans* (Müller) Context: NW quadrant, ditch, 8.	1	
7	*Ostrea edulis* (L.) Context: NW quadrant, bank,	1	fragment, common oyster topsoil.(?Romano-British : NT)
8	*Pomatias elegans* (Müller) *Vertigo pygmaea* (Draparnaud) *Pupilla muscorum* (L.) *Vallonia costata* (Müller) *Cepaea nemoralis* (L.) *Helicella virgata* (da Costa) *Helicella itala* (L.) Context: NW quadrant, ditch, 7.	1 1 2 1 1 4 14+	00300, mid-banded modern
9	*Pomatias elegans* (Müller) Context: NW quadrant, ditch, 7.	1	
10	*Helicella itala* (L.) Context: NW quadrant, ditch, 7.	1	
11	*Pupilla muscorum* (L.) *Cepaea nemoralis* (L.) Context: NW quadrant, ditch, 7.	1 2	yellow 00000, both
12	*Cepaea nemoralis* (L.) Context: NW quadrant, ditch, 3.	1	00000, probably yellow; inside of shell with full gloss
13	*Helicella itala* (L.) Context: NW quadrant, ditch, 3.	1	
14	*Helicella itala* (L.) Context: NW quadrant, ditch floor, 1.	2	
15	*Cepaea nemoralis* (L.) Context: NW quadrant, ditch, 3.	1	yellow 00000
16	*Pomatias elegans* (Müller) Context: SW quadrant, bank, 11.		
17	*Cepaea nemoralis* (L.) *Helicella virgata* (da Costa) *Helicella itala* (L.) Context: SW quadrant, ditch, 6.	3 4 4	one 00000, not yellow, one 00300, one 00300S, perhaps pink modern
18	*Cepaea nemoralis* (L.) Context: SW quadrant, ditch, 7.	1	poorly preserved, markings uncertain
19	*Pomatias elegans* (Müller) Context: SW quadrant, bank, 11.	2	
20	*Helicella virgata* (da Costa) Context: SW quadrant, bank, 11.	1	modern
21	*Pomatias elegans* (Müller) *Cepaea nemoralis* (L.) *Helicella itala* (L.) Context: SW quadrant, bank, 11.	1 1 1	poorly preserved
22	*Pomatias elegans* (Müller) *Pupilla muscorum* (L.) *Clausilia bidentata* (Ström) *Cepaea hortensis* (Müller) *Cepaea nemoralis* (L.) *Helicella virgata* (da Costa) *Helicella itala* (L.) Context: SW quadrant, bank, 11.	13+ 2 1 3 5 4 21	all five-banded – 1 (23) (45); 1 (23)45; 12345 one pink 00000 with periostracum, modern, two are 00000, ancient; one is 00300, one is 00300S modern

	Mollusc	*Number Preserved*	*Comment*
23	*Pomatias elegans* (Müller)	2	
	Vallonia sp (probably *costata*)	1	
	Cepaea hortensis (Müller)	1	five-banded 1(23)45
	Cepaea nemoralis (L.)	1	00300
	Context: SW quadrant, bank, 11.		
24	*Pomatias elegans* (Müller)	5	
	Cochlicopa sp	1	
	Pupilla muscorum	1	
	Vallonia costata (Müller)	1	
	Vallonia excentrica Sterki	1	
	Cepaea hortensis (Müller)	1	12345
	Cepaea nemoralis (L.)	5	one ?00000, badly preserved; one is ?yellow 00000; two are 00000; one is 00300S
	Helicella itala (L.)	3	
	Retinella radiatula (Alder)	2	
	Context: SE quadrant, central area, topsoil.		
25	*Cepaea nemoralis* (L.)	1	five-banded (1234)5
	Helicella itala (L.)	1	
	Context: SW quadrant, eccentric mound, base of Robbing 3.		
26	*Cepaea hortensis* (Müller)	1	five-banded 1(2345)
	Context: SE quadrant, eccentric mound, base of Robbing 1.		
27	*Pomatias elegans* (Müller)	31+	
	Helicella itala (L.)	2	
	Discus rotundatus (Müller)	1	
	Context: eccentric mound, base of Robbing 3, with Cremation 3.		
28	*Vertigo pygmaea* (Draparnaud)	1	
	Pupilla muscorum (L.)	17	
	Vallonia costata (Müller)	2	
	Vallonia excentrica Sterki	3	
	Context: SW quadrant, central area, pit, 14.		

Site III

29	*Pomatias elegans* (Müller)	3	
	Pupilla muscorum (L.)	1	
	Cepaea nemoralis (L.)	3	one is heavy spread-banded S, probably 00300S; two are 00000, one perhaps pink
	Helicella virgata (da Costa)	2	modern
	Helicella itala (L.)	2	
	Context: base of topsoil.		
30	*Pomatias elegans* (Müller)	3	
	Helicella itala (L.)	26	
	Context: S quadrant, Secondary Burial 2.		
31	*Pomatias elegans* (Müller)	2	
	Cepaea nemoralis (L.)	1	00000
	Helicella itala (L.)	3	
	Context: N quadrant, core of mound, 11.		
32	*Vallonia costata* (Müller)	1	
	Cepaea nemoralis (L.)	1	00000, probably yellow
	Helicella virgata (da Costa)	1	modern
	Helicella itala (L.)	2	
	Context: S quadrant, berm, 7.		
33	*Pomatias elegans* (Müller)	3	
	Cepaea hortensis (Müller)	1	1(234)5
	Helicella itala (L.)	1	
	Context: S quadrant, area of cremation pyre, base of 10.		

Mollusc	Number Preserved	Comment
34	*Helicigona lapicida* (L.)	2	

Also two protoconchs (embryonic shells), not identified.
Context: S quadrant, berm, 7.

| 35 | *Pomatias elegans* (Müller) | 1 | |

Context: S quadrant, floor of ditch.

| 36 | *Ostrea edulis* (L.) | 1 | fragment |

Context: S quadrant, Secondary Burial 2.

37	*Pomatias elegans* (Müller)	15	
	Carychium sp	2	
	Cochlicopa sp	5	
	Pupilla muscorum (L.)	6	
	Vallonia costata (Müller)	4	
	Vallonia excentrica Sterki	4	
	Cepaea hortensis (Müller)	1	1(23)45
	Cepaea nemoralis (L.)	1	00000 perhaps yellow
	Helicella itala (L.)	31	
	Discus rotundatus (Müller)	1	

Context: Mound, area of cremation pyre, base of 10.

| 38 | *Pomatias elegans* (Müller) | 1 | |

Context: W quadrant, mound, base of 10.

| 39 | *Pomatias elegans* (Müller) | 1 | |
| | *Helicella itala* (L.) | 7 | |

Context: S quadrant, Secondary Burial 1, in urn.

| 40 | *Pomatias elegans* (Müller) | 20 | |

Context: S quadrant, Secondary Burial 2, in largest urn.

Site XI

41	*Pomatias elegans* (Müller)	9+	
	Cepaea hortensis (Müller)	4	three are 12345; one is 10345
	Cepaea nemoralis (L.)	7	all unbanded 00000
	Cepaea sp juvenile	1	00000

Context: NW quadrant, mound, 5.

| 42 | *Cepaea nemoralis* (L.) | 2 | both probably yellow, |

Context: SE quadrant, on chalk bedrock.   one 00000, one 00300

Site XV

| 43 | *Pomatias elegans* (Müller) | 3 | |
| | *Cepaea nemoralis* (L.) | 1 | 00000 |

Context: NE quadrant, in primary cremation pit.

44	*Pomatias elegans* (Müller)	3	
	Vallonia costata (Müller)	1	
	Helicella itala (L.)	1	

Context: SE quadrant, base of topsoil.

Site XVII

45	*Pomatias elegans* (Müller)	36	
	Carichium sp	1	
	Vallonia costata (Müller)	1	
	Cepaea nemoralis (L.)	1	pink 00000
	Helicella itala (L.)	2	

Context: base of mound, in central burial pit.

Site XX

	Mollusc	Number Preserved	Comment
46	*Pomatias elegans* (Müller)	2	
	Cepaea nemoralis (L.)	1	yellow 00300, no periostracum but very well preserved
	Helicella itala (L.)	5	
	Retinella radiatula (Alder)	1	

Context: ditch, section 8, 23.

Table 32 Contents of snail samples

Species	Unquestioned Samples	Probably Good	Certainly Recent, Modern or Suspect
Pomatias elegans	109	7	33
Carychium sp	3	–	–
Cochlicopa sp	5	-	3
Vertigo pygmaea	–	1	1
Pupilla muscorum	7	17	11
Vallonia costata	5	2	6
Vallonia excentrica	4	3	1
Clausilia bidentata	–	–	1
Helicigona lapicida	–	–	2
Cepaea hortensis	7	1	5
	all five-banded	five-banded	all five-banded
Cepaea nemoralis	16	4	24
	1 badly preserved	2 00000	2 badly preserved
	14 00000	2 00300	9 00000
	1 five-banded, might be S		8 00300
			5 00300S (1 might be 12345S)
Helicella virgata	–	–	19
Helicella itala	78	9	52
Discus rotundatus	2	–	–
Retinella radiatula	–	1	2
Ostrea edulis	1	–	1

COMMENTS

Of the samples reported above, the following are suspect because either they contain obviously modern snails, or they have *Helicella virgata* which is not yet reliably reported before about 1200 AD (M P Kerney, pers comm), or they are at the same depth in the same formation as some of these:

3, 4, 5, 7, 8, 16, 17, 19, 20, 21, 22, 23, 24, 29, 32, 34. 44 is presumably also shallow.

From the data given with the samples, there seems no reason to doubt the dating of the snails in the following samples, either because of the given depth at which they were found or because (where depth is not stated) of their associations (eg 'in urn'):

1, 2, 6, 9, 10, 11, 12, 13, 14, 15, 18, 25, 26, 27, 28, 30, 31, 33, 35, 36, 37, 38, 39, 40, 41, 42, 43, 45, 46.

The contents of the samples are given, the samples being grouped as above, in Table 32.

Of the above species, *Carychium, Cochlicopa, Vertigo pygmaea, Clausilia bidentata*, the two species of *Cepaea, Discus rotundatus* and *Retinella radiatula* are very widespread. (The morphs of *Cepaea nemoralis* are discussed later.) All the others are characteristic of definitely dry and highly calcareous ground, and *Pupilla muscorum, Vallonia costata* and *excentrica*, and *Helicella itala* and *virgata* in addition are indicators of very open grassy country. If all the unquestioned samples are of barrow age, then it can be said definitely that the vegetation on Snail Down then was very similar to what is there now, though the occurrence of a little scattered hawthorn or juniper scrub cannot be ruled out. There is a very noticeable absence of several species which are widespread at the present day but on the downs seem to prefer fairly lush vegetation such as long grass and weeds and so are often associated with cultivation or human disturbance at least, eg *Hygromia striolata* and *hispida*,

Table 33   Wood species represented by charcoal from barrow contexts

	Corylus	*Fraxinus*	Pomoideae	*Prunus*	*Quercus*
Site I Disc-barrow					
Cremation 1, primary	–	–	–	–	+
Cremation 3	–	–	–	–	+
Cremation 4	–	–	–	–	+
Sweepings pit	–	–	–	+	–
Floor of ditch surrounding barrow	–	–	–	–	+
Site II Saucer-barrow					
Eccentric pit, cremation 6	–	+	–	+	+
Site III Bell-barrow					
Secondary Burial 1 (Cremation 8), urn contents	–	–	+	+	+
Floor of ditch	–	+	–	–	–
Funeral pyre (Fig 12 for location of lettered logs)	–	–	–	–	log 1(A)
Funeral pyre	–	–	–	–	log 1a(B)
Funeral pyre	–	–	–	–	log 1b(C)
Funeral pyre	–	log 2(L)	–	–	–
Funeral pyre	–	–	–	log 3(M)	–
Funeral pyre	–	–	–	–	log 4(J)
Funeral pyre	–	–	–	log 5(K)	–
Funeral pyre	–	–	–	–	log 6(E)
Funeral pyre	–	–	–	–	log 7(D)
Funeral pyre	–	–	–	–	log 8(F–H)
Site XIV Scraped-up bowl-barrow					
Primary cremation pit	–	–	+	–	+
Site XVII Bowl-barrow					
Primary cremation pit	–	+	–	+	–
Pit A, SW quadrant	–	+	–	+	–
Pit C	–	–	–	+	–
Site XIX Double bell-barrow					
Core of main mound	–	–	–	–	+

T THE SNAIL DOWN RADIOCARBON DATES

PAUL ASHBEE, WITH ALEX BAYLISS

Eleven radiocarbon dates, produced by the National Physics Laboratory, AERE Harwell (through A J Walker), the University of Oxford Radiocarbon Accelerator Unit (through R A Housley), and the Scottish Universities Research and Reactor Centre (through G T Cook), were obtained from charcoal fragments (Table 34) and human bones from seven of the barrows. The results are summarised in the following tables.

Table 34	Snail Down: charcoal species used for radiocarbon dates			
Barrow	*Laboratory Code No*	*Species*	*Weight in grams*	*Comments*
II	GU-5301	*Corylus sp.*	1.1	Off-centre burial
		Pomoideae	2.8	
		Quercus sp.	7.2	
		Total	11.1	
III	NPL-141 NPL-S61 NPL-S13	*Quercus* sp.		Funeral pyre associated with central burial
	GU-5302	Pomoideae	0.1	Burial on berm of barrow
		Prunus avium/padus type	0.1	
		Quercus sp.	1.5	
		Unidentified charcoal	4.4	
		Total	6.1	
XIV	OxA-4178	*Fraxinus* sp.	1.9	Insufficient for conventional dating. *Fraxinus* (young wood) *c* 0.02g sent for accelerator dating
		Quercus sp.	0.1	
		Total	2.0	
XVII	GU-5303	*Corylus* sp.	7.7	Central burial
		Pomoideae	2.3	
		Prunus avium/padus type	1.5	
		Total	11.5	
	OxA-4179	*Corylus sp.*	0.1	Peripheral deposit. Insufficient for conventional accelerator dating. Pomoideae *c* 0.07g sent for dating.
		Pomoideae	2.2	
		Unidentified charcoal	1.2	
		Total	3.5	
XIX	GU-5304	*Quercus* sp.	9.2	Near base of mound

Table 35 Snail Down: radiocarbon dates

Barrow	Sample location	Laboratory code No	Radiocarbon Age BP
II	Eccentric burial pit	GU-5301	5690 ± 90
III	Central pyre	NPL-141	3490 ± 90
		HAR-61	3540 ± 140
		HAR-13	3500 ± 110
	Secondary Burial 1	GU-5302	3440 ± 90
XIV	Burial pit beneath barrow	OxA-4178	3555 ± 75
XV	Secondary inhumation burial	GU-5305	2920 ± 70
XVII	Central burial pit	GU-5303	5310 ± 70
	Peripheral pit	OxA-4179	3480 ± 70
XIX	Within larger mound of double bell-barrow	GU-5304	3330 ± 80
XXII	Peripheral secondary inhumation on berm of bell-barrow	OxA-4211	3485 ± 110

The dates have been calibrated following the Trondheim Convention (Mook 1986; Pearson and Stuiver 1986, 839–862; Pearson, Pilcher *et al* 1986) and their age ranges at one (1) sigma and two (2) sigma are tabled in Table 36 together with the probability distributions of these dates.

Apart from the two anomalous results (Site II, GU-5301; Site XVII, GU-5303), and that from Site XV (GU-5305), the dates in radiometric years (BP) cannot be statistically separated (Ward and Wilson 1978). Indeed, there is no evidence that they do not simply reproduce determinations of the same chronological event. Thus it could be contended that the separation in time of those barrows from which samples were taken would be impracticable, if not impossible. Despite this stricture, certain tendencies emerge. Thus Site III could, in general terms, be a little later than Site XIV; Site XIX, the double bell-barrow, might have been raised subsequent to the establishment of Site XXII, the adjacent single bell-barrow. In general terms, these inherent possibilities might be seen as following observed trends (Piggott 1973, 374–375; Coles and Harding 1979, 267–268; Ashbee 1981, 32; *ibid* 1985, 83–84; *ibid* 1986, 85). Nonetheless, it should not be overlooked that Site XIV had beneath it an all-but unfurnished cremation burial and that Sites XIX and XXII are both bell-barrows. Here at Snail Down, however, any radiocarbon dates which might give a generalised Beaker horizon, which the Wessex phenomenon, distinguished by its specialised barrows, overlaps and succeeds, are absent. This observation of possible tendencies is therefore tentative at best.

Despite the difficulties inherent in determining a sequence of barrow line and cluster development, the general date that emerges, of the order of *c* 1800 cal BC, is of considerable importance. This is because it has recently been shown by RCHME that some of the barrows may have been sited in association with ancient fields (Fig 2). Such has for long been suspected (Bowen 1961, 30), and was deemed possible on Snail Down because of the contiguity of barrows to boundary ditches observable on classic aerial photographs (Pl 1). It has also been established at Amesbury (Ashbee 1985, 84, fig 44). The Amesbury barrows overlying ancient fields were not, however, those

from which radiocarbon dates were obtained, although their nature and siting is not in question. As a result of the Snail Down dates it is possible to say that established field systems were probably in being before 1800–1900 BC.

One date, 1875–1440 cal BC (GU-5304 3330 ± 80 BP) is of particular interest in that it pertains to the larger mound of a double bell-barrow, Site XIX. It is from charcoal (*Quercus* sp.) found among ancient turves and topsoil some four feet below its crown. This earthen core, originally enveloped by chalk from the ditch, had been broken away by the passage of armoured vehicles when the barrows were a military training area. Clearly the implication of such a single date must be treated with reserve and extended argument should not be based upon it. Single radiocarbon dates from barrows and cairns are still the rule, however, and comparisons must be made. Charcoal fragments (*Acer* sp.) were incorporated, with occupation earth, into the loam core of the Amesbury G58 bell-barrow (Ashbee 1985, 43) and their assay yielded the radiocarbon date 1870–1420 cal BC (HAR-6226 3310 ± 80 BP). Snail Down Site XIX's calibrated age ranges (GU-5304 3330 ± 80 BP) at 1 sigma are BC 1737–1521 and at 2 sigma BC 1875–1440. For Amesbury Barrow G58 (HAR-6226 3310 ± 80 BP), the calibrated age ranges are at 1 sigma BC 1760–1575 and at 2 sigma BC 1860–1495. With barrow construction and incorporations in mind, loam core samples of charcoal from Milton Lilbourne (Ashbee 1986) Barrows 2 and 4, also bell-barrows, were dated. The two samples from Barrow 2 are HAR-6456 3420 ± 80 BP, 1940–1520 cal BC and HAR-6472 3590 ± 80 BP, 2200–1740 cal BC and that from Barrow 4 is HAR-6455 3380 ± 80 BP, 1890–1510 cal BC. They cannot be satisfactorily separated from either the Amesbury G58 date or that from Snail Down Site XIX in terms of radiocarbon results (Ward and Wilson 1978), although, in general terms, it is quite likely that Barrow 2 at Milton Lilbourne is earlier than Snail Down XIX (76% confidence) and Amesbury G58 (81% confidence).

Structures beneath barrows are of importance for dating, as it is far from clear whether the raising of a barrow was a continual process or one where the stages were separated by perhaps lengthy periods of time. Snail Down Site III is significant in this respect, in that dates

Table 36   Snail Down radiocarbon dates: calibrated age ranges

Barrow

II   *GU-5301   5690 ± 90 BP*
          Calibrated Age Ranges
          1σ cal BC 4715–4460
          2σ cal BC 4780–4350

III   *NPL-141   3490 ± 90 BP*
          Calibrated Age Ranges
          1σ cal BC 1935–1695
          2σ cal BC 2115–1610
          HAR-61   3540 ± 140 BP
          Calibrated Age Ranges
          1σ cal BC 2125–1695
          2σ cal BC 2290–1520
          HAR-13   3500 ± 110 BP
          Calibrated Age Ranges
          1σ cal BC 2010–1690
          2σ cal BC 2140–1530
          GU-5302   3440 ± 90 BP
          Calibrated Age Ranges
          1σ cal BC 1886–1673
          2σ cal BC 2020–1520

XIV   *OxA-4178   3555 ± 75 BP*
          Calibrated Age Ranges
          1σ cal BC 2028–1777
          2σ cal BC 2135–1699

XV   *GU-5305   2920 ± 70BP*
          Calibrated Age Ranges
          1σ cal BC 1261–1008
          2σ cal BC 1383–920

XVII   *GU-5303   5310 ± 70 BP*
          Calibrated Age Ranges
          1σ cal BC 4241–4007
          2σ cal BC 4340–3990
          OxA-4179   3480 ± 70 BP
          Calibrated Age Ranges
          1σ cal BC 1896–1705
          2σ cal BC 2020–1640

XIX   *GU-5304   3330 ± 80 BP*
          Calibrated Age Ranges
          1σ cal BC 1737–1521
          2σ cal BC 1875–1440

XXII   *OxA-4211   3485 ± 110 BP*
          Calibrated Age Ranges
          1σ cal BC 1950–1680
          2σ cal BC 2134–1520

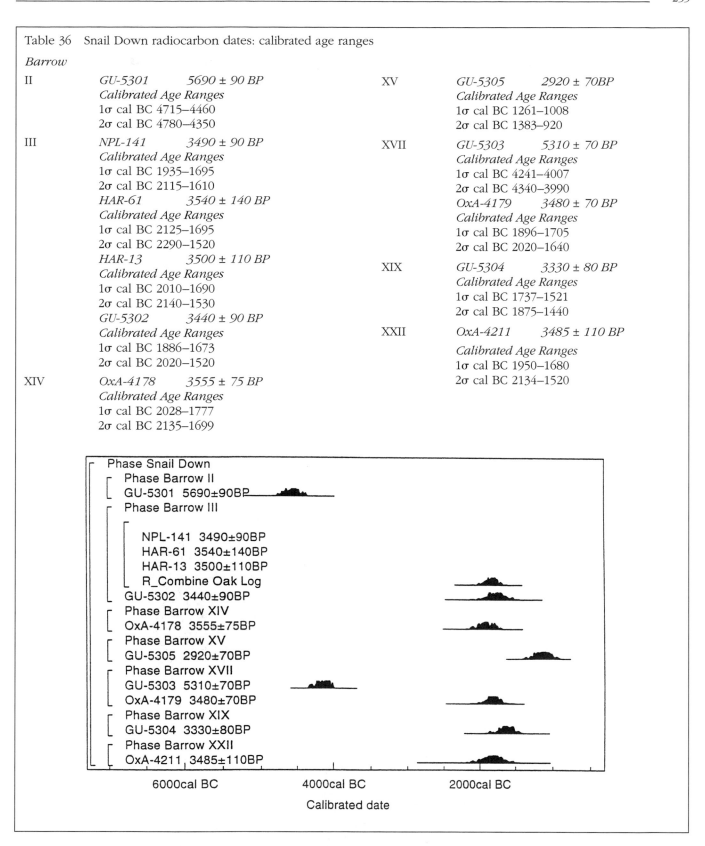

were obtained for the remains of a pyre beneath the mound, which can be compared with one from charcoal accompanying a secondary cremation in a pit beneath a flint cairn, on its berm. Between 1967 and 1972, three radiocarbon dates, one produced by the National Physical Laboratory, Teddington and two at AERE Harwell, were obtained from charcoal taken from the primary pyre or burned structure. This charcoal (*Quercus* sp.) yielded the date NPL-141 3490 ± 90 BP and confirmatory dates, HAR-61 3540 ± 140 BP and HAR-13 3500 ± 110 BP. If these be considered as a single date, it can usefully be compared with the date GU-5302 3440 ± 90 BP obtained from charcoal, which was an amalgam of species from the burial on the berm. Whereas it is customary and convenient to consider such dates in terms of their central value rather than their error terms, it would be dangerous to claim a dating difference, although it is not unreasonable to suppose that a peripheral interment is in succession to one at the centre of a given barrow. In more general terms, like other aspects of Snail Down's dates, they are commensurate with the Amesbury (Ashbee 1985, 83) and Milton Lilbourne (Ashbee 1986, 81) series.

Bone samples were assayed from two of the burials, those beneath Sites XV and XXII. The first, a skeleton in general articulation, despite some displacement by rabbits (Pl 40), was thought to be of Romano-British or even Anglo-Saxon date (see further below). In contrast, the second, a contracted male skeleton (Pl 57) associated with beads, found added to a small mound on the berm of this substantial bell-barrow, yielded the date 2140–1520 cal BC (OxA-4211; 3485 ± 110 BP). This accelerated date from a rib-bone is in harmony with the general pattern emerging from Snail Down's charcoals, which reflects care in excavation and lengthy protection in Wiltshire Heritage Museum. Besides the nature of this date and its application to archaeological considerations, it is perhaps the earliest for a palaeopathological condition, an haemangeomatic tumor (Section A).

As well as providing insights into barrow groups, structure, pre-raising usages and interments, the Snail Down dates allow some far-reaching inferences regarding the patterns of earlier Bronze Age artefacts and their relative inter-relationships. As is sometimes the case when handling a muster of radiocarbon dates from a given archaeological context, anomalies become apparent. Thus for Snail Down Site II, the assay of charcoal from the occupation debris associated with the cremation burial of a youthful person, which included Food Vessel sherds (D7, Fig 44), the surprising result GU-5301 5690 ± 90 BP emerged. Food Vessels, in general terms, are coeval with late Beakers and thus a date of the order of c 2000 cal BC might have been expected. This anomalous date, 4780–4350 cal BC, is more appropriate to the earliest Neolithic or even later Mesolithic phenomena. When inconsistent dates emerge, and let it be said that laboratories are sensitive to the problems that they pose and are greatly concerned by them, an explanation, although not always convincing, may lie in the possible re-use of pieces of already very ancient timber. The sample GU-5301 had been processed in 1993 during the 3rd International Readiocarbon Intercomparison (Scott *et al* 1998) which showed the Scottish Universities Research and Reactor Centre to be consistent with the consensus. It was, for its greater part, oak (*Quercus* sp.) which has a long life-span, is durable and, because it is laborious to work, subject to re-use. However, two millennia have to be accounted for, and, although there is evidence for possible survivals (Ashbee *et al* 1989, 71), the inconsistency cannot be realistically explained by this alone. Similar difficulties surround the dates from the central and peripheral burials of Site XVII, both of which were accompanied by substantial pieces of Collared Urns. The Collared Urn tradition appears to have obtained between 2200 and 1300 cal BC, although survivals may be more numerous than is generally allowed (Longworth 1984, 79); the date of 2030–1630 cal BC (OxA-4179, 3480 ± 70 BP), obtained from charcoal, mostly Pomoideae, in a peripheral pit,

together with the packed-in sherds of an incomplete collared Accessory Vessel (D22, Fig 47), would be comfortably within these limits. On the other hand, charcoal, largely *Corylus* sp. from the central interment of cremated bones yielded and, again, a broken Collared Urn (D23, Fig 47), yielded the date of 4350–3990 cal BC (GU-5303 5310 ± 70 BP). Hazel (*Corylus* sp.) is usually thought of as a bush but in wildwood conditions it can be a canopy tree (Rackham 1976, 68). Thus, like the oak from Site II, the charcoal could also have been from ancient timber.

Although these exceptionally early radiocarbon dates from Sites II and XVII at Snail Down appear as anomalous, there are two factors regarding them that should be borne in mind. First, the burial of occupation debris with Food Vessel sherds, and the interment of cremated bones with the smashed Collared Urn, could be considered as continuations of an aspect of depositional practices from earlier Neolithic times (Ashbee 1986, 73; Thomas 1991, 56–78; Case 1992, 425). Secondly, there are early radiocarbon dates from not dissimilar contexts. Two good examples are the charcoal from the primary fill of a ring-ditch at Roxton, in Bedfordshire (Taylor and Woodward 1985) 7010–6170 cal BC (HAR-998) and the oak charcoal from the 'fire-trench' beneath the Ystrad-Hynod, Powys, cairn (Ap Simon 1974) 4660–4160 cal BC (NPL-242 5530 ± 95 BP). An even earlier date 7290–6720 cal BC (HAR-645 8100 ± 70 BP) was obtained from charcoal in a peripheral pit beneath the turf mound of Barrow 1 at Harting, in Sussex (Drewett 1976, 129, Figs 3, 4) which, on account of flintwork close by, was considered as from Mesolithic activity. In the light of the seemingly continued depositional usages and Snail Down's two exceptionally early radiocarbon dates, it is apposite to consider whether or not groups and lines of barrows and cairns were sited in specific locations which were marked by much earlier usages and that, for particular reasons, ancient remnants were incorporated ?

Three of Snail Down's barrows (III, XIX, XXII) have, from their various interments, produced grave furniture appropriate to the Wessex earlier Bronze Age phenomenon (Piggott 1938), and although distant from the classic nexus of the series, which is still lacking direct dates (Piggott 1971, 55), are of great value in that they provide further dates for specific combinations. These grave groups consist of two categories: two furnished with beads (XXII and III) and one (Site XIX) with an ogival dagger, a decorated double ring-headed pin and an Accessory Cup, now lost, which accompanied a cremation in a monoxylous timber coffin, disinterred in 1806 (Section M).

The date of 2590–1980 cal BC (OxA-4211 3485 ± 110 BP), obtained from a rib-bone, for the amber beads and perforated cockle-shell (Section K) which furnished the peripheral contracted inhumation burial on the berm of Barrow XXII, a bell-barrow with added small mound, can be compared with the date 2280–1740 cal BC (HAR-1237 3620 ± 90 BP) from *Quercus* sp. charcoal from the burnt area beneath Amesbury Barrow G39. Here the grave furniture, removed in c 1808 (Hoare 1812, 159; Ashbee 1981), comprised amber and jet beads together with a V-perforated jet button. These buttons are normally found in later-phase Beaker contexts (Piggott 1963, 78; Clarke 1970, II, 448) which also embrace the fusiform jet beads. This

Snail Down date is clearly separable from that of the not dissimilar Amesbury G39 assemblage (HAR-1237, probably after OXA-4211, 94% certain). However, with the contracted burial, in Beaker mode, in mind, it could be seen as the continuum of a particular style of burial.

A cremation burial in the berm of the bell-barrow site III was furnished also with beads of amber and jet, together with faience (Section K). In this instance it is important to observe that this faience bead was of the glassy kind, so far met with as furnishing the secondary burial in the Mound of the Hostages, at Tara, in Ireland (O'Riordain 1956). The date 2030–1520 cal BC from associated charcoal, GU-5302 3440 ± 90 BP, can be compared with that from Milton Lilbourne 1, the disc-barrow where charcoal from the SE grave, examined by Thurnam during the nineteenth century (Ashbee 1986, 35), yielded the date 2030–1440 cal BC (HAR-6471 3400 ± 110 BP). Disc-barrows have for long been considered as containing female interments (Grinsell 1958, 101) and faience beads of the segmented tubular type come almost wholly from cremation graves mostly in such barrows (Piggott 1973, 366). Indeed, this Snail Down Barrow III date would not be out of place in the Milton Lilbourne series – the nine dates from disc-, bell- and bowl- barrows – even when consolidated and combined with those from Amesbury (Ashbee 1986, 84). Furthermore, it could accord with dates obtained from various aspects of barrows and cairns in distant parts of Britain, notably those for a cairn group on Shaugh Moor, Dartmoor (Smith and Wainwright 1978, 446; Wainwright *et al* 1979, 24). Charcoal from a central pit, with faience beads, below ring-cairn 2 yielded the date 2020–1520 cal BC (HAR-2220 3430 ± 90 BP). Also to be taken into consideration are the following, mostly Food Vessel and Collared Urn, dates: Harland Edge, Beeley Moor, Derbyshire (Riley 1967), where charcoal with a Food Vessel beneath a cairn gave 2190–1420 cal BC (BM-178 3440 ± 150 BP); Eriswell, in Suffolk (Dymond 1966; *ibid* 1974), where charcoal from an ancient surface dated a Collared Urn to 2140–1510 cal BC (BM-315 3470 ± 115 BP); Easington, in Yorkshire (Baker *et al* 1971), where large timbers, beneath the wash of a mound, with Beaker associations, emerged as 2030–1520 cal BC (BM-269 3450 ± 90 BP); Brenig, in Denbighshire (Lynch 1993), where a carbonised plank from a ? mortuary house proved to be 1940–1520 cal BC (HAR-799 3420 ± 80 BP); Ascot, in Buckinghamshire (Bradley and Keith-Lucas 1975), where charcoal from the surface of an ancient pre-barrow soil gave 1930–1530 cal BC (HAR-478 3430 ± 70 BP); Tallington, in Lincolnshire (Simpson 1976), where bone from a coffin burial, with a Food Vessel, was 2190–1320 cal BC (UB-450 3410 ± 165 BP); and Cow Common (Swell 8), in Gloucestershire (Saville 1979), where the oak (*Quercus* sp.) charcoal around a cremation pit proved to be 1950–1520 cal BC (HAR-1325 3430 ± 80 BP). In the light of this broad and not inconsistent pattern, it could be contended that the bead-furnished burial in the berm of Snail Down Barrow III is early in its series and that, by implication, the bell-barrow must precede it.

Snail Down's richly furnished monoxylous timber coffin burial beneath the larger mound of XIX, the double bell-barrow, has a general counterpart in the monoxylous timber coffin burial containing a cremation with an attendant Accessory Cup beneath Barrow 4, one of the larger

Milton Lilbourne bell-barrows (Ashbee 1986, 41–52, figs 20, 21, 22, 23, 25). From the loam core of the barrow as well as the charcoal spread and a baulk of timber which guarded the south end of the coffin, five radiocarbon dates were obtained: HAR-6455, 3380 ± 80; HAR-6453, 3580 ± 80; HAR-6454, 3780 ± 80 BP; HAR-6457, 3590 ± 90 BP; and HAR-6458, 3460 ± 80 (Haddon-Reece in Ashbee *ibid*, 81–84). Their average, of the order of 3490 ± 60 BP (2120–1680 cal BC), makes this example clearly older than the loam core of Snail Down Barrow XIX, which was 1880–1430 cal BC (GU-5304 3330 ± 80 BP). On the other hand, moving out from Wiltshire to the few dates that we have for ogival dagger graves which have been styled *Camerton-Snowshill* and latterly *Aldbourne-Edmondsham* (Burgess 1980, 104, fig 3.6), this date has easier, although perhaps not entirely satisfactory, bed-fellows. The dagger-grave dates are Earl's Barton, Northamptonshire, 1520–1320 cal BC (BM-680 3169 ± 51 BP) and 1670–1390 cal BC (BM-681 3214 ± 64 BP); Edmondsham, Dorset, 1440–1220 cal BC (BM-708 3069 ± 45 BP) and 1940–1682 cal BC (BM-709 3477 ± 52 BP); and Hove, Sussex, 1600–1400 cal BC (BM-682 3189 ± 46 BP). When considering such a pattern it should not be overlooked that by this time the great henges of Wessex were either established or in the process of modification (Ashbee 1986, 84).

Besides the insights into the temporal qualities of the barrows, their arrangements and deposits, the Snail Down radiocarbon dates are a valuable addition to our understanding of the sequential nature of the Wessex phenomenon. Any appreciation of this must be provisional because there are no direct radiocarbon dates for the burials from Colt Hoare's excavations which were the basis of the seminal study (Piggott 1938). As has been stressed (Ashbee *ibid*), most relevant dates have been from outside the geographical focus; assessments of time-scales are from extrapolation. Before radiocarbon dates became available, indeed almost at the outset of its study, the Wessex phenomenon was divided into two phases, based upon a clear separation of the daggers (ApSimon 1954). Thus the *Bush Barrow* (Wessex I) daggers and their associations belong to that part of our earlier Bronze Age which corresponds with Reinecke's A1 division, while the *Camerton-Snowshill* (Wessex II) ogival daggers, pins, and other artefacts are later because they correspond to Reinecke's A2/B1 division. Although, in typological terms, these associations still hold good, it is contended that during the *Bush Barrow* phase the connections were with Brittany, while, in *Camerton-Snowshill* times, there were close links with Central Europe (Gerloff 1975, 70–128).

In general terms, Wessex aggrandisement began during the currency of later Beakers and Food Vessels and the seemingly short-lived *Bush Barrow* phase followed. Its funerary sheet gold could have been produced by no more than two goldsmiths with a span of half-a-century (Coles and Taylor 1971). This, however, need mean no more than a brief time-span for deposition and it could have been only an incident within a wider phase. The dates, cited above, from the charcoal close by the Earl's Barton, Northamptonshire, *Camerton-Snowshill* dagger were, when calibrated, expected to indicate the end of the Wessex episode (McKerrell 1972, 296). Further dates, also cited above, for such daggers, have since emerged and they appear to cluster within the limited period *c*

1550–1200 cal BC. Although the span of the *Bush Barrow* phase is nebulous, estimates can be made. In the light of the single date from Amesbury Barrow G39, the suggested dates that have emerged for the initial *Bush Barrow* phase are *c* 2100–1700 cal BC, some 400 years, and for the *Camerton-Snowshill* sequence *c* 1700–1400 cal BC, a further 250 years (Burgess 1980, 98–111). With this limited cluster of dagger dates, the later phase could be envisaged as extending to embrace the later Wilsford shaft sinking (Ashbee *et al* 1989, 68–71). All in all, it may emerge that the definition of what we term *Wessex* grave furniture may have continued for a longer time than has been allowed (Ashbee 1981, 32).

Snail Down's bell- and disc-barrows, recognised as an integral part of the Wessex phenomenon from the outset (Piggott 1938, 90), together with the grave furniture enumerated above, accord well with the tentative chronological considerations that have been outlined. Apart from that from Site XIX, which augments the list of *Camerton-Snowshill* dagger dates, the remainder cluster about 1800 cal BC, which is appropriate to the initial *Bush Barrow* phase. This, as has been indicated, overlaps with later Beakers, Food Vessels and Collared Urns, these last being a feature of certain Wessex assemblages (Piggott 1938, 90, fig 21). It will be remembered that Collared Urns were found in Site XVII. By and large, these Snail Down dates, although comparable with those from Amesbury and Milton Lilbourne (Ashbee 1985, 83; *ibid* 1986, 81) may converge more closely. This, in the light of the patterns examined above, allows the possibility that the deposition of grave furniture and the subsequent raising of barrows, seen often as a process of gradual accretion, need not have been an even process. Indeed, it could be contended that, via the radiocarbon dates, we are witness to what was a notable event in earlier Bronze Age Wessex.

Whereas, with one exception, the Snail Down radiocarbon dates have significantly augmented our appreciation of *Wessex*, in that something of the developmental sequence can be seen, the single date 1390–910 cal BC (GU-5305 2920 ± 70 BP), obtained from human bone taken from an inhumation burial beneath the crown of Site XV, stands apart. In the light of pieces of Romano-British pottery found within the rabbit-disturbed mound, and the many unfurnished intrusive inhumation burials in Wiltshire's barrows, which have for long been thought of as of that period, or Pagan Saxon, the burial was, at the time of excavation, thought of also as Romano-British. This date, however, albeit a single one, and thus statisti-cally uncertain, could call into question the nature and age of some of these subsequent burials in barrows (Grinsell 1957, 242–245; Bonney 1973, 474; Harding 1974, 113). Indeed, it has for long been tacitly recognised that, because of poor records or a lack of association, a large proportion has had to be regarded as of uncertain origin.

This general horizon, the last Bronze Age and the earliest Iron Age, is defined in Wessex, on the one hand, by the older dates 1260–900 cal BC (BM-694 2867 ± 55 BP), 1260–850 cal BC (BM-695 2854 ± 63 BP), of the reasonable spread (BM-692/699) of radiocarbon dates from the Simons Ground Deverel Rimbury cemeteries on the southern heath-lands of Dorset (White 1982, 41), and, on the other, by dates obtained from bone and antler, 1390–830 cal BC (I-5971 2875 ± 90 BP), 1420–900 cal BC (I-5973 2935 ± 90 BP), associated with early activity on the site of South Cadbury Castle, in Somerset (Barrett *et al* 2000, 370–372). Although traces of activity and settlement of the later Bronze Age in the vicinity of Stonehenge are tenuous, it could be claimed, on the grounds, for example, of the series of dates from the Wilsford Shaft (Ashbee *et al*, 1989, 70, fig 64), that there was continuing activity in the area until Iron Age times and the establishment of the chain of hill-forts around and within the area (Cunliffe 1991, 312–357, fig 14.1). Sidbury, close by Snail Down, is an example, whose crucial link with surrounding fields and boundary ditches has been established by the Reading Survey (Bradley *et al* 1994).

Barrow excavation in places distant from Wessex has unearthed inhumation burials from which radiocarbon dates, comparable with that from Snail Down's Site XV, have been obtained. Human foot bones from what was thought to be a disturbed primary inhumation burial beneath a barrow at Tallington, in Lincolnshire (Simpson 1976, 217) yielded the date 1040–540 cal BC (UB-453 2675 ± 100 BP). Bone from a secondary inhumation within a ring-ditch at Warren Farm, Wolverton, in Buckinghamshire (Green 1975), produced the date 1430–990 cal BC (HAR-341 2990 ± 80 BP).

Although a single radiocarbon date is far from con-clusive, nonetheless this particular date of 1390–910 cal BC (GU-5305 2920 ± 70 BP) for the secondary inhumation burial from Site XV, within a small associated cemetery, is of importance in that it provides a possible insight into the nature of later Bronze Age burials. Indeed, interment in barrows may have developed at this time and, eventually, complemented the various inhumation forms, many inse-curely dated, which are a feature of Iron Age southern England (Whimster 1977).

U EXCAVATION MEMENTOES LEFT BY HOARE AND CUNNINGTON

Nicholas Thomas*, with a note by Antony Gunstone

U1 **Flat copper-alloy uniface disc**, possibly of brass; edge in part rounded, in part slightly ridged. Obverse inscribed in raised letters OPENED BY W^m.CUNNINGTON 1805. Diam 31.5mm; th 2mm. DM 373. Snail Down Site II, floor of central burial pit.

U2 **George III halfpenny, 1799** (British Museum Catalogue no 1248/1251). Snail Down Site 1, eccentric tump, associated with Robbing 1.

Description by Anthony Gunstone

The coin belongs to a large issue of halfpennies and farthings struck for the Government by Matthew Boulton at the Soho Mint, Birmingham, in 1799. It was the only halfpenny in circulation for the first six years of the nineteenth century and would certainly have been readily available for use as a souvenir of an excavation.

Conscious of the need to record for posterity precisely where they had dug, Hoare and Cunnington sometimes deposited one of three types of excavation disc or plaque on the floor of their trench before filling it in. Since such trenches usually exposed a burial pit, the floor of that was where they placed their record (cf U1 above). Occasionally the act was restricted to a George III halfpenny taken from the pocket, the most suitable copper coin of the realm in circulation at that time (cf U2 above). To them, it mattered not that the date on the coin seldom coincided with the date of the excavation. One disc and one halfpenny were the yield from Snail Down 1953–1957, out of the nine barrows whose centres were excavated: of which three had not been dug into by Hoare. Post-war excavation has shown that Hoare and Cunnington were generally sparing with these often well-made tokens. 'We have left in several of them (barrows) tokens in lead and copper, stating they had been investigated' (Hoare 1829, 6).

Three types of token are known so far to have been used by Hoare and Cunnington, as Paul Robinson has explained (1976, 15–16):

1. a circular disc cast with a raised inscription like that from Snail Down II, U1. Flat, plain reverse. A specimen cleaned at Wiltshire Heritage Museum about 1954 showed the yellower colour suggestive of brass. Diameter 31.5mm; th 2–3mm.

2. a thicker, more obviously copper-coloured uniface disc with obverse slightly less in diameter than the reverse; the former inscribed OPENED BY R.C.H., deeply cast not impressed into the surface of the flan. Flat, plain reverse. Diam 32.5mm; th 3mm.

3. a square cutting from lead sheet, bearing on one side initials and date incused untidily into the surface. At least one known with a D and a C back to front. 41.5 × 41.5 or 41.5 × 41 or 42mm; 3mm thick. In *Tumuli Wiltunenses* Hoare illustrates the type as a blank (1829, 6). Presumably dates and initials were added as the need arose. The punches used appear to be common to all the lead plaques recorded to date.

So far, three different dates have been found on these various records, 1804, 1805 and 1807. The year 1805 alone appears on the first type: all three dates have been recorded on the lead plaques. Type 2 was cast with initials alone.

Apart from the full name – Wm. Cunnington – on type 1, type 2 invariably carries Hoare's initials with stops, R. C. H.; unstopped initials RCH and WC have been recorded on the lead plaques.

Together with unused examples in the Stourhead Collection at Wiltshire Heritage Museum, and at Salisbury and Bristol Museums, the following finds of discs, plaques and halfpennies have been reported over the years while excavating barrows previously dug into by Hoare and Cunnington:

*This section owes much to Dr Paul Robinson, Curator of the Wiltshire Heritage Museum. The note on the coin, V2, was kindly prepared by the late A J H Gunstone FSA, who dug at Snail Down as a schoolboy in 1955 and was the writer's friend and colleague at Birmingham Museum and Art Gallery before becoming Director, Lincolnshire Museums. The writer has in preparation a comprehensive study of these mementoes which will be published elsewhere.

Type 1

Snail Down Site II	This Section, U1; Wiltshire Heritage Museum, DZSWS: 1955.213.
Wilsford G33	E Proudfoot, pers comm; Salisbury Museum.
Wilsford cum Lake G52 and G53	Smith 1991, 11, 21 (fig 7), 23, (fig 9); two discs, Wiltshire Heritage Museum, DZSWS: 1964.12.
Wiltshire Heritage Museum	Annable and Simpson 1964, opp p 1. DZSWS: 1955.213.
Wiltshire Heritage Museum, 'found in a barrow'	Presented by the Rev^d G H Engleheart at an unknown date. DZSWS: 1992.320
Bristol Museum and Art Gallery	BRSMG 0.3672; formerly Wiltshire Heritage Museum, DZSWS: 1955.213.

Type 2

Pound Down, Bishops Cannings ?G53	Hoare 1819, 92, No 4; Thurnam 1860, 321.
Wiltshire Heritage Museum	Annable and Simpson 1964, opp p. 1; three examples, DZSWS: 1955.213.
Bristol City Museum and Art Gallery	BRSMG 0.3673; formerly DZSWS: 1955.213.
Salisbury and South Wiltshire Museum	97/1972; formerly DZSWS: 1955.213.

Type 3

Amesbury G51	
(a) OPEND/1804/WC	Cunnington 1975, pl 30; Ashbee 1978, 19, pl 8.
(b) OPEND/1805/WC	Ashbee, *ibid.* Both Wiltshire Heritage Museum, DZSWS: 1968.24.
Possibly North Down	
Group, Bishops Cannings	
G9 OPEN'D/1804/WC	Thurnam 1860, 319 and fig.
(note apostrophe)	
Another barrow in this group	
OPEND/1804/WC	*ibid*
Rolleston Down,	
Winterbourne Stoke G43	
OPEND/1804/WC	Ozanne 1972, 44. Wiltshire Heritage Museum?
Dorset: Oakley Down bowl-barrow	
OPEND/1804/WC	White and Reed 1971, 163 Priest's House Museum, Wimborne Minster (no number).
Wiltshire Heritage Museum	
(a) OPEND/1804/WC	Ashbee 1960, pl IIa; DZSWS: 1955.213.
(b) OPEND/1805/WC	Robinson 1976; DZSWS: 1955.213.
(D and C back to front)	
(c) OPEND/1807/RCH	Ashbee *ibid*; DZSWS: 1955.213.
Salisbury and South Wiltshire Museum	
OPEND/1807/RCH	96/1972, formerly DZSWS: 1955.213.

Halfpennies

Snail Down, Site I	This Section, U2.
Bishops Cannings G9 (described as a halfpenny of George III)	Thurnam 1860, 319. Now lost.
Codford Down No 5 (described by Steele as a 1799 penny)	Annable 1958, 9. ?Now lost.
Rolleston Down G43 (two halfpennies)	Ozanne 1972, 44. Wiltshire Heritage Museum?
Wilsford G1	E Proudfoot, pers comm; Salisbury Museum.
(dated 1773)	

Plate 36   Site XV, post ring in SW quadrant, looking E. Note rabbit-ridd

In 1965 (Thomas, 143, 147), the writer suggested that excavation discs were probably used only when a notable grave-group had been recovered. Deposit of a halfpenny or halfpenny trade token, or nothing at all, was the usual reaction to an unaccompanied cremation and this proposal seems to remain true, as U2 from Snail Down I confirmed. It was his belief that Matthew Boulton may have been commissioned to strike the superior disc, our type 1. This suggestion has been supported by Robinson (1976, 15), but documentary or other firm proof has yet to be established.

R H Cunnington has emphasised that, until 1804, Hoare and his collaborator William Cunnington made do with current coins, usually halfpence, from Matthew Boulton's great re-issue of coppers for the nation. Then they introduced their first dated plaques, the square, rough-and-ready inscribed sheet-lead clippings, our type 3 (R H Cunnington 1954, 221). In a letter of March 1805 Hoare reminds Cunnington to bring a good supply of 'leaden tokens' for the Woodyates (S Wilts) campaign of that year, in a specially made leather bag (*ibid* 1975, 72). Hoare himself explained it to the readers of *Ancient Wiltshire*: at Barrows 1, 2 and 4 at Fovant, '…we deposited new Bolton (*sic*) half-pennies and square pieces of lead stamped 'Opened 1804. W.C.' and in one of them a Southampton half-penny, W. Beavis' (1812, 237–238). The act of deposition often did not quite match up, in its dating, to Hoare's wholly commend-able desire to show posterity that he and Cunnington had been there already, in such-and-such a year.

During the course of our work on Snail Down, Charles Thomas persuaded a shopkeeper in Collingbourne Ducis to allow him to select fresh, appropriately dated pennies from her till, which we deposited in the burial pits of Sites I–III and in some of our cuttings across the linear ditch (Sites VI and VII) and elsewhere, leaving our mark in what was, by then, a well-established tradition.

Plate 37   Site XV, post hole 35 with packing flint (rabbit burrow below

V A STUDY OF
STRIPPED I

SALISBURY PLAIN TRAINING ARE

The existence of the stripped barrow 2249 (S
Snail Down was brought to the attention of th
secretary, A Summers, in 1983. In view of the i
increasingly rare, undisturbed chalk dow
seemed a great opportunity to study this area
detail. The previous history was confirmed by
who had seen the site during the excavatio
Thomas in 1953 and had visited it occasional
the following twenty-five years. She had obse
very slow rate of colonisation from bare chalk
covering of vegetation with bare patches. Su
enquiries recently revealed that H C Bowen
Royal Commission on the Historical Monu
England, had requested a study of the flora w
carried out by T C E Wells, of Monk
Experimental Station, in 1970. He suggested tha
be made at ten-year intervals.

The SPTA Botany group were unawar
paper, but sought advice from the Area Region
of the Nature Conservancy Council, S Lane, and
with B Gillam and members of the Botan
discussed a monitoring programme.

The subsequent scheme was based on
quadrats running E to W across the disc-barro
with two star signs on adjacent barrows. The qu
not include the ditch, which had a closed vegetat
due to silting and hence enjoyed greater hum
the bared chalk. The quadrats were marked w
corners driven into the chalk, and the mob
frames were subdivided into 25 smaller squares.

The vegetation of each quadrat was o
squared paper so that individual plants could b
exactly, or, where dense growth occurred, the

Plate 50   Site XVII, sherds of incomplete Collared Vessel D22, packed into pit A at W end of E/W baulk. Scale, inches. Looking NE. See Figure 29 (Nicholas Thomas).

Plate 51   Site XVIII, rabbit-damaged mound, section 1, looking N (Nicholas Thomas).

Plate 52   Site XVIII, E face of ditch, section 3 (Nicholas Thomas).

Plate 53   Site XIX, cuttings across mounds and intervening space, looking SE. Stake rings around mounds indicated (Nicholas Thomas),

Plate 54   Site XIX, cutting in N mound, E face. Stakes defining its edge, one in profile pushed out by pressure of mound. Smaller scale, inches/centimetres (Nicholas Thomas).

Plate 55   Site XIX, cutting across ditch NW of N mound, section 2, NE face (Nicholas Thomas).

Plate 56   Site XXII, W face section 1, showing pit containing Inhumation 2. Scale, inches/centimetres. See Figure 36 (Bret Guthrie).

Plate 57   Site XXII, crouched Early Bronze Age Inhumation 2 fully exposed. Left scale, inches/centimetres. Looking E (Bret Guthrie).

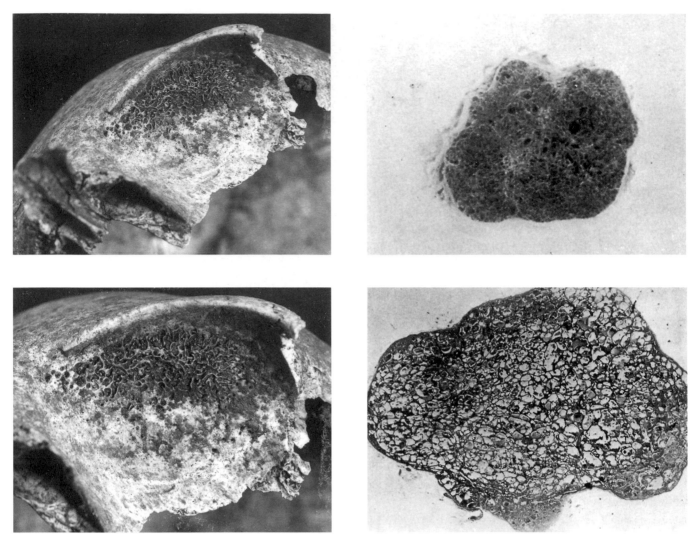

Plate 58   Site XXII, traces of the tumour haemangioma in left orbit of Inhumation 2. Possibly the earliest recorded instance of this condition (Anthony Duggan).

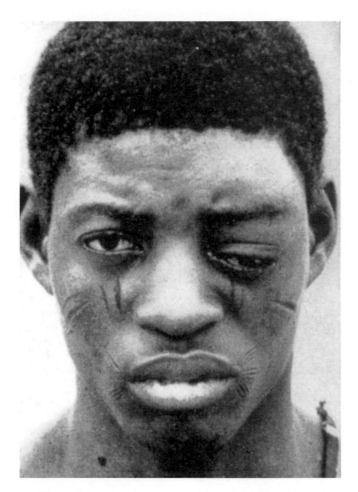

Plate 59   Haemangioma arising in upper part of left orbit of male TIV, Northern Nigeria (F C Rogers, 'Eye diseases in the African continent', *American Journal of Opthalmology*, 45, 1958).

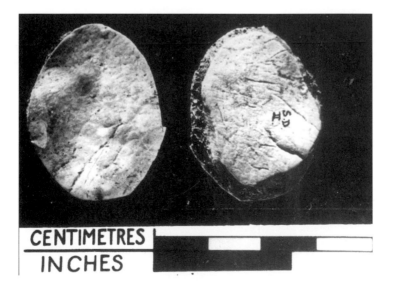

Plate 60   Site II, trepanned cranial disc. Note point where surgical cutting overlapped (Maurice Cookson).

A

B

C

D

Plate 61   Metallographic analysis of copper-alloy awls from Site I, Site II and Barrow III, Marshfield (Glos), to determine whether structures altered by inclusion in funeral pyres: a, b, L2; c, L1; d, Marshfield. Scales: a x 250, b x 750, c x 250, d x 150 (E C Ellwood).

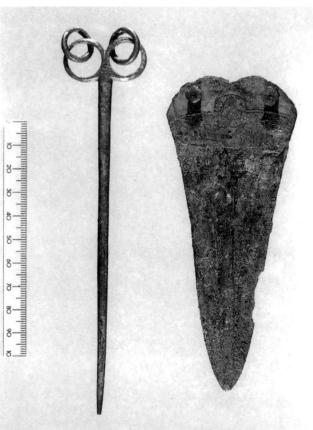

Plates 62 and 63   Copper-alloy ogival dagger, M1, and ring-headed pin, M2, Site XIX. Dagger retains evidence for lined wooden scabbard and handle, with cloth impression on one rivet. Cleaning has revealed decoration on head of pin. Scale, centimetres (Wiltshire Heritage Museum).

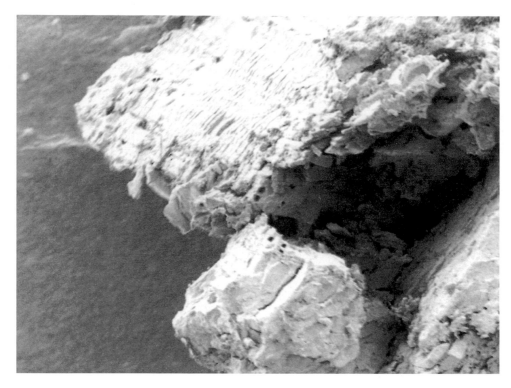

Plate 64A   Site XIX, cross-section of the wood from the sheath mouth of M1, covering one year's growth. Magnification c 180x (English Heritage).

Plate 64B   Tangental section of the wood from M1; note the large vessels in the early wood and ray cells replaced by copper salts. The wood structure has been lost. Magnification c 250x (English Heritage).

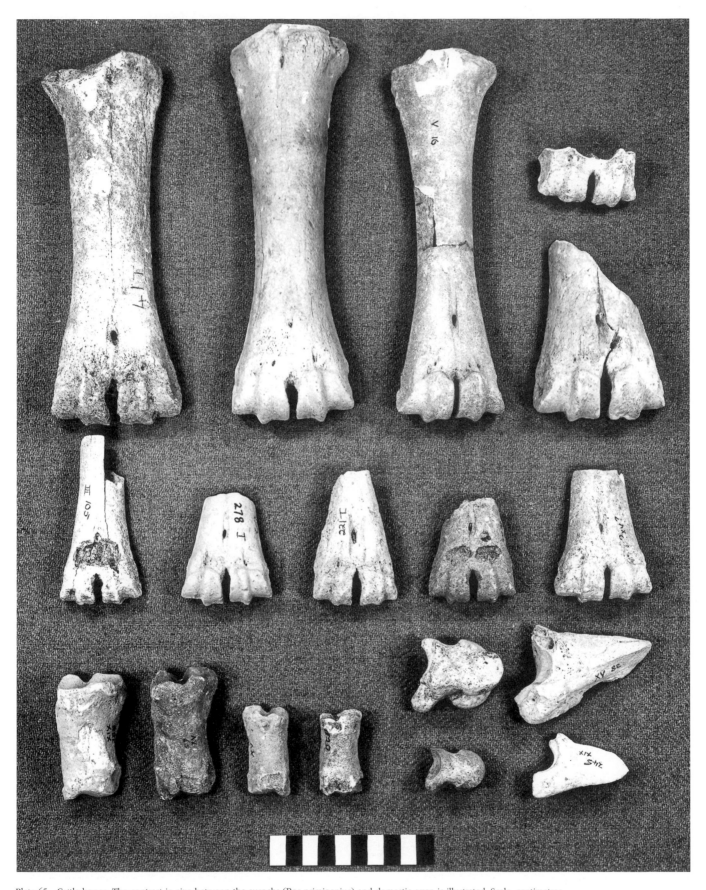

Plate 65   Cattle bones. The contrast in size between the aurochs (Bos primigenius) and domestic oxen is illustrated. Scale, centimetres.
Top row: metacarpal bones of aurochs, one certainly from a cow and an unfused epiphysis from a calf.
Middle row: metacarpals from domestic animals.
Bottom row: contrasting groups of phalanges and hoof cores, the larger being aurochs and the smaller being domestic cattle (Juliet Clutton-Brock, Peter A Jewell)

Plate 66   Metacarpal of a domestic ox with epiphyses chewed away. The heavy gnawing of the ends is most likely to have been done by a dog. Scale, centimetres (Juliet Clutton-Brock, Peter A Jewell).

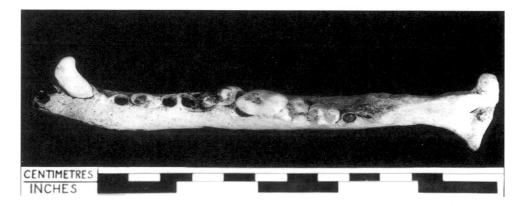

Plate 67   Dog: both left and right rami of this mandible were found in the primary silt in the ditch of Site III. The mandible is complete except for some teeth. The size of the jaw and degree of crowding of the teeth is typical of all the dog jaws from Snail Down. Periodontal disease of the bone can be seen around the inside edges of the sockets of the carnassial tooth and the third and fourth premolars (Juliet Clutton-Brock, Peter A Jewell).

PART 3: SNAIL DOWN, THE ANATOMY OF A BRONZE AGE BARROW CEMETERY AND ITS PEOPLE

Nicholas Thomas

It is ... the record of what men did in a long past time at a particular spot: and therefore since thought governs action, what they were thinking.
Cyril Fox, *Life and Death in the Bronze Age*, xxvii

In Part 3, barrows on Snail Down are identified by their site number allocated during the course of the excavations of 1953, 1955 and 1957 (thus Site III, the bell-barrow excavated in 1955); or else by Salisbury Plain Training area (SPTA) number. These numberings are shown in Tables 1 and 2 (see pages 7 and 8). Other Wiltshire barrows are given their numbering by parish as in the *Victoria County History of Wiltshire*, I, pt 1 (Grinsell 1957). Unless stated otherwise, barrows referred to are in Wiltshire. Part 3 includes a series of fifteen schedules listing comparative barrow features. Each begins with Wiltshire, then proceeds to Dorset and, variously, to other southern and south-western counties, thence northwards and north-east, followed by sites in Wales, Scotland and the Continent. These lists are not claimed to be comprehensive.

1 THE CHOICE OF SNAIL DOWN FOR A BARROW CEMETERY

The excavations revealed sufficient structural uniformity and common burial practices for us to be confident that the barrow cemetery on Snail Down was the burial ground of a single community. We also suppose, though it was unsubstantiated by excavation, that this barrow group stood within sight or at least within reasonable distance of the permanent settlement – the home farms – of those buried there. The important but smaller barrow cemetery just eastward, on Cow Down (Thomas 1976, 22, fig 10), may have served a separate community, each farming adjacent parts of a region relatively rich in land for pasture and arable, having water from the Bourne close by, woodland in that valley and local surface outcrops of workable flint.

A suggestion that barrow groups (which we also refer to as cemeteries), but not necessarily isolated barrows, were developed within the home territory of a community has been well made by H S Green, among others, when discussing barrow locations around Milton Keynes (1975, 126–130). On this reckoning, the Snail Down settlements are not likely to have been to the north: there is dead ground within 200m of Site XX. The cemetery seems to face south-east, where the Bourne runs. Cow Down, on the contrary, may have belonged to people settled a little up river, towards Collingbourne Ducis, even though its alignment points, in one direction, towards Sidbury Hill. These are the two quite different directions towards which the eye is drawn when viewing the landscape from one cemetery or the other.

If, on the contrary, a community used its burial ground to impress its claim upon that part of the downland, it might locate its barrows deliberately within sight of those of a neighbouring community rather than towards its own dwellings. The Snail Down barrows certainly can be seen from Cow Down.

Settlement hereabouts had been prolonged. An earlier Neolithic site, possibly including a flint mine, may have existed on or near Sidbury Hill. Flaked flint axes, one partly ground, found there by J V S Megaw are evidence for that (Megaw 1967), while a small quantity of earlier Neolithic wares from Snail Down confirms the presence of those pioneer farmers around the northern slopes of the Hill. On Weather Hill, about one mile west of Snail Down, two long barrows have been recorded, Fittleton G5 and G5a (Grinsell 1957, 140). Only a little further afield is the substantial Collingbourne Kingston long barrow (G21) on Fairmile Down, north-east of that village (Grinsell 1957, 140; Burl 1987, Pl 14). Eastwards, the long barrows on Wick Down and west of Leckford Bottom, Collingbourne Ducis (G23, G24) were first noticed by Grinsell (*ibid*), but he classified them as doubtful. A double-entrance henge monument lies within 1.3km (0.8 mile) of the centre of the cemetery. It lies to the north-west, outside Weather Hill Firs (SU 207526 and McOmish *et al* 2002, fig 2.18). Its users may have included those who were responsible for the sherds of Peterborough and Grooved Wares at several of the Snail Down barrows. Alternatively, they could have been the people living in the transient-looking settlement located beneath Sites X–XIV, who used Beakers, Grooved Ware and characteristic domestic wares and made flint and stone tools. The small fields recorded in Figure 2 among the Snail Down barrows may also have belonged to the Beaker settlement.

purpose completed, it was filled and left as a scraped-up barrow (Smith and Simpson, 1966, 132–133).

The stone-embanked enclosure incorporated in West Overton G6b is perhaps the nearest that Wessex communities came to building the kinds of stone ring-cairn and platform-cairn found widespread in south-west and northern England, in Wales and Ireland (Lynch, 1974, 1975, 1979, 1986). As Francis Lynch has also recognised, her 'Variant Circles' find their chalk land counterpart in pond-barrows (Lynch 1979, 7). For all of them, enclosure and gathering place were more important than burial ground. While in use, the emphasis upon spreading and depositing charcoal was more apparent within the stone circles than in pond-barrows. Then, having run their allotted span, the tradition was to fill them, converting enclosure to mound, as happened at Brenig 51 (Denbighs: Lynch 1975, 20). In marked contrast, pond-barrows seem to have been left to become overgrown and weathered when no longer in use.

A feature of Sites I and III was the occurrence of large trough-shaped pits whose chalk or earthy fillings gave no indication of their original use (Figs 3, 9, Pl 7). The eccentric mound of the disc-barrow, Site I, covered the largest of these. Its clean chalk-rubble fill suggested that it had not been left open for long before re-filling and concealment beneath a small mound. Around the outer edge of the ditch of the bell-barrow, Site III, three pits had been evenly spaced out and left to silt up naturally. All could have been used to contain corpses. At Site I, the pit's digging might possibly have preceded construction of the disc-barrow. The pits around Site III followed the building of that barrow: their contents, if human, would have been destined for subsequent burial as secondary interments there or elsewhere. Only two secondary cremation burials were found in Site III: but there were close neighbours which could have received these corpses or their ashes for burial.

Building the bowl-barrow Site XVII began with a timber structure, irregular in its ground plan but possibly forming a platform. If so, it could have supported a corpse. The posts, perhaps with the corpse an added attraction, drew birds of prey such as buzzards to perch and digest their kill (Section Q).

A notable phenomenon at Snail Down was the discovery of isolated pieces of unburnt human bone and teeth, some of them from primary positions in barrows and all from sites whose burials had been after cremation. Four barrows yielded such remains:

1. Site I. Skull fragments, scapula. Ditch and central plateau
2. Site III. Incisor tooth. Immediately N of central funeral pyre
3. Site XIX. Molar tooth. N mound, core
4. Site XX. Mainly skull fragments. Middle layers in ditch, cuttings A, F, section 8.

These occurrences reinforce the suggestion of extended burial practice at Snail Down. Since the adult incisor tooth found unburnt beside the funeral pyre at Site III could have slipped from the skull of the female cremated there, this would suggest either that the corpse had been allowed to reach an advanced stage of decay in that location before cremation; or else that heavily decayed remains of the corpse had been brought from elsewhere

for cremation on the site of this bell-barrow and one tooth at least had escaped the flames. Such an explanation could account also for the adult molar tooth within the N mound of Site XIX, since burnt timbers at the base of the south, presumably contemporary, mound may have come from a pyre in the immediate vicinity. With no cremation on the site of Site I, however, it is less easy to explain the isolated, unburnt bones found lying about there. Site XX seems to have been a cenotaph.

It may be simplest to accept that during the lifetime of such a barrow cemetery, bodies, and fragments from bodies long since committed to the flames of the pyre and subsequent burial, will have been much in evidence, whether they awaited cremation or lay about as apparently unconsidered witnesses of burials past.

Extended pre-burial ritual, including the exposure of corpses, has been documented at many barrow sites in Britain and there is no need to seek further than Wiltshire and Dorset for evidence. Bird pellets were found at Earl's Farm Down, Amesbury, G70 (Christie 1964, 44, 45), where a corpse had lain exposed. Here a prominent post provided buzzards with the kind of perch they like to use after a successful hunt for food.

Several inhumation burials have been recorded where the corpse was incomplete. Others have been found at least in part disarticulated, all of it clear evidence that in the earlier Bronze Age it was still common practice to expose the dead over lengthy periods before burial; and that different attitudes affected bodies and body parts. The primary burial beneath a bell-barrow at Sutton Veney comprised a corpse that seems to have been dismembered (Johnston 1980, 34–36). When placed upon its bier, the body sections had been distributed approximately correctly, without disguising their dismembered state. Disarticulated bones were found in remains of a coffin at Site A, Down Farm, Pewsey (Vatcher 1960, 341–343); a dismembered skeleton lay in a pit beneath a disc-barrow at Earl's Farm Down, G61a (Ashbee 1985, 48–51).

Careful examination of two cremations from a scraped-up bowl-barrow, G45, at Greenland Farm, Winterbourne Stoke (Christie 1970, 72–73) established that neither corpse had been complete before cremation. In Dorset, at barrow B, Litton Cheney, a young man's hands had been put first into the grave and his body then extended over them (Wacher 1959, 164). S and C M Piggott (1944, 68–69) noted that the corpse buried in Crichel Down barrow 5 had been trussed so tightly that a number of bones had become disjointed: such damage was unlikely to have occurred unless the body had already decomposed.

It was Ashbee's view that the pit containing a mortuary house, which he discovered beneath bowl-barrow G51 among the Cursus group near Stonehenge, had been left open during the course of at least one winter before the mound was raised over it (Ashbee 1978, 5). The same observation was made by Proudfoot of the central grave pit beneath bell-barrow 2 at Edmondsham, Dorset (1963, 400). Likewise at Beaulieu barrow II (Hants), a mortuary house within a pit had reached a state of collapse before the burial mound was built over it (C M Piggott 1943, 6–9). To the mortuary house beneath Beaulieu barrow II can be added a second mortuary house in that cemetery, beneath barrow IX (ibid, 17–19). Construction of such houses implies that their purpose was to hold a corpse for a period before burial, as well as becoming the house of the dead after the barrow was built to cover it.

Timber structures have also been found whose purpose may have been the exposure of corpses, like the proposed platform at Site XVII. Greenlands Farm, Winterbourne Stoke G39 covered a central stake structure that possibly served this purpose, after which it was burnt (Gingell 1988, 52).

At Crichel Down barrow 11, the area around the deep central burial shaft had been trampled and disturbed, suggesting to the excavators (S and C M Piggott 1944, 74) that it had suffered prolonged exposure to the weather before being sealed beneath its burial mound.

Often slight and sometimes inconclusive though the indications may be, enough has now been unearthed from Bronze Age (and earlier) sites in the British Isles to convince us that burial was usually a seasonal, extended, community activity, not necessarily related to the ergonomics of agriculture; and that extensive evidence exists to show that corpses could reach their final resting places incomplete and in a state of decay.

It should be emphasised, however, that apparent states of decay through exposure might indicate, on the contrary, that differing attitudes existed to the disposal of bodies and body parts. Incompleteness may reflect a *need* to bury parts only of a corpse, rather than represent the loss of parts during the process of exposure.

5 THE BURIAL PROCESS: THE DEAD AT SNAIL DOWN

Table 37 is a record of the Bronze Age men, women and children including babies found at Snail Down, 1953–1957, first those associated with the barrows of Phases 2–5, Figure 61, then a group of the later Bronze Age, Phase 6, from Sites V and XV. All are cremations unless stated otherwise. A primary burial has not yet been found in Sites V, VIII or XXII. Burials recorded by Hoare are set out in Table 38.

So far, possibly 28 cremations and four inhumations (one a foetus) of the earlier Bronze Age have been reported or recovered. Five other inhumations, from Site XV and one from Site V, belong to the later Bronze Age.

Table 37　Bronze Age men, women and children including babies found at Snail Down 1952–1957.

Site 1953–1957	Burials listed in Part 2, Section A	Adult Male	Adult Female	Child Age 2–12	Baby Age 0–2 F – Fetus	Sex unknown A= Adult C = Cenotaph
I	1					1
I	2					1
I	3	?1				
I	4	?1				
II	5		?1			
II	6		?1			
II	1 (inhumation)				F	1
III	7		?1			
III	8			1		1
III	9				1	1
IV						1
XIV	10		?1			
XV	11					A
XVI	12					1
XVI	13					1
XVI	14			?1		1
XVII	15	1				
XVIII						1
XIX						2
XX						C
XXI						1
XXII	2 (inhumation)	1				
Later Bronze Age inhumations						
V	8			1		1
XV	3		1			
XV	4		?1			
XV	5					A
XV	6					A
XV	7				1	1

Table 38 Burials, age and sex unknown, recorded by Hoare in Snail Down barrows not excavated in 1953–1957 (cf Table 1 above).			
Hoare Number	Cremation	Inhumation	Cenotaph C
1(1)	1		
1(2)		?1	
2			C
3		1	
5			C
6	1 + box		
7 or 8	1		
9(1)			?C
9(2)	1		
10			
15	?1		
17	1		
19	1		
21			C
26	?1		

The jaw and thigh bone found by Hoare close to the surface in 2209 (2) cannot be attributed to a period, nor can the human bones from Site I and from the ditch of Site XX. Sexing cremated bones is notoriously difficult. Nevertheless Dr Cornwall and his colleagues have succeeded in identifying four that may be female and three possibly that were of men. One inhumation was of a young male. Since perhaps 24 Early Bronze Age burials are of unknown sex, it is not possible to draw conclusions about the Snail Down community in the way that Green has been able to do following excavation of a ring-ditch at Milton Keynes (Bucks: 1975, 129–130). There the preponderance of females, children and babies suggested that the ring-ditch might have been the burial place for the home ground, where womenfolk and the young were more likely to reside. Their men and youths he expected to be frequently away; and buried away from home if death came. All that can be noted of the burials from Snail Down is that so far the bones of a foetus, two babies and three children, two of them of the later Bronze Age, have been recorded; and that this is a relatively low proportion of the very young for a cemetery of this size. The rare instances of foetal burials are noted in Section A.

Because of the rarity of inhumations at Snail Down, it is necessary to look closely at the burial of the youth in the little mound on the berm of Site XXII. Since this structural feature of a bell-barrow may be unique, and may also have been an addition, the discovery of an inhumation *added* to it as a secondary burial sets that grave apart from the mainstream of burial practice within the Snail Down community. One suggestion is that the youth from Site XXII may not have belonged to the Snail Down community: may, perhaps, have been travelling through the area when ill health (Section A) finally brought about his death. What would be more likely, in those circumstances, than interment in an already added mound to a fine bell-barrow, subject, no doubt, to the approval of those who controlled the burial ground? That the little necklace buried with the boy included a sea shell of a kind unrecorded hitherto from a burial, hints at a possible seaside home

ground for him, perhaps to the south, about Southampton water, or north-westwards towards the Bristol Channel. The fashionable amber beads, however scanty, suggest some association with the wealth that is apparent among Wessex communities. Was his presence here related to a visit to Stonehenge, or to exchange of goods? Remove this youth, then, from the Snail Down community, and their close adherence to the rite of cremation becomes even more marked.

There is no dispute, however, about Hoare's discovery of an inhumation burial in 2205 (his 3), the small bowl-barrow at the western end of one of the two alignments constituting the main layout of Snail Down (Fig 2A). He reported that an unaccompanied skeleton was found, not, apparently, in a grave. He failed to comment upon its posture, emphasising instead the contrast between this interment, which lacked grave-goods, and the fine series of bone tools and one bronze object (Section M, M4-M14, Fig 56) occurring in the adjacent barrow, 2207, within a pit which contained no human remains.

Eleven of the Snail Down barrows have received complete excavation. Twenty-one were examined by the antiquarian's means of a central pit or trench; six were found by Hoare to have covered empty burial pits. Fifteen burials occurred in those barrows cleared completely. The absence of human bones from Sites X-XIII need not mean that they were cenotaphs. Their ruin by rabbits, whose burrows often extended into chalk bedrock, may have eliminated all trace of bones, even those buried in graves.

Total excavation of the remaining 21 barrows (including 2244 but not 2209) might not add substantially to the number who were interred at Snail Down. Among that select group it seems to have been the custom to bury no more than three or four within one mound, including secondary graves: for the most part, one burial per structure was normal. The total number of people buried at Snail Down in the earlier Bronze Age might not have exceeded fifty. Whether this represents a small community, or, perhaps more likely, strict selection of those entitled to receive barrow burial, we have at present no means of telling.

SNAIL DOWN

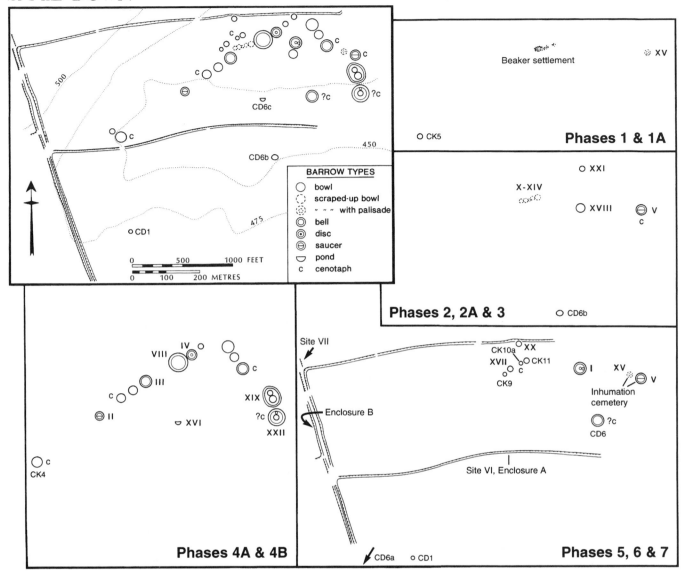

Fig 61 The Snail Down barrow cemetery and earthworks; proposed development.

6 THE BURIAL PROCESS: CREMATION AND FUNERAL PYRES

At Snail Down, as elsewhere during the earlier Bronze Age, some corpses were cremated within the area of the cemetery and their ashes picked out and buried in an adjacent pit; others had been burnt elsewhere and their bones brought to the site of the barrow in a container.

The mound of Site III was found to have preserved the lowest layer of charred oak and other wood from what we believe to have been a carefully laid, probably square or rectangular funeral pyre. Before the flames had died down or been quenched, the area must have become black with wood ash, as well as hot enough to have burned the subsoil red and yellow with its intensity. Those involved in the next stage, searching among the

ash and burnt embers, scattering some in the process, to recover the cremated bones, must also have become hot and blackened from their work, unless the pyre was left to burn out and cool naturally.

Ample evidence for a funeral pyre was also recovered by Hoare from beneath 2231 (his 9) although no primary cremation burial was found in this small bowl-barrow; and from the large bell-barrow 2254 (his 26), where once again he failed to locate an interment. Sites IV, 2253 (his 17) and 2254 yielded enough wood ash for Hoare to remark upon it; and to suggest that there, too, corpses had been burnt *in situ*.

Examination of charcoals associated with cremations at Snail Down has revealed (Section S) that the following woods at least were used in the pyres: hazel, apple/hawthorn/rowan/whitebeam type, wild cherry/bird-cherry type, oak and ash. Evidence from other barrows cited below suggests that these were the woods usually selected for burning the dead.

Since 1945, published excavation of at least eleven barrows in Wiltshire has produced evidence of heavy burning on the ancient land surface that probably represents cremation at the barrow site.

Barrows overlying the site of a funeral pyre

Wiltshire

Amesbury G39 (Ashbee 1981, 7–9, fig 6). Oval area 13½ft across, oak.
Amesbury G61, New Barn Down (Ashbee 1985, 54–55). Oval, 15 × 23ft. Oak, ash and apple.
Amesbury G71, Earl's Farm Down (Christie 1967, 343–345, fig 3). 8 x 10ft, oak, ash.
Lamb Down, Codford, Site C (Vatcher 1963, 422, fig 5). 6 × 8ft, ash.
Lamb Down, Codford, Site F (*ibid*, 425). 8 × 8ft, ash.
Milton Lilbourne triple barrow G2–4 (Ashbee 1986, 46, fig 20). 17 × 12ft, oak.
Shrewton, Net Down h (Green & Rollo-Smith 1984, 270, fig 8, 271). *C* 7 × 7 ft. Wood not identified.
Shrewton, Net Down L (*ibid*, 279–281, fig 13). *C* 8 x 8 ft. Wood not identified.
Shrewton, Rollestone Field 23a (*ibid*, 282, fig 14, 285). *C* 7 × 8ft. Wood not identified.
Wilsford cum Lake G51 (Smith 1991, 16–17, fig 4). *C* 5 × 6ft, wood not identified.
Winterbourne Stoke G38 (Vatcher 1962, 241; Vatcher and Vatcher 1976, 273; Gingell 1988, 48). Apparently a heaped-up pyre comprising the whole mound.

From elsewhere in England and Wales since 1945, pyres or substantial bonfires have been found beneath round barrows, among which the following are of note:

Dorset

Edmondsham (Proudfoot 1963, 398–400). 3½ × 3ft but originally larger. Oak.
Oakley Down (White and Reed 1971, 160). Possibly pre-barrow. No dimensions given.

Hampshire

Micheldever Wood (Fasham 1979, 14). c 10 × 6½ft, oak, blackthorn, hazel, hawthorn, cereal straw.

Somerset

Tynings Farm T11 (Taylor 1951, 140, fig 25, 145–146). 4ft across, oak, at least 10 logs or boards, up to 3 deep; but possibly a bonfire, not a pyre.

Berkshire

Down (Richards 1991, 12). Circular burnt area, *c* 5ft across. Wood not identified.
Farncombe Down (Rahtz 1962, 4). 5ft triangular area, oak.

Gloucestershire

Marshfield barrow III (Gettins *et al* 1953, 26, fig 2). About 4ft square with further scatter. Wood not identified.

Oxfordshire

Radley Barrow 7 (Atkinson 1954, 28, 30–31). 5ft square, swept clean.
Stanton Harcourt King Barrow (Harden and Treweeks 1945, 24–25, 30). 9 × 11ft, ash.

Suffolk

Poor's Heath, Risby (Vatcher and Vatcher 1976, 269–272, fig 3). 25 × 18ft, oak.

Cheshire

Gallowsclough Hill (Forde-Johnston 1960, 78). Oval mound of ashy sand, charcoal, 5 × 4ft, perhaps covering pyre.

Derbyshire

Swarkeston Lowes Barrow 4 (Greenfield 1960, 7). 10½ × 10¾ft. Oak.

Denbighshire

Brenig Barrows 40 (Lynch 1974, 28–30 and plan), 4¼ × 3¼ft. Burnt ?platform or mortuary house. Oak.
Brenig Barrow 42 (*ibid*, 22–23 and plan). About 5ft square. Wood not identified.

The size, shape and constituents of a funeral pyre would have been influenced by the combustibles available and the energy and traditions of the community who built it. The rectangular layout of mainly oak logs, saplings and twigs at Snail Down Site III, which measured about 7 x 3½ft, is narrower than most but broadly comparable. At Site III and elsewhere, a much larger area was covered with wood ash and included at least one timber cast aside presumably in the search for burnt bone, as we found also at Site XIX. At Stanton Harcourt King Barrow (Harden and Treweeks 1945, 24–25, 30), the pyre had been formed around a vertical post that may also have been used, initially, as a laying-out marker for the barrow that was to follow. The size and shape of the pyre would also have been affected by the way in which the body was to be arranged upon it – extended or contracted. At Shalbourne Barrow 2 (Johnston 1963, 369), the relatively unburnt state of skull and toe bones suggests that the corpse had been extended. The shape of the pyre at Site III hints at a similar disposition.

Not every pyre, according to surviving records, had basal timbers as substantial as some of those at Site III. But the logs at Swarkeston Lowes 4, with their charred surfaces and hollow interiors, were remarkably similar (Greenfield 1960, 7).

There is still inadequate evidence for the original height of a pyre. Remains of the huge one within the mound of Bulford Barrow 3 found by Hawley (1910, 619–620) was a rare survival: its 7ft stack of oak and ash logs, laid horizontally as well as vertically, eventually collapsed during excavation, burying one of the workers to his shoulders in wood ash. That this represents the burning of a small building remains a possibility.

Oak was the favoured wood, with straw and a variety of small scrub and twigs to get the blaze going. Vatcher remarked upon the unusual use of ash alone for the pyre beneath barrow F at Lamb Down (1963).

Most barrow-site pyres were fired, as at Site III, in order to burn one corpse and were then sealed by the barrow mound that followed. Extended use of a pyre site, making it a crematorium, has been established at Risby (Suffolk: Vatcher and Vatcher 1976, 270–272), where the excavators estimated that the site may have been used for two centuries. The bonfire site forming part of phase III at Earl's Farm Down, Amesbury G71 (Christie 1967, 343–345, fig 3) may also indicate a crematorium.

The task of carrying out a cremation possibly fell to the dead person's family. Lasting no doubt for several hours, it would have involved stoking and watching; in the process getting hot and dirty. The enigmatic line of fencing immediately NW of the pyre at Site III might have acted as some kind of barrier between those charged with the work and members of the community less intimately related, there only as witnesses.

7 THE BURIAL PROCESS: CARE OF THE HUMAN ASHES

Excavation has not yet revealed whether the pyre was allowed to go out and cool of its own accord, or else extinguished artificially. Whichever method was adopted, the next task was to collect the burned bones of the corpse. Leaving them among the ashes and sealing the whole area beneath a mound was not unknown, for example at Minning Low (Derbys: Bateman 1861, 57) and Loanhead of Daviot (Aberdeens: Kilbride Jones 1936, 282). But it was not the norm. In collecting bone, although much finely comminuted human ash remained in the pyre, the main pieces were removed and wood ash and burnt soil with them. Two problems of burial procedure then arose. Should the cremation be buried with its charcoal and burnt soil, or carefully cleaned; and should the larger burnt bones be further broken up before burial?

State of cremations at Snail Down

Site I   Cremations 1, 2, 4. Free of charcoal.
          Cremation 3. Free of charcoal, but charcoal occurred above it; all in a disturbed context.
          Burnt human bone (?associated with one of the above). With charcoal, burnt soil, in own pit.
Site II   Central cremation. Small amount of charcoal.
          Off-centre cremation. Much charcoal, burnt soil, domestic rubbish, potsherds.
Site III Central cremation. Free of charcoal (but replaced by Hoare).
          Secondary cremation 1. Much charcoal.
          Secondary cremation 2. Free of charcoal (but scattered in ancient times).
Site XIV Primary cremation. Some charcoal.
Site XV   Primary cremation. Free of charcoal.
Site XVI Token cremation. Some wood ash.
Site XVII Central cremation. Much charcoal, burnt soil and ashy material in pit and scattered on ancient land surface round about it.
Site IV   ?Primary cremation. ? Much charcoal ('ashes').
2253   ?Primary cremation. ? Much charcoal ('ashes').

At Snail Down, some cremations were buried with wood ash, burnt soil, even domestic rubbish, others were clearly cleaned before interment. At Bevan's Quarry, Temple Guiting (Glos: O'Neil 1967, 19–20), the excavator remarked upon the dirtiness of the cremations, noting also that several had been buried still hot. This unusual state for the bones was recorded also at West Overton G6b (Smith and Simpson 1966, 128–129). Undamaged, often delicate objects like amber beads, buried with cremations, showed that bones were usually cold by the time they were ready for burial.

It seems a safe assumption, judging by the state of most Bronze Age cremations, that in preparing burnt human bones for burial, long bones, skull and pelvis were often broken into smaller pieces as soon as they were cool. At Snail Down, there was a slight but definite variation in the extent to which this had been done.

In order to preserve the burned bones for burial, they had to be kept together in a container. Except where an urn or wooden box was used, a bag, whether of leather or textile, was the favoured receptacle. Even when cremations like 2 and 4 at Site I had been incorporated within the make-up of a mound, their compactness is best explained by the use of a bag. At Site XIV the cremation on the floor of the burial pit was elongated, one end more pointed as if that was the mouth of the bag, squeezed tight by the person who had carried it to the pit. In so doing, the more compact and heavy bone ash and smallest pieces had been shaken down to the bottom of the bag. The bones concentrated into only a small part of the central burial pit in Site XVII may have been deposited there in a bag, or at least emptied out of a container into the half-filled pit. The same was true of Secondary Burial 1 (Cremation 8) in Site III.

Recent excavations have produced evidence, mainly from southern England, for cremation containers in barrows.

Cremation containers in barrows

Wiltshire

Amesbury G58, New Barn Down (Ashbee 1985, 43). Bones sorted in bag by being carried.
Amesbury G61a, New Barn Down (Ashbee 1985, 51). Similar. Grave goods outside bag.
Amesbury G71, Earl's Farm Down (Christie 1967, 344). Possible container.
Amesbury G133, King Barrow Ridge (Gingell 1988, 36–39). Cloth bag within Collared Urn.

Avebury G55 (Smith 1965, 31). Oblong bone mass: bag or box. Another cremation (1) tipped out of a container.

Durrington G7 (Richards 1990, 175). Triangular mass, bag or basket. In central burial pit accompanying primary inhumation.

Milton Lilbourne triple barrow G2–4 (Ashbee 1986, 33, fig 9). Elongated bone mass: bag.

West Overton G6b (Smith and Simpson 1966, 127, 128). (1) Bones sorted in bag. (2) Hot cremation in charred basket. (3) Bones in bag within urn.

Shrewton, Net Down 5c, 5d, 5f (Green & Rollo-Smith 1984, 265, 269). Evidence for organic containers.

Shrewton, Net Down 5L (*ibid*, 279–280). Organic container secured by bead necklace.

Shrewton, Rollestone Field 25 (*ibid*, 287). Cremation perhaps in a bag in pit.

Winterbourne Stoke G30 (Christie 1963, 378). Dome-shaped bone mass suggested container.

Winterbourne Stoke G47, Greenlands Farm (Gingell 1988, 60). Leather garment or bag.

Dorset

Edmondsham (Proudfoot 1963, 405). Circular container.

Kingston Russell Barrow 6N (Bailey *et al* 1980, 28, pl V). Bag within an urn.

Winterbourne Steepleton, Sheep Down (Atkinson *et al* 1951, 7, fig 3). Basket or wooden keg.

Hampshire and the Isle of Wight

Arreton Down, Isle of Wight (Alexander and Ozannes 1960, 269). Basket.

Beaulieu Barrow III (C M Piggott 1943, 10). Moss wrapping.

Beaulieu Barrow IV (*ibid*, 13). Moss wrapping bound into a bundle.

Bishops Waltham, Great Barrow (Ashbee 1958, 149). Bones sorted in a bag.

Micheldever Wood triple barrow (Fasham 1979, 11). Circular container for cremation.

Berkshire

Hodcott Down (Richards 1991, 12). Tight-packed, probably in a leather bag.

Gloucestershire

Marshfield Barrow III (Gettins *et al* 1953, 26–27, pl 1a). Bag on ancient land surface.

Cheshire

Gallowsclough Hill (Forde-Johnston 1960, 77, 80). Possible bag.

Denbighshire

Brenig Barrow 45 (Lynch 1974, 14). ?Wooden container.

Not every cremation brought to the site of burial was finally interred in its container. It seems likely that the cremation buried off-centre in Site II had been emptied into the lower half of its double pit.

8 THE BURIAL PROCESS: TREATMENT OF THE PYRE REMAINS

With the cremated bone removed from the timbers and ashes of the pyre, burial ceremonial had to draw to a dignified conclusion the role played by the pyre. At Site III, the basal logs and small wood, as well as charred timbers cast aside in the search for cremated bone (and perhaps as a means of hastening extinction of the flames), were left exactly as they had been and sealed beneath the mound when the barrow was built. By contrast, care seems to have been taken to sweep clean the pyre site found beneath Radley barrow 7 (Oxon: Atkinson 1954, 28, 30–31). The sweepings, incorporating inevitably a certain quantity of burnt human bone, had been put carefully into a small pit dug into the pyre floor. Leaving large lumps of charred wood as at Site III, or Swarkeston Lowes (Derbys: Greenfield 1960, 7, pl 3), was not common practice.

In most cremation burials the pyre was built away from the site of the barrow. Such pyres could have been nearer, perhaps, to the home of the deceased than to the traditional burial ground. At Site II, the intact off-centre burial had been in a double pit, bones in the lower part, then a sealing with material that had the character of rubbish from the home – animal bones, dirty soil, sherds of a Food Vessel (Section D, D7). At Site I, a small pit appeared to contain pyre sweepings, a practice found elsewhere when the pyre had been located away from the barrow site, for example Upper Chamberlain's Farm, Eriswell (Suffolk: Dymond 1976, 4). Evidently it was important to bring at least a token from the pyre to the burial place.

Ash- or charcoal-filled pits have been recorded from several barrows in the region and beyond.

Charcoal-filled pits beneath barrows

Wiltshire

Burderop Down, Chiseldon (Passmore 1929, 242). Charcoal. With bones of large bird.

Down Farm, Pewsey, Sites C, D (Vatcher 1960, 346). Ash-filled pits.

Milton Lilbourne triple barrow G4 (Ashbee 1986, 52). Charcoal, but possibly not prehistoric.

Tan Hill, All Cannings G1 (Thurnam 1860, 325). Ashes.

West Overton G6b (Smith and Simpson 1966, 126, 127). Hawthorn charcoal in one pit; blackthorn and hazel in another.

Wilsford cum Lake G51 (Smith 1991, 16–17, fig 4). Pyre sweepings as well as main cremation: wood not identified.

Hampshire

Moor Green (Ashbee and Dimbleby 1976, 9). Oak, charcoal from large timbers.

Devon

Shaugh Moor cairn group (Wainwright *et al* 1979, 10–28). Charcoal, mainly oak.

Gloucestershire

Marshfield Barrow III (Gettins *et al* 1953, 27–28). Charcoal, cremated bone.

Oxfordshire

Radley Barrow 7 (Atkinson 1954, 28, 30–31). Wood ash, small burnt bone.
Stanton Harcourt King Barrow (Harden and Treweeks 1945, 30). Wood ash.

9 THE BURIAL PROCESS: THE BURIAL PIT AND ITS COVER

In southern England at least, it was usual to inter cremated human bones, whether contained in a bag, an urn or some other receptacle – or quite loose – in a burial pit. The opposite practice, where the cremation was laid or heaped upon the ancient land surface, was much rarer. A few barrows have preserved evidence for this less complex ritual.

Cremations interred on the ancient land surface

Wiltshire

Amesbury G39 (Ashbee 1981, 9). Cremation beside site of pyre.

Dorset

Crichel Down Barrow 2 (S and C M Piggott 1944, 64–65, fig 10). Central, beside post hole.

Crichel Down Barrow 9 (*ibid*, 72, fig 19). Three cremations on land surface, around central cremation in scooped grave.

Hampshire

Beaulieu Barrows I and III (C M Piggott 1943, 5, 10, figs 3, 6). At or near barrow centres, on ancient land surface; III wrapped in moss and compacted. Stoney Cross Barrows II and V (*ibid*, 20, 22). Both on ancient land surface, beneath turf core of each barrow.

Surrey

Deerleap Wood, Wotton (Corcoran 1963, 7). Possible inhumation on ancient land surface.

Gloucestershire

Marshfield Barrow III (Gettins *et al* 1953, 26–27, pl 1a). Kidney-shaped mass with grave-goods placed on top.

Pits dug to contain cremated bones were usually approximately circular in plan, with sides roughly vertical and floor flat. The slightly conical burial pit beneath Crichel Down 15 (Dorset) is unusual (S and C M Piggott 1944, 76). Evidence for the use of antlers and even of stone and bronze axes in the cutting of burial pits has been recorded. These generally carefully fashioned pits were awkward to dig. Cutting and prizing away the chalk in an increasingly restricted space must have been the work of just one or two people, scraping out the spoil with their hands. Some pits, like that beneath saucer-barrow 2 at Fosbury, near Shalbourne (Johnston 1963, 364), were no more than shallow scoops. The average cremation pit measured 2–3ft in diameter and penetrated solid chalk to a depth of 1–2ft. At Earl's Farm Down G70 (Christie 1964, 36, pl 111) the cremation pit, with its circularity, its 2ft depth and the signs of vertical tool marks down its sides can be cited as a classic example of a well-formed container pit for a human cremation of the Early Bronze Age.

The series of primary and secondary cremation pits at Snail Down (excluding Sites II and XVI) had the following dimensions shown in Table 39.

The oval burial pit beneath Site XIV was considerably larger than the others exposed during the course of our excavations. The pits from Sites III(2) and XVII were

Site	Primary/ Secondary	Chalk-surface Dimensions	Depth from top of chalk	Tool Marks
I	Primary	3 × 3½ft	1¾ft	
III	Primary	4¼ × 3½ft	6in	
III	Secondary 1	2ft 2in diam	1⅓ft	
III	Secondary 2	1ft 7in diam	7in	
XIV	Primary	7 × 5½ft	1½ft	
XV	Primary	3½ × 3ft	1¼ft	
XVII	Primary	2ft diam	1½ft	axe/adze

Table 39   Cremation pit sizes, Snail Down

rather smaller than the others. They varied less in depth, having mostly been carved some 1–½ft into solid chalk. The primary pit beneath Site III had hardly penetrated natural chalk and it is possible that when Hoare found it, his own clearing of its contents may have extended it into the chalk as well as altering its shape.

The two burial pits from Site II were exceptional. Their dimensions were as follows:

II	Primary	3½ft diam	2½ft deep
II	Off-centre	3¼ × 3½ft diam	2½ × 2¾ft deep

Like the miniature version in Site XVI – 1?ft diam, 1?ft depth, and the even smaller one, Pit 5, in Site II, 1?ft diameter, 1ft deep, each comprised an upper pit through whose floor a smaller hole had been cut (Figs 8, 28).

Reference has already been made (Site XVI) to recent finds of similar pits-within-pits from Rollestone Field, and from Down Farm, Woodcutts (Dorset): here attention can be drawn to further instances of this specialised shape, at Amesbury G61 and G72, bowl- and saucer-barrows respectively (Ashbee 1985, 58, 67 and fig 30). Each cremation had been deposited in the lower pit. It is possible to see something of a pit-within-a-pit in the funnel-shaped pit 4/6 lying outside Site 4 at City Farm, Hanborough (Oxon) and containing in its lower section an upright Collared Urn holding a washed cremation (Case *et al* 1966, 30). A much earlier discovery of this highly specialised shape of burial pit was made by Figg at Crowlink Barrow, Friston (Sussex: 1852, 207–212). This lower pit contained part of a human jaw, above it a cremation with charcoal. The double pit was comparable in size to Site II. A larger version occurred beneath Long Crichel barrow 7 (Dorset: Green *et al* 1983, 44, fig 4). Here the upper pit measured 8¼ × 6ft, depth 3ft; the lower pit was 5ft across and 3ft in depth.

Saucer-shaped depressions carved into the floors of one secondary burial pit in Site III (Fig 13; Pl 21) and in the central cremation pit beneath Site XVII (Fig 31, Pl 49) may possibly have been expressing something of the same ritual.

Digging the cremation (or inhumation) pit must have constituted one of the most personal episodes in a Bronze Age burial ceremony. Although, as Site XVII suggested, it may not always have been followed immediately by the barrow building – concealment of the burial area by a mound of pre-determined shape – the assumption must be that pit digging and deposition of the bones, with whatever grave goods, was the climax of a ceremony that may have lasted for many days.

We have indicated the range of pits that was available within the Bronze Age burial tradition and the care which was usually devoted to their formation. In no barrows was this more clearly expressed than in Snail Down Sites III and XVII. At Site III, in a procedure that lacks precise parallel (but see below), the ancient topsoil – part of the land surface covered with ash and burnt soil from the pyre alongside – was removed first and heaped around the southern edge of the pit; and subsoil from the second stage of pit forming went in an arc around its northern edge (Fig 12; Pl 17). It seems to convey an appreciation, however instinctive, of the make-up of the soil beneath their feet, fertile humus on top, then the more sterile chalky subsoil separating it from white bedrock. The same

discrimination was revealed at Site XVII, topsoil to the east, chalk heaped at the north, well clear of the burial pit's edge (Fig 31; Pl 45). Other instances known to the writer of the separation of humus and subsoil as part of burial procedure include the King Barrow, Stanton Harcourt (Harden and Treweeks 1945, 30) and Edmondsham (Dorset: Proudfoot 1963, 396, fig 3). At the King Barrow, during the re-filling of a pit dug to receive ashes from a funeral pyre, the subsoil gravel was returned to the pit first, burnt humus going back on top, in the correct natural order of soil formation. At Edmondsham, the large central grave, holding only a cremation, had been refilled in a distinctive sequence, turf first and then chalk, in reverse of nature. Such care taken to separate one from the other was surely only what an experienced farmer might show, and yet it has been documented so rarely in excavation.

The phenomenon of a spoil heap deliberately left beside the burial (or other) pit and preserved by the barrow's mound has been noted many times in Britain and elsewhere.

Spoil heaps beside burial pits under barrows

Wiltshire

Amesbury G71, Earl's Farm Down (Christie 1967, 339–340). Residual spoil after pit re-filled.

Bishops Cannings G81 (Robertson-Mackay 1980, 138, fig 2). Upcast piled immediately to the N and NE.

Down Farm, Pewsey, Sites A, B (Vatcher 1960, 341, 343). Spoil at Site A piled round pit; possibly also at Site B.

Knighton Hill, Broad Chalke (Rahtz 1970, 81). Main upcast piled on E side of pit before being shovelled back.

Shrewton, Net Down 5f (Green & Rollo-Smith 1984, 269–270, fig 8). Upcast NE of central Pit 1.

Shrewton, New Down 5i (*ibid*, 273–274, fig 10). Upcast S of Pit 1.

Shrewton, New Down 5j (*ibid*, 273). Residue of upcast left around pit's edge.

Shrewton, Rollestone Down 23 (*ibid*, 281–283, fig 14). Upcast E of Pit 1.

Sutton Veney (Johnston 1980, 33). Spoil piled around pit.

Winterbourne Stoke G47 (Gingell 1988, 60). Spoil around, then partly pulled back into pit.

Dorset

Canford Heath (Ashbee 1956, 45–46, Figs 2, 3). Possible spoil heap beside central pit.

Crichel Down Barrow 11 (S and C M Piggott 1944, pl XIV). Chalk rubble heaped around edge of deep burial shaft.

Launceston Down Barrow 5 (Green *et al* 1983, 41) . Primary grave refilled with its own spoil.

Launceston Down Barrow 7 (*ibid*, 46, fig 5). Upcast left around central inhumation pit.

Litton Cheney Barrow B (Wacher 1959, 164). Spoil heaped around N side of pit but much returned.

Simons Ground Barrow F (White 1982, 12, fig 11). Spoil heaped on N side of pit.

Hampshire

Beaulieu Barrow IV (C M Piggott 1943, 12). Spoil spread as a floor around NW half of pit.

Hurn, near Christchurch, Barrow 1 (C M Piggott 1943a, 252). Spoil returned to pit and also heaped over as a gravel cairn.

Cornwall

Watch Hill, St Stephen-in-Brannel (Miles 1975, 10–11). Upcast around central pit.

Berkshire

Hodcott Down Barrow a (Richards 1991, 12, 13, fig 9). Spoil in an extended heap eastwards from edge of cremation pit.

Oxfordshire

Radley Barrow 2 (Atkinson 1954, 18–19). Some spoil to one side of pit, the rest spread over it after re-filling.

Suffolk

Poor's Heath, Risby (Vatcher and Vatcher 1976, 267–269, fig 3). Spoil thrown neatly to SW of grave and not used for its re-fill. Other early burial pits also with spoil heaps.

Derbyshire

Swarkeston Lowes Barrow 4 (Greenfield 1960, 4). Some upcast piled around coffin pit.

Denbighshire

Brenig Barrow 41 (Lynch 1974, 26 and plan). Shale upcast around central pit in wide spreads.

North Yorkshire

Little Ouseburn Barrow (Rahtz 1989, 23, figs 9, 10). Upcast around central pit, bearing footprints.

Tayside (Perthshire)

Pitnacree (Coles and Simpson 1965, 40–41, pl XI). Especially clear evidence for upcast left beside a post pit.

FRANCE

Kervingar (Plouarzel, Brittany: Giot 1960, 135, fig 37). Spoil heap beside burial vault beneath Armorican round barrow.

HOLLAND

The Eight Beatitudes, Barrows 1, 16 (Glasbergen 1954, 33, pls 111, XVII). Spoil in a spread around central pits.

During a number of recent barrow excavations it has been recorded that the spoil from a burial pit was used to re-fill the pit or to act as packing round a coffin or other related feature. In some of these instances the upcast was so completely re-used that no trace remained of a spoil heap like those listed above. This would apply certainly to the large pit from Snail Down Site I, whose clean chalk filling appeared to have been replaced very soon after its excavation. It was sealed beneath the disc-barrow's second mound which, like the central mound, is most likely to have been derived from the substantial surrounding barrow ditch.

At Earl's Farm Down G70 (Christie 1964, 36), the spoil from the main cremation pit may have been used to pack the hole of a large post standing beside it. The excavation of West Overton G6b (Smith and Simpson 1966, 127) showed that the central grave had been refilled by its own spoil. The same could also be said for the central cremation pit at Radley Barrow 4a (Williams 1948, 5), whose re-filling was derived entirely from what had just been dug out. So too the pit beside the funeral pyre beneath the Stanton Harcourt King Barrow (Harden and Treweeks 1945, 30).

Overall, however, it seems to have been more usual to dispose elsewhere of the spoil from a burial pit, leaving no trace of it either in the pit's subsequent re-fill or upon the ancient land surface preserved by the barrow mound. At Snail Down, pit spoil was lacking entirely from around the central burial at Site I and from both pits at Site II. No spoil occurred in the vicinity of the pits beneath Sites XIV and XV, but the condition of both mounds through rabbit burrows and rabbiting was such that this lack of evidence must not be treated as conclusive. Tank damage may also have removed traces of spoil from the first secondary burial at Site III.

The stage during burial ceremonial at which a pit was dug to receive corpse or cremation followed no set rule. At Snail Down Site XVII, the cremation pit may have been dug some little time before the burial was made. Indeed the large Collared Urn subsequently smashed in it could have been set there for a while before removal and the enactment of other events prior to breaking and final burial. At Site III it was clear that the pit had been dug soon after the pyre had been fired and burnt bones collected: the pit's spoil sealed a burnt land surface and incorporated much burnt material. Although Site III reflected normal procedure when a cremation pit was sited beside its pyre, this appeared to have been broken at Norton Bavant G1Oc (Goddard 1917, 400), where it was recorded that the pit had been dug before lighting the pyre.

At Snail Down it seems to have been traditional to locate the primary grave pit as near to the centre of the final structure as possible. The pit beneath the central mound of Site I may have replaced a laying out marker there; and was located close to the hole left by such a peg at Site III. The same can be shown for Sites II and XVII. Assuming that Sites XIV and XV were early barrows on the Down (Fig 61), it should be noted that their burial pits had been planned noticeably off-centre (Figs 21, 25). The secondary or additional burials found during the excavations of 1953–1957, like other features found beneath the mounds, all lay to the south-west, except for the inhumation added to Site XXII. These rules of positioning were noted by Green among round barrows in the Great Ouse Valley, where the primary burials were located invariably to the west of his barrows' central point (1975, 129). At Snail Down as among the ring-ditch builders at Milton Keynes, tradition ruled the location of all burials beneath or made as additions to the barrow mounds.

The central pit of Site V and that of Secondary Cremation I at Site III, had both been sealed by a covering that may have stood proud of the surrounding land surface. A South Wales parallel has already been cited for the puddled chalk cover to the ritual pit at Site V. Other carefully made pit covers have been recorded in recent years from Wiltshire and Dorset.

Covers for burial pits

Wiltshire

> Amesbury G133, King Barrow Ridge (Gingell 1988, 36). Chalk crust covering small ritual pit at centre.
> Shrewton, Net Down 5a (Green & Rollo-Smith 1984, 260). Chalk upcast returned to seal burial pit.
> Shrewton, Net Down 5f (*ibid*, 269). Chalk upcast and turf used to seal burial pit.
> Shrewton, Net Down 5L (*ibid*, 279, fig 13). Two burial pits sealed with chalk capping.
> Wilsford cum Lake G51 (Smith 1991,17, fig 4). Phase 3 cremation pit sealed by chalk rubble.

Dorset

> Kinson Barrow 2 (Knocker 1959, 135). Central pit had traces of clayey sand sealing.
> Simons Ground Barrow F (White 1982, 12, fig 11). Sandstone block in mouth of pit.

Perhaps surprisingly, such covers to burial pits in Wessex are rarely recorded, as the shortness of this list indicates. They seem to be different in concept from coverings – or lids placed over the mouths of urns, like the slab of Purbeck limestone sealing the top of a Deverel Rimbury urn and sheltering an Accessory Vessel placed beside it found with the central cremation burial at Barrow 3, Crichel Down (S and C M Piggott 1944, 67, fig 13). Other urn coverings, including wood (Crichel Down again, barrow 10: *ibid*, 73, fig 20), and cloth, have been recorded from time to time as evidence of this approach to the ritual need perceived by some communities to seal a pit or its content or both. More frequently found are small flint cairns, of the kind that sealed Secondary Burial 1 at Site III and originally covered – before being dispersed anciently – Secondary Burial 2 there. Post-1945 discoveries of such protective cairns from Wiltshire and Dorset have been recorded.

Cairns covering graves in Wiltshire and Dorset

Wiltshire

> Amesbury G71, Earl's Farm Down (Christie 1967, 343–344, fig 4). Cairn over child inhumation.
> Amesbury G72, Earl's Farm Down (Ashbee 1985, 64). Cairn over central grave, protecting upstanding urn.
> Knighton Hill, Broad Chalke (Rahtz 1970, 79, fig 6). Cairn over central cremation pit, protecting upstanding Deverel Rimbury urn.
> Shrewton, Net Down 5a, 5j (Green and Rollo-Smith 1984, 262, 273). Flint cairns heaped over burial pits: sarsen included in 5a.
> Woodford G13, Heale Hill (Gingell 1988, 31). Probable cairn over central inhumation grave.

Dorset

> Crichel Down Barrows 3 and 8 (S and C M Piggott 1944, 66, 71, figs 13, 17). Cairns covering central burial area.
> Frampton Barrow 2 (Forde-Johnston 1959, 123–124). Layer of flints sealing secondary inhumation grave.
> Long Bredy (Eogan 1978, 43). Large flint cairn beneath chalk mound.

10 THE BURIAL PROCESS: THE GRAVE-GOODS

For numbers and variety of barrow types, for the great size of some of them and the majesty of their layout within an imposing landscape, Snail Down is one of the finest Bronze Age barrow cemeteries in Britain. Yet none of this is mirrored in the grave-goods that accompanied the bones of those buried there. What has been found, first by Hoare in 1805 and then during 1953–1957, is set down in Table 40.

The only grave-group that might be described as chieftainly came from the central grave of Site XIX in 1805: within a wooden coffin, a cremation was accompanied by a small ogival dagger in its scabbard (Gerloff 1975, 105, No 184) and a decorated copper alloy ring-headed pin, also cased (Fig 57: Annable and Simpson 1964, Nos 193, 194). Now missing is the Accessory Cup, in fragments, that was also recorded. Well-made barbed and tanged flint arrowheads, antler-surrounded cremation and a pebble (Fig 58: Annable and Simpson 1964, 57 and 112, Nos 396–398) marked Hoare's Hunter's Barrow (2253) as the grave of somebody almost equally of note. At the western extreme of the cemetery, barrow 2207, a cenotaph (see Section 11 below), covered an unusually extensive offering of bone points and pins, a bone version of a shale or amber spacer plate (unless it be a copy of an archer's wrist guard), a grooved whetstone and a copper alloy axe-chisel fitted into a bone handle (Fig 56: N Thomas 1954, 317–320, fig 2; Annable and Simpson 1964, 57 and 112, Nos 382–389). With these, but now lost, Hoare reported finding three stone hones, one of them possibly another grooved whetstone. This grave must have been that of a master craftsman.

Two groups of grave-goods consisted of token offerings of beads. Between them, Sites III (2) and XXII (2) included shell, shale, jet, amber, stone and a single faience bead (Fig 54); an unassociated shale dumb-bell-shaped one from Site XV may have been derived from the off centre cremation burial (Figs 26, 54; K8).

The pottery with which some of the graves were provided was generally of good quality, the urns from Sites III (2), XVII and XVIII being outstanding (Figs 45, 47, 43). At the other end of the scale a Bipartite Vessel buried with Site III (3) (Fig 46, D13) is as basic an example of Bronze Age ceramics as you could dread to find. Most of these vessels were there as containers and may not have been considered as grave-goods. More obviously an offering was the Accessory Cup D4 from Site II, found by Hoare with another, of which only a rim sherd has survived, together with a copper alloy awl (Fig 44, D4, D5; fig 55, L2).

Metal awls, like the one found with the cremation from Sites I (2) and II(1), have been cited as pins used to fasten the bag in which the cremation lay, though they seem much too short for that. As for the cranial disc from Site II (2) (Fig 38; Pl 60), its inclusion is understandable enough if its extraction had caused the death of the person whose burnt bones it accompanied.

To the less obviously spectacular category of grave goods belonged the flint scraper and perhaps the two sherds placed in the cremation pit beneath Site XIV, and the worked flint found among the cremated bones at the centre of Site III (contained originally in an Urn).

When the grave finds are considered in relation to their position within the cemetery, it might not be totally coincidental that barrows 2207, 2253 and Site XIX, containing the three richest groups of offerings, fall at each end and near the middle of the cemetery, as if carefully shared out among the apparently more modestly provided graves. Yet to have arranged that, when the development of the cemetery must have been spread at least over generations, would have been difficult.

Outside the environs of Stonehenge, the finds from a great barrow cemetery like Snail Down are not unduly insignificant: comparable groups of barrows like Oakley Down (Dorset:Woodward 2000, fig 28) or Barrow Hills Field, Radley (Oxon: Barclay and Halpin 1999, *passim*)) were generally furnished for the after life in apparent moderation, while usually having in each a small number of graves whose offerings stood out for their obvious richness.

Deliberate breakage of pottery (Site XVII: Pl 47) and the careful burial of sherds (Sites II (2), XIV, XVII (Pl 50) and possibly XVI and XIX); and the concentrated group of high-quality Collared Urn sherds (D8) found just above the ancient land surface close to the central burial in Site III (Figs 10, 45) was a feature of pottery treatment at Snail Down that has not been recorded so strikingly in other extensively excavated barrow cemeteries. As a recurring burial trait here it offers a powerful argument for continuity of funeral practice over several decades and, for the same reason, it supports our belief (Section 18 below) that Snail Down was the burial ground for a single community.

Broken objects in graves have been commented upon many times, especially by scholars like L V Grinsell (1975, chap 7). Positive evidence for the violent smashing of an urn has so far been recorded only from Snail Down. Much more frequent has been the finding of fragmentary pottery and metalwork whose damaged state invites description as ritual (ie deliberate) breakage.

Evidence for ritual breakage of grave goods

Wiltshire

Amesbury G58, New Barn Down (Ashbee 1985, 67–69). Top of dagger handle broken off.

Amesbury G70, Earl's Farm Down (Christie 1964, 38). Sherds of urn and Accessory Cup suggested deliberate breakage.

Bishops Cannings G61 (Thurnam 1860, 323). Sherds mixed with cremation.

Down Farm, Pewsey, Site A, G4 (Vatcher 1960, 343). Inclusion of sherds of ?deliberately broken urn with inhumation.

Knighton Hill, Broad Chalke (Rahtz 1970, 78, 81). Deverel Rimbury urn buried as fragments with cremation.

Near Knook Barrow, Heytesbury (R H Cunnington 1954, 220–221). Metal dagger buried in two pieces with a cremation in an urn. William Cunnington's first excavation, c 1798.

Lamb Down, Codford St Mary, Site F (Vatcher 1963, 425). Urn sherds scattered around cremation on ancient land surface.

Ogborne St Andrew Barrow 6 (Cunnington 1881, 69). Cist containing cremation and Food Vessel sherds.

Sutton Veney (Johnston 1980, 33, 34, fig 4). Shattered Food Vessel (not necessarily deliberate) buried with inhumation.

Winterbourne Stoke G45, Greenland Farm (Christie 1970, 67). Urn sherds crushed into a ritual deposit of flints.

Dorset

Crichel Down Barrow 1 (S and C M Piggott 1944, 63). Urn burnt after breaking.

Crichel Down Barrow 7 (*ibid*, 69). Urn sherds in soil around pit.

Down Farm (Barrett *et al* 1991, 128). Broken, incomplete Food Vessel in post hole associated with pond-barrow.

Oakley Down (White and Reed 1971, 160). Large, fragmentary Collared Urn in central cremation pit.

Hampshire

Rockbourne Down (S and C M Piggott 1945, 157–159, figs 5, 6). Food offering in Food Vessel entirely lacking its upper half.

Oxfordshire

Ashville Trading Estate, Abingdon, cremation 1032 (Parrington 1978, 9–10, pl IV). Pit containing cremation, pyre material and Collared Vessel buried as sherds.

Table 40   Grave-goods associated with burials and barrows; (2) indicates secondary or satellite burials or contexts

	I (2)	I (2)	II (2)(2)	II (2)	III	III	V	VIII	X	XI	XII	XIII	XIV	XV	XV (2)	XVII	XVII (2)	XVIII	XIX	XX	XXII (2)	2207	2253
POTTERY																							
Peterborough Ware, sherds	X				X	X			X	X	X	X	X	X		X		X	X				
Beaker, sherds	X			X	X	X			X	X	X	X	X	X		X		X	X	X			
Grooved Ware, sherds					X	X		X	X											X			
Collared Urn					?	2										X		X					
Collared Vessel						X						X						X					
Collared Vessel, sherds	X				X	X				X	X	X	X				X						
Bipartite Vessel						X																	
Food Vessel	X		X	X									X										
Food Vessel, sherds	X		X	X																			
Accessory Cup				2																			
Accessory Vessel, sherds				2									X										
STONE, FLINT																							
Axe-head, stone				X																			
Whetstone, grooved																						2	X
Whetstone																						2	5
Pebble																							
Arrowhead, flint																							
Scraper, flint					X								X										
COPPER ALLOY																							
Dagger, ogival																			X				
Pin, ring-headed																			X				
Awl		X		X																			
Axe, miniature																						X	
Unidentified					X																		
BONE, ANTLER																							
Handle, axe																						X	
Pin, perforated																						X	
Pin																						3	
Plate																						X	X
Wreath, antler																							
BEADS																							
Faience						X								?									
Amber						X															2		
Jet						3																	
Jet-shale						X									?								
Shell						X															X		
Stone						X																	
DOG																							X
BURIAL DETAIL																							
Trepanned disc																							
Cremation	X		X		X	X						X	X	X		X		X	?2				X
Inhumation	3		X	X	2		X							5							X		
Cenotaph																						?	

South Glamorgan

Sutton 268' Llandow (Fox 1959, 67). Sherds of Beaker, packed around skull of central burial.

Gwynedd

Druids' Circle 277, Penmaenmawr (Griffiths 1960, 316–317). Pit containing empty, broken Food Vessel.

Derbyshire

Doll Tor, Stanton Moor (Heathcote 1939, 117). Broken urns (?Collared) associated with cremations. Swarkeston Lowes Barrow 4 (Greenfield 1960, 7). Upper filling of cremation pit contained sherds of incomplete Collared Urn.

The order in which grave-goods were placed with the interment in its pit, the positioning of objects in the grave, these were significant considerations, unlikely to have been left to chance. The beads found associated with Secondary Burial 1 (Cremation 8) at Site III make the point: two little amber beads and one of faience were among the bones close to the base of the urn; shale beads lay at a higher level. As the flint cairn was heaped over the urn in its pit another shale bead, dumb-bell-shaped, was added to complete the gift. An almost identical bead, found beneath Skeleton I (Inhumation 3) (later Bronze Age) added to Site XV, may have been a similar late offering, although it might have come originally from the off-centre primary burial. When Hoare opened the Hunter's Barrow (2253: Hoare 1812, 183–184) he found the skeleton of what must have been the dead man's dog nearly six feet above the burial that had been placed upon the barrow's floor, the original land surface. Here an antler "wreath" had been arranged around burnt bones probably contained in a bag, or else emptied out of a bag so neatly that the pile they made was worthy of note. The offering – five flint arrowheads and a pebble – had been put among the bones. Why five arrowheads? Such a small number has been recorded many times with skeletons accompanied by Beakers: it seems to have represented the average and surprisingly frugal contents of a quiver of that time (Clark 1963, 77).

The saucer-shaped hollows carefully scraped out of the floors of cremation pits containing urns at Sites III (2) and XVII indicated where the urns' bases were to be set – precisely. Thus was it done at the former. Thus may it have been done also at XVII, if it be allowed that the large urn smashed there had originally stood for a time in its pit before further burial ceremonial required its removal. When the final act took place, first the pit floor with its urn-base depression was covered with some burial deposit: only then was the urn put back and smashed; and followed by the cremated bones and final pit-filling. This carefully thought-out order of deposition was matched at the barrow at Knighton Hill, Broad Chalke. Ash and some burnt human bone filled the lowest part of the pit; the urn and its cremation then followed (Rahtz 1970, 78–79).

When Hoare excavated Site XVIII, he found that the elegant Collared Urn (Fig 43, D24) had been placed deliberately at the edge of a substantial cremation pit (Hoare 1812, 184). So too with the central burial at Site II. The Accessory Cup D4, recovered complete (Fig 44), had evidently been placed near the top of the piled cremation: lower down among the bones a second vessel was added with an awl (Fig 44, D5, L2). And whereas the upper vessel appears to have been placed without particular ceremony, Hoare describes how the lower one had a wall of bones carefully placed around it as if for its protection (Hoare 1812, 182).

Excavation of the central burial beneath the larger mound of Site XIX revealed a wooden coffin deposited on the ancient land surface, which had been packed with a cremation and grave goods before burial. That task might have been done at the man's home and the burial and complete offering brought to the barrow site. Possibly for this reason the copper alloy dagger and ring-headed pin (Fig 57) had each been sheathed, and wrapped with cloth as an added protection (Hoare 1812, 185; see also Section M).

All the Collared Urns containing cremations uncovered so far at Snail Down have been found upright. Only a Food Vessel, D3, possibly containing an offering, has been unearthed lying inverted (Fig 8; Pl 12).

11 THE BURIAL PROCESS: CENOTAPHS AND RITUAL BARROWS

Consideration of grave-goods and burial methods brings us to the phenomenon of the so-called cenotaph barrows, of which there appear to have been at least five at Snail Down. Hoare concealed his frustration and almost disbelief when failing to find central burials, by classifying each as a *tumulus honorarius* or *cenotaphium* (1812, 186): Warne found another Latin term for the phenomenon, *tumulus inanis* (1866, Communications from personal friends, 23), preferring, one suspects, the derivative silly to the Latin empty. For Sir Cyril Fox it was no strange thing to find such an 'empty' barrow, as he did at Six Wells 267' (South Glam: 1959, 152). He proposed a new class for it, 'ritual barrow', and saw the type as the final covering mound – barrow-like – for a structure in which rituals were performed for whatever purpose, until, in due time, that activity had to cease and the place be sealed. At Six Wells 267' the structure covered by the mound was a timber circle twenty-eight feet across that may have been a building; to Fox, a 'ritual hut'. It contained a small, dome-covered cylindrical pit akin to the covered pit at Site V (Fig 17; Pls 27, 28), whose earthy clay contents defied analysis. The Six Wells structure's timbers had been drawn out before this sanctified area was hidden and preserved beneath a mound.

Some non-sepulchral barrows may, then, be regarded as a formalised means of preserving a sacred place for posterity, their original purpose perhaps removed from burial practice. Where established by complete excavation, the term *ritual barrow* can be accepted.

For some such barrows, the mound itself seems to have been what the builders required. Lynch (1974, 39–41) has suggested that Barrow 47 among her Brenig (Denbighs) series was more likely to have been a territorial marker, its position on a promontory laying dramatic claim to the land around it.

Cenotaph may reasonably be used to describe several barrows whose recorded contents proclaim burial, without the presence of a corpse. For the barrow at Crig-a-Mennis, Liskey (Cornwall), Christie (1960, 88–89) argued that, in the absence of a burial, the presence of two *empty* Cornish urns (of outstanding quality) can best be explained as tokens for dead people, perhaps drowned at sea, in which direction the causeway across the barrow's ditch was directed. When death struck while away from home, burial would probably have taken place wherever that was, accounting, in part, possibly, for the existence of some isolated barrows. We have tentatively attributed the intrusive inhumation of a youth in Site XXII to such an emergency; the isolated bowl-barrow 2209 (Fig 2A) might have been the covering for another stranger. Commemoration of distant burial could have been an important reason for a cenotaph barrow, especially when the community was sufficiently strong to maintain a cemetery of the magnitude of Snail Down.

An essential criterion in the establishment of a cenotaph by excavation must be that examination of the mound was comprehensive. This cannot be claimed for the seven mounds at Snail Down opened by Hoare and listed below, since his method was usually restricted to a central pit or square, sometimes undermining its sides to expose further ancient ground. Only rarely, as at Bush Barrow (Wilsford (S) G5), did he drive in a trench from the mound's edge*. At Snail Down his work was as superficial and centre-focused as usual. Yet to uncover a grave pit, and not to find either form of burial seems at least reasonably strong evidence that the barrow was commemorating a person whose body had not been there to inter.

Though Sites X–XIII were extensively excavated without result, we have preferred to omit them from consideration as cenotaphs. Their rabbit- and rabbitter-riddled state left too many grounds for doubt, nor were they examined completely during our excavations, as the plan, Fig 21, makes clear. More extensive work at the better-preserved Site XIV revealed an off-central burial. This leaves Site V for consideration, since an extensive but still incomplete excavation uncovered central features resembling those beneath Fox's ritual barrow at Six Wells 267'. It too may have been a cenotaph and we

include it in our table below. Yet the special shape of this earthwork, which we have likened to the ring-ditches of the Upper Thames and elsewhere, may require it to be regarded as yet another type of burial-free ritual structure.

Site XXII is included in Table 41 because Hoare found no evidence for burial despite a substantial central excavation.

Of these, 2207 yielded important grave goods in an otherwise empty pit (Fig 56). The central areas of the other cenotaph barrows cleared by Hoare were featureless.

Except for 2257, the possible Snail Down cenotaphs are concentrated in the western half of the cemetery; we argue below that 2207 may have been a key mound in the development of the cemetery's layout (below, section 17; Fig 61).

Besides those at Snail Down, other examples of apparent cenotaphs and ritual barrows have been recorded in recent years as follows.

Apparent cenotaph and ritual barrows

Wiltshire

> Amesbury G132, King Barrow Ridge (Gingell 1988, 39–40).
> Down Farm, Pewsey, Site B (Vatcher 1960, 343–345). But possibly robbed.
> Milton Lilbourne triple barrow, G2–4 (Ashbee 1986, 38).

Dorset

> Canford Heath (Ashbee 1956, 45–47).
> Canford Heath, Poole, Barrow 24 (Hawsey and Shackley 1980, 42).
> Crichel Down Barrow 4 (S and C M Piggott 1944, 67).
> Crichel Down Barrow 8 (*ibid*, 71).
> Kinson, near Bournemouth (Knocker 1959, 135–137).
> Portesham (Thompson and Ashbee 1957, 126). Skeleton possibly destroyed by acid soil.
> Simons Ground, Hampreston, Site B (White 1982, 5–6, fig 4).

			SITES	
Barrow type	Hoare Numbers	SPTA	(1953–57) Bowl	Grave Goods
Bowl	11	2229	XX	
Bowl	2	2207		●
Bowl	9	2231		
Bowl	5	2216		
Bell	21	2257		
Ring-ditch	23	2266	V	
Bell with added mound 11	25	2269	XXII	

Table 41   Possible cenotaph or ritual barrows at Snail Down

*This is suggested by perusal of air photographs as well as by Hoare's published description of the excavation (1812, 202-205) and the extended cutting that it must have involved.

Hampshire and the Isle of Wight

Hurn Barrow 2 (C M Piggott, 1943a, 256–257).
Ashy Down Barrow 9, (Drewett 1972, 41–42).

West Sussex

West Heath, Harting, Barrows I–IV (Drewett 1976, 127–136, 142). Acid soil may have destroyed burials.

Cornwall

Carloggas, Barrow III (Miles 1975, 45–50).
Crig-a-Mennis, Liskey (Christie 1960, 88–89).
Davidstow Moor (Christie 1988, 31–51).

Berkshire

Farncombe Down (Rahtz 1962, 4).

Oxfordshire

Radley Barrow 6 (Williams 1948, 12–13).

Yorkshire (NR)

Kildale Moor cairns (Ashbee 1957). Acid soil may have destroyed all burials: none found.

South Glamorgan

Six Wells 267' (Fox 1959, 152).

Denbighshire

Brenig Barrow 47 (Lynch 1974, 39–41)

12 THE BURIAL PROCESS; THE MOURNERS

Only beneath Site III was there a suggestion that provision had been made for mourners or other members of the community. North-west of the area of the funeral pyre lay a row of stake holes with a central gap, (Figs 9, 12) which in all probability was part of the burial ceremonial there and not a residue from the nearby pre-barrow Beaker settlement. Regular in layout (unlike the settlement stakeholes) and suggestively close to the area of the burial pit, they invite explanation in terms of the cremation that took place beside them. It seems improbable that a line of fencing would have been erected to control or encourage a draught for the pyre. It is possible that this fence – if such it is – may have been erected as a symbolic barrier to restrict access, or a view of the pyre, between those closely related to the deceased and charged with the burning and disposal of her ashes, and others who were less directly concerned. More remotely still, the fence with its gap might have been erected to represent one wall of a token house, with an entrance whence the dead began her last journey. For the rest, the record remains tantalisingly silent.

13 BARROW BUILDING: LOCATION AND PLANNING

Choosing the position for an addition to the cemetery would have been one of two fundamental considerations at the time of a funeral. The other was the burial rite – cremation or inhumation? – and therefore the location of the funeral pyre in the event of a body-burning. For the Snail Down people cremation was the preference. Site III, and the presence of much charcoal in some of Hoare's sites, suggest that cremation at the designated barrow space was not unusual. For other cremations we have no means of knowing where the burnings took place. An almost noticeable rarity of scraps of charcoal from the barrows excavated in the fifties suggests that, if not at the site of the barrow, pyres were located away from Snail Down.

At an early stage in the development of the cemetery it must have been decided to locate barrows in an alignment between 2207 and Site XXI (Figs 2, 2A, 61). Less rigidity was attached to the south-easterly alignment, or spread, between Sites XXI and XXII; and for a few, barrows were allowed almost anywhere within that angle as long as it was close to either of the lines. Evidently Site XVI had to remain isolated: and 2254 was placed centrally between it and Site XXII. No mounds were built on the gently rising ground to the south, except for our discovery, 2244, whose potential significance has been remarked upon (Section1) and to which we shall return (Section 17). Barrows 2217 and 2216, with Site III, are spaced symmetrically, leaving a gap between 2216 and Site II for another barrow of roughly equivalent size. Otherwise, spacing was irregular. Three pairs of barrows almost touch: VIII and IV, I and XVIII, XIX and XXII. Sites X–XIV are contiguous: and there appears to have been thought-out spacing in the alignment between 2220 and 2235. When the centre of Site III had to be located on the ground, careful calculation would thus have been necessary to settle its diameter, assuming that 2217 and Site XIV were already built (Section 17).

At Snail Down the barrow-building tradition was for circularity. Only Sites V, XVIII, 2255 and 2244 seem to have been oval or (XVIII) sub-circular. Circular barrow building had to start by driving in a peg (as in Site III, Fig 9) and marking out the line of the ditch by cord of selected radius. Where the barrow was to be a bell (eg Site III), or have an outer bank like the two discs and saucer (Sites I, IV and II), concentric rings had also to be marked on the ground which incorporated a ditch width calculated to produce sufficient turf and chalk for mounds and banks. We have no reason to believe that any of the Snail Down mounds had been augmented by spoil gathered from elsewhere. To work out the yield of a ditch of chosen diameter so as to build a mound of preconceived size was a difficult computation, not always achieved. At Rollestone Down G43, a bell-barrow, a slot had been cut through the floor of its ditch which Ozanne interpreted as an afterthought since the ditch, as originally dug, had not yielded enough spoil for the outer bank that was part of the barrow's original design (Ozanne 1972, 54–55).

When a berm had to be allowed for, as at Site III, calculation of mound height and diameter *vis-à-vis* diameter, width and depth of ditch needed to be particularly accurate, especially if the berm was to retain its turf.

Laying-out stakes and other barrow-builders' markers have been recorded within the region and beyond.

Laying-out stakes and other barrow-builders' markers

Wiltshire

Amesbury G51, Stonehenge Cursus Group (Ashbee 1978, 8, fig 2). Barrow ditch with four causeways symmetrical to centre.
Amesbury G70, Earl's Farm Down (Christie 1964, 35, 42, fig 2). Central post (set up in a post hole) possibly for ritual as well as laying out barrow.
Avebury G55 (Smith 1965, 26–28, 40, fig 1). Mound not central to ditch (other examples noted in report).
Lamb Down, Codford, Site C (Vatcher 1963, 422, fig 3). Single central stake, extending up into mound.
Winterbourne Stoke G30 (Christie 1963, 377, fig 3). Of four central stakes, the only one withdrawn lay at the exact centre.
Winterbourne Stoke G45, Greenland Farm (Christie 1970, 67). Flint blocks used to lay out scraped-up barrow.
Sutton Veney (Johnston 1980, 31, 33, fig 2). Burial pit exactly south of the barrow centre.

Dorset

Crichel Down Barrow 9 (S and C M Piggott 1944, 71, fig 19). Shallow ?laying out ditch followed inner edge of true ditch.

Oxfordshire

Stanton Harcourt King Barrow (Harden and Treweeks 1945, 25, fig 8). Pyre post probably also for laying out.
City Farm, Hanborough, Site 4 (Case *et al* 1966, 29). Stake central to two ditch circles.

Denbighshire

Brenig Barrow 51 (Lynch 1975, 19). Central stake, possibly a permanent feature of the circle.

At the planning stage a decision would have been required about the need for a post ring, whether out of structural necessity as at Site XIX (to prevent the two mounds from coalescing too quickly), or symbolic, perhaps, of a ditch, as at Site XV; or decorative, if such poles were painted or carved or supported other adornment. If required, timbers had to be gathered and prepared, their quantity depending upon the proposed diameter of the mound they were to enclose.

So too had someone to decree whether the barrow mound was to be derived from a surrounding ditch or else scraped up from round about, using mainly turf and topsoil. Such a form of barrow would have created much untidiness in a cemetery like Snail Down, where it is our belief that ordered external appearance was important (Sections 14, 15). This is an argument for considering Sites X-XV as early within its development (Section 17; Fig 61).

Excavation in Wiltshire and beyond has established the existence of scraped-up barrow mounds. At Brenig 41 (Denbighs: Lynch 1974, 23) part of the turf core had been brought up from the valley floor some distance away. Evidence for scraped-up or ditchless barrows is relatively rare.

Scraped-up or ditchless barrows

Wiltshire

Amesbury G73, Earl's Farm Down (Thomas 1956a, 239).
Bishops Cannings G62 and G62a (Proudfoot 1965, 133).
Down Farm, Pewsey, Sites A, B (Vatcher 1960, 340–345, fig 2).
Fosbury 4, near Shalbourne (Johnston 1963, 366–367, fig 5).
Lamb Down, Codford St Mary, Sites B, C (Vatcher 1963, 420, 422, fig 5).
Overton Hill G6b (Smith and Simpson 1966, 122–125, fig 1).
Wilsford cum Lake G52-G54 (Smith 1991, 19–26, figs 9, 10).
Winterbourne Stoke G45, Greenland Farm (Christie 1970, 64–67, fig 2).
Woodford G13, Heale Hill (Gingell 1988, 31, fig 9).

Dorset

Crichel Down Barrows 4, 7, 12–18 (S and C M Piggott 1944, 67, 69, 74–77, figs 16, 21, 24, 26).
Litton Cheney Barrow b (Wacher 1959, 163–165). Mound scraped-up: penannular ditch for outer bank and final mound covering.

Hampshire and the Isle of Wight

Arreton Down, Isle of Wight (Alexander and Ozannes 1960, 269, fig 3).
Ashy Down Barrow 9, (Drewett 1972, 41–42).
Beaulieu Barrows I, VII (C M Piggott 1943, 5–6, fig 3).
Hurn, Christchurch, Barrows 1–3 (C M Piggott 1943a).
Stoney Cross Barrow I (C M Piggott 1943, 20, fig 15).

Sussex

Minstead, West Sussex (Drewett 1975, 56–58).
West Heath, Harting, Barrows II, V, VI, VIII, IX (Drewett 1976, 131; *ibid* 1985, *passim*).

Derbyshire

Swarkeston Lowes Barrow 4 (Greenfield 1961, 4). First-phase barrow ditchless.

Cheshire

Gallowsclough Hill (Forde-Johnston 1961, 81). Ditchless.

Denbighshire

Brenig Barrow 41 (Lynch 1974, 23). Turves from surrounding area and valley bottom.

Finally, as a symbol whose importance we can only guess at, the form of the barrow had to be decided. Snail Down comprises:

bowl-barrows	14
bell-barrows	4
double bell-barrow	1
bell-barrow with added mound	1
disc-barrow	1
disc-barrow with two mounds	1
saucer-barrow	1
pond-barrow	1
scraped-up mounds	5
scraped-up mound with stake ring	1
ring-ditch	1
small oval ring-ditch	1

Of these 32 barrows, only three are truly monumental by Wessex standards, Sites VIII, XIX and XXII. They are all bell-barrows with noticeably wide berms. Three other bell-barrows, Site III, 2257 and 2254 are of more modest size while still constituting major funerary monuments. One of them was a cenotaph. The two disc-barrows are similar in diameter to bells like Site III. As enclosed spaces they would have been impressive. The rest of the barrows today lack outstanding visual significance.

Barrow excavators like Drewett (1976, 141–142) have attempted to identify one particular mound within a cemetery as having had special importance and often, therefore, being of notable size. For Drewett, Barrow 3 among the West Heath, Harting (Sussex) group was the Founder Barrow. At Snail Down, Site VIII dominates the main northeast/south-west element of the cemetery, and seems to have been closely associated with Site IV, whose ditch it appears to intersect. Sites XIX and XXII assume a commanding role in the apparently less carefully planned eastern alignment. Of all sites, VIII stands as dominant, in a dominating position. Yet Hoare christened Site XXII the King Barrow (1812, 185). We return to this matter below (Section 17).

14 BARROW BUILDING: CONSTRUCTION

Barrow excavation over many years has revealed, often dramatically, how the work was done. In chalk country the successive stages usually come to light with extraordi-

nary clarity. Yet sands and gravels, sometimes preserving associated turves and soils, can also present striking evidence for the barrow-building techniques and processes of Bronze Age communities.

Excavation of Site III revealed every stage of construction. We pick up the sequence at the point where the pyre had been extinguished, a central cremation pit carefully dug (though the resulting shape was none too regular) and a substantial urn set in it, collar probably protruding above ground: container for a woman's ashes. Already, we must suppose, the initial planning with central peg and cord had been done for the central features. Pyre, pit and enigmatic line of fencing were part of the scheme and it would not have been easy (or even dignified) to execute the laying out after those activities.

The extent of the berm, beginning where the outer edge of the mound was to occur, would probably have been indicated on the ground at the preliminary lay-out stage, as also the inner and outer edges – the width – of the ditch. Piles of turf or large flints, small heaps of chalk, pegs could have been the leader's means of showing where the digging was to be done. At Site XIX, two circles of stakes, diameters and spacing between stakes carefully calculated, would have been driven in; at Site XV the same, though with greater delicacy if those posts, not structurally necessary unless to support a fence, had been decorated. Mound building could then begin.

Many barrow excavations have revealed evidence for gang work. This was never clear at Snail Down. The only suggestion came at Site III at the point where the turf mound neared completion and the chalk covering was to be applied next. At their junction (eg Pl 16), some workers had started to expose natural chalk in the ditch and to heap it upon the turf and soil core while others were still moving soil. This interleaving of chalk and subsoil as the ditch diggers gradually struck bedrock affords compelling commentary upon their varying degrees of effort.

When digging a ditch to form a barrow on downland chalk as firm as that at Snail Down, the resulting spoil would consist invariably of turf with soil adhering to its roots, then loam below that, mixed with flints and chalk chips, the latter increasing in density with depth: and finally, as a third general level, the undisturbed chalk. The top of this would be grooved and holed by bush and tree roots and natural weathering. But an inch or two below that surface the chalk is firm and pure white. At Snail Down it lies horizontally bedded in layers about one or two inches thick, with short vertical lines of cleavage here and there (Pl 6).

At all levels from turf downwards it is not and probably never was difficult to dig and extract in this area of downland.

Only at Site III was the sequence of barrow building absolutely clear. As both cross-sections establish (Figs 10, 11; Pl 14), first the turf was cut from along the course of the proposed ditch and piled, grass uppermost, like Site XIX, to form a slightly oval heap exactly over the central burial pit and sealing the area of the pyre. Placing the first turves into and around the pit, probably in such a way as to protect the urn it held, would have required care. As ditch digging proceeded, we visualise groups of (antler) pick people and (wood or animal shoulder blade) shovellers – the hands also used for that – filling baskets first with subsoil, then mixed chalk and soils and finally pure chalk, gradually heaping up the mound over its turf core until the pre-determined height and diameter were reached. The sequence in our archaeological record is clear. The result was a white mound, a grassed berm and a chalk-white ditch flat floored and vertical sided (Pl 13).

There was a wealth of difference between this structural design and that adopted for Sites XVII and XIX. There seems to have been little attempt to create a solid chalk crust over XVII. Whereas a concentration of chalk rubble was noticeable around the edge of the mound, the make-up of the inner two-thirds never appeared as more than a soil through which chalk rubble was sparsely diffused (Pl 43). The barrow's ditch was of modest proportions. To have covered the mound with a dense jacket of chalk would have involved perhaps twice the effort in bedrock digging. Possibly that effort was not available. Perhaps the design did not require it. Site III and neighbouring Site XVII were thus a contrast in earthwork.

Site XIX, with its fairly substantial ditch, was left by its builders a more consciously whitened monument though here again the effect was less dramatic than at Site III. The main mound (Pl 53) was white all over, though thin: the smaller mound retained only the slightest of chalky coverings. The space between the two mounds, in contrast, held a considerable chalk deposit. Assuming that the purpose of the mounds' surrounding stake rings was to inhibit coalescence and maintain the special nature of a double bell-barrow, we must suppose that the chalk now levelling up the space between the mounds had been derived from both chalky coverings by weathering. It had not survived solid like that sealing Site III. Possibly the latter had received some final treatment, trampling for example, that had solidified the chalk until virtually weatherproof. For whatever reason, these three sites were left by their builders in different states of whiteness. And if Site III must have remained white for generations, weeds and grasses would have colonised the others much more quickly. From this evidence at Snail Down it must be accepted that not every barrow built in chalk country was left with a long-life pure-white mound.

Many archaeologists, Stukeley possibly the first among them (1740, 44), have noted or commented upon the white coverings to barrows built upon chalk. Grinsell attempted a comprehensive Wessex list in 1941 (105), and the coloured effects achieved by barrow builders in other environments. Of his excavation of Barrow 3 at Bulford (1910, 618) Col Hawley wrote: "In its new state it must have presented the appearance of a white dome . ... in this instance it must have taken years for wind-driven soil to collect and grass to grow upon it'. Of a bell-barrow at Portesham (Dorset) Ashbee's description is almost lyrical, calling its outer layer all yellow and grey '...like Saturn and its ring from the opposite hill-side' (Thompson and Ashbee 1957, 126). Many twentieth-century barrow excavations have revealed the outward appearance of mounds.

Evidence for the original outward appearance of barrow mounds

Wiltshire

Amesbury G39 (Ashbee 1981, 9–13). Chalk envelope.

Amesbury G51, Stonehenge Cursus Group (Ashbee 1978, 10–12). Chalk 9–12in thick.

Amesbury G58, Earl's Farm Down (Ashbee 1985, 44–45). Chalk envelope.

Amesbury G61, New Barn Down (*ibid*, 62). Chalk envelope.

Amesbury G70, Earl's Farm Down (Christie 1964, 33–34). Chalk envelope, may not have extended over top of mound.

Amesbury G71, Earl's Farm Down (Christie 1967, 342, 347). Chalk envelope sealed mound and flint kerb in phases 2 and 3.

Amesbury G74, Earl's Farm Down (Thomas 1956a, 238). A hard chalk capping.

Bulford Barrow 3 (Hawley 1910, 618). Chalk 2ft thick: surface hard in places.

Knighton Hill, Broad Chalke (Rahtz 1970, 77–78). Chalk envelope.

Milton Lilbourne triple barrow (Ashbee 1986, 39, 49, fig 25). Chalk envelopes.

Shalbourne barrow 1 (Johnston 1963, 362). Chalk core covered by flints, then loam, and finally a chalk envelope.

Sutton Veney (Johnston 1980, 33). Chalk envelope.

Wilsford cum Lake G51 (Smith 1991, 14, 16). Chalk mound in phase 1; chalk envelope over core of occupation earth in phase 2.

Winterbourne Stoke G32, Greenlands Farm (Gingell 1988, 43). Chalk envelope.

Winterbourne Stoke G38, Greenlands Farm (*ibid*, 48). Chalk envelope.

Winterbourne Stoke G39, Greenlands Farm (*ibid*, 51). Chalk envelope.

Woodford G12, Heale Hill (Gingell 1988, 24). Chalk envelope.

Dorset

Crichel Down barrow 2 (S and C M Piggott 1944, 65–66). Earthy chalk mound over turf core.

Crichel Down barrow 3 (*ibid*, 66–67). Chalk envelope over flint cairn.

Frampton barrow 1 (Forde-Johnston 1959, 115). Chalk envelope 2½ft thick.

Hardy Monument, Blackdown (Thompson and Ashbee 1957, 126). Yellow gravel envelope over turf core.

Kingston Russell barrow 6g (Bailey *et al* 1980, 21). Thin chalk envelope.

Litton Cheney barrow B (Wacher 1959, 164–165). Thin chalk envelope over scraped-up mound.

Poole barrow 1 (Case 1953, 148). Gravel envelope over turf core.

Poole barrow 2 (*ibid*, 154). Gravel envelope over turf core.

Hampshire

Beaulieu Barrow II (C M Piggott 1943, 7). Orange gravel envelope over turf core.

Beaulieu Barrow III (*ibid*, 9). Gravelly clay envelope over turf core.

Beaulieu Barrow IV (*ibid*, 13). Gravelly clay envelope over turf core.

Micheldever Wood triple barrow (Fasham 1979, 11–15). Edging of chalk lumps; flint nodules as capping to loam core.

Sussex

West Heath, Harting, barrow I (Drewett 1976, 129). Orange sand over turf core.

West Heath, Harting, barrow IV (*ibid* 1976, 134). Orange sand over turf core.

Surrey

Deerleap Wood, Wotton (Corcoran 1963, 3–4). Orange sand subsoil heaped around edge of bell-barrow mound for visual effect.

Berkshire

Farncombe Down (Rahtz 1962, 11, fig 4). Chalk envelope 2ft thick over turf core.

Oxfordshire

Radley barrow 3 (Atkinson 1954, 23). Gravel-capped earth core.

Radley barrow 4/4a (Williams 1948, 3). Gravel-capped turf core.

Radley barrow 7 (Atkinson 1954, 28). Gravel-capped earth core.

Suffolk

Poor's Heath, Risby (Vatcher and Vatcher 1976, 265–266). Chalk envelope over chalk and sand mound.

Cheshire

Gallowsclough Hill (Forde-Johnston 1961, 75, 81). Salmon-pink sand over clay mound.

In describing Site XVIII, attention has been drawn to the striking contrast in shape between the slot-like ditches around that mound and around Site XXI, with the broad, flat-floored ditches surrounding every other barrow tested so far at Snail Down. The former are notably rare, as C M Piggott emphasised in a summary of ditch profiles recorded among the barrows she excavated on Beaulieu Heath in the New Forest (1943, 23). A list of barrows with this style of ditch from the Wessex region, excavated within recent years, shows how rare they are in chalk country, and usually not possible on gravel because of the material's instability.

Barrows with narrow, slot-like, surrounding ditches

Wiltshire

Amesbury G51, Stonehenge Cursus Group (Ashbee 1978, figs 3, 4): 2½ft deep, 2ft wide at floor. Floor pecked to make smooth.

Amesbury G61 (Ashbee 1985, fig 18): 4½ft deep, 2ft wide at floor.

Amesbury G70, Earl's Farm Down (Christie 1964, fig 3): 4ft deep, 2ft wide at floor.

Winterbourne Stoke G38, Greenlands Farm (Gingell 1988, fig 27). 4ft deep, 1¾ft wide at floor.

Winterbourne Stoke G39, Greenlands Farm (*ibid*, fig 30). 4½ft deep, 1¾ft wide at floor.

Winterbourne Stoke G43, Rollestone Down (Ozanne 1972, fig 5). Inner ditch 2ft deep, less than 2ft wide at floor.

Woodford G12, Heale Hill (Musty and Stone 1956, fig 1). 2ft deep, 2ft wide at floor.

Hampshire

Beaulieu Barrow V (C M Piggott 1943, 13). 3¼ft deep, 1¾ft wide at floor.

By the beginning of the second millennium BC the virtually universal rule in barrow-ditch digging was to make the floor flat and walls near vertical, with roughly a right angle at their junction. Where the subsoil was of gravel, this was physically impossible and a completed ditch profile had to be broadly U- or V-shaped. The same profile was aimed at frequently in clay subsoils. If there was a hard bedrock, especially any kind of limestone, flat floor and vertical walls were usually the features they received. The ditch enclosing barrow 6 on Charmy Down, above Bath, or that around Sutton 268', South Glamorgan, represent the tendency (Grimes 1960, fig 94; Fox 1959, fig 42). On Snail Down, at Site I, the unusual skill with which the horizontal bedding of the chalk had been worked to the advantage of the diggers enabled them to produce a ditch exceptionally broad, flat floored and vertical sided, even by their community's standards (Pls 4, 5). Around Site II the chalk was not everywhere as evenly bedded and as a result the barrow ditch lacked that precise angle between wall and floor (Pl 9).

The Snail Down ditch profiles followed this tradition, just as surely as the chalk-cut U-shaped ditch around bowl-barrow G12 at Heale Hill, Woodford (Gingell 1988, 26, fig 4) departed from it.

At Amesbury G51, a bell-barrow within the Stonehenge Cursus Group, the ditch diggers had pecked the chalk surface to make it flat: but they had eschewed the vertical wall tradition in favour of slight batter, perhaps to slow the silting process (Ashbee 1978, 10). Those who built the bowl-barrow G46 at Winterbourne Stoke made the inner wall of their ditch a little less steep than the outer one to facilitate basketing spoil on to the mound within (Gingell 1988, 57, fig 33).

Stake or post rings, all approximately circular, were recorded around the edges of three Snail Down barrows, Sites XV, XVI and XIX. Ashbee placed Site XV in category A2 of his classification of stake and post circles in British round barrows (Ashbee 1959), a single ring with closely spaced stakes or posts. Sites XVI and XIX, excavated after his study, belong to the same category. Spaces between these timbers were generally 1¾-2½ft (*c* 0.5–0.7m). At Sites XV and XIX, the rings edged the mounds. In this they differed from Site XVI, where the ring defined the inner edge of the pond-barrow's surrounding bank.

The Snail Down rings each served a different purpose. At Site XV, the mound was low and unlikely to have required any form of structural retainer. Moreover the ring was of posts set in holes. It may be permissible to see here a circle of sturdy uprights, perhaps carved and painted, whose purpose was visual, enhancing the appearance of an otherwise unspectacular mound.

At Site XIX the purpose was different. As section 1 (Fig 34) and Plate 54 make clear, rings of short stakes had been driven in around the mounds' edges to retain their shape and preserve the double bell-barrow's defining berm. Such rings would also have helped to maintain the space between the mounds. During the barrow's *floruit*, stakes had been forced outwards by pressure of mound-spread. These two rings were structural.

The pond-barrow, Site XVI, included a stake ring which had been set around the inner edge of its bank in order to maintain the chalky white hollow within. It seems likely that the stakes here belonged to a shallow, bank-retaining fence. No evidence was found to indicate whether the timbers at Sites XV and XIX had supported fencing or been joined in any other way.

A feature emphasising continuity of building tradition within the cemetery was the use of stake or post rings in barrows belonging to different phases (Fig 61). It is also noticeable how, so far, the use of these rings appears to be concentrated in the south-eastern part of Snail Down.

A number of stake and – more rarely – post rings have been recorded since Ashbee's list of 1959.

Stake and post rings discovered beneath barrows since Ashbee's list published in 1959

Wiltshire

Amesbury G61, New Barn Down (Ashbee 1985, 52–58). Stake ring surrounding stake structure.

Amesbury G71, Earl's Farm Down (Christie 1967, 337–347). Phase 2, four concentric stake rings.

Shrewton, New Down 5d (Green and Rollo-Smith 1984, 265–267). Central double stake ring and passage, off-centre single stake ring.

Winterbourne Stoke G38, Greenlands Farm (Gingell 1988, 47–50, fig 26). Stake ring.

Winterbourne Stoke G39, Greenlands Farm (*ibid*, 50–55, fig 29). Stake ring.

Winterbourne Stoke G47, Greenlands Farm (*ibid*, 58–63, fig 36). Disc-barrow. Stake ring around central mound, with passage.

Dorset

Fordington Farm, Dorchester (Bellamy 1992, 111–112, fig 4). Four concentric ovoid rings.

Hampshire and the Isle of Wight

Buckskin, Barrow II, Basingstoke (Allen *et al* 1995, 161, fig 2). Bell-barrow. Two concentric stake rings around central pre-barrow mound, random stake arcs possibly associated. Outer ring perhaps a hurdle revetment for central turf platform.

Buckskin, Barrow A, Basingstoke (*ibid*, 158). Stake ring and avenue.

Apse Down, Isle of Wright (*ibid*, 182; Tomalin 1979). Stake ring.

Gallibury Down, Isle of Wight (Tomalin 1979, 275–276). Single stake rings in periods 1 and 3.

Kent

Wouldham 1, Tonbridge and Malling (Cruse and Harrison 1984, 83, fig 2, 93–95). ?Palisade in temporary penannular ditch.

Cornwall

Davidstow Moor I (Christie 1988, 32–38). Stake ring; double fence ring around crest of mound.

Davidstow Moor XXVI (*ibid*, 109–116). Possible post ring.

Berkshire

Charnham Lane, Hungerford (Ford 1991, part 2, 180). Possible post or stake ring enclosing a burial feature.

Hodcott Down (Richards 1991, 12). Two stake rings.

Lincolnshire

Little Duke Farm, Deeping St Nicholas (French 1994). First phase, multiple stake rings; second phase, post ring in trench.

Tallington, Site 16 (Simpson 1976, 221–229). Second phase, four concentric stake rings placed around first-phase mound.

Northamptonshire

Maxey (Pryor and French 1985, 62–66). Oval barrow ditch containing ring of contiguous posts.

Leicestershire

Piper Hole Farm, Eaton (Clay 1980, 27–32). Multiple stake rings.

Sproxton (*ibid*, 1–14). First phase, wide-spaced stake ring; second phase, four concentric stake rings.

Powys

Four Crosses, Llandrysilio, Site 1 (Warrilow *et al*, 1986, 55–57). Five concentric stake rings surrounding stake structure or possible ring.

Ibid, Site 5 (*ibid*, 63–68). Phase 3, stake ring set along line of phase 2 ditch.

Trelystan, Longmountain, Barrows 1, 2 (Britnell 1982, 139–161). Barrow 1, phase 2, three roughly concentric stake rings; Barrow 2, five concentric stake rings.

Yorkshire

Cowlam Wold, Barrow 1, Humberside (Watts and Rahtz 1984, 6–14). Second phase, double stake ring.

15 BARROW BUILT: BRONZE AGE MAINTENANCE

After their construction, how long did barrows in chalk country or in any other environment remain new-built in appearance – white, or gravel yellow or rocky granular? Scraped-up bowl-barrows and cairns of other materials were left with their edges probably in close contact with whatever undergrowth the area supported. Sites X–XIV may have become grassed-over within less than a decade. But where a mound had been heaped up from a surrounding ditch, the undisturbed downland was kept at bay by it, only wind-blown seeds spreading on to the mound with ease. Indeed an upstanding mound might trap flying weed seeds to a special extent. Yet if that mound was chalk-crusted, only a small proportion of weeds would take root. The greening process might be very slow, especially if the surface of the chalk crust or other covering had been well trodden down, as it may have been on Site III. Where the burial mound was a bell-barrow, and its berm left to grass, that would be a direct and important source for re-colonisation of the mound as well as the ditch. To have kept a bell-barrow mound white might therefore have been a harder task than the maintenance of a bowl-barrow's whiteness.

A form of gardening may have been followed to maintain the continued whiteness of mounds and ditches. At Site II, where the ditch runs under the modern Track T1 (Fig 6; Pl 9), analysis of the silt on the ditch floor by I W Cornwall hinted at the possibility that it had been kept clean for a certain time, or else cleared out after a period of silting. Ashbee also was willing to consider the possibility that the ditch of disc-barrow Amesbury G61a had been scoured on occasion, though the evidence he uncovered was ambiguous, and slight at best (Ashbee 1985, 46). It might have been that, after building, which probably involved some sort of consecration, a form of taboo kept the community away from its barrows, leaving them to become overgrown as nature willed. In contrast, the universal practice of secondary burial, well attested at Snail Down, can be said to imply that each barrow continued to be its own cemetery, available for additional burials. On balance it is not unreasonable to suppose that the Snail Down community, like others, maintained for a time the original appearance of at least some of their burial mounds.

Site I was not restored after excavation: it remains almost as it was left in August 1953, except for the central pit features that were re-filled with chalky soil. The outlines of the quadrant system are still clear. Excavators' spoil heaps around the edges of the quadrant system became colonised with weeds within ten years and are down again to thick, downland turf. Within, weeds and grasses, blocked from the central platform by the broad surrounding ditch, have only just begun colonisation (Pl 8). The central area revealed completely in 1953 retains its essential chalkiness, dulled only by a thin, patchy spread of weeds. Soil re-filling the burial features in 1953, in contrast, has encouraged an outwards spread of weed from each, mainly mosses, with good turf established in the three pits. The re-filling of the large pit beneath the eccentric mound has slumped, revealing the upper walls and edge as almost pure chalk and providing a much-reduced soil area over the pit floor for what is now a fairly well-developed turf. In 1953 Site II was re-covered with a light spread of spoil which filled its ditch and central pits and left a thin chalky soil over the central plateau. The site of the outer bank was levelled by Army bulldozer, not re-built. The outer parts of the surrounding spoil heaps were left. A thin downland soil profile with turf and weeds now covers Site II, removing all whiteness. The surviving spoil heaps are covered with a fully developed downland turf.

16 BARROW BUILT: SUBSEQUENT USE

Barrows at Snail Down received secondary burials and offerings of pottery (and perhaps thus food), which encourage us to consider what else happened among the barrows in between the building of new ones. Sir Cyril Fox was convinced that the surrounding ditches, as well as circular settings of stakes, implied dancing, whether at the funeral (within or outside circular stake settings, perhaps, before they were covered by barrow mounds), or afterwards in the ditch, whose often carefully flattened floor provided admirable inducement. Indeed, at Sutton 268' (South Glamorgan: Fox 1959, 98) he interpreted a hard-pan layer around the outer edge of the first-phase mound as the result of prolonged dancing or shuffling. Despite the narrowness of the ditch of Earl's Farm Down, Amesbury G70, Christie (1964, 31, 41) thought that there were traces of foot marks in sludge on its floor. At Snail Down Site I we entertained the same suspicion concerning the origin of chalk sludge in parts of that ditch. In due course, when rain produced the same effect upon the floor after our excavation had restored it to its original appearance, the idea had reluctantly to be abandoned. Yet despite the occurrence of more than one group of sharp, freshly knapped flint flakes upon the ditch floor of Site I, and small patches of charcoal in similar locations at Site II, the impression remained that such superbly made circular earthworks provided a perfect setting for dancing, even if, lacking entrances, start and finish would have involved an undignified jump down and scramble out again.

Lack of stratification left it in doubt whether the Food Vessel D3 had been deposited in Site II (Pl 12) during the course of the initial burial ceremony, or added afterwards as an instance of continuing regard for the barrow and its burials. For the same reason, it could not be proved that the off-centre burial pit at Site II was contemporary with that at the centre: a strong likelihood only, since they shared an unusual shape. Nor could we tell whether interment of the foetus in Site II was contemporary with the two adult burials there. Since the cremations were of women, it seems at least possible that the new-born baby belonged to one of them.

There was no doubt that at least Pit A at the NW edge of Site XVII (Fig 29; Pl 50) had been dug some while after the barrow's construction, in order to receive the broken, incomplete remains of the small Collared Vessel D22 (Fig 47). Here was an unequivocal post-barrow offering. Its character – concern for the disposal of broken pottery – echoed the smashed urn at the barrow's centre. The discovery, so frequently, of secondary burials and other additions to barrow mounds may have discouraged archaeologists from entertaining the possibility that offerings like pots of food or drink – even flowers – were sometimes left *on top* of a barrow. The broken, abraided and incomplete Collared Vessel carefully buried at the mound's edge of Site XVII could represent the final disposal of an offering originally left on its top.

Burl has made the intriguing proposal (1987, 196–197) that Pits A-C, with their broken Collared Vessel, scraps of cremated human bone and charcoal respectively, reproduce in miniature the sequence of events during the original burial process at this barrow – funeral pyre, cremation, smashing of a pot. This interpretation seems to echo the findings of Kilbride-Jones at Loanhead of Daviot, a recumbent stone circle in Aberdeenshire (1936, 297–298).

Site III carried most evidence for usage after the barrow had been completed. First its three enigmatic boat-shaped pits dug at almost equal intervals around the outer circumference of the ditch, just clear of its edge and left to silt up naturally: their shape made them suitable as laying-out places for the dead. Had Snail Down III become a resting place in due course for three secondary burials, there would have been a suggestive correlation with the pits: but only two such burials were found. One had been sealed beneath a flint cairn, a clear statement about its present and future sanctity. The other was quite different. First established in an inadequate-sized pit, it seems subsequently to have been exhumed, cremation scattered about and urn replaced, unbroken and carefully wedged upright by two small vessels, perhaps added to the burial pit just for this purpose.

In 1971, Stuart Piggott discussed the possibility that tomb-robbing may have occurred in periods earlier than the Iron Age, where its existence among Halstatt tombs in Germany has been documented (Piggott 1971, 54). His Archaeological Survey and Policy for Wiltshire suggests that evidence for tomb-robbing be sought among British Bronze Age barrow burials; the curious ritual exposed at Site III, Secondary Burial 2 (Cremation 9), might possibly represent such an occurrence. Against it should be set the careful way in which Collared Urn D11 was replaced intact and wedged upright by Accessory Vessels D12 and D13 (Pl 23), although such could possibly be seen as a gesture of repentance by the guilty parties. On balance we prefer to see the strange circumstances surrounding this burial as an instance of a return to a grave for a ritual – but otherwise inexplicable – act.

The inhumation inserted into the small mound on the berm of Site XXII, was an Early Bronze Age secondary burial like those occupying a similar position – on the berm – at Site III. Less to be expected, because of its later Bronze Age date, was the small inhumation cemetery added to Sites XV and V, its corpses originally entombed beneath piles of flints.

17 THE SNAIL DOWN BARROW CEMETERY: CHRONOLOGY

Figure 61 illustrates the seven earliest phases which we propose for Snail Down. For clarity, the extensive remains of ancient fields within the area (Fig 2) have been omitted. Despite considerable overlapping, these phases are to be regarded as broadly chronological; and, as we admit below, the mounds in Phase 2 might belong to Phase 5. Radiocarbon determinations (Section T) have suggested that Phases 1–5 could have occurred within a timespan of 150–600 years.

Phase I

The first use of Snail Down seems to have been domestic, beginning probably in the third millennium with earlier Neolithic pottery. The weathered Cornish greenstone axe from beneath Site II (Fig 53, J1) might belong to this episode. Oak of the fifth millennium Cal BC used for the cremations in Sites II and XVII (Section T) offers the possibility that Neolithic occupation hereabouts may go back to the beginnings of agriculture in southern Britain. Peterborough and Grooved Ware sherds, concentrated at Sites XV and XIX, but occurring elsewhere, show that later Neolithic activity continued on the Down. Beneath Sites III and X-XIV, the discovery of much Beaker ware, fine vessels alongside domestic cooking pots, and with it a representative flint industry as well as a fragment of a battle-axe of Group XIV camptonite from the Nuneaton (Warwicks) region (Shotton 1959, 135–137), coincided with the sort of apparently flimsy, stake-built structures that are commonly associated with such material (Gibson 1982, 307–315 and *passim*). The widest date range of the Snail Down Beakers, and thus at least the later part of Phase 1, could be *c* 2400–1700 cal BC.

Phase IA

Site XV, a scraped-up earth mound within a ring of posts, and perhaps also the inhumation burial beneath 2205 (Fig 2A) may have belonged to the Beaker-associated settlement beneath Sites X–XIV, located, as they are, at a discreet distance from that living area. The unassociated shale bead from Site XV (K8; Fig 54) would have been a more appropriate association with material from Phase 4 and is indeed closely matched by a bead from Site III, Secondary Burial 1 (Cremation 8), associated there with a segmented bead of faience (Fig 54). But the presence of notable Grooved Ware at Site XV makes it difficult to place this mound in a later phase (it would have to be Phase 4 on grounds of location): we therefore propose that it is the earliest barrow within the Snail Down cemetery area, with 2205 close chronologically and culturally. Burial rites of inhumation as well as cremation were evidently acceptable to the Snail Down community at that time.

Phase 2

Principally because they are scraped-up barrows like Site XV, we place Sites X–XIV in this Phase. They occur where they do because, as so often among barrow builders, structural contact with a former Beaker settlement seems to have been important. These mounds exactly overlie such an occupation area (Figs 21, 61). Their builders had abandoned – or here chose not to employ – post circles to retain their shape. If these mounds were raised before Sites III and VIII, their presence would account for the gap between those two bells. If, on the contrary, they belong to Phase 5 not 2, the space between III and VIII is curious, though having parallels elsewhere in the cemetery: between Site II and 2216 for instance, and 2257 and Site XIX. An offering of two adjoining Collared Urn sherds in the cremation pit beneath XIV places that grave nearer to Phase 4 than Phase 1 and 1A, but so does the jet-shale bead from Site XV of Phase 1A. In any case, Collared Urn sherds (though none with traces of rim or collar) appear to have been associated with Beaker wares in that settlement.

Phase 2A

Sites V and 2244 at present remain enigmas. Both apparently ring-ditches and oval in plan, there may be an association between them. If 2244 can be accepted as a focus at least for the barrows of Phase 4, it must be among the earliest barrows on the Down. Discovered in 1953, it is unexcavated. Barrow ditch tradition in which vertical sides and wide flat floor were striking features of Phases 4 and 5 is present in Site V. The location of Sites XV and V could account for the space between the Phase 4B sites of 2257 and XIX. The survey (Fig 2) suggests that the ditch of Site XIX cuts the ditch of Site V. We therefore give primacy to XV and V: and believe that 2244 may be contemporary with Site V or even earlier.

Phase 3

So far, excavation has revealed that the builders of Sites XVIII and XXI introduced a tradition of slot-like barrow ditches that sets them apart from the mounds of Phases 4 and 5, and from Site V. Barrows from elsewhere in Wessex, whose mounds had been heaped from this kind of ditch, show a tendency to belong more readily to the later Neolithic than to the earlier Bronze Age. The Collared Urn D24 recovered by Hoare from Site XVIII (Fig 43) belongs to Longworth's primary series (1961, 295, no 72) and its status is confirmed in his discussion of the Snail Down urn material above (Section D).

Within the cemetery's layout, Site XXI occurs at the north-east end of the principal alignment of mounds which, we argue below, belongs to the next and most important phases of cemetery development, 4A and 4B. Since the south-west end of this alignment may also occur where it does because of the prior existence of 2205, of our Phase 1A, then 2205 and Site XXI may both be early mounds on the Down, between which the major barrow building of Phase 4A was to be aligned.

Phase 4, A and B

The way in which Snail Down was to evolve into one of the great barrow cemeteries of Bronze Age Britain was decided now. In a decision somehow enshrined, the community must have established where future barrows were to go. First, we believe, there was to be a north-east/south-west alignment whose ends were already marked by 2205 (Phase 1A) and Site XXI (Phase 3). The true south-west end of this line was 2207 (Fig 2A). Apparently a cenotaph, its relatively rich deposit of offerings (Fig 56) in a pit might possibly be said to suggest dedication. Barrows would be built along this line as burial became necessary. The broad space between Site II and 2207 allowed for additional barrows whose building, in the event, never occurred. This alignment afforded a suitable association with Sites X-XIV and the Beaker settlement they covered. It came to be dominated by Site VIII, the most substantial barrow in the cemetery and, through its position, the most commanding. A second, less accurately maintained alignment was to run south-east from Site XXI, whose position thus became critically important to the whole scheme. Once again barrows would be built, as death brought the need, along this line, whose south-east end had no early anchor, unless the outstanding bell-barrow with added mound (Site XXII; Fig 2A) was among the first to be built in this Phase. A primary burial has not yet been located beneath it; and radiocarbon determination (Section T) has hinted with 86.7% confidence that Site XIX may have been built before Site XXII.

Barrow 2244, of Phase 2A, falls accurately within the angle formed by these two alignments and it may be no coincidence that it is almost equidistant from Sites II and XXII. Our belief is that there was some compelling relationship between the mass of Snail Down (Phase 4) and this small, oval, possible ring-ditch that faces it and yet is separated from it by a shallow gully.

It is not possible to be certain which alignment came first, Phase 4A or 4B. They could have developed at the same time. Since one is so much more exact in its line than the other, that one may at least have been conceived first. Radiocarbon determinations (Section T) suggest that Site III may have been built before Site XIX, and also before inhumation 2 was added to Site XXII.

The pond-barrow, Site XVI, is attributed to Phase 4A because of the resemblance of its pit-within-a-pit to the two burial pits and the empty miniature version in the saucer-barrow Site II.

Ashbee (Section T) has considered at length the implications of the Snail Down radiocarbon series for the period of the Wessex Culture which enfolds Phases 4A, 4B and much of 5 at the cemetery.

Phase 5

The heart of Snail Down was its two alignments of Phase 4A/4B, its great Wessex Early Bronze Age period. Phase 5 saw infilling which could have been broadly contemporary with Phase 4 and might have included Site I, a disc-barrow of specialised Wessex form. An extra minor alignment, 2220, Site XVII, 2231 and 2235 (Fig 2A), must have enjoyed some relationship with the earlier Sites X-XIV parallel immediately to the south. They (2220–2235) could have been added in this Phase. Barrow 2235 appears to overlie the earthen edge of 2231. Site XVII is likely to have been built later than Site III because of the feature that linked its central, primary burial pit to Secondary Burial I at the bell-barrow, the saucer-shaped depression scraped into the floor of each pit. Continued use of such an inconspicuous yet notable feature nevertheless suggests closeness in time between the two burials.

Since Site XX and 2254 lie furthest from the Phase 4 alignments, it is proposed that they were among the last to be added during Phase 5. Similarly, 2209 seems to lie outside the Snail Down cemetery.

Alternative phasing

We cannot rule out the possibility that the space between Sites III and VIII reflected some still visible remains of the Beaker settlement rather than the mounds of X-XIV. The latter could then have occurred as infilling in Phase 5, about the time when secondary burials were being added to Site III. Since its relatively strong association with Grooved Ware should assign Site XV to an early period (Phase 1A) within the cemetery, then for Sites X–XIV to belong to Phase 5 would imply a return to a scraped-up mound tradition after the mass of ditch-encircled mounds of Phase 4 had been built. In view of the evidence for continuity at the cemetery (see Section 18 below), such a change seems unlikely; and the radiocarbon determination hints at the opposite order.

Phase 6

A radiocarbon determination for Skeleton III (Inhumation 4) added to Site XV (GU-5305; 2920 ± 70 BP, *c* 1260–900 cal BC), places it within the later Bronze Age, towards the end of the second millennium BC. It seems likely that the scattered remains of four other skeletons from Site XV and the one from Site V nearby are contemporary with Skeleton 3. Apparently they represent a small inhumation cemetery added to existing barrows (Sites XV, V) of a kind and from a period rarely recorded in Britain. The significance of this little burial ground is commented upon by Ashbee (Section T).

Phase 7

The boundary or enclosure ditches radiating from Sidbury Hill (Fig 1) have been designated Sites VI and VII where they form Enclosure A surrounding the barrows (Fig 2). The Reading survey (Bradley *et al* 1994) has suggested that these, in their final form (Site VI) may be attributed to the Middle Iron Age, beginning within the sixth century BC. Yet Enclosure A incorporates changes to its ditch profile which indicate that in origin this system must go back in time (Site VII), perhaps sufficiently far to become broadly contemporary with the later Bronze Age burials in Sites XV and V of our Phase 6.

From its inception, Enclosure A overlay fields (Fig 2), some of which could even be contemporary with the Beaker settlement covered by Sites X–XIV. We have not attempted to attribute these ancient field remains to any of our phases. It is clear, however, that Sites VI and VII belong to the final stages of a complex farming regime, wherein mixed agriculture, closely influenced by changing land division and ownership, was practised hereabouts for two prehistoric millennia and more.

Phase 8

Romano-British people may have established a farm to the north of the cemetery; there was, perhaps a barn, part of Site IX, (though it may be no more than a small field); and allowed their farm vehicles to wear tracks across the Down which encroached upon the ditch around Site XX and the berm of Site III. A broad scatter of their potsherds, with some later Roman coins, indicates manuring and other agricultural work hereabouts, with heightened activity during the later first century and again towards the end of our Roman history.

Phase 9

Evidence from excavation for use of the Down in post-Roman times is negligible. Trackways continued to be used, even extended. Two medieval iron arrowheads (Fig 59, N2, N3) from shafts loosed during hunting expeditions, are all that were recovered from such a long span of history. And, later, a sheep's broken bronze rumbler bell and a clay pipe from Georgian times (Fig 59, N5, N12). Then came the antiquaries Sir Richard Colt Hoare and William Cunnington, the date 1805, and perhaps the following year also (R H Cunnington 1975, 73, 88). They lodged in the Crown Hotel, Everleigh; in a paddock behind whose buildings our own excavation team pitched its tents and cooked its food in 1955 and 1957.

Phase 10

Finally, as the clouds of war gathered in the late thirties of our own time, Snail Down was turned over to tank-training. Allen's air photograph of 4 June 1939 (Pl 1) shows harm beginning to be done, the cemetery's two main alignments proving irresistible to young men learning to go to war in armoured fighting vehicles. A swathe of damage was inflicted by tank tracks across a major axis of each barrow in the two alignments of Phase 4: turf ripped off, chalk crust, even upper levels removed and the earthy core of each mound exposed to wind and rain (Plates 2, 3). In these circumstances, in 1952 a three year programme of rescue excavation was undertaken, selecting specific types of barrow and aiming at total excavation (the objectives are explained in the Introduction).

The excavations of 1953–57 re-affirmed the importance and majesty of the Snail Down barrow cemetery and today every effort is made to protect it. The enemy now is rabbits, who do more internal damage than ever the training for tank warfare did.

18 SNAIL DOWN: A COMMUNITY BURIAL GROUND?

We believe that the data obtained during three seasons of excavation and fieldwork in the 1950s supports the proposal that Snail Down was used by one community or, at the very least, by people maintaining a common burial tradition. It contained variety. But evidence for common practices recurred with sufficient frequency for us to be confident that one broad set of tenets was guiding people whenever the need for burial on Snail Down arose.

A series of common traits emerged from the excavations which forms the basis of this argument. They are illustrated graphically in Figure 62, which is best understood by working from the left-hand column of sites.

Phase 1A   **Site XV(1)** was linked to Sites X-XIV (Phase 2) through the choice of scraped-up mounds. Its only burial was the probable source of a type of jet-shale bead (K8) whose exact fellow (K1) occurred with Secondary Burial 1 in Site III, (III(2) in Fig 62: Phase 4A). The post ring surrounding Site XV(1) was matched by the stake rings of Site XIX (Phase 4B). Their proximity within the cemetery should also be noted.

Phase 2   **Site XIV** included evidence for an interest in the careful incorporation of broken pottery with its primary burial that reflects the inclusion of potsherds in one burial pit at Site II (Phase 4A) and, much more dramatically, in primary and secondary positions at Site XVII (Phase 5).

Phase 2A   **Sites V(1) and 2244** were built with an oval ground plan; external banks added to their mutual resemblance. The survey (Fig 2) has suggested that 2257, a bowl-barrow located close to Site V and given to Phase 4B, may also have originally been oval in plan.

Site V(1) yielded a pit whose mouth had been sealed (with puddled chalk), which recalled the flint pit-coverings over the two secondary burials at Site III (Phase 4A) and perhaps also over the central grave pit of Site II (disturbed and replaced by Hoare: Phase 4A). The W pit in Site V, though smaller, resembled the pit beneath the eccentric mound of Site I (Phase 5).

Phase 3   **Sites XVIII and XXI** were encircled by slot-like ditches so far without parallel at Snail down.

Phase 4A   **Site II** contained two cremation graves and a third, much smaller and not used for burial, whose particular configurations, pits-within-pits, were found only at Site XVI (Phase 4A). The inclusion of a group of base sherds of a Food Vessel (D7) with the burnt bones in its off-centre burial pit link Site II with Sites XIV (Phase 2) and XVII (Phase 5).

Site III(1). The mound covered a central burial pit, the spoil from whose original digging had been carefully disposed, topsoil to the south, subsoil to the north, just as it had been at Site XVII (Phase 5), save that there humus

was piled to the east. Large pits dug symmetrically around the outer edge of the ditch recall the even larger pit beneath the eccentric mound of Site I (Phase 5).

Site III, Secondary Burial 1 (Cremation 8), was covered by a flint cairn like that originally placed over Site III, Secondary Burial 2 (Cremation 9), and probably over the central burial pit at Site II (all Phase 4A). These pit covers could be following a practice seen also on the chalk covering to a pit at Site V(1) (Phase 2A). The saucer-shaped hollow carved in the floor of the burial pit for Secondary Burial 1 at Site III is exactly matched by a depression carved in the floor of the central burial pit of Site XVII (Phase 5).

Site XVI yielded a pit-within-a-pit which mirrors the three such pits from Site II (Phase 4A).

Phase 4B   **Sites XIX and XXII** were each double barrows, XIX built certainly to this plan, XXII containing, uniquely, a small mound on the berm within its ditch which may also have been original. In this generally rare elaboration in barrow architecture, these sites reflect the two small, probably contemporary mounds of Site I (Phase 5). The stake rings rammed home to maintain the specialised shape of XIX recall the post ring, raised perhaps for a different purpose, around XV (Phase 1A). It is noteworthy that post/stake encircled barrows, as well as double barrows, occur close together at Snail Down. Figures 61 and 62 show that cenotaph barrows occur in Phases 4A and 4B and possibly 2A, as well as in 5.

Phase 5   **Site I** whose double mounds link it to Sites XIX and XXII, has associations with Site III (Phase 4A) through the great pit beneath the eccentric mound. The generally oval shape of this and the three carefully spaced pits outside the ditch of III may have served similar purposes in burial ceremonial.

Site XVII produced features that link it with Sites II and XIV (Phases 4A and 2 respectively) – potsherds – and with III (Phase 4A), in their equally careful disposal of spoil during the digging of burial pits.

Community practice as well as broader, regional influence is also to be seen in the addition from time to time of specialised Wessex barrow forms at Snail Down. They appear in Phases 4A (saucer, bell, pond and disc), 4B (bell and double bells) and 5 (bell and double disc). The spread within our proposed phasing is wide. The occurrence of several possible cenotaph barrows in Phases 2A, 4 and 5 also suggests regular practice at this burial ground. Finally, as we have already considered at some length, where Early Bronze Age inhumation is found at Snail Down it is so noticeably contrary to custom there that it reinforces graphically the preference for cremation within this cemetery during its Early Bronze Age phases. The interment of an unburnt foetus at Site II should not, perhaps, be counted as normal inhumation.

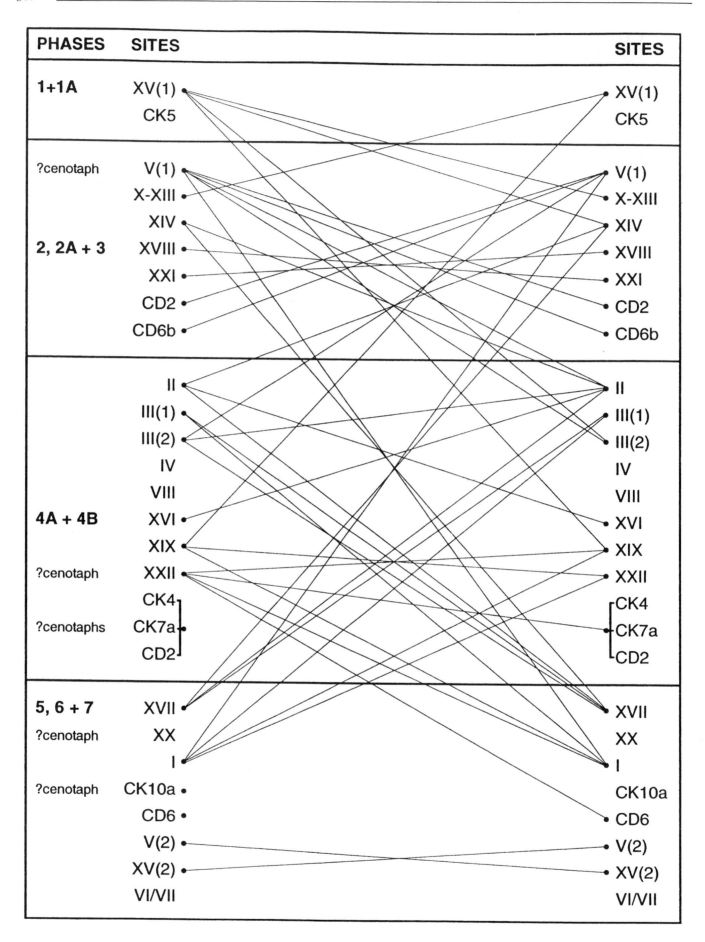

Fig 62   The barrow cemetery: phases and linking features.

We believe that the evidence we have set out is sufficiently strong to warrant the proposition that one community or closely associated group of people was responsible for the evolution of Snail Down.

There is at present no indication of how local this community was. A perforated sea shell (K11) found with the inhumation added to the extra mound of Site XXII must have come from over fifty miles away: and Longworth has indicated a north-west Welsh parallel for the unusual decoration on the Collared Urn D24 from XVIII. Otherwise, the grave goods and other Bronze Age finds from Snail Down are typical of material from other barrows on Salisbury Plain; they are not exotic. Snail Down is, physically, part of its landscape, looking perhaps towards the Bourne for its people's home farms; and to Sidbury Hill for an outstanding landmark – and perhaps much more than that – which must have dominated their world.

The relatively small number of people buried at Snail Down is in marked contrast with the size of many of the barrows and the majesty of their arrangement. From this we would argue that use of the cemetery was restricted, but whether the men and women, with a few of their children were leading members of the community or chosen from some other criteria we cannot show. Grave goods hardly substantiate the former: only three barrows (one a cenotaph) yielded objects that could be supposed to represent wealth or prestige. But outside the Stonehenge region this need cause no surprise. At Site III, Secondary Burial 1 (Cremation 8) had at least been furnished with beads made of valued materials, faience probably the most highly prized of all. The urns from Sites III, XVII and XVIII were of high quality: and the operation of trepanning, which probably caused the death of a person buried in Site II, must have called for expertise that had, perhaps, to be brought in from elsewhere, at whatever cost (Section A). When Hoare named our Site XXII as the King Barrow, his estimation of its importance, and, by implication, the importance of whoever lay beneath it, need not have been too fanciful.

Bibliography

The date that follows the author's name is the date of printing, the year for which the volume (if a periodical) was published, if different, is put first in brackets.

Abbreviations:

BAR - British Archaeological Reports.

HMSO – Her Majesty's Stationery Office.

RCHME – Royal Commission on the Historical Monuments of England.

SMR – Sites and Monument Record

VCH – The Victoria History of the Counties of England; A History of Wiltshire, Volume I, Part I (1957).

WANHM – The Wiltshire Archaeological and Natural History Magazine.

WANHS – Wiltshire Archaeological and Natural History Society.

Abbreviated titles of current periodicals and series are those recommended by the Council for British Archaeology (*Signposts for Archaeological Publication*, 3rd ed, 1991).

Abercromby, the Hon J, 1912, *A Study of the Bronze Age Pottery of Great Britain and Ireland and its Associated Grave-Goods* (2 vols). Oxford

Alexander, J A, Ozanne, P C, and Ozanne, A, 1960, Report on the investigation of a round barrow on Arreton Down, Isle of Wight, *Proc Prehist Soc*, **26**, 263–302

Allen, M J, Morris, M and Clark, R H, 1995, Food for the living: a reassessment of a Bronze Age barrow at Buckskin, Basingstoke, Hampshire, *Proc Prehist Soc*, **61, 157–189**

Annable, F K, (1957) 1958, Excavation and field-work in Wiltshire: 1957, *WANHM*, **57,** 2–17

Annable, F K, (1958/1959) 1959, Excavation and field-work in Wiltshire: 1958, *WANHM*, **57**, 227–239

Annable, F K, 1962 A Romano-British pottery in Savernake Forest, kilns 1–2, *WANHM*, **58**, 143–155

Annable, F K, 1966a, A late first-century well at *CVNETIO*, *WANHM*, **61**, 9–24

Annable, F K, 1966b, Romano-British interments at Potterne and Bradford-on-Avon, *WANHM*, **61**, 95–96

Annable, F K and Simpson, D D A, 1964, *Guide Catalogue of the Neolithic and Bronze Age Collections in Devizes Museum*. Devizes

Applebaum, S, (1954) 1955, The agriculture of the British Early Iron Age as exemplified at Figheldean Down, Wiltshire, *Proc Prehist Soc*, **20**, 103–114

ApSimon, A M, 1954, Dagger graves in the 'Wessex' Bronze Age, *Annu Rep Univ of Lond Insti of Arch*, **10**, 37–62

ApSimon, A M, (1973) 1974, The excavation of a Bronze Age barrow and a menhir at Ystrad-Hynod, Llanidloes (Mont), 1965–66, *Archaeol Cambrensis*, **122**, 35–54

Ashbee, P, (1954) 1956, The excavation of a round barrow on Canford Heath, Dorset, 1951, *Proc Dorset Natur Hist Archaeol Soc*, **76**, 39–50

Ashbee, P, 1957, Excavations on Kildale Moor, North Riding of Yorkshire, 1953, *Yorkshire Archaeol J*, **39**, 179–192

Ashbee, P, (1957)1958, The Great Barrow at Bishop's Waltham, Hampshire, *Proc Prehist Soc*, **23**, 137–166

Ashbee, P, (1957) 1959, Stake and post circles in British round barrows, *Archaeol J*, **114**, 1–9

Ashbee, P, 1960, *The Bronze Age Round Barrow in Britain*. London: Phoenix House

Ashbee, P, 1966, The Fussell's Lodge long barrow excavations 1957, *Archaeologia*, **100**, 1–80

Ashbee, P, (1975/1976) 1978, Amesbury barrow 51: excavations, 1960, *WANHM*, **70/71**, 1–60

Ashbee P, (1979/1980) 1981, Amesbury barrow 39: excavations 1960, *WANHM*, **74/75**, 3–34

Ashbee, P, (1984) 1985, The excavation of Amesbury barrows 58, 61a, 61, 72, *WANHM*, **79**, 39–91

Ashbee, P, 1986, The excavation of Milton Lilbourne barrows 1–5, *WANHM*, **80**, 23–96

Ashbee, P and Dimbleby, G W, (1974) 1976, The Moor Green barrow, West End, Hampshire: excavations, 1961. With contribution by A M ApSimon, *Proc Hampshire Fld Club Archaeol Soc*, **31**, 5–18

Ashbee, P, Bell, M and Proudfoot E, 1989, *Wilsford Shaft: excavations 1960–2*. English Heritage Archaeological Report no 11. London: English Heritage

Aspinall, A, Warren, S E, Crummett, J G and Newton, R G, 1972, Neutron activation analysis of faience beads, *Archaeometry*, **14**, 27–40

Aspinall, A and Warren, S E, 1973, "The problem of faience beads'. Lecture delivered at a conference held in Newcastle, January 1973

Atkinson, D R, 1965, Clay tobacco pipes and pipemakers of Marlborough, *WANHM*, **60**, 85–95

Atkinson, D R, 1970, Clay tobacco pipes and pipemakers of Salisbury, Wiltshire, *WANHM*, **65**, 177–189

Atkinson, R J C, (1952/1953) 1954, Excavations in Barrow Hills Field, Radley, Berks, 1944–45, *Oxoniensia*, **17/18**, 14–35

Atkinson, R J C, 1956, *Stonehenge*. London: Hamish Hamilton

Atkinson, R J C, 1957, Worms and weathering, *Antiquity*, **31**, 219–233

Atkinson, R J C, Brailsford, J W and Wakefield, H G, 1951, A pond barrow at Winterbourne Steepleton, Dorset, *Archaeol J*, **108**, 1–24

Atkinson, R J C, Piggott, C M and Sandars, N K, 1951a, *Excavations at Dorchester, Oxon*, Oxford: Ashmolean Museum

Bailey, C J, Smith, S and Tomalin, D, 1980, Excavation of three round barrows in the parish of Kingston Russell, *Proc Dorset Natur Hist Archaeol Soc*, **102**, 19–31

Baker, H, Burleigh, R and Meeks, N, 1971, British Museum natural radiocarbon measurements, VII, *Radiocarbon*, **13**, 157–188

Banks, C, 1961, Report on the recently discovered remains of the Wild Ox (*Bos primigenius Bojanus*) from East Ham, *London Natur*, **41**, 54–59

Barclay, A and Halpin, C, 1999, *Excavations at Barrow Hills, Radley, Oxfordshire. Volume I: The Neolithic and Bronze Age Monument Complex.* Oxford Archaeological Unit Thames Valley Landscapes, Volume **11**. Oxford

Barrett, J, Bradley, R and Green, M, 1991, *Landscape, Monuments and Society: The Prehistory of Cranborne Chase.* Cambridge: Cambridge University Press

Barrett, John C, Freeman, P W M and Woodward, Ann, 2000, *Cadbury Castle, Somerset.* English Heritage Archaeological Report, **20**, London: English Heritage

Bateman, T, 1861, *Ten Years' Diggings in Celtic and Saxon Grave Hills, the Counties of Derby, Stafford and York, 1848–1858.* London: Derby

Beck, C and Shennan, S, 1991, *Amber in Prehistoric Britain.* Oxbow Monograph **8**. Oxford

Beck, H C and Stone, J F S, 1936, Faience beads of the British Bronze Age, *Archaeologia*, **85**, 203–252

Bell, M, Fowler, P J and Hillson, S W 1996, *The Experimental Earthwork Project, 1960–1962.* CBA Research Report **100**. York: CBA

Bellamy, P S, (1991) 1992, The excavations of Fordington Farm round barrow, *Dorset Natur Hist Archaeol Soc Proc*, **113**, 107–132

Biek, L, 1963, *Archaeology and the Microscope.* London: Lutterworth Press

Boessneck, J, 1969, Osteological differences between sheep (*Ovis aries* Linne') and goat (*Capra hircus* Linne'), in (eds) D Brothwell and E Higgs, *Science in Archaeology, a Comprehensive Survey of Progress and Research*. 331–358. London: Thames and Hudson

Boessneck, J, Müller H H and Teichert, M, 1964, OsteologischeUnterscheidungskerkmale swischen Schaf (*Ovis aries* Linne') und Zeige (*Capra hircus* Linne'), *Kuhn-Archiv*, **78**, 1–2, 1–129

Bonney, D J, 1973, The Pagan Saxon period, *c* 500–700, in (ed) E Crittall, *A History of Wiltshire*, **1**, pt **2**, 468–484. London: Institute of Historical Research, Victoria County Histories

Bowen, H C, 1961, *Ancient Fields.* London: British Association For the Advancement of Science

Bowen, H C, 1978, Celtic fields and ranch boundaries in Wessex, in (ed) Susan Limbrey and J G Evans, *The Effect of Man on the Landscape: the Lowland Zone*, 115–123. CBA Res Rep **21**. London: CBA

Bradley, R, Entwistle, R and Raymond, F, 1994, *Prehistoric Land Divisions on Salisbury Plain. The Work of the Wessex Linear Ditches Project.* English Heritage Archaeological Report **2**. London: English Heritage

Bradley, R and Keith-Lucas, M, 1975, Excavation and pollen analysis on a bell-barrow at Ascot, *J Archaeol Sci*, **2**, 95–108

Britnell, W, 1982, The excavation of two round barrows at Trelystan, Powys, *Proc Prehist Soc*, **48**, 133–201

Britton, D, 1961, A study of the composition of Wessex Culture bronzes – (based on spectroscopic analysis by E E Richards), *Archaeometry*, **4**, 39–52

Brothwell, D R, 1981, *Digging up Bones.* London: British Museum (Natural History)

Burgess, C, 1980, *The Age of Stonehenge.* London: Dent

Burl, A, 1987, *The Stonehenge People.* London: Dent

Burstow, G P and Holleyman, G A, (1957) 1958, Late Bronze Age settlement on Itford Hill, Sussex, *Proc Prehist Soc*, **23**, 167–212

Bussell, G D, Pollard, A M and Baird, D C, (1981) 1982, The characterisation of Early Bronze Age jet and jet-like material by X-ray fluorescence, *WANHM*, **76**, 27–32

Carson, R A G, Hill, P V and Kent, J P C, 1960, *Late-Roman Bronze Coinage AD 324–498.* London: Spink.

Case, H J, (1952) 1953, The excavation of two round barrows at Poole, Dorset, *Proc Prehist Soc*, **18**, 148–159

Case, H J, (1956/1957) 1957, The Lambourn Seven barrows, *Berks Archaeol J*, **55**, 15–31

Case, H J, 1992, Review of 'Rethinking the Neolithic' by Julian Thomas, *Proc Prehist Soc*, **58**, 424–425

Case, H J, 1995, Some Wiltshire Beakers and their contexts, *WANHM*, **88**, 1–17

Case, H J, Bayne, B, Steele, S, Avery, G and Sutermeister, H, (1964/1965) 1966, Excavations at City Farm, Hanborough, Oxon, *Oxoniensia*, **29/30**, 1–98

Case, H J and Whittle, A W R, 1982, *Settlement Patterns in the Oxford Region: Excavations at the Abingdon Causewayed Enclosure and Other Sites.* CBA Research Report No **44**. Oxford: CBA and Ashmolean Museum

Christie, P M, 1960, Crig-a-Mennis: a Bronze Age barrow at Liskey, Perranzabuloe, Cornwall, *Proc Prehist Soc*, **26**, 76–97

Christie, P M, 1963, The Stonehenge Cursus, *WANHM*, **58**, 370–382

Christie, P M, 1964, A Bronze Age round barrow on Earl's Farm Down, Amesbury, *WANHM*, **59**, 30–45

Christie, P M, 1967, A barrow-cemetery of the second millennium BC in Wiltshire, *Proc Prehist Soc*, **33**, 336–366

Christie, P M, 1970, A round barrow on Greenland Farm, Winterbourne Stoke, *WANHM*, **65**, 64–73

Christie, P M, 1988, A barrow cemetery on Davidstow Moor, Cornwall: Wartime excavations by C K Croft Andrew, *Cornish Archaeol*, **27**, 27–110

Clark, J G D, 1941, *Prehistoric England.* London: Batsford

Clark, J G D, 1954, *Excavations at Star Carr.* Cambridge: Cambridge University Press

Clark, J G D, 1963, Neolithic bows from Somerset, England, and the prehistory of archery in North-West Europe, *Proc Prehist Soc*, **29**, 50–98

Clarke, D L, 1970, *Beaker Pottery of Great Britain and Ireland.* Cambridge: Cambridge University Press

Clarke, D V, Cowie, T G and Foxon, A, 1985, *Symbols of Power at the Time of Stonehenge*. Edinburgh: National Museum of Antiquities of Scotland

Clay P, 1980, *Two Multi-Phase Barrow Sites at Sproxton and Eaton, Leicestershire*. Leicestershire Museums, Art Galleries and Records Service Archaeological Report No **2**. Leicester

Clay, R C C, 1924, An Early Iron Age site on Fyfield Bavant Down, *WANHM*, **42**, 457–496

Clay, R C C, (1925/1927) 1927, The barrows on Marleycombe Hill, Bowerchalke, *WANHM*, **43**, 548–556.

Clayton, P, 1976, *Archeological Sites of Britain*. London: Batsford.

Cleal, R M J and Allen, M J, 1994, Investigation of tree-damaged barrows on King Barrow Ridge and Luxenborough Plantation, Amesbury, *WANHM*, **87**, 54–84

Cleal, R M J and Raymond, F, 1990, The Prehistoric Pottery, in J C Richards, *The Stonehenge Environs Project*, 233–246. English Heritage Archaeological Report No **16**. London: English Heritage

Clifford, E M, 1938, The excavation of Nympsfield long barrow, Gloucestershire, *Proc Prehist Soc*, **4**, 188–213

Clutton-Brock, J, 1962, Near Eastern canids and the affinities of Natufian dogs, *Z. Tierzüchtung u. Züchtungsbiologie*, **76**, 326–333

Clutton-Brock, J, 1962a, An Analysis of Mammalian Faunas from Prehistoric Sites in India and Western Asia. Unpublished PhD thesis, University of London, 133

Clutton-Brock, J and Burleigh, R, 1991, The skull of a Neolithic horse from Grimes Graves, Norfolk, England, in (eds) R Meadow and H – P Uerpmann, *Equids in the Ancient World*, **II**, (in press). Wiesbaden: Ludwig Reichert

Coles, J M and Harding, A F, 1979, *The Bronze Age in Europe*. London: Methuen

Coles, J M and Simpson, D D A, 1965, The excavation of a Neolithic round barrow at Pitnacree, Perthshire, Scotland, *Proc Prehist Soc*, **31**, 34–57

Coles, J M and Taylor, J J, 1971, The Wessex Culture: a minimal view, *Antiquity*, **45**, 6–14

Collins, A E P and Evans, E E, 1968, A cist burial at Carrickinab, Co Down, *Ulster J Archaeol, 3 Ser*, **31**, 16–24

Collis, J, 1983, *Wigber Low Derbyshire: A Bronze Age and Anglian Burial Site in the White Peak*. Sheffield: University of Sheffield

Corcoran, J X W P, 1963, Excavation of the bell-barrow in Deerleap Wood, Wotton, *Surrey Archaeol Collect*, **60**, 1–18

Crawford, O G S, 1928, *Air Survey and Archaeology*. Ordnance Survey Professional Papers, New Series No **7**. London: HMSO

Crawford, O G S, 1953, *Archaeology in the Field*. London: Phoenix House

Crawford, O G S and Keiller, A, 1928, *Wessex from the Air*. Oxford: Oxford University Press

Cruse, R J and Harrison, A C, (1983) 1984, Excavation at Hill Road, Wouldham, *Arch Cant*, **99**, 81–108

Cunliffe, B W, 1991, *Iron Age Communities in Britain*. London: Routledge and Kegan Paul

Cunnington, H, 1881, A description of three barrows opened on the occasion of the visit of the Wiltshire Archaeological and Natural History Society to Marlborough, August, 1879, *WANHM*, **19**, 67–74

Cunnington, M E, 1923, *The Early Iron Age Inhabited Site at All Cannings Cross Farm, Wiltshire*. Devizes: Simpson

Cunnington, M E, 1929, *Woodhenge*. Devizes: Simpson

Cunnington, M E and Goddard, E H, 1934, *Catalogue of Antiquities in the Museum of the Wiltshire Archaeological and Natural History Society at Devizes. Part II*. Devizes: Devizes Museum

Cunnington, R H, (1953/1954) 1954, The Cunningtons of Wiltshire, *WANHM*, **55**, 211–236

Cunnington, R H, 1975, *From Antiquary to Archaeologist*. Aylesbury: Shire Publications

Cunnington, W and Goddard, E H, 1896, *Catalogue of the Antiquities in the Museum of the Wiltshire Archaeological and Natural History Society at Devizes. Part I: The Stourhead Collection*. Devizes: Devizes Museum

Curwen, E C, 1954, *The Archaeology of Sussex*. London: Methuen

Drew, C D and Piggott, S, 1936, The excavation of long barrow 163a on Thickthorn Down, Dorset, *Proc Prehist Soc*, **2**, 77–96

Drewett, P L, (1970) 1972, The excavation of two round barrows and associated fieldwork on Ashy Down, Isle of Wight, 1969. *Proc Hampshire Fld Club Archaeol Soc*, **27**, 33–56

Drewett, P L, 1975, The excavation of a turf barrow at Minstead, West Sussex, 1973, *Sussex Archaeol Collect*, **113**, 54–65

Drewett, P L, 1976, The excavation of four round barrows of the second millennium BC at West Heath, Harting, 1973–5, *Sussex Archaeol Collect*, **114**, 126–150

Drewett, P L, 1985, The excavation of barrows V-IX at West Heath, Harting, 1980, *Sussex Archaeol Collect*, 123, 35–60

Dupertius, C W and Hadden, J A, 1951, On the reconstruction of stature from long bones, *American Journ Physical Anthropol*, **9**, 15–53

Dyer, J F, 1961, Dray's Ditches, Bedfordshire and Early Iron Age territorial boundaries in the eastern Chilterns, *Antiq J*, **41**, 32–43

Dyer, J F, 1981, *The Penguin Guide to Prehistoric England and Wales*. London: Allen Lane

Dyer, J F, 1997, *Ancient Britain*. London: Routledge

Dyer, J F, 2001, *Discovering Prehistoric England*, Princes Risborough: Shire Publications

Dymond, D P, 1966, Ritual monuments at Rudston, E Yorkshire, England, *Proc Prehist Soc*, **32**, 86–95

Dymond, D P, (1973) 1976, The excavation of a prehistoric site at Upper Chamberlain's Farm, Eriswell, *Proc Suffolk Inst Archaeol Hist*, **33**, 1–18

Edwards, D A (ed), 1984, Discovery from the Air: G W G Allen. *Aerial Archaeol*, **10**, fig 55

Eogan, G, 1978, The excavation of a round barrow at Long Bredy, Dorset, *Proc Dorset Natur Hist Archaeol Soc*, **100**, 43–53

Evans, J, 1872, *The Ancient Stone Implements, Weapons, and Ornaments, of Great Britain*. London: Longmans

Evans, J, 1881, *The Ancient Bronze Implements, Weapons, and Ornaments, of Great Britain and Ireland*. London: Longmans.

Evens, E D, Grinsell, L V, Piggott, S and Wallis, F S, 1962, Fourth report of the sub-committee of the South-West Group of Museums and Art Galleries (England) on the petrological identification of stone axes, *Proc Prehist Soc*, **28**, 209–266

Evens, E D, Smith, I F and Wallis, F S, 1972, The Petrological Identification of Stone Implements from South-West England. Fifth Report of the Sub-Committee of the South-Western Federation of Museums and Art Galleries, *Proc Prehist Soc*, **38**, 235–275

Fasham, P J, (1978) 1979, The excavation of a triple barrow in Micheldever Wood, Hampshire, *Proc Hampshire Fld Club Archaeol Soc*, **35**, 5–40

Field, N, 1985, A multi-phased barrow and possible henge monument at West Ashby, Lincolnshire, *Proc Prehist Soc*, **51**, 103–136

Figg, W, 1852, On the opening of a barrow at Crowlink in Friston, *Sussex Archaeol Collect*, **5**, 207–212

Fleming, A, 1971, Territorial patterns in Bronze Age Wessex, *Proc Prehist Soc*, **37**, pt **1**, 138–166

Ford, S, 1987, Chronological and functional aspects of flint assemblages, in (eds) A G Brown and M R Edmonds, *Lithic Analysis and Later British Prehistory*, 67–85. BAR, British Series, **162**, Oxford

Ford, S, 1991, An Early Bronze Age pit circle from Charnham Lane, Hungerford, Berkshire, *Proc Prehist Soc*, **57**, pt **2**, 179–181

Ford, S, Bradley, R, Hawkes, J and Fisher, P, 1984, Flint working in the metal age, *Oxford J of Archaeol*, **3**, 157–173

Forde-Johnston, J, 1959, The excavation of two barrows at Frampton in Dorset, *Proc Dorset Natur Hist Archaeol Soc*, **80**, 111–132

Forde-Johnson, J, (1960) 1961, The excavation of a round barrow at Gallowsclough Hill, Delamere Forest, Cheshire, *Trans Lancashire Cheshire Antiq Soc*, **70**, 74–83

Fowler, P J, 1967, *Wessex*. London: Heinemann

Fox, A and Stone, J F S, 1951, A necklace from a barrow in North Molton Parish, North Devon, *Antiq J*, **31**, 25–31

Fox, Sir C, 1959, *Life and Death in the Bronze Age*. London: Routledge and Kegan Paul

French, C A I, 1994, *Excavation of the Deeping St Nicholas Barrow Complex, South Lincolnshire*. Lincolnshire Archaeol and Heritage Rep Ser, No **1**. Lincoln: Heritage Trust of Lincolnshire

Gerloff, S, 1975, *The Early Bronze Age Daggers in Great Britain*. Prähistorische Bronzefunde, **6 (2)**. Munich

Gettins, G L, Taylor, H and Grinsell, L V, 1953, The Marshfield barrows, *Trans Bristol Gloucestershire Archaeol Soc*, **72**, 23–44

Gibson, A M, 1982, *Beaker Domestic Sites: a Study of the Domestic Pottery of the Late Third and Early Second Millennia BC in the British Isles*. BAR, British Series, **107**. Oxford

Gibson, A M, 1986, *Neolithic and Bronze Age Pottery*. Princes Risborough: Shire Publications

Gibson, A M and Kinnes, I A, 1997, On the urns of a dilemma: C14 and the Peterborough problem, *Oxford J Archaeol*, **16(1),** 65–72

Gibson, A M, Kinnes, I A, *et al*, forthcoming, Results of the British Museum Radiocarbon Dating Programme for British Beakers

Gifford, J, 1957, The physique of Wiltshire, in (eds) R B Pugh and E Crittall, *A History of Wiltshire*, Volume **1**, **Part 1**, 1–20. London: Institute of Historical Research, Victoria County Histories

Gingell, C J, (1987) 1988, An earthwork near Badbury Rings in Dorset, *Proc Dorset Natur Hist Archaeol Soc*, **109**, 65–78

Gingell, C, 1988, Twelve Wiltshire round barrows. Excavations in 1959 and 1961 by F de M and H L Vatcher, *WANHM*, **82**, 19–76

Gingell, C, 1992, *The Marlborough Downs: A Later Bronze Age Landscape and its Origins*. WANHS Monograph **1**. Stroud

Giot, P R, 1960, *Brittany*. London: Thames and Hudson

Glasbergen, W, 1954, Barrow excavations in the Eight Beatitudes. The Bronze Age cemetery between Totefout and Halve Mijl, North Brabant. I. The excavations, *Palaeohistoria*, **II**, 1–134

Goddard, E H, 1912, Notes on implements of the Bronze Age found in Wiltshire, with a list of all known examples found in the County, *WANHM*, **37**, 92–158

Goddard, E H, 1914, A list of prehistoric, Roman and Pagan Saxon antiquities in the county of Wilts, *WANHM*, **38**, 153–378

Goddard, E H, 1917, Notes: 'MS. Collections for Wilts', by C H P Wyndham, *WANHM*, **39**, 395–401

Good, G L and Tabraham, C J, 1981, Excavations at Threave Castle, Galloway, 1974–1978, *Medieval Archaeol*, **25**, 90–140

Gover, J E B, Mawer, A and Stenton, F M, 1939, *The Place-Names of Wiltshire*. Engl Place-Name Soc, **XVI**

Green, C, Lynch, F and White, H, (1982) 1983, The excavation of two round barrows on Launceston Down, Dorset (Long Crichel 5 and 7), *Proc Dorset Natur Hist Archaeol Soc*, **104**, 39–58

Green, C and Rollo-Smith, S, 1984, The excavation of eighteen round barrows near Shrewton, Wiltshire, *Proc Prehist Soc*, **50**, 255–318

Green, H S, (1974) 1975, Early Bronze Age burial, territory and population in Milton Keynes, Buckinghamshire, and the Great Ouse valley, *Archaeol J*, **131**, 75–139

Green, H S, 1980, *The Flint Arrowheads of the British Isles*. BAR, British Series, **75**. Oxford

Green, H S, 2000, *A landscape revealed; 10000 years on a chalkland farm*. Stroud: Tempus

Greene, K, (1974) 1976, A group of Roman pottery from Wanborough, Wiltshire, *WANHM*, **69**, 51–66

Greenfield, E, 1960, The excavation of Barrow 4 at Swarkeston, Derbyshire, *Journ Derbyshire Archaeol Natur Hist Soc*, **80**, 1–48

Griffiths, W E, 1960, The excavation of stone circles near Penmaenmawr, North Wales, *Proc Prehist Soc*, **26**, 303–339

Grimes, F W, 1938, A barrow on Breach Farm, Llanbleddian, Glamorgan, *Proc Prehist Soc*, **4**, 107–121

Grimes, F W, 1960, *Excavations on Defence Sites, 1939–45*. London: HMSO

Grinsell, L V, 1934, Bell-barrows, *Proc Prehist Soc East Anglia*, **VII**, 203–230

Grinsell, L V, 1941, The Bronze Age round barrows of Wessex, *Proc Prehist Soc*, **7**, 73–113

Grinsell, L V, 1953, *The Ancient Burial-Mounds of England*, 2nd Ed. London: Methuen

Grinsell, L V, 1957, Archaeological gazetteer, in (eds) R B Pugh and E Crittall, *A History of Wiltshire*, Volume **I**, **Part 1**, 21–279. London: Institute of Historical Research, Victoria County Histories

Grinsell, L V, 1958, *The Archaeology of Wessex*. London: Methuen

Grinsell, L V, 1959, *Dorset Barrows*. Dorchester: Dorset Natural History and Archaeological Society

Grinsell, L V, 1974, Disc-barrows, *Proc Prehist Soc*, **40**, 79–112

Grinsell, L V, 1975, *Barrow, Pyramid and Tomb*. London: Thames and Hudson

Grinsell, L V, 1989, *An Archaeological Autobiography*. Gloucester: Alan Sutton

Grinsell, L V and Dyer, J F, 1971, *Discovering Regional Archaeology, Wessex*. Tring: Shire Publications

Guido, M, Henderson, J, Cable, M, Bayley, J and Biek, L, 1984, A Bronze Age glass bead from Wilsford, Wiltshire: Barrow G42 in the Lake Group, *Proc Prehist Soc*, **50**, 245–254

Hamlin, A and Case, H J, 1963, Excavations of ring-ditches and other sites at Stanton Harcourt; notes on the finds and on ring-ditches in the Oxford region, *Oxoniensia, 28, 1–52*

Hansford Worth, R, 1937, Dartmoor Excavation Committee, Thirteenth Report, *Rep Trans Devonshire Ass*, **69**, 143–150

Harcourt, R, 1974, The dog in Prehistoric and Early Historic Britain, *J Archaeol Sci*, **1**, 151–175

Harden, D B and Treweeks, R C, 1945, Excavations at Stanton Harcourt, Oxon, 1940, *Oxoniensia*, **10**, 16–41

Harding, A and Warren, S E, 1973, Early Bronze Age faience beads from Central Europe, *Antiquity*, **47**, 64–66

Harding, D W, 1974, *The Iron Age in Lowland Britain*. London: Routledge and Kegan Paul

Hawkes, C F C, (1939) 1940, The excavations at Quarley Hill, 1938, *Proc Hampshire Fld Club Archaeol Soc*, **14**, 136–194

Hawkes, J, 1954, *A Guide to the Prehistoric and Roman Monuments in England and Wales*. London: Chatto and Windus

Hawley, W, 1910, Notes on barrows in south Wilts, *WANHM*, **36**, 615–628

Hawsey, I and Shackley, M, 1980, The excavation of a Bronze Age round barrow on Canford Heath, Poole, Dorset (SZ 01889586), *Proc Dorset Natur Hist Archaeol Soc, 102, 33–42*

Healey, E, (forthcoming), *Stone Tools: A Glossary of Post-Glacial Lithics*. The Lithics Studies Society Occasional Paper No **4**

Healey, E and Robertson Mackay R, 1983, The lithics industries from Staines causewayed enclosure and their relationship to other Earlier Neolithic industries in southern Britain, *Lithics*, **4**, 1–27

Heathcote, J P, 1939, Excavations on Stanton Moor. Excavations at Doll Tor. The Nine Stones, Harthill Moor, *Derbyshire Archaeol J*, **13**, 105–128

Henshall, A S, 1968, Scottish dagger graves, in (eds) J M Coles and D D A Simpson, *Studies in Ancient Europe*, 173–195. Leicester: Leicester University Press

Hoare, Sir R C, 1812, *The Ancient History of South Wiltshire*. London: Miller

Hoare, Sir R C, 1819, *The Ancient History of North Wiltshire*. London

Hoare, Sir R C, 1829, *Tumuli Wiltunenses; a Guide to the Barrows on the Plains of Stonehenge*. Shaftesbury

Hodges, H W M, 1964, *Artefacts*. London: John Baker

Hughes, G, 2000, *The Lockington Gold Hoard*. Oxford: Oxbow Books

Jenkins, J G, 1961, *The English Farm Wagon*. Reading: University of Reading

Jewell, P A, 1958, Buzzards and barrows, *S African Archaeol Bull*, **52**, 153–155

Jewell, P A, 1962, Changes in size and type of cattle from prehistoric to medieval times in Britain, *Z Tierzüchtung u. Züchtungsbiologie*, **77**, 159–167

Jewell, P A (ed), 1963, *The Experimental Earthwork on Overton Down, Wiltshire 1960*. London: British Association for the Advancement of Science

Jewell, P A, 1963a, Cattle from British archaeological sites, in *Man and Cattle, Symposium, 1961*, 89–91. Roy Anth Inst London

Johnston, D E, 1963, A group of barrows near Shalbourne, Wilts, *WANHM*, **58**, 362–369

Johnston, D E, (1977/1978) 1980, The excavation of a bell-barrow at Sutton Veney, Wilts, *WANHM*, **72/73**, 29–50

Kilbride-Jones, H E,1936, A Late Bronze Age cemetery: being an account of the excavations of 1935 at Loanhead of Daviot, Aberdeenshire, on Behalf of HM Office of Works, *Proc Soc Antiq Scot*, **70**, 278–310

King, J D, 1948, The influence of diet on parodontal disease, *Nutritional Abstracts and Reviews*, **17**, 569–590

Kinnes, I A, Gibson, A M, Ambers, J, Bowman, S, Leese, M and Boast, R, 1991, Radiocarbon dating and British Beakers: the British Museum Programme, *Scott Archaeol Rev*, **8**, 35–68

Kinnes, I A and Longworth, I H, 1985, *Catalogue of the Excavated Prehistoric and Romano-British Material in the Greenwell Collection*. London: British Museum

Knocker, G M, 1959, Excavation of three round barrows at Kinson, near Bournemouth, *Proc Dorset Natur Hist Archaeol Soc*, **80**, 133–145

Lanting, J N and van der Waals, J D, 1972, British Beakers as seen from the Continent, *Helinium*, **12**, 20–46

Longworth, I H, 1961, The origins and development of the primary series in the collared urn tradition in England and Wales, *Proc Prehist Soc*, **27**, 263–306

Longworth, I H, 1984, *Collared Urns of the Bronze Age in Great Britain and Ireland*. Cambridge: Cambridge University Press

Lucas, A, 1948, *Ancient Egyptian Materials and Industries*. London

Lukis, W C, 1867, Notes on barrow diggings in the parish of Collingbourne Ducis, *WANHM*, **10**, 85–103

Lynch, F, 1970, *Prehistoric Anglesey*. Llangefni: Anglesey Antiquarian Society

Lynch, F, 1974, Brenig Valley excavations 1973, *Trans Denbighshire Hist Soc*, **23**, 9–64

Lynch, F, 1975, Brenig Valley excavations 1974, *Trans Denbighshire Hist Soc*, **24**, 13–37

Lynch, F, 1979, Ring cairns in Britain and Ireland: their design and purpose (The Oliver Davies Lecture for 1979), *Ulster J Archaeol 3 ser*, **42**, 1–19

Lynch, F, 1986, Excavation of a kerb circle and ring cairn on Cefn Caer Euni, Merioneth, *Archaeol Cambrensis*, **135**, 81–120

Lynch, F, 1993, *Excavations in the Brenig Valley: a Mesolithic and Bronze Age Landscape in North Wales.* Cambrian Archaeol Monographs **5**. Cambrian Archaeological Association

Margary, I D, 1973, *Roman Roads in Britain.* London: John Baker

Mawer, A and Stenton, F M, with assistance from Gover, J E B, 1929, *The Place-Names of Sussex, Part 1, Rapes of Chichester, Arundel and Bramber.* Engl Place-Name Soc, **VI**.

McKerrell, H, 1972, On the origins of British faience beads and some aspects of the Wessex-Mycenae relationship, *Proc Prehist Soc*, **38**, 286–301

McComish, D, Field, D and Brown, G, 2002, *The Field Archaeology of the Salisbury Plain Training Area.* London: English Heritage

Mattingly, H, 1968 *A Catalogue of the Roman Coins in the British Museum: The Coins of the Roman Empire, Vol. IV, Antoninus Pins to Commodus,* 2nd Edition, London

Megaw, J V S, 1967, Notes on Iron Age and Neolithic material from Sidbury Camp, *WANHM*, **62**, 115–117

Miles, H, 1975, Barrows on the St Austell granite, Cornwall, *Cornish Archaeol*, **14**, 5–81

Miller, G S, 1912, *Catalogue of the Mammals of Western Asia.* London: British Museum (Natural History)

Mook, W G, 1986, Business meeting: Recommendations/Resolutions, adopted by the Twelfth International Radiocarbon Conference, *Radiocarbon*, **28**, 799

Moore, C N and Cummins, W A, 1974, Petrological identification of implements from Derbyshire and Leicestershire, *Proc Prehist Soc*, **40**, 59–78

Moore, N W, 1957, The past and present status of the buzzard in the British Isles, *British Birds*, **50**, 173–197

Mortimer, J R, 1905, *Forty Years' Researches in British and Saxon Burial Mounds of East Yorkshire.* London: Brown

Musty, J W G and Stone, J F S, 1956, An Early Bronze Age barrow and Late Bronze Age urnfield on Heale Hill, Middle Woodford, *WANHM*, **56**, 253–261

Newell, R S, (1931) 1932, Barrow 85 Amesbury (Goddard's List). Lat 51° 9' 32.7' Long 1°44' 44.8', *WANHM*, **45**, 432–458

Olivier, A C H, 1987, Excavation of a Bronze Age funerary cairn at Manor Farm, near Borwick, North Lancashire, *Proc Prehist Soc*, **53**, 129–186

O'Neil, BHStJ, 1952, The excavation of Knaekyboy Cairn, St Martin's, Isles of Scilly, 1956–58, *Antiq J*, **32**, 21–34

O'Neil, H E, 1967, Bevan's Quarry round barrow, Temple Guiting, Gloucestershire, 1964, *Trans Bristol Gloucestershire Archaeol Soc*, **86**, 16–41

O'Riordáin, S P, 1956, A burial with faience beads at Tara, *Proc Prehist Soc*, **21**, 163–173

Ozanne, P, 1972, The excavation of a round barrow on Rollestone Down, Winterbourne Stoke, Wiltshire, *WANHM*, **67**, 43–60

Parke, A L, (1953) 1955, The excavation of a bell-barrow, Oakley Down, Wimbourne St Giles, *Proc Dorset Natur Hist Archaeol Soc*, **75**, 36–44

Parker, S, Roberts, C and Manchester, K, 1986, A review of British trepanations with reports on two new cases, *Ossa*, **12**, 141–158

Parrington, M, 1978, *The Excavation of an Iron Age Settlement, Bronze Age Ring-Ditches and Roman Features at Ashville Trading Estate, Abingdon (Oxfordshire) 1974–76.* Oxfordshire Archaeological Unit Report **1**. CBA Research Report **28**. London

Passmore, A D, (1927–1929) 1929, Fieldwork in N Wilts, 1926–28, *WANHM*, **44**, 240–245

Pearson, G W, Pilcher, J R, Baillie, M G L, Corbett, D M and Qua, F, 1986, High precision ^{14}C measurement of Irish oaks to show the natural ^{14}C variations from AD 1840–5210 BC, *Radiocarbon*, **28**, 911–934

Pearson, G W and Stuiver, M, 1986, High precision calibration of the radiocarbon time-scale, 500–2500 BC, in (eds) M Stuiver and R S Kra, International ^{14}C conference, 12th Proceedings, *Radiocarbon*, **28**, 239–262

Perry, J S, 1943, Reproduction in the Water vole (*Arvicola amphibius* Linne'), *Proc Zool Soc London*, **126**, 166–167

Phillips, P and Thomas J, 1989, The pit deposit at Ash Hill long barrow, in (ed) P Phillips, *Archaeology and Landscape Studies in North Lincolnshire* Pt 1: *Excavations at North Lincolnshire Long Barrows*, 39–56. BAR, British Series, **208(i)**, Oxford

Piggott, C M, 1942, Five Late Bronze Age enclosures in North Wiltshire, *Proc Prehist Soc*, **8**, 48–61

Piggott, C M, 1943, Excavation of fifteen barrows in the New Forest, 1941–2, *Proc Prehist Soc*, **9**, 1–27

Piggott, C M, 1943a, Three turf barrows at Hurn, near Christchurch, *Proc Hampshire Fld Club Archaeol Soc*, **15**, 248–262

Piggott, S, 1938, The Early Bronze Age in Wessex, *Proc Prehist Soc*, **4**, 52–106

Piggott, S, 1940, A trepanned skull of the Beaker period from Dorset and the practice of trepanning in prehistoric Europe, *Proc Prehist Soc*, **6**, 112–132

Piggott, S, 1962, From Salisbury Plain to South Siberia, *WANHM*, **58**, 93–97

Piggott, S, 1962a, *The West Kennet Long Barrow.* London: HMSO

Piggott, S, 1963, Abercromby and after: the Beaker cultures of Britain re-examined, in (eds) I Ll Foster and L Alcock, *Culture and Environment, Essays in Honour of Sir Cyril Fox*, 53–91. London: Routledge and Kegan Paul

Piggott, S, 1971, An archaeological survey and policy for Wiltshire: Part III, Neolithic and Bronze Age, *WANHM*, **66**, 47–57

Piggott, S, 1973, The Wessex Culture and the final phase of Bronze Age technology, in (ed) E Crittall, *A History of Wiltshire*, Volume **I**, part **2**, 281–407. London: Institute of Historical Research, Victoria County Histories

Piggott, S and Piggott, C M, 1944, Excavation of barrows on Crichel and Launceston Downs, Dorset, *Archaeologia*, **90**, 47–80

Piggott, S and Piggott, C M, 1945, The excavation of a barrow on Rockbourne Down, *Proc Hampshire Fld Club Archaeol Soc*, **16**, 156–162

Pitt-Rivers, A H L F, 1890, *King John's House, Tollard Royal, Wilts.* Privately printed

Pitts, M and Jacobi, R M, 1979, Some aspects of change in flaked stone industries of the Mesolithic and Neolithic in southern Britain, *Journ Archaeol Science*, **6**, 163–177

Proudfoot, E V W, 1963, Report on the excavation of a bell-barrow in the parish of Edmondsham, Dorset, England, 1959, *Proc Prehist Soc*, **29**, 395–425

Proudfoot, E V W, 1965, Excavation and fieldwork in Wiltshire, 1964, *WANHM*, **60**, 132–133

Pryor, F, French, C, Crowther, D, Simpson G and Taylor, M, 1985, *Archaeology and Environment in the Lower Welland Valley*. East Anglian Archaeol Report No **27**, (Fenland Project No 1). Cambridge: Cambridgeshire Archaeological Committee

Pugh, C W, 1953, *The Wiltshire Archaeological and Natural History Society 1853–1953*. Devizes

Rackham, O, 1976, *Trees and woodland in the British Landscape*. London: Weidenfeld and Nicolson

Rahtz, P A, 1962, Farncombe Down barrow, Berkshire, *Berks Archaeol J*, **60**, 1–24

Rahtz, P A, 1962a, Neolithic and Beaker sites at Downton, near Salisbury, Wiltshire, *WANHM*, **58**, 116–141

Rahtz, P A, 1970, Excavations on Knighton Hill, Broad Chalke, 1959, *WANHM*, **65**, 74–88

Rahtz, P A, 1989, *Little Ouseburn Barrow, 1958. Round Hill, an Early Bronze Age Barrow at Little Ouseburn, North Yorkshire, England*. York University Publications **7**. York

Raymond, F, 1994, The Pottery, in R Bradley, R Entwistle and F Raymond, *Prehistoric Land Divisions on Salisbury Plain; The Work of the Wessex Linear Ditches Project*, 69–90. English Heritage Archaeological Projects, **2**. London

Richards, J, 1990, *The Stonehenge Environs Project*. English Heritage Archaeological Report no **16**

Richards, J (1986–90) 1991, Death and the past environment, *Berks Archaeol J*, **73**, 1–42

Riley, D N, (1966) 1967, An Early Bronze Age cairn on Harland Edge, Beeley Moor, Derbyshire, *Derbyshire Archaeol J*, **86**, 31–53

Robertson-Mackay, M E,1980, A 'head and hoofs' burial beneath a round barrow, with other Neolithic and Bronze Age sites, on Hemp Knoll, near Avebury, Wiltshire, *Proc Prehist Soc*, **46**, 123–176

Robinson, P H, 1976, 19th and 20th Century Wiltshire trade checks, bonuses and advertisement tickets etc in Devizes Museum, *WA and NHS Bi-Annual Bulletin*, No **21**, Autumn, 12–16

Roe, F E S, 1966, The battle-axe series in Britain, *Proc Prehist Soc*, **32**, 199–245

RCHME, 1979, *Stonehenge and its Environs*. Royal Commission on Historical Monuments, England. Edinburgh: University Press

Russel, A D, 1990, Two Beaker burials from Chilbolton, Hampshire, *Proc Prehist Soc*, **56**, 153–172

Saville, A, 1979, *Recent Work at Cow Common Bronze Age Cemetery, Gloucestershire*. Committee for Rescue Archaeology in Avon, Gloucestershire and Somerset Occa Pap No **6**. Bristol

Saville, A, 1980, On the measurement of struck flakes and flake tools, *Lithics*, **1**, 16–21

Saville, A, (1977, 1978) 1980a, Five flint assemblages from excavated sites in Wiltshire, *WANHM*, **72/73**, 1–28

Scott, E M, Harkness, D D and Cook, G T, 1998, Interlaboratory comparisons; lessons learned, *Radiocarbon*, **40**, 331–340

Shawcross, F W and Higgs, E S, (1960) 1961, The Excavation of a *Bos primigenius* at Lowe's Farm, Littleport, *Proc Camb Ant Soc*, **54**, 3–16

Shotton, F W, 1959, New petrological groups based on axes from the West Midlands, *Proc Prehist Soc*, **25**, 135–143

Simpson, D D A, 1971, Beaker houses and settlements in Britain, in (ed) D D A Simpson, *Economy and Settlement in Neolithic and Early Bronze Age Europe*, 131–152. Leicester: Leicester University Press

Simpson, W G, 1976, A barrow cemetery of the second millennium BC at Tallington, Lincolnshire, *Proc Prehist Soc*, **42**, 215–239

Smith, I F, 1965, Excavation of a bell-barrow, Avebury G55, *WANHM*, **60**, 24–46

Smith, I F, 1965a, *Windmill Hill and Avebury: Excavations by Alexander Keiller, 1925–1939*. Oxford: Clarendon Press

Smith, I F, 1991, Round barrows Wilsford Cum Lake G51-G54: excavations by Ernest Greenfield in 1958, *WANHM*, **84**, 11–39

Smith, I F and Simpson, D D A, 1966, Excavation of a round barrow on Overton Hill, North Wiltshire, England, *Proc Prehist Soc*, **32**, 122–155

Smith, K and Wainwright, G J, 1978, South Dartmoor, Devon, *Proc Prehist Soc*, **44**, 446–447

Southern, H N, 1954, Tawny owls and their prey, *Ibis*, **96**, 348–410

Southern, H N and Crowcroft, W P, 1956, Terrestrial habits of the water vole (*Arvicola amphibius*), *Proc Zool Soc London*, **126**, 166–167

Spindler, K, 1994, *The Man in the Ice*. London: Weidenfeld and Nicolson

Stevens, F, (1932–1934) 1934, 'The Highfield pit dwellings', Fisherton, Salisbury, excavated May, 1866, to September, 1869, *WANHM*, **46**, 579–624

Stevenson, M D, (1983–1986) 1987, Bronze age funerary deposits in the Royston area, *Herts Arch*, **9**, 8–14

Stone, J F S, (1930–1932) 1932, Saxon interments on Roche Court Down, Winterslow, *WANHM*, **45**, 568–582

Stone, J F S, (1935–1937) 1937, Excavations at Easton Down, Winterslow, 1933–1934, *WANHM*, **47**, 68–80

Stone, J F S, (1935–1937) 1937a, An unrecorded group of barrows and other earthworks at Ford, Laverstock, *WANHM*, **47**, 406–411

Stone, J F S, (1935–1937) 1937b, An enclosure on Boscombe Down East, *WANHM*, **47**, 466–489

Stone, J F S, (1935–1937) 1937c, A Late Bronze Age habitation site on Thorny Down, Winterbourne Gunner, S Wilts, *WANHM*, **47**, 640–660

Stone, J F S, 1958, *Wessex before the Celts*. London: Thames and Hudson

Stone, J F S and Thomas, L C, 1957, The use and distribution of faience in the ancient East and prehistoric Europe, *Proc Prehist Soc*, **22**, 37–84

Stourhead Coll, See Cunnington, W and Goddard, EH, 1896

Stukeley, W, 1740, *Stonehenge a Temple restor'd to the British Druids*. London

Swan, V G, 1973, Aspects of the New Forest late-Roman pottery industry, in (ed) A Detsicas, *Current Research in Romano-British Coarse Pottery*, 117–134. CBA Research Report **10**. London

Swan, V G, 1975, Oare reconsidered and the origins of Savernake Ware in Wiltshire, *Britannia,* **VI**, 37–61

Taylor, A F and Woodward, P J, 1985, A Bronze Age barrow cemetery and associated settlement at Roxton, Bedfordshire, *Archaeol J,* **142**, 73–149

Taylor, H, (1949–1950) 1951, The Tynings Farm barrow group. Third report. *Proc Univ Bristol Spelaeol Soc,* **6**, 111–173

Thomas, A C, 1954, Folklore from a Wiltshire village, *Folklore,* **65**, 165–168

Thomas, J, 1991, *Rethinking the Neolithic.* Cambridge: Cambridge University Press

Thomas, N, 1954, Notes on some Early Bronze Age grave groups in Devizes Museum, *WANHM,* **55**, 311–332

Thomas, N, 1956, Museum report, 1954–55, *WANHM,* **56**, 172–184

Thomas, N, 1956a, Excavation and field-work in Wiltshire: 1956, *WANHM,* **56**, 231–252

Thomas, N, 1965, Reviews: Guide Catalogue of the Neolithic and Bronze Age Collections in Devizes Museum, *WANHM,* **60**, 142–147

Thomas, N, 1966, Notes on some Early Bronze Age objects in Devizes Museum, *WANHM,* **61**, 1–8

Thomas, N, 1976, *A Guide to Prehistoric England,* 2nd Ed. London: Batsford

Thomas, N, 2003, Frederick Kenneth Annable – 'Ken' – BA, FSA, FMA, 1922–2002: a Memoir, *WANHM,* 96, 1–6

Thomas, N and Thomas, A C, 1956, Excavations at Snail Down, Everleigh; 1953, 1955. Interim report, *WANHM,* **56**, 127–148

Thomas N and Thomas, A C,1958, Excavation and field-work in Wiltshire: 1957, by F K Annable, *WANHM,* **57**, 5–8

Thomas, S, 1965, *Pre-Roman Britain.* London: Studio Vista

Thompson, M W and Ashbee, P, 1957, Excavation of a barrow near the Hardy Monument, Blackdown, Portesham, Dorset, *Proc Prehist Soc,* **23**, 124–136

Thurnam, J, 1860, Barrows on the downs of north Wilts, examination of, in 1853–57, *WANHM,* **6**, 317–336

Thurnam, J, 1871, On ancient British barrows, especially those of Wiltshire and the adjoining counties, (Part II, round barrows), *Archaeologia,* **43(2)**, 285–544

Tomalin, D J, 1979, Barrow excavation in the Isle of Wight, *Curr Archaeol,* **68**, 273–276

Vatcher, F de M, 1960, The excavation of a group of barrows at Down Farm, Pewsey, Wilts, *WANHM,* **57**, 339–351

Vatcher, F de M, 1962, Excavation and fieldwork in Wiltshire, 1961, *WANHM,* **58**, 241

Vatcher, F de M, 1963, The excavation of the barrows on Lamb Down, Codford St Mary, *WANHM,* **58**, 417–441

Vatcher, F de M and Vatcher, H L, 1976, The excavation of a round barrow near Poor's Heath, Risby, Suffolk, *Proc Prehist Soc,* **42**, 263–292

Wacher, J S, (1958) 1959, Litton Cheney excavations, 1956, *Proc Dorset Natur Hist Archaeol Soc,* **80**, 160–177

Wacher, J S, 1964, Excavations at Breedon-on-the-Hill, Leicestershire, 1957, *Antiq J,* **44**, 122–142

Wainwright, G J, 1979, *Mount Pleasant, Dorset: Excavations 1970–1971.* Rep Res Comm Soc Antiq London, **37**. Dorking

Wainwright, G J, Fleming, A and Smith, K, 1979, The Shaugh Moor project: first report, *Proc Prehist Soc,* **45**, 1–33

Wainwright, G J and Longworth, I H, 1971, *Durrington Walls: Excavations 1966–1968.* Rep Res Comm Soc Antiq London, **29**. Dorking

Ward, A H, 1988, Survey and excavation of ring cairns in SE Dyfed and on Gower, West Glamorgan, *Proc Prehist Soc,* **54**, 153–172

Ward, G K and Wilson, S R, 1978, Procedures for comparing and combining radiocarbon age determinations: a critique, *Archaeometry,* **20**, 19–31

Ward-Perkins, J B, 1940, *London Museum Catalogues: No 7. Medieval Catalogue.* London: Lancaster House

Warne, C, 1866, *The Celtic Tumuli of Dorset.* London

Warrilow, J L, 1980, *Bronze Age Miniature Accessory Vessels in South-West England.* Unpublished Undergraduate Thesis, University College, Cardiff

Warrilow, W, Owen, G and Britnell, W, 1986, Eight ring-ditches at Four Crosses, Llandysilio, Powys, 1981–85, *Proc Prehist Soc,* **52**, 53–87

Watts, L and Rahtz, P,1984, *Cowlam Wold Barrows.* York Univ Archaeol Publ **3**. York: Department of Archaeology, University of York

Wheeler, R E M, 1943, *Maiden Castle, Dorset.* Rep Res Comm Soc Antiq London, **12**, Oxford

Whimster, R P, 1977, Iron Age burial in southern Britain, *Proc Prehist Soc,* **43**, 317–327

White, D A, 1982, *The Bronze Age Cremation Cemeteries at Simons Ground, Dorset.* Dorset Natur Hist Archaeol Soc, Monograph **3**. Dorchester

White, D A and Reed, R, 1971, The excavation of a bowl barrow at Oakley Down, Dorset, 1968, *Proc Dorset Natur Hist Archaeol Soc,* **92**, 159–167

Whittle, A, 1997, *Sacred Mound, Holy Rings.* Oxbow Monograph **74**. Exeter: Short Run Press

Whittle, A, Atkinson, R J C, Chambers, R and Thomas, N, 1992, The Neolithic and Early Bronze Age complex at Dorchester on Thames, Oxon, excavations, 1947–1952 and 1981, *Proc Prehist Soc,* **58**, 143–201

Williams, A, 1948, Excavations in Barrow Hills Field, Radley, Berkshire, 1944, *Oxoniensia,* **13**, 1–17

Wilson, G, 1980, Methods of flint measurement, *Lithics,* **1**, 15–16

Woodbridge, K, 1970, *Landscape and Antiquity.* Oxford: Clarendon Press

Woodward, A, 2000, *British Barrows. A Matter of Life and Death.* Stroud: Tempus Publishing Ltd

Wymer, J J, 1966, Excavations of the Lambourn long barrow, 1964, *Berkshire Archaeol J,* **62**, 1–16

Young, R, 1987, *Lithics and subsistence in North-East England.* BAR, British Series, **161**, Oxford

Index

Compiled by Peter Ellis

Note: page numbers in italics denote illustrations

WILTSHIRE ARCHAEOLOGICAL AND NATURAL HISTORY SOCIETY MONOGRAPH SERIES

1. *The Marlborough Downs: a later Bronze Age landscape and its origins*, by Christopher Gingell, 1992, ISBN 0 947723 04 8.

2. *Ludgershall Castle, Wiltshire, a report on the excavations by Peter Addyman, 1964-1972*, compiled and edited by Peter Ellis, 2000, ISBN 0 947723 07 2.